86-1256

86-1256

PRACTICAL MEASUREMENTS FOR EVALUATION IN PHYSICAL EDUCATION

FOURTH EDITION

BARRY L. JOHNSON

Corpus Christi State University
Corpus Christi, Texas

JACK K. NELSON

Louisiana State University
Baton Rouge, Louisiana

Burgess Publishing

A Division of Burgess International Group, Inc.

Development editor: Anne E. Heller

Assistant development editor: Charlene J. Brown

Copy editor: J. Leslie Reindl

Production coordinator: Melinda Berndt

Text and cover design: Terry Dugan

Library of Congress Cataloging in Publication Data

Johnson, Barry L.
    Practical measurements for evaluation in physical education.

    Includes bibliographies and index.
    1. Physical fitness—Testing. I. Nelson, Jack K.
II. Title.
GV436.J6 1986   613.7'076   85-28049
ISBN 0-8087-1094-X

Burgess Publishing
7110 Ohms Lane
Edina, MN 55435

JIHGFEDCBA

CONTENTS

PREFACE

The fourth edition of *Practical Measurements for Evaluation in Physical Education* follows the preceding editions in its practical approach to measurement. The basic purposes are the same:

1. To develop within the prospective physical education teacher a greater understanding and appreciation of the need for and the application of tests and measurements in the evaluation process
2. To offer practical and economical tests in the various performance areas that can be used by the average physical education teacher in a variety of school situations
3. To attempt to define and discuss the different abilities, to present brief summaries of pertinent research findings, and to identify problems involved in isolating and measuring the specific components of performance

The fourth edition contains the same number of chapters, but has extensive revisions. Some of the major revisions deserve special mention. Chapter 3, Basic Statistical Techniques, has been reorganized and expanded. Fundamental statistical techniques and concepts are presented in the first section. The second section deals with statistical techniques for the teacher, including graph construction, correlation, and simple, expedient ways to construct percentile norms and T scores. The third section is aimed more toward research and test construction. It describes t tests, analysis of variance, regression, and intraclass correlation. The last section introduces the reader to use of the computer. The basic steps in analyzing data by means of a computer are described; the versatility and practical uses of microcomputers are discussed. A sample computer input and output is included in Appendix E.

Another major addition is the inclusion of measurement of motor performance for the handicapped in Chapter 18. Some practical tests and resources are presented for measuring motor performance of mentally retarded persons, of children with auditory and visual impairment, and of emotionally disturbed children.

The chapter on anthropometric measurement, body build, and body composition (Chapter 10)

has been thoroughly revised and expanded. Chapter 21, The Measurement of Knowledge, has also been enlarged, with increased attention given to written test construction and evaluation.

Most of the chapters have been brought up to date with current reviews of literature concerning the various areas of measurement. The basic approach and coverage, however, remain essentially the same with regard to practical measurements for evaluation. Other good tests are available in the different areas in addition to the ones we present. Tests requiring expensive equipment have been generally excluded. Therefore, the reader must not be lulled into complacency with the idea that the tests presented in this text, or in any other, are the only ones available, or that they are necessarily the best measures in each area or situation or both.

To become effective in any endeavor, we must know where we are going and have some means of assessing how well our goals have been achieved. Our hope is that the readers of this book, whether they are undergraduate or graduate students or teachers in the field, will develop an attitude toward evaluation that transcends the mere use of tests. The theme of this book is that the person who is doing the evaluating, not the test or the measuring device, is the key to successful evaluation. A test with reportedly high validity and reliability coefficients may be utterly worthless if it is not administered and interpreted correctly.

We wish to express our gratitude to the many individuals who have contributed so much in the preparation of this book. We wish to thank our colleagues and students who have given generously of their time to help in testing and constructing norms. We are grateful to the many authors and publishers who have permitted use of their materials. We are also indebted to the Literary Executor of the late Sir Ronald A. Fisher, F.R.S., to Dr. Frank Yates, F.R.S., and to Longman Group Ltd., London, for permission to reprint Table III from their book *Statistical Tables for Biological, Agricultural and Medical Research* (6th ed., 1974).

CHAPTER 1

ORIENTATION TOWARD MEASUREMENT AND EVALUATION IN PHYSICAL EDUCATION

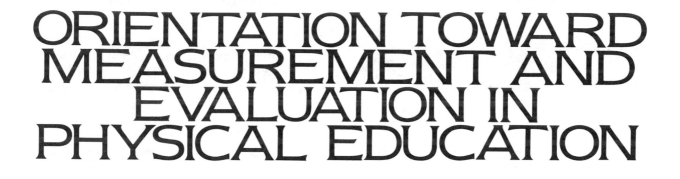

OBJECTIVES

After reading this chapter, the student should be able to:

1. Distinguish among the terms *tests, measurements, evaluation,* and *research*
2. List the different reasons for using tests and

measurements in the evaluation process in physical education

3. Appreciate how the principles of measurement and evaluation can guide and give greater meaning to the total physical education program

---

The physical educator must have a sound philosophical perspective to become skilled in evaluation processes. As educators, we identify our students as our single most important concern, and we lead, guide, and direct them toward the objectives of our field. We are constantly aware of the general goals that the physical education profession has set forth, and we realize that it is through the attainment of these goals that we can best produce graduates who will become worthy and effective citizens of our society. The goals are:

Neuromuscular development—Development of motor abilities such as agility, balance, power, speed, kinesthetic perception, reaction time, coordination, and sports or dance skills

Organic development—Proper physical growth and development, including such physical fitness components as flexibility, strength, muscular endurance, cardiovascular endurance, and body composition

Social and emotional development—Development of qualities such as sportsmanship,

character, leadership, and healthy attitudes toward physical activity, fitness, and sports

Acquisition of knowledge and understanding—Learning about movement, physical activities, fitness, and sports topics generally including historical background, values of participation, game rules, strategies, game courtesies, performance techniques, and principles of conditioning and the importance of fitness for life

Evaluation of progress in the achievement of these goals requires knowledge and skills in different areas of human behavior. Because general goals are stated in broad terms, they are vague and difficult to evaluate. Thus, behavioral objectives are formulated to specify the behavior that reflects successful achievement of general goals. Specific measurements are required to determine to what extent the behavioral objectives are achieved. Objectives will be further discussed later.

In the final analysis, we use evaluation processes to determine the effectiveness of physical education. Moreover, evaluation is related to philosophical perspective, since it indicates the extent to which goals are accomplished.

Probably the most common misconception concerning evaluation in physical education is that it is employed only in grading. Certainly grading is an important matter, and one that has been discussed and debated copiously. Chapter 5 is devoted to this topic. Yet, despite its prominence, grading is by no means the only, nor the most important, reason for using evaluation.

BASIC TERMS

Before we explore more fully other purposes of evaluation, we will identify and discuss certain basic terms.

TEST. A test is a form of assessment used to measure the acquisition and retention of knowledge or ability in some physical or mental endeavor. A teacher commonly measures students' knowledge and understanding about a sport or activity through use of a teacher-made test. On the other hand, the teacher might measure basketball skill through use of a standardized test such as the AAHPERD basketball skills test. A test of knowledge, skill, or affective behavior is a tool of measurement that provides data for evaluation.

MEASUREMENT. Measurement is an aid in the evaluation process. In measurement, various tools and techniques are used to collect data. A test is a specific type of measurement. Height and weight are examples of measurements that are not tests.

EVALUATION. Evaluation is much broader than tests and measurements. It is a subjective decision-making process in which collected measurements are assessed to ascertain the extent to which objectives are being accomplished.

FORMATIVE EVALUATION. The term *formative* as applied to evaluation refers to the gathering and evaluation of information about a student's progress throughout the unit of instruction. This type of evaluation serves as feedback to the student and teacher; it enhances the educational process and increases the chance for successful learning.

SUMMATIVE EVALUATION. Summative evaluation is that evaluation conducted at the end of a unit. An example is the determination of grades at the end of a course.

RESEARCH. Research is a careful investigation conducted to extend knowledge or to explore further and verify that which has already been explored. Research demands sound measurement techniques. Scientifically constructed tools and tests in the field of physical education are frequently used to collect data for research purposes.

From the preceding, we can see that a test is merely one type of measurement, while measurement itself involves all the tools that may be employed in the collection of data. Tests and measurements provide information about a specific act that has taken place at a specific time. Evaluation is a more general concept giving meaning to the tests and measurements conducted. To make an intelligent evaluation, one must know the desired objectives, know which tools are the most effective for the collection of data, and make unbiased judgments concerning the educational significance of the results.

Researchers must use scientifically constructed tests and measuring instruments to reach valid conclusions. Thus, tests and measuring instruments are basic tools of research; the measurements course should be thought of as one of the prerequisites for research. Through research, the physical educator is able to devise more effective means of measurement and evaluation. Consequently, each area complements the other.

NEED FOR MEASUREMENT AND EVALUATION

Measurement and evaluation are employed for many reasons. Moreover, the interpretation and use of the information obtained may have varied applications. For example, a test that is given for the purpose of improving the learning process may be put to further use by the teacher in grading or in interpreting the program to pupils, administrators, teachers, and other interested groups.

Measurement is the basis of technology, and no program can gain professional acceptance or public respect without it. The proper use of measurement and evaluation in physical education programs provides several vital services in the teaching and learning process. Some of these are as follows.

1. Motivation. Students are more interested in learning and advancing to a higher performance level when they know what the goal is and when they receive feedback con-

cerning their progress toward the goal. The use of *formative* measurement and evaluation techniques during the unit maintains student interest, while the use of *summative* measurement and evaluation at the end of the unit informs students of their performance relative to other students, which fosters continued interest and motivation.

2. Diagnosis and Prescription. Measurement can be used as an aid in pinpointing weaknesses in performance. When weaknesses are revealed, the physical educator evaluates the specific training techniques available and prescribes the most suitable technique to aid the student in improving performance.

3. Selection for Team Membership or Special Activities. Measurement and evaluation are the most effective objective ways to select the best performers from the many who hope to make the team or participate in special activities. Everyone has equal opportunity when selection is based on the results of a sound evaluation process. An attempt to choose without measurement is an invitation to criticism and resentment.

4. Determination of Status for Grades. Evaluation at the end of a unit or course is an integral part of the grading process. The teacher must be ever cognizant of the far-reaching effect grades can have on students in their future endeavors. Consequently, summative evaluation must be handled carefully to ensure that the permanent records accurately reflect each student's true status and level of achievement for the course.

5. Aiding of Skill Learning. In most school situations, facilities are inadequate for the class size. An innovative teacher can often increase the teaching space by making use of a wall, hallway, stage, and other small spaces as testing stations. With these stations, students can practice the activity and increase their skills. Moreover, regular testing throughout the unit enhances the reliability of the tests when they are given at the end of the unit for summative evaluation.

6. Determination of Teaching Effectiveness. How well or how poorly a class performs on a unit test may be a good indicator of the effectiveness of the teaching. Unbiased evaluation of the results of measurement can help teachers identify their own strengths and weaknesses and thereby improve their future instructional effectiveness.

7. Public Relations. Parents, teachers, administrators, and the local public in general are interested in how well students perform. Outstanding and unusual performance as indicated by measurements can be used to develop interest, pride, and recognition within the school and community. Such performance has also served at times as effective ammunition against attempts to curtail or eliminate physical education requirements.

8. Aiding of Research. Careful measurement provides data that can be assembled and evaluated for educational significance. Research is an important responsibility of any outstanding program, since it provides valuable information about offerings, teaching techniques, and body of knowledge in general.

9. Construction of Norms and Scoring Scales. Measurement provides data that can be used in establishing norms or scoring scales or both. Such devices are valuable to teachers in that raw scores can be quickly evaluated qualitatively. Norms enable the teacher to compare students' performance on different tests and against different populations such as local, regional, or national groups. Norms and scoring scales provide great motivation and interest for students, who are usually eager to learn how well they have performed.

10. Classification. Teachers may arrange students into homogeneous groups through measurements of performance or traits or both. Such classifications may enhance teaching or learning in certain courses and can without doubt provide for greater safety in such courses as swimming, gymnastics, and scuba diving.

11. Program Evaluation. Teachers and administrators frequently use test results to evaluate the program and thereby determine the need for change. Some courses, for example, may prove to be costly in terms of equipment expense and administrative time, or perhaps unproductive in strengthening identified weaknesses. If, for example, the

test results reveal that the students perform consistently at a high level in an activity, it may be that the activity could be deleted or alternated with another. If students perform poorly on skills tests in an activity, perhaps more time needs to be spent on that activity or the activity should be dropped if the equipment, facilities, or class schedule is judged to be inadequate. For the enterprising teacher and administrator, measurement plays an important role in assessing the quality of the program and pointing to the need for change.

PRINCIPLES OF MEASUREMENT AND EVALUATION

A program of measurement and evaluation is most effective when sound principles are developed, understood, and followed as they relate to personal philosophy of education and life. Although the principles discussed here provide greater depth and meaning to the total physical education program, each must be evaluated in terms of personal philosophy and the philosophy of the school in which one is employed.

Measurement and Evaluation Should Be Used as a Means to an End. Measurement and evaluation should not be ends in themselves. Testing for the sake of testing is not only a waste of time but also an actual obstruction to the total educational process. When measurements are conducted, the resulting data should have a definite use. Measurement and evaluation are the means by which teachers accomplish the task of educating students.

Measurement and Evaluation Should Be Related to Goals and Objectives. Measurement should be conducted for the purpose of evaluating the outcomes of physical education in light of educational goals. Examples of general goals in physical education were given on the first page of this chapter. General goals are stated in broad terms and are sometimes vague. The trend today has been to narrow general goals down to specific objectives stated in more meaningful behavioral terms. For example, the general goal that deals with neuromuscular development might be narrowed to a behavioral objective as follows:

General goal	Development of neuromuscular skill
General objective	Development of balance
Intermediate objective	Static balance performance in upright standing position
Behavioral objective	To balance statically for at least 20 sec on one of three trials of the Bass stick test

Balance is only one of many components of neuromuscular skills, and static balance as just described is only one of thousands of behavioral objectives that could be formulated to give meaning and show progress to the general goal.

Measurement and Evaluation Should Be Used to Determine the Value of Equipment, Materials, and Methods. Measurement should provide a special service in the physical education program in improving teaching methods and in determining the efficacy of certain physical education equipment and materials. Through repeated measurements and analysis, it is possible to identify and eliminate inferior equipment and materials as well as to abandon certain methods that are counterproductive to the growth of the program.

Measurement and Evaluation Should Use Both Objective and Subjective Techniques. Considerable advantage is to be gained in having a number of objective measures in the evaluation program, particularly in the process of awarding grades. Students, parents, and administrators readily understand and appreciate objective measures, and consequently such measures are more easily defended than subjective ones.

However, physical education teachers can never abandon subjective evaluation, nor should they even try. Certain performances require qualitative rather than quantitative evaluation. However, the teacher should be alert to the fact that when subjective measurement is called for, every effort should be made to make the evaluation as objective as possible. The use of certain criteria and carefully prepared rating forms can aid in this endeavor. It is commonly accepted that no amount of objective measurement will replace sound judgment, nor is anything wrong with subjective judgment when the tester is qualified to evaluate the quality being measured. In a sports skill such as tennis or basketball, for example, no objective test can measure all the factors involved in actual competition. Some qualities are more accurately measured than others, and the amount of objectivity varies accordingly. If a test item is capable of being measured easily, such as in units of time or distance, it usually will have high objectivity. On the other hand, if it is hard to quantify, as in the case of judging a trampoline performance or assessing attitude, then lower objectivity is acceptable.

Measurement and Evaluation Are Normally Preceded by Instruction and Practice. Unless the performance test is designed to measure initial status, it normally should follow a period of instruction and practice to ensure the student's safety and familiarity with the test items. Moreover, the reliability (and thus validity) of any test is much improved when students are familiar with the test items and have overcome initial variations in performance owing to learning, release of inhibitions, and other factors (Nelson and Dorociak 1982). In many cases, observation and sound judgment are sufficient at the beginning of an instructional unit to enable the teacher to evaluate subjectively the students' initial status without using valuable teaching time for or unnerving students with formal testing. When an early test is necessary, however, the directions must be quite clear and performance hazards eliminated. Moreover, it is a wasteful practice to measure students at the beginning of a semester and then fail to follow through by identifying specific weaknesses, prescribing certain activities to overcome the deficiencies, and then using the prescription.

Measurement and Evaluation Should Be Conducted in a Professional Manner. In measurement programs, testing conditions must be exactly alike for all students within the group to ensure reliability and validity, since a change in conditions may produce different results. If a teacher attempts to motivate some students during a test with words of encouragement or special information, he or she should treat all students in the same manner. This also means that test directions should be explicit and be rigidly followed to ensure accurate scores. Performances can vary greatly as a result of special instructions, goals, and conditions (Johnson and Nelson 1967; Nelson 1978).

Measurement and Evaluation Should Be Conducted by Trained Personnel. When possible, well-trained experienced personnel should provide the leadership for developing comprehensive measurement and evaluation programs. Through such leadership, the measurement and evaluation process can be upgraded in any program. Moreover, teachers must constantly strive to improve the tests and other measuring instruments and evaluate their usefulness in the educational process. Since no measurement is infallible, *we must recognize that the person who is doing the evaluating, not the measuring device*

itself, is the key to successful evaluation. A test with reported high validity and reliability may be worthless if it is not administered and interpreted correctly. Thus, in matters of measurement and evaluation, well-trained leadership can greatly facilitate the effectiveness of any program.

Measurement and Evaluation Use Criterion-Referenced Standards and Norm-Referenced Standards. Evaluation is the process of giving meaning to measurement by judging it against some standard. Two commonly used standards today are criterion referenced and norm referenced.

Criterion-referenced standards are concerned with the degree to which a student achieves a level of competence; they require that the competence level be defined in explicit terms. For example, a criterion-referenced standard for sixth grade girls might be the ability to perform 35 bent-knee sit-ups in 2 min. Students who meet this standard are judged to have achieved an acceptable level of abdominal strength and endurance. Thus, a criterion-referenced standard is useful when it is desirable that all students achieve a given level of competence. Such a standard is frequently used in formative evaluation, whereby the student is given information as to the degree of mastery at various points in the instructional unit.

Norm-referenced standards are based on statistical procedures and are used to judge individual performance in relation to performance of others in the same population. For example, a norm-referenced standard might be that a student who performs 55 sit-ups in 2 min is at the 95th percentile. In other words, 55 sit-ups is a greater number than that performed by 95% of students of the same age and sex. Norm-referenced standards are most often used in summative evaluation to indicate the relative degree of achievement of the students at the end of the unit.

In using the criterion-referenced standard, the teacher must establish realistic levels of competence that most students can reasonably attain within various time limits during the course. If this is done, this type of standard provides a motivationally and educationally sound approach to achievement. A limitation of this standard is, however, that the teacher knows only when students have met an acceptable performance level—not how high a level they could actually attain. Thus, in using the criterion-referenced standard, the teacher should also try to motivate students to strive for the highest possible level for their age and sex.

Measurement and Evaluation Should Be Used for Both Formative and Summative Purposes. A skillful teacher uses formative evaluation throughout the instructional unit. It promotes high levels of learning among all students and pinpoints areas in which further development and learning are needed. It is usually based on specific objectives (such as to hold a headstand for 5 sec) and uses criterion-referenced standards. Summative evaluation is used to determine whether broad objectives have been achieved and the degree of achievement. Thus, norm-referenced standards are usually involved in summative evaluation.

The most effective evaluation program includes both formative and summative procedures. This ensures that some measurement is used throughout the unit of instruction to facilitate the learning process.

Measurement and Evaluation Consider the Whole Individual and the Environment. Evaluation should be interpreted in terms of the whole individual in relation to the environment. A student who has done exceptionally well for several months but suddenly begins to do poorly owing to circumstances beyond his or her control (such as emotional distress over the death of a family member) should be evaluated on a different basis from students whose performances have been consistent throughout the semester. For example, the student might be given more time to complete course requirements and perhaps a second chance on the first one or two assignments done poorly. One must remember that a test is not infallible, and test results must be viewed in light of the total evaluation process.

Measurement and Evaluation in the Physical Education Program Must Function Soundly Within the School Philosophy. The physical education program must make every attempt to function harmoniously within the educational philosophy of the school and on an equal basis with other subjects in its conducting of a sound measurement and evaluation program. Not uncommonly, however, a school's philosophy is at variance with a teacher's personal philosophy.

When this happens, it is best for the teacher to seek ways to resolve the conflict. Three possibilities are the effecting of a change in the school philosophy, the modification of personal philosophy, or a move to a different school with a more compatible philosophy. Since school boards consist of representatives of the general public, teachers and administrators must attempt to educate the board members concerning policies and procedures that reflect a sound philosophical basis in a democratic society.

BIBLIOGRAPHY

AAHPERD, *Skills Test Manual: Basketball*. Reston, Va.: AAHPERD, 1966.

Bloom, B. S., et al., *A Taxonomy of Education Objectives: Handbook 1, The Cognitive Domain*. New York: David McKay, 1956.

Bloom, B. S., et al., *Handbook on Formative and Summative Evaluation of Student Learning*. New York: McGraw-Hill, 1971.

Bucher, C. A., *Administration of Physical Education and Athletic Programs*. 7th ed. St. Louis: C. V. Mosby, 1977.

Jewett, A. E., et al., "Educational Change Through a Taxonomy for Writing Physical Education Objectives." *Quest* 16:32–38, 1971.

Johnson, B. L., and J. K. Nelson, "The Effects of Applying Different Motivational Techniques During Training and in Testing Upon Strength Performance." *Research Quarterly* 38:630–636, December 1967.

May, R. E., "A Dean of Education Speaks." *JOHPER* 36:624–626, September 1965.

McCloy, C. H., and N. D. Young, *Tests and Measurements in Health and Physical Education*. New York: Appleton-Century-Crofts, 1954.

Nash, J. B., *Physical Education: Interpretations and Objectives*. New York: A. S. Barnes, 1948.

Nelson, J. K., "Motivating Effects of the Use of Norms and Goals with Endurance Tests." *Research Quarterly* 49:317–321, 1978.

Nelson, J. K., and J. J. Dorociak, "Reducing Administration Time While Improving Reliability and Validity of Fitness Tests." *JOHPERD* 53(1): 63–65, 1982.

CHAPTER 2

A BRIEF HISTORICAL OVERVIEW OF MEASUREMENT AND EVALUATION

OBJECTIVES

After reading this chapter, the student should be able to:

1. Identify the major areas of measurement in physical education
2. Appreciate the contributions of individuals and organizations to measurement and evaluation in physical education
3. Recognize the names of early leaders in the various areas of measurement in physical education

Knowing the efforts of predecessors in one's own professional field of study not only allows a better understanding of measurement and evaluation but also prepares one for professional meetings in which the names of historical figures and prominent tests are often mentioned. The brief history presented here includes some of the important contributions in specific areas of measurement and evaluation.

PHYSICAL FITNESS MEASUREMENT

Physical fitness has always been one of the foremost goals of physical education. The measurement of physical fitness and methods of developing fitness have been topics of national concern through the years. The medical doctors who constituted the early leadership in the profession were initially attracted to physical education because of their interest in physical fitness. It was mutual interest in physical fitness and other physical measurements that prompted the meetings leading to the formation of our national organization, now known as the American Alliance for Health, Physical Education, Recreation and Dance (AAHPERD).[1]

A great deal of credit must be given to the Turner societies in the 1800s for promoting an interest in the development and maintenance of physical fitness through gymnastic exercise programs. The Turners were mainly German immigrants who fled to the United States in the 1840s because of political pressures in Europe. Turnvereins were established throughout much of the East and the Midwest. These societies took advantage of every opportunity to sell their programs of gymnastics and physical fitness to the schools. As a result of their efforts, gymnastics and developmental exercises made up the greater part of the physical education programs around the nation until the early 1900s. Then team games became increasingly popular, and these and lighter

---

1. This organization formerly was called the American Alliance for Health, Physical Education and Recreation (AAHPER). In 1980, its name was changed to reflect its growing involvement in dance. The abbreviation AAHPERD will be used for all references to the organization in this text, regardless of its actual name at the time.

recreational-type activities began to crowd out the more formal physical development programs.

Draft statistics in World War I focused national attention on the need for increased physical fitness of American youth. Consequently, the states passed laws making physical education mandatory in the schools. In the 1920s and 1930s, the natural play movement spearheaded by Wood, Hetherington, and others brought about a decrease in emphasis on physical fitness, and again it was war that generated national concern over the need for fitness. During World War II, the Army, Navy, and Air Force established their own physical fitness test batteries, and considerable research was done on this subject. After the war, the nation relaxed again, only to be jarred awake by the startling results of the Kraus–Weber test, which showed American children to be decidedly inferior to European children in minimum muscular fitness. As a result, in 1956 President Eisenhower established the President's Council on Youth Fitness, which was to focus national attention on the need for physical fitness programs in the schools.

In 1958, the AAHPERD Youth Fitness Test with accompanying national norms was developed for boys and girls in grades 5 through 12. In 1965 and again in 1975, the test went through revisions, but it never escaped the criticism of many researchers who desired a separation of motor fitness items from physical fitness items.

Recent attempts at physical fitness test construction have drawn closer to the concept that a physical fitness test should include the components of strength, flexibility, muscular endurance, cardiovascular endurance, and body composition. The AAHPERD Health Related Physical Fitness Test (1980) meets these criteria except for a strength test item. Background work on the five components, as well as on several others, is discussed in this chapter. The reader is referred to Chapter 11 for further discussion of physical fitness and the AAHPERD Health Related Physical Fitness Test battery.

Anthropometrics and Body Composition Measurement

Most of the earliest research in physical education dealt with the structure and proportions of the body (anthropometrics). Measurements are known to have been made even in ancient India and Greece. Not until the mid 1800s, however, did researchers begin reporting their data. In 1860, Cromwell completed a study on the growth of schoolchildren and discovered that boys were shorter and lighter than girls during the approximate ages of 11 to 14 (Baldwin 1914). Edward Hitchcock, of Amherst College, is generally recognized as the leading figure in anthropometric testing between 1860 and 1880 (Bovard et al. 1950).

Following up on the earlier work of Cromwell and Hitchcock were D. A. Sargent and D. W. Hastings. Sargent's work was noteworthy in the 1880s and the 1890s; it involved strength measurements of men and women college students at Harvard.

Other contributions made in anthropometrics include McCloy's Classification Index, which is based on age, height, and weight; Wetzel's grid technique, which uses age, height, and weight measures to plot and evaluate growth and development on a grid with seven physique channels; Pryor's width–weight tables, which use the width of the pelvic crest, the width of the chest, and standing height to determine normal weight; and Meredith's height–weight chart, which identifies normal and abnormal growth patterns.

Concerning the establishment of body types, several contributors should be mentioned. E. Kretschmer, one of the earliest workers in this field, classified individuals into asthenic (thin), athletic (muscular), and pyknic (fat) categories, and attempted to relate body type to personality. W. H. Sheldon and associates, influenced by Kretschmer, refined the latter's system of classification and Sheldon began a life's work of studying the ramifications of somatotypes. Sheldon's three basic body components were termed ectomorphy (characterized by leanness), mesomorphy (characterized by muscular hardness), and endomorphy (characterized by heavy softness). F. A. Sills introduced a fourth somatotype called omomorphy, characterized by a V-type build with large shoulders and chest and small hips and legs. T. K. Cureton, Jr. (1947) devised a simple physique rating scale that could be used by the nonexpert in establishing the general physique type on the basis of subjective rating of external fat, muscular, and skeletal development.

More recently, emphasis has shifted toward measurement and evaluation of percent of body fat in relation to muscle mass. John Piscopo and James Baley (1980) have identified some anthropometric and body composition characteristics that influence fitness and motor performance. Various skin fold calipers have been manufactured and used in the estimation of body fat, with the Lange skin fold caliper and Flick Fat-O-Meter being widely used in the United States. A more sophisticated measuring technique, underwater (hydrostatic) weighing, continues to be regarded as the most accurate measure of body composition. With skin fold measures being added to AAHPERD's Health Related Physical Fitness Test, the evaluation of body composition has been included as an established component of physical fitness.

Cardiovascular Endurance Measurement

The measurement and evaluation of cardiovascular endurance have become a major part of physical fitness testing. Since the popularization of aerobics by Kenneth Cooper, jogging, swimming, and cycling tests for time or distance have been widely used. Moreover, serious interest prevails in the simple measures of resting pulse rate, training heart rate, and recovery pulse rate in gaining personal information regarding the effect of cardiovascular training on the body.

Early studies and tests of cardiovascular function were perhaps stimulated by the work of Angelo Mosso, an Italian physiologist, in 1884. Mosso noted that an efficient circulatory system improved the performance of muscles.

In 1905, W. C. Crampton developed a rating scale for the changes that occur in cardiac rate and arterial pressure when a person assumes an erect position from a lying-down position as an indication of general physical condition. This test influenced the work of other investigators, including McCurdy, Meylan, Foster, Barach, and Barringer (Bovard et al. 1950; Burton-Opitz 1922; McCloy 1930). In 1920, E. C. Schneider reported findings concerning a rather comprehensive test that had been used to assess fatigue and physical condition. The test was used to determine the physical state of aviators in World War I by the Air Force (Bovard et al. 1950).

In 1925, J. M. Campbell published a test involving breath holding and recovery after exercise. This preliminary study later developed into the Campbell Pulse Ratio Test. W. W. Tuttle, influenced by Campbell's work, developed the Tuttle Pulse Ratio Test and conducted a considerable amount of cardiovascular research during the 1930s.

In 1943, the Harvard Step Test was developed by Lucien Brouha and associates to determine the general capacity of the body to adapt and recover from work. The work consisted of stepping up and down on a bench at a prescribed cadence. Pulse rate was taken at set intervals after exercise to measure recovery. This test has been extensively used in testing and research programs.

In addition to McCurdy, Brouha, and Tuttle, other outstanding contributors to cardiovascular research are Cureton, L. Larson, P. Karpovich (Bovard et al. 1950), and C. McCloy, to name but a few. In recent years, cardiovascular research and measurement have become somewhat more sophisticated with the increased use of laboratory instrumentation for the analysis of circulatory and respiratory responses under various test conditions. For example, the measurement of maximal oxygen consumption has become routine in physical education laboratories.

Cooper did extensive research in an attempt to establish a rating scale for the relative values of activities in terms of circulorespiratory conditioning. His research showed the importance of such activities as running, swimming, cycling, walking, handball, basketball, squash, and others in the development of circulorespiratory endurance. Cooper recommended a simple 12-minute run–walk scale for people to evaluate their own condition.

Flexibility Measurement

Formal tests of flexibility did not appear in the professional literature until 1941, when Cureton published a battery of practical performance-oriented tests that subsequently became widely used. Later, McCloy changed the tests from absolute, or performance-oriented, tests to relative tests. All of Cureton's tests, with the exception of the ankle flexibility test, were linear measures. The ankle flexibility test relied on the use of a protractor to secure the measure in terms of degrees of rotation.

Jack Leighton developed the flexometer in 1942. This instrument evolved from a modification of the goniometer, which made possible the measurement of many joint movements.

The popularity of the hip flexion exercise, in which students attempt to keep knees straight and touch fingers to toes, was evidenced by the development of several test modifications. Cureton's 1930 version, which he called the forward-bending-of-trunk test, was followed by the Scott–French bobbing test, which involved a bench and attached scale so that students could reach lower than their toes. In 1952, Katherine Wells and Evelyn Dillon published a sit-and-reach test with a horizontal, elevated scale that provided scores in negative and positive units. In 1966, B. L. Johnson modified the Wells and Dillon test to result in all positive scores by merely lining a student's heels on the 15-in. mark of a yardstick and having the student reach as far down the stick as possible. Specific directions and local norms were later established, ranging from as low as 4 in. to as high as 32 in. This version, the modified sit-and-reach test, was subsequently published without permission in *The Official YMCA Physical Fitness Handbook* (Myers 1975) and is now frequently and erroneously referred to as the YMCA trunk flexion test (Gooding 1976; Pollock 1976).

Four sports and dance-oriented flexibility tests were also developed in 1966 (Johnson 1966). The tests related to gymnastics, certain types of dance, and swimming. In 1972, seeking to attain more exact measures, B. L. Johnson developed a testing instrument called a flexomeasure. The device was then modified for use with seven different flexibility tests in 1977. Other contributions may be found in Chapter 6.

Strength Measurement

D. A. Sargent provided the chief impetus for strength measurement during the early years of the profession. The dynamometer and the spirometer were developed and used for testing in Sargent's intercollegiate strength test (Bovard et al. 1950). The universal dynamometer, developed in 1894 by J. H. Kellogg, was used to test the static or isometric strength of a large number of muscles. Then, in 1915, E. G. Martin developed a resistance strength test to measure the strength of muscle groups with a flat-faced-type spring balance (Bovard et al. 1950). In 1925, F. R. Rogers refined the intercollegiate strength test and validated it as a measure of general athletic ability. Rogers also created the physical fitness index (PFI), and devised a new statistical technique for determining norms of physical achievement (Bovard et al. 1950). He later showed how his PFI program could be adapted to the physical needs of the individual. McCloy developed a strength test that he thought was an improvement over the Rogers' strength test in terms of administration, scoring, and validity. This test left out the lung capacity test, which McCloy did not consider a strength measure (McCloy and Young 1954). Chinups and dips, which were items in Sargent's, Rogers', and McCloy's strength tests, were not exclu-

sively strength items, but were muscular endurance items as well. Thus, only three items of these early strength tests were pure measures of strength—back strength, leg strength, and grip strength.

In 1928, Edwin R. Elbel found that strength could be increased by short static (isometric) contraction exercises. However, interest in isometric exercises seemed to remain dormant for the next two decades. In fact, it was not until 1953, when the startling results of Hettinger and Muller's experiments on isometric strength training were published, that a new era in strength training began. As mentioned previously, static strength testing was not new, as evidenced by the early use of the dynamometer and the comprehensive measurement of strength by H. Harrison Clarke with the tensiometer, an instrument originally designed to measure aircraft cable tension, which Clarke adapted to measure strength of various muscle groups.

Muscular Endurance Measurement

The history of muscular endurance measurement closely parallels that of muscular strength testing. Hitchcock and Sargent compiled extensive data on muscular endurance of the arms and shoulders of college men in the latter half of the nineteenth century (Bovard et al. 1950). In 1884, Mosso invented the ergograph and helped to establish the relationship between physical condition and muscular activity. Mosso also pointed out that the body's ability to do work depends on adequate nutrition and that fatigue of one set of muscles affects others as well (Burton-Opitz 1922). In 1922, an adaptation of Mosso's ergograph made it possible to study successive muscular contractions on a smoke drum. Clarke and other researchers have conducted a number of studies on the Kelso–Hellebrandt ergograph, using larger muscle groups than were used with the earlier ergograph of Mosso. Test items such as pull-ups and dips that combine both strength and endurance have been used as strength measures or muscular endurance measures or both on many physical fitness tests and motor ability tests.

MOTOR ABILITY MEASUREMENT

Motor ability measurement includes a broad range of performance abilities such as agility, balance, kinesthetic perception, power, reaction time, rhythmic coordination and dance, and speed of movement. A historical overview of measurement in these areas follows.

Agility Measurement

Agility measurement as a specific area does not have a long or extensive background. However, contributions made in this area include (1) Royal H. Burpee's test of agility (known as the Burpee test) developed in 1935 and used extensively by the Armed Services during World War II under the name "squat thrust test"; (2) McCloy's scholarly endeavors in the area of motor ability, including agility measurement (McCloy and Young 1954); (3) the analysis of agility tests by Young, Gates and Sheffield, and Sierakowski in the 1930s and 1940s, (4) agility tests modified and developed by Johnson and Nelson in the late 1960s in the form of the quadrant jump test and the LSU agility test; and (5) Kirby's SEMO agility test published in 1971.

Balance Measurement

Balance measurement is another area that does not have a long or extensive background. Ruth Bass is probably the most widely known contributor in this area, with her practical tests of static and dynamic balance published in 1939. Other practical tests were modified and developed by Johnson and Nelson in the late 1960s. Then, in the 1970s, Johnson developed the levelometer board with seven tests of static or dynamic balance or both (Johnson 1979). Some of the tests mentioned are covered in Chapter 14.

Kinesthetic Perception Measurement

Numerous studies have attempted to measure and evaluate different forms of kinesthetic perception. The study of kinesthesis has posed a special enigma to physical educators owing to the acknowledged importance of kinesthesis in physical performance and its elusiveness in resisting measurement and even definition. Special mention should be made of M. Gladys Scott for her work in this area. Other researchers who have made significant contributions are Bass, Henry, McCloy, Russell, Slater–Hammel, Wiebe, Witte, and Young. Other contributions are noted in Appendix C.

Power Measurement

Although power has been measured in athletic events through the centuries, it was not given a great deal of attention by physical educators until after Sargent's publication in 1921 of "The Physical Test of a Man." Then McCloy (1932), working with Sargent's vertical jump test, found significant correlations with the total point score in the 100-yard dash, the running high jump, the standing broad jump, and the 8-pound shot put. Other noteworthy contributors in this area were Capen and Chui, who conducted studies revealing the importance of strength gains in increasing velocity, and Bovard and Cozens, who designed the leap meter for measuring vertical jump power. In the 1960s, Glencross experimented in this area in an attempt to develop and validate tests of power. New tests of power reflecting the direction of Glencross' efforts were reported by Margaria and associates in 1966 and by Johnson in 1969.

Rhythm and Dance Measurement

This area of measurement has been plagued by a lack of experimentation for the development of objective and practical tests. While the well-known Seashore tests have been extensively used in research, they have not been practical for physical education measurement. Moreover, objective instruments for measuring rhythm have been devised but their use is not feasible for many teachers. However, special mention should be made of I. F. Waglow, Eloise Lemon, Elizabeth Sherbon, and Dudley Ashton for constructing tests that can be useful to teachers of rhythm and dance. Other contributors to this area of measurement are found in Chapter 17.

Speed and Reaction Time Measurement

Numerous studies have been conducted in physical education, psychology, and other fields on various facets of reaction time and speed of movement. Psychologists have been primarily concerned with response time as it relates to learning, whereas physical education researchers have been mainly concerned with methods of improving speed of movement and reaction time and with how these factors influence physical performance. Although a number of variables affect measurement of speed and reaction time (e.g., motivation, set, sensory discrimination, and practice), the measuring devices are generally quite precise. The leadership and research of F. M. Henry in this area of measurement are recognized as a prime factor in many of the studies that followed his work. Other contributions are found in Chapter 15.

General Motor Ability Measurement

Sargent pioneered testing in the area of general motor ability in the 1880s for the purpose of assessing athletic ability in men. In 1901, Sargent developed a test consisting of six simple exercises that were to be executed in a 30-min period without rest. Several years later, Meylan, of Columbia University, developed a comprehensive physical ability test that included running, jumping, vaulting, and climbing (Bovard et al. 1950). In 1924, J. H. McCurdy served as chairman of the National Committee on Motor Ability Tests, which established a number of such tests. In 1927, David K. Brace developed his Brace Motor Ability Test for classifying and measuring achievement. McCloy suggested that Brace's test was basically a motor educability test, and after much research, McCloy revised the Brace test in 1931 in an attempt to increase its validity as a measure of motor educability. This revision is now known as the Iowa Brace Test. In 1932, the Johnson Motor Educability Test, named after Granville Johnson, the originator of the test battery, was designed for the purpose of sectioning classes into homogeneous groups. Research revealed that it had some predictive value as a general motor educability test, particularly with regard to success in the learning of tumbling skills (Johnson and Nelson 1979). Other contributions to this area of measurement include Kenneth Hill's motor educability test for junior high school boys, Aileen Carpenter's study of motor ability and motor capacity, and Arthur Adams' sports type motor educability test. McCloy combined size, maturity, power, motor educability, and large muscle speed into a general motor capacity test that sought to assess innate potential in the area of motor ability. This was undoubtedly the most comprehensive effort to predict potential for physical achievement in a fashion similar to the way intelligence tests are used. A number of other motor ability tests have been devised, but space does not permit adequate discussion here. This area of measurement is covered in Chapter 19.

Sports Skills Measurement

Among the earliest reported sports skills tests were the Athletic Badge tests devised in 1913 by the Playground and Recreation Association of America. The test items pertained to the sports of volleyball, tennis, baseball, and basketball. In 1918, Hetherington developed tests for the California decathlon, which made use of a graduated score plan (Bovard et al. 1950). In 1924, Brace reported a six-item skill test in basketball (Bovard et al. 1950), and a year later Beall completed an experimental study in tennis to determine a battery of tests for that sport. Increasing interest in testing of sports skills was evident in the 1930s, and throughout the following 30 years, many fine tests were proposed, developed, and used by physical educators. However, for many years a need had often been expressed for nationally standardized tests. This lack of national standards had frequently been cited as one of physical education's biggest failings. In response to this need, AAHPERD initiated a sports skills test project in 1959 to determine standards for at least 15 sport activities. This project began under the direction of the Research Council of AAHPERD, with Brace serving as test consultant and Sills as chairman. The resulting tests and norms have made it possible to evaluate skill performance more effectively, bring about greater motivation, and improve teaching. An AAHPERD committee is now charged with the task of revising the skills tests and developing new ones. Many of these tests are presented in Chapter 16.

OTHER MEASUREMENT AREAS

Several measurement areas are distinctly different from the components and abilities previously mentioned. These include knowledge (cognitive), posture, and social qualities and attitudes.

Knowledge Measurement

Among the earliest published sports knowledge tests was a basketball knowledge test published by J. G. Bliss in 1929. Since that date, numerous sports knowledge tests have been constructed and published. Unlike other subject areas, standardized tests have not been available on a commercial basis; consequently, physical educators have had to prepare their own or locate tests from the literature to duplicate. Outstanding contributors to the literature in the area of sports knowledge tests are Esther French, Catherine Snell, Katherine Ley, Gail Hennis, Rosemary Fisher, and Jack Hewitt. Further contributions and references for this area of measurement are in Chapter 21.

Posture Measurement

The earliest contributions made in posture measurement were in the form of records and anthropometric charts by Hitchcock, Sargent, J. W. Seaver, Luther H. Gulick, Thomas D. Wood, Delphine Hanna, and others. During the 1930s and 1940s, a great deal of interest was shown in developing methods of measuring and evaluating posture. Studies were presented that reported the use of such instruments as the Cureton–Gunby conformateur, Korbs' comparograph, the posturemeter, the scoliometer, x-ray machine, pedograph, camera, and rating scales. Difficulty in devising practical, objective instruments for assessing posture, plus the lack of definite criteria as to what good posture should entail for different individuals, resulted in a drop in the number of reported studies on the topic in the 1950s. Nevertheless, articles on posture have continued to appear in the professional literature, indicating a constant concern with the importance of good posture.

Social Qualities and Attitudes Measurement

McCloy focused attention on the measurement of social qualities by physical educators in an article that appeared during the first year of publication of the *Research Quarterly,* 1930. In 1936, O'Neel and Blanchard published separate behavior rating scales for use in physical education. Despite a dearth of objective measurement in this area, an imposing number of studies have been published and new measuring instruments have been reported in the last 30 years. Physical educators have long recognized that continuous attempts should be made to measure social qualities if social development is to be one of physical education's objectives. The work of J. L. Moreno and Helen Jennings in sociometric measurement has been of great value to physical educators as well as counselors and other teachers. The late Charles C. Cowell made splendid contributions to measurement of social qualities in physical education. Considerable progress has been made in attitude assessment; Carlos Wear, Gerald Kenyon, and others have been prominent in this area.

CONCLUSIONS

Physical education has been extremely fortunate to have excellent and inspiring leadership in the areas of research and measurement, and the quantity and quality of research in physical education have continued to improve.

Scientific endeavors in all fields have had rather crude beginnings. To confirm this phenomenon, we need only recall the primitive practices in early medicine, the simple but awkward designs of the early automobiles, and the hilarious first attempts of men to fly. Yet, when one considers the tremendous advances that have been made in these fields in the last quarter of a century, the prognosis for progress in evaluation in physical education should indeed be encouraging. Physical education is a relatively new field. This is attested to by the fact that many of the persons named in this chapter as being early leaders in the area of measurement are still active today or only recently have retired or died.

The history of measurement in physical education reveals that in some areas, research efforts have not been reported for 20 or 30 years. The profession must continue to seek new and better ways of measuring those traits that physical educators have already had some success in measuring and, at the same time, must make renewed and vigorous efforts to assess those qualities that heretofore have baffled attempts at measurement.

With new and more precise measuring devices, improved methods of analyzing data, increased emphasis on research in graduate study, and the fact that more persons are seeking advanced degrees, the future indeed looks bright.

BIBLIOGRAPHY

AAHPERD Health Related Physical Fitness Test Manual. Reston, Va.: AAHPERD, 1980.

Baldwin, B. T., *Physical Growth and School Progress.* Washington, D.C.: Bureau of Education Bulletin No. 10, 1914, p. 143.

Beall, E., "Essential Qualities in Certain Aspects of Physical Education With Ways of Measuring and Developing Same." Unpublished master's thesis, University of California, 1925.

Blanchard, B. E., "A Behavior Frequency Rating Scale for the Measurement of Character and Personality in Physical Education Classroom Situations." *Research Quarterly* 6:56–66, May 1936.

Bliss, J. G., *Basketball*. Philadelphia: Lea & Febiger, 1929.

Bovard, J. F., and F. W. Cozens, *The Leap Meter: An Investigation Into the Possibilities of the Sargent Test as a Measure of General Athletic Ability*. Eugene, Ore.: University of Oregon Press, 1928.

Bovard, J. F., et al., *Tests and Measurements in Physical Education*. Philadelphia: W. B. Saunders, 1950.

Brouha, L., "The Step Test: A Simple Method of Measuring Physical Fitness for Muscular Work in Young Men." *Research Quarterly* 14:31–35, March 1943.

Burton-Opitz, R., "Tests of Physical Efficiency." *American Physical Education Review* 27:153–159, April 1922.

Capen, E. K., "The Effect of Systematic Weight Training on Power, Strength, and Endurance." *Research Quarterly* 21:83–93, May 1950.

Chui, E., "The Effect of Systematic Weight Training on Athletic Power." *Research Quarterly* 21:188–194, October 1950.

Cooper, K. H., *The New Aerobics*. New York: Bantam Books, 1970.

Cowell, C. C., "Validating an Index of Social Adjustment for High School Use." *Research Quarterly* 29:7–18, March 1958.

Crampton, W. C., "A Test of Condition." *Medical News* 88:529, September 1905.

Cureton, T. K., Jr., "Objective Test of Swimming." Unpublished master's thesis, Springfield College, Springfield, Mass, 1930.

——— , "Flexibility as an Aspect of Physical Fitness." *Research Quarterly Supplement* 12:388–390, May 1941.

——— , *Physical Fitness Appraisal and Guidance*. St. Louis: C. V. Mosby, 1947.

Fisher, R. B., "Tests in Selected Physical Education Service Courses in a College." Microcarded doctoral dissertation, State University of Iowa, Iowa City, 1950, p. 72.

French, E., "The Construction of Knowledge Tests in Selected Professional Courses in Physical Education." *Research Quarterly* 14:406–424, 1943.

Gates, D. D., and R. P. Sheffield, "Tests of Direction as Measurements of Different Kinds of Motor Ability in Boys of the Seventh, Eighth, and Ninth Grades." *Research Quarterly* 11:136–147, October 1940.

Glencross, D. J., "The Nature of the Vertical Jump Test and the Standing Broad Jump." *Research Quarterly* 37:353–359, October 1966.

Gooding, J., "Measure Your Own Physical Quotient." *Reader's Digest,* October 1976, pp. 178–182.

Hennis, G. M., "Construction of Knowledge Tests in Selected Physical Education Activities for College Women." *Research Quarterly* 27:301–309, October 1956.

Hettinger, T., and E. A. Muller, "Muskelleistung und Muskeltraining." *Arbeitsphysiologie* 15:111–126, 1953.

Hewitt, J. E., "Hewitt's Comprehensive Tennis Knowledge Test." *Research Quarterly* 35:147–155, May 1964.

Jennings, H., *Sociometry in Group Relations*. Washington, D.C.: American Council on Education, 1948, 1959.

Jensen, C. R., and C. Hirst, *Measurement in Physical Education and Athletics*. New York: Macmillan, 1980, p. 14.

Johnson, B. L., "Practical Tests of Flexibility." Unpublished study, 1966, available from Brown and Littleman, Portland, Tex.

——— , "The Establishment of a Vertical Arm Pull Test (Work)." *Research Quarterly* 40:237–239, March 1969.

——— , *Practical Flexibility Measurement With the Flexomeasure*. Portland, Tex.: Brown and Littleman, 1977.

——— , *Balance Challenger Test Booklet*. Portland, Tex.: Brown and Littleman, 1979.

Johnson, B. L., and J. K. Nelson, *Practical Measurements for Evaluation in Physical Education*. Minneapolis: Burgess, 1979.

Kretschmer, E., *Physique and Character*. New York: Harcourt Brace Jovanovich, 1925.

Leighton, J., "A Simple Objective and Reliable Measure of Flexibility." *Research Quarterly* 13:205–216, May 1942.

Ley, K. L., "Constructing Objective Test Items to Measure High School Levels of Achievement in Selected Physical Education Activities." Microcarded doctoral dissertation, University of Iowa, Iowa City, 1960, p. 25.

Margaria, R., et al., "Measurement of Muscular Power (Anaerobics) in Man." *Journal of Applied Physiology* 21:1662–1664, September 1966.

McCloy, C. H., "Athletic Handicapping by Age, Height, and Weight." *American Physical Education Review* 32:635–642, November 1927.

——— , "Character Building Through Physical Education." *Research Quarterly* 1:41, October 1930.

——— , "Recent Studies in the Sargent Jump." *Research Quarterly* 3:235, May 1932.

——— , and N. D. Young, *Tests and Measurements in Health and Physical Education*. New York: Appleton-Century-Crofts, 1954.

McCurdy, J. H., "Adolescent Changes in Heart Rate and Blood Pressure." *American Physical Education Review* 15:421, June 1910.

Meredith, H. V., *Physical Growth Records for Boys and Physical Growth Records for Girls*. Washington, D.C.: National Education Association, 1947.

Moreno, J. L., "Who Shall Survive? A New Problem to the Problem of Human Relationships." Washington, D.C.: Nervous and Mental Disease Publishing Co., 1934.

Myers, C. R., *The Official YMCA Physical Fitness Handbook*. New York: Popular Library, 1975, p. 103.

O'Neel, E. W., "A Behavior Frequency Rating Scale for the Measurement of Character and Personality in High School Physical Education Classes for Boys." *Research Quarterly* 7:67, May 1936.

Piscopo, J., and J. A. Baley, *Kinesiology: The Science of Movement*. New York: John Wiley, 1981, pp. 120–121.

Pollock, M., "An Aerobics Fitness Program for Adults." *JOPER* 47:15–17, November-December 1976.

Pryor, H. B., *Width–Weight Tables*. Stanford, Calif.: Stanford University Press, 1940.

Reilly, F. J., *New Rational Athletics for Boys and Girls*. Boston: D. C. Heath, 1916, p. 191.

Sargent, D. A., "Twenty Years' Progress in Efficiency Tests." *American Physical Education Review* 18:452, October 1913.

——— , "The Physical Test of a Man." *American Physical Education Review* 26:188–194, April 1921.

Schneider, E. C., "A Cardiovascular Rating as a Measure of Physical Fatigue and Efficiency." *JAMA* 74:1507, May 1920.

Scott, M. G., and E. French, *Evaluation in Physical Education*. St. Louis: C. V. Mosby, 1950.

Seaver, J. W., *Anthropometry and Physical Examination*. Meriden, Conn.: Curtis-Way, 1909, pp. 14–15.

Sheldon, W. H., et al., *The Varieties of Human Physique*. New York: Harper, 1940.

Sierakowski, F., "A Study of Change of Direction Tests for High School Girls." Master's thesis, State University of Iowa, Iowa City, 1940.

Sills, F. A., "A Factor Analysis of Somatotypes and Their Relationship to Achievement in Motor Skills." *Research Quarterly* 21:424–437, December 1950.

Wells, K. F., and E. K. Dillon, "The Sit and Reach—A Test of Back and Leg Flexibility." *Research Quarterly* 23:118, March 1952.

Wetzel, N. C., "Physical Fitness in Terms of Physique, Development, and Basal Metabolism." *JAMA* 116:1187–1195, March 1941.

Young, K. E., "An Analytic Study of the Tests of Change of Direction." Master's thesis, State University of Iowa, Iowa City, 1937.

CHAPTER 3

BASIC STATISTICAL TECHNIQUES

OBJECTIVES

After reading this chapter, the student should be able to:

1. Define what is meant by the terms *measures of central tendency* and *measures of variability,* and give two examples of each

2. Construct a frequency polygon for a set of scores

3. Convert raw scores to percentiles and *T* scores

4. Explain what is meant by positive and negative correlation, and interpret the meaningfulness of a correlation in terms of percentage of variation

5. Understand the concept of the *t* test and analysis of variance with regard to comparisons among groups

6. Understand the difference between interclass (*r*) and intraclass (*R*) methods of determining reliability

7. Follow the formulas to calculate the various values presented in this chapter

---

Two essential steps in evaluation are the analysis and the presentation of the results of tests and measurements. Physical educators can spend hours carefully and skillfully measuring, but if they are unable to organize and analyze the data collected, they cannot effectively use the information to evaluate the program. This brings us to the subject of statistical analysis.

Mention of the word *statistics* usually causes dismay on the part of the prospective teacher. There may be a number of reasons for this attitude—a poor background in mathematics, intimidation by the terminology and formulas, and so on—but whatever the reason, the situation is unfortunate. When faced with the part of teacher preparation that includes statistics, many students simply endure the course and are quite sure that they will never use the computations in their teaching. Thus, they enter the field minus a valuable tool.

With the recalcitrant student in mind, we will attempt to present this portion of the evaluation process as simply and as practicably as possible. We will use what has often been called the cookbook approach, wherein students need not understand the derivation of the formulas, which may be likened to recipes. Instead, they merely follow the steps to achieve the end product. Our objective is to give students the confidence to use the basic statistical tools required for effective evaluation. Basic knowledge of statistics and of statistical techniques is useful in the following ways:

1. It is needed for the conduct of research and the reporting of results.

2. It enables the teacher to better understand and profit from professional literature, especially research publications.

3. It is needed for evaluation of available tests on a scientific basis.

4. It makes test data more meaningful and aids in the understanding and interpretation of scores.

5. It can be of considerable help in the grading process.

6. It is necessary for test construction.

This chapter is divided into four major parts. Part I, Fundamentals of Statistics, includes basic concepts, symbols, definitions, and the calculation of measures of central tendency and variability. Part II, Statistical Techniques for the Teacher, covers techniques for making graphs, the development of percentile and T-score norms, and the calculation and interpretation of correlation. The title of the third part, Basic Techniques for Test Construction and Research, may be misleading in that the section makes no attempt to provide comprehensive coverage of statistics for all kinds of test construction and research. It deals only with basic tools such as correlation and prediction, t tests, and analysis of variance. The last part is an introduction to use of the computer in measurement and evaluation.

Sample problems are given at the end of the chapter.

I. FUNDAMENTALS OF STATISTICS

Before we discuss fundamental statistical concepts, we will identify a few terms.

BASIC TERMS

STATISTICS.   A means by which a set of data may be described and interpreted in a meaningful manner; also a method by which data may be analyzed and inferences and conclusions drawn

POPULATION.   All of the possible subjects within a defined group, for example, all the tenth grade boys in a particular high school (or the whole nation, for that matter)

SAMPLE.   A part of a population. In the population example, a sample could be a selected group of the tenth grade boys from a particular school

RANDOM SAMPLE.   A sample in which every member of the specified population has an equal chance of being selected

UNGROUPED DATA.   Raw scores presented as they were recorded, no attempt being made to arrange them into a more meaningful or convenient form

GROUPED DATA.   Scores that have been arranged in some manner such as from high to low or into classes or categories to give more meaning to the data or to facilitate further calculations

FREQUENCY DISTRIBUTION.   A method of grouping data; a table that presents the raw scores or intervals of scores and the frequencies with which the raw scores occur

UNGROUPED VERSUS GROUPED DATA

In the past in most educational statistics textbooks, the major emphasis was on the use of grouped data, and certainly there are still some advantages in working with frequency distributions. Before the age of calculators, grouped scores were generally faster to use even though the procedures were indirect and complicated. Today, however, the use of pocket calculators is widespread among students from grade school through graduate study. A number of inexpensive calculators are available that provide the mathematical functions required by the average physical education teacher. Consequently, the frequency distribution has greatly diminished in importance. In keeping with this change, practically all of the statistical techniques in this text will involve ungrouped data and the so-called computer methods of computation.

MEASURES OF CENTRAL TENDENCY

One of the first questions students ask on seeing their own score is, "What was the average?" They ask this unaware that they are now dealing in statistics. They merely want to know how they stand in relation to the rest of the group. Even without a formal course in statistics, they know from past school experiences that there usually are a few high scores, a few low scores, and a lot of middle scores. The average tells them how most of the class did. This, then, is a measure of central tendency. It is a single score that best represents all the scores. The three basic measures of central tendency are the mean, the median, and the mode.

The Mean

The mean is simply the arithmetic average. It is computed by adding all the scores and then dividing by the number of scores involved. The symbol for the mean of a population is μ, and for a sample, $\overline{X}$. The mean is by far the most commonly used measure of central tendency and, for the most part, the most reliable. The main weakness of the mean is that, with a small sample, extreme scores have a misleading effect. In the following group of scores the mean is 10, and it is representative of the group:

$$
\begin{array}{c}
12 \\
11 \\
10 \\
9 \\
\underline{8} \\
\end{array}
\quad \overline{X} = \frac{\Sigma X}{N} = \frac{50}{5} = 10
$$

$\Sigma X^1 = 50$

However, if we change the highest score from 12 to 30 in this group of scores, the mean becomes 13.6, which raises the measure of central tendency considerably.

$$
\begin{array}{c}
30 \\
11 \\
10 \\
9 \\
\underline{8} \\
\end{array}
\quad \overline{X} = \frac{\Sigma X}{N} = \frac{68}{5} = 13.6
$$

$\Sigma X = 68$

The mean of 13.6 is not representative of the group, since it is higher than every score but one. Although this example may be a bit extreme, it illustrates the point that one should always consider the number of cases and look at the data, rather than blindly trust statistics. To be a good measure of central tendency, the mean should be in the middle of the scores.

The Median

The median is that point in the distribution at which 50% of the scores lie above it and 50% lie below it. In other words, it is the midpoint, or 50th percentile. In calculating the median, one must put the scores in order from high to low, then calculate the point that separates the upper

and lower halves. This point is calculated by use of the formula $(N + 1)/2$. (This point is the *position* of the median, not the median itself.) If the point is between two scores, one obtains it by calculating the average of the two scores. For example, we have the eight scores 49, 58, 56, 49, 55, 46, 41, 53. We first put them in order:

$$
\begin{array}{l}
58 \\
56 \\
55 \\
53 \\
49 \\
49 \\
46 \\
41 \\
\end{array}
\quad \leftarrow 4.5\text{th score}
$$

$$
\begin{array}{l}
\text{Position of the median} \\
= \dfrac{N + 1}{2} \\
= \dfrac{8 + 1}{2} \\
= \dfrac{9}{2} \\
= 4.5\text{th score}
\end{array}
$$

The score value for the median thus lies between scores 53 and 49, so we compute it by averaging the two scores: $53 + 49/2 = 51$. Hence, 51 is that point above which and below which lie 50% of the scores.

Extreme scores do not greatly affect the median. Using the same five scores with which we demonstrated the influence of extreme scores on the mean, we find that the position is $(5 + 1)/2 = 6/2 = 3\text{rd score}$:

$$
\begin{array}{ll}
12 & 30 \\
11 & 11 \\
10 = \text{median} & 10 = \text{median} \\
9 & 9 \\
8 & 8 \\
\end{array}
$$

With a large number of scores, the mean is not influenced a great deal by extreme scores either. In fact, the median is the preferred measure of central tendency only when the scores do not conform to the normal distribution. In other words, if the scores cluster at either end of the distribution, the median may be a better central tendency measure. When scores cluster at the upper or lower ends, rather than the middle, the distribution is said to be *skewed*. We will discuss skewness later in the chapter.

The Mode

This measure of central tendency is defined as the score that occurs most frequently. It is a rough measure and is used more for description than for exact analysis. The word *mode* is sometimes used in describing fashions; it simply indicates what most people are wearing. In fact, it is probably in this context that we in physical education are most likely to have use for the mode. For example, when uniforms have to be ordered, it is valuable to know what sizes are the most prevalent.

---

1. The symbol Σ, the Greek letter *sigma*, means summation; X stands for scores; thus ΣX means the sum of scores.

To locate the mode when scores are ungrouped, the teacher needs merely to locate the score (or scores, for there may be more than one mode) that appears the most often. Because there may be more than one mode, this measure is the least reliable of the three measures of central tendency that are generally used. When data follow a typical normal curve, the mean, the median, and the mode fall at the same point.

MEASURES OF VARIABILITY

Variability may be defined as the scatter or spread of scores from a point of central tendency. When we measure the variability of a group of scores, we are determining the amount of scatter or spread in the scores. This information tells us how homogeneous or heterogeneous a group is. While two groups may have the same mean or median, they may differ considerably in variability. For example, if five students score 84, 80, 78, 75, and 73 on a test, their mean score is 78. Another group of five students score 98, 95, 78, 65, and 54, and their mean score is also 78. However, there is an obvious difference between the two groups in the variability of their scores.

The measures of variability discussed in this text are the range, standard deviation, and variance.

The Range

While the range is the simplest measure of variability, it is crude and limited in that it is completely dependent on the two most extreme scores in a group of scores. Generally speaking, a large range usually indicates a large degree of vari-

ability. The range is defined as the difference between the highest and lowest scores in a set of data. Technically, the formula is: (high score − low score) + 1. The addition of 1 is necessary to include both the highest and lowest scores within the range. Since the range considers only the two extreme scores out of the entire frequency distribution, it is a weak measure of variability.

The Standard Deviation

The standard deviation is probably the best of several measures of variability. It reflects the magnitude of the deviations of the scores from the mean.

Measures of variability augment measures of central tendency in providing more information about a group of scores. It was stated earlier that one of the first questions a student asks concerning a test is, "What is the average?" A second question is, "What is the highest (or lowest) score?" The student has learned that the range tells how the scores varied and, consequently, more about individual performance in relation to the class. However, the standard deviation is a much more precise measure of variability than the range, and it is thus frequently employed in research and measurement. The mean and standard deviation provide a great deal of information about a set of scores.

The following set of scores will be used to demonstrate the calculation of the standard deviation: 12, 8, 7, 16, 6, 2, 20, 10, 8, 1, 4, 10, 8, 6, 2. Table 3.1 shows the steps involved.

In the table the scores are ungrouped, that is, they have not been arranged in any specific order.

Table 3.1. Calculation of Mean and Standard Deviation From Ungrouped Scores

SCORE (X)	SCORE SQUARED (X^2)	CALCULATIONS
12	144	
8	64	$\text{Mean } (\overline{X}) = \dfrac{\Sigma X}{N} = \dfrac{120}{15} = 8$
7	49	
16	256	
6	36	$\text{Standard deviation } (s) = \sqrt{\dfrac{N\Sigma X^2 - (\Sigma X)^2}{N(N-1)}}$
2	4	
20	400	
10	100	$= \sqrt{\dfrac{15(1338) - (120)^2}{15(15-1)}}$
8	64	
1	1	
4	16	$= \sqrt{\dfrac{20{,}070 - 14{,}400}{15(14)}}$
10	100	
8	64	
6	36	$= \sqrt{\dfrac{5670}{210}}$
2	4	
$\Sigma X = 120$	$\Sigma X^2 = 1338$	$= \sqrt{27}$
		$= 5.2$

The steps in computing the standard deviation are as follows:

Step 1. Add the scores. The result is ΣX. When there are many numbers or when the numbers are large or both, a calculator or an adding machine is of immeasurable help.

Step 2. Square each score. Most pocket calculators simplify this process. If the calculator has a memory key, both the ΣX and the ΣX^2 can be obtained in one operation.

Step 3. Insert the data into the following formula[2]:

$$s = \sqrt{\frac{N \Sigma X^2 - (\Sigma X)^2}{N(N - 1)}}$$

To calculate the standard deviation, square root must be computed. Most calculators have square root keys. A description of the steps involved in computing square root is provided in Appendix B.

The formula just given is the so-called computer method. The standard deviation is actually the square root of the sum of the squared deviations of the scores from the mean divided by the number of scores ($N - 1$ for a sample). The formula is:

$$s = \sqrt{\frac{\Sigma X^2}{N - 1}}$$

While this may seem simpler than the first formula, it really is not. With this formula each score has to be subtracted from the mean, which is laborious when there are many scores. Moreover, the mean is usually not a whole number, so all the deviations are decimal fractions with plus and minus values. These deviations then have to be squared and summed. So, despite the longer formula with the computer method, the calculations are much simpler. With the computer method, the mean is assumed to be zero; each raw score is then that amount of deviation from zero. The correction for the assumed mean is what makes the formula longer.

The Variance

Another common measure of variability is variance. It is the standard deviation squared. It is computed as a part of analysis of variance procedures and is frequently referred to as mean square (MS). Actually, the definition of variance is "the mean of the squared deviations from the mean." The symbol for variance of a population is σ^2 and of a sample is s^2.

The Normal Curve

The normal curve is a theoretical distribution of scores based on probability. The basis for most statistical methods is the assumption of a normal distribution. The normal curve is bell shaped and symmetrical (Figure 3.1) and based on an infinite number of cases.

Statistical methods that assume the characteristics of the normal probability curve are called *parametric* methods. When data cannot be assumed to conform to a normal distribution, *nonparametric* statistical techniques are used.

Many human traits have a normal distribution, because they occur according to the laws of chance. Heredity, environment, social conditions, and other factors produce these traits. Actually, very few distributions are perfectly normal. However, if the number of cases in a distribution is sufficiently large, many of the traits measured occur in a frequency that follows the shape of the normal curve quite closely. The concept of what is normal, or average, is based on this phenomenon. For example, in a population of 10-year-old boys of a particular race and location, some boys will be very short, some very tall, and most about the same size. The same is true for strength, speed, neuromuscular skills, mental abilities, and other traits.

In the normal distribution, one standard deviation above and below the mean encompasses the middle 68.26% or approximately two thirds of the scores. Two standard deviations above and below the mean include approximately 95% of the scores, and three standard deviations account for over 99% of the distribution (Figure 3.1).

We will come back to the normal curve and its properties when we discuss standard scores.

Skewness

In many instances a set of scores will not have the normal curve shape. Because of the laws of chance, some samples can be expected to have a disproportionately large number of high scores or low scores (or both). When the scores are clustered at one or the other end of the distribution, the curve is said to be *skewed*.

Figure 3.2 illustrates *positive* skewness, in which the scores are clustered at the lower end of the

---

2. The symbol for the standard deviation of a population is the lowercase Greek letter sigma, σ, and of a sample it is s.

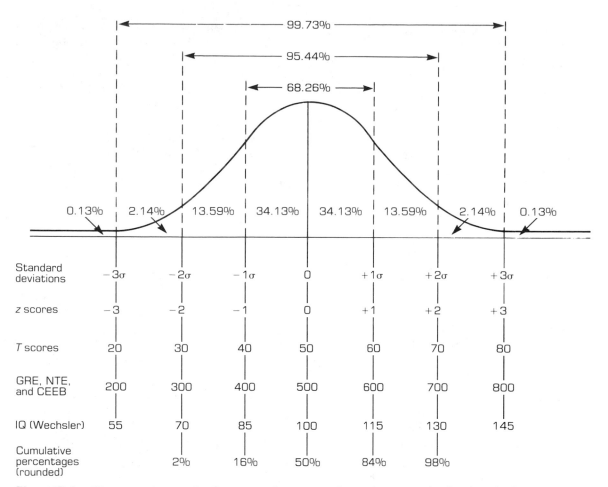

Figure 3.1. The normal curve (and comparative scores for various standardized scales)

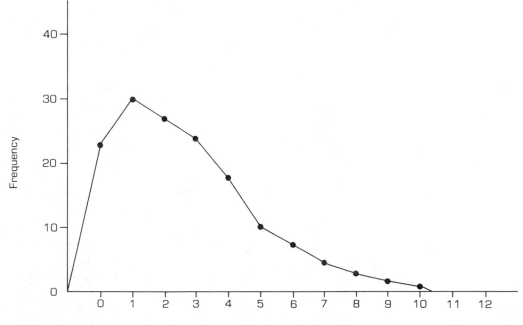

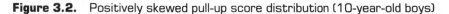

Figure 3.2. Positively skewed pull-up score distribution (10-year-old boys)

scale. In Figure 3.3, the scores are predominantly at the upper end of the distribution, and thus the curve is *negatively* skewed. If the tail of the curve is to the right, the skew is positive; if the tail points to the left, it is negative. In Figure 3.2 the performance of 10-year-old boys in pull-ups forms a positively skewed curve, since most boys that age cannot do many pull-ups (30% cannot do any and 55% cannot do more than one). In fact, pull-up performance tends to be positively skewed at any age. However, Figure 3.3 also represents pull-up performance but with a select population (competitive gymnasts) who typically possess tremendous arm and shoulder strength relative to their body weight. Consequently, their scores cluster at the upper end of the scale, and the distribution is negatively skewed.

There are terms to describe the amount of pointedness or flatness of frequency distributions, and there are mathematical techniques for measuring the amount of skewness. The reader is directed to the references at the end of the chapter.

II. STATISTICAL TECHNIQUES FOR THE TEACHER

FREQUENCY DISTRIBUTION

With a large number of scores, and especially when the range of scores is large, the organization of scores from high to low is best done by constructing a frequency distribution using step intervals.

A step interval is merely a small range of scores, such as scores from 96 to 100. In this case, the size of the step interval is 5. In other words, all scores of 96, 97, 98, 99, and 100 are placed in this interval. The next lower step interval would be from 91 to 95, and the next from 86 to 90, and so on. Once the scores are placed in a step interval, they lose their individual identity. Consequently, when scores are put in step intervals they are called grouped data.

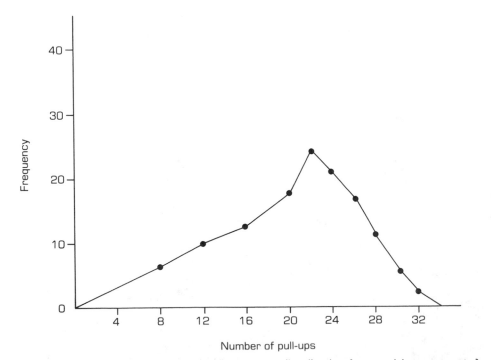

Figure 3.3. Negatively skewed pull-up score distribution (competitive gymnasts)

The following steps may be used in setting up a frequency distribution:

Step 1. Establish the range of scores (high score − low score + 1). For the following push-up scores, the highest score is 55 and the lowest is 4; the range is 55 − 4 + 1 = 52:

26, 55, 20, 6, 16, 29, 42, 13, 27, 35, 31, 26, 4, 22, 15, 29, 37, 28, 24, 17, 25, 38, 25, 32, 10, 17, 27, 20, 21, 15, 34, 28, 30, 16, 23, 25, 27, 30, 22, 17, 12, 41, 36, 24, 25, 18, 26, 30, 20, 18, 47, 32, 25, 12, 9, 31, 38, 34, 22, 37.

Step 2. Determine the size and number of step intervals. Generally, one should try to keep the number of step intervals between 10 and 20. An expedient way to determine the size of the interval is to divide the range by 15. Hence, 52/15 = 3.5, which, when rounded off, is 4. With a step interval of size 4, there are 12 step intervals for this range of scores.

Step 3. Set up the step intervals. The highest step interval must include the highest score, and if the size of the step interval is an even number, the lowest score in the step interval should be a multiple of the interval size. If the size of the step interval is an odd number, the middle score of the step interval should be a multiple of the interval size. With 4 as the size of the step interval for the push-up scores, a step interval of 52 to 55 is selected as the top interval, since it contains the highest score (55) and since the lowest score of the step interval (52) is a multiple of 4. The next step interval is 48 to 51, then 44 to 47, and so on. Table 3.2 shows the frequency distribution for the 60 scores.

Step 4. Tabulate raw scores. After the step intervals have been established, tally each raw score in the proper interval until all scores have been tallied, and then compute the frequency column as shown in the table.

The frequency distribution provides the teacher with immediate information concerning the range, a rough indication of the measure of central tendency, and the general manner in which the scores were distributed.

Table 3.2. Frequency Distribution

INTERVAL	TALLIES	FREQUENCY
52–55	I	1
48–51	0	0
44–47	I	1
40–43	II	2
36–39	IIII	5
32–35	IIII	5
28–31	IIII IIII	9
24–27	IIII IIII III	13
20–23	IIII III	8
16–19	IIII II	7
12–15	IIII	5
8–11	II	2
4–7	II	2
		$N = 60$

GRAPHING PROCEDURES

The teacher may wish to analyze scores visually by plotting performances on a graph. A graph has a horizontal axis *(X)*, called the *abscissa,* and a vertical axis *(Y)*, called the *ordinate.* The height of the vertical axis should be about three fourths the length of the horizontal axis. Also, the vertical axis *(Y)* should begin with zero. This is quite standard for graphing; if a graph does not conform to these proportions, it can be greatly distorted and thus misrepresent the distribution. Graphs can be of different types. One of the most commonly used is the *frequency polygon.*

Frequency Polygon

In Figure 3.4 we have plotted the sit-and-reach test scores of 100 college women. We have simply tallied the number of students who achieved each of the sit-and-reach distances from 22 to 44 cm. In many cases, however, it is more convenient to group scores into intervals (i.e., to develop a frequency distribution). In Figure 3.5 we have taken the same data but have grouped the sit-and-reach test scores into intervals of 2 cm each. Thus, in the first interval (22–23 cm), there were two students; three students scored 24 or 25 cm, and so forth.

Figure 3.5 resembles Figure 3.4 except it is a little "smoother." It illustrates the fact that when scores are grouped into a frequency distribution, some specific information about scores is lost. Furthermore, grouping data may distort the distribution to some extent, but with a sufficient number of scores the amount of distortion is minimal.

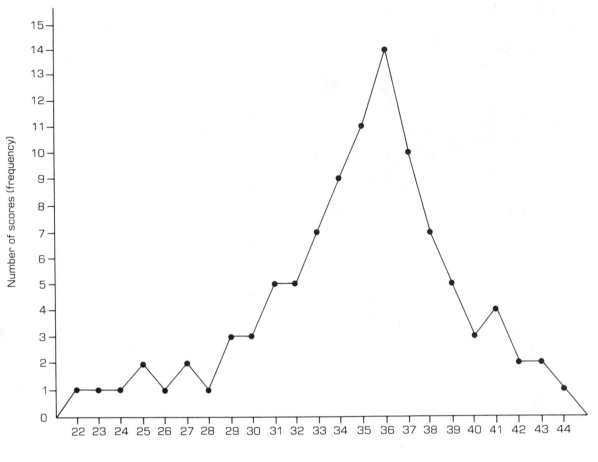

Figure 3.4.   Frequency polygon of sit-and-reach test scores of 100 college women

Frequency polygons are often used to show and compare two or more distributions. In Figure 3.6 the distributions of college men and women's scores in the sit-and-reach test are shown. The comparative characteristics of each distribution can be seen at a glance. When distributions are to be compared, they should have about the same number of scores.

There are many examples of the use of graphs to compare two or more performances, such as trained and untrained subjects' cardiovascular responses before, during, and after exercise; older and younger children's learning curves; different experimental and control groups' performances at various stages of an experiment; and visually impaired, auditory impaired, and non-handicapped children's motor proficiency scores over practice trials, to cite but a few. Graphs are also used to illustrate relationships between different measurements, as we will demonstrate when we introduce regression later in this chapter.

Histogram

The histogram is basically a bar graph in which the height of each column represents the frequency of scores. Like the frequency polygon, the histogram provides a quick picture of the distribution. The same proportionate dimensions of the ordinate (Y axis) and abscissa (X axis) hold (i.e., the vertical axis should be three fourths the length of the horizontal axis). The Y axis should begin at zero, and some blank space should be left at each end of the graph. The largest frequency should not quite reach the top of the graph, so that the data are "within the picture."

The scores are represented along the X axis in any chosen step intervals. In Figure 3.7 we have grouped the women's sit-and-reach test scores into step intervals of two, as we did in Figure 3.5. Instead of having points denoting frequency of scores as in the polygon, we draw lines parallel to the X axis at the heights of the various frequencies.

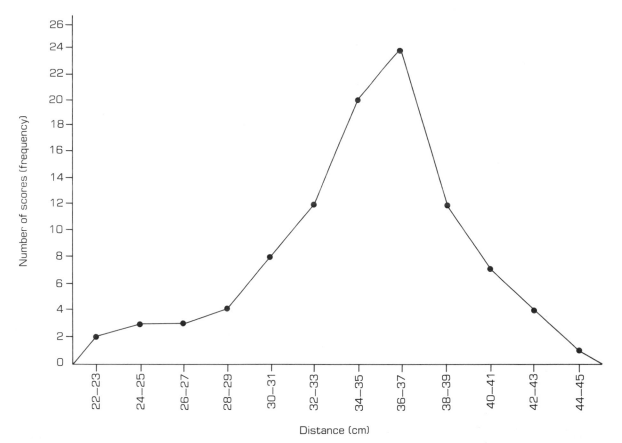

Figure 3.5.   Frequency polygon of sit-and-reach test scores of 100 college women when scores are grouped into step intervals

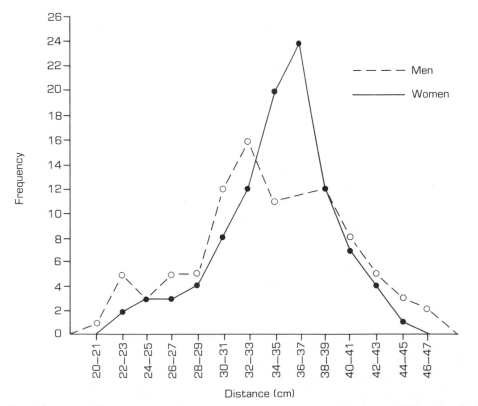

Figure 3.6.   Frequency polygon of two distributions of sit-and-reach test scores (100 college women and 100 college men)

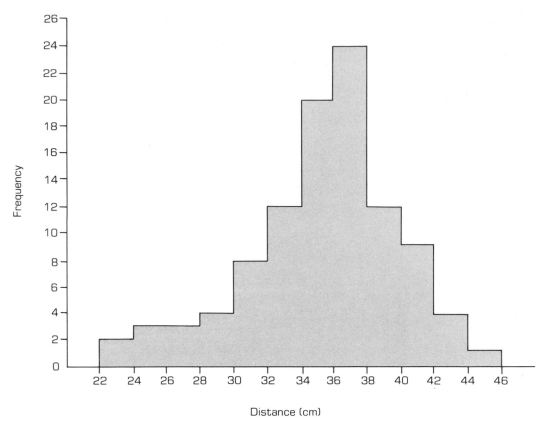

Figure 3.7.   Histogram of sit-and-reach test scores of 100 college women

PERCENTILES AND STANDARD SCORES

All teachers should have a basic understanding of norms and be able to construct their own norms. Steps in constructing two types of norms, percentiles and standard scores (*T* scores), are described here.

Percentiles

One of the more common ways of presenting norms is by percentiles. The physical educator frequently has occasion to use percentiles, since many standardized tests (e.g., the AAHPERD Youth Fitness Test, the AAHPERD Health Related Physical Fitness Test, and the AAHPERD Sports Skills Test) present scores in this manner. Generally speaking, students are fairly well oriented in the interpretation of percentiles.

A percentile score informs students what proportion of individuals of the same population (e.g., the same age, sex, ability level) scored below them. For example, a percentile rank of 80 on a test means that 80% of the people taking the test had lower scores, and 20% had higher scores. With percentiles (as with other norms), scores from different tests can be compared to show how a student performed in relation to the other students taking each test.

In most statistics and tests and measurements books, percentiles are calculated from a frequency distribution. This method is described in Appendix D. However, we are going to demonstrate a much simpler technique. Once one is familiar with the steps, one can construct percentile norms for a couple of hundred scores in less than a half hour. The steps are described and illustrated in Tables 3.3 through 3.7.

Step 1.   Tally the raw scores on a prepared tally sheet. You can develop your own sheets for various tests. The tally sheet used for the sit-up scores in Table 3.3 is quite versatile in that it can accommodate any scores from 0 to 100, or 0.1 to 10.0, or 0.01 to 1.00. In a test such as the 9-minute run, if the highest score is 2570 yd and the lowest is 1300, start with the highest and make columns of numbers (in 10-yd intervals) down to 1300. Do the same for any test for which you wish to calculate percentiles. The tallying of scores is a painstaking task. It

Table 3.3. Constructing Percentile Norms: Tallying the Scores (Step 1) (1-Minute Sit-up Scores for 80 13-Year-Old Girls)

43	25	38	32	18	26	28	32	28	42	60	55	39	46	36	38
29	19	30	23	23	38	36	27	33	27	39	36	35	49	41	50
32	22	50	27	15	16	46	31	44	33	35	51	46	35	24	20
32	12	28	30	20	31	26	34	29	35	37	25	36	38	40	48
52	24	33	31	40	34	39	42	39	30	48	37	49	40	36	37

Tally Sheet

Score	Tally	Score	Tally	Score	Tally	Score	Tally	
100		75		50	||	25	||	
99		74		49	||	24	||	
98		73		48	||	23	||	
97		72		47		22	|	
96		71		46	|||	21		
95		70		45		20	|||	
94		69		44	|	19		
93		68		43	|	18	|	
92		67		42	||	17		
91		66		41	|	16	|	
90		65		40	|||	15	|	
89		64		39	||||	14		
88		63		38	||||	13		
87		62		37	|||	12	|	
86		61		36	JHT	11		
85		60	|	35	||||	10		
84		59		34	||	9		
83		58		33	|||	8		
82		57		32	||||	7		
81		56		31	JHT	6		
80		55	|	30	|||	5		
79		54		29	||	4		
78		53		28	||	3		
77		52	|	27	||	2		
76		51	|	26	||	1		

helps to make a check mark at each raw score as it is tallied.

Step 2. Make a cumulative frequency column. Starting with the poorest score (usually the lowest), progressively record the number of persons receiving the scores, as scores accumulate at each obtained score (Table 3.4). For example, one girl scored 12, two girls scored 15 and below,

Table 3.4. Constructing Percentile Norms: Setting up the Cumulative Frequency Column (Step 2)

Score	Tally	Cum	Score	Tally	Cum	Score	Tally	Cum	Score	Tally	Cum
100			75			50	II	(76)	25	II	(14)
99			74			49	II	(74)	24	II	(12)
98			73			48	II	(72)	23	II	(10)
97			72			47			22	I	(8)
96			71			46	III	(70)	21		
95			70			45			20	III	(7)
94			69			44	I	(67)	19		
93			68			43	I	(66)	18	I	(4)
92			67			42	II	(65)	17		
91			66			41	I	(63)	16	I	(3)
90			65			40	III	(62)	15	I	(2)
89			64			39	IIII	(59)	14		
88			63			38	IIII	(55)	13		
87			62			37	III	(51)	12	I	(1)
86			61			36	JHT	(48)	11		
85			60	I	(80)	35	IIII	(43)	10		
84			59			34	II	(39)	9		
83			58			33	III	(37)	8		
82			57			32	IIII	(34)	7		
81			56			31	JHT	(30)	6		
80			55	I	(79)	30	III	(25)	5		
79			54			29	II	(22)	4		
78			53			28	II	(20)	3		
77			52	I	(78)	27	II	(18)	2		
76			51	I	(77)	26	II	(16)	1		

seven scored 20 and below, and so forth. When you reach the highest score you should have accounted for the total *N* (in this case 80 students). *Note:* If the measurement is one in which lower scores are better, such as times for races or heart rate after exercise, be sure either to construct your tally sheet with the lowest raw scores at the top or to start your cumulative frequency column at the top rather than at the bottom.

Step 3. Calculate the number of scores needed for each percentile rank by multiplying the desired percentages by the total number of scores. In most percentile norm tables, only every 5th percentile is represented, such as 95, 90, 85, and so on. The 99th percentile and the 1st percentile are also frequently given (the 100th and 0 percentiles are theoretically impossible, since a score cannot be better than or lower than itself). In Table 3.5, each desired percentile is multiplied by 80. If there are 150 students, multiply 150 by 0.99, 0.95, 0.90, and so on to get the *number* of scores that represents each percentile rank.

Table 3.5. Constructing Percentile Norms: Determining the Number of Scores Needed for Each Percentile With 80 Scores (Step 3)

%	NO. SCORES NEEDED	RAW SCORE	%	NO. SCORES NEEDED	RAW SCORE	%	NO. SCORES NEEDED	RAW SCORE
99	79.2	___	65	52	___	30	24	___
95	76	___	60	48	___	25	20	___
90	72	___	55	44	___	20	16	___
85	68	___	50	40	___	15	12	___
80	64	___	45	36	___	10	8	___
75	60	___	40	32	___	5	4	___
70	56	___	35	28	___	1	.8	___

Thus, the 60th percentile represents the 48th score (0.60 × 80 = 48), the 35th percentile is the 28th score (0.35 × 80 = 28), and so on.

Step 4. Locate the cumulative value that coincides with each of the percentile points and place the raw score that the value represents next to the percentile. In Table 3.6, for example, the 90th percentile is the 72nd score from the bottom. From the cumulative frequencies we see that the 72nd score is located at raw score 48; thus, a score of 48 is the 90th percentile. For the 25th percentile, the 20th score is found at raw score 28, and so on. Note that when the desired cumulative value is somewhere between the existing values, we use the higher (better) score. For example, for the 50th percentile we need to find the 40th score. Looking at the cumulative frequencies, we see that 39 students scored 34 sit-ups and below, and 43 scored 35 and below. Consequently, the 40th score is one of the four raw scores of 35. Thus, 35 is the 50th percentile.

Step 5. Delete the "Number of Scores Needed" column and you now have percentile norms for 1-minute sit-ups for these 13-year-old girls (Table 3.7). For long-term use, it is desirable to have stable norms that can be used for evaluating sit-up performance at this age level in the future. In this case, accumulate at least a couple of hundred scores or so; then construct the table of norms.

In interpreting a percentile table, there are three things to remember:

1. The percentile rank for a given score tells what percentage of people scored at or less than the score. As an illustration, in Table 3.7 a student who scored 40 sit-ups did better than 75% of the 13-year-old girls who took that test (25% did more than 40 sit-ups).

2. If a student's score falls between two percentiles, the lower percentile is used. For example, in Table 3.7 a girl who did 34 sit-ups would be assigned to the 45th percentile. One cannot interpolate between the 45th and 50th percentiles because raw scores may not be equally spaced.

3. If a raw score falls at more than one percentile, the higher percentile is used. In Table 3.7 a score of 36 represents both the 55th and 60th percentiles, so the higher (60th) percentile is assigned.

The 25th percentile is referred to as the first quartile (Q_1), and the 75th percentile is the third quartile (Q_3). The difference between these two points is the interquartile range. It encompasses the middle 50% of the scores, and these points are sometimes used as cutoff scores for screening purposes.

A principal weakness of percentiles is that they do not represent equal distances between score units, and in the normal curve the scores are clustered around the middle. In fact, more than 68% of the scores fall between plus and minus 1 standard deviation from the mean. Consequently, a small change in raw scores in the middle of the

Table 3.6. Constructing Percentile Norms: Locating the Raw Score That Represents Each Percentile (Step 4)

100		75		50	II (76)	25	II (14)
99		74		49	II (74)	24	II (12)
98		73		48	II (72)	23	II (10)
97		72		47		22	I (8)
96		71		46	III (70)	21	
95		70		45		20	III (7)
94		69		44	I (67)	19	
93		68		43	I (66)	18	I (4)
92		67		42	II (65)	17	
91		66		41	I (63)	16	I (3)
90		65		40	III (62)	15	I (2)
89		64		39	IIII (59)	14	
88		63		38	IIII (55)	13	
87		62		37	III (51)	12	I (1)
86		61		36	卌 (48)	11	
85		60	I (80)	35	IIII (43)	10	
84		59		34	II (39)	9	
83		58		33	III (37)	8	
82		57		32	IIII (34)	7	
81		56		31	卌 (30)	6	
80		55	I (79)	30	III (25)	5	
79		54		29	II (22)	4	
78		53		28	II (20)	3	
77		52	I (78)	27	II (18)	2	
76		51	I (77)	26	II (16)	1	

%	NO. SCORES NEEDED	RAW SCORE	%	NO. SCORES NEEDED	RAW SCORE	%	NO. SCORES NEEDED	RAW SCORE
99	79.2	60	65	52	38	30	24	30
95	76	50	60	48	36	25	20	28
90	72	48	55	44	36	20	16	26
85	68	46	50	40	35	15	12	24
80	64	42	45	36	33	10	8	22
75	60	40	40	32	32	5	4	18
70	56	39	35	28	31	1	.8	12

Table 3.7. Constructing Percentile Norms: The Completed Table (Step 5)

PERCENTILE	NUMBER OF SIT-UPS
99	60
95	50
90	48
85	46
80	42
75	40
70	39
65	38
60	36
55	36
50	35
45	33
40	32
35	31
30	30
25	28
20	26
15	24
10	22
5	18
1	12

distribution results in a rather large change in percentile points. Likewise, a relatively large change in raw scores is needed to produce a change in percentiles at the ends of the scale. In Table 3.7, for example, an increase of one sit-up (from 35 to 36) results in an increase of 10 percentile points (from 50 to 60). At the lower end of the distribution, an increase of ten sit-ups (from 12 to 22) is needed to change 9 percentile points (from 1 to 10); at the upper end, an increase of 12 sit-ups is necessary for improvement from the 90th to 99th percentile.

Since percentile ranks are ordinal data and change at different rates, the averaging of percentiles is not mathematically sound. Thus, a teacher should not try to total or average the percentile scores of students on different tests in order to arrive at a total or average score or grade. Also, in percentile norms it is quite likely that extreme scores may be encountered in the future that cannot be placed on the scale. For these reasons, percentiles are not as statistically sound as some other types of norms such as the T scale and other standard scores.

Standard Scores

Many of the measurements taken by physical educators are in different units. For example, scores may be recorded in seconds, as in the 50-yard dash; in feet, as in the softball throw; or in rep-

etitions, as in sit-ups. Moreover, the physical educator measures strength in pounds, records the number of times a student volleys a tennis ball against a wall, scores the vertical jump in inches, charts the zone in which a golf ball lands, and uses written test scores, ratings, game scores, and various and sundry other units of measurement.

The combining of scores from separate tests has often posed a difficult problem for teachers who lack the knowledge (or the desire, or both) to transform raw scores into some form of standard score.

z Scores

z Scores are scores expressed in terms of standard deviations from the mean. The mean of z scores is zero; thus scores below the mean are expressed as negative values and scores above the mean as positive values. The formula for computing z scores is:

$$z \text{ score} = \frac{\text{raw score} - \text{mean of scores}}{\text{standard deviation}}$$

If, for example, the mean for the vertical jump is 16 in. and the standard deviation is 7, what is the z score for a jump of 14 in.? Using the formula:

$$z = \frac{14 - 16}{7} = -0.29$$

a jump of 9 in. would be a z score of -1.0; a jump of 26.5 in. would equal a z score of 1.5, and so on.

Specific scores on different tests may be readily and meaningfully compared by simply using z scores (assuming that the test distributions are similar). If a girl had a score of 15 sec on the flexed-arm hang and ran 1840 yd in the 9-minute run, how can these performances be compared? If the means are 10 sec and 1560 yd, respectively, the girl was above average on both tests, but how much above? Was she better on one test than the other? z Scores can be used to answer these questions. For example, if the mean is 10 sec and the standard deviation is 5 for the flexed-arm hang, her score of 15 sec represents a z score of 1.00.

$$z = \frac{15 - 10}{5} = 1.00$$

On the 9-minute run, with a mean of 1560 yd and a standard deviation of 280, we see that her score of 1840 yd is also a z score of 1.00.

$$z = \frac{1840 - 1560}{280} = 1.00$$

Thus, the performances are similar in that each score is 1.00 standard deviation above the mean. If we refer back to Figure 3.1, the normal distribution, we can see that both scores are better than 84% of the scores (50 + 34.13%). A table of percentages of the total area under the normal probability curve can be found in any statistics book. Thus, a tester can determine the percentage of scores above and below a particular score by converting the raw score to a z score and consulting the table. He or she can also see what percentage of a population lies between certain scores and can determine the probability that a particular score will occur.

The z score is the basis of all standard scores such as the T scale. Most testers do not use z scores for norms simply because they are awkward to deal with in that the numbers are usually small, involve decimals, and are expressed in both positive and negative values.

T Scores

The T scale converts raw scores into normalized standard scores with a mean of 50 and a standard deviation of 10. Figure 3.1 shows the relationship of T scores to z scores. A z score of 0.00 is equal to a T score of 50; a z score of −1.00 is a T score of 40, and so on. One can see that since plus and minus 3 standard deviations encompass more than 99% of the scores (99.73%) in the normal distribution, most scores will fall between T scores of 80 and 20. In fact, many norm tables present only this range of T scores. T scores represent equivalent points in the distribution; thus, they are comparable for different tests, since the reference is always to a standard scale of 100 units that is based on the normal curve.

T scores can be constructed by any of several methods. The T score for any specific raw score can be determined by the following formula:

$$T \text{ score} = 50 + \frac{10}{s} (X - \overline{X})$$

where s is the standard deviation of the raw scores, X is the specific score in question, and $\overline{X}$ is the mean of the group of scores. One can see that we are simply calculating a z score, multiplying this by 10, and adding 50. To illustrate, suppose a student made a score of 94 on a test for which the mean was 80 and the standard deviation 20. Substituting in the formula, we have:

$$
\begin{aligned}
T &= 50 + \frac{10}{20} (94 - 80) \\
&= 50 + 0.5 (14) \\
&= 50 + 7 \\
&= 57
\end{aligned}
$$

Any T could be computed in this way.

However, another approach that we feel offers a relatively easy and expedient method of establishing a T scale from a set of raw scores is described as follows. For purposes of illustration, we will use sit-and-reach test scores of 100 college men.

Step 1. Compute the mean and standard deviation. The mean of the 100 scores is 33.4 cm, and the standard deviation is 7.3 cm.

Step 2. Multiply the standard deviation by 0.1. This gives us a T value of 0.73. We multiplied by 0.1 because the standard deviation for the T scale is 10. So each T score from 0 to 100 is one tenth of the standard deviation.

Step 3. Prepare a table of numbers (T scores) from 0 to 100. The mean of the raw scores is then placed next to the T score of 50. In Table 3.8 we have placed the mean sit-and-reach score of 33.4 cm next to 50.

Step 4. Next add the value obtained in step 2 (0.1 × standard deviation), which in our example is 0.73, to the mean and to each subsequent number to represent T scores of 51 to 100 (Table 3.8). Then subtract the T value from the mean and from each number thereafter to determine the T scores 49 to 0 (Table 3.8). Remember that with some measures such as timed events and heart rate, lower scores are better. Therefore, you should subtract the T values toward 100 and add those toward 0.00 (i.e., lower time = higher T score).

Step 5. Round off the scores to correspond to actual raw scores. In other words, if the sit-and-reach test is scored only to the nearest centimeter, you do not need to use decimals; round off to the nearest centimeter. Table 3.9 shows the finished T scale.

After the scores are rounded off, whether spaces are left in the T scale or more than one raw score is given for different T scores is mostly a matter

Table 3.8. Constructing a *T* Scale for Sit-and-Reach (S-R) Test Scores for College Men[a]

T SCORE	S-R SCORE	T SCORE	S-R SCORE	T SCORE	S-R SCORE	T SCORE	S-R SCORE	
100	69.90	75	51.65	50	33.40	25	15.15	
99	69.17	74	50.92	49	32.67	24	14.42	
98	68.44	73	50.19	48	31.94	23	13.69	
97	67.71	72	49.46	47	31.21	22	12.96	
96	66.98	71	48.73	46	30.48	21	12.23	
95	66.25	70	48.00	45	29.75	20	11.50	
94	65.52	69	47.27	44	29.02	19	10.77	
93	64.79	68	46.54	43	28.29	18	10.04	
92	64.06	67	45.81	42	27.56	17	9.31	
91	66.33	66	45.08	41	26.83	16	8.58	
90	62.60	65	44.35	40	26.10	15	7.85	
89	61.87	64	43.62	39	25.37	14	7.12	
88	61.14	63	42.89	38	24.64	13	6.39	
87	60.41	62	42.16	37	23.91	12	5.66	
86	59.68	61	41.43	36	23.18	11	4.93	
85	58.95	60	40.70	35	22.45	10	4.20	
84	58.22	59	39.97	34	21.72	9	3.41	
83	57.49	58	39.24	33	20.99	8	2.74	
82	56.76	57	38.51	32	20.26	7	2.01	
81	56.03	56	37.78	31	19.53	6	1.28	
80	55.30	55	37.05	30	18.80	5	.55	
79	54.57	54	36.32	29	18.07	4	0	
78	53.84	53	35.59	28	17.34	3		
77	53.11	52	34.86	27	16.61	2		
76	52.38	51	34.13	26	15.88	1		

[a]Mean = 33.4 cm, s = 7.3 cm, T = 0.73 cm.

of choice. The main thing is the inclusion of all possible raw scores within the *T* scale, even if all raw scores are not contained in the original sample of scores. The *T* scale is usually being projected for future use, not just for the scores used in developing it in one instance.

The fact that it is rare for students to have *T* scores over 80 or below 20 may give rise to some confusion on the part of the student who is accustomed to thinking that scores in the 60s are poor and those in the 70s only fair. Thus, the teacher must have a basic understanding of the *T* scale and the normal curve, and must educate students adequately concerning *T* scores. Earlier we pointed out that percentiles are used to a great extent because of their ease of interpretation, yet they have several shortcomings. *T* scores overcome the disadvantages of percentiles, but they are harder to interpret. Table 3.10 shows the relationship of *T* scores to percentiles in a normal distribution.

Table 3.9.   Completed *T* Scale for Sit-and-Reach (S-R) Test Scores for College Men

T SCORE	S-R SCORE	*T* SCORE	S-R SCORE	*T* SCORE	S-R SCORE	*T* SCORE	S-R SCORE	
100	70	75	52	50		25	15	
99	69	74	51	49	33	24		
98		73	50	48	32	23	14	
97	68	72		47	31	22	13	
96	67	71	49	46		21	12	
95	66	70	48	45	30	20		
94		69	47	44	29	19	11	
93	65	68		43	28	18	10	
92	64	67	46	42		17	9	
91	63	66	45	41	27	16		
90		65	44	40	26	15	8	
89	62	64		39		14	7	
88	61	63	43	38	25	13	6	
87		62	42	37	24	12		
86	60	61		36	23	11	5	
85	59	60	41	35		10	4	
84	58	59	40	34	22	9		
83		58	39	33	21	8	3	
82	57	57		32	20	7	2	
81	56	56	38	31		6	1	
80	55	55	37	30	19	5		
79		54	36	29	18	4	0	
78	54	53		28	17	3		
77	53	52	35	27		2		
76		51	34	26	16	1		

The percentile ranks are not exact; they have been rounded to whole numbers for simplicity. The table may be of some value to the teacher in explaining *T* scores to students and parents.

The physical education teacher should periodically revise the *T* scale. As more scores are accumulated, the mean and standard deviation should be computed again to verify their accuracy, and if warranted a new *T* scale should be constructed. The *T* scale will not change markedly once it has been established with a sufficient number of observations (at least 200). This is true also for percentiles and any other type of norms. The physical educator would be remiss, however, if he or she did not continue to inspect and evaluate the norms, just as it is necessary regularly to evaluate the total tests and measurements program.

Percentiles, *T* scores, and other standard scores represent valuable tools for the teacher. Their application to grading is discussed in Chapter 5. Besides being used for grading, they may be used in the construction of a test battery, in establish-

Table 3.10. Comparative Percentile Ranks[a] for *T* Scores

T	PERCENTILE	*T*	PERCENTILE
80	99.9	49	46
75	99	48	42
70	98	47	38
68	96	46	34
66	95	45	31
65	93	44	27
64	92	43	24
63	90	42	21
62	88	41	18
61	86	40	16
60	84	39	14
59	82	38	12
58	79	37	10
57	76	36	8
56	73	35	7
55	69	34	6
54	66	33	5
53	62	32	4
52	58	31	3
51	54	30	2
50	50	25	1

[a]Percentiles are rounded to whole numbers.

ing a profile assessing performance in various areas, for diagnosis, and for any of the many occasions when it is desirable to compare scores from different tests.

CORRELATION

Correlation refers to the relationship of one variable to another. Physical educators and coaches frequently would like to know the relationships between various abilities and performances. For example, a coach may want to know if there is any relationship between leg strength and speed of a lineman's charge. The physical educator may wish to know the relationship between performance in a distance run and performance on a step test. Moreover, an understanding of correlation is necessary in determining validity, reliability, and objectivity as steps in test construction and in evaluating tests already published.

The Pearson product moment correlation (r) is most commonly used in determining relationships. The numerical relationship may vary between $+1$ and -1, or from a perfect positive relationship to a perfect negative relationship. If a group of men were tested on strength and power and the strongest men were nearly always best in power performance, a high positive correlation could be expected. However, if as strength increased, power tended to decrease, a high negative correlation could be expected. If two sets of data are totally unrelated, the correlation coefficient will be 0. In practice, the coefficient seldom is $+1$, -1, or 0 because of the many uncontrolled factors that influence the two variables being correlated. The problem of interpreting correlation coefficients (as to what is high, low, and average) is sometimes difficult.

Probably one of the most important factors regarding the size of the coefficient has to do with the purpose for which the correlation is computed. For example, a coefficient of correlation of .65 may be considered quite high when a specific measurement such as leg strength is correlated with performance in a particular sport. On the other hand, a coefficient of .65 is quite low when the correlation is between the scores made on the odd- and even-numbered questions on a written examination. Certain arbitrary terms or designations as to what correlations are considered high, average, and low are sometimes given. The following scale is an example of interpretation of coefficients of correlation in general terms:

$r = .00$ (no relationship)

$r = \pm.01$ to $\pm.20$ (low relationship)

$r = \pm.20$ to $\pm.50$ (slight to fair relationship)

$r = \pm.50$ to $\pm.70$ (substantial relationship)

$r = \pm.71$ to $\pm.99$ (high to very high relationship)

$r = \pm1.00$ (perfect relationship)

Such rankings are merely rough guides and, as stated previously, their worth depends on the purposes for which the computation was done. For instance, for demonstrating reliability of a test, a correlation coefficient of at least .80 is desired and should preferably be higher. Methods of establishing test reliability will be discussed in Chapters 4 and 21.

In essence, if the purpose is to predict future performance, the coefficient of correlation must be much higher than if the purpose is just to establish a relationship between two traits. This, however, leads to another misconception concerning the characteristics of correlation, one that can be rather dangerous: that a correlation shows causation. Suppose that a rather high correlation is found between physical fitness and scholastic achievement. The conclusion might erroneously be made that academic achievement is a result of physical fitness. Although some causation may be present, the correlation itself does not support this assumption. In any correlation, several factors may be responsible for both performances. In the previous example, a more absurd interpretation would be that gains in scholastic achievement would result in improved physical fitness.

One of several ways of interpreting coefficients of correlation is by means of the *coefficient of determination* (Garrett 1958). In this method, one merely squares the *r* and the resulting r^2 represents the proportion of variance in one variable that can be accounted for by the other variable. To illustrate, suppose that the coefficient of correlation between the *X* variable speed, as measured by a sprint, and the *Y* variable agility, as measured by a shuttle run, is $r = .80$. Then $r^2 = .64$. This is interpreted as indicating that 64% of the variance in the agility score is accounted for by the variability in the speed score. This method points out rather strongly that a high coefficient of correlation is needed to reveal a marked degree of association. An *r* of .30 indicates only 9% association, and an *r* of .40 only 16%. On the other hand, when the *r* is very high, the degree of association is also high. To illustrate, an *r* of .97 indicates that 94% of the variability in one variable is accounted for by the variance in the other variable.

One further precaution should be mentioned regarding correlation. The coefficient of correlation should not be interpreted as a percentage of perfect relationship. While the meaning of statistical significance is beyond the scope of this book, we must emphasize that in relation to the coefficient of determination, an *r* of .50 is not half as large as an *r* of 1.00, and an *r* of .75 is not merely three times as large as an *r* of .25. By using the coefficient of determination (r^2), we can see that an *r* of 1.00 is four times as strong as an *r* of .50, and that an *r* of .75 is nine times as large as an *r* of .25.

Rank–Difference Method of Correlation

The rank–difference method is a nonparametric statistical technique, which can be used with scores that do not conform to normal distribution. It involves ordinal (ranked) scores and is a convenient tool for teachers who want to obtain a quick measure of relationship between two sets of scores involving a small number of subjects. This method uses the rank that each student attains on each test, and the relationship is established in terms of the degree of difference *(D)* between

rankings. The symbol for this coefficient is the Greek *rho* (ρ), and the formula is:

$$\rho = 1.00 - \frac{6\,(\Sigma D^2)}{N\,(N^2 - 1)}$$

The steps involved in computing the correlation coefficient by this method are illustrated by the data presented in Table 3.11. In this example, we have devised a skills test in badminton and wish to establish the validity (the degree to which the test measures what it is supposed to measure) of the test. Students completed a round-robin tournament in badminton and were ranked according to their order of finish in the tournament. If the test is valid, those persons who were most successful in the tournament should score the highest on the skills test, and the losers the lowest. For purposes of illustration, only 15 subjects are used.

Step 1. Rank the scores on both tests. Notice that in the rankings for the skills test there are two persons with a rank of 3.5 and three with a rank of 10. In the first instance, two students scored the same on the skills test, and therefore deserve the same rank. However, they take up two positions, 3 and 4. An average is computed (3 + 4 = 7 ÷ 2 = 3.5), and both students are given the rank of 3.5. Four places have been accounted for now, so the next rank is 5.

Similarly, three students had identical scores of 10 and take up positions 9, 10, and 11. An average is again computed (9 + 10 + 11 = 30 ÷ 3 = 10), and the rank of 10 is assigned to each. The next rank after these three is 12. The last rank should equal *N* (unless the last rank is tied).

Step 2. Determine the differences between the rankings on the two tests and enter in column *D*. Since these differences are to be squared, the plus or minus is not important except as a check to see that the ranking and subtraction are correct (the sum of the *D* column is 0.00).

Step 3. Square each number in the difference *(D)* column and total these values (ΣD^2).

Step 4. Find the coefficient of correlation by substituting the obtained values into the formula.

In the hypothetical example given there was a very high degree of validity for the badminton

Table 3.11. Rank–Difference Method of Correlation

SUBJECT	SKILL TEST SCORE	TOURNAMENT GAMES WON	RANK IN SKILL TEST	RANK IN TOURNAMENT	DIFFERENCE, D	D^2
1	20	14	1	1	0	0
2	16	12	2	3	1	1
3	12	13	3.5	2	1.5	2.25
4	12	10	3.5	5	1.5	2.25
5	10	11	5	4	1	1
6	9	6	6	9	3	9
7	8	9	7	6	1	1
8	7	8	8	7	1	1
9	6	5	10	10	0	0
10	6	7	10	8	2	4
11	6	4	10	11	1	1
12	5	0	12	15	3	9
13	4	2	13	13	0	0
14	3	3	14	12	2	4
15	2	1	15	14	1	1
$N = 15$						36.50

$$\rho = 1 - \frac{6(\Sigma D^2)}{N(N^2 - 1)} = 1 - \frac{6\,(36.50)}{15\,(15^2 - 1)}$$

$$= 1 - \frac{219}{(15)\,(224)} = 1 - \frac{219}{3360} = 1 - .07$$

$$\rho = .93$$

skills test. It should be pointed out that the relationship between skills test scores and number of tournament games won could also have been established by use of the product–moment method. The rank–difference method is quick and simple, but it becomes impractical with a large number of scores.

Product–Moment Method With Ungrouped Data

In Table 3.12, push-up scores *(X)* and fitness index scores *(Y)* from the Harvard Step Test are shown for 15 students. The following steps describe the procedures for determining the relationship between push-up performance and cardiovascular fitness using the product–moment method of correlation. The symbol for the product–moment coefficient of correlation is *r.*

Step 1. Compute the mean for each set of scores. The mean for push-ups $(\overline{X})$ is found to be 22 and for the step test scores $(\overline{Y})$, 73.

Step 2. Subtract the mean $(\overline{X})$ from each score in column *X* and enter in column *x*. Similarly, subtract the mean $(\overline{Y})$ from the scores in column *Y* to form column *y*.

Step 3. Square each value in columns *x* and *y* and enter as x^2 and y^2, respectively. Obtain the sum for each column $(\Sigma x^2 = 734, \Sigma y^2 = 1714)$.

Step 4. Multiply *x* and *y* values. The *xy* column represents the product–moment values, or the distance of each student's scores from the mean of each set of scores. Note that there is a column for positive cross products and a column for negative values. Find the algebraic sum of these two columns $(\Sigma xy = 777)$. If the column of negative cross products were larger, the correlation would be negative.

Step 5. Substitute the obtained values into the formula, and determine the coefficient of correlation $(r = .69)$.

Another method may be used with ungrouped data, which is actually less laborious but involves a more imposing-looking formula. This method is to assume the means to be 0 and to use the raw scores as deviations and then a correction factor. This method employs the same principle as that outlined in calculating standard deviation from ungrouped data. The formula is:

$$r = \frac{N\,(\Sigma XY) - (\Sigma X)(\Sigma Y)}{\sqrt{N(\Sigma X^2) - (\Sigma X)^2}\ \sqrt{N(\Sigma Y^2) - (\Sigma Y)^2}}$$

Table 3.12. Calculation of the Coefficient of Correlation for Ungrouped Scores by the Product—Moment Method

STUDENT	PUSH-UP X	STEP TEST Y	x	y	x^2	y^2	xy (+)	xy (−)
1	28	84	6	11	36	121	66	
2	23	74	1	1	1	1	1	
3	13	57	−9	−16	81	256	144	
4	16	63	−6	−10	36	100	60	
5	17	80	−5	7	25	49		−35
6	24	72	2	−1	4	1		−2
7	25	70	3	−3	9	9		−9
8	26	65	4	−8	16	64		−32
9	10	59	−12	−14	144	196	168	
10	33	91	11	18	121	324	198	
11	25	73	3	0	9	0		
12	20	60	−2	−13	4	169	26	
13	18	73	−4	0	16	0		
14	16	83	−6	10	36	100		−60
15	36	91	14	18	196	324	252	
$N = 15$	$\Sigma X = 330$	$\Sigma Y = 1095$			$\Sigma x^2 = 734$	$\Sigma y^2 = 1714$	915	−138
	$\overline{X} = 22$	$\overline{Y} = 73$					$\Sigma xy = 777$	

$$r = \frac{\Sigma xy}{\sqrt{(\Sigma x^2)(\Sigma y^2)}} = \frac{777}{\sqrt{(734)(1714)}} = \frac{777}{\sqrt{1,258,076}} = \frac{777}{1122} = .69$$

To illustrate, Table 3.13 shows the body weights and the scores (in seconds) for the flexed-arm hang test for ten girls 12 years of age. In calculating the coefficient of correlation by this method, each score is squared, the cross products of the X and Y scores are computed, and the resulting total of each column is inserted into the formula. In this example, a high negative correlation is obtained. This indicates that the heavier girls were not able to hang on the bar as long as the lighter girls. In other words, the greater the body weight, the poorer the performance on this test.

Table 3.13. Calculation of the Coefficient of Correlation for Ungrouped Scores Using Deviations Taken From Zero (Computer Method)

STUDENT	WEIGHT X	FLEXED-ARM HANG TEST Y	X^2	Y^2	XY
A	80	35	6,400	1225	2,800
B	117	10	13,689	100	1,170
C	96	19	9,216	361	1,824
D	85	22	7,225	484	1,870
E	92	25	8,464	625	2,300
F	100	15	10,000	225	1,500
G	130	5	16,900	25	650
H	125	8	15,625	64	1,000
I	93	15	8,649	225	1,395
J	88	20	7,744	400	1,760
$N = 10$	$\Sigma X = 1006$	$\Sigma Y = 174$	$\Sigma X^2 = 103,912$	$\Sigma Y^2 = 3734$	$\Sigma XY = 16,269$
	$(\Sigma X)^2 = 1,012,036$	$(\Sigma Y)^2 = 30,276$			

$$r = \frac{N(\Sigma XY) - (\Sigma X)(\Sigma Y)}{\sqrt{N(\Sigma X^2) - (\Sigma X)^2}\sqrt{N(\Sigma Y^2) - (\Sigma Y)^2}} = \frac{10(16269) - (1006)(174)}{\sqrt{10(103,912) - (1006)^2}\sqrt{10(3734) - (174)^2}}$$

$$= \frac{162,690 - 175,044}{\sqrt{27,084}\sqrt{7064}} = \frac{-12,354}{13,860} = -.89$$

III. BASIC TECHNIQUES FOR TEST CONSTRUCTION AND RESEARCH

In this section, some of the preceding concepts and techniques will be expanded. The use of correlation in predicting performance and ways of comparing performances to determine whether there are significant differences between groups or between initial and final tests will be discussed. Lastly, reliability by analysis of variance will be determined.

CORRELATION AND PREDICTION

The ability to predict some behavior or quality (i.e., variable) on the basis of another measure (another variable) depends on a relationship having been established between the predictor variable and the variable being predicted (the criterion). The closer the relationship the more accurate the prediction.

Simple (Zero Order) Correlation (r)

Let us first use a hypothetical example of a perfect relationship between two variables, height and weight. Figure 3.8 shows the height and weight of eight 11-year-old boys and the means and standard deviations of the group from which this sample was drawn. Since the $r = 1.00$, weight can be predicted perfectly if height is known.

First, let us examine the relationship and the prediction by the use of z scores. For example, Student A is 57.5 in. tall, which is a z score of -0.5. Remember the formula for z scores:

$$z = \frac{X - \overline{X}}{s} = \frac{57.5 - 60}{5} = -0.5$$

The boy weighs 95 lb, which is also a z score of -0.5:

$$z = \frac{95 - 105}{20} = -0.5$$

Student B has a z score of 1.00 for both height and weight. In turn, the two variables of every student are the same z score distance from the mean. This constitutes perfect correlation, which is illustrated by the straight line in Figure 3.8. Consequently, a boy 70 in. tall (z score of 2.00) should weigh 145 lb, because this weight also has a z score of 2.00. We can simply plot it on the table, thus extending the line.

In prediction one does not actually compute z scores. However, correlation can be computed by the use of z scores:

$$r = \frac{\Sigma[(zx)(zy)]}{N}$$

For prediction, a regression formula is used. The basic prediction (regression) formula for a straight line is:

$$\hat{Y} = a + bX$$

where $\hat{Y}$ is the predicted Y score, a is the Y intercept, b is the slope of the line, and X is any predictor (X) score.

The intercept refers to the point where the regression line crosses the Y (vertical) axis. It is the predicted $\hat{Y}$ value when X is zero. The b value indicates the degree of slope of the regression line. It signifies the amount of change in Y that accompanies a change of one unit of X. The formulas for a (the Y intercept) and b (the slope of the line) are as follows:

$$b = r\left(\frac{s_y}{s_x}\right)$$

where r is the correlation between X and Y, s_y is the standard deviation of the Y scores, and s_x is the standard deviation of the X scores.

$$a = \overline{Y} - b\overline{X}$$

where $\overline{Y}$ is the mean of the Y scores and $\overline{X}$ is the mean of the X scores.

The regression formula is used to predict the weight of the boy just mentioned (who was 70 in. tall) using the data in Figure 3.8, in which the correlation is 1.00. The computation of the formula is presented in the table; the regression equation is $\hat{Y} = -135 + 4X$. This can be used to predict body weight for any height. In our case $X = 70$ and thus $\hat{Y} = -135 + 4(70) = -135 + 280 = 145$.

Hence, the predicted weight is 145 lb, and we are "positive" of the prediction because in this hypothetical example the relationship of the predictor variable X (height) and the criterion variable Y (weight) is perfect.

Figure 3.9 portrays a more realistic relationship ($r = .72$) between height and weight. When a correlation is not perfect (and most likely we

GROUP HEIGHT (IN.)	GROUP WEIGHT (LB.)	
$\bar{X} = 60$	$\bar{Y} = 105$	$r = 1.00$
$s_x = 5$	$s_y = 20$	

SAMPLE OF EIGHT STUDENTS FROM DISTRIBUTION		
Student	X (ht)	Y (wt)
A	57.5	95
B	65	125
C	60	105
D	52.5	75
E	55	85
F	67.5	135
G	50	65
H	62.5	115

REGRESSION EQUATION

$$\hat{Y} = a + bX$$

$$b = r\left(\frac{s_y}{s_x}\right) = 1.00\left(\frac{20}{5}\right) = 4.00$$

$$a = \bar{Y} - b\bar{X} = 105 - 4(60)$$
$$= -135$$
$$\hat{Y} = -135 + 4X$$

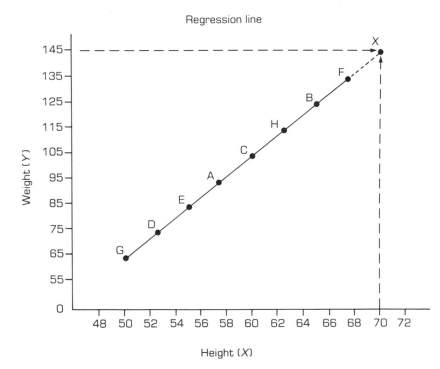

Regression line

Figure 3.8.   Regression line and equation for height and weight of boys $(r = 1.00)$

will never find a perfect correlation), the dots on the graph do not follow a straight line. Connecting the dots results in jagged, sometimes even circular, patterns. However, the best-fitting straight line that will provide the most accurate $\hat{Y}$ value for any given X score can be calculated (Figure 3.9). This is done by selecting a low X score and a high X score and calculating the predicted $\hat{Y}$ value for each using the prediction formula. The resulting two points are then connected to form the predicted regression line.

As an example, 57 is used for the low X score and 63 is chosen for the high X score (Figure 3.9). The calculation of the regression equation (shown in the figure) provides the predicted weights $(\hat{Y})$ for heights of 57 and 63 in. as follows:

GROUP HEIGHT (IN.)	GROUP WEIGHT (LB.)	
$X = 60$	$Y = 102.5$	$r = .72$
$s_x = 3.1$	$s_y = 20.6$	

SAMPLE OF EIGHT STUDENTS FROM DISTRIBUTION		
Student	X (ht)	Y (wt)
A	58	90
B	63	96
C	59	110
D	62	136
E	56	78
F	65	120
G	57	78
H	60	112

REGRESSION EQUATION

$$\hat{Y} = a + bX$$

$$b = r\left(\frac{s_y}{s_x}\right) = .72\left(\frac{20.6}{3.1}\right) = 4.8$$

$$a = \overline{Y} - b\overline{X} = 102.5 - 4.8(60)$$
$$= -185.5$$

$$\hat{Y} = -185.5 + 4.8X$$

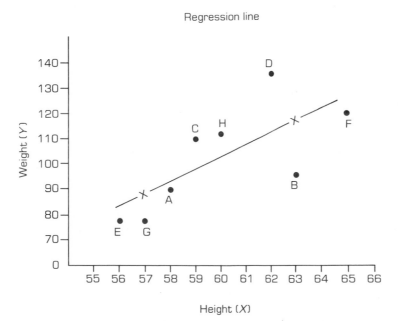

Regression line

Figure 3.9. Regression line and equation for height and weight of boys ($r = .72$)

$$\hat{Y} = a + bX$$
$$\hat{Y} = -185.5 + 4.8X \text{ (from Figure 3.9)}$$
$$\hat{Y} = -185.5 + 4.8(57) = 88.1 \text{ lb}$$
$$\hat{Y} = -185.5 + 4.8(63) = 116.9 \text{ lb}$$

These predicted $\hat{Y}$ values are placed on the graph in Figure 3.9 as shown by the "x" points, and the line of best fit is drawn. Notice that the points that represent the scores for the eight boys do not

fall on the line. The degree of closeness to the line depends on the size of the *r*. When *r* is high, the dots are close to the line, and the lower the *r* the farther away are the points. The distance of the points from the line represents the *error of prediction*.

When we calculated the line of best fit, we took two boys' heights and predicted their weights. Boy G, who was 57 in. tall, was predicted to weigh 88.1 lb. From Figure 3.8, we can see that he actually weighs 78 lb. This difference of the actual (78) minus the predicted (88.1) is -10.1 lb. Boy B weighs 110 lb, but his predicted weight was 116.9 lb, a difference of -6.9. These differences (or errors) are often called *residual scores*. We could calculate residual scores for all of the students and compute the standard deviation of the residuals and this would be the *standard error of prediction*, or *standard error of estimate*. However, we can compute the standard error more easily by the formula:

$$SE = s_y \sqrt{1.00 - r^2}$$

For our example, it would be:

$$20.6\sqrt{1.00 - .72^2} = 14.3$$

Remember, when we introduced correlation in the second section of this chapter we used r^2 to indicate the amount of association or commonality between two measures. If the r is high, the r^2 is high and indicates that a great deal of the performance on one variable is associated with scores on the other. Thus, $1.00 - r^2$ is error in the sense that it is unexplained variance of scores, or the amount one variable is not associated with the other. The r^2 then largely determines the error of prediction. The standard error of prediction is interpreted the same way as standard deviation. In other words, about 68% of the actual Y values will fall between the predicted value $(\hat{Y})$ and plus and minus the standard error. It is 68% certain that a person who is 55 in. tall will weigh between 64.2 and 92.8 lb. To get that range, the predicted $\hat{Y}$ score of 78.5 lb is calculated first. Then the standard error of 14.3 is subtracted and added to get the "confidence band." The higher the correlation, the smaller the error. For example, if the correlation were .92 instead of .72, the standard error would be only 8.1 lb. If the r were 1.00, there would be no error of prediction.

All prediction formulas should provide the user with the standard error as well as the coefficient of correlation. The size of the standard error is very meaningful information in evaluating the accuracy of any prediction formula.

Multiple Correlation (R)

In multiple correlation and multiple regression, there are a criterion (Y) and two or more predictor (X) variables. In physical education measurement, multiple regression is used more than simple regression, which involves only one predictor. It stands to reason that $\hat{Y}$ will be more accurately predicted if more than one predictor is used.

In predicting body density from underwater weighing (from which one can estimate percent fat), the estimate will be better if several skin fold measures are used than if just one is used. The number of predictors a tester eventually selects is determined by the increase in the size of the correlation (R) between the criterion and the predictors with increasing number of predictors, as well as by administrative considerations such as testing time and amount of equipment needed. Therefore, in the example of body fat prediction, if the size of the R does not greatly increase when four skin fold measures rather than three are used, we most likely would sacrifice a little accuracy for administrative considerations and use just three body sites.

Multiple correlation takes into account not only the relationship between each of the X variables and the criterion but also the interrelationships among the X variables themselves. The multiple regression formula then adjusts for these interrelationships. If there were no relationships among the X variables, one could simply predict in an additive fashion, but of course this never is the case.

The multiple regression formula is

$$\hat{Y} = a + b_1(X_1) + \ldots b_n(X_n)$$

It consists of a Y intercept and b (slope of the line) values for each of the X variables, providing a prediction of $\hat{Y}$ based on a linear composite of the predictor variables. To illustrate, Behnke and Wilmore presented the following regression equation for predicting body density (BD) of young men from four skin fold (SF) measurements and height (ht):

$$
\begin{aligned}
BD(\hat{Y}) = \; & 1.06671 + 0.00098(\text{ht}) \\
& - 0.00027(\text{suprailiac SF}) \\
& - 0.00071(\text{abdominal SF}) \\
& - 0.00040(\text{thigh SF}) \\
& + 0.00074(\text{knee SF})
\end{aligned}
$$

The R was .81 and the standard error of estimate was 0.0075 g/ml.

They also presented a formula predicting body density from just two skin fold sites:

$$
\begin{aligned}
BD(\hat{Y}) = \; & 1.08543 - 0.00086(\text{abdominal SF}) \\
& - 0.00040(\text{thigh SF})
\end{aligned}
$$

For this formula, the R was .80 and the standard error was 0.0076 g/ml. Here very little accuracy was lost; some administration time was saved by using only two skin fold measures instead of four, plus the height measurement.

t TEST AND ANALYSIS OF VARIANCE

At times the physical educator or coach may like to compare methods of training or teaching or the performance of different groups or to determine whether significant improvement resulted from a particular training program. To do this, the significance of the observed difference between means must be determined. The word *significance* is of critical importance in such comparisons, because it refers to samples actually measured rather than to the entire population. Consequently, one must determine whether an observed difference may be attributed to chance error of sampling or may be a real (significant) difference.

It should be understood that successive samples from a population would not be expected to have identical means. In fact, if 1000 samples were drawn, their means would approximate a normal curve. Differences between sample means also approximate a normal distribution, and a test of the significance of the difference between means must be applied.

The Null Hypothesis

The null hypothesis is commonly used for statistically testing the significance of the difference between means. The null hypothesis states that there is no real difference between means, and that any observed difference is due to sampling error. Therefore, any difference between means must be of a certain magnitude before the null hypothesis can be rejected and the difference concluded to be real. If the difference is not large enough, the investigator fails to reject the null hypothesis and must conclude that the difference is due to sampling error.

The t Test

The *t* test may be used to determine the significance of the difference between two sample means. The *t* distribution is based on the concept that a normal distribution results when a large number of samples are drawn. However, when the size of samples is small, the probability of rejecting a test hypothesis, usually the null hypothesis, decreases.

It is beyond the scope of this book to provide a comprehensive explanation of the *t* distribution and hypothesis testing, but a simple example will convey the basic concept of the *t* distribution. Before adopting a new method of teaching, a teacher would want to be reasonably sure that the new method was superior to the old method. Consequently, he or she would hesitate to change methods because of a favorable study that involved only a few subjects rather than a large sample. It is only common sense that a large sample will more closely approximate the population from which it is drawn than will a small sample. The *t* distribution is based on this premise. Therefore, in essence, the difference between sample means must be larger when samples are small than when they are large for the difference to be significant. The *t* values are shown in Table 3.14. It should be pointed out that the values in the table are not the observed differences but rather the ratio between the observed differences and the reliability estimates (standard errors) of the sample means in approximating the true means of their respective population (or populations). The column "Degrees of Freedom" refers to the size of the sample, or more specifically to $n - 1$. As was mentioned before, the *t* value necessary for significance is larger when the sample (degrees of freedom) is small.

The other two columns in the table are headed .05 and .01. The .05 level of probability means that the chance is only 5 out of 100 that a difference as large as was obtained could be attributed to chance error of sampling. At the .01 level, the chance of sampling error is only 1 in 100. Thus, one can be more confident that the difference is real at the .01 level than at the .05; the *t* values needed at the .01 level are therefore greater than those needed for the .05 level. It should be mentioned that other probability levels may be used but the .05 and .01 levels are most common.

t Test for Significance of Difference Between Means in Independent (Uncorrelated) Samples

On many occasions the investigator wishes to compare two groups that represent independent samples. A physical educator may want to compare running times of two groups trained by different methods, or perhaps the physical fitness scores of two groups of students, one of which had a required physical education program and the other did not (or possibly social adjustment inventory scores of boys against the scores of

Table 3.14. *t* Values for Determining Significance

DEGREES OF FREEDOM	PROBABILITY (*t*) .05	.01	DEGREES OF FREEDOM	PROBABILITY (*t*) .05	.01
1	12.71	63.66	19	2.09	2.86
2	4.30	9.92	20	2.09	2.84
3	3.18	5.84	21	2.08	2.83
4	2.78	4.60	22	2.07	2.82
5	2.57	4.03	23	2.07	2.81
6	2.45	3.71	24	2.06	2.80
7	2.36	3.50	25	2.06	2.79
8	2.31	3.36	26	2.06	2.78
9	2.26	3.25	27	2.05	2.77
10	2.23	3.17	28	2.05	2.76
11	2.20	3.11	29	2.04	2.76
12	2.18	3.06	30	2.04	2.75
13	2.16	3.01	40	2.02	2.70
14	2.14	2.98	60	2.00	2.66
15	2.13	2.95	120	1.98	2.62
16	2.12	2.92	∞	1.96	2.58
17	2.11	2.90			
18	2.10	2.88			

Table 3.14 is taken from Table III of R. A. Fisher and F. Yates, *Statistical Tables for Biological, Agricultural and Medical Research.* Published by Longman Group Ltd. London (previously published by Oliver & Boyd Ltd. Edinburgh) and by permission of the authors and publishers.

girls). In each comparison, the samples are drawn from independent populations; hence, the means are considered uncorrelated.

To illustrate the steps involved in a comparison of independent samples, let us suppose that to establish evidence of validity for a basketball skills test, the test is administered to two groups having a known difference in basketball playing ability. One sample is composed of varsity players and the other of intramural players. For convenience, let there be small numbers of subjects in the groups. The steps that follow are computed in Table 3.15.

Step 1. Compute the mean and standard deviation for each set of scores.

Step 2. Square the standard deviations to compute the variances (s^2) for the two groups.

Step 3. Insert the values in the formulas and compute the *t* ratio.

Step 4. The number of degrees of freedom (df) is $N - 2$, since 1 df is lost in calculating each mean. With eight subjects in each group, the df is $16 - 2 = 14$.

Step 5. Refer to the *t* values in Table 3.14. With 14 df, the *t* of 4.51 is greater than the *t* of 2.14 needed for significance at the .05 level of probability and also greater than the 2.98 needed for significance at the .01 level.

The *t* is therefore significant at the .01 level of probability. Hence, only 1 time out of 100 would we expect to get a difference as large as was obtained between varsity and intramural players owing to chance (sampling error). The null hypothesis is rejected; we may conclude that the test demonstrates construct validity. (See Chapter 4 for a discussion of construct validity.)

t Test for Significance of Difference Between Scores of Correlated Samples

When two groups consist of the same subjects, such as initial and final test scores, scores on trial 1 and trial 2, or of opposite conditions such as dehydrated and hydrated, one should not use the *t* test for independent (uncorrelated) groups. These groups are not independent; they comprise the same people. The two sets of scores are highly correlated, so the *t* test for determining the significance of the difference between scores of correlated samples must be used.

For illustration, assume that a muscular endurance test was administered to ten students and that a week later they were tested again in the presence of spectators, march music, and other forms of motivation. Was there significant improvement because of the motivational techniques? To determine this, the following steps are used (Table 3.16).

Table 3.15. t Test for Independent Groups

GROUP I (VARSITY PLAYERS)		GROUP II (INTRAMURAL PLAYERS)	
Scores (X_1)	X_1^2	Scores (X_2)	X_2^2
10	100	3	9
16	256	1	1
5	25	2	4
6	36	0	0
12	144	4	16
8	64	1	1
9	81	5	25
6	36	4	16
$\Sigma X_1 = 72$	$\Sigma X_1^2 = 742$	$\Sigma X_2 = 20$	$\Sigma X_2^2 = 72$

$$\overline{X}_1 = \frac{\Sigma X_1}{n_1} = \frac{72}{8} = 9 \qquad\qquad \overline{X}_2 = \frac{\Sigma X_2}{n_2} = \frac{20}{8} = 2.5$$

$$s_1 = \sqrt{\frac{N_1 \Sigma X_1^2 - (\Sigma X_1)^2}{N_1 (N_1 - 1)}} \qquad\qquad s_2 = \sqrt{\frac{N_2 \Sigma X_2^2 - (\Sigma X_2)^2}{N_2 (N_2 - 1)}}$$

$$s_1 = \sqrt{\frac{(8)742 - (72)^2}{8(7)}} = 3.66 \qquad\qquad s_2 = \sqrt{\frac{(8)72 - (20)^2}{8(7)}} = 1.77$$

$$s_1^2 = (3.66)^2 = 13.40 \qquad\qquad s_2^2 = (1.77)^2 = 3.13$$

$$t = \frac{\overline{X}_1 - \overline{X}_2}{\sqrt{\dfrac{s_1^2 (n_1 - 1) + s_2^2 (n_2 - 1)}{n_1 + n_2 - 2} \times \dfrac{n_1 + n_2}{n_1 n_2}}} = \frac{9 - 2.5}{\sqrt{\dfrac{13.40(7) + 3.13(7)}{8 + 8 - 2} \times \dfrac{8 + 8}{(8)(8)}}} =$$

$$t = \frac{6.5}{1.44} = 4.51$$

Step 1. List the pairs of scores. Remember, each person was tested twice. You must place the two scores side by side in order to subtract one from the other to form a difference column.

Step 2. Compute the mean difference $(\overline{D})$.

Step 3. Establish a deviation column (d) by subtracting the mean difference from each difference score $(D - \overline{D})$.

Step 4. Square the deviations and total them to get the Σd^2.

Step 5. Compute the standard deviation of the differences by the formula:

$$s_D = \sqrt{\frac{\Sigma d^2}{n - 1}}$$

Step 6. Compute the standard error of the mean difference by the formula:

$$SE_{\overline{D}} = \frac{s_D}{\sqrt{n}}$$

Step 7. Calculate the t value by the formula:

$$t = \frac{\overline{D}}{SE_{\overline{D}}}$$

Step 8. Refer to the t table (Table 3.14) with $n - 1$ df ($10 - 1 = 9$). The t of 5.33 surpasses the t of 3.25 needed for significance at the .01 level of probability. Hence, we may conclude that the application of special motivational techniques significantly improved endurance performance in this sample.

Analysis of Variance and the *F* Test

In testing the null hypothesis for the difference between sample means, the F test may be used to determine the significance of the difference. Remember, a t test may also be employed for this purpose when just two groups are to be compared. In fact, when there are just two groups, F is equal to t^2.

Analysis of variance is more versatile than the t test in that it can be employed when there are more than two groups to be compared; it can be

Table 3.16. t Test for Scores From Correlated Samples

REGULAR ENDURANCE TEST	MOTIVATED ENDURANCE TEST	DIFFERENCE (D)	d	d²
45	54	9	1	1
33	50	17	9	81
59	58	−1	−9	81
32	38	6	−2	4
30	42	12	4	16
27	35	8	0	0
29	38	9	1	1
59	66	7	−1	1
44	48	4	−4	16
40	49	9	1	1
		80		$\Sigma d^2 = 202$

$$\text{Mean difference } \overline{D} = \frac{\Sigma D}{n} = \frac{80}{10} = 8$$

$$s_D = \sqrt{\frac{\Sigma d^2}{n-1}} \qquad SE_{\overline{D}} = \frac{s_D}{\sqrt{n}} \qquad t = \frac{\overline{D}}{SE_{\overline{D}}}$$

$$s_D = \sqrt{\frac{202}{10-1}} \qquad SE_{\overline{D}} = \frac{4.74}{\sqrt{10}} \qquad t = \frac{8}{1.5}$$

$$s_D = \sqrt{22.44} \qquad SE_{\overline{D}} = \frac{4.74}{3.16} \qquad t = 5.33$$

$$s_D = 4.74 \qquad SE_{\overline{D}} = 1.5$$

utilized when there is more than one variable to be analyzed; and the procedures are used in computing intraclass reliability coefficients, which will be described later in the chapter.

Analysis of Variance for Comparing Independent Samples

To illustrate the steps involved in analysis of variance for comparing two independent groups, performances on the modified OSU (Ohio State University) Step Test by a group of sedentary adults who have just completed a nine-week course involving brisk walking are compared with performances of a similar sample of subjects who have been participating in bowling.

The mean of the walking group is 9 innings, and the mean of the bowling subjects is 5. Is the mean difference significant?

The reader is already acquainted with the bulk of the computations, since some of the procedures are identical to the computer method for correlation and standard deviation. The steps are illustrated in Table 3.17.

Step 1. Sum the raw scores (ΣX) and the squared raw scores (ΣX^2) for each group.

Step 2. Add the two raw score sums together to get a grand ΣX.

Step 3. Add the two squared raw score sums together to get a grand ΣX^2.

Step 4. Compute the total sum of squares (SS_T) by the formula:

$$SS_T = \text{grand } \Sigma X^2 - \frac{(\text{grand } \Sigma X)^2}{\text{total } N}$$

Note: The last half of the equation represents the correction (C) factor, which is necessary because the raw scores are used rather than deviations of the scores from the mean. The formula could be written:

$$SS_T = \text{grand } \Sigma X^2 - C$$

Step 5. Obtain the between-groups sum of squares (SS_B). This is computed by the formula:

$$SS_B = \frac{(\Sigma X_1)^2}{n_1} + \frac{(\Sigma X_2)^2}{n_2} - C$$

Step 6. Obtain the within-groups sum of squares (SS_W). This is obtained by simply subtracting the between-groups sum of squares from the total sum of squares:

$$SS_W = SS_T - SS_B$$

Table 3.17. Analysis of Variance for Independent Groups: Performance on Modified OSU Step Test

GROUP I (WALKING)			GROUP II (BOWLING)		
X_1	X_1^2		X_2	X_2^2	
10	100		3	9	
16	256		6	36	
5	25		2	4	
6	36		3	9	
12	144		7	49	
8	64	$\overline{X}_1 = \dfrac{\Sigma X_1}{n_1} = \dfrac{72}{8} = 9$	6	36	$\overline{X}_2 = \dfrac{\Sigma X_2}{n_2} = \dfrac{50}{10} = 5$
9	81		10	100	
6	36		1	1	
Step 1: $\Sigma X_1 = 72$	$\Sigma X_1^2 = 742$		8	64	
			4	16	
			Step 1: $\Sigma X_2 = 50$	$\Sigma X_2^2 = 324$	

Step 2: grand $\Sigma X = 72 + 50 = 122$

Step 3: grand $\Sigma X^2 = 742 + 324 = 1066$

Step 4: SS_T grand $\Sigma X^2 - \dfrac{(\text{grand } \Sigma X)^2}{\text{total } N} = 1066 - \dfrac{(122)^2}{18} = 1066 - 826.9 = 239.1$

Step 5: $SS_B = \dfrac{(\Sigma X_1)^2}{n_1} + \dfrac{(\Sigma X_2)^2}{n_2} - C = \dfrac{(72)^2}{8} + \dfrac{(50)^2}{10} - 826.9 = 898 - 826.9 = 71.1$

Step 6: $SS_W = SS_T - SS_B = 239.1 - 71.1 = 168$

Step 7: $MS_B = \dfrac{SS_B}{k - 1} = \dfrac{71.1}{2 - 1} = 71.1$

Step 8: $MS_W = \dfrac{SS_W}{N - k} = \dfrac{168}{18 - 2} = 10.5$

Step 9: $F = \dfrac{MS_B}{MS_W} = \dfrac{71.1}{10.5} = 6.77$

Step 7. Find the variance, or mean square (MS), for the between-groups sum of squares. This is found by dividing the SS_B by the degrees of freedom, which is the number of groups minus 1. The symbol for groups is usually given as k. Express the computation as

$$MS_B = \frac{SS_B}{k - 1}$$

If, for example, there are four groups, the degrees of freedom would be $k - 1 = 4 - 1 = 3$.

Step 8. Find the variance for the within-groups component (MS_W). This is determined by dividing the sum of squares for within groups by its degrees of freedom, which is the total number of subjects (N) minus the number of groups (k):

$$MS_W = \frac{SS_W}{N - k}$$

Step 9. Compute the F ratio. This is done by dividing the MS for the between-groups component by the MS for the within-groups component:

$$F = \frac{MS_B}{MS_W}$$

Step 10. Determine whether the F ratio is significant (whether there is a real difference at the .05 level between the walking and bowling groups). To do this, consult Table K.1 in Appendix K. The criterion value used to determine whether the F is significant is found by locating the *column* in the table with the degrees of freedom (df) of the between-groups MS. The table heading for columns is "Numerator Degrees of Freedom." In this problem, the df for between groups is $k - 1$, that is, $2 - 1 = 1$. Next, find the *row* that corresponds to the within-groups df, which is $N - k$ (18 − 2).

The rows are entitled "Denominator Degrees of Freedom" in the table. The intersection of the appropriate column and row for 1 and 16 df is 4.49 for the .05 level of probability. The F of 6.77 exceeds the value necessary to reject the null hypothesis at the .05 level of significance, and we can therefore conclude that there is a significant difference between the walking and bowling groups in favor of walking. In research publications, the summary of the analysis of variance is usually shown by a table similar to Table 3.18.

F Distribution and Tests of Significance

It is beyond the scope of this book to provide a comprehensive explanation of the F distribution and hypothesis testing. As a general statement, the probability of rejection of the null hypothesis is heavily dependent on variability within samples and on sample size.

It is evident from the F ratio that if there is a large within-groups variance (MS_W) in relation to the between-groups variance (MS_B), the size of the F will be decreased. This situation is much more likely to occur with small samples than with large samples, since the within-groups variance is calculated by dividing the within-groups sum of squares by ($N - k$) df. Consequently, a larger denominator would reduce the variance, provided that the within-groups sum of squares was not proportionately larger. However, the variability within groups is also influenced by sample size insofar as larger samples tend to approximate the population more closely, which in turn reduces the size of the variance. Another term often used for within-groups variance is *sampling error.*

An examination of the F tables in Appendix K reveals that the values needed for significance are greater with small samples (as reflected by $N - k$) than for larger samples. The reader is referred to a basic statistics textbook for a discussion of

type I and type II errors with regard to hypothesis testing. A type I error is when the null hypothesis is rejected when it is true; in other words, when one concludes that there is a significant difference between two samples when actually there is none. The type II error is when the hypothesis is accepted when it should be rejected.

A researcher can reduce the probability of committing a type I error by establishing a higher level of significance. For example, accepting significance at the .10 level (alpha level) means that one is willing to be wrong (i.e., conclude that there is a difference when the difference is actually due to chance or sampling error) 10 times out of 100. By setting the alpha level at the .05 level, the decision will be incorrect only 5 times out of 100, and at the .01 level, it will be incorrect once out of 100 times.

The alpha level should be set at the onset of a study. The .05 and .01 alpha levels are the two most frequently used in research. A type I error is usually more serious than a type II. The probability of making a type II error increases as the probability of making a type I error is reduced. One of the most effective ways to reduce the chance of type II error is to secure larger samples. As was stated earlier, a larger sample often automatically reduces the within-groups variance because it tends to approximate the population more closely.

The F tables in Appendix K are based on this premise, which is why a higher F is needed with small samples than with large. The tables are constructed to reduce the probability of committing a type I error. The F values needed for significance are in turn larger for the .05 level of significance than for the .10 alpha level, and the F values needed for the .01 level are greater still.

Analysis of Variance for Comparing Correlated (Paired) Samples

For illustrative purposes, let us determine whether a particular conditioning exercise program is effective in producing significant im-

Table 3.18. Summary of Analysis of Variance Comparison of Step Test Performance of Walking and Bowling Groups

SOURCE OF VARIATION	SUM OF SQUARES	DEGREES OF FREEDOM	MEAN SQUARE	F
Between	71.1	1	71.1	6.77[a]
Within	168.0	16	10.5	
Total	239.1	17		

[a]Significant at the .05 level.

provement in physical fitness. A fitness test was administered to a group of ten students at the beginning of a semester and again at the end of the semester after the students had participated in the exercise program. The average improvement in the physical fitness test was 2. (Small numbers are used simply for ease of presentation.) In actual practice, if the difference were very small, one would probably not bother to test it for significance. Furthermore, in a real situation, one would want to use an adequate number of subjects for increased confidence in any inferences that might be drawn from the results.

The initial and final fitness test scores for the ten subjects are shown in Table 3.19.

This comparison requires a slightly different procedure from the previous one, which involved two independent groups. Although this study also seeks to test the significance of the difference

between two sets of scores, the same people comprise the two groups. Therefore, the two scores are correlated, because we would expect each subject's final score to be related to his or her initial score regardless of treatment. (The same relationship would be found in a study using matched groups.) This poses a problem in that a considerable amount of the within-groups (error) sum of squares can be attributed to the pairing of scores because of the "carryover" of differences within the groups from the initial to the final test. Hence, this presents a new source of variation that has to be computed.

The steps in the analysis of variance for correlated (or repeated) measures are as follows:

Step 1. Obtain the ΣX and the ΣX^2 and compute the total sum of squares (SS_T) exactly as done in Table 3.17.

Table 3.19. Analysis of Variance for Correlated Groups (Repeated Measures)

INITIAL TEST	FINAL TEST	Σ ROWS	(Σ ROWS)²
5	6	11	121
3	5	8	64
4	9	13	169
8	10	18	324
1	4	5	25
6	5	11	121
2	6	8	64
5 $\overline{X} = 4.0$	7 $\overline{X} = 6.0$	12	144
2	3	5	25
4	5	9	81
$\Sigma X = \overline{40}$	$\Sigma X = \overline{60}$	grand $\Sigma X = \overline{100}$	(Σ rows)² = $\overline{1138}$

$$\Sigma X^2 = (5^2 + 3^2 + 4^2 + \ldots + 5^2) = 602$$

Step 1: $SS_T = \Sigma X^2 - C = 602 - \dfrac{(100)^2}{20} = 602 - 500 = 102$

Step 2: $SS_B = \dfrac{(\Sigma X)^2}{n_1} + \dfrac{(\Sigma X_2)^2}{n_2} - C = \dfrac{(40)^2}{10} + \dfrac{(60)^2}{10} - 500 = 520 - 500 = 20$

Step 3: $SS_R = \dfrac{(X_{11} + X_{12})^2 + (X_{21} + X_{22})^2 + \ldots + (X_{n1} + X_{n2})^2}{\text{(number or measures)}} - C$

$\qquad = \dfrac{(5 + 6)^2 + (3 + 5)^2 + \ldots + (4 + 5)^2}{2} - 500 = 569 - 500 = 69$

Step 4: $SS_E = SS_T - SS_B - SS_R = 102 - 20 - 69 = 13$

Step 5: $MS_B = \dfrac{SS_B}{k - 1} = \dfrac{20}{1} = 20$

Step 6: $MS_R = \dfrac{SS_R}{R - 1} = \dfrac{69}{9} = 7.67$

Step 7: $MS_E = \dfrac{SS_E}{(k - 1)(R - 1)} = \dfrac{13}{(1)(9)} = 1.44$

Step 8: $F = \dfrac{MS_B}{MS_E} = \dfrac{20}{1.44} = 13.89$

Step 2. Compute between-groups sum of squares (SS_B) in the same manner as in the previous example.

Step 3. Compute the sum of squares due to the pairing effect of the test–retest. This is done by adding the initial and final test scores for each subject, squaring the sums, and then adding all the squared sums for the ten subjects. The sum of the rows squared is divided by K (2), since two scores make up each sum. The usual correction factor *(C)* is then subtracted. Label the resulting sum of squares for subjects or rows, SS_R.

$$SS_R = \frac{(ER_1)^2 + (ER_2)^2 \ldots + (ER_n)^2}{K} - C$$

Step 4. Compute the error sum of squares (SS_E). The error is often referred to as *residual* or *interaction*.

$$SS_E = SS_T - SS_B - SS_R$$

Step 5. Compute the variance for between groups as in Table 3.19.

$$MS_B = \frac{SS_B}{k - 1}$$

Step 6. Compute the variance, or mean square, for subjects by dividing the SS_R by its degrees of freedom, which is one less than the number of subjects, or rows.

$$MS_R = \frac{SS_R}{R - 1}$$

Step 7. Obtain the error (or residual or interaction) of MS by dividing the SS_E by $(k - 1)(R - 1)$ degrees of freedom.

$$MS_E = \frac{SS_E}{(k - 1)(R - 1)}$$

Step 8. Compute the *F* ratio.

$$F = \frac{MS_B}{MS_E}$$

Step 9. Consult Table K.2 in Appendix K for appropriate degrees of freedom for numerator and denominator, in this case 1 and 9 df. The *F* required at the .01 alpha level is 10.56. Since the *F* ratio surpassed this, one can reject the null hypothesis at the .01 level and conclude that significant improvement in physical fitness was attained through the conditioning exercise program.

Table 3.20 summarizes the analysis of variance for the fitness gains.

Note: If the researcher had computed the analysis of variance for independent groups, the *F* would not have been significant, and the researcher would have committed a type II error.

Other Forms of Analysis of Variance

Analysis of variance in its simplest form has been presented. A number of more complex designs are used to detect different sources of variation. Our examples have used only two groups (or sets of scores). Analysis of variance can be performed with any number of groups. In fact, the main advantage of analysis of variance over the *t* test is that the *t* test cannot be used when more than two means are to be compared, because the means are no longer independent and the probability of committing type I error is increased.

When an analysis of variance is performed with three or more groups, the *F* test does not indicate where the differences are but only whether there are differences among the groups. Consequently, one must employ further analysis such as orthogonal comparisons or a multiple-range test such as the Scheffé, the Tukey hsd, the Duncan multiple range, or Newman–Keuls. The reader is referred

Table 3.20. Summary of Analysis of Variance for Improvements in Physical Fitness as a Result of a Conditioning Program

SOURCE OF VARIATION	SUM OF SQUARES	DEGREES OF FREEDOM	MEAN SQUARE	F
Subjects (rows)	69	9	7.67	
Between groups	20	1	20.00	13.89[a]
Error	13	9	1.44	
Total	102	19		

[a]Significant at the .01 level.

to Clarke and Clarke, Glass and Stanley, or Morehouse and Stull for discussion of the multiple-range tests. Steel and Torrie cover orthogonal comparisons.

When two or more variables are to be compared, two-way analysis of variance procedures allow comparisons of the main effects plus the interaction of variables, which enables the investigator to determine the effects of one variable in the presence of another.

Covariance is an extension of analysis of variance that permits statistical adjustment of groups by adjustment of the final means for any differences in initial means. In all analysis of variance designs, the basic model is the same, which is the division or partitioning of the total variation in scores into different components—or sources of variation—between and within groups.

Analysis of Variance for Estimating Reliability

The concept of reliability is discussed in Chapter 4. It refers to the repeatability of performance. Obviously, a test would be of little value if it did not yield consistent results if the same individuals were to take it more than once. Traditionally, product–moment correlation has been employed to estimate the reliability of a test by correlating the scores of a group of subjects on one day (or test administration) with the same subjects' scores on another day (or trial).

Safrit provided a comprehensive discussion of the limitations of the product–moment correlation coefficient for this purpose. Baumgartner and Jackson also discussed and documented reasons for the impropriety of the product–moment correlation for test reliability and objectivity. They cited three main weaknesses:

1. The product–moment correlation is a bivariate statistic, whereas reliability and objectivity estimates are univariate. In other words, product–moment correlation is designed to establish the relationship between two variables such as chinning performance and body weight. Reliability, on the other hand, deals with only one variable, and concerns the consistency of subjects on repeated measures of the same test. Similarly, objectivity involves one test (or variable) scored by two or more testers; thus, it too is a univariate statistic.

2. Product–moment correlation is limited to just two variables. Frequently, more than two trials are given and the tester is interested in know-

ing the reliability of multiple trials, or he or she wants to know the objectivity of judges when there are more than two. For example, if a test calls for three trials, the tester must either give three more trials with the average of each set used for the correlation, or give one additional trial so that the average of the first two trials can be correlated with the average of the last two trials. In either case, one or more extra trials must be given just for reliability purposes.

3. The product–moment correlation does not permit as thorough an examination of the different sources of variability on multiple trials as does the intraclass correlation coefficient by analysis of variance. In the previous example, if one correlates the average of the first three trials with the average of the last three trials, one would not take into consideration the trial-to-trial variation within each set of trials.

Analysis of Variance for Intraclass Correlation

The symbol R will be used for the intraclass correlation coefficient. It will be quickly obvious that the steps in computing R are nearly identical to the analysis of variance calculations previously covered.

A number of different statistical designs can be employed to analyze different sources of variance. As with practically all statistical techniques, opinions differ as to the relative merits of each design. The reader is again referred to Safrit for a more comprehensive discussion and pertinent references.

One design will suffice for the majority of test situations in which the tester wishes to estimate the reliability of a test (or the objectivity of judges). In the following example, the tester seeks to determine the reliability of four trials on a vertical jump test for girls. For simplicity, only five subjects will be used. The steps are illustrated in Table 3.21. Steps 1 through 7 are the same as the steps in analysis of variance for paired measures presented in Table 3.19.

Step 1. Compute the total SS.

Step 2. Compute the SS for trials (columns), which we have referred to as between groups in previous examples.

Step 3. Compute the sum of squares for subjects (rows).

Table 3.21. Intraclass Correlation for the Reliability of Four Trials on the Vertical Jump

SUBJECT	TRIAL 1	TRIAL 2	TRIAL 3	TRIAL 4	Σ Rows	$(\Sigma$ Rows$)^2$
A	8	9	11	10	38	1444
B	8	7	6	5	26	676
C	12	15	17	19	63	3969
D	9	13	12	15	49	2401
E	12	10	10	8	40	1600
ΣX:	49	54	56	57	grand ΣX: 216	10,090

$$\Sigma X^2 = (8^2 + 8^2 + 12^2 + \ldots + 8^2) = 2586$$

Step 1: $SS_T = 2586 - \dfrac{(216)^2}{20} = 2586 - 2332.8 = 253.2$

Step 2: $SS_B \text{ (trials)} = \dfrac{(49)^2 + (54)^2 + (56)^2 + (57)^2}{5} - 2332.8 = 7.6$

Step 3: $SS_R \text{ (subjects)} = \dfrac{10,090}{4} - 2332.8 = 2522.5 - 2332.8 = 189.7$

Step 4: $SS_E \text{ (interaction)} = 253.2 - 7.6 - 189.7 = 55.9$

Step 5: $MS_B \text{ (trials)} = \dfrac{SS_B}{k-1} = \dfrac{7.6}{4-1} = 2.53$

Step 6: $MS_R \text{ (subjects)} = \dfrac{SS_R}{R-1} = \dfrac{189.7}{5-1} = 47.43$

Step 7: $MS_E \text{ (interaction)} = \dfrac{SS_E}{(k-1)(R-1)} = \dfrac{55.9}{(3)(4)} = 4.66$

Step 8: $(F \text{ trials}) = \dfrac{MS_B}{MS_E} = \dfrac{2.53}{4.66} = .54$

Step 9: $R = \dfrac{MS_{(subjects)} - MS_{(error)}}{MS_{(subjects)}}$

$MS_{(subjects)} = 47.43 \quad MS_{(error)} = \dfrac{SS_{trials} + SS_{interaction}}{df_{trials} + df_{interaction}} = \dfrac{7.6 + 55.9}{3 + 12} = 4.23$

$R = \dfrac{47.43 - 4.23}{47.43} = .91$

Step 4. Compute the SS for interaction (designated as SS_E in Table 3.19).

Step 5. Compute the mean square for trials (MS_B).

Step 6. Compute the mean square for subjects (MS_R).

Step 7. Compute the mean square for interaction (MS_E).

Step 8. Compute the F test for trials (Table 3.22). This step determines whether there were significant differences among the trials. There are varying opinions as to what should be done if a significant difference is found. On the one hand, it can be argued that the performance should be consistent from one

trial to the next; any trial-to-trial variance should be attributed to measurement error.

On the other hand, it has been observed on numerous occasions that performances may improve with increased trials owing to a learning effect or release of inhibitions or both. Thus, it is contended that this source of variance should be removed from the estimate of reliability.

The tester thus must decide whether to include or remove any significant trial-to-trial variability from the error component. Authorities are not in agreement on the issue. In most instances, however, common sense should be able

Table 3.22.   Summary of Analysis of Variance for Reliability Estimate

SOURCE OF VARIATION	SUM OF SQUARES	DEGREES OF FREEDOM	MEAN SQUARE	F
Subjects	189.7	4	47.43	
Trials	7.6	3	2.53	.54[a]
Interaction	55.9	12	4.66	
Total	253.2	19		

[a]Not significant at the .05 level.

to dictate the decision or at least offer logical alternatives.

First, it should interest the tester whether there are significant differences among trials. If there are no differences, the variance for trials is simply included as part of the measurement error. If differences are found, the tester should analyze the scores to detect any trend such as a learning phenomenon. If the differences appear to be random, the trial variability should not be removed but should be considered measurement error.

Baumgartner and Jackson advocated a procedure in which, if a significant F for trials is found, the tester discards any trials that are quite dissimilar from the rest of the trials. A new analysis is performed with the remaining trials and another F is computed, until no significant trial differences are found. This procedure seems most appropriate when a trend is apparent in the data, such as when subjects show early improvement and then level off. For example, if five trials on a shuttle run agility test yielded a significant F for trials with means of 11.6, 11.2, 10.7, 10.6, and 10.7 sec, the tester might logically discard the first two trials and compute another analysis with the last three trials. If no significant trial differences are found with the new analysis, the tester then includes whatever variance was found for trials in the error component. Moreover, this procedure would indicate that the subjects should be given some practice trials prior to test trials.

Step 9.   Compute R. The formula for R reflects a ratio of true score variance to observed score variance. Theoretically, any observed score consists of the true score plus error score. (Sources of error will be discussed in some detail in Chapter 4.) People do not perform identically, however, on every trial, a fact partially due to measurement error. In theory, any single score can be considered as representing true score plus whatever measurement error exists. Furthermore, the variance of a group of observed scores equals the variance of the true scores plus the variance of the error scores.

Reliability *(R)* can be defined as the true score variance divided by the observed score variance. In estimating R from a set of scores, the formula is:

$$R = \frac{MS_{(subjects)} - MS_{(error)}}{MS_{(subjects)}}$$

Note: Since we have suggested that between-trial variance be included as measurement error, either with or without adjustments for trend (step 8), the mean square for error will consist of the *combined* sum of squares for trials and interaction divided by the degrees of freedom for *both* trials and interaction, that is:

$$MS_E = \frac{SS_B + SS_E}{df_B + df_E}$$

In the example in Table 3.22, the F for trials was not significant, so the variance for trials was included with the error variance and R was computed to be .91 (Table 3.21). The same procedures could have been applied for the objectivity of different testers or judges. Instead of trials, the columns in Table 3.21 would be testers or judges.

IV. USING THE COMPUTER

A few years ago, doctoral students and research professors were the only persons in physical education who used computers to any extent. This has changed rapidly, reflecting the change in society. Computerized information is now a routine part of most phases of our daily lives. In education, elementary school children are being introduced to computer operation, and desktop microcomputers are a common sight in the classroom. In 1980, nearly a half million personal computers were sold in the United States. Interestingly, children have accepted and learned to use computers more readily than adults.

Physical educators can utilize computers for measurement and evaluation purposes in many ways. Most public school teachers have the opportunity to use computers. The majority of school systems have computer facilities or easy access to them through a nearby university or industry. However, in this book we will not present a detailed description of the use of computers in physical education. We will merely provide a general introduction to computer operation and will briefly discuss microcomputers and ways in which physical education teachers, coaches, or both might use computer services. Readers are urged to familiarize themselves with computer operation so they can use the computer effectively for measurement needs.

THE COMPUTER

Computer machinery and instrumentation are referred to as hardware. The computer can process a tremendous amount of information in a very short time, and it can store a vast amount of data. The user must supply the data and also tell the computer what to do with it. Fortunately, for our purposes we don't have to be computer experts to tell the computer what to do with the data. We have only to select the appropriate program (software) already written by a computer expert, and run it on the computer.

INPUT OF DATA

The user transmits data and gives commands to the computer in any of several ways: by cards, by a terminal, by optical scanner sheets, or by microcomputer.

Cards

The use of cards is nearly obsolete. In this method, a typewriter-like keypunch machine is used to record data on cards. Subject identification number, gender, age, grade, or other relevant information is coded by punching out (by typing) numbers and letters. Some of the cards are coded to tell the computer certain information such as user identification, what statistical program to run, and how the computer is to read the columns with regard to number of variables and where the decimals are. A card is prepared for each person tested. The computer can handle hundreds of cards in a matter of seconds.

Terminal

The most popular way of transmitting information to the computer is through a terminal. A terminal usually consists of a typewriter keyboard with a television screen. The terminal is connected to the host computer (mainframe) by a phone line. The data and program instructions for the computer are transmitted electronically to the computer. Data are typed into the terminal and appear on a video screen, so that they can be checked and edited before being sent to the computer. An advantage of the terminal is that it can be located a considerable distance from the computer.

Optical Scanner Sheets

This method of feeding information to the computer is used in physical education mostly for written tests, questionnaires, and other inventories. Every student has at one time or another marked answers to multiple-choice questions by darkening answer spaces on a scanner sheet. The scanner sheet is read by the computer by means of different light patterns, which trigger electrical impulses to the computer. With this method, students' scores can be fed to the computer without having to put them on cards or type them on a terminal. There is a sheet for each student. Of course, one has to tell the computer what to do with the data. Physical performance tests can also be scored with optical scanner sheets.

Microcomputer

Data can be submitted to the mainframe from a microcomputer by means of a *modem*. A modem is an attachment that enables the microcomputer to communicate with other computers by phone. Data can be entered directly in the same manner as with a terminal, or it can be stored and entered on a disk. The latter method has obvious advantages in that scores can be amassed, edited, and entered all at one time. The use of microcomputers in measurement in physical education is discussed later in this chapter.

PROGRAMS

The term *programming* has been used several times in the foregoing discussion with regard to giving instructions to the computer. A computer can perform only those operations that it has been directed to do. Instructions are given to the computer in the form of a program, and the process of doing so is called programming. A professional programmer has to learn computer languages, which consist of various algebraically oriented commands. Some languages are FORTRAN, PASCAL, COBOL, and BASIC. Programs are the "software" of the computer system.

One does not have to be proficient in programming to use computers because "canned" programs are available for many applications. For test analysis, there are programs that enable one to analyze data by a variety of statistical techniques such as correlation, regression, multiple correlation, *t* test, analysis of variance, covariance, and factor analysis. The programs also can present the data graphically. Furthermore, the programs provide instructions on how to alter and custom-tailor existing programs to best fit the purpose. The three statistical program packages that are often used in physical education are SPSS (Statistical Package for the Social Sciences) (Nie et al., 1975), SAS (Statistical Analysis System) (Barr et al., 1976), and BMD (Biomedical Computer Programs) (Dixon, 1974).

These three packages have a number of similarities, but each has its own specific terminology and ways of describing the data and requesting the analysis. Each has a manual that can be followed quite easily.

BASIC STEPS IN COMPUTER ANALYSIS OF DATA

Step 1. Before collecting the data, it is a good idea to consult with someone at the computer center (or any knowledgeable individual, such as a colleague who is familiar with the operations). This person most likely will be able to give you some tips on how to record and arrange the data to save time and effort later.

Step 2. Collect the data, making sure that you obtain all the necessary information such as age if needed, grade, and so on.

Step 3. Record the data on the recommended form or coding sheet as directed by the "consultant." You can thus allocate the correct number of columns for the various items of information and scores, which will make subsequent transmission of data to the computer a simple process.

Step 4. Consult with a computer center operator again for instructions on how to use the terminal.

Step 5. Give commands to the computer by typing them on the terminal typewriter. There are certain statements and commands that have to be given to the computer to get the data analyzed.

    a. The first thing to do is to identify yourself in the prescribed manner for the particular computer center. The computer operator will explain how to do this. You will need a user identification and perhaps a password.

    b. You will then tell the computer what statistical program package to use, such as SAS, SPSS, or BMD.

    c. You also need to name the analysis or job, so that it can be identified later. For example, you may wish to store it, or you may have several sets of data to analyze.

    d. Give the appropriate job control language (JCL) commands. These commands specify how the computer is to read the data, what the variables are, the nature of the scores, the decimals, whether there are minus values, and so on, according to the format of the particular packaged program.

Step 6. Enter the data, for example, the scores to be analyzed.

Step 7. Tell the computer what statistical analysis you want and any other operations to be performed such as correlations by age, plotting or charting of the data, and perhaps sorting and printing of certain data sets.

Step 8. Submit the job to the computer.

Appendix E gives a sample of the program commands for a Statistical Analysis System (SAS) correlation analysis.

MICROCOMPUTERS

The use of small desktop computers, called microcomputers, has increased tremendously. Some of the reasons for the great interest among researchers and educators in microcomputers are their simplicity of use, their decreased cost, and their packaging of large amounts of computing power in increasingly smaller packages.

The microcomputer has become a significant tool in computer-assisted instruction in the classroom from elementary school through college. There is every indication that microcomputers will become more and more popular in the near future. Some authors have predicted that the microcomputer will soon be a common fixture in teachers' offices just as the hand calculator is now.

Microcomputers are evaluated on features such as (1) size of the memory, (2) availability and quality of software (for analysis of data, record keeping, word processing), (3) peripherals available (storage capacity, printers, modems for communicating with other computers, and input devices), (4) size and clarity of graphics capabilities, (5) screen display (number of characters × lines), (6) keyboard style and features, (7) potential for expansion and communication with other computers, and (8) computer languages used for programming. Cost and service capabilities are obviously other important considerations.

Microcomputers are easy to use. For most operations it is simply a matter of turning the computer on, selecting and inserting the disk that has the desired statistical analysis program, responding to a few questions about the nature of the data (number of variables, number of subjects, etc.), entering the data by typing each person's score or scores, and then simply recording or printing the results of the analysis.

There are many ways that a physical educator can use microcomputers for measurement. Because of its portability, a microcomputer can be taken to the gymnasium to assist in test scoring. For example, a microcomputer can be of immense help in computations such as regression formulas for predicting percent body fat from skin fold measurements, computing relative strength by dividing body weight into amount of weight lifted, averaging scores on several trials, and computing weighted total standard scores.

The calculation of standard scores and norms can be greatly facilitated with a microcomputer. Norm data can be stored and new data then added for revising norms. Intraclass reliability and validity coefficients can be calculated. The physical educator can compute correlations between measures and develop regression equations; t tests and analysis of variance can be performed to compare groups. The microcomputer can make graphs and charts to display test data, to illustrate comparative performances from year to year, for example. Fitness scores and norms can be computed and stored on disks.

A microcomputer with a word processor and printer can be of tremendous help in constructing and revising written tests. Test items can be stored and retrieved for use in making new tests or alternate forms of a test. The entire test can be "pieced together" by the word processor. In addition, the microcomputer can be used in item analysis.

Coaches also can find many uses for microcomputers. Conditioning data such as strength, power, speed, agility, and body composition measurements can be rapidly analyzed and profiled. Practice data, game statistics, and scouting information can be stored, retrieved, and processed. The possibilities are endless.

The growing importance of computers is an inescapable feature of modern life. Physical education teachers should welcome and take advantage of the fruits of these technologic advances to improve their measurement and evaluation programs.

PROBLEMS

1. Find the mean, median, and mode for the following scores: 10, 17, 9, 5, 3, 15, 4, 8, 10, 20, 9, 7, 9, 3, 6.

2. Compute the mean and standard deviation for the following sets of scores:
   a. 13, 11, 6, 3, 15, 10, 5, 8, 7, 12, 1, 7, 8, 8, 11, 2, 7, 8, 8, 6, 9, 10, 8, 9, 8.
   b. 9, 12, 15, 11, 10, 7, 20, 15, 11, 12, 15, 20, 10, 8.
   c. 18, 21, 17, 18, 10, 23, 18, 25, 15, 22, 20, 18, 12, 20, 12, 21, 20, 15, 17, 18.

3. Construct T scales for the three sets of data in problem 2.

4. Rank the following 12 students on right and left grip strength and compute a rank–order correlation between the two variables:

STUDENT	GRIP STRENGTH (kg)	
	Right	Left
A	32	30
B	42	36
C	39	33
D	35	37
E	40	37
F	31	27
G	30	35
H	38	36
I	42	38
J	34	32
K	38	39
L	43	40

5. Using the same raw scores as in problem 4, compute the product–moment correlation using the deviation method.

6. Construct percentile norms for the following physical fitness test scores:

60	50	40
64	62	46
55	43	74
42	58	50
80	49	61
54	59	68
58	75	54
53	57	44
48	56	70
71	33	52
55	52	55
46	65	40

7. Determine the correlation between grip strength *(X)* and results of a tennis wall volley test *(Y)* using the computer method.

X	Y	X	Y	X	Y
107	25	153	19	117	15
130	30	110	10	115	23
143	44	148	24	100	26
112	34	121	38	155	31
88	6	98	22	106	16
124	14	141	18	113	19
104	12	165	29	103	38
120	28	110	21	95	13
118	20	104	25	112	28
102	9	122	24	129	22

8. Use a *t* test for independent groups to compare the mean performance on a volleyball wall volley test of Group A, whose members practiced 45 min daily, with Group B, whose members practiced two days per week for 1½ hr each day. Test the mean difference for significance at the .05 level.

GROUP A	GROUP B
30	26
38	27
36	34
29	24
35	23
37	32
28	25
40	20
35	22
32	19
	23

9. Compare groups A and B in problem 8 with analysis of variance for independent groups. What is the relationship between the *F* ratio you obtain to the *t* value you computed in question 8?

10. Determine whether the following students in a beginning badminton class made significant improvement in a cardiovascular fitness test by analysis of variance with repeated measures.

STUDENT	PRETEST	POSTTEST
A	60	65
B	43	50
C	65	65
D	64	72
E	76	80
F	81	80
G	59	63
H	69	66
I	72	74
J	58	57

11. Calculate the reliability of three trials on a volleyball skills test using the intraclass correlation technique.

SUBJECT	TRIAL 1	TRIAL 2	TRIAL 3
A	3	6	4
B	6	8	2
C	5	5	3
D	10	9	12
E	4	7	6
F	18	15	16
G	1	7	3

BIBLIOGRAPHY

Barr, A. J., et al., *A User's Guide to SAS 76*. Cary, N.C.: Statistical Analysis System Institute, 1976.

Bartz, A. E., *Basic Statistical Concepts in Education and the Sciences*. Minneapolis: Burgess, 1976.

Baumgartner, T. A., and A. S. Jackson, *Measurement for Evaluation in Physical Education*. 2nd ed. Dubuque, Iowa: William C. Brown, 1982.

Behnke, A. R., and J. H. Wilmore, *Evaluation and Regulation of Body Build and Composition*. Englewood Cliffs, N.J.: Prentice-Hall, 1974.

Clarke, H. H., and D. H. Clarke, *Advanced Statistics With Applications to Physical Education*. Englewood Cliffs, N.J.: Prentice-Hall, 1972.

Dixon, W. J., Ed., *BMD: Biomedical Computer Programs*. Berkeley, Calif.: University of California Press, 1974.

Garrett, H. E., *Statistics in Psychology and Education*. 5th ed. New York: Longmans, Green, 1958, p. 179.

Glass, G. V., and J. C. Stanley, *Statistical Methods in Education and Psychology*. Englewood Cliffs, N.J.: Prentice-Hall, 1970.

Helwig, J. T., *SAS Introductory Guide*. Cary, N.C.: Statistical Analysis System Institute, 1978.

Lindgren, B. W., *Basic Ideas of Statistics*. New York: Macmillan, 1975.

Morehouse, C. A., and G. A. Stull, *Statistical Principles and Procedures With Applications for Physical Education*. Philadelphia: Lea & Febiger, 1975.

Nie, N. H., et al., *SPSS: Statistical Package for the Social Sciences*. 2nd ed. New York: McGraw-Hill, 1975.

Safrit, M. J., Ed., *Reliability Theory*. Reston, Va.: AAHPERD, 1976.

Steel, R. G. D., and J. H. Torrie, *Principles and Procedures of Statistics*. New York: McGraw-Hill, 1960.

Weber, J. C., and D. R. Lamb. *Statistics and Research in Physical Education*. St. Louis: C. V. Mosby, 1970.

CHAPTER 4

TEST EVALUATION, CONSTRUCTION, AND ADMINISTRATION

OBJECTIVES

After reading this chapter, the student should be able to:

1. Identify sound criteria for the evaluation and selection of tests in physical education

2. Describe and apply the steps involved in the construction of a motor performance test

3. Apply the principles of test administration in measuring motor performance

---

For physical education teachers to evaluate effectively tests that are available for use in their program, they should have knowledge about the construction of tests. Included in the procedures for test construction are the criteria by which a test may be judged. This information enables teachers to acquire confidence in their efforts to establish their own tests.

BASIC CONCEPTS IN TEST EVALUATION

Four of the most basic concepts involved in test construction and evaluation are *validity, reliability, objectivity,* and *norms.*

Validity

Validity refers to the degree to which a test measures what it was designed to measure. To the beginner in the field of tests and measurements, this concept may seem so basic that it scarcely deserves mention. Nevertheless, many tests are found to be rather weak in this most basic consideration. Probably every student has had the unnerving experience of being given a test that seems to pertain to some course other than the one in which he or she is enrolled. In such cases

the test fails in content validity by not being related to the material that has been covered in the course.

Another example of poor test validity is the case of the student who can beat everyone in the class, say in badminton, but whose grade is lowered because he does poorly on one skill test (say, bouncing the shuttle off a wall). In this instance the teacher, in his or her zeal to employ objective measures, has overlooked their main function—to supplement other means of evaluation. In addition to the teacher's misuse of the test, the test itself did not represent an accurate measure of ability to play badminton. We should hasten to say that, in many cases, volleying tests demonstrate high validity. The point we are attempting to make with this example is that the test constituted a somewhat artificial setting, and it touched on only a small facet of the game. For a test to be valid, a critical analysis must be made as to the nature of the activity it is to measure and the skills and special abilities that are involved.

Since testing has different purposes, and since validity refers to the degree to which a test achieves its purpose, it follows that there are different types of validity. We will briefly describe four kinds of validity and ways by which validity may be established. There may be considerable overlap among the different types of validity, depending on the purpose or purposes for using a test.

Face Validity

A test has face validity if it appears to measure the ability in question. Some measurement specialists do not like the term *face validity*. The term *logical validity* is often used when a test obviously involves the skill or ability that is being evaluated. A test that calls for a student to walk along a narrow board or beam is obviously a test of dynamic balance. A test that requires a subject to run rapidly in and around closely spaced obstacles can be considered to have face validity as an agility test, and so on. While face validity does not lend itself to any type of statistical treatment, it is an important concept that unfortunately is often overlooked by testers in search of highly objective measures.

A tester should always be cognizant of face validity, since it is of paramount importance from the student's point of view. More will be said about face validity as we discuss other concepts of validity as well as the other functional criteria for judging the worth of a test.

Content Validity

Whether a test possesses content validity is a subjective judgment. Content validity is, however, fundamental for tests that aim to measure what students have learned in a class. It must be kept in mind that a test represents a sampling of test items from a so-called universe of possible test items. Unfortunately, it sometimes becomes a guessing game on the part of the students, who hope that the teacher will select a sample of items that corresponds to what they have been studying. A big difference between the test and the students' expectations may indicate either poor communication with respect to the course objectives or poor test construction. Content validity applies to physical performance tests as well as to written tests. If, for example, 90% of the instruction in beginning tennis concentrated on forehand and backhand ground strokes and service, skills tests should attempt to assess these skills if they are to demonstrate content validity. It stands to reason that face validity of the test item serves to reinforce content validity in skills testing.

Criterion Validity

Sometimes a test is used to predict future performance or is used in place of another test that is perhaps longer or requires more elaborate equipment or facilities. The terms *predictive validity* and *concurrent validity* also have been used to designate these concepts. Both are based on a criterion that is considered to represent the performance or characteristics in question. A college entrance examination is an example of a test that attempts to predict success in college, which is the criterion. Motor-educability tests were developed in physical education a number of years ago. It was hoped that such tests would predict the ease with which the student could learn motor skills. Obviously, the identification of the proper criterion is of critical importance. As a general rule, the use of more than one criterion is recommended.

Often it may be advantageous in terms of time, equipment, facilities, or other conditions for a physical educator to be able to use a shorter, less elaborate, or less rigorous test. For example, suppose that a teacher wishes to measure cardiorespiratory fitness. The most valid measure of this parameter is generally acknowledged to be maximal oxygen consumption, which requires expensive equipment for the necessary gas analysis, considerable time for individual testing, and subjects who are willing to exercise maximally. Thus, a test that does not require such expensive equipment and can employ mass testing and submaximal exercise is desirable. The construction of such a test may employ maximal oxygen consumption as the criterion.

Results of round-robin tournaments, judges' ratings, or both are sometimes used as criteria for sports skills tests. The tournaments and ratings take considerable time, scheduling, and special arrangements, and therefore the use of skills tests would be advantageous if their results could be demonstrated to be suitable criteria.

The degree of association of a measure with the criterion is usually evaluated statistically by correlation. In Chapter 3 we cautioned that correlation does not imply causation. A test may correlate with the criterion, but the reason may not be apparent. It could well be that another factor or several factors are associated with both variables and are the cause of the relationship. A former colleague who had been a tennis coach for many years maintained that he could devise a test of throwing apples in a basket that would correlate as highly with tennis-playing ability as some of the tennis skills tests. Although he never followed through with this claim, he was undoubtedly basing his assertion on the fact that there are probably some underlying motor abilities necessary for successfully throwing apples into a basket that also contribute to success in tennis. Another example is the Knox Penny Cup

Test that consists of a person running and dropping a penny in one of three cups that are painted different colors and placed in a row on the floor. As the student runs toward the three cups, the tester calls out a color, thereby requiring the student to make a rapid choice of action. The author of the test reported a very high correlation with the criterion of basketball-playing ability. In this case, the choice–response factor that is probably being measured by the Penny Cup Test is also a factor in basketball, and this might account for the correlation. However, the test completely fails with respect to face validity and content validity and would likely not be accepted by students as a measure of basketball skill. Face validity should never be ignored in test construction, and the potential user of a test must not be totally concerned with (or misled by) statistical evidence of validity.

Construct Validity

The term *construct validity* refers to the degree to which performances on a test correspond to the abilities or traits that the test purports to measure. Construct validity can be established in different ways, but methodology is mostly based on testing the theory that underlies the parameter. For example, the LSU (Louisiana State University) Step Test presented in Chapter 9 consists of five pulse counts: before exercise, immediately after exercise, and 1, 2, and 3 min into recovery. The test is based on the constructs that these pulse measures do reflect differences in cardiorespiratory fitness; that is, a person with a high degree of fitness generally has a lower pulse rate at rest, the pulse count is lower after a standard workout, and the recovery rate is faster. Consequently, if the test is valid, conditioned individuals should have a lower profile of pulse counts than unconditioned subjects.

An experimental study could be set up to establish construct validity based on the underlying theory as follows: All subjects are given the step test and then assigned to groups. One group serves as control and does not undergo any conditioning, another group engages in a physical conditioning program, and perhaps another group is given an exercise program of greater or lesser intensity or duration. The step test can be said to demonstrate construct validity if it reflects the expected gains in cardiovascular fitness as a result of the conditioning programs. The degree to which it can distinguish between levels of fitness may be eval-uated by whether it reveals a difference between the two exercise programs.

Another method by which construct validity can be estimated is by correlation of the test with another test of its kind, since a cardiovascular test could be expected to correlate with other cardiovascular tests. Construct validity may also be appropriate, however, when no measures of the ability in question are widely accepted as valid tests. An example might be perceptual motor ability, for which there is no acknowledged criterion measure such as is maximal oxygen consumption for cardiovascular fitness. It would be logical, then, for a tester to examine the constructs underlying perceptual motor performance and seek to evaluate his or her test in light of these constructs.

Reliability

Reliability may be thought of as the repeatability of test results. A student's scores should not differ markedly on repeated administrations of the same test. Some measurements must be exactly the same each time to be considered reliable, while other measurements are allowed more leeway. For example, a scale reading would not be acceptable at all if it were not the same each time a specified weight was placed on the scale. On the other hand, a student could not be expected to obtain the exact same score on a golf test involving the hitting of balls into numbered circles. In the latter example, too many factors are involved that tend to reduce the probability of identical scores.

Reliability and validity are interrelated. In fact, reliability is a necessary part of validity, because if consistent measurements cannot be achieved, the test cannot be considered valid. To illustrate, suppose that a physical education teacher wishes to measure leg strength. Using a dynamometer and belt arrangement, she is able to obtain an accurate measure of force exerted by the legs. However, the exact angle at which the leg extension test is performed is difficult to determine. Consequently, although the teacher obtains an accurate (and valid) measure of a particular student's leg lift at a specified angle, she may find considerable variation in his scores on subsequent tests because of her difficulty in establishing the correct angle—resulting in a low reliability coefficient. Furthermore, when she tests a group of students for leg strength, her inability to establish the same angle for everyone results in an invalid measure of the group's leg strength at the desired position.

On the other hand, a test can be reliable and yet be not valid. Suppose that, in an attempt to isolate and measure leg strength, a teacher has students push upward on a bar placed on their shoulders and attached to a dynamometer. Regardless of the fact that consistent (reliable) scores are obtained on repeated tests, the test is invalid, because the amount that each student can lift is limited by the amount of weight that the back can support. Consequently, the strength of the legs, which is much greater than that of the back, is not being isolated.

In Chapter 3 we made the point that theoretically any observed score contains the subject's true score plus measurement error. Therefore, reliability is defined as the true score variance divided by the observed score variance. Measurement error encompasses many things, some of which are obvious while others may be more obscure.

Possible influences on a student's performance from one occasion to another on the same test (sources of measurement error) include the clarity and consistency of instructions, the number of trials given, the subject's state of health, the subject's concentration and determination, whether spectators are present, the subject's conception of the importance of the test (i.e., the many factors encompassed under student motivation), the length of the test, fatigue, environmental effects of temperature and humidity, the scoring procedures, whether knowledge of results is given, differences in test administration procedures, and the length of time between trials. Ordinarily, the concept of reliability assumes that the time interval between a test and retest is not long enough to allow real changes in ability that might be attributed to maturation, learning, forgetting, or changes in physical condition.

A tester can establish reliability in different ways. The test–retest method is often preferable in physical performance tasks. A test–retest could be given on the same day or on different days. One would expect higher reliability coefficients for the former situation than the latter (unless fatigue is a factor), since the variables influencing performance would be more likely to be comparable when the test is given twice on the same day. The reader is referred to Chapter 3 for a discussion of intraclass correlation coefficients.

The reliability of written tests and tests that have a number of trials, such as reaction time tests and some accuracy tests, is sometimes determined by what is called the split-halves technique. This method usually involves a division of the test into a set of odd-numbered trials or items and a set of even-numbered trials or items. The two sets are correlated. Then, because the test has been halved, the correlation is stepped up by the Spearman–Brown formula (see Chapter 21). This technique is not as appropriate as the intraclass correlation coefficient, since it uses a bivariate statistic for a univariate situation. Moreover, a split-halves correlation and a step-up procedure usually produce a spuriously high r.

In addition to the many factors associated with the test situation and the subject's physical and emotional condition, reliability is affected by the spread or variance of the scores. Unless there is a reasonable distribution of performances among the subjects, the trial-to-trial reliability coefficient will be low. A teaching technique that is sometimes employed to demonstrate this point is to have students guess what the correlation would be in this example:

Five individuals were tested on two separate days on the standing broad jump. Each person jumped 6 ft the first day and 6 ft the second. What is the test–retest reliability?

Most students will guess that the R (or r) will be 1.00, or perfect. Actually, it will be 0.00, because there is no scatter or spread of scores within the sets of data. (Try it with either R or r.)

The length of a test is an important factor. Generally speaking, the more trials, the higher the reliability. Common sense indicates that we could find a more reliable estimate of a student's true ability in free-throw shooting if we gave the student 30 trials rather than only 2 or 3. Another generality is that performances that call for near maximal exertion, such as strength or power measures, require fewer trials for reliability purposes than do performances that demand more precise neuromuscular responses, such as accuracy tasks.

Objectivity

Objectivity of a test pertains primarily to the clarity of the directions for administering and scoring the test. High objectivity is obtained when different teachers give a test to the same individuals and obtain approximately the same results. Naturally, the assumption is that the testers are equally competent. Objectivity is a part of reliability, or a form of it. Testing and scoring are two major sources of potential problems regarding the reliability of any test. As with any testing situation, the competency of the tester and the skill and care with which he or she administers the test are determining factors in obtaining reliable and thus valid results. Objectivity is dependent to a large extent on how complete and clear are the test instructions. For example, for the timing of a race, if directions are not clear as to when the watch should be started—at the sound of the gun or when the smoke is seen—there is increased likelihood for error. Moreover, if procedures for scoring are not standardized, some testers will record scores to the nearest half second, others to the nearest tenth of a second, and so on.

Norms

Norms are values considered representative of a specified population. A test that has accompanying norms is definitely desirable. Norms provide information that enables the student and teacher to interpret the student's score in relation to the scores made by other individuals in the same population. An understanding of what constitutes the "same population" is necessary for intelligent use of norm tables.

Norms are usually based on age, grade, height, or weight or various combinations of these characteristics. In norm tables for physical performance there are separate scales for boys and girls; in written tests this distinction is usually not made. The important factor is that norm tables are interpreted in light of the specific group from which the norms were compiled. For example, a standing broad jump of 8 ft would not be impressive at all if done by a college athlete, whereas it would be an outstanding achievement if performed by a 10-year-old boy.

To evaluate performance in relation to a set of norms, one must first evaluate the adequacy of the norms. Several factors should be considered.

1. The number of subjects used in establishing the norms should be sufficiently large. Although sheer numbers do not guarantee accuracy, in general the larger the sample, the more likely that it will approximate the population.

2. The norms should represent the performance of the population for which the test was devised. It would not be appropriate to compile norms from a select group (such as physical education majors) to represent all college students in a physical performance test. Similarly, the user of norms should not evaluate the performance of his

or her students on the basis of norms designed for a different population.

3. The geographic distribution that norms represent should be taken into account. Considerable variation in performance is often found among students in different geographic locations. For the most part, local norms are of more value to the teacher than are national norms.

4. The clarity of the directions for test administration and scoring is definitely involved in the evaluation of the accompanying norms. If the testing and scoring procedures that the teacher uses are not identical to those that the testers who compiled the norms employed, the norms are worthless.

5. Norms are only temporary and must be revised periodically. Certain traits, characteristics, and abilities of children today differ from those of children a number of years ago. Consequently, the date on which the norms were established should be considered and weighed accordingly.

ADDITIONAL CRITERIA FOR THE SELECTION AND EVALUATION OF TESTS

In addition to the basic concepts of validity, reliability, objectivity, and norms, several other features should be considerations in the selection and evaluation of tests. These are presented here in the form of questions that one might ask before selecting a particular test as part of the evaluation program.

1. *Is the Test Easy to Administer?*   Ease of administration involves many things, including time, equipment, space, and number of testers needed. The administrative feasibility of a test extends to the attitude that the tester, and certainly the students, have toward the test. Some physical fitness tests, for example, are so rigorous that some students who do them actually become ill and others suffer from soreness for days afterward. In such a case, the test could have high validity, reliability, and objectivity coefficients; it could possess any number of desirable test characteristics, such as economy of time, space, or equipment; but it would still be unacceptable. Thus, ease of administration encompasses the entire realm of administrative considerations, including attitude in

relation to the contribution that the test can make to the program.

2. *Does the Test Require Expensive Equipment?* A formidable item to consider in any school testing program is cost. Undoubtedly, if a school had unlimited resources it could use elaborate instruments, machines, and electronic devices to measure human performance with great precision. In reality, however, the physical education budget rarely permits the purchase of expensive equipment that is only applicable to a specific test. Some tests must be excluded for exactly this reason. One of the outstanding features of the AAHPERD Youth Fitness Test is that it requires almost no equipment. Occasionally a teacher may have to compromise to some extent by selecting a test having less accuracy than another but requiring less equipment.

3. *Can the Test Be Administered in a Relatively Short Time?* A perpetual problem that confronts most physical educators is the numerous encroachments on class time. Recognizing this, most authorities recommend that tests and measurements programs consume no more than 10% of the total instructional time. Therefore, any single test battery must be evaluated in terms of economy of time as well as of money. This often presents the teacher with a dilemma. For a test to meet the demands of validity and reliability, a sufficient number of trials must be given, which may consume more time than the teacher wishes to spend. Attempts to compromise, by reducing the number of test items or trials or both, usually result in a serious loss in validity and reliability, thereby reducing the intended worth of the test. The problem is compounded in short activity units, in which time for instruction and practice is at a premium.

4. *Can the Test Be Used as a Drill During Practice Sessions?* Although this feature of a test is not always desirable, its presence can offer a partial solution to the problem of economy of time as well as of other test criteria. For example, the more familiar students are with a test, the less time the teacher needs to explain the administration and scoring procedures. In addition, practice of the test serves to reduce the effects of insight

into the nature of the test, which may cause a rather pronounced improvement in scores in the middle or later portions of the test.

If the test is a measure of skills that represent the actual abilities required in the activity, its use as a form of practice would seem to be logical and desirable. This line of reasoning is based on the principle of content validity—in other words, students should be tested on what they have practiced. On the other hand, if the test skill is artificial and the student practices it more than the actual activity, the test is not suitable as a drill during practice sessions.

5. *Does the Test Require Several Trained Testers?* Since some test batteries contain a number of individual test items, in the interest of time it is almost imperative that more than one person be called on to administer the test. Furthermore, some test items require more skill and experience to administer than others, and thus training and practice are needed. If more than one person is to give the same test, standardized directions and objectivity coefficients should be established.

The utilization of several testers requires considerable planning and organization. Naturally, arrangements must be made to have the testers available at the proper time. Pretest meetings are usually required, and various other details of coordination need to be accomplished.

Thus far it would appear that tests that call for several testers are undesirable. At times, however, tests of this nature are of immense value. One such instance is when large-scale comprehensive evaluation is advocated, as is sometimes the case for physical fitness testing at various times during the school year. Generally, placement and screening tests are most effectively administered in this way.

To summarize, whenever the abilities that are to be measured necessitate the use of several test items, or when a particular test item requires a specialist to administer it, the use of trained testers is not only expedient but also necessary. On the other hand, teachers who must evaluate students in various activities ordinarily do not have other staff members or trained assistants available and must bear this in mind in the selection of tests. While the use of students as testers may be profitable to the student testers as well as to the teacher, their use is not always administratively feasible or desirable.

6. *Can the Test Be Easily and Objectively Scored?* Certainly this criterion has been mentioned or alluded to a number of times in the foregoing discussion. Nevertheless, it calls for further comment. Specifically, one should consider whether (a) a test requires another person to act as an opponent, a thrower, a server, and so forth, (b) the students can test and score themselves during practice sessions, and (c) the scores adequately distinguish among different levels of skill.

The first consideration, concerning the involvement of another individual in the performance of the student, represents somewhat of a paradox in the construction of a performance test. In most sports, the skill of the opponent has a direct bearing on an individual's performance. In activities such as tennis, badminton, handball, volleyball, and football, to name but a few, the quality of the performance of a player is relative to the skill of the opponent. In other sports such as golf, archery, and bowling, a person's performance can be immediately assessed by score alone (playing conditions being equal for everyone, of course). Therefore, in many activities a performance test simply cannot take into account the influence that is rendered by the competitive situation.

Recognizing this restriction, the makers of performance tests have attempted to isolate the skills that are involved and to measure them independently. However, if the isolated skills call for the services of another individual, acting either as an opponent or as a teammate, then objectivity is reduced. To illustrate, in an attempt to duplicate the actual activity, it may be desirable to have someone serve the shuttlecock to the person being tested on the high clear stroke, or pitch to a student being tested on batting, or run a pass pattern to test an individual's skill at passing a football. In these cases it is obvious that the skill of the helping individual could greatly affect the student's score. This is not to say that tests of this type are inferior. On the contrary, if the helper is sufficiently skilled and his or her performance is constant for each subject, this method of evaluation can be efficient and

valid. The helper might well be the teacher, but problems arise in the planning and organizing of a testing arrangement such as this, including sufficient number of trials and fatigue on the part of the teacher.

In the effort to avoid the influence of another person and to preserve high objectivity, there is danger of an artificial situation being created. A student hitting a softball from a batting tee, or bouncing the ball himself or herself before stroking in tennis, is an example of a situation not found in the actual game condition. This, then, is the paradox inherent in performance test construction—scientific precision versus gamelike conditions.

A second consideration in scoring a test is whether students can test and score themselves. Although this feature of a test is not always applicable, it is usually of considerable importance when the test is to be used as a teaching aid. For instance, a wall volley drill in tennis might be employed as a regularly scheduled exercise and rainy-day activity for development of proficiency in the basic strokes. It also might be one of the measuring devices used in evaluation. In this situation, students could benefit from self-testing throughout the course if they are provided with a record of progress, while at the same time the practice blocks the possible negative effects of their confronting a unique test situation at the end of the unit.

A third aspect of scoring relates to the precision with which test scores can differentiate among persons of different abilities. This consideration overlaps with so many other characteristics of testing that it will only be mentioned briefly here. Tests that stress speed sometimes encourage poor form. Some wall volley tests are examples of this, in that a higher score may be achieved if the person stands very close to the wall and uses mainly wrist action rather than the desired stroking movement.

In some tests, the units of measurement are not fine enough to reflect various levels of ability. A classic example is an agility test in which students score a point each time they cross a center line as they run from one side of the court to the other. Because of the distance involved and the limited opportunity for earning of points, most of the scores fall within a range of about 3 points. Other examples include test items scored on a pass–fail basis and tests using targets with widely spaced point values.

Related to this are tests designed to measure accuracy in the hitting of a ball or a shuttlecock into particular scoring zones on a court. Several tests employ a rope or string placed above the net, or at other spots on the floor, to separate the skilled player who correctly places the shot from the sloppy performer who might hit the same scoring zone but with a poor shot that would be unsuccessful against an actual opponent. Similarly, attention should be given to the probable action of a real opponent when zones are marked on a playing court. For instance, areas that are just barely out-of-bounds might be given some point value if logically the opponent would not let a ball (or a shuttlecock, or other game missile) land in that area for fear that it might fall good. In addition, it should be assumed that the more highly skilled players will deliberately hit shots that land close to boundary lines, as these are ordinarily the hardest to return. Therefore, it does not seem appropriate to penalize good players by denying them points for barely missing in what would probably be a good shot in an actual game.

7. *Is the Test Challenging and Meaningful?* Of vital importance to the success of any testing program is the attitude with which the students approach the tests. Generally speaking, most students like to be tested. The challenge of the task, the information that is derived, and the curiosity and competitive nature of the individual are some of the factors that produce a favorable testing situation. On the other hand, students can learn to dread tests for any number of reasons. The student may be made to feel inferior and the object of ridicule by the test, may feel inadequately prepared, may place too much importance on the results, or may regard the test as being unfair, too strenuous, too easy, or perhaps meaningless.

The physical educator should seek to capitalize on the motivating properties that are generally inherent in physical performance tests. The tests and the conditions in which they are given should be carefully considered with regard to student enjoyment. This is a time when the physical education teacher has an excellent opportunity to establish a favorable teacher–student relationship through encouragement and individual attention.

The test itself must be challenging. For this it must offer sufficient latitude in scoring to accommodate large differences in ability. A disadvantage of a test such as pull-ups is that almost always one or more students in the class cannot do a single pull-up and therefore receive a score of zero. Similarly, a test should allow opportunity to record improvement. Referring again to pull-ups, a student may have improved during the course to the point where he can just about pull himself up to chin level, which for him might represent a significant gain in strength, but he still receives a zero. At the other extreme are tests that have a performance ceiling, which make no provision for better scores after a particular level has been attained.

Related closely to the challenging aspect of a test is the degree to which it is meaningful. Performance tests should involve the actual skills that are used in the activity, and the skills should be measured as much as possible in gamelike situations. A softball test in which the student is asked to catch a ball that is thrown out of a second-story window can hardly be considered realistic. The teacher would have difficulty convincing students that their ability to play softball was being assessed in such an ungamelike situation.

Test selection, then, calls for coupling of scientific considerations with common sense. There is no substitute for good judgment. The physical educator must be constantly alert to the needs and interests of the students as these pertain to tests and measurements as well as to the program under study.

STEPS IN TEST CONSTRUCTION

When published tests are either unavailable or not exactly suitable for a particular situation, it becomes necessary for the physical educator to construct his or her own test. Although it is not imperative that a teacher read books on tests and measurements to devise a test for self-use, the construction of a test that is scientifically sound does require skillful analysis and technical training. Moreover, many teachers are reluctant to try their hand at formulating tests because they lack confidence in their ingenuity and their knowledge of test construction.

The following steps are suggested to guide the physical educator in devising a physical performance test that will adhere to the criteria of validity, reliability, and other basic principles.

First Step

The first step is to analyze the game or physical qualities in question to determine the skills or factors to be measured. This, of course, necessitates a thorough understanding of what is involved in the physical performance that is being evaluated. A mere listing of the components of the activity is insufficient. The relative importance of each component must be determined. Naturally, some abilities involving strategy and reaction to an opponent are ordinarily not considered in this analysis because of the difficulty in measuring those qualities objectively.

Second Step

The second step is to select test items that measure the qualities in step 1. Unquestionably, this is one of the most crucial steps in the entire test construction procedure. The items must be chosen with regard to their importance as well as their propensity to be measured accurately.

The test items may be selected from other established tests, may be chosen by a jury of experts, or may be determined arbitrarily after analysis of the performance in question. If the test pertains to a sport, the test item should conform as much as possible to the actual game situation and not be taken out of context. If the test is for physical fitness or motor ability, the test item should not favor persons of a particular size and penalize others unless body size is a factor in performance, such as obesity being incompatible with physical fitness.

The test items generally should stress good form as well as the main scoring criteria. It has been observed that in some tests the student can achieve a higher score by using an unorthodox style rather than the prescribed form.

The literature contains numerous test items that have been used for measuring various components of physical fitness. When numerous test items are available, the test maker might choose test items in relation to established criteria, such as restrictions on time, equipment, space, or other considerations pertinent to the local situation.

That the test item is only a sample of the total performance or quality must be thoroughly understood by the teacher when formulating the test and especially when evaluating the results. In devising the test items, care must be taken to isolate as much as possible the desired ability. If the test situation is too complicated, the results may be misleading. This is particularly true when a test item is to be used for diagnostic purposes. To illustrate, if the teacher is attempting to measure arm and shoulder girdle strength, a test item such as the shot put would not be suitable because of the uncontrolled variables of past experience and technique. On the other hand, test makers sometimes make the mistake of isolating a skill or trait to such an extreme that the test item becomes meaningless.

Third Step

The third step is to establish the exact procedures for the administration and scoring of the test. In accomplishing this obvious step, the physical educator must resort to a certain amount of trial and error. The best-laid plans on paper may be totally inoperable in practice. Furthermore, the directions for testing and scoring may appear to be perfectly clear when the test is tried on only one or two subjects. However, marked revisions may be necessary after the test is given to a number of people, owing to differences in the way the directions may be interpreted or perhaps to unanticipated levels of performance.

The clarity and simplicity of directions bear directly on the reliability and objectivity of a test. The test maker should strive to establish procedures that facilitate the administration of the test both from the standpoint of the tester and the subject. Validity is also obviously impaired if the student does not fully understand the directions.

Fourth Step

The fourth step is to determine the reliability of each test item. As described previously, a reliability coefficient can be calculated on the basis of any number of trials, by a test–retest situation, or by the split-halves method. The following are some considerations in accomplishing this step:

1. The subjects who are selected for testing should be representative of the population for whom the test is intended.

2. In establishing the score value to be used to indicate the performance of each subject for each of the trials or test administrations, care should be taken to obtain an appropriate measure. In other words, a sufficient number of trials should be given, the test directions should be made perfectly clear, and ample opportunity should be afforded each person to become accustomed to the

test itself. These suggestions have been mentioned before, but are important enough to state again.

A further consideration with regard to scoring and reliability pertains to the question of whether one should use the average score or the best score. For example, should one use the best of three trials on a standing long jump or the average of the three trials? The decision probably involves several factors, including convenience of scoring on the part of the tester in that the best score is easier to extract than the average. Some argue that one ultimately wants the student's best performance; others maintain that the best score may not be representative of the student's typical performance. The type of test is definitely a factor. In reaction-time testing, for example, the best score may be the result of anticipation of the stimulus and thus may actually be a false score.

With regard to reliability, most research findings have shown that the average score is more reliable than the best score.

3. Chapter 3 discusses correlation and factors to consider in the interpretation of a specific coefficient of correlation. Test makers generally recommend that a test should have a reliability coefficient of at least .70 to be acceptable. Naturally, the higher the coefficient the better. Some authorities feel that a coefficient of at least .85 is needed to satisfy the criterion of reliability. Certainly one should not expect perfect correlation, owing to normal variations in performance from one time to the next.

Low reliability coefficients often call for revisions in the test item or for its elimination. Sometimes the simple inclusion of more trials greatly improves the reliability. Some types of physical performance have less reliable results than others. Tests of kinesthesis, for example, generally are very low in reliability owing to the nature of the test items.

One final admonition for teachers who are judging tests on the basis of coefficients of reliability, validity, and objectivity: *These values mean nothing if the person using the test is not a competent tester. A particular test can be highly reliable when administered by one person but completely unreliable if given by a careless or untrained tester. Furthermore, a skilled, conscientious per-*

son can obtain a higher reliability coefficient than that which is published.

Fifth Step

The fifth step is to compute the objectivity of each test item. This step is not always performed, depending on how the test is going to be used and by whom. This step could be done at the same time that reliability is being assessed. Another term for objectivity is *intertester reliability.* Objectivity is assessed by having two or more competent testers administer the test to the same students. Through intraclass R the objectivity coefficient can be computed to determine the extent of agreement between the different test administrators. Most of the considerations that were discussed regarding reliability are applicable here. Needless to say, objectivity is directly related to the skill and integrity of the testers as well as to the clarity and simplicity of the instructions and scoring procedures of the test.

Sixth Step

The sixth step is to establish validity. This procedure in test construction may be approached in several ways. The test maker may wish to use a combination of methods. The most common procedures are as follows:

1. The students' performance on the new test is correlated with their scores on a previously validated test. If a high correlation is obtained, the test maker can claim that the new test is valid. It should be obvious, however, that this procedure has certain weaknesses. In the first place, the validity coefficient only demonstrates the degree to which the new test coincides with the other test; consequently, the former can only be shown to be as valid as the latter, never more valid. Usually the teacher has decided to develop a new test because the established test is more time consuming or costly or does not lend itself as well to the teaching situation.

2. If the test in question is designed to measure performance in an activity such as tennis, badminton, or handball, the scores on the test are correlated with the results of a singles round-robin tournament. If the test is valid, the persons placing highest in the tournament should score highest on the test, the poorest players should have the lowest scores, and so on through the different levels of ability. A round-robin tournament

consumes a great deal of time, however, because it usually requires a large number of games (number of games $= N[N-1]/2$). For example, with only 20 participants, 190 games are required!

3. In some activities, such as team sports, round-robin tournaments are not feasible. However, the ratings of experts can be used as the criterion to which the performance on a test is correlated. The experts must be selected with care, but at the same time the services of nationally known figures are not needed for this purpose. To illustrate, if the test pertains to performance in basketball, the varsity basketball coaches could certainly be considered qualified to rate skills, provided ample opportunity is allowed for observation of each student. In addition, scales that are suitably graduated must be devised to differentiate between various levels of ability. For example, specific point values are usually given for arbitrary standards of performance, such as 5 for excellent; 4, good; 3, average. If there are several judges, the average rating is ordinarily correlated with the score made on the performance test. Judges' ratings can be used in validating individual activities as well as team sports.

4. Another approach involves comparison of performance of persons with known levels of ability. In this method individuals are assigned to groups that supposedly represent different degrees of proficiency. The formation of the groups may be done through ratings by competent judges, such as a coach rating his or her varsity players, or through simply selecting whole groups of performers on the basis of their status as a group. For instance, the varsity may be assumed to represent the highest level of ability, the junior varsity next, the freshmen next, intramural players next, and finally, perhaps, physical education students just beginning the activity. After the test has been administered to all subjects, the test performances of the different groups are compared to determine the degree to which the test differentiated among the assumed levels of ability.

   A variation of this approach involves the use of a number of teams that are considered to represent different degrees of skill on the basis of their order of finish in a tournament or their conference standings. It can be readily seen that there are bound to be some erroneous assumptions as to the various levels of ability because of upsets, unusual circumstances, and the indistinguishable clustering effect found at the middle of any performance scale that conforms to normal distribution.

5. The last method of determining validity that will be presented here involves the use of a composite score of all the test items in the battery as the performance criterion. Frequently, physical fitness tests are established in this manner. The scores for the various test items that were selected as measures of the basic components are converted to standard scores that are then added. This total is assumed to represent physical fitness, or motor ability, or sports skills, or whatever is being tested. Each test item is then correlated with the criterion (total score) and with each of the other items. Multiple correlation can then be employed to select the test battery, which is composed of the test items that correlate highest with the criterion and lowest with one another. The latter is necessary because a test item that correlates highly with another one is considered to measure the same thing and is therefore superfluous. Consequently, if two test items are found to be highly related, the one that correlates highest with the criterion would be selected.

   If there are a considerable number of test items, this process can select the least number of items to comprise the test battery. Regression equations can also be used to predict the individual's score on all items on the basis of his or her scores on the selected items.

The basic procedures just described can be used to establish the validity of each test item in any battery. In cases where the composite score is not considered appropriate, the items can be correlated with judges' ratings, tournament standings, established tests, and so on to determine the validity of each item. The items should then also be intercorrelated to eliminate duplication.

Seventh Step

The next step is to revise the test in light of the findings of the steps just described, and finalize the written instructions for administering and scoring the test.

Eighth Step

The eighth and last step is to construct norms. A large number of subjects who are representative of the population for whom the test is intended should be given the test and their scores recorded. The scores can then be converted to percentiles or T scores (or whatever suitable score form is wanted). Norms for each test item should be prepared, as well as norms for the composite or total score, if appropriate.

CRITERION-REFERENCED MEASUREMENT

Much of the discussion in this chapter has pertained to norm-referenced measurement, at least with respect to methods for establishing validity and reliability and the importance of a test's ability to distinguish among students. However, there has been considerable interest in recent years in criterion-referenced measurement, in which the primary interest is whether a student has achieved a specified objective.

In norm-referenced testing, we assess students' relative performance. For example, in fitness testing we may be interested in how our students compare with other students, perhaps nationally or just within our state or school system. In such instances, a raw score such as 41 sit-ups has no meaning until we can compare it with other scores. For a 13-year-old girl, 41 sit-ups is better than the score of 75% of girls at that age, whereas 41 sit-ups is only the median score for 13-year-old boys. We strive to select or construct test items that provide the best (maximum) discrimination among performances, and we develop norms so that students can see how they perform relative to others.

Norm-referenced measurement is the basis for the grading system in most schools and colleges in the United States. Critics of norm-referenced measurement (or at least overreliance on its use) claim that this type of measurement is not effective in the diagnosis of student weaknesses and of weaknesses in the instructional program. Testers and students tend to place too much importance on test results. The tests themselves often contain trivial or irrelevant items that are used mostly to achieve greater variance among scores. There is concern that norm-referenced measurement causes overemphasis on competition rather than promoting cooperation and support among students in helping one another achieve the course objectives.

Criterion-referenced measurement became popular in the 1960s. It emphasizes behavioral objectives, competence-based instruction, and programmed learning. Its use is more prevalent in elementary physical education programs than in the higher grades. In criterion-referenced measurement, the major concern is whether individuals reach an established level of performance regardless of how well other individuals do. This form of mastery–nonmastery evaluation is used in a number of areas such as driver training, pilot training, typing and shorthand proficiency, becoming a Morse code operator, certification as a sports official, and various licensing practices in medicine, law, and other professions. The Red Cross swimming tests use criterion-referenced testing to determine proficiency categories. Hills used perhaps the ultimate example of criterion-referenced testing—parachute packing. Relative packing performance does not matter; the criterion is whether the parachute opens. When parachutists have to pack their own chute, mastery takes on a very real meaning.

Although parachute packing is an extreme example, it does emphasize a very desirable end product of criterion-referenced instruction: that the student become responsible for his or her own learning and progress. As a matter of fact, criterion-referenced instruction and measurement are theoretically ideal. All students proceed at their own pace. Those who learn quickly can advance to higher levels, while the slower learner is given more time to achieve the established level of performance. Unfortunately, our school and grading systems are not structured for individual pacing.

PROBLEMS ASSOCIATED WITH CRITERION-REFERENCED MEASUREMENT

Basically our school structure is such that 12 years are needed for a student to achieve a high school education. Our grading system is mostly norm referenced, with A, B, C, D, and F designating relative levels of performance. A teacher who gives all students high grades for mastery will very soon be reprimanded by the administration. Pass–fail grading can be used, but it lacks the capacity for providing sufficient information as to achievement of the various objectives.

Our schools are not presently able to cope with remedial instruction. In the criterion-referenced approach to learning, we are proceeding on the assumption that most students can master the material if given enough time. But how much time can we allow?

Frequent measurement is basic to the success of criterion-referenced instruction. Therefore, valid and reliable tests are imperative (as with any instructional program). However, because of the need for frequent evaluation, the instructional time required for testing poses a major problem. The increased use of computers could do a great deal in this respect, but the burden of continual testing and follow-up of students with respect to mastery and retention of the many specific objectives may be overwhelming for most teachers. The simplest approach in this respect may be to group specific objectives into units and then test only for the established criteria for the unit (Hills 1976).

An important point is that in criterion-referenced instruction the teacher does not just teach the "answers" to the test questions. The test that represents the established criteria should demand thorough understanding or skill or both if it is to denote mastery. Herein lies a problem in that some teachers are deceived into thinking that criterion-referenced tests are easy to construct; hence, some very poor tests are masquerading as criterion-referenced measurement instruments.

One of the most difficult problems in criterion-referenced measurement is to decide on the level of achievement that represents mastery. In most instances an attainment level is arbitrarily set, and justification for setting that particular score is rarely given. Another problem is the number of test items needed to assess appropriately a specific behavioral domain (Udinsky, Osterlind, and Lynch, 1981).

Validity

The validity of criterion-referenced tests may be established in some of the same ways as in norm-referenced tests. Known differences between groups may be used in some instances, and comparison of test results before and after instruction can certainly be appropriate. Safrit (1981) described some statistical approaches that have been used. She pointed out that the very nature of criterion-referenced measurement does not lend itself to the traditional methods of establishing validity and reliability used in norm-referenced tests, because the latter tests are based on individual differences. Logical validity and content validity have been assumed for many criterion-referenced tests.

Reliability

Theoretically, if criterion-referenced instruction were successful every student would have a low score on the pretest and all students would achieve mastery on the posttest. The standard deviation would be zero if the usual methods for establishing reliability were followed. Essentially, the tester wishes to know how consistently the criterion-referenced test places students into mastery–nonmastery categories. Safrit and Stamm compared different methods of estimating reliability for criterion-referenced measurement of achievement in the psychomotor domain. The Swaminathan–Hambleton–Algina estimate of P was calculated for bowling scores on two separate days (this method could be used with alternate test forms also). Single administration estimates of reliability developed by Huynh and Subkoviak were computed by Safrit and Stamm and found to be comparable indicators of the P derived from the test–retest method.

More research is needed on ways to improve and demonstrate the validity and reliability of criterion-referenced measurement. Undoubtedly, this measurement technique has an important place in our education system. It is important to realize that norm-referenced and criterion-referenced measurement techniques are used for different purposes and that both are appropriate for those purposes. All educators are responsible for becoming more knowledgeable about the strengths and weaknesses of both techniques and for trying to use each more effectively.

TEST ADMINISTRATION

Several recommendations pertinent to test administration, scoring procedures, and suggestions for standardization have already been presented in this chapter. Specific pointers are also given in later chapters with the directions for each of the tests presented in those chapters. However, some general test administration recommendations will be given here.

The Boy Scout motto, "be prepared," could easily pertain to test administration. Sloppy, inaccurate testing, or perhaps even the lack of testing by some physical education teachers, may well be due to neglect of planning and organization or to ignorance of the effort needed for a good testing program.

Preparation for testing includes attention to many details such as method of recording scores, arrangement of testing stations, collection of necessary equipment, and training of testers.

Method of Recording Scores

Whether to use score sheets or score cards may seem a trivial question, but it can be an important factor and requires considerable forethought. Does one want score cards that each student can carry from station to station or score sheets at each test station?

The score card has the advantage that it facilitates recording of scores, and the tester does not have to look through a list of names. It also can be helpful from the standpoint that students are allowed more time to examine and reflect on their performance on the different tests.

The score sheet has the advantage of lessening the possibility of loss of scores, which may occur when a score card is mislaid or not turned in. The score sheet also reduces the possibility of students "altering" their scores.

Arrangement of Testing Stations

The arrangement of testing stations requires careful deliberation, since several factors may be important. Of primary consideration is the possible effect of fatigue. Strenuous tests should not be placed back to back, or a distance run should not be scheduled first.

Test stations may have to be arranged in light of available equipment. For example, if stopwatches are needed for three tests and only two stopwatches are available, obviously one test needs to be scheduled on another day.

The tester must be mindful of the time required for each test; tests that take a particularly long time to administer may be handled best by using two or more test stations.

Training of Testers

The training of testers is a vital step in tests that have several stations. One can never assume that a person is a competent tester just because he or she has read and understood the test instructions. It is strongly advised that practice sessions be held with a sample of subjects to help clarify directions and standardize procedures. Also, testers should be given as much information as possible concerning measurement of the particular abilities to which they are assigned.

Practice of Test Items

Familiarity with and practice of the test items by students have been stressed previously. Failure to allow for these represents a major source of measurement error. This assertion can be tested by giving a test item to a sample of subjects, even a fairly familiar item such as a standing long jump, and allowing several trials. Almost invariably improvement is observed with each trial. It is simply common sense that familiarity with a test increases reliability. In a distance run, for example, a student requires practice to learn his or her optimal pace. In an agility test, subsequent trials yield better scores because of learning and improved technique in running the pattern. The same phenomenon can be observed in most types of performances.

It is highly recommended that students be allowed to get into some degree of condition before being subjected to rigorous fitness tests. Failure to do this is not only unwise from a medical standpoint but also is likely to promote fear, resentment, and improper attitudes toward fitness and physical education.

Standardization of Instructions

This is another important and often overlooked administrative detail. Care must be taken that some students are not given additional or different information concerning what is considered adequate or good performance, suggested goals, and so on. Sometimes a tester will attempt to motivate students by giving false norms, such as by telling them that younger students performed better or by mentioning an "average" score that is actually extremely high. Research has shown that although such tactics sometimes do promote better performances, they may also have an adverse effect, such as when students stop trying in order to rationalize failure as being due to not trying rather than a lack of ability.

Collection of Necessary Equipment

The competent tester will make a careful, detailed checklist of test equipment, floor-marking materials, measuring tapes, pencils, stopwatches, and other needed items. Much time is wasted when the tester must hurry about after the start of the class period to locate some small but necessary item such as chalk for a vertical jump test. A mental rehearsal of each test item is advised.

Moreover, it is wise to store test materials that can be readily set up when a test is to be given, rather than "starting from scratch" each time. A sample materials-and-supplies checklist is provided in Appendix G.

Interpretation of Test Results

Last, but of fundamental importance, is scoring and interpretation of test results. In some tests calculations are required, such as the division of body weight into strength scores. Much time and effort are saved if someone performs the calculations as each person is tested instead of the calculations being done after the testing for perhaps hundreds of scores.

Interpretation and diagnosis are often sadly neglected. The use of up-to-date local norms helps to a considerable extent, especially when students are knowledgeable as to what the norms mean and have ready access to them. If testing is to have real value, however, there should be follow-up. After initial screening, further testing may be indicated to construct a more comprehensive and accurate profile of a student's status.

Finally, it is hoped that after a student's strengths and weaknesses have been identified through sound testing, a carefully planned program of activities will be prescribed in keeping with the student's needs.

CONCLUSION

Much more could be said about test construction, test selection and evaluation, and administration. Certainly these represent the very essence of the tests and measurements program. Separate coverage could have been accorded the construction of written tests, attitude scales, social adjustment inventories, and other measuring tools, but these are simply not within the scope of this chapter. The interested reader is referred to Chapters 20 and 21 and to other sources that pertain to knowledge test construction, the devising of attitude scales, and other measuring tools. The primary consideration in evaluating any test and the basic steps in constructing a test of any type are the same.

The underlying message of this chapter and in fact the theme of the entire book pertains to the intelligent application of tests and measuring tools. An evaluating device can only be valid, reliable, and objective if it is used properly. Norms yield worthwhile information only when the tests are administered and scored in the same way for each individual and only when the individuals are from the same population. With these thoughts in mind we are ready to turn our attention to the discussion and presentation of some practical measurements for evaluation in specific areas in physical education.

BIBLIOGRAPHY

American Psychological Association, *Standards for Educational and Psychological Tests*. Washington, D.C.: American Psychological Association, 1974.

Cronbach, L. J., *Essentials of Psychological Testing*. 3rd ed. New York: Harper and Row, 1970.

Hills, J. R., *Measurement and Evaluation in the Classroom*. Columbus, Ohio: Charles E. Merrill, 1976.

Huynh, H., "On the Reliability of Decisions in Domain-Referenced Testing." *Journal of Educational Measurement* 13:253–264, 1976.

Mehrens, W., and R. Ebel, Eds., *Principles of Educational and Psychological Measurement*. Skokie, Ill.: Rand McNally, 1967.

Safrit, M. J., Ed., *Reliability Theory*. Reston, Va.: AAHPERD, 1976.

———, *Evaluation in Physical Education*. 2nd ed. Englewood Cliffs, N.J.: Prentice-Hall, 1981.

———, and C. L. Stamm, "Reliability Estimates for Criterion-Referenced Measures in the Psychomotor Domain." *Research Quarterly for Exercise and Sport* 51:359–368, May 1980.

Subkoviak, M. J., "Estimating Reliability From a Single Administration of a Criterion-Referenced Test." *Journal of Educational Measurement* 13: 265–276, 1976.

Swaminathan, H., R. K. Hambleton, and J. Algina, "Reliability of Criterion-Referenced Tests: A Decision-Theoretic Formulation." *Journal of Educational Measurement* 11:263–267, 1974.

Udinsky, B. F., S. J. Osterlind, and S. W. Lynch, *Evaluation Resource Handbook*. San Diego: Edits Publishers, 1981.

CHAPTER 5

GRADING IN PHYSICAL EDUCATION

OBJECTIVES

After reading this chapter, the student should be able to:

1. Understand the basic philosophical considerations that influence grading in physical education

2. Describe different methods of assigning grades in physical education

3. Determine an overall grade in a unit while giving proper weight to the different objectives of the course

PHILOSOPHICAL CONCEPTS OF GRADING

Educators are in close agreement concerning the importance of basing measurement and evaluation on the objectives that guide the educative process. However, great variation exists among educators regarding how to evaluate, grade, and interpret progress to pupils, parents, and school administrators. Moreover, the entire process of measurement, evaluation, and grade placement has gone through tumultuous times in recent years, with students demanding alternative grading systems and some educators advocating the need for schools without failure. Thus, the first part of this chapter considers some of the concepts behind grading, while the last part deals with the basic mechanics of arriving at the final grade.

Educational Objectives

The objectives most commonly listed as worthy of pursuit in physical education are (1) neuromuscular skill, (2) physical fitness, (3) social development, and (4) acquisition of knowledge. While some educators in the field measure each objective as nearly equally as possible in determining grades, others support the use of only two or three that they consider unique to physical education. For example, Duncan supported sports and dance skills and physical development as the unique objectives in the field. From this viewpoint, social and mental fitness objectives are important but the physical educator's primary emphasis is not directed toward them.

Unfortunately, some physical educators tend to completely ignore the more widely recognized objectives and award grades on the basis of such administrative details as the number of absences, the number of times students failed to dress out, the number of times they were tardy, and whether they took showers after activity. Rather than grading on the number of absences, a wiser administrative procedure might be to require students to repeat any course that has been missed a certain number of times. Otherwise, students who are penalized for missing a few classes may be penalized twice in that they may make a poor showing on test days owing to previous absences. On the other hand, students who miss a few classes (not enough to have to repeat) but still do well on test days should not be penalized at all. This is the usual situation in other subject areas. As educators we should be primarily concerned with measuring educational objectives, not administrative objectives.

Improvement Versus Status

Some physical educators become quite concerned as to whether they should grade on improvement or class status. While some teachers feel that improvement (progress made between the initial and the final test) is of utmost importance in determining grades, most physical educators support the concept of grading on relative achievement, commensurate with grading practices in other subject areas. Moreover, many teachers wish to avoid the following disadvantages of grading on improvement in physical education:

1. Such grading is time consuming in that it requires the same test to be given twice (once before instruction and again after instruction).

2. In some skill and fitness activities, giving the test before instruction may be dangerous if students are in poor condition. In addition, beginners' performances are inconsistent; tests given at the beginning of a unit tend to be unreliable.

3. When students know or suspect that improvement is a basis for grading, they will perform at a minimal level on the first test to show improvement on the second test.

4. When all students do their best on both tests, the weaker students with low initial scores usually have an advantage in that their potential for improvement is greater. Thus, students with less knowledge and skills may receive higher grades.

5. Improvement-based grading is not compatible with experiences apt to occur in real life. For example, a member of a sales organization might be the person with the greatest improvement during a 12-month period but may still be the lowest on the staff in total sales. Consequently, he or she receives less commission than the others and probably will still be the least likely to receive a promotion.

6. Similarly, improvement-based grading is not in accordance with grading in other subject areas. In subjects such as math, English, and history, the usual procedure is to total the points achieved on the various tests and reports and to assign grades based on those totals. Obviously, the students with the higher totals receive the higher grades.

Effort Versus Performance

Although most educators laud diligent effort, they tend to reward actual performance. For example, a salesman works hard five days a week and earns a certain salary, while another salesman works only two days a week selling the same products and earns three times as much. We find the same situation in sports. One youngster may work hard seven days a week but still place second in a track meet, behind a youngster who practices less. Certainly we admire and encourage supreme effort, but we cannot overlook actual relative performance in assigning grades.

Many physical educators find it difficult to award high grades to gifted students who attend class less and work less than other students but who score exceedingly well on test days. If we wish to parallel the awarding of grades with real-life situations and thus prepare students to face the future realistically, we must give prime consideration to actual performance. Moreover, we must recognize that some students, no matter how much effort they exert, may never achieve above-average performance.

Future Growth Versus Present Status

Another philosophical consideration is whether a student's future growth and development should be taken into account in grading. It has been said that whatever exists in any amount can be measured; by the same reasoning, one can say that what does not yet exist cannot be measured. Education is fundamentally aimed at the student's future growth and development (Bovard, Cozens, and Hagman 1950). However, evaluation in which potential is considered is much more difficult than evaluation concerned only with the student's present status (Brubacher 1962). Some educators try to compromise by placing primary emphasis on the student's demonstrated competence and then making adjustments when there is evidence of future growth and development. Such adjustments are decidedly qualitative judgments, and the issue of fairness to all students may be raised.

Ability to Repeat Versus Ability to Work With the Material

Still another point of interest is whether we should evaluate students' ability to repeat what has been presented or be concerned with what they can do with what they have learned. One of the most widely held views is that learning is the successful acquisition of skills and knowledge that the student has set out to learn. This is sometimes called the *input* method, in which the teacher is the transmitter of the information or skill and the student's mind and body represent a sort of reservoir until such time as the student is called on to reproduce the information or skill on a test (Bovard, Cozens, and Hagman 1950). However, others support the *output* method, and strive to present important concepts or general ideas and then grade on how well the student can work with what has been learned insofar as showing comprehension and application of new ideas, improved concepts, patterns, skills, or movement.

Teaching for Testing Versus Teaching for Learning

Sometimes an educator may resolve to evaluate only those things that can be measured quantitatively (Barrow and McGee 1964). Moreover, he or she may tend to teach only those facts and skills that can be isolated for scientific measurement and grading. This is unfortunate, for many other things need to be covered. A common pitfall for teachers is to teach only information that will appear on a nationally standardized test, so that the class ranks high on norm comparisons. While this may boost the teacher's ego and make him or her appear an outstanding teacher, the practice is built on a false assumption and cannot be condoned.

Independent Class Status Grading Versus Grouped Class Status Grading

Although most educators teach different sections of the same course identically and group the sections together for assigning grades, they should recognize certain classes might have advantages over others. For example, in a conditioning course in which cardiovascular endurance is a major objective, sections meeting three times a week may have an advantage over sections meeting twice a week, since a person can jog only so much per period in developing endurance. Moreover, time of day, weather conditions, and other factors may have a more advantageous or detrimental influence on one course section than on another. Thus, the educator may feel it important to consider each course section as an independent unit and evaluate each student according to ability and opportunity to achieve the objectives in that section. The main drawback to grading each section

independently is that individual grades may depend on the section to which the student is assigned. For example, if the student happens to be in a section with a disproportionate number of high-ability students, he or she may receive an average or low grade (if grading is norm referenced), whereas the same performance may warrant an A in another section.

The same can be true of different schools and of different course sections within a school. There is no sure way to standardize all conditions so that an A grade in one course section is an A in all course sections, an A in one school is also an A in another school, and an A under one teacher is an A under a different teacher.

Since unique circumstances surround each course section, some educators believe that the best they can do is to determine which students in a course section accumulated the most points and assign them an A, which students accumulated enough points for a B, and so on down to the lowest group for that course section. Each section is treated independently. On the other hand, if class sections are grouped for grading purposes, the teacher must assume that all students had equal opportunity to achieve and that all conditions were equally favorable for each section. While such equalization may be possible, it could prove most difficult to achieve in many situations.

Multiple Observation for Grading

A teacher should not rely solely on one method of evaluation or on a single instrument in collecting scores for determining grades. It would seem much more desirable to use a combination of grading components that take into account course objectives, the various facets of performance, and the multiple needs of the students. It is not enough merely to test skill performance through objective tests and subjective ratings; the teacher should also measure knowledge and may consider evaluating physical fitness to determine the overall grade.

Failure Versus Automatic Promotion

In the early decades of this century, educators commonly used a failing grade to retain students who had not demonstrated satisfactory progress in learning. While most students passed, there were always a few who did not. Promotion in those days was not always guaranteed. In the past few decades, however, many teachers have argued that it is of little value to fail students, since they tend to learn no more on the second attempt (Ebel 1980). Moreover, the impact of failure is more detrimental emotionally and socially than the advantages gained by the demand for account-ability.

Thus, many educators have forsaken the fail-ure–retention system in favor of the social or automatic promotion. The emphasis in education has shifted away from subject matter to learning conditions and processes. In a child-centered education, educators view motivation and the pursuit of unique interests as being more signif-icant than failure. The premise has been to keep children with their classmates and that "every child is a success."

In the past few years, scores on college admis-sion tests and standardized achievement tests have been declining. Students graduate from high school who cannot read, write, or perform elementary arithmetic. Colleges have been forced to establish remedial programs. Legislatures in many states have found it desirable to establish testing pro-grams for minimum competency. The public has reached a point where it is no longer willing to accept that there is no reported failure.

Reporting of Grades

The final grade for a course should be based on total points accumulated. For example, an instructor queried by a student might report as follows:

> You had a total of 225 points, which ranks you fifth of the 30 students in the class. This places you within the B-grade range.

This type of reporting is quite different from the justification needed for grades used for dis-cipline or for high grades given to low-level per-formers and low grades to high-level performers. It is a matter-of-fact presentation: "Here are the test results, reports, and other assignments com-pleted and these are the points you accumulated."

Principles of Grading

By way of summary, it is important that basic principles of grading be recognized and followed:

1. Grading in physical education should be commensurate with grading in other subject areas of the school.
2. Measurement and evaluation for grading purposes must be based on the educational objectives of the course rather than on trivial or insignificant rules and procedures.
3. Grades should be assigned on the basis of the number of points accumulated in a course, reflecting the student's achievement in meet-ing the objectives.
4. The awarding of grades should parallel real-life situations, in which honors, promotions, and rewards are the result of achievement. Grading thereby prepares students for life after graduation.
5. Grades should be based on a sufficient num-ber of observations. In physical education, grades should be based on more than one objective.
6. Promotion should not be automatic. In well-planned physical education programs, a majority of students are successful. How-ever, such programs also can identify stu-dents who have failed to make sufficient progress in learning.

DETERMINATION OF GRADES

Determining grades is one of the most per-plexing problems that physical educators face. Since grades should be the result of accurate eval-uations of students' achievement toward the major objectives, varied evidence must be collected and weighted to assure validity and fairness. The pri-mary purpose of grading is to report to the stu-dents, their parents, and administrators an eval-uation of the students' achievement. The logical steps necessary for effectively determining grades in physical education are discussed in this section.

Selection and Weighting of Course Objectives

In physical education classes, the instructor must rely on logic and philosophy to determine which objectives are most important in accor-dance with the nature of the activity and the needs of the student. The emphasis varies from one instructor to another and from course to course. Thus, one instructor may select and weight the objectives in a particular course as follows: phys-ical fitness, 50%; skill, 25%; and knowledge, 25%. In this case, social development was not consid-ered as making up part of the grade; instead, the teacher might elect to use the results of social measurement for guidance purposes. Another instructor might feel that skills should make up 40% of the grade; physical fitness, 25%; knowledge, 25%; and social development, 10%. As can be seen from these examples, the amount of weight an objective carries in evaluation depends on the philosophy of the teacher as well as on the particular course that is being taught.

Selection and Administration of Tests for the Instructional Unit

An adequate but reasonable number of tests should be selected to assess student progress over the course of the instructional unit. Tests should be selected on the basis of the weighted objectives for the course and the type of activity in which the students engaged during the instructional unit. The data in Table 5.1 represent scores of eight tests that were administered during a 6-week softball unit. Four tests are skill items (representing 50% of the unit grade), two tests are physical fitness items (representing 25% of the grade), one test is for knowledge (representing 12.5% of the grade), and one test is for social measurement (representing 12.5% of the grade). In the illustration, each test item is considered to have equal weight; therefore, each item is worth 12.5%. Consequently, once raw scores have been converted to scale scores or some type of standard score, the teacher can merely total the standard scores and convert them into letter grades. Obviously, that each item has equal weight would not always be the case. Some items may be weighted more heavily than others, so they would be multiplied by that weight before the grand total is computed.

Treatment of Raw Scores

Since raw scores from different tests are not directly comparable, they must be changed to some type of score that reduces such variables as time, distance, and rating scores to a common denominator, such as standard scores (discussed in Chapter 3) and rating scale scores.

Rating Scale Scores

This method is recommended for use with small classes (30 students or less). It is expedient and can be used by those with a limited background in statistics. The steps are as follows:

Step 1. Record raw scores for each test item after the student's name. In between items leave a space for each item's scale score, to be recorded later.

Example:

NAME	PULL-UPS (NUMBER)	SCALE SCORE	12-MINUTE RUN—WALK (MILES)	SCALE SCORE
A.L.	17		2.0	
A.D.	8		2.2	
A.J.	10		2.4	
B.B.	5		1.0	
B.C.	19		1.5	
B.D.	14		2.1	
C.C.	6		1.3	
C.D.	12		1.6	
C.E.	16		1.8	
D.E.	3		2.5	

Step 2. Rank the raw scores from high to low and assign 5 points to the highest 10% of scores, 4 points to the next 20% of scores, 3 points to the next 40% of scores, 2 points to the next 20% of scores, and 1 point to the lowest 10% of scores.

Example:

Table 5.1. Comparative Grades for 6-Week Softball Unit by Two Different Methods

Name	6-Week Skill Test—50% (AAHPERD Items)								Physical Fitness—25%				Knowledge—12½%		Social Development—12½%		Computations		Grading Method	
	Accuracy Throw	T Score	Fungo Hitting	T Score	Speed Throw	T Score	Fielding Ground Balls	T Score	Squat Thrusts (3 Trials)	T Score	1-Mile Run	T Score	Knowledge Test	T Score	Social Test	T Score	Total T Score	Average T Score	Curve Method	Absolute Method
1 A.L.	25	72	39	66	14.2	57	20	63	291	80	6.3	55	97	68	89	62	523	65	A	A
2 A.D.	16	54	34	60	17.6	45	18	57	176	46	6.8	49	80	53	96	68	432	54	B	C
3 A.J.	12	46	28	53	15.6	48	14	43	195	51	6.5	52	65	39	78	52	384	48	C	D
4 B.B.	11	44	19	41	15.3	53	18	57	180	47	6.4	53	90	62	68	42	399	50	C	C
5 B.C.	17	56	28	53	13.9	58	17	53	190	50	6.6	51	66	40	87	60	421	53	C	C
6 B.D.	14	50	21	44	18.3	43	20	63	249	64	6.9	48	72	45	77	51	408	51	C	C
7 C.C.	23	68	17	39	14.5	56	15	47	171	45	6.5	52	88	60	93	65	432	54	B	C
8 C.D.	15	52	37	63	15.6	52	18	57	185	49	6.7	50	64	38	65	40	401	50	C	C
9 C.E.	10	42	26	50	13.2	60	17	53	163	43	7.0	47	78	51	79	53	399	50	C	C
10 D.E.	13	48	15	36	14.8	45	16	50	235	63	6.0	58	96	67	72	46	413	52	C	C
11 D.I.	13	48	32	58	18.9	41	20	63	155	40	7.0	47	71	44	95	67	408	51	C	C
12 D.K.	21	64	11	31	14.8	55	12	37	190	50	6.7	50	77	50	74	48	385	48	C	D
13 E.E.	19	60	34	60	14.9	54	18	57	220	59	5.6	62	87	59	83	56	467	58	A	B
14 E.L.	9	40	40	68	12.8	61	10	30	226	60	7.1	45	68	42	86	59	405	51	C	C
15 E.M.	12	46	29	54	19.9	38	20	63	195	51	6.5	52	76	49	56	32	385	48	C	D
16 F.G.	8	38	14	35	16.2	50	17	53	141	36	7.7	39	95	66	76	50	367	46	D	D
17 F.H.	4	30	31	56	14.9	46	9	27	218	58	6.0	58	75	48	63	47	370	49	C	D
18 F.P.	19	60	25	49	16.7	48	19	60	198	52	6.4	53	85	57	83	56	435	54	B	D
19 G.G.	13	48	36	63	16.2	50	6	17	117	29	6.6	51	58	33	70	44	335	42	D	F
20 G.Z.	7	36	13	34	12.1	64	17	53	213	57	6.1	57	75	48	66	40	389	49	C	D
21 G.J.	12	46	30	55	21.2	33	17	53	185	49	10.6	7	84	56	73	47	346	43	D	D
22 H.I.	18	58	23	46	15.3	47	19	60	180	47	6.7	50	60	35	61	36	379	47	D	D
23 H.M.	6	34	35	61	26.1	17	9	27	207	55	6.2	56	73	46	85	58	354	46	D	D
24 H.O.	11	44	21	44	17.2	47	16	50	198	52	6.7	50	63	37	72	46	370	46	D	D
25 I.K.	17	56	29	54	10.0	71	19	60	203	54	6.3	55	75	48	58	34	442	54	B	C

PULL-UPS (NUMBER)	SCALE SCORE	12-MINUTE RUN–WALK (MILES)	SCALE SCORE
19	5 points	2.5	5 points
17	4 points	2.4	4 points
16		2.2	
14		2.1	
12	3 points	2.0	3 points
10		1.8	
8		1.6	
6	2 points	1.5	2 points
5		1.3	
3	1 point	1.0	1 point

Step 3. If the test item is to be weighted for extra points, multiply the weight of the item times the scale score.

Example: In this case the teacher decides to give the pull-up test a weight of 2 and the 12-minute run–walk a weight of 3. Thus, A.L., with 17 pull-ups, would have 4 scale points times 2 for a total of 8 points for pull-ups; and 3 scale points times 3 for a total of 9 points for the 12-minute run test.

Step 4. Transfer scale points or weighted scale points into the score book.

Example:

NAME	PULL-UPS (NUMBER)	SCALE SCORE	12-MINUTE RUN–WALK (MILES)	SCALE SCORE
A.L.	17	8	2.0	9
A.D.	8	6	2.2	12
A.J.	10	6	2.4	12
B.B.	5	4	1.0	3
B.C.	19	10	1.5	6
B.D.	14	6	2.1	9
C.C.	6	4	1.3	6
C.D.	12	6	1.6	9
C.E.	16	8	1.8	9
D.E.	3	2	2.5	15

Converting Total Points or Average Points Into Letter Grades

Once all of the different test items have been numerically scored, treated, and totaled, it usually becomes necessary to convert total points or average points into letter grades of A, B, C, D, and F for the report card. Converting total or average points into letter grades may involve one or more of several methods. The methods of curve grading and grading by absolute standards are discussed here using average *T* scores from tests of skill, fitness, knowledge, and behavior for a unit on softball (Table 5.1).

GRADING ON AN ABSOLUTE STANDARD

In this method, the teacher or the school sets up standards for the different letter grades, such as 95–100 = A, 85–94 = B, 76–84 = C, 66–75 = D, and below 65 = F. For this system to work satisfactorily, the measuring instruments must be accurate, or the teacher will sometimes have to adjust the difficulty of tests so that the majority of students do not end up with extremely high or low grades. Table 5.2 shows the computations necessary for converting the average *T* scores from Table 5.1 into percentages for the

Table 5.2. Converting Average T Scores Into Percentages for the Absolute Scale[a]

$$\frac{65}{65}(100) = 100$$

$$\frac{58}{65}(100) = 89$$

$$\frac{54}{65}(100) = 83$$

$$\frac{48}{65}(100) = 74$$

$$\frac{50}{65}(100) = 77$$

$$\frac{53}{65}(100) = 82$$

$$\frac{51}{65}(100) = 78$$

$$\frac{48}{65}(100) = 74$$

$$\frac{54}{65}(100) = 83$$

$$\frac{46}{65}(100) = 71$$

$$\frac{54}{65}(100) = 83$$

ABSOLUTE SCALE[b]	FREQUENCY	GRADE
95–100	1	A
85– 94	1	B
76– 84	12	C
66– 75	10	D
0– 65	1	F
	$N = 25$	

[a]T scores of ten students listed in Table 5.1.
[b]When all 25 percentages are computed, grading by absolute standards results in a large number of Cs and Ds.

scale. The highest average T score of 65 is treated as the highest possible score in order to raise the other scores enough to fit into the scale.

Some disadvantages to absolute grading are the frequent need for additional computations after final average scores have been computed, in order to fit some scores into the absolute scale pattern, and the fact that allowances are not made when differences are slight, such as a 1-point difference between an A and a B.

CURVE GRADING

Curve grading is based on the mean and standard deviation of a group of scores. Although many teachers indicate that they grade on a curve, few actually find the mean and standard deviation that are needed for true curve grading.

The steps necessary for curve grading are:

Step 1. Compute the mean and standard deviation for the set of scores.

Step 2. If using the common five-letter grading system (A, B, C, D, and F), assign the grades a standard deviation range, as follows:

A = more than $1.5\,s$ above the mean

B = between $+0.5\,s$ and $+1.5\,s$ above the mean

C = between $-0.5\,s$ and $+0.5\,s$ from the mean

D = between $-0.5\,s$ and $-1.5\,s$ below the mean

F = more than $1.5\,s$ below the mean

To illustrate the application of this method of assigning grades, we will use the average of the total T scores from the softball unit from Table 5.1. The mean is 50.1 and the standard deviation is 4.4.

Step 3. Determine the C range (since the C range extends above and below the mean, its determination facilitates calculation of the other grade ranges). In this example,

$$C = \overline{X} \pm 0.5\,s = 50.1 \pm 0.5(4.4) =$$
$$50.1 \pm 2.2 = 47.9\text{--}52.3$$

Step 4. Establish the B range. The lower limit is known (52.4), since the upper limit of the C range is 52.3. The upper limit of the B range is:

$$B = \overline{X} + 1.5\,s = 50.1 + 1.5(4.4) =$$
$$50.1 + 6.6 = 56.7$$

Thus, the B range is 52.4–56.7.

Step 5. Determine the A range. This is simply 56.8 and above, that is, over $1.5\,s$ above the mean.

Step 6. Determine the D range in exactly the same way the B range was determined, except subtracting from the mean rather than adding. The upper limit of the D range (47.8) is known, since the lower limit of the C range is 47.9. The lower limit of D is:

$$D = \overline{X} - 1.5\,s = 50.1 - 1.5(4.4) =$$
$$50.1 - 6.6 = 43.5$$

Thus, the D range is 43.5–47.8.

Step 7. Determine the F range. This is any grade 43.4 or lower (i.e., more than 1.5 s below the mean).

Step 8. Set up the completed scale:

A = 56.8 and above

B = 52.4–56.7

C = 47.9–52.3

D = 43.5–47.8

F = 43.4 and below

Note: With this procedure, the teacher actually has to multiply the standard deviation by only two values: 0.5 and 1.5. The rest of the procedure involves simply adding and subtracting these values from the mean.

Step 9. Establish the frequency and percentage of scores from the grade range, as shown in Table 5.3. In this table there is a column entitled "Theoretical Percentage." These percentages are taken from tabled values of the percentages of scores in the normal probability curve that fall ±0.5 standard deviations and ±1.5 standard deviations from the mean.

When the obtained grade distribution percentages are compared with the theoretical (normal curve) percentages in Table 5.3, the percentages are not too dissimilar. The major difference is that the example has considerably more C grades and fewer Bs and Ds. However, it should be pointed out that strict curve grading is usually inappropriate with a small number of students.

The main advantage of this type of grading is that grades are based on the standard deviation, which makes it a standard score method. One disadvantage is that some students will get As and some Fs, regardless of how "typical" the sample. Yet, overall, this method is probably the most reliable, particularly with fairly large numbers.

Grading by Observation of Scores

This method is quite simple in that final scores are merely listed down a page in high-to-low order and after close observation, lines are drawn between the natural breaks in the scores, which frequently separate upper and lower groups from the large average group (Table 5.4). If a break does not appear within a reasonable distance, judgment must be used in determining where the cut-off point is between two grades. In cases where scores run close together, some teachers find it satisfactory and fair to designate the top score of the scores they would normally consider in the C group as a B −, and the next lower score is considered a C. (Teachers might have a better basis for determining the cut-off points if they calculate the mean first.)

Usually a rough guide should be followed in determining how many As, Bs, Cs, Ds, and Fs should be given. For example, the highest 10% of the scores could be assigned As, the next 20% Bs, the next 40% Cs, the next 20% Ds, and the lowest 10% Fs. This system imposes somewhat of a normal curve on the students, and yet with small classes, the actual performances may not approach normality. Thus, the percentages given for As, Bs, Cs, Ds, and Fs need not be followed slavishly but should be used merely as a guide. If the class appears to be especially good, the teacher may assign more high grades and less low grades, and vice versa if the class is below par.

Assigning grades by observation of scores allows the teacher to relate the performance of a student to that of classmates who have been through the same procedure. The teacher is free to use his or her judgment in assigning grades with both individual capacity and standards in mind.

Contract Grading

Bloom and colleagues suggested that the physical education teacher could preestablish what performance scores would indicate competence.

Table 5.3. Example of Frequency and Percentage of Grades When Determined by Curve Method

GRADE	FREQUENCY	PERCENTAGE	THEORETICAL PERCENTAGE
A	2	8	7
B	5	20	24
C	12	48	38
D	4	16	24
F	2	8	7

Table 5.4. Grading by Observation of Scores
(N = 25)

6-WEEKS' TOTAL POINTS (TENNIS UNIT)	
94 92	A
88 87 84 83 80	B
77 77 76 76 76 75 75 72 70 69 69	C
65 65 64 63 61	D
57 53	F

The student and teacher could agree on certain criteria for achievement in determining various grades. One criterion might be the student's achieving a certain score on skills tests or writing a certain number of papers, or the teacher's making a prescribed number of observations of performances. There may be different options for attaining different grade levels (e.g., five papers for an A, four for a B, and so forth). The major weakness of this system is the heavy focus on quantitative criteria and the lack of qualitative evaluation of competency.

With contract grading, all students could receive a grade of A in a course, depending on such factors as the abilities of the students and the pedagogical process of the instructor. In this method, grades are determined from pretest criteria rather than from actual test data.

Determining the Final Letter Grade From Subarea Letter Grades

To this point our discussion has centered on accumulation of points in various testing areas (objectives) and then, as a last step, assignment of the letter grade. Some teachers prefer, however, to establish letter grades for each major objective and then make a decision as to the final letter grade. Two examples are given in Figure 5.1 whereby subarea letter grades are converted into a total value and then compared with a grade and value scale for the final grade.

SUMMARY

Grades should reflect achievement toward the objectives of the unit of instruction, not administrative aspects of behavior such as tardinesses and absences. The steps in grading for a unit of instruction are as follows:

Step 1. Establish sound objectives or goals for the unit.

Step 2. Determine the importance or weight of each objective before instruction begins.

Step 3. Select and administer a practical number of tests during the unit of instruction.

Step 4. Analyze raw scores and derive either grand total points or average points.

Step 5. Convert total or average points into letter grades by one of the following methods:
   a.   Absolute standards
   b.   Curve grading
   c.   Observation of scores

Of paramount importance is that students are informed as to the method of grading and the weighting of objectives at the beginning of the unit. Although there are many varied methods of grading, probably no one method best fits all situations. However, the physical educator should make every effort to establish a fair and sound method of testing and grading that will fit into the evaluation policies of the school.

BIBLIOGRAPHY

Barrow, H. M., and R. McGee, *A Practical Approach to Measurement in Physical Education.* Philadelphia: Lea & Febiger, 1964.

Bayles, E. E., "The Philosophical Approach to Educational Measurement." *Educational Administration and Supervision* 26:455–461, September 1940.

Bloom, B., et al., *Formative and Summative Evaluation.* New York: McGraw-Hill, 1971.

Example 1. Weighting of Objectives

Skills	50% = .50
Knowledge	25% = .25
Fitness	15% = .15
Social	10% = .10

Subarea Grade:

Objective	Grade	Points		Percent	Point Value
Skills	B+	9	×	.50	4.5
Knowledge	C−	4	×	.25	1.0
Fitness	B	8	×	.15	1.2
Social	C	5	×	.10	0.5
				Total =	7.2

Final Grade: B− (from Grade and Value Scale)

Grade and Value Scale

Grade	Value
A+	12
A	11
A−	10
B+	9
B	8
B−	7
C+	6
C	5
C−	4
D+	3
D	2
D−	1
F	0

Example 2. Weighting of Objectives

Skills	40% = .40
Knowledge	20% = .20
Fitness	30% = .30
Social	10% = .10

Subarea Grade:

Objective	Grade	Points		Percent	Point Value
Skills	C−	4	×	.40	1.6
Knowledge	B+	9	×	.20	1.8
Fitness	D	2	×	.30	.6
Social	A	11	×	.10	1.1
				Total =	5.1

Final Grade: C (from Grade and Value Scale)

Figure 5.1. Determination of final letter grade from subarea letter grades on the basis of different weighting of objectives

Bovard, J. F., F. W. Cozens, and E. P. Hagman, *Tests and Measurements in Physical Education.* 3rd ed. Philadelphia: W. B. Saunders, 1950, pp. 3−4.

Brubacher, J. S., *Modern Philosophies of Education.* 3rd ed. New York: McGraw-Hill, 1962, p. 253.

Dewey, J., "Progressive Eduation and the Science of Education." *Progressive Education* 5:200, August 1928.

————, *The Sources of a Science of Education.* New York: Liveright, 1929, pp. 64−65.

Duncan, R. O., "Fundamental Issues in Our Profession." *JOHPER* 35:19−22, May 1964.

Ebel, R. L., "The Failure of Schools Without Failure." *Phi Delta Kappa*, February 1980, pp. 386−388.

Fabricius, H., "Grading in Physical Education." *JOHPER* 38:36−37, May 1967.

Garrett, H. E., *Statistics in Psychology and Education.* 6th ed. New York: David McKay, 1966.

Hanson, D. L., "Grading in Physical Education." *JOHPER* 38:37, May 1967.

Kilpatrick, W. H., *A Reconstructed Theory of the Educative Process.* New York: Columbia University Press, 1935, pp. 29−30.

Larson, L. A., and R. D. Yocom, *Measurement and Evaluation in Physical, Health, and Recreation Education.* St. Louis: C. V. Mosby, 1951.

Mathews, D. K., *Measurement in Physical Education.* Philadelphia: W. B. Saunders, 1963, pp. 313−328.

Remmers, H. H., et al., *A Practical Introduction to Measurement and Evaluation.* New York: Harper and Row, 1965, pp. 286−302.

Singer, R., "Grading in Physical Education." *JOHPER* 38:38−39, May 1967.

Smith, F. M., and S. Adams, *Educational Measurement for the Classroom Teacher.* New York: Harper and Row, 1966, pp. 194−199.

Solley, W. H., "Grading in Physical Education." *JOHPER* 38:35−36, May 1967.

CHAPTER 6

THE MEASUREMENT OF FLEXIBILITY

OBJECTIVES

After reading this chapter, the student should be able to:

1. Define flexibility and differentiate between relative and absolute flexibility tests
2. Understand the specific nature of flexibility

and recognize some of the problems involved in its measurement

3. Follow the directions for administering practical tests of flexibility

Flexibility, as a component of physical fitness, is the ability to move the body and its parts through a wide range of motion without undue strain to the articulations and muscle attachments. Flexibility is usually discussed in terms such as *flexion,* in which the angle of the body with its articulations is decreased through movement; *extension,* in which the angle of the body with its articulations is increased through movement; *hyperextension,* in which the angle of a joint is extended beyond its normal range; *double-jointedness,* a nonexistent condition but nevertheless a term used with reference to a person with unusual flexibility in certain positions; and finally, *"muscle-boundness,"* an unfortunate term used to describe inflexibility in an individual who has well-developed muscles. Regardless of how it is defined or described, flexibility provides a further dimension in performance, allowing a higher degree of freedom and ease of movement, and has important implications for safety from injury.

Flexibility measurement brings to light concepts that must be identified for proper selection and scoring of available flexibility tests. For example, there are two types of flexibililty tests:

1. Relative flexibility tests, those designed to

be relative to the length or width of a specific body part. In these tests one measures not only the movement but also the length or width of an influencing body part.

2. Absolute flexibility tests, those in which one measures only the desired movement in relation to an absolute performance goal. For example, on the splits, one determines the distance between the floor and the performer's seat (Johnson 1978).

Flexibility scores may be reported as a result of *linear measurement,* in which scores occur in inches or millimeters as determined from use of a tape measure, yardstick, or flexomeasure, or of *rotary measurement,* in which scores occur in degrees of rotation as determined by the use of a protractor, goniometer, or flexometer. Although flexibility correlates minimally with some motor abilities, it is usually considered an important factor in certain activities, as exemplified by the diver flexing and extending in the air or by the swimmer executing the butterfly stroke with the dolphin fishtail kick. It is difficult to determine how much flexion–extension is needed by an individual, and the teacher and student together must evaluate the degree needed in each joint in terms of ease of performance and safety in the activity or for the part of the body that is involved. Flexibility is usually mentioned as an attribute of physical fitness. A loss in flexibility is frequently one of the first signs of the body's getting out of shape.

USES OF FLEXIBILITY TESTS

Flexibility tests are used in physical education classes in several ways:

1. As a factor in physical fitness tests
2. As a means for determining students' potential in certain sport activities
3. As a means for determining achievement and skill grades when flexibility performance is a specific objective in the teaching unit
4. As a means for diagnosing the extent of a previous injury or the cause of poor posture

PROBLEMS IN MEASUREMENT OF FLEXIBILITY

Several problems are apparent in conscientious measurement of flexibility. First, the teacher or coach must decide whether the test should be *relative* to the length or width of a body part or *absolute,* a measure of what the student can do related to a predetermined goal of performance. Generally, the absolute method is desirable when flexibility training and testing are for purposes of sports performance. In the earlier example of the splits, in absolute flexibility testing one is saying, "I don't care how tall or short you are, I just want to know how close you can lower your seat to the floor."

Second, flexibility is highly specific. A person can be quite flexible in one body area and only slightly flexible in another. Thus, there is a limitation in including only one flexibility item in a physical fitness test battery. While the item might be ideal for some students, it could be the worst possible selection for others. Therefore, one really needs to present a choice of one out of three flexibility items to allow each student to perform the one that he or she can do most successfully.

Third, certain practical tests, such as the front-to-rear splits and the shoulder rotation, are time consuming owing to the difficulty elementary students have in understanding the correct position. However, this problem can be minimized by having demonstrators available or pictures posted to help prepare students prior to testing.

Fourth, since warm-up exercises substantially improve flexibility performance, students must be allowed several warm-up trials before being tested, for their scores to be reliable.

And finally, there is a need for scoring scales and norms at the elementary, junior high, and senior high levels.

PRACTICAL TESTS OF FLEXIBILITY

The Leighton Flexometer (Leighton 1942) and the electrogoniometer (Adrian, Tipton, and Karpovich 1965) (Figure 6.1) are usually regarded as the most accurate instruments for the measurement of flexibility; however, many tests may be accurately and satisfactorily given with use of an inexpensive instrument, the aluminum flexomeasure (Johnson 1977b), in schools that do not have the more expensive equipment.[1]

AAHPERD Sit-and-Reach Test (AAHPERD 1980)

Objective: To evaluate the flexibility (extensibility) of the low back and posterior thighs.

Age Level: Ages 5 to 17 (and adulthood).

Sex: Satisfactory for both boys and girls.

Validity and Reliability: The technical manual (AAHPERD 1984) states that this test was chosen because it has been noted in clinical settings that persons with low-back problems often have a restricted range of motion in the hamstring muscles and low back. The validity of the test is thus supported by logic. Reliability coefficients have ranged from .84 to .98.

Equipment: A specially constructed box (Figure 6.2) with a measurement scale with 23 cm at the level of the feet.

Directions: Students remove their shoes and sit down at the testing box with their knees fully extended and feet shoulder-width apart, placed against the end board. The arms are extended forward and the hands are placed on top of each other. The student reaches forward, palms down, along the measuring board four times and holds the maximum reach on the fourth trial. The maximum reach must be held for 1 sec.

---

1. Various flexibility instruments are available for use in flexibility measurement. Information on specific instruments is available as follows: *Electrogoniometer:* Electrogoniometer Manual, Springfield College, Department of Health, Physical Education, and Recreation, Springfield, MA 01109. *Flexomeasure:* Instructions and performance norms, B & L Products Company, P.O. Box 473, Portland, TX 78374. *Goniometer:* Rehabilitation Products, Evanston, IL 60201. *Leighton Flexometer:* Country Technology, Inc., P.O. Box 87, Gays Mills, WI 54631.

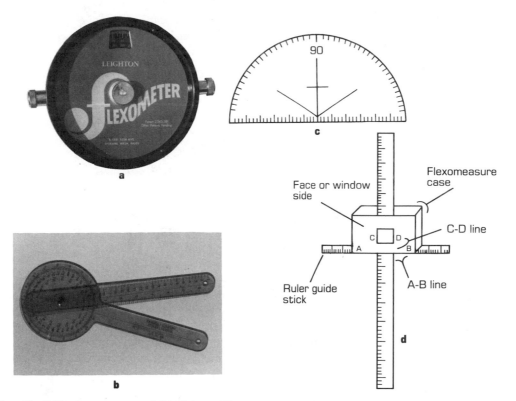

Figure 6.1.   Flexibility instruments: (a) Leighton Flexometer. (b) Goniometer. (c) Protractor. (d) Flexomeasure

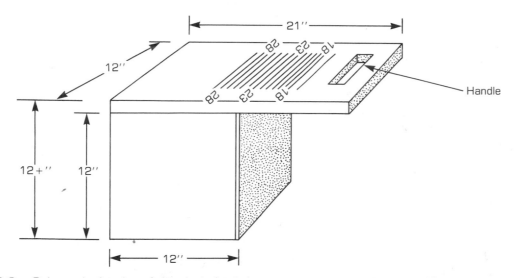

Figure 6.2.   Schematic drawing of the sit-and-reach test measurement apparatus (Source: *AAHPERD Health Related Physical Fitness Test Manual*. Reston, Va.: AAHPERD, 1980. Used by permission)

Scoring: The score is the farthest point reached on the fourth trial, to the nearest centimeter. The most distant point must be touched with *both* hands. If the hands reach unevenly, a new trial is given. The tester should place one hand on the subject's knees to make sure that the knees are fully extended. Percentile norms for boys and girls are available for ages 5 to 17+ (Table 6.1).

Additional Pointers:

1.   The manual emphasizes the need for warm-up, which should include slow, sustained static stretching of the low back and posterior thighs.

2.   The trial is repeated if the knees bend or the hands become uneven.

Table 6.1. Percentile Norms in Centimeters for Sit-and-Reach Test

PERCENTILE	AGE												
	5	6	7	8	9	10	11	12	13	14	15	16	17+
	GIRLS												
95	34	34	34	36	35	35	37	40	43	44	46	46	44
75	30	30	31	31	31	31	32	34	36	38	41	39	40
50	27	27	27	28	28	28	29	30	31	33	36	34	35
25	23	23	24	23	23	24	24	25	24	28	31	30	31
5	18	18	16	17	17	16	16	15	17	18	19	14	22
	BOYS												
95	32	34	33	34	34	33	34	35	36	39	41	42	45
75	29	29	28	29	29	28	29	29	30	33	34	36	40
50	25	26	25	25	25	25	25	26	26	28	30	30	34
25	22	22	22	22	22	20	21	21	20	23	24	25	28
5	17	16	16	16	16	12	12	13	12	15	13	11	15

Source: Adapted from *AAHPERD Health Related Physical Fitness Test Manual.* Reston, Va.: AAHPERD, 1980. Used by permission.

3. A bench with a metric ruler can be used in place of the prescribed test apparatus.

4. The test apparatus should be placed against a wall to prevent it from slipping.

Test Interpretation: A score above the 50th percentile is considered normal. Scores below P_{50} represent poor flexibility in the posterior thighs or low back or posterior hip. Students scoring below the 25th percentile should be given a remedial program. Exercises to improve flexibility are provided in the manual. In preadolescence and during the adolescent growth spurt (age 10–14), it is normal for many boys and girls to not be able to reach the 23-cm level, because the legs become proportionally longer in relation to the trunk during this period (Table 6.1).

Modified Sit-and-Reach Test (Johnson 1977b)

Objective: To measure the development of hip and back flexion as well as extension of the hamstring muscles of the legs. The object is to see how far the fingertips can be extended beyond the foot line with the legs straight.

Sports Specificity: Vaulting, diving, and trampoline skills; straight-arm, straight-leg press to handstand in floor exercise; other gymnastic skills.

Age Level: Age 6 through college age.

Sex: Satisfactory for both boys and girls.

Reliability: An *r* of .94 was found when the best score of three trials was recorded from separate testings and correlated.

Objectivity: An *r* of .99 was found when the

scores from an experienced tester were correlated with scores from an inexperienced tester.

Validity: Face validity is accepted for this test.

Equipment: Flexomeasure case with yardstick and tape (Figure 6.1). (See Appendix I for alternate test without flexomeasure.)

Directions: The tester lines up the 15-in. mark of the yardstick with a line on the floor and tapes the ends of the stick to the floor so that the flexomeasure case (window side) is face down. The student sits down and lines up the heels with the near edge of the 15-in. mark and slides the seat back beyond the zero end of the yardstick. A partner should stand and brace his or her toes against the student's heels. Also, an assistant should stand on each side to hold the student's knees in a locked position as the student prepares to stretch. With heels not more than 5 in. apart, the student slowly stretches forward while pushing the flexomeasure case as far down the stick as possible with the fingertips of both hands (Figure 6.3). The reading is taken at the near edge of the flexomeasure case.

Scoring: The best of three trials measured to the nearest quarter of an inch is the test score. Table 6.2 shows norms for this test.

Bridge-up Test (Johnson 1977b)

Objective: To measure hyperextension of the spine.

Sports Specificity: Butterfly event; high jump event; balance beam and floor exercise skills in gymnastics; modern dance and ballet movements.

Age Level: Age 6 through college age.

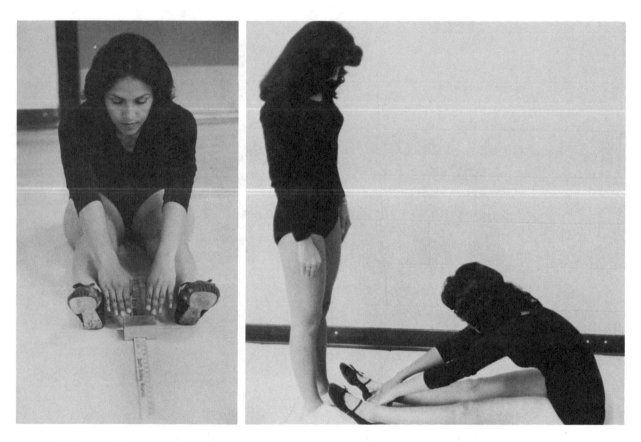

Figure 6.3.   Modified sit-and-reach test

Table 6.2.   Norms in Inches for Modified Sit-and-Reach Test, College Students[a]

PERFORMANCE LEVEL	MEN	WOMEN
Advanced	23¾ and above	25¾ and above
Advanced intermediate	21¼–23½	22½–25½
Intermediate	18¾–21	20 –22¼
Advanced beginner	17 –18½	18 –19¾
Beginner	16¾ and below	17¾ and below

[a]Based on the scores of 100 men and 100 women at Corpus Christi State University, Corpus Christi, Tex., 1977.

Sex: Satisfactory for both boys and girls.

Reliability: An *r* of .97 was found when the best score of three trials was recorded from separate testings and correlated.

Objectivity: An *r* of .99 was found when the scores from an experienced tester were correlated with scores from an inexperienced tester.

Validity: Face validity is acceptable for this test when students are strong enough to extend the body from the floor.

Equipment: Flexomeasure case with yardstick and ruler guide inserted. The A–B line of the case must be nearest the zero end of the yardstick. (See Appendix I for alternate test without flexomeasure.)

Directions: The student assumes a supine (back-lying) position on the floor (or a mat) and tilts the head back, pushing upward and arching the back while walking the hands and feet as close together as possible. A partner, located at one side, places the zero end of the yardstick on the mat or floor and slides the flexomeasure case vertically upward until the ruler guide touches the highest point of the arched spine (Figure 6.4). The reading (to the

Figure 6.4.   Bridge-up test

nearest quarter of an inch) is taken in the case window at the lower (C–D) line.

Scoring: The best score (to the nearest quarter of an inch) of three trials is recorded and then subtracted from the student's standing height (floor to navel). The smaller the difference, the better the performance (Table 6.3). Example

> Standing height: 46 in. (floor to navel)
> Best arch: 30 in.
> Score: 16 in.

Additional Pointers:

1.   The thumbs should be next to the ears as the student pushes the body upward from the floor.

2.   If the student is too weak to push upward,

the head may remain on the floor as the back is arched for the measurement.

3.   The student should be cautioned to not strain unduly in arching. It is best that students train over an extended period of time and thus avoid injury.

4.   The tester should slide the case upward rapidly to get the correct reading, since this exercise is difficult for some individuals to hold.

Front-to-Rear Splits Test (Johnson 1978)

Objective: To measure the extension of the legs from front to rear. The object is to get the crotch as close to the floor as possible.

Table 6.3.   Norms for Bridge-up Test, College Students[a]

PERFORMANCE LEVEL	MEN		WOMEN	
	Inches	Centimeters	Inches	Centimeters
Advanced	12.5 and below	31.8 and below	11.75 and below	29.8 and below
Advanced intermediate	16.25–12.75	41.3–32.4	15.00–12.00	38.1–30.5
Intermediate	20.75–16.50	52.7–41.9	17.75–15.25	45.1–38.7
Advanced beginner	28.25–21.00	71.8–53.3	20.75–18.00	52.7–45.7
Beginner	28.50 and above	72.4 and above	21.50 and above	54.6 and above

[a]Based on the scores of 100 men and 100 women at Corpus Christi State University, Corpus Christi, Tex., 1977.

Sports and Dance Specificity: Hurdling event; floor exercise and balance beam events; dance leaps (e.g., figure skating, ballet, and modern dance).

Age Level: Any age from 6 through college age.

Sex: Satisfactory for both boys and girls.

Reliability: An *r* of .91 was found when the best score of three trials was recorded from separate testings and correlated.

Objectivity: An *r* of .99 was found when the scores from an experienced tester were correlated with scores from an inexperienced tester.

Validity: Face validity is accepted for this test.

Equipment: Flexomeasure case with yardstick and ruler guide inserted. The A–B line of the case must be nearest the zero end of the yardstick (Figure 6.5).

Directions: From a standing position, the student extends the legs apart from the front to rear and lowers the crotch as near the floor as possible (Figure 6.6). The motion should be slow and steady, without bouncing. During lowering, an assistant should be positioned behind the student with the zero end of the yardstick on the floor. When the lowest point is reached, the case is raised upward until the ruler guide rests under the crotch. The reading to the nearest quarter of an inch is taken in the case window at the lower (C–D) line.

Scoring: The best score of three trials is recorded as the performance score. Table 6.4 shows norms for this test.

Additional Pointers:

1. The knees must be locked at the moment of measurement.
2. The performer's hands may touch the floor for balance during the test.

Side Splits Test (Johnson 1977b)

Objective: To measure extension in spreading the legs apart. The object is to get the crotch as close to the floor as possible.

Sports and Dance Specificity: Vaulting, floor exercise, and balance beam events; modern and ballet dance.

Age Level: Age 6 through college age.

Sex: Satisfactory for both boys and girls.

Reliability: An *r* of .92 was found when the best score of three trials was recorded from separate testings and correlated.

Figure 6.5.   Flexomeasure position for splits test

Objectivity: An *r* of .99 was found when the scores from an experienced tester were correlated with scores from an inexperienced tester.

Validity: Face validity is accepted for this test.

Equipment: Same as for the front-to-rear splits test.

Directions: Same as for the front-to-rear splits test except the legs are extended side to side until the crotch is as near the floor as possible (Figure 6.7).

Scoring: The best score of three trials is recorded as the performance score. Table 6.5 shows norms for this test.

Additional Pointers:

1. The knees must be locked at the moment of measurement.
2. The performer's hands may touch the floor for balance during the test.
3. The performer's hips must not shift past the vertical during the measurement.

Shoulder-and-Wrist Elevation Test (Johnson 1977b)

Objective: To measure shoulder and wrist flexibility. *Note:* Since it is difficult to elevate the shoulders in this test without extending the wrists, the movements of these two joints are combined for the score.

Figure 6.6. Front splits

Table 6.4. Norms for Front-to-Rear Splits Test, College Students[a]

PERFORMANCE LEVEL	MEN		WOMEN	
	Inches	Centimeters	Inches	Centimeters
Advanced	2 — 0	5.1–0	1½–0	3.8–0
Advanced intermediate	6¼— 2¼	15.9–5.7	4½–1¾	11.4— 4.4
Intermediate	12¼— 6½	31.1–16.5	8 —4¾	20.3–12.1
Advanced beginner	15¾–12½	40.0–31.8	9¾–8¼	24.8–21.0
Beginner	16 and above	40.6 and above	10 and above	25.4 and above

[a]Based on the scores of 100 men and 100 women at Corpus Christi State University, Corpus Christi, Tex., 1977.

Sports Specificity: Gymnastics (bars and floor exercise skills); butterfly stroke in swimming; wrestling.

Age Level: Age 6 through college age.

Sex: Satisfactory for both boys and girls.

Reliability: An *r* of .93 was found when the best score of three trials was recorded from separate testings and correlated.

Objectivity: An *r* of .99 was found when the scores from an experienced tester were correlated with scores from an inexperienced tester.

Validity: Face validity is accepted for this test.

Figure 6.7.   Side splits

Table 6.5.   Norms in Inches for Side Splits Test, College Students[a]

PERFORMANCE LEVEL	MEN	WOMEN
Advanced	3 – 0	2¾– 0
Advanced intermediate	8 – 3¼	7½– 3
Intermediate	17½– 8¼	16¾– 7¾
Advanced beginner	22½–17¾	21½–17
Beginner	22¾ and above	21¾ and above

[a]Based on the scores of 100 men and 100 women at Corpus Christi State University, Corpus Christi, Tex., 1977.

Equipment: Flexomeasure case with yardstick and ruler guide inserted plus one extra yardstick. The A–B line of the case must be nearest the zero end of the yardstick. (See Appendix I for alternate test without flexomeasure.)

Directions: The student assumes a prone (face-down) position with the arms straight over the head and grasps the extra yardstick with the hands about shoulder-width apart. He or she then raises the stick upward as high as possible while keeping the chin on the floor and elbows straight. As the stick is raised, an assistant positioned in front keeps the zero end of the yardstick on the floor. When the highest point is reached, the assistant raises the case vertically upward until the ruler guide rests under the raised yardstick and at the midpoint between the hands (Figure 6.8). The reading to the nearest quarter of an inch is taken in the case window at the lower C–D line. The student's arm length is measured from the acromion process (top of the arm at the joint) to the middle fingertip. The zero end of the flexomeasure yardstick is placed next to the middle fingertip (as the arm hangs down) and the case is raised until the A–B line rests on the acromion process. The reading is taken to the nearest quarter of an inch at the A–B line at the bottom of the case.

Scoring: The best lift of three trials is subtracted from arm length. The closer arm lift approaches

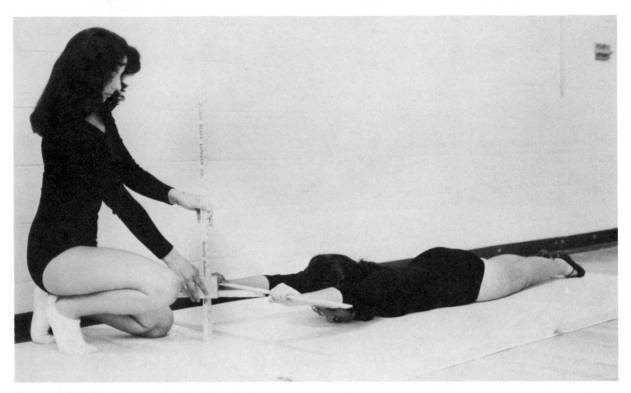

Figure 6.8.   Shoulder-and-wrist elevation test

arm length, the better the score. Thus, a score of zero would be perfect (Table 6.6). Example

Arm length: 30 in.
  Best lift: 16 in.
    Score: 14 in.

Additional Pointer: Although some individuals are so flexible that they can move the stick beyond the highest vertical point (arms perpendicular to the floor), the measurement must be taken at the highest vertical point.

Trunk-and-Neck Extension Test (Johnson 1978)

Objective: To measure ability to extend the trunk and neck.

Sports Specificity: Gymnastics (floor exercise, beam); butterfly stroke in swimming; wrestling.

Age Level: Age 6 through college age.

Sex: Satisfactory for both boys and girls.

Reliability: An *r* of .90 was found when the best score of three trials was recorded from separate testings and correlated.

Objectivity: An *r* of .99 was found when the scores from an experienced tester were correlated with scores from an inexperienced tester.

Validity: Face validity is accepted for this test.

Equipment: Flexomeasure case with yardstick and ruler guide inserted. The A–B line of the case must be nearest the zero end of the yardstick.

Table 6.6.   Norms in Inches for Shoulder-and-Wrist Elevation Test, College Students[a]

PERFORMANCE LEVEL	MEN	WOMEN
Advanced	6 – 0	5½– 0
Advanced intermediate	8¼– 6¼	7½– 5¾
Intermediate	11½– 8½	10¾– 7¾
Advanced beginner	12½–11¾	11¾–11
Beginner	12¾ and above	12 and above

[a]Based on the scores of 100 men and 100 women at Corpus Christi State University, Corpus Christi, Tex., 1977.

(See Appendix I for an alternate test without flexomeasure.)

Directions: An assistant measures the student's trunk and neck length by taking the distance to the nearest quarter of an inch between the tip of the nose and the seat of the chair in which the student is sitting. The chin must be level as the zero end of the yardstick is placed between the legs and on the seat level of the chair. Next, the flexomeasure case is raised until the bottom of the ruler guide touches the tip of the nose. The assistant should record the reading at the bottom of the case (the A–B line). The student then assumes a prone (facedown) position on a mat, and with the hands resting at the small of the back, raises the trunk upward as high as possible from the floor. A partner should hold the student's hips by placing his or her hands on the back of the thighs (base of the buttocks). The assistant, located to the front, places the zero end of the yardstick on the mat and slides the flexomeasure case vertically upward until the upper edge of the ruler guide touches the tip of the student's nose (Figure 6.9). The reading to the nearest quarter of an inch is taken in the case window at the lower (C–D) line.

Scoring: The best of three lifts is subtracted from trunk and neck length. The closer the trunk lift is to the estimated trunk and neck length, the better the score. Thus, a score of zero would be perfect (Table 6.7). Example

Trunk and neck length: 32 in.
Best trunk lift: 15 in.
Score: 17 in.

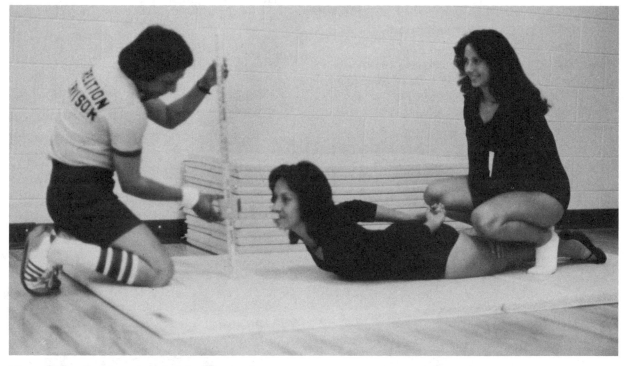

Figure 6.9.　Trunk-and-neck extension test

Table 6.7.　Norms in Inches for Trunk-and-Neck Extension Test, College Students[a]

PERFORMANCE LEVEL	MEN	WOMEN
Advanced	3–0	2 –0
Advanced intermediate	6–3¼	5¾–2¼
Intermediate	8–6¼	7¾–6
Advanced beginner	10–8¼	9¾–8
Beginner	10¼ and above	10 and above

[a]Based on the scores of 100 men and 100 women at Corpus Christi State University, Corpus Christi, Tex., 1977.

Shoulder Rotation Test (Johnson and Garcia 1977)

Objective: To measure the extent to which the shoulders will rotate with as narrow a grip of the hands as possible.

Sports Specificity: Butterfly, crawl, and back-crawl strokes in swimming; dislocate and inlocate on the rings, uneven bars, and horizontal bars in gymnastics.

Age Level: Age 6 through college age.

Sex: Satisfactory for both boys and girls.

Reliability: An *r* of .97 was found when the best score of three trials was recorded from separate testings and correlated.

Objectivity: An *r* of .99 was found when the scores from an experienced tester were correlated with scores from an inexperienced tester.

Validity: Face validity is accepted for this test.

Equipment: Flexomeasure with yardstick and guide stick inserted and 60 in. of rope.

Directions: The student grasps one end of the rope with the left hand and grasps the rope a few inches away with the right hand. Both arms are then extended to full length in front of the chest and the rope is rotated over the head. As resistance is met in rotating the shoulders, the student lets the rope slide in the grip of the right hand so that the arms can spread and allow lowering of the rope until it is resting across the back (Figure 6.10). Keeping the arms locked, the student rotates to the starting position and the number of inches of rope between the thumbs of the hands is then measured. The least amount of distance indicates a better level of performance. An assistant measures the maximum shoulder width across the back of the student from deltoid to deltoid with the flexomeasure.

Scoring: The shoulder width is subtracted from the total inches of the best score of three trials. Thus, the lower the score, the better the performance (Table 6.8). Example

Best trial: 30 in.
Shoulder width: 19 in.
Score: 11 in.

 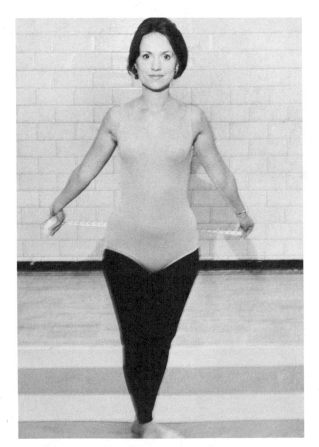

Figure 6.10.   Shoulder rotation test

Table 6.8. Norms in Inches for Shoulder Rotation Test, College Students[a]

PERFORMANCE LEVEL	MEN	WOMEN
Advanced	7 —Less	5 —Less
Advanced intermediate	11½— 7¼	9¾— 5¼
Intermediate	14½—11¾	13 —10
Advanced beginner	19¾—14¾	17¾—13¼
Beginner	20 and above	18 and above

[a]Based on the scores of 100 men and 100 women at Corpus Christi State University, Corpus Christi, Tex., 1977.

Ankle Extension (Plantar Flexion) Test (Johnson 1977b)

Objective: To measure ankle extension (plantar flexion).

Sports and Dance Specificity: Swimming; diving; gymnastics; dance and jumping events. In gymnastics, dance, and diving, ankle extension adds to the beauty of movement, while in swimming and jumping it adds to mechanical efficiency.

Age Level: Age 6 through college age.

Sex: Satisfactory for both boys and girls.

Reliability: An r of .88 was found when the best score of three trials was recorded from separate testings and correlated.

Objectivity: An r of .99 was found when the scores from an experienced tester were correlated with scores from an inexperienced tester.

Validity: Face validity is accepted for this test.

Equipment: Flexomeasure case with yardstick and ruler guide inserted. The A–B line of the case must be nearest the zero end of the yardstick. (See Appendix I for an alternate test without flexomeasure.)

Directions: The student removes his or her shoes and takes a sitting position on the floor with the right leg as straight as possible. An assistant places the zero end of the yardstick on the floor and slides the case downward until the ruler guide is resting across the lowest point of the shin bone. The student extends the ankle and the assistant repeats the measurement at the highest point of the foot (either the toes or instep) during maximum extension. The procedure is repeated for the left foot. The difference between the upper foot line (during extension) and the lower shin bone line is recorded to the nearest one eighth of an inch for each foot (Figure 6.11).

Scoring: The right foot difference is averaged with the left foot difference and the score is compared with the scale in Table 6.9.

Ankle Flexion (Dorsiflexion) Test (Johnson and Garcia 1977)

Objective: To measure ankle flexion and stretch the gastrocnemius (calf) and heel cord.

Sports Specificity: Forward landings from horizontal distance jumps and vaults; excess lean as in the flight in the ski jump.

Age Level: Age 6 through college age.

Sex: Satisfactory for both boys and girls.

Reliability: An r of .88 was found when the best score of three trials was recorded from separate testings and correlated.

Objectivity: An r of .99 was found when the scores from an experienced tester were correlated with scores from an inexperienced tester.

Validity: Face validity is accepted for this test.

Equipment: A yardstick or measuring tape.

Directions: The student stands as far back from a wall as possible, keeping the heels flat on the floor, and leans into the wall touching the wall with the hands, chin, and chest. The hands may be extended against the wall as the chin and chest touch the wall but the body and knees must be kept straight. An assistant measures the distance between the toe line and the wall (after the best lean forward is made with heels flat on floor) (Figure 6.12). The assistant measures standing body height from floor to chin.

Scoring: The distance of the best lean out of three to the nearest quarter of an inch is subtracted from standing body height (floor to chin) and performance is compared with the scale in Table 6.10. The closer the lean distance gets to standing height, the better the score. Thus, a score of zero would be perfect. Example

Standing height: 53 in. (floor to chin)
Best lean: 33 in.
Score: 20 in.

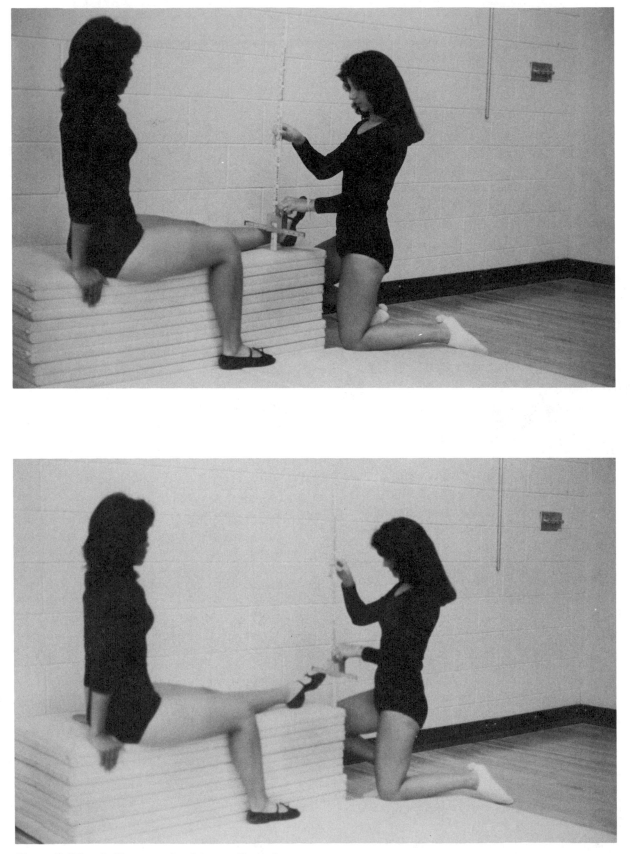

Figure 6.11.   Ankle extension (plantar flexion) test

Table 6.9. Norms in Inches for Ankle Extension (Plantar Flexion) Test, College Students[a]

PERFORMANCE LEVEL	MEN	WOMEN
Advanced	¾ and below	½ and below
Advanced intermediate	1½—1	1¼—¾
Intermediate	2 —1¾	1¾—1½
Advanced beginner	3 —2¼	2¼—2
Beginner	3¼ and above	2½ and above

[a]Based on the scores of 100 men and 100 women at Corpus Christi State University, Corpus Christi, Tex., 1977.

Figure 6.12. Ankle flexion (dorsiflexion) test

Table 6.10. Norms in Inches, for Ankle Flexion (Dorsiflexion) Test, College Students[a]

PERFORMANCE LEVEL	MEN	WOMEN
Advanced	26½ and below	24¼ and below
Advanced intermediate	29½—26¾	26½—24½
Intermediate	32½—29¾	30¼—26¾
Advanced beginner	35¼—32¾	31¾—30½
Beginner	35½ and above	32 and above

[a]Based on scores obtained from Mike Morgan, Corpus Christi State University, Corpus Christi, Tex., 1976.

FINDINGS AND CONCLUSIONS FROM FLEXIBILITY MEASUREMENT AND RESEARCH

Flexibility does not exist as a general characteristic but rather as a highly specific ability of individual joints of the body (Dickinson 1968; Harris 1969; Hupprich and Sigerseth 1950). Thus, a person who is very flexible in one joint may be average in another and quite inflexible in still a third.

There is opposing evidence regarding age and flexibility. Most research has shown that flexibility increases until early adolescence, when a leveling off or decrease begins (Hupprich and Sigerseth 1950; Phillips et al. 1955). Clarke reported that the decline begins around 10 years of age for males and 12 years of age for females. Milne, Seefeldt, and Reuschlein found a significant decrease in flexibility in children from kindergarten age to grade two. Evidence also shows that older adults have less flexibility than younger adults. The decrease in activity that characterizes aging is probably responsible for much of this loss. Loss of flexibility can contribute to postural problems such as lordosis, swayback, scoliosis, round shoulders, and forward head position (Falls 1980; Londeree 1981).

In general, girls are more flexible than boys (Hall 1956; Milne, Seefeldt, and Reuschlein 1976; Phillips et al. 1955). Anatomical and regular activity and movement pattern differences between the sexes may account for the flexibility differences (Corbin and Noble 1980).

Generally, body size is not related to flexibility. However, Krahenbuhl and Martin reported a negative relationship between flexibility and body surface area. Muscle size apparently has very little influence on flexibility (Jones 1977).

Like other components of physical fitness, flexibility can be improved through training. Numerous independent studies reveal significant improvement as a result of regular training (Bennett 1956; deVries 1962; Fieldman 1966; McCue 1953; Nelson, Johnson, and Smith 1982).

Flexibility training is frequently recommended as an aid in preventing muscle and connective tissue injuries. Coaches, trainers, and others concerned with athletics maintain that stretching plays an important role in reducing and sometimes eliminating soreness (Schultz 1979; deVries 1961). Wilkerson concluded that muscle soreness of football players during early season workouts seemed to be minimized by a stretching program.

Specific flexibility training procedures involving static stretch and ballistic stretch methods have been studied, with significant gains reported for each (deVries 1962; Kusinitz and Keeney 1958; Marchbank 1970). Proprioceptive neuromuscular function (PNF) has been shown to be effective in increasing flexibility (Corbin and Noble 1980; Rogers 1978). It involves contraction of the muscle to be stretched and then contraction of the antagonist during the stretching. All stretching techniques increase flexibility; no technique has been shown to be most effective. Most authorities recommend static stretching as being the safest yet effective method (Beaulieu 1981; Cooper and Fair 1978; Schultz 1979; de Vries 1962).

In a study by Frey, the sauna was investigated for effects, if any, on hip flexion. Only one of three hip flexion tests showed any significant improvement in results from this type of heat application. However, the application of heat and allowance of some cooling before use of static stretch techniques is a normal procedure in physical therapy. This cooling procedure apparently was not done in Frey's study and this could possibly explain the lack of significant improvement found on the two straight-leg flexion tests. Fieldman (1968) reported that hip flexion performance improved when the test was preceded by a pretrial of the same test and the improvement was even greater when related warm-up exercises were administered prior to the test.

Nelson and Dorociak found a test–retest reliability coefficient of .96 for the sit-and-reach test when students practiced the item prior to testing. A coefficient of .41 was obtained with subjects who did not practice.

Concerning the effects of physical education activities and sports on flexibility, the following findings have been reported: gymnastics and tumbling activities brought significant increases in flexibility for certain body parts (Derk 1971; Nelson, Johnson, and Smith 1983); exercycling (Angle 1963) and modern dance participation (Bennett 1956) also increased flexibility in certain areas. General physical education activities were superior to weight training and isometric training for increasing flexibility (Rallis 1965), but weight training did not decrease flexibility performance (Kusinitz and Keeney 1958; Massey and Chaudet 1956).

Professional concern has existed for many years regarding the relationship, if any, that exists between anthropometric measures and flexibility. While Mathews (1957, 1959), Fieldman (1966), and Harvey and Scott found no significant relationship, Broer and Galles found that students with a longer trunk-plus-arm measurement have a significant advantage on the hip flexion test. McCloy's quotient (McCloy and Young 1954) was devised to take into account the lengths of influencing body parts in certain flexibility tests. Controversy still exists on the question, and it is therefore important for the teacher or coach to determine whether the end results of flexibility measurement are best obtained through the use of relative or absolute flexibility tests.

BIBLIOGRAPHY

AAHPERD Health Related Physical Fitness Test Manual. Reston, Va.: AAHPERD, 1980.

AAHPERD Technical Manual Health Related Physical Fitness. Reston, Va.: AAHPERD, 1984.

Adrian, M., C. M. Tipton, and P. V. Karpovich, *Electrogoniometer Manual.* Springfield, Mass.: Physiological Research Laboratory, Springfield College, 1965.

Angle, N. K., "The Effect of a Progressive Program of Exercise Using the Exercycle on the Flexibility of College Women." Unpublished master's thesis, University of Washington at Seattle, 1963.

Beaulieu, J. E., "Developing a Stretching Program." *The Physician and Sportsmedicine* 9:59–69, November 1981.

Bennett, C. L., "Relative Contributions of Modern Dance, Folk Dance, Basketball, and Swimming to Motor Abilities of College Women." *Research Quarterly* 27:261, October 1956.

Broer, M., and N. Galles, "Importance of Relationship Between Various Body Measurements in Performance of the Toe-Touch Test." *Research Quarterly* 29:262, October 1958.

Clarke, H. H., Ed., "Joint and Body Range of Movement." *Physical Fitness Research Digest* 5:16–18, 1975.

Cooper, D. L., and J. Fair, "Developing and Testing Flexibility." *The Physician and Sportsmedicine* 6:137–138, October 1978.

Corbin, C. B., and L. Noble, "Flexibility: A Major Component of Physical Fitness." *JOPERD* 51:23–24, June 1980.

Derk, G. M., "The Changes Occurring in Strength and Flexibility During Competitive Gymnastics Season Involving High School Boys." Unpublished master's thesis, University of Kansas, Lawrence, 1971.

deVries, H. A., "Prevention of Muscular Distress After Exercise." *Research Quarterly* 32:177–185, March 1961.

———, "Evaluation of Static Stretching Procedures for Improvement of Flexibility." *Research Quarterly* 33:222–229, May 1962.

Dickinson, R. V., "The Specificity of Flexibility." *Research Quarterly* 39:792–794, October 1968.

Falls, H. B., "Modern Concepts of Physical Fitness." *JOPERD* 51(4):25–27, 1980.

Fieldman, H., "Effects of Selected Extensibility Exercises on the Flexibility of the Hip Joint." *Research Quarterly* 37:326–331, October 1966.

———, "Relative Contribution of the Back and Hamstring Muscles in the Performance of the Toe-Touch Test After Selected Extensibility Exercises." *Research Quarterly* 39:518–523, October 1968.

Frey, H. J., "A Comparative Study of the Effects of Static Stretching Sauna, Warm-up, Cold Applications, Exercise Warm-ups on Flexibility of the Hip Joint." Microcarded doctoral dissertation, University of Utah, Salt Lake City, 1970.

Hall, D. M., "Standardization of Flexibility Tests for 4-H Club Members." *Research Quarterly* 27:296–300, October 1956.

Harris, M. L., "A Factor Analytic Study of Flexibility." *Research Quarterly* 40:62–67, May 1969.

Harvey, V. P., and G. D. Scott, "Reliability of a Measure of Forward Flexibility and its Relation to Physical Dimensions of College Women." *Research Quarterly* 38:28–33, March 1967.

Hupprich, F. L., and P. Sigerseth, "The Specificity of Flexibility in Girls." *Research Quarterly* 21:32, March 1950.

Johnson, B. L., *Gymnastics for the Beginner: A Coeducational Approach.* Manchaca, Tex.: Sterling Swift, 1976, pp. 6–8.

———, *Flexibility Tests and Scoring Scales for Elementary Schools.* Portland, Tex.: Brown and Littleman, 1977a.

———, *Practical Flexibility Measurement With the Flexomeasure.* Portland, Tex.: Brown and Littleman, 1977b.

———, "Flexibility Assessment." In S. N. Blair, Ed., *SDAAHPERD Proceedings*, 1978, pp. 63–79.

———, and M. J. Garcia, *Fitness and Performance for Everyone.* Portland, Tex.: Brown and Littleman, 1977, pp. 56–67.

Jones, A., "Flexibility as a Result of Exercise." *Athletic Journal* 57(3):32–40, 1977.

Krahenbuhl, G. S., and S. L. Martin, "Adolescent Body Size and Flexibility." *Research Quarterly* 48:797–799, December 1977.

Kusinitz, I., and C. E. Keeney, "Effects of Progressive Weight Training on Health and Physical

Fitness of Adolescent Boys." *Research Quarterly* 29:294, October 1958.

Leighton, J., "A Simple Objective and Reliable Measure of Flexibility." *Research Quarterly* 13:205–216, May 1942.

Londeree, B. R., "Strength Testing." *JOPERD* 52:44–46, September 1981.

Marchbank, W. J., "A Study of the Johnson Shoulder Rotation Test." Unpublished study, Northeast Louisiana University, Monroe, 1970.

Massey, B. H., and N. L. Chaudet, "Effects of Systematic, Heavy Resistive Exercise on Range of Joint Movement in Young Male Adults." *Research Quarterly* 27:50, March 1956.

Mathews, D., "Hip Flexibility of Elementary School Boys as Related to Body Segments." *Research Quarterly* 30:302, October 1959.

————, et al., "Hip Flexibility of College Women as Related to Length of Body Segments." *Research Quarterly* 28:355, December 1957.

McCloy, C. H., and N. D. Young, *Test and Measurements in Health and Physical Education.* New York: Appleton-Century-Crofts, 1954, p. 227.

McCue, B. F., "Flexibility Measurements of College Women." *Research Quarterly* 24:323–324, October 1953.

Milne, C., V. Seefeldt, and P. Reuschlein, "Relationship Between Grade, Sex, Race, and Motor Performance in Young Children." *Research Quarterly* 47:726–730, December 1976.

Nelson, J. K., and J. J. Dorociak, "Reducing Administration Time While Improving Reliability and Validity of Fitness Tests." *JOPERD* 53:63–65, January 1982.

————, B. L. Johnson, and G. C. Smith, "Physical Characteristics, Hip Flexibility and Arm Strength of Female Gymnasts Classified by Intensity of Training Across Three Age Levels." *Journal of Sports Medicine and Physical Fitness* 23:95–101, March 1983.

Phillips, M., et al., "Analysis of Results from the Kraus-Weber Test of Minimum Muscular Fitness in Children." *Research Quarterly* 26:322, October 1955.

Rallis, S., "A Comparison of Three Training Programs and Their Effects on Five Physical Fitness Components." Unpublished master's thesis, Wayne State University, Detroit, 1965.

Rogers, J. L., "PNF: A New Way to Improve Flexibility." *Track Technique* 74:2345–2347, 1978.

Schultz, P., "Flexibility: Day of the Static Stretch." *The Physician and Sportsmedicine* 7:109–114, 117, November 1979.

Wells, K. F., and E. K. Dillon, "The Sit and Reach—A Test of Back and Leg Flexibility." *Research Quarterly* 23:118, March 1952.

Wilkerson, G. B., "Developing Flexibility by Overcoming the Stretch Reflex." *The Physician and Sportsmedicine* 9:189–191, September 1981.

CHAPTER 7

THE MEASUREMENT OF STRENGTH

OBJECTIVES

After reading this chapter, the student should be able to:

1. Define stength and differentiate between isometric, isotonic, and isokinetic strength
2. Distinguish between absolute and relative strength measurement
3. Understand and anticipate some of the administrative problems involved in measuring strength
4. Follow the directions for administering tests of strength

Strength is frequently recognized by physical educators as the most important factor in the performance of physical skills. While strength may be defined generally as the muscular force exerted against movable and immovable objects, it is best measured by tests that require one maximum effort for a given movement or position. The two types of muscular contraction most frequently measured in physical education classes are dynamic (isotonic) and static (isometric). In isotonic contraction, muscular force moves an object of resistance; the contraction takes place over a range of movement. In isometric contraction, muscular force is exerted over a brief period (usually 6 to 10 sec) without movement of the object of resistance or the body joints involved. Both types of contraction may be easily and inexpensively measured in the average school situation. While a certain degree of strength is necessary in performing daily activities and sports skills, we regard a high degree of strength as a luxury that makes for greater ease of performance and for a feeling of vitality well worth the effort necessary to acquire and maintain it.

Since strength is a physical fitness component, it should be related to each individual and thus be measured in relation to the person's body weight. A person who weighs 150 lb and can lift 175 lb should be considered stronger per body weight than an individual who weighs 225 lb and can lift 230 lb. The 150-lb person would score $175 \div 150 = 1.17$, while the 225-lb person would score $230 \div 225 = 1.02$. These scores mean that the lighter person is stronger per body pound than the heavier person, and that the heavier person, to attain a higher state of fitness strength, must either lose some body weight or develop additional strength or both.

Because strength and power are terms often used interchangeably (particularly with regard to isotonic strength), we want to present some observations that should help distinguish between them.

1. Strength is a component of power. Power also includes the components of time and distance.
2. While in both power and isotonic strength tests an object of resistance is moved through a range of motion, the isotonic strength test differs in the following respects:
   a. The object of resistance is always near if not at maximum load.

b. The object of resistance is never released with the expectation of gaining height or distance.

c. The range of movement is not as exaggerated or as complete.

d. Measurement is based on the amount of weight moved through a specified range and not on distance or time elements.

USES OF STRENGTH TESTS

Several ways in which strength tests could be used in physical education classes are as follows:

1. As a factor in physical fitness tests

2. As a means for determining potential in specific sports activities

3. As a means for determining achievement and grades in conditioning and weight-training classes

4. As a means for evaluating the possible solutions to overcoming poor postural positions or for pinpointing areas of weakness that need strengthening for better performance

5. As a means for motivating students through the feeling of accomplishment and satisfaction with strength increases

PROBLEMS ASSOCIATED WITH STRENGTH TESTING

Several of the problems and limitations associated with the measurement of strength are listed and discussed here.

1. The muscular strength tests most frequently used during the past few decades have included test items of dubious validity. For example, the inclusion of the lung capacity measure in the Rogers strength test has been debated many times over the years. Also, inclusion of muscular endurance items, such as pull-ups and dips for maximum repetition, has added to the confusion concerning strength test results and their interpretation.

2. A number of tests provide accurate strength measurement but require expensive equipment; consequently, many schools are unable to include such tests in their physical education program.

3. At the present time, measurement of abdominal strength has been quite limited. Many of the better-known strength tests have avoided this area entirely, although abdominal strength is important in various activities. The sit-up test with maximum (or near maximum) resistance behind the neck, presented in this chapter, represents only one attempt at assessing abdominal strength.

4. Different grip widths produce different strength performance results (Stumiller 1976). Thus, it is important to specify that grip be at shoulder width in testing.

5. In measuring static strength, establishment of precisely the same position or angle is difficult for certain exercises and for all subjects. Differences in the amount of musculature and fatty tissue and different lengths of body segments pose special problems for accurate testing. It is imperative that such tests start at the same angle and from the same reference point for each student. For example, specific phrases such as "starting with the elbows at a 90-degree angle" or "starting with the bar between the eyebrows and the hairline" are necessary if comparisons are to be made within a group or with established norms. Furthermore, in using any type of gauge such as the scale device that does not have a memory pointer (a pointer that remains in place after pressure is released), the tester must keep his or her eyes at the same level as the scale to secure an accurate reading.

PRACTICAL TESTS OF RELATIVE STRENGTH

Only a few tests of strength that are practical in terms of time, equipment, and cost are presented here. When special testing instruments are necessary for these tests, the cost is not unreasonable for most schools. Unfortunately, it is not feasible for us to present all the strength exercises that are practical for measurement. Tests are grouped under the headings "Isotonic Strength Tests," "Spring Scale Strength Tests," and "Isometric Strength Tests." All are scored with relation to body weight.

Isotonic Strength Tests (Johnson 1966a)

The objective of isotonic strength tests is to measure strength through a complete range of movement. Specific tests discussed here are the pull-up test, the dip test, the bench squat test, the sit-up test, the bench press, and the standing vertical arm press test.

In general, students should be allowed to become familiar with these tests through the use of similar weight-training exercises at least several days prior to testing. Then two trials are allowed for each test. When students are not familiar with the tests to be given, usually more than two trials are needed to determine maximum effort for each test. Thus, a greater amount of time is needed for testing.

The student (or testing team) should load the bar or strap to be used with weight plates. If the student successfully completes the movement on the first trial, he or she can add more weight and try to attain a higher score on the second trial. If the student is unsuccessful in completing the first trial, some of the weight is removed for the second trial. Should the second trial be unsuccessful also, the student should take a short rest and then try again with a further reduced load. Several weight bars and straps should be available so that as one student finishes, the next one will have the weights adjusted and be ready for testing.

Students should warm up before reporting to the testing station, but they should be cautioned not to overwork. All students should use a shoulder-width grip in such tests as pull-ups, dips, bench press, and vertical press.

For scoring, the better score of two trials is divided by body weight and the result is recorded. If the student does not desire to take a second trial, the first score is used.

Pull-up Test

Objective: To measure the strength of the arms and shoulders in the pull-up movement.

Age Level: Age 12 through college age.

Sex: Recommended for boys only.

Reliability: An r of .99 was found when scores were recorded on separate days from students familiar with the exercise.

Objectivity: An r of .99 was reported by Ronald Taylor, Northeast Louisiana University, Monroe, 1972.

Validity: Face validity is accepted for this test.

Equipment and Materials: A horizontal bar raised to a height so that all subjects hang with their feet off the floor; several 2½-, 5-, 10-, and 25-lb weight plates; a rope or strap to secure the weights to the waist of the performer; a chair for the performer to stand on in taking the preliminary position on the bar.

Directions: After securing the desired amount of weight to the waist, the student steps on the chair and takes a firm grasp (palms facing away from face) on the bar. As the student assumes a straight-arm hang, the chair is removed while he pulls himself upward until the chin is above the bar (Figure 7.1). As he moves down, the chair is replaced under his feet. The student may step down and readjust the weights before repeating the exercise for the second trial.

Scoring: The better score of two trials is recorded in terms of the amount of extra weight satisfactorily lifted. A student who cannot execute the exercise with more than his own body weight receives zero. The norms in Table 7.1 represent the best score divided by body weight before and after training.

Safety: The performer should be assisted to and from the chair as he mounts and dismounts with the extra weight.

Additional Pointers:

1. The performer should refrain from lifting the legs or using a swinging action to get upward.

2. The tester may extend his or her arm horizontally across the performer's thighs to prevent lifting of the legs during the pull-up.

3. For individuals who cannot chin their own body weight, the following procedure may be used in terms of measurement and motivation: Hang a tape (cloth) measure from the bar so that it bisects the point of the performer's chin as he pulls and slides the chin upward along the tape. Score the performer in terms of the number of inches between the chin and the top of the bar. For example, the best non-chinner might get his chin 1 in. from the top of the bar and consequently score a −1, whereas a weaker performer might lack 6 in. and receive a −6 as his score.

Dip Test

Objective: To measure the strength of the arms and shoulders in the dip movement (a vertical lowering and push-up movement).

Age Level: Age 12 through college age.

Sex: Recommended for boys only.

Reliability: An r of .98 was found when scores were recorded on separate days from students familiar with the exercise.

Objectivity: An r of .99 was reported by Charles Prestidge, Northeast Louisiana University, Monroe, 1972.

Figure 7.1.   Pull-up test

Table 7.1.   Norms for Pull-up Test for College Men Before and After 9 Weeks of Training[a]

PERFORMANCE LEVEL	SCORE	
	Before Training	After Training
Advanced	.42 and above	.56 and above
Advanced intermediate	.31—.41	.41—.55
Intermediate	.16—.30	.20—.40
Advanced beginner	.06—.15	.09—.19
Beginner	.00—.05	.00—.08

[a]Based on the scores of 80 men, Corpus Christi State University, Corpus Christi, Tex., 1976. Raw scores are figured by dividing body weight into the additional weight successfully used in the test.

Equipment and Materials: Two parallel bars raised to a height that all subjects are supported freely above the ground (in the lowered bent-arm support position); weight plates, straps, and a chair as in the pull-up test.

Directions: After securing the desired amount of weight to his waist, the student steps on the chair and takes a secure grip on the bars. As he assumes a straight-arm support position, the chair is removed and the student lowers himself until his elbows form a right angle (Figure 7.2). As the student pushes up to a straight-arm support position, the chair is replaced under his feet. The student may step down and readjust the weights before he repeats the exercise.

Scoring: Same as for the pull-up test. Norms are shown in Table 7.2 for college men before and after training.

Safety: Same as for the pull-up test.

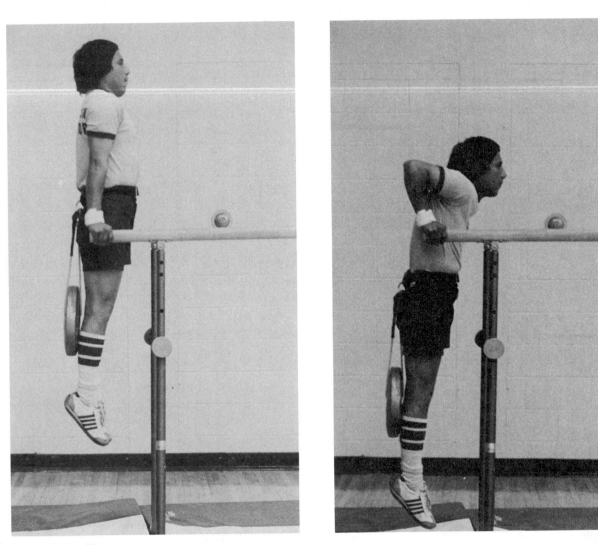

Figure 7.2.   Dip test

Table 7.2.   Norms for Dip Test for College Men Before and After 9 Weeks of Training[a]

PERFORMANCE LEVEL	SCORE	
	Before Training	After Training
Advanced	.60 and above	.74 and above
Advanced intermediate	.46–.59	.61–.73
Intermediate	.23–.45	.36–.60
Advanced beginner	.10–.22	.21–.35
Beginner	.00–.09	.00–.20

[a]Based on the scores of 80 men, Corpus Christi State University, Corpus Christi, Tex., 1976. Raw scores are figured by dividing body weight into the additional weight successfully used in the test.

Additional Pointers:

1. The performer should refrain from swinging or kicking in returning to the straight-arm support position.

2. The tester should extend his or her fist upward from the bar so that the performer's shoulder will touch it when the elbows form the right angle.

3. For students who cannot push to a straight-arm support position with their own body weight, the following procedure may be used in terms of measurement and motivation: Attach a scale alongside the parallel bars (marked off in 1-in. intervals). Mark on the scale the performer's shoulder location (point of the acromion process) while in the straight-arm support position. Score the performer in terms of the number of inches he raises his shoulders (point of the acromion process) from the straight-arm position on the push upward.

Bench Squat Test

Objective: To measure the strength of the legs and back in lowering to and rising from a sitting position.

Age Level: Age 12 through college age.

Sex: Recommended for both boys and girls.

Reliability: An r of .95 was found when scores were recorded on separate days from students familiar with the exercise.

Objectivity: An r of .99 was reported by Mike Recio, Northeast Louisiana University, Monroe, 1972.

Validity: Face validity is accepted for this test.

Equipment and Materials: An adjustable bench, fold-up mats, or box to get the seat level adjusted to lower patella (kneecap) level; a barbell; weight plates; and a thick towel to pad the bar.

Directions: After the student adjusts the desired amount of weight on the bar, two assistants place the bar on the shoulders (and behind the neck) of the student as he or she stands near the edge of the mats or bench. With the feet a comfortable distance apart and a firm grasp of the hands on the bar, the student lowers to an erect sitting position on the mats or bench (Figure 7.3). Then, without rocking back and forth, the student returns to the standing position. The performer may readjust the weights for the second trial.

Scoring: The total weight of the barbell (including the collars) satisfactorily lifted in the better lift of two trials is divided by body weight to get the score. The norms in Table 7.3 represent performance before and after training.

Safety: The two assistants should stand at each end of the barbell and be ready to catch the bar in the event the performer overleans or starts to fall.

Additional Pointers:

1. The performer should sit on the near edge of the bench or mats so that he will not have to rock back and forth to get up.

2. The seat level of bench, mats, or beverage cases should be adjusted to the lower patella level before the squat is executed.

Sit-up Test (Knees Bent)

Objective: To measure the strength of the abdominal muscles and trunk flexors.

Age Level: Age 12 through college age.

Sex: Satisfactory for both boys and girls.

Reliability: An r of .91 was found when scores were recorded on separate days from students familiar with the exercise.

Objectivity: An r of .98 was reported by Mary Jane Garcia, Northeast Louisiana University, Monroe, 1972.

Validity: Face validity is accepted for this test.

Equipment and Materials: A mat; a bar 5 or 6 ft in length; a dumbbell bar; an assortment of weight plates; a 12-in. ruler; and tape.

Directions: The student may execute the sit-up with either a weight plate, a dumbbell, or if necessary, a barbell behind the neck. Should a dumbbell or barbell be used, the attached weight plates must not have a greater circumference than standard 5-lb plates. After selecting the desired amount of weight, the performer places it on a mat so that when in the supine position, he or she can grasp the weight easily and hold it to the back of the neck. The performer then assumes a supine position and flexes the knees over the 12-in. ruler while sliding the heels as close to the seat as possible. He or she holds the ruler tightly under the knees until instructed to slowly slide the feet forward. At the point where the ruler drops to the mat, the tester marks the heel line and seat line to indicate how far the feet should remain from the seat during the exercise (Figure 7.4).

Scoring: Same as for pull-up test. Table 7.4 shows norms for this test for college students.

Safety: An assistant should be ready to remove the weight at the completion of the lift.

Figure 7.3. Bench squat test

Table 7.3. Norms for Bench Squat Test for College Students Before and After 9 Weeks of Training[a]

PERFORMANCE LEVEL	SCORE	
	Men	Women
BEFORE TRAINING[b]		
Advanced	1.61 and above	1.29 and above
Advanced intermediate	1.38–1.60	1.11–1.28
Intermediate	.94–1.37	.87–1.10
Advanced beginner	.81– .93	.68– .86
Beginner	.00– .80	.00– .67
AFTER TRAINING[c]		
Advanced	2.09 and above	1.56 and above
Advanced intermediate	1.76–2.08	1.32–1.55
Intermediate	1.19–1.75	.92–1.31
Advanced beginner	.91–1.18	.71– .91
Beginner	.00– .90	.00– .70

[a]Raw scores are figured by dividing body weight into the additional weight successfully used in the test.
[b]Based on the scores of 80 men and 80 women, Corpus Christi State University, Corpus Christi, Tex., 1976.
[c]Based on a limited number of scores from physical education weight-training classes at Corpus Christi State University, Corpus Christi, Tex., 1976.

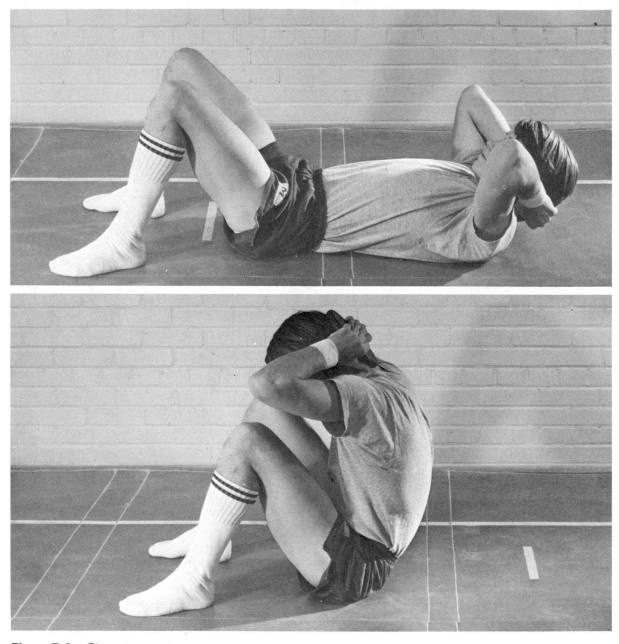

Figure 7.4. Sit-up test

Table 7.4. Norms for Sit-up Test (Knees Bent), College Students[a]

PERFORMANCE LEVEL	SCORE	
	Men	Women
Advanced	.34 and above	.20 and above
Advanced intermediate	.29–.33	.16–.19
Intermediate	.18–.28	.11–.15
Advanced beginner	.12–.17	.06–.10
Beginner	.00–.11	.00–.05

[a]Based on the scores of 111 men and 80 women, Corpus Christi State University, Corpus Christi, Tex., 1976. Raw scores are figured by dividing body weight into the additional weight successfully used in the test.

Additional Pointer: If the ruler is taped at the seat line, the performer can maintain distance between the seat and heel line better. The assistant must firmly secure the performer's feet to the floor.

Bench Press Test

Objective: To measure strength of arm and shoulder extension in a push-up movement.

Age Level: Age 12 through college age.

Sex: Satisfactory for both boys and girls.

Reliability: An r of .93 was found when scores were recorded on separate days from students familiar with the exercise.

Objectivity: An r of .97 was reported by Dixie Bennett and Steve Long, Northeast Louisiana University, Monroe, 1972.

Validity: Face validity is accepted for this test.

Equipment and Materials: A bench; a weight bar 5 or 6 ft in length; and enough weight plates to be more than sufficient for the strongest student.

Directions: After adjusting the desired amount of weight on the bar, the student assumes a supine position on the bench and two assistants place the bar in his or her hands and across the chest. With the hands approximately shoulder-width apart, the performer extends the arms, pressing the bar to a "locked out" (elbows straight) position (Figure 7.5). The two assistants remove the bar on completion of the trial. The performer may readjust the weight for the second trial.

Scoring: The total weight correctly lifted in the better of two trials is divided by body weight to get the score. Table 7.5 provides norms for college students before and after training.

Safety: The two assistants should remain ready to take the barbell at any time during the trial.

Standing Vertical Arm Press Test

Objective: To measure strength of arm and shoulder extension in a vertical overhead press movement.

Age Level: Age 12 through college age.

Sex: Recommended for boys only.

Reliability: An r of .98 was found for this test with a group of students who were familiar with the exercise. The best score of two trials, conducted on separate days, was recorded as the test score.

Objectivity: An r of .99 was reported by Charles Prestidge, Northeast Louisiana University, Monroe, 1972.

Validity: Face validity is accepted for this test.

Equipment and Materials: A weight bar 5 or 6 ft in length and enough weight plates to be more than sufficient for the strongest student.

Directions: After adjusting the desired amount of weight on the bar, the performer assumes a standing position (feet a comfortable distance apart for balance) and two assistants place the bar in the performer's hands at the front chest position. With a forward grasp (palms facing away), the performer extends the arms upward, pressing the bar to a "locked out" (elbows-straight) position (Figure 7.6). The weight is held steady for a count of 3 to show control, after which it is lowered to the floor. The performer may readjust the weights for the second trial.

Scoring: Same as for the bench squat test. Table 7.6 shows norms for college men before and after training.

Safety: The two assistants should remain ready to catch the barbell at any time during the trial.

Additional Pointer: The performer must avoid flexing at the knees and hips during the press. Arching of the lower back is dangerous and is not allowed.

Spring Scale Strength Tests (Johnson 1966b)

The objective of spring scale strength tests is to measure strength through a limited range of motion. Specific tests discussed here are the overhead pull test, the two-hand push test, and the press test. These tests are recommended for girls in place of the pull-up test, the dip test, and the standing vertical arm press test previously presented for boys only. However, boys may use the spring scale tests too.

All three tests require the same equipment, which consists of a Viking scale (measuring to 300 lb); a heavy-duty eye hook (for overhead attachment); an exercise bar with a screw hook; a small foot platform with a heavy-duty eye hook; and two 18-in. chain sections and one 5-ft chain section.[1]

In general, students should be allowed to become familiar with the spring scale tests at least several days prior to testing. On testing, each student should be allowed two trials (if she so desires), in which she can register the maximum amount of weight possible for each test. Students

---

1. All equipment is available at reasonable cost from B & L Products, P.O. Box 473, Portland, TX 78374.

Figure 7.5. Bench press test

Table 7.5. Norms for Bench Press Test for College Students Before and After 9 Weeks of Training[a]

PERFORMANCE LEVEL	SCORE	
	Men	Women
BEFORE TRAINING[b]		
Advanced	1.20 and above	.48 and above
Advanced intermediate	.99–1.19	.41–.47
Intermediate	.79– .98	.30–.40
Advanced beginner	.69– .78	.21–.29
Beginner	.00– .68	.00–.20
AFTER TRAINING[c]		
Advanced	1.33 and above	.57 and above
Advanced intermediate	1.18–1.32	.52–.56
Intermediate	.96–1.17	.41–.51
Advanced beginner	.85– .95	.37–.40
Beginner	.00– .84	.00–.36

[a]Raw scores are figured by dividing body weight into the additional weight successfully used in the test.

[b]Based on the scores of 80 men and 65 women, Corpus Christi State University, Corpus Christi, Tex., 1976.

[c]Based on a limited number of scores from physical education weight-training classes at Corpus Christi State University, Corpus Christi, Tex., 1976.

Figure 7.6. Standing vertical arm press test

Table 7.6. Norms for Standing Vertical Arm Press Test for College Men Before and After 9 Weeks of Training

PERFORMANCE LEVEL	SCORE	
	Before Training[a]	After Training[b]
Advanced	.92 and above	1.08 and above
Advanced intermediate	.80—.91	.97—1.07
Intermediate	.58—.79	.71— .96
Advanced beginner	.47—.57	.59— .70
Beginner	.00—.46	.00— .58

[a]Based on the scores of 80 men, Corpus Christi State University, Corpus Christi, Tex., 1976. Raw scores are figured by dividing body weight into the additional weight successfully used in the test.
[b]Based on a limited number of scores from a physical education weight-training class, Corpus Christi State University, Corpus Christi, Tex., 1976.

should warm up before reporting to the testing station, but they should be cautioned not to overwork.

All students should use a shoulder-width grip on each test. Foot stance marks should be placed on the floor so that they will assume the same position each time they execute the tests and so that they will be pulling or pushing in a vertical direction. The tester should keep his or her eyes at the same level as the scale to determine the maximum amount of weight registered. If a regular training program is to be conducted, paint marks of different colors along the links of the chain will help each girl to quickly identify her particular link for each exercise.

The better score of two trials is divided by body weight and the result is recorded as the test score.

Overhead Pull Test

Objective: To measure the strength of the arms and shoulders in the pull-up movement.

Age Level: Age 12 through college age.

Sex: Recommended for girls in place of the pull-up test, but boys may use the test too.

Reliability: An *r* of .98 was found for this test when students were tested, allowed a short rest, and then retested.

Objectivity: An objectivity coefficient of .99 was obtained by John Huntsman, Northeast Louisiana University, Monroe, 1969.

Validity: Face validity is accepted for this test.

Equipment and Materials: The spring scale rig as previously described. Figure 7.7 illustrates the arrangement for the overhead pull test.

Directions: The tester should hook the bar to that part of the chain that will allow the student to start the pull from a straight-arm position but with all the body weight resting on the feet. The student's feet should be flat on the floor and about 12 in. apart. With a forward grasp on the bar (hands about shoulder-width apart) (Figure 7.8), the student pulls the bar downward without bending the knees or hips or turning the body. The student must bend only at the elbows and keep both feet on the floor while maintaining an erect posture. An assistant should hold the performer's hips so that the feet do not leave the floor. The performer may rest a few seconds and then repeat the exercise.

Scoring: Keeping the eyes on the level of the scale, the tester records the greatest number of pounds pulled by means of a steady pressure. The better score of two trials is divided by body weight and recorded as the test score. Table 7.7 shows norms for college women.

Additional Pointer: The tester should make sure that the student understands that the pull is to be a steady one rather than a hard or fast jerk.

Two-Hand Push Test

Objective: To measure the strength of the arms and shoulders in a downward push movement.

Age Level: Age 12 through college age.

Sex: Recommended for girls in place of the dip test. Satisfactory for men when a 300-lb scale is used.

Reliability: An *r* of .97 was found for this test when students were tested, allowed a short rest, and then retested.

Objectivity: An *r* of .99 was obtained by John Huntsman, Northeast Louisiana University, Monroe, 1969.

Validity: Face validity is accepted for this test.

Equipment and Materials: Same as for the overhead pull test.

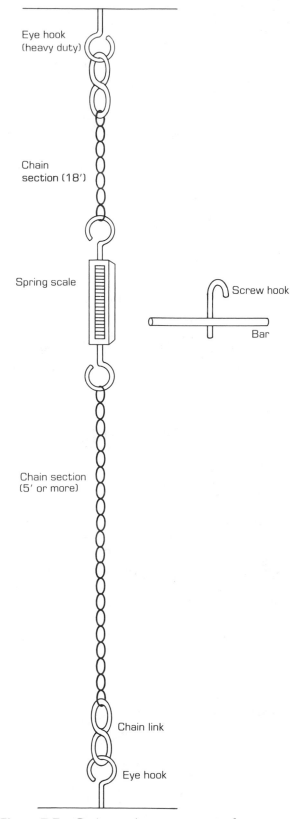

Eye hook
(heavy duty)

Chain
section (18')

Spring scale

Screw hook

Bar

Chain section
(5' or more)

Chain link

Eye hook

Figure 7.7. Spring scale arrangements for overhead pull test

Figure 7.8. Overhead pull test

Table 7.7. Norms for Overhead Pull Test, College Women[a]

PERFORMANCE LEVEL	SCORE
Advanced	1.15 and above
Advanced intermediate	1.04–1.14
Intermediate	.85–1.03
Advanced beginner	.76– .84
Beginner	.00– .75

[a]Based on the scores of 80 women, Corpus Christi State University, Corpus Christi, Tex., 1976. Raw scores are figured by dividing body weight into the amount of weight registered on the spring scale.

Directions: The tester hooks the bar attachment to that part of the chain that will allow the bar to run horizontally across the navel of the performer. With the body weight distributed equally over the feet, the performer pushes the bar vertically downward by attempting to straighten out the arms. The feet must remain flat on the floor during the test; an assistant should hold the student's hips to keep the feet down (Figure 7.9).

Scoring: Keeping the eyes on the level of the scale, the tester records the greatest number of pounds pushed by means of a steady pressure. The better score of two trials is divided by body weight and recorded for the test score. Table 7.8 shows norms for college students.

Figure 7.9. Two-hand push test

Additional Pointer: The head of the performer must not lean over to the side of the chain but must remain directly in front and in line with it.

Press Test

Objective: To measure the strength of arm extension in a vertical overhead press movement.

Age Level: Age 12 through college age.

Sex: Recommended for girls in place of the standing vertical arm press test with a barbell. Boys may take this test too.

Reliability: An r of .96 was found for this test when students were tested, allowed a short rest, and then retested.

Objectivity: An r of .99 was obtained by John Huntsman, Northeast Louisiana University, Monroe, 1969.

Validity: Face validity is accepted for this test.

Equipment and Materials: Same as for the overhead pull test. The S hooks are no longer required, as shown in Figure 7.10.

Directions: The tester hooks the bar to that part of the chain that allows the student to start the push with the bar located in front of the forehead (between the eyebrows and the hairline) (Figure 7.10). Keeping the feet flat on the floor, the student presses the bar vertically upward by attempting to straighten out the arms. Palms should be forward on the grasp. The performer may rest a few seconds and then repeat the trial.

Scoring: Same as for the two-hand push test. Table 7.9 shows norms for college women.

Additional Pointer: The performer should stand facing the back side of the scale so that the tester can simultaneously observe the body position and the score.

ABSOLUTE STRENGTH TESTS

Olympic Lifts

The competitive sport of weight lifting was incorporated into the Olympic Games in 1896. It was designed for men, and until the present time there is no known record of women ever competing in this sport. Originally, there were three Olympic lifts, but in recent years the military press lift was dropped from competition owing to the difficulty of judging it. The two remaining lifts are presented here. For these two tests, world records are recognized in accordance with body weight categories.

Table 7.8. Norms for Two-Hand Push Test, College Students[a]

PERFORMANCE LEVEL	SCORE	
	Men	Women
Advanced	1.16 and above	.99 and above
Advanced intermediate	1.07–1.15	.92–.98
Intermediate	.90–1.06	.64–.91
Advanced beginner	.81–.89	.52–.63
Beginner	.00–.80	.00–.51

[a]Based on the scores of 200 men and 150 women, Corpus Christi State University, Corpus Christi, Tex., 1977. Raw scores are figured by dividing body weight into the amount of weight registered on the spring scale.

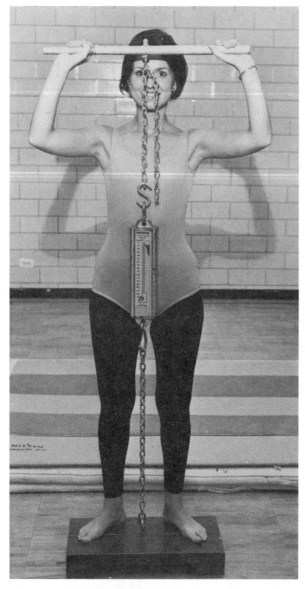

Figure 7.10.   Press test

Table 7.9. Norms for Press Test, College Women[a]

PERFORMANCE LEVEL	SCORE
Excellent	.56 and above
Good	.48—.54
Average	.34—.47
Poor	.27—.33
Very poor	.00—.26

[a]Based on the scores of 100 women as reported by Ronald Taylor, Northeast Louisiana University, Monroe, La., 1972. Raw scores are figured by dividing body weight into the amount of weight registered on the spring scale.

body other than the feet may touch the floor during the lift. The weight must be maintained overhead with arms and legs extended in a steady position for a 2-sec count. The feet must be aligned during the hold position (Figure 7.11).

Scoring: The best lift of three trials is recorded as the score. Table 7.10 shows samples of world-class scores.

Safety: Spotters or assistants should be available to help the performer in the event of difficulty.

Additional Pointers:

1.   The turning of the wrists must not take place until the bar has passed the top of the performer's head.

2.   The performer may recover from the split or squat phase of the performance in his own time.

3.   The lift must meet all international standards for correct performance to stand as a record.

Two-Hand Clean-and-Jerk Lift

General Description: The strength of the performer is measured by his ability to lift the bar from the floor to the chest and then in a second exertion extend the bar vertically overhead by the use of the arms and legs.

Equipment and Materials: Same as for the two-hands snatch lift.

Directions: The performer grasps the bar (palms downward) and pulls it in a single movement from the ground to the shoulders, while splitting or bending the legs. The performer recovers to an alignment of the feet in his own time. He then bends the legs and extends them as well as the arms so as to push the bar to a vertically extended position overhead (Figure 7.12). He returns the feet to the same line again. The performer must hold the weight overhead for a 2-sec. count.

Two-Hand Snatch Lift

General Description: The strength of the performer is measured by his ability to lift the bar in one movement from the floor to an arms-extended position overhead.

Equipment and Materials: An official weight-lifting barbell 7 ft in length and 1 in. in diameter and official weights graduated in pounds or kilograms.

Directions: The performer grasps the bar (palms downward) and pulls it in a single movement from the ground to full extension of the arms vertically above the head, while either splitting or bending the legs. The bar must pass with continuous movement along the body, and no part of the

Figure 7.11. Two-hand snatch lift

Table 7.10. Sample World Class Scores[a] for Two-Hand Snatch Lift and Clean-and-Jerk Lift

WEIGHT CLASS	TWO-HAND SNATCH LIFT		CLEAN-AND-JERK LIFT	
	Pounds	Kilograms	Pounds	Kilograms
Fly (to 114½ lb or 51.3 kg)	233	104.4	308	138.0
Bantam (to 123½ lb or 55.3 kg)	259	116.0	333	149.2
Feather (to 132¼ lb or 59.2 kg)	277	124.1	349	156.4
Light (to 148¾ lb or 66.6 kg)	303	135.7	391	175.2
Middle (to 165¼ lb or 74.0 kg)	336	150.5	418	187.3
Light-heavy (to 181¾ lb or 81.4 kg)	359	160.8	446	199.8
Middle-heavy (to 198¼ lb or 88.8 kg)	386	172.9	471	211.0
Heavy (to 242½ lb or 108.6 kg)	391	175.2	493	220.9
Super-heavy (over 242½ lb or 108.6 kg)	410	183.7	531	237.9

[a]Scores are merely sample scores, not necessarily world records.

Scoring: The best lift of three trials is recorded as the score. Table 7.10 shows samples of world-class scores.

Safety: Two assistants should be available to help the performer in the event of difficulty.

Additional Pointers:

1. The performer must hold the weight motionless for the 2-sec count.

2. The lift must meet all international standards for correct performance to stand as a record.

Power Lifts

Power lifting is a relatively new type of weight-lifting competition composed of the squat lift, the bench press lift, and the dead lift. It was organized in 1965 as a competitive sport for men. For women interested in strength testing, we recommend the tests presented under the heading "Practical Tests of Relative Strength," although power-lift competition is now held for women. The three power lifts are described here with sample world class scores. World records are recognized in body weight categories.

Squat Lift

General Description: The strength of the performer is measured by his ability to squat downward with a weight resting behind the shoulders and to then return to the standing position.

Equipment and Materials: An official weight-lifting barbell 7 ft in length and 1 in. in diameter and official weights graduated in pounds or kilograms.

Figure 7.12. Two-hand clean-and-jerk lift

Directions: The performer assumes a motionless upright position with the barbell across the shoulders in a horizontal position, not more than 1 in. below the top of the deltoids, with hands gripping the bar and feet flat on the floor. The performer then bends the knees, lowering the body until the tops of the thighs are parallel with the floor (Figure 7.13). He returns to the upright standing position at will, without double bouncing. After remaining motionless for a 2-sec count, the performer returns the barbell to the rack.

Scoring: The best lift of three trials is recorded as the score. Table 7.11 shows sample world-class scores.

Safety: Padding may be applied to the bar but must not exceed 30 cm in width and 5 cm in thickness. Spotters or assistants should be ready to help the performer in the event of difficulty.

Additional Pointers:

1. The use of a wedge at the heels or toes is forbidden.

2. The lifter must not rise on his toes or heels during the performance.

3. The lifter must not shift the bar or the feet during the performance.

4. Failure of the performer to assume an upright position at the start and completion of the lift is a cause for disqualification.

5. The performance must meet all international standards of power-lifting competition to stand as a record.

Bench Press Lift

General Description: The strength of the performer's arm and shoulder extension is measured

Figure 7.13. Squat lift (Photo courtesy of Public Information Offices, Corpus Christi State University, Corpus Christi, Texas)

Table 7.11. Sample World Class Scores[a] in Pounds for Squat Lift, Bench Press Lift, and Dead Lift

WEIGHT CLASS (lb)	SQUAT LIFT	BENCH PRESS LIFT	DEAD LIFT
Fly (to 114.5)	480	303	458
Bantam (to 123.5)	441	265	513
Feather (to 132.25)	502	310	551
Light (to 148.75)	573	369	615
Middle (to 165.25)	705	452	705
Light-heavy (to 181.75)	744	524	777
Middle-heavy (to 198.25)	772	485	744
100 kg (to 220.5)	783	525	777
Heavy (to 242.5)	870	550	821
Heavyweight (to 275)	865	600	882
Super heavyweight (276+)	974	625	890

[a]Scores are merely sample scores, not necessarily world records.

by his ability to press a weight upward while lying on a bench.

Equipment and Materials: An official barbell and weights as described in the squat lift plus a flat, level bench between 25 and 30 cm wide.

Directions: The performer assumes either a complete extended supine position on the bench or a position with only the head and trunk (including buttocks) extended on the bench and the feet flat on the floor. The bar is then placed across his chest (Figure 7.14). When the bar is resting motionless, the performer presses the bar vertically to straight-arm's length and holds it motionless for a 2-sec count. The performer's hands must not be wider apart than 81 cm measured between the forefingers.

Scoring: The best lift of three attempts is recorded as the score. Table 7.11 shows sample world-class scores.

Figure 7.14.   Bench press test (Photo courtesy of Public Information Offices, Corpus Christi State University, Corpus Christi, Texas)

Safety: Two or more assistants must be ready to help the performer in the event of difficulty.

Additional Pointers:

1. The lifter must not raise himself or shift position from the bench or move the feet during the lift.
2. There must be no excessive pressure of the bar against the performer's chest or heaving or bouncing of the bar from the chest.
3. The lift must meet all international standards of power-lifting competition to stand as a record.

Dead Lift

General Description: The strength of the performer is measured by his ability to lift a barbell from the floor to an erect standing position.

Equipment and Materials: Same as for the squat lift.

Directions: The bar is laid horizontally in front of the performer's feet. Gripping the bar in an optional grasp with both hands (Figure 7.15a), the performer lifts the bar with one continuous motion until he reaches an erect standing posi-

tion. At this point, the knees are locked and the shoulders thrust back (Figure 7.15b). The bar must be held for a 2-sec count.

Scoring: The best lift of three trials is recorded as the score. Table 7.11 shows sample world-class scores.

Safety: Two spotters should be available to assist the performer in the event of loss of balance or inability to control the weight.

Additional Pointers:

1. The lifter must not rise on the toes or heels or shift the feet during the lift.
2. The lifter must not support the bar on the thighs.
3. The lift must meet all international standards of power-lifting competition to stand as a record.

ISOMETRIC STRENGTH TESTS

The objective of isometric strength tests is the measurement of strength without movement of the resistance or the joints involved. Several instruments are used.

Figure 7.15.   Dead lift. **(a)** Starting position   **(b)** Standing position (Photo courtesy of Public Information Offices, Corpus Christi State University, Corpus Christi, Texas)

Tensiometer (Clarke 1948; Clarke and Munro 1970)

The tensiometer is an instrument that indicates the pounds of pressure exerted (Figure 7.16). The large tensiometer measures up to 300 lb; a smaller tensiometer is used when measurements are expected below 30 lb, owing to the inaccuracy of the lower end of the 300-lb instrument. The smaller tensiometer measures accurately from 0 to 100 lb. The reliability of the tensiometer is quite high; objectivity coefficients for practically all tests were in the .90s. The instrument can be purchased from the Pacific Scientific Company, Inc., of Los Angeles. The equipment required for various tests with the tensiometer includes a strap with D ring, a pair of cables with adjusters, a goniometer to establish correct joint angles, and a specially constructed table for various exercise positions.

Grip Dynamometer

The grip dynamometer is used to measure the grip strength of the hand. It has an adjustable handle to fit the size of the hand and a maximum needle indicator for ease of scoring (Figure 7.17). The scoring dial is marked off in kilograms, from 0 to 100. Reliability coefficients have been reported in the .90s. The instrument may be purchased from the C. H. Stoelting Company of Chicago. Norms for both boys and girls have been established with the Smedley grip dynamometer (Table 7.12).

Back and Leg Dynamometer

This instrument consists of a scale that measures from 0 to 2500 lb in 10-lb increments attached to a strong platform, with a chain and bar attachment for individual adjustments according to height (Figure 7.18). Satisfactory reliability has been reported for tests with this instrument, Rs ranging from .86 into the .90s. The main drawback of this instrument is the expense involved for a limited number of exercises. The instrument may be purchased from the Nissen Corporation of Cedar Rapids, Iowa.

Grip Strength Indicator Test

Objective: To measure the combined strength of the hands.

Directions: The student grasps the Hanson scale[1] with the thumbs along the top center edge of each

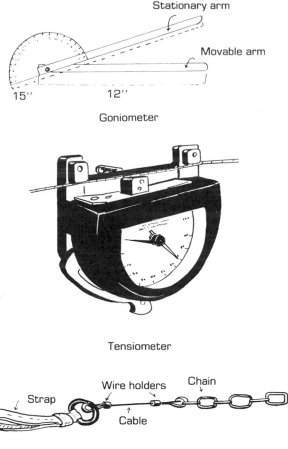

Figure 7.16. Tensiometer with attachments and goniometer

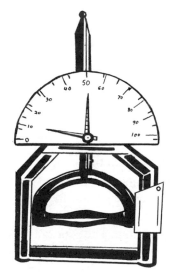

Figure 7.17. Grip dynamometer

side and the fingers clutching underneath. He or she squeezes steadily as hard as possible with both hands and notes the pounds exerted on the

---

1. The Hanson scale is available from B & L Products, P.O. Box 473, Portland, TX 78374.

Table 7.12. Norms for Strength of Grip in Kilograms (Smedley Instrument)[a]

AGE	BOYS		GIRLS	
	Right Hand	Left Hand	Right Hand	Left Hand
6	9.21	8.48	8.36	7.74
7	10.74	10.11	9.88	9.24
8	12.41	11.67	11.16	10.48
9	14.34	13.47	12.77	11.97
10	16.52	15.59	14.65	13.72
11	18.85	17.72	16.54	15.52
12	21.24	19.71	18.92	17.78
13	24.44	22.51	21.84	20.39
14	28.42	26.22	24.79	22.92
15	33.39	30.88	27.00	24.92
16	39.37	36.39	28.70	26.56
17	44.74	40.96	29.56	27.43
18	49.28	45.01	29.75	27.66

[a]Based on 2788 boys and 3471 girls in Chicago.

Figure 7.18. Back and leg dynamometer

scale (Figure 7.19). The performer then weighs himself or herself on the same scale.

Scoring: The amount squeezed on the scale is divided by body weight for the score. Norms are shown in Table 7.13.

Additional Pointer: The squeeze must not be fast or jerky or the reading will be distorted.

Heavy-Duty Spring Scale

The heavy-duty spring scale is seldom used but can be employed most effectively in a strength-testing program. With the scale placed under an isometric rack, accurate measurements can be

recorded for the military press, the bench press, the curl, and other exercises. In any exercise in which the student is required to push or lift upward, the maximum amount read on the scale is recorded and then body weight is subtracted from that figure. For the leg press, a bar may be inserted underneath the scale; a belt is then attached to both ends of the bar and is placed over the subject's hips for the lift. The large scale, which provides motivation, can easily be seen by both the tester and the subject. The reliability for this instrument has been reported in the .90s.

ISOKINETIC STRENGTH MEASUREMENT

Isokinetic strength measurement requires a special device with an automatic governor to control the resistance and speed at which the subject operates the machine (Figure 7.20).[2] Isokinetic strength training develops strength through the full range of motion. In other words, it combines the advantages of isometric and isotonic training. In the lifting of a barbell or dumbbell (as in isotonic training), resistance is not equal at each point in the movement owing to momentum and coordinating movements. In isometric training, the muscle receives only one point of maximum resistance at a time. However, the isokinetic

2. The instrument shown in Figure 7.20 is available from Mini-Gym Exercise Equipment, P.O. Box 266, 909 W. Lexington, Independence, MO 64051.

Figure 7.19. Grip strength indicator test with the Hanson scale

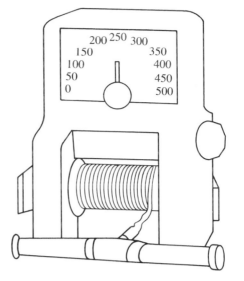

Figure 7.20. Isokinetic Mini Gym, Model 180

FINDINGS AND CONCLUSIONS FROM STRENGTH MEASUREMENT AND RESEARCH

machine adjusts automatically to each exertion throughout its full range.

When isokinetic machines are available, they may be preferred over standard barbells and weight-lifting equipment owing to the possibility of greater strength development for the time involved. However, standard weight-lifting equipment is effective and may remain more economical for many years to come.

Prior to 1950, both coaches and athletes believed that weight training did not produce the type of strength necessary for superior sports performance and, furthermore, that such training hindered speed of movement. However, since 1950 a number of studies have shown that strength can be greatly increased through weight training, and also that speed of movement may be enhanced (Endres 1953; Mosely et al. 1953; Wilkin 1952; Zorbas and Karpovich 1951). Consequently, weight training is now a vital part of most athletic conditioning programs.

Strength, like all abilities, is quite specific to the type of strength (Berger 1962a) and to the movements (Gardner 1963) and muscle groups (H. Clarke 1973) involved. Through factor analysis, Jackson and associates identified three factors associated with isotonic strength performances on the Universal Gym when height and weight were held constant: factor I, upper extremities

Table 7.13. Norms for Grip Strength (Two Hands) (Hanson Scale)[a]

PERFORMANCE LEVEL	MEN	WOMEN
Advanced	.99 and above	.82 and above
Advanced intermediate	.86–.98	.66–.81
Intermediate	.75–.85	.57–.65
Advanced beginner	.59–.74	.44–.56
Beginner	.00–.58	.00–.42

[a]Raw scores are figured by dividing body weight into the amount exerted.

and trunk; II, lower extremities; and III, trunk and lower extremities. The strength tests having the highest relationships with the three factors were: the military and bench presses for factor I, upper and lower leg presses for factor II, and lateral flexion for factor III.

Although Ebel in 1928 was probably the first to note that strength could be increased by short static contraction (isometric) exercises, it was not until the highly publicized experiments of Hettinger and Muller in 1953 that mass interest was aroused in this type of training. Since then, numerous studies have indicated that strength can be significantly increased by isometric exercise (Gardner 1963; Rarick and Larson 1958; Titlow 1977; Wolbers and Sills 1956).

Once it was clearly understood that both isometric and isotonic exercises could increase strength, investigators turned their attention to a comparison of the two systems. The results of such endeavors show, in general, no significant difference in the amount of strength developed by the two programs (Adamson 1961; Chui 1964; Rasch 1957; Titlow 1977). Usually differences in the two programs have been specific to the manner in which the strength was tested, either by isotonic means or by isometric measurement (Berger 1962a).

While comparisons of isometric and isotonic strength have abated, further studies have compared isokinetic with isotonic strength training (Titlow 1977) and strength training machines such as the Nautilus and Universal Gym with traditional barbell (free weights) programs (Coleman 1977; Sanders 1980). All programs have been shown to be effective, with no meaningful differences between methods. Stone and O'Bryant reported the results of a series of experiments that demonstrated the effectiveness of a model of training (periodization) based on Eastern European weight-lifting programs over the so-called traditional methods.

Numerous studies have investigated various combinations of sets and repetitions for increasing strength through weight training (Berger 1962b; Berger and Hardage 1967; D. H. Clarke 1973; Wilkin 1952). Although provision of days of rest from strength training, such as every other day, is common practice, recent studies have evidenced greater improvement (or at least no decrement) with greater frequency of training, up to 5 days a week (Gillam 1981; Gregory 1981; Westcott 1979a).

Strength differences between the sexes are commonly observed. The extent of biologic versus sociocultural effects, however, is not known. In prepubescent strength performance, sex-role expectations are believed to be very influencial (Corbin and Nix 1979). Rees and Andres found no differences in grip strength between boys and girls ages 4 to 6, yet nearly three fourths of the children felt that boys were stronger. Such stereotyping is considered detrimental for the potential of girls to perform in physical activities (Harris 1977). Weight training appears to produce similar responses in women and men; however, increases in muscle girth are far greater in males than in females (Brown and Wilmore 1974; Jackson, Watkins, and Patton 1980; Wilmore 1974).

A great deal of interest has been focused on the use of anabolic steroids. Most of the studies done on this topic have found no significant, consistent effect on lean body mass, muscle girth, or strength (Lamb 1980; Loughton and Ruhling 1977). Controversy exists over whether the studies have used sufficient dosage (Harvey et al. 1976) and have controlled for placebo effect (Ariel and Savilla 1972) and diet. Certainly there are potential serious health hazards associated with long-term administration of steroids, and their use is strongly condemned (American College of Sports Medicine 1979).

Weight training can produce a significant decrease in body fat and an increase in lean body weight (Gettman et al. 1978), even though total body weight may increase, decrease, or remain the same (Mayhew and Gross 1974; Wilmore 1974).

It is generally acknowledged that strength is best increased through high resistance and few repetitions, while endurance is improved most effectively with the reverse (low resistance and many repetitions). Research findings have not always supported this axiom. DeLateur and colleagues found that subjects training for strength gained as much endurance as endurance-trained subjects, and the latter gained as much strength as strength-trained subjects. Clarke and Stull and Stull and Clarke found that both endurance training (low resistance, many repetitions) and strength training (high resistance, few repetitions) produced increased strength. On the other hand, Anderson and Kearney reported highest strength gains from the traditional strength-training regimen, although improvements in strength were noted in endurance-trained subjects and in a combination program of medium resistance and a medium number of repetitions.

Several studies have dealt with the relationship between strength and endurance. Absolute strength obviously is related to absolute endurance (Ebel 1928; Tuttle et al. 1966), and relative strength is related to relative endurance (Johnson and Morgan 1976; Stumiller and Johnson 1976). Carlson and McCraw found significant negative correlations between isometric strength and relative isometric endurance, as did Tuttle. Others have found no relationship (Start and Graham 1964).

Various publications have contained evidence as to the effectiveness of strength training on improved performances such as in speed of movement (Chui 1964; Johnson 1964; Whitley and Smith 1966); power (Bangerter 1968; Blattner and Noble 1979; Chui 1950; Moulds et al. 1979); sprinting, jumping, and throwing (Gillespie 1978; Jarver 1980; Perrin 1972); football (Riley 1978); and soccer (Godik 1976).

Concerning strength and academic achievement, Clarke and Jarman (1961) found that high-strength groups had a consistent tendency to have higher means on standard achievement tests and grade point averages. Other studies (Tinkle and Montoye 1961; Wessel and Nelson 1961) revealed that persons who had greater strength as measured by grip strength had significantly better grades in physical education courses.

Studies have indicated the effects of motivation on strength performance (Marcel 1961; Nelson 1962). Johnson and Nelson reported that subjects receiving motivation during isometric training showed significant increases in strength in proportion to the amount of motivation. They further noted that a special motivational testing situation (which included marching music, spectators, photographers, and competition) significantly increased the strength performance scores of the training groups over the performance level achieved during training. There can be no doubt that strength testing and strength training are greatly influenced by motivation.

BIBLIOGRAPHY

Adamson, G. F., "Effects of Isometric and Isotonic Exercise on Elbow Flexor and Spine Extensor Muscle Groups." In *Health and Fitness in the Modern World,* Chicago: Athletic Institute, 1961, p. 172.

American College of Sports Medicine, "Position Statement on the Use and Abuse of Anabolic-Androgenic Steroids in Sports." *Medicine and Science in Sports*: XI-XII, 1977.

Anderson, T., and J. Kearney, "Effects of Three Resistance Training Programs on Muscular Strength and Absolute and Relative Endurance." *Research Quarterly for Exercise and Sport* 53:1–7, March 1982.

Ariel, G., and W. Savilla, "Anabolic Steroids: The Physiological Effects of Placebos." *Medicine and Science in Sports* 4:124–126, 1972.

Bangerter, B., "Contributive Components in the Vertical Jump." *Research Quarterly* 39:432–436, October 1968.

Berger, R. A., "Comparison of Static and Dynamic Strength." *Research Quarterly* 33:329, October 1962a.

———, "Optimum Repetitions for the Development of Strength." *Research Quarterly* 33:334–338, October 1962b.

———, and B. Hardage, "Effect of Maximum Loads for Each of Ten Repetitions on Strength Improvement." *Research Quarterly* 38:715–718, December 1967.

Blattner, S. E., and L. Noble, "Relative Effects of Isokinetic and Plyometric Training on Vertical Jumping Performance." *Research Quarterly* 50:583–588, December 1979.

Brown, C. H., and J. H. Wilmore, "The Effects of Maximal Resistance Training on Strength and Body Composition of Women Athletes." *Medicine and Science in Sports* 6:174–177, 1974.

Carlson, R. B, and L. W. McCraw, "Isometric Strength and Relative Isometric Endurance." *Research Quarterly* 42:244–250, October 1971.

Chui, E., "Effect of Weight Training on Athletic Power." *Research Quarterly* 21:188, October 1950.

———, "Effects of Isometric and Dynamic Weight-Training Exercises Upon Strength and Speed of Movement." *Research Quarterly* 35:246–257, October 1964.

Clarke, D. H., "Adaptations in Strength and Muscular Endurance Resulting From Exercise." *Exercise and Sport Science Reviews* 1:73–102, 1973.

———, and G. A. Stull, "Endurance Training as a Determinant of Strength and Fatigability." *Research Quarterly* 41:19–26, 1970.

Clarke, H., "Objective Strength Tests of Affected Muscle Groups Involved in Orthopedic Disabilities." *Research Quarterly* 19:118–147, May 1948.

———, Ed., "Toward a Better Understanding of Muscular Strength." *Physical Fitness Research Digest*, Series 3 (1), January 1973.

———, and B. O. Jarman, "Scholastic Achievement of Boys 9, 12 and 15 Years of Age as Related to Various Strength and Growth Measures." *Research Quarterly* 32:155, May 1961.

————, and R. A. Munroe, "Cable Tension Strength Test Batteries." Microcarded publication, University of Oregon, Eugene, 1970.

Coleman, A. E., "Nautilus Versus Universal Gym Strength Training in Adult Males." *American Corrective Therapy Journal* 31:103–107, 1977.

Corbin, C. A., and C. Nix, "Sex-Typing of Physical Activities and Success Predictions of Children Before and After Cross-Sex Competition." *Journal of Sport Psychology* 1:43–52, 1979.

DeLateur, B. J., J. F. Lehmann, and W. E. Fordyce, "A Test of the DeLorme Axiom." *Archives of Physical Medicine and Rehabilitation* 49:245–248, 1968.

Ebel, E. R., "A Study in Short Static Strength of Muscles." Unpublished master's thesis, International YMCA College, Springfield, Mass., July 1928, p. 64.

Eckert, H. M., and J. Day, "Relationship Between Strength and Workload in Pushups." *Research Quarterly* 38:380–383, October 1967.

Endres, J. P., "The Effect of Weight Training Exercise Upon the Speed of Muscular Movement." Microcarded master's thesis, University of Wisconsin, 1953, pp. 29–31.

Gardner, G. W., "Specificity of Strength Changes of the Exercised and Non-exercised Limb Following Isometric Training." *Research Quarterly* 34:99–100, March 1963.

Gettman, L. R., J. J. Ayres, M. L. Pollock, and A. Jackson, "The Effect of Circuit Weight Training on Strength, Cardiorespiratory Functions and Body Composition of Adult Men." *Medicine and Science in Sports* 10:171–176, 1978.

Gillam, G. M., "Effects of Frequency of Weight Training on Muscle Strength Enhancement." *Journal of Sports Medicine and Physical Fitness* 21:432–436, 1981.

Gillespie, J., "Triple Jump Peaking." *Track Technique* 73:2313–2314, 1978.

Godik, M., "The Preparatory Period." *Yessis Review* 11:85–88, 1976.

Gregory, L. W., "Some Observations on Strength Training and Assessment." *Journal of Sports Medicine and Physical Fitness* 21:130–137, 1981.

Harris, D., "Physical Sex Differences: A Matter of Degree." In M. Adrien and J. Brame, Eds., *NAGWS Research Reports III*. Reston, Va: AAHPERD, 1977.

Harvey, G. R., et al., "Anabolic Effects of Methandienone in Men Undergoing Athletic Training." *Lancet* 2(7988):699–702, 1976.

Hettinger, T., and E. A. Muller, "Muskelleistung und Muskeltraining." *Arbeitsphysiologie* 15:111–126, 1953.

Hosler, W. W., "Electromyographic and Girth Considerations Relative to Strength Training." *Perceptual and Motor Skills* 44:293–294, 1977.

Jackson, A., M. Watkins, and R. W. Patton, "A Factor Analysis of Twelve Selected Maximal Isotonic Strength Performances on the Universal Gym." *Medicine and Science in Sports and Exercise* 12:274–277, 1980.

Jarver, J., Ed., *The Throws*. Los Altos, Calif.: Tafnew Press, 1980.

Johnson, B. L., "A Comparison of Isometric and Isotonic Exercises Upon the Improvement of Velocity and Distance as Measured by a Vertical Rope Climb Test." Unpublished master's thesis, Louisiana State University, Baton Rouge, 1964.

————, "Isotonic Strength Tests." Unpublished study, Northeast Louisiana University, 1966a.

————, "Spring Scale Strength Tests: Measuring Strength Through a Limited Range of Motion." Unpublished study, Northeast Louisiana University, 1966b.

————, and M. D. Morgan, "Relationship of Relative Bench Press Strength to Relative Push-Up Endurance." Unpublished study, Corpus Christi State University, Corpus Christi, Tex., 1976.

————, and J. K. Nelson, "The Effects of Applying Different Motivational Techiques During Training and in Testing Upon Strength Performance." *Research Quarterly* 38:630–636, December 1967.

Lamb, D. R., "Anabolic Steroids and Strength and Power Related Athletic Events." *JOPERD*, 51:58–59, February 1980.

Loughton, S. J., and R. O. Ruhling, "Human Strength and Endurance Responses to Anabolic Steroid and Training." *Journal of Sports Medicine and Physical Fitness* 17:285–297, 1977.

Marcel, N. A., "The Effect of Knowledge of Results as a Motivation on Physical Performance." Unpublished study, Louisiana State University, Baton Rouge, 1961.

Mayhew, J. L., and P. M. Gross, "Body Composition Changes in Young Women With High Resistance Weight Training." *Research Quarterly* 45:433–440, December 1974.

Mosely, J. W., et al., "Weight Training in Relation to Strength, Speed, and Coordination." *Research Quarterly* 24:308–315, October 1953.

Moulds, B., D. R. Carter, J. Coleman, and M. Stone, "Physical Responses of a Woman's Basketball Team to a Preseason Conditioning Program." In J. Terauds, Ed., *Science in Sports*, Del Mar, Calif.: Academic Publishers, 1979, pp. 203–210.

Nelson, J. K., "An Analysis of the Effects of Applying Various Motivational Situations to College Men Subjected to a Stressful Physical Performance." Microcarded doctoral dissertation, University of Oregon, Eugene, 1962.

————, B. L. Johnson, and G. C. Smith, "Physical Characteristics, Hip Flexibility and Arm Strength of Female Gymnasts Classified by Intensity of Training Across Three Age Levels." *Journal of Sports Medicine and Physical Fitness* 23(1):95–101, 1983.

O'Bryant, H. S., "Periodization: A Hypothetical Training Model for Strength and Power." Unpublished doctoral dissertation, Louisiana State University, Baton Rouge, 1982.

Perrin, B., "A Power, Simulation, and Sensation Training Program." *Athletic Journal* 53:19–25, 34–36, 66, 1972.

Rarick, L., and G. L. Larson, "Observations on Frequency and Intensity of Isometric Muscular Effort in Developing Muscular Strength." *Research Quarterly* 29:333–341, October 1958.

Rasch, P. J., "Relationship Between Maximum Isometric Tension and Maximum Isotonic Elbow Flexion." *Research Quarterly* 28:85, March 1957.

————, and L. E. Morehouse, "Effects of Static and Dynamic Exercises on Muscular Strength and Hypertrophy." *Journal of Applied Physiology* 11:25, July 1957.

Rees, R. C., and F. F. Andres, "Strength Differences: Real and Imagined." *JOPERD* 51:61, February 1980.

Riley, D., "In Season Strength Training: Key to Peak Performance." *Scholastic Coach* 47:55–56, 164–165, 1978.

Sanders, M. T., "Comparison of Two Methods of Training on the Development of Muscular Strength and Endurance." *Journal of Orthopedic Sports Physical Therapist* 1:210–213, 1980.

Start, K. B., and J. S. Graham, "Relationship Between Relative and Absolute Isometric Endurance of an Isolated Muscle Group." *Research Quarterly* 35:193–204, May 1964.

Stone, M. H., "A Hypothetical Model for Strength Training." *Journal of Sports Medicine and Physical Fitness* 21:342–351, 1981.

Stull, A. G., and D. H. Clarke, "High-Resistance, Low-Repetition Training as a Determiner of Strength and Fatigability." *Research Quarterly* 41:189–193, May 1970.

Stumiller, B., "The Effect of Three Different Grip Widths on Strength Performance." Unpublished study, Corpus Christi State University, Corpus Christi, Tex., 1976.

————, and B. L. Johnson, "The Relationship of Relative Strength to Relative Endurance." Unpublished study, Corpus Christi State University, Corpus Christi, Tex., 1976.

Tinkle, W. F., and H. J. Montoye, "Relationship Between Grip Strength and Achievement in Physical Education Among College Men." *Research Quarterly* 32:242, May 1961.

Titlow, L. W., "Comparative Effects of Isometric, Isotonic, and Isokinetic Training on Strength Maintenance." Unpublished doctoral dissertation, Texas A & M University, College Station, 1977.

Tuttle, W. W., et al., "Relation of Maximum Back and Leg Strength to Back and Leg Strength Endurance." *Research Quarterly* 26:96–106, March 1955.

Werschoshanskij, J., and W. Semjonow, "Strength Training for Sprinters." *Athletic Coach* 7:5–9, 1973.

Wessel, J. A., and R. C. Nelson, "Relationship Between Grip Strength and Achievement in Physical Education Among College Women." *Research Quarterly* 32:244, May 1961.

Westcott, W. L., "Weight Training: A Daily Activity." JOPER 76(3):58, 1979a.

————, "Female Responses to Weight Training." JOPER 77(2):31–33, 1979b.

Whitley, J. D., and L. E. Smith, "Influence of Three Different Training Programs on Strength and Speed of a Limb Movement." *Research Quarterly* 37:142, March 1966.

Wilkin, B. M., "The Effect of Weight Training on Speed of Movement." *Research Quarterly* 23:361–369, October 1952.

Wilmore, J. H., "Alterations in Strength, Body Composition, and Anthropometric Measurements Consequent to a 10 Week Weight Training Program." *Medicine and Science in Sports* 6:133–138, 1974.

————, "Body Composition and Strength Development." *JOPER* 46:38–40, 1975.

Withers, R. T., "Effect of Varied Weight-Training Loads on the Strength of University Freshmen." *Research Quarterly* 41:110–114, March 1970.

Wolbers, C. P., and F. D. Sills, "Development of Strength in High School Boys by Static Muscle Contraction." *Research Quarterly* 27:446, December 1956.

Zorbas, W. S., and P. V. Karpovich, "The Effect of Weight Lifting Upon the Speed of Muscular Contraction." *Research Quarterly* 22:145–148, May 1951.

CHAPTER 8

THE MEASUREMENT OF MUSCULAR ENDURANCE

OBJECTIVES

After reading this chapter, the student should be able to:

1. Define muscular endurance and differentiate between isometric and isotonic endurance

2. Distinguish between absolute and relative endurance measurement

3. Understand and anticipate some of the administrative problems involved in measuring endurance

4. Follow the directions for administering practical tests of muscular endurance

Muscular endurance may be dynamic or static. It concerns the ability of a muscle to repeat movements against submaximal resistance or pressure or to maintain a certain degree of tension over time. Muscular endurance tests are of three basic types, and each type may be *relative* or *absolute*. In a *relative* endurance test, the muscles work with a load that is proportionate to the maximum strength of a particular muscle group (Rasch 1956) or to body weight.[1] In an *absolute* endurance test, all subjects use a set load. The load therefore has no definite relationship to maximum strength of the individual (Start and Graham 1964) or to body weight.

The three types of muscular endurance tests are:

1. *Dynamic Tests.* The performer executes identical repetitions of a movement through a designated distance and over either an unlimited amount of time or a specified time interval. The score is the number of correct executions completed. Examples of such tests include barbell exercises with submaximal loads, push-ups, pull-ups, and sit-ups.

2. *Repetitive Static Tests.* The performer executes repetitions of force against a static measuring device, and the score is the number of times the force equals a certain percentage of either the maximum strength of the muscles involved or body weight. An example is the number of times a performer can squeeze 80 lb or more on a grip strength dynamometer. The test is usually over when the performer fails to squeeze the prescribed load or falls behind the desired cadence. While some authors identify this type of test as a dynamic test, movement over a distance is not a factor.

3. *Timed Static Tests.* The performer maintains one continuous muscle contraction rather than executing a series of contractions, and the score is the amount of time the weight is held. An example is the flexed-arm hang test for girls (AAHPERD 1976).

---

1. We recommend relative endurance tests that are based on proportional amount of body weight rather than on percentage of maximum strength, since maximum strength is known to fluctuate and to depend on many variables. The tester can be certain of the maximum body weight measure, whereas he or she can never know for sure whether the effort on a strength measure is maximal. Moreover, most common muscular endurance tests (e.g., pull-ups, dips, push-ups) are relative endurance tests, since individuals work with their own body weight. Johnson and Garcia have further illustrated this in a relative strength–relative endurance continuum.

Tests of muscular endurance are quite practical for the majority of schools and have been widely used in physical fitness testing programs. Such tests differ from strength tests in that the score is the number of repetitions executed (or the length of time a set tension was maintained) and not the maximum amount of weight lifted or force exerted.

While muscular endurance is closely associated with strength, it is also associated with the number of active capillaries within the working muscles. Because of this association, muscular endurance tests are sometimes confused with circulorespiratory endurance tests. However, muscular endurance tests primarily tax the skeletal muscles involved, whereas the circulorespiratory endurance items primarily tax the efficiency of the heart and lungs.

USES OF MUSCULAR ENDURANCE TESTS

Muscular endurance tests can be employed in physical education classes in several ways:

1. As a factor in physical fitness tests
2. As a means to motivate students to improve their status within the class
3. As a measure for determining achievement and grades when muscular endurance is a specific objective in a physical activity class
4. As a means to indicate an individual's readiness for vigorous activity

PROBLEMS ASSOCIATED WITH MUSCULAR ENDURANCE TESTING

Several problems are associated with muscular endurance testing:

1. Definite guidelines must be followed in the scoring of muscular endurance tests, since slight deviations from the correct form and procedure may greatly affect final results.
2. Since motivational factors greatly influence results, it is most important that the tester standardize as much as possible motivational factors during testing, so that all students are scored on the same basis. Furthermore, if scores are to be used as norms, a notation should be made if a special type of motivation is utilized. Nelson (1978) has shown that supplementary instructions relating to norms and goals influence performance.
3. Certain muscular endurance tests take a considerable amount of time to administer and, as a result, a time limit is sometimes placed on them. However, this is not always justifiable, since low correlations are often found between the timed and untimed tests. Perhaps a better approach would be to use barbell plates equal to a certain percentage of the performer's body weight so that the repetitions will not be so numerous. Clarke and associates (1954) suggested, in their studies on ergography, that a load and cadence that accomplish the most work in a relatively short amount of time be considered as a criterion.
4. On some occasions, testers have used dynamic muscular endurance exercises in a training program but have measured the effectiveness of these exercises with a static endurance test, and vice versa. It should be recognized, however, that the most valid measure of dynamic endurance training is the dynamic endurance test; likewise, the most valid measure of static endurance training is the static endurance test.
5. Many of the norms presently used are out of date or were set up on a limited number of cases. Thus, new norms are needed for both old and new tests.
6. Because of the decided dependence of strength on some endurance items, such as push-ups and pull-ups, the use of the term *endurance* in these measures is sometimes difficult to defend. Obviously, if a person lacks sufficient strength to do one pull-up, we cannot validly conclude that the person has no endurance. In such instances, measures employing repetitive lifting of submaximal weights or static endurance tests are recommended.

PRACTICAL TESTS OF MUSCULAR ENDURANCE

Several practical tests of muscular endurance in terms of time, equipment, and cost are presented here.

Sit-ups (Bent Knees) (Johnson 1967)

Objective: To measure the endurance of the abdominal muscles.

Age Level: Age 10 through college age.

Sex: Satisfactory for both boys and girls.

Reliability: An *r* as high as .94 has been reported for this test.

Objectivity: An *r* of .98 was found for this test.

Validity: Face validity is accepted for this test.

Equipment and Materials: A mat and yardstick.

Directions: From a supine position, the performer flexes the knees over the yardstick while sliding the heels as close to the seat as possible. The performer holds the yardstick tightly under the knees until instructed to slowly slide the feet forward. At the point where the yardstick drops to the mat, the tester marks the heel line and seat line to indicate how far the feet should remain from the seat during the bent-knee sit-up exercise (Figure 8.1). The performer interlaces the fingers behind the neck and performs sit-ups, alternating a left-elbow touch to the inside right knee and a right-elbow touch to the inside left knee (Figure 8.2). The exercise is repeated as many times as possible.

Scoring: The total number of repetitions is recorded for the score. However, repetitions should not be counted when fingertips do not maintain contact behind the head, when the knee is not touched, or when the performer pushes off the floor with the elbow. Norms before and after training are shown for college students in Table 8.1 and after training only for high school students in Table 8.2.

Additional Pointers:

1. The feet should rest flat on the floor and may be separated a few inches.

2. The back of the hands should touch the mat before each sit-up.

3. Taping the yardstick to the floor at the seat line helps the performer maintain proper distance between seat and feet.

AAHPERD Modified Sit-ups (AAHPERD 1980)

In the AAHPERD Health Related Physical Fitness Test, sit-ups are executed with knees flexed, heels 12 to 18 in. from the buttocks, and arms crossed on the chest with the hands on opposite shoulders. The subject curls up to a sitting position touching the elbows to the thighs (Figure 8.3) and then returns to the down position until the midback makes contact with the testing surface. The arms must remain in contact with the chest throughout the exercise. The number of correct sit-ups done in 1 min is the score.

Norms for boys and girls ages 5 to 18 are provided in Table 8.3.

Flexed-Arm Hang (AAHPERD 1976)

Objective: To measure the endurance of the arms and shoulder girdle in the flexed-arm hang position.

Age Level: Age 10 through college age.

Sex: Presented for girls. The test can be used quite effectively for boys who cannot chin themselves, however, thereby enabling the tester to obtain some objective measure of arm and shoulder endurance and providing a record of progress.

Reliability: An *r* as high as .90 has been reported for this test.

Objectivity: An *r* of .99 was obtained for this test.

Validity: Face validity is accepted for this test.

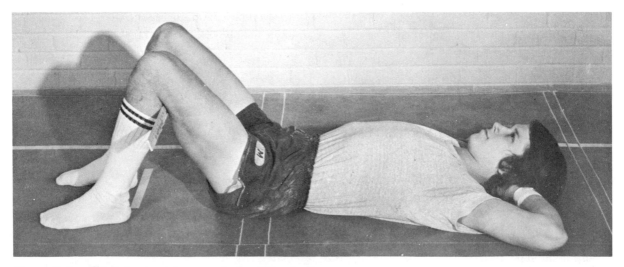

Figure 8.1.   Obtaining bent-knee angle for sit-up test

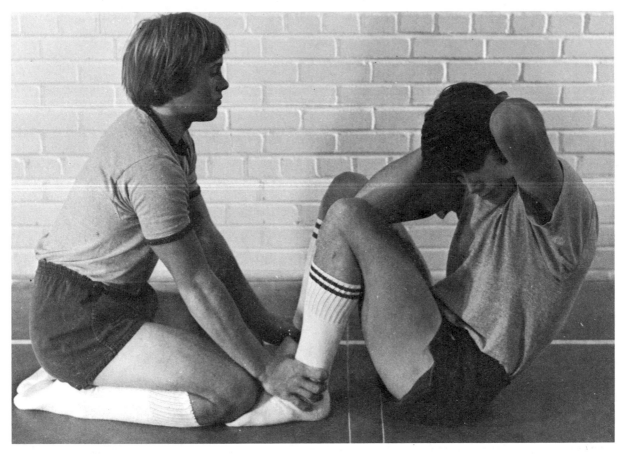

Figure 8.2.   Sit-up test (bent knee)

Table 8.1.   Raw Score Norms for Sit-ups (Bent Knees) for College Students Before and After 9 Weeks of Training[a]

PERFORMANCE LEVEL	SCORE BEFORE TRAINING		SCORE AFTER TRAINING	
	Men	Women	Men	Women
Advanced	66 and above	49 and above	96 and above	57 and above
Advanced intermediate	53–65	37–48	79–95	41–56
Intermediate	34–52	21–36	44–78	27–40
Advanced beginner	25–33	13–20	31–43	18–26
Beginner	0–24	0–12	0–30	0–17

[a]Based on 85 scores for men and 80 scores for women obtained at Corpus Christi State University, Corpus Christi, Tex., 1976.

Table 8.2.   Raw Score Norms for Sit-ups (Bent Knees) for High School Students Following 9 Weeks of Training[a]

PERFORMANCE LEVEL	NUMBER OF SIT-UPS	
	Boys	Girls
Advanced	78 and above	75 and above
Advanced intermediate	56–77	51–74
Intermediate	41–55	36–50
Advanced beginner	26–40	16–35
Beginner	0–25	0–15

[a]Based on 91 scores for boys and 116 scores for girls obtained by Terry Witt at Flour Bluff High School, Corpus Christi, Tex., 1977.

Figure 8.3.   Modified sit-up

Equipment and Materials: A horizontal bar 1½ in. in diameter raised to a height so that the tallest girl cannot touch the ground from the flexed-arm hang position (if standard equipment is not available, a piece of pipe or a doorway gym bar can be used) and a stopwatch.

Directions: With the assistance of two spotters, the performer raises the body off the floor so that the chin is above the bars and the elbows are flexed, using an overhand grip (Figure 8.4). The performer holds this position for as long as possible.

Scoring: The number of seconds to the nearest second that the performer maintains the proper position is recorded as the score. Table 8.4 shows norms for girls aged 9 to 17 years.

Additional Pointers:

1. The time should be started as soon as the subject starts in the flexed-arm hang position.

2. The time should be stopped as soon as the chin touches the bar, tilts backward, or drops below the bar.

3. A variation of this test, which is a little easier to score, is to time from the beginning of the flexed-arm hang position until the arms are fully extended. There is no difficulty in determining when the person reaches full extension, which ordinarily occurs suddenly after the subject has hung for a while in a partially flexed position. The time is rarely over 2 min for boys and is usually under 1 min for girls.

Pull-ups (AAHPERD 1976)

Objective: To measure the muscular endurance of the arms and shoulder girdle in pulling the body upward.

Age Level: Age 10 through college age.

Sex: Satisfactory as a test for boys only.

Reliability: An *r* as high as .87 has been reported for this test when subjects were tested on separate days.

Objectivity: An *r* of .99 was obtained by Mike Recio, Northeast Louisiana University, Monroe, 1972.

Validity: Face validity is accepted for this test.

Equipment and Materials: A horizontal bar 1½ in. in diameter raised to a height so that the tallest performer cannot touch the ground from the hanging position (if standard equipment is not available, a piece of pipe or the rungs of a ladder can be used).

Table 8.3.   Norms for Modified Sit-ups

PERCENTILE	AGE												
	5	6	7	8	9	10	11	12	13	14	15	16	17+
						GIRLS							
95	28	35	40	44	44	47	50	52	51	51	56	54	54
75	24	28	31	35	35	39	40	41	41	42	43	42	44
50	19	22	25	29	29	32	34	36	35	35	37	33	37
25	12	14	20	22	23	25	28	30	29	30	30	29	31
5	2	6	10	12	14	15	19	19	18	20	20	20	19
						BOYS							
95	30	36	42	48	47	50	51	56	58	59	59	61	62
75	23	26	33	37	38	40	42	46	48	49	49	51	52
50	18	20	26	30	32	34	37	39	41	42	44	45	46
25	11	15	19	25	25	27	30	31	35	36	38	38	38
5	2	6	10	15	15	15	17	19	25	27	28	28	25

Source: Adapted from *AAHPERD Health Related Physical Fitness Test Manual.* Reston, Va.: AAHPERD, 1980. Used by permission.

Figure 8.4. Flexed-arm hang

Directions: The performer assumes the hanging position with the overhand grasp (palms forward) and pulls the body upward until the chin is over the bar (Figure 8.5). After each chin-up, he returns to a fully extended hanging position. The exercise should be repeated as many times as possible.

Scoring: The score is the number of completed pull-ups. Table 8.5 shows norms for boys aged 9 to 17.

Additional Pointers:

1. Only one trial is allowed unless it is obvious that the student can do better with a second chance.

2. Swinging and snap-up movements must be avoided. The tester may check this by holding an extended arm across the front of the performer's thighs.

3. The knees must not be flexed during the pull, and kicking motions must be avoided.

4. Although the palms-forward grasp is customarily prescribed in physical fitness batteries, there is no logical reason why it rather than the reverse (palms-inward) grasp should be employed, other than the fact that the forward grasp is more difficult. As a matter of fact, since the reverse grip yields more repetitions, it might actually be a better measure in terms of distribution of scores. As McCloy and Young pointed out, the overhand grip became standard in World War II when the Armed Forces decreed that it was similar to the grip needed in climbing a fence. These authors adroitly commented that the reverse grip is the one used in the climbing of a rope.

Baumgartner Modified Pull-up Test (Baumgartner and Jackson 1982)

Objective: To measure arm and shoulder girdle strength or endurance or both.

Age Level: Elementary school age to college age.

Sex: Satisfactory for both boys and girls.

Reliability: Intraclass reliability estimates over .90 have been reported.

Validity: Face, or logical, validity is assumed, since the test consists of pulling the body weight with the arms until exhaustion. Jackson and associates proposed construct validity for the test, since males performed significantly better than females.

Table 8.4. Norms in Seconds for Flexed-Arm Hang, Girls

PERCENTILE	AGE							
	9–10	11	12	13	14	15	16	17+
95	42	39	33	34	35	36	31	34
75	18	20	18	16	21	18	15	17
50	9	10	9	8	9	9	7	8
25	3	3	3	3	3	4	3	3
5	0	0	0	0	0	0	0	0

Source: Adapted from *AAHPERD Youth Fitness Test Manual*. Reston, Va.: AAHPERD, 1976. Used by permission.

Figure 8.5. Pull-up

Table 8.5. Raw Score Norms for Pull-ups, Boys

PERCENTILE	AGE							
	9–10	11	12	13	14	15	16	17+
95	9	8	9	10	12	15	14	15
75	3	4	4	5	7	9	10	10
50	1	2	2	3	4	6	7	7
25	0	0	0	1	2	3	4	4
5	0	0	0	0	0	0	1	0

Source: Adapted from *AAHPERD Youth Fitness Test Manual*. Reston, Va.:
AAHPERD, 1976. Used by permission.

Equipment: A pull-up board, constructed from two 10-ft boards, each 2 in. × 12 in., fastened together with three 12-in. hinges (which permits the board to be folded in half for transportation and storage); a pull-up bar, made from ¾-in. plumbing pipe, with vertical uprights 6 in. high and a bar 18 in. long; a four-wheel scooter board, 24 in. long, 18 in. wide, and ½ in. thick, with nonrotating wheels 2 in. in diameter, and a 2-in. angle iron mounted underneath near the top (this is used to hook over a bar, such as a doorway pull-up bar 5 ft from the floor, which gives the board a 30-degree angle from the floor).

Directions: The student lies prone on the inclined board, and the scooter board is placed under the student's midsection. Usually, the top edge of the scooter board is placed just below the sternum, but if the subject has very long or heavy legs, it may be placed lower. The tester and an assistant push the subject on the scooter board up to the top of the board. The subject then grasps the bar with an overhand grip, hands shoulder-width apart. The test is administered like the regular pull-up test. The subject is cautioned to pull evenly with both arms and to not drag the toes.

Scoring: The total number of completed repetitions is the score. Norms for college women are provided in the original reference and in Baumgartner and Jackson. Jackson and associates gathered norms for 345 boys and 318 girls between the ages of 9 and 11 (Table 8.6).

Half-Squat Jump Test

Objective: To measure the endurance of the muscles of the legs.

Age Level: Age 10 through college age.

Sex: Satisfactory for both boys and girls.

Reliability: An *r* of .82 was reported by Charles Prestidge, Northeast Louisiana University, Monroe, 1972.

Objectivity: An *r* of .99 was reported by Mike Recio, Northeast Louisiana University, Monroe, 1972.

Validity: Face validity is accepted for this test.

Equipment and Materials: Adjustable bench, chair, fold-up mats, cold drink cases, or anything that can be stacked to measure to the lower patella (kneecap) level of the knees.

Directions: An assistant adjusts the seat level of the bench, chair, or whatever is available to the lower patella (kneecap) level of the student (Figure 8.6). The student then turns away from the

Table 8.6. Norms for Baumgartner Modified Pull-ups, Boys and Girls aged 9 to 11 Years[a]

PERCENTILE	NUMBER OF PULL-UPS	
	Boys	Girls
95	52	41
90	47	38
85	42	33
80	40	30
75	39	28
70	35	26
65	33	25
60	31	23
55	30	21
50	28	20
45	27	19
40	25	18
35	24	17
30	23	16
25	20	14
20	19	13
15	17	12
10	15	11
5	12	9

[a]Data from 345 boys and 318 girls from Denton, Tex., public schools.
Source: Jackson, A., L. Bruya, W. Baun, P. Richardson, R. Weinberg, and I. Caton. Baumgartner's Modified Pull-up Test for Male and Female Elementary School Aged Children. *Research Quarterly for Exercise and Sport* 53:163–164, June 1982, published by AAHPERD. Reprinted by permission.

bench, clasps the hands behind the head, and puts one foot slightly ahead of the other. He or she squats down until the buttocks touch the surface of the seat level and jumps upward, extending the legs (knees straight) and switching the position of the feet (Figure 8.7). The exercise is repeated as many times as possible.

Scoring: One point is scored for each correct repetition. Table 8.7 shows norms for college students.

Additional Pointers:

1. If the performer stops to rest, scoring is terminated.

2. The feet must come off the floor on each jump, and the legs must be extended.

3. The performer's buttocks must touch the horizontal seat level on each repetition for it to be scored.

Push-ups

Objective: To measure the endurance of the arms and shoulder girdle.

Age Level: Age 10 through college age.

Sex: Satisfactory for boys only.

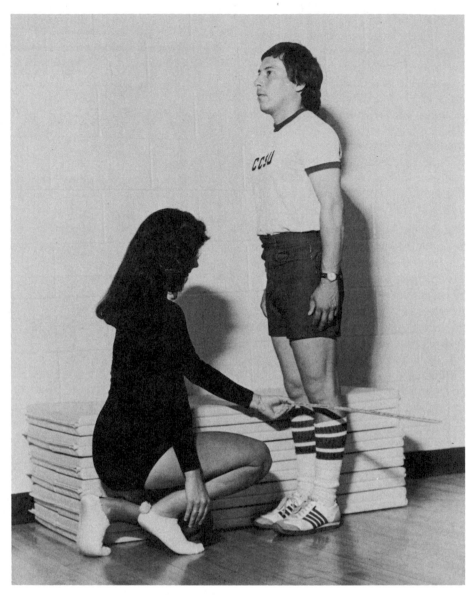

Figure 8.6. Determining distance for the half-squat jump test

Reliability: We could not find a coefficient of reliability reported for this test.

Objectivity: An r of .99 was reported by Mike Recio, Northeast Louisiana University, Monroe, 1972.

Validity: Face validity is accepted for this test.

Equipment and Materials: A mat on the floor.

Directions: From a straight-arm front-leaning rest position with hands on the floor, under the shoulders, the performer lowers the body until the chest touches the mat and then pushes upward to the straight-arm support position (Figure 8.8). The exercise is repeated as long as possible without rest. The body must not sag or pike upward but maintain a straight line throughout the exercise.

Scoring: The score is the number of correct push-ups executed. Tables 8.8 and 8.9 show norms for boys and men, respectively.

Additional Pointers:

1. The score is terminated if the performer stops to rest.

2. If the chest does not touch the mat or if the arms are not completely extended on an execution, the trial does not count.

3. To rigidly supervise the correct execution of the test, the tester or an assistant should lie on the right side of the performer and place his or her right hand, palm upward, under the performer's chest. The tester's left hand should be placed lightly on the performer's

Figure 8.7.   Half-squat jump

Table 8.7.   Raw Score Norms for Half-Squat Jump Test, College Students[a]

PERFORMANCE LEVEL	NUMBER OF JUMPS	
	Men	Women
Advanced	86 and above	44 and above
Advanced intermediate	66–85	34–43
Intermediate	37–65	22–33
Advanced beginner	19–36	15–21
Beginner	0–18	0–14

[a]Based on the scores of 200 men, as reported by M. C. Gomez, Corpus Christi State University, Corpus Christi, Tex., 1974, and 100 women, as reported by Charles Prestidge, Northeast Louisiana University, Monroe, La., 1972.

elbow. In this manner the tester can easily determine if the chest was lowered enough and if the arms reached complete extension.

Modified Push-ups

Objective: To measure the endurance of the arms and shoulder girdle.

Age Level: Age 10 through college age.

Sex: Satisfactory for girls only.

Reliability: An *r* as high as .93 has been reported for this test.

Validity: Validity as high as .72 has been reported with the Rogers' Short Index (Stumiller and Johnson 1976).

Equipment and Materials: A mat on the floor.

Figure 8.8. Push-up

Directions: With the knees bent at right angles and the hands on the floor directly under the shoulders, the performer lowers the body to the floor until the chest touches and then pushes back to the starting position (Figure 8.9). She does as many repetitions as possible without rest. The body must not sag but maintain a straight line throughout the trial.

Scoring: The score is the number of correct push-ups executed. Tables 8.10 and 8.11 show norms for girls and college women, respectively.

Additional Pointers:

1. Scoring is terminated if the performer stops to rest.

2. If the chest does not touch the mat or if the

Table 8.8. T Score Norms for Push-ups, Sixth, Seventh, and Eighth Grade Boys[a]

T SCORE	NUMBER OF PUSH-UPS		
	6th Grade	7th Grade	8th Grade
80	39 and above	40 and above	49 and above
75	34–38	36–39	44–48
70	30–33	32–35	39–43
65	25–29	28–31	34–38
60	21–24	24–27	29–33
55	16–20	20–23	24–28
50	12–15	16–19	19–23
45	7–11	12–15	14–18
40	3–6	8–11	9–13
35	0–2	4–7	4–8
30		0–3	0–3

[a]Based on the scores of 161 sixth grade boys, 167 seventh grade boys, and 149 eighth grade boys, Baton Rouge, La., 1972.

Table 8.9. Scale Point Norms for Push-ups, Men

SCALE POINTS	NUMBER OF PUSH-UPS	
	Age Under 30	Age Over 30
100	60	50
95	58	48
90	56	46
85	54	44
80	53	43
75	50	40
70	48	38
65	46	36
60	44	34
55	42	32
50	40	30
45	38	28
40	36	26
35	34	24
30	32	22
25	30	20
20	28	18

Source: J. T. Fisher, "Marine Corps Physical Fitness Programs." *Journal of Physical Education* 65:120, March-April, 1968.

arms are not completely extended on an execution, the trial does not count.

Endurance Dips

Objective: To measure the endurance of the arms and shoulder girdle.

Age Level: Age 10 through college age.

Sex: Satisfactory for boys only.

Reliability: An r as high as .90 has been reported for this test when subjects were tested on separate days.

Objectivity: An r of .99 was reported by Mike

Recio, Northeast Louisiana University, Monroe, 1972.

Validity: Face validity is accepted for this test.

Equipment and Materials: Two parallel bars raised to a height so that each subject is supported freely above the ground in a lowered bent-arm support position.

Directions: The performer assumes a straight-arm support position between the bars and then lowers the body until the elbows form a right angle (Figure 8.10). He then pushes back to a straight-arm support position and continues for as many repetitions as possible.

Figure 8.9. Modified push-up

Table 8.10. Minimum Standard Raw Scores for Modified Push-ups, Girls[a]

AGE	SCORE
6–7	4
8–9	7
10–11	9
12–13	10
14–15	12
16–18	14

[a]Scores from Quaker Oats-American Athletic Union (AAU) Physical Fitness Pentathlon Event. National Standards were designed by the AAU for each age group.

Table 8.11. Raw Score Norms for Modified Push-ups, College Women[a]

PERFORMANCE LEVEL	NUMBER OF PUSH-UPS
Advanced	31 and above
Advanced intermediate	25–30
Intermediate	13–24
Advanced beginner	7–12
Beginner	0–6

[a]Based on the scores of 50 women, Corpus Christi State University, Corpus Christi, Tex., 1977.

Scoring: The score is the number of correct dips executed. Table 8.12 shows norms for college men.

Additional Pointers:

1. Scoring is terminated if the performer stops to rest.

2. The performer should refrain from swinging or kicking in returning to the straight-arm support position.

3. The tester should extend his or her fist upward from inside the bar so that the performer's shoulder will touch it, which notifies both student and tester that the elbows reached the right angle.

4. The tester's other arm can be held across the front of the performer's thighs in the event of swinging, and at other times the tester can lightly grasp the performer's elbow to stress full arm extension.

5. Having the parallel bars lower at one end than the other facilitates the testing of subjects of different heights.

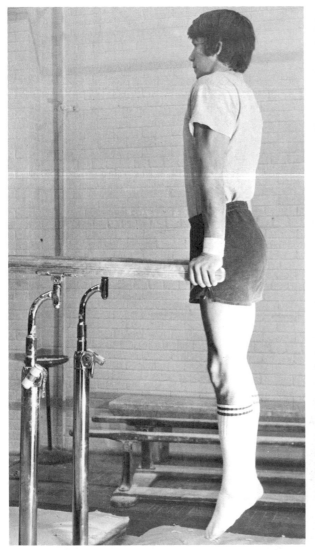

Figure 8.10. Endurance dip

Table 8.12. Raw Score Norms for Endurance Dips, College Men[a]

PERFORMANCE LEVEL	NUMBER OF DIPS
Advanced	25 and above
Advanced intermediate	18–24
Intermediate	9–17
Advanced beginner	4–8
Beginner	0–3

[a]Based on scores reported from physical education classes at the University of Florida, Gainesville, Fla., and at East Texas State University, Commerce, Tex.

Burpee (Squat Thrust)

Objective: To measure the general muscular endurance of the body.

Age Level: Age 10 through college age.

Sex: Satisfactory for both boys and girls.

Reliability: An r of .97 was found for this test when subjects were tested on separate days.

Validity: Face validity is accepted for this test.

Equipment and Materials: A mat on the floor.

Directions: From a standing position, the student bends at the knees and waist and places the hands on the floor in front of the feet (Figure 8.11a), thrusts the legs backward to a front leaning rest position (Figure 8.11b), returns to the squat position as in the first count (Figure 8.11c), and stands erect (Figure 8.11d). From the signal "go," the exercise is repeated at a constant rate of movement for as long as possible.

Scoring: The score is the number of correct repetitions. The score is recorded to the nearest whole number. Table 8.13 shows norms for college students.

Equipment and Materials: A single bar raised to a height so that the tallest girl cannot touch the floor when in the lowest position.

Directions: The performer starts from a straight-arm support position on the bar by lowering downward until the elbows form approximately a right angle (Figure 8.12). She then pushes back to the straight-arm support position and continues the exercise for as many repetitions as possible. It is permissible for the student to slide the body against the bar during the upward and downward phases of the exercise.

Scoring: The total number of repetitions is recorded for the score. However, repetitions should not be counted when the elbows do not bend sufficiently on the lowering phase of the exercise or

Start

a

b

d

Additional Pointers:

1. Scoring is terminated if the performer stops to rest.
2. Incorrect repetitions are not counted toward the score.
3. Persons with low-back problems should not be tested.

One-Bar Dip Test for Endurance

Objective: To measure the endurance of the arms and shoulder girdle.

Age Level: Age 12 through college age.

Sex: Recommended for girls.

Reliability: An *r* of .81 was found for this test when 20 students were tested on separate days.

Objectivity: An *r* of .96 was obtained when two testers independently scored 20 students on the test.

Validity: Face validity is accepted for this test.

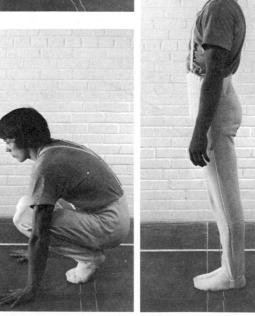

c

Figure 8.11. Burpee (squat thrust)

Table 8.13. Raw Score Norms for Burpee (Squat Thrust) Test, College Students[a]

PERFORMANCE LEVEL	NUMBER OF SQUAT THRUSTS	
	Men	Women
Advanced	94 and above	46 and above
Advanced intermediate	70–93	38–45
Intermediate	39–69	20–37
Advanced beginner	22–38	12–19
Beginner	0–21	0–11

[a]Based on a limited number of scores from physical education classes at Corpus Christi State University, Corpus Christi, Tex., 1976.

Figure 8.12. One-bar dip

when they do not fully extend on the press phase. Table 8.14 shows norms for college women.

Repetitive Press Test With Spring Scale (Johnson 1967)

Objective: To measure the endurance of the arms and shoulders in a mid-military press-type exercise.

Age Level: Age 15 through college age.

Sex: Satisfactory for both boys and girls.

Reliability: An *r* of .92 was found when girls were tested at one third of their body weight.

Validity: Face validity is accepted for this test.

Equipment and Materials: A Viking spring scale

Table 8.14. Raw Score Norms for One-Bar Dip Test for College Women Before and After 9 Weeks of Training

PERFORMANCE LEVEL	SCORE	
	Before Training[a]	After Training[b]
Advanced	9 and above	25 and above
Advanced intermediate	7–8	19–24
Intermediate	4–6	12–18
Advanced beginner	2–3	7–11
Beginner	0–1	0–6

[a]Based on the scores of 100 women as reported by Mike Recio, Northeast Louisiana University, Monroe, La., 1972.
[b]Based on a limited number of scores of women, 1972.

(measuring to 300 lb); a heavy-duty eye hook; an exercise bar with a screw hook; a small but sturdy wooden foot platform with a heavy-duty eye hook; and two 18-in. chain sections and one 5-ft chain section.

Directions: The tester should hook the bar to that part of the chain that allows the student to start the push with the bar in front of the forehead between the eyebrows and the hairline. With the feet flat on the floor, the student presses the bar vertically upward by attempting to straighten out the arms. Palms should be forward. The male performer must register at least one half of his body weight and the female one third of her weight on the scale at approximately 2 sec at a cadence of push-one, push-two, and so on for as many repetitions as possible. The press must be steady each time until it reaches the desired score. The tester should maintain the cadence and reset the dial indicator before each press. (See Figure 7.10.)

Scoring: The score is the number of times the performer can register the needle indicator above one half of body weight (boys) or one third of body weight (girls). Table 8.15 shows norms for college students.

Additional Pointers:

1. The test is terminated on the third successive failure to register the proper score.

2. Scoring is terminated when the performer is unable to keep up with the cadence.

3. An alternate test is to use one half of the male performer's maximum strength press and one third of the female performer's. However, maximum strength is much more variable from day to day than is body weight. Also, the tester never knows for certain when he or she has secured maximum effort from the student.

Handstand Push-ups Against Wall

Objective: To measure the endurance of the arms and shoulders in pressing the body in a handstand position.

Age Level: Age 12 through college age.

Sex: Recommended for boys only.

Reliability: An *r* of .83 was obtained when students were tested on separate days.

Objectivity: An *r* of .98 was obtained when two testers independently scored 20 students.

Table 8.15. Raw Score Norms for the Repetitive Press Test With Spring Scale, College Students[a]

PERFORMANCE LEVEL	NUMBER OF PRESSES	
	Men	Women
Advanced	47 and above	44 and above
Advanced intermediate	34–46	31–43
Intermediate	18–33	11–30
Advanced beginner	7–17	2–10
Beginner	0–6	0–1

[a]Based on the scores of 100 men, as reported by Ronald Taylor, Northeast Louisiana University, Monroe, La., 1972, and 100 women, as reported by Dixie Bennett, Northeast Louisiana University, Monroe, La., 1972.

Validity: Face validity is accepted for this test.

Equipment and Materials: A mat placed on the floor and against a smooth-surfaced wall.

Directions: The performer places his hands on the mat (approximately 1 ft from the wall and shoulder-width apart) and kicks upward into a handstand with the heels resting against the wall. He then bends at the elbows, allowing the body to lower until the tip of the nose touches the mat (Figure 8.13). He then pushes the body back to its original position by extending the elbows until they lock. The movement is repeated as many times as possible. A spotter (assistant) should place two fingers against each knee of the performer and assist the performer in maintaining balance as he does the exercise.

Scoring: The score is the number of successful push-ups from a touch of the nose to a lock-out position of the elbows. Table 8.16 shows norms for college men.

Table 8.16. Raw Score Norms for Handstand Push-up Test Against Wall, College Men[a]

PERFORMANCE LEVEL	NUMBER OF HANDSTANDS
Advanced	18 and above
Advanced intermediate	11—17
Intermediate	4—10
Advanced beginner	2—3
Beginner	0—1

[a]Based on the scores of 30 men, Corpus Christi State University, Corpus Christi, Tex., 1975.

Additional Pointers:

1. A spotter should assist the performer in getting into and out of the handstand position.

2. The performer's hands should be flat on the mat with fingers pointing directly toward the wall during the exercise.

Figure 8.13. Handstand push-up

3. The exercise is terminated if the performer hesitates to rest.

FINDINGS AND CONCLUSIONS FROM MUSCULAR ENDURANCE MEASUREMENT AND RESEARCH

Muscular endurance has been the subject of a multitude of studies. Moreover, endurance performance has been studied in a variety of ways. For example, in some studies endurance is tested isometrically, either with maximal or submaximal contractions repeated at a set cadence for as long as possible (D. H. Clarke 1973; Grose 1958; Rich 1960). In other studies endurance is tested dynamically, by exercises done with a load that is some proportion of maximal isotonic strength (Hansen 1963b; Mathews and Kruse 1957; Walters et al. 1960) or a proportion of maximal isometric strength (Baer et al. 1955; Clarke et al. 1954; Nelson 1962, 1978). Still other studies have used a load relative to maximal isometric strength that the subject holds statically for as long as possible (Hansen 1963a; Martens and Sharkey 1966; Start and Holmes 1963; Start and Graham 1964). Undoubtedly, some of the conflicting findings can be attributed to the many ways endurance has been studied.

Kroll delivered the 1981 C. H. McCloy Research Lecture on the analysis of local muscular fatigue patterns. The comprehensive review focused on fatigue patterns relative to level of strength in males and females, recovery and over-recovery patterns, the quick jump in strength phenomenon, psychologic factors, and muscle fiber type composition.

H. H. Clarke summarized numerous studies on the relationship between strength and endurance (1973) and on the endurance of the arm and shoulder-girdle muscles (1978). D. H. Clarke (1973) provided an extensive review of studies related to adaptations in strength and muscular endurance resulting from exercise. Weight training has long been used in developing both strength and endurance. Research has substantiated its effectiveness (Berger 1960; Dennison et al. 1961; Kusinitz and Keeney 1958; Stull and Clarke 1970). Several studies have reported that isotonic exercises are more effective than isometric exercises in the development of muscular endurance (McCraw and Burnham 1966; Petersen 1960; Wallace 1958). Other researchers have found both isotonic and isometric programs to be equally effective (Baer et al. 1955; D. H. Clarke 1973; Dennison et al. 1961; Howell et al. 1962).

Endurance performance is definitely influenced by motivation. Various motivational techniques such as competition, goals, verbal exhortation, and exaggerated importance of the task have been studied; most have brought about increases in endurance performance (Gerdes 1958; Hall 1951; Johnson 1963; Nelson 1962). Nelson (1978) investigated the influence of different motivational instructions, such as the use of goals and of real and fictitious norms, on endurance testing. All treatment groups surpassed the control (no supplementary information). The highest and most varied performance was evidenced by subjects who were given ego-threatening norms that were actually far above their capabilities. Hypnosis has been shown to improve endurance performance in some instances (Hyvarinen, Komi, and Puhakka 1977; Johnson and Kramer 1960, 1961).

Intuitively, warm-up prior to vigorous performance is considered important. However, research results have not borne out its importance. No significant effect was observed as a result of passive heating of the muscle (Sedgwick and Wahalen 1956) or of active warm-up with use of hypnosis to control the psychologic variable (Massey et al. 1961).

Bilateral training has been shown to be effective in increasing the strength of the untrained limb, but improvement in muscular endurance is more resistant to cross transfer (Mathews et al. 1956). However, one study reported that when endurance in the trained limb was increased to a very high level, endurance in the untrained limb improved to about 28% of that level (Hodgkins 1961).

Torranin, Smith, and Byrd investigated the effects of rapid thermal dehydration and rehydration on isometric and isotonic muscular endurance. Endurance performance on the hand grip, arm curl, bench press, and leg press significantly decreased following dehydration.

The relationship between strength and endurance has been studied by various researchers, with inconclusive results, as indicated in Chapter 7. In view of the recent interest in isokinetic strength training, Barnes analyzed the relationship between isokinetic strength and isokinetic endurance and found no correlation when endurance was defined as the total number of repetitions performed in a workout. A low but significant relationship was found between isokinetic strength and endurance when endurance was defined as total foot-pounds of work done. Heyward found no significant difference between strong and weak women in endurance of exercise at various percentages of maximal strength. Kroll and associates found that power-trained athletes fatigued faster than endurance-trained athletes on isometric endurance performances. Higher maximum isometric strength was associated with a faster rate of fatigue.

Clarkson and colleagues reported that muscle fiber type did not relate to either isokinetic strength or endurance. The endurance performance decline in peak torque within treatments (different angular velocities) was related to initial strength; however, the decline in strength and the pattern of fatigue across treatments were unrelated to initial strength.

Clarke (1962) studied the role of contraction duration of the hand-gripping muscles in muscular fatigue. Using a constant 1-sec rest interval, he found that the contraction duration varied between 1 and 4 sec. He concluded that greater control of muscular endurance is afforded by regulation of the rate of energy expenditure by monitoring the rate of contraction rather than by varying the duration of contraction.

Gabbard, Patterson, and Elledge compared combinations of forearm positions (pronated, supinated, and semipronated) and grips (thumb over and thumb under) on pull-up and straight-arm hang performances. In pull-up performance, the supinated and the semipronated positions were superior to the more commonly used pronated position. This finding is in agreement with previous research (DeWitt 1944; Fatyol 1980; Piscopo 1974; Rasch 1956) and biomechanical analysis (Luttgens and Wells 1982). For the straight-arm hang, the pronated and the semipronated forearm positions with thumb under the bar were the most effective. With regard to thumb position, the trends led the authors to recommend the thumb over the bar for pull-ups and the thumb under the bar for the straight-arm hang.

Kipping or kicking actions increase pull-up performance and must be controlled during testing (DeWitt 1944). Similarly, the straight-body position should be specified in the testing instructions for the flexed-arm hang, since piking at the hips or bending of the knees can result in a significantly higher score (Stumiller and Johnson 1976).

Excess weight is a handicap in the performance of relative endurance tests, such as push-ups, pull-ups, and squat jumps (Loveless 1952; Sills and Everett 1953).

Gabbard, Kirby, and Patterson investigated the feasibility of using the straight-arm hang as a muscular endurance test for children 2 to 6 years of age. The test was deemed reliable for 4- to 5-year-olds but questionable for younger children.

Karpovich and associates found low correlations between sit-ups and leg lifts and between timed sit-ups and untimed sit-ups, which indicates that such items should not be used interchangeably in test batteries.

BIBLIOGRAPHY

AAHPERD Health Related Physical Fitness Test Manual. Reston, Va.: AAHPERD, 1980.

AAHPERD Youth Fitness Test Manual. Reston, Va.: AAHPERD, 1976.

Baer, A. D., et al., "Effects of Various Exercise Programs on Isometric Tension, Endurance, and Reaction Time in the Human." *Archives of Physical Medicine and Rehabilitation* 36:495–502, 1955.

Barnes, W. S., "The Relationship Between Maximum Isokinetic Strength and Isokinetic Endurance." *Research Quarterly for Exercise and Sport* 51:714-717, December 1980.

Baumgartner, T. A., "Modified Pull-up Test." *Research Quarterly* 49:80–84, March 1978.

————, and A. S. Jackson, *Measurement for Evaluation in Physical Education.* 2nd ed. Dubuque, Iowa: William C. Brown, 1982, pp. 209–210.

Berger, R. A., "The Effect of Varied Weight Training Programs on Strength and Endurance." Microcarded master's thesis, University of Illinois, Urbana-Champaign, 1960.

Clarke, D. H., "Strength Recovery From Static and Dynamic Muscular Fatigue." *Research Quarterly* 33:349–355, October 1962.

————, "Adaptations in Strength and Muscular Endurance Resulting From Exercise." In J. H. Wilmore, Ed., *Exercise and Sport Sciences Reviews.* New York: Academic Press, 1973, pp. 74–102.

————, and G. A. Stull, "Endurance Training as a Determinant of Strength and Fatigability." *Research Quarterly* 41:19–26, 1970.

Clarke, H. H., Ed., "Toward a Better Understanding of Muscular Strength." *Physical Fitness Research Digest,* Series 3, January 1973.

————, "Endurance of Arm and Shoulder-Girdle Muscles." *Physical Fitness Research Digest,* Series 8, October, 1978.

————, et al., "Strength and Endurance (Conditioning) Effects of Exhaustive Exercise of the Elbow Flexor Muscles." *Journal of the*

Association of Physical and Mental Rehabilitation 8:184–188, 1954.

Clarkson, P. M., J. Johnson, D. Dextradeur, W. Leszczynski, J. Wai, and A. Melchoionda, "The Relationship Among Isokinetic Endurance, Initial Strength Level, and Fiber Type." *Research Quarterly for Exercise and Sport* 53:15–19, March 1982.

Dennison, J. D., et al., "Effect of Isometric and Isotonic Exercise Programs Upon Muscular Endurance." *Research Quarterly* 32:348–353, October 1961.

DeWitt, R. T., "A Comparative Study of Three Types of Chinning Tests." *Research Quarterly* 15:249–251, October 1944.

Fatyol, T., "Hand Grips and Pull-up Performance." Unpublished study, Louisiana State University, Baton Rouge, 1980.

Gabbard, C., T. Kirby, and P. Patterson, "Reliability of the Straight-Arm Hang for Testing Muscular Endurance Among Children 2 to 5." *Research Quarterly* 50:735–738, December 1979.

———, P. Patterson, and J. Elledge, "Grip and Forearm Position Effects on Tests of Static and Dynamic Upper Body Endurance." *Research Quarterly for Exercise and Sport* 52:174–179, May 1981.

Gerdes, G. R., "The Effects of Various Motivational Techniques Upon Performance in Selected Physical Tests." Microcarded doctoral dissertation, Indiana University, Bloomington, 1958, pp. 88–92.

Grose, J. E., "Depression of Muscle Fatigue Curves by Heat and Cold." *Research Quarterly* 29:19–31, March 1958.

Hall, D. M., "Endurance Tests for 4-H Club Members." *Research Quarterly* 22:48, March 1951.

Hansen, J. W., "The Effect of Sustained Isometric Muscle Contraction on Various Muscle Functions." *Internationale Zeitschrift für Angewandte Physiologie Einschliesslisch Arbeitsphysiologie* 19:430–434, 1963a.

———, "The Training Effect of Dynamic Maximal Resistance Exercises." *Internationale Zeitschrift für Angewandte Physiologie Einschliesslisch Arbeitsphysiologie* 19:420–424, 1963b.

Heyward, V., "Relative Endurance of High- and Low-Strength Women." *Research Quarterly for Exercise and Sport* 51:486–493, October 1980.

Hodgkins, J., "Influence of Unilateral Endurance Training on Contri-lateral Limb." *Journal of Applied Physiology* 16:991–993, 1961.

Howell, M. L., et al., "Effect of Isometric and Isotonic Exercise Programs Upon Muscular Endurance." *Research Quarterly* 33:539, December 1962.

Hyvarinen, J., P. V. Komi, and P. Puhakka, "Endurance of Muscle Contraction Under Hypnosis." *Acta Physiologica Scandinavica* 100:485–487, 1977.

Jackson, A., L. Bruya, W. Baun, P. Richardson, R. Weinberg, and I. Caton, "Baumgartner's Modified Pull-up Test for Male and Female Elementary School Aged Children." *Research Quarterly for Exercise and Sport* 53:163–164, June 1982.

Johnson, B. L., "The Effect of Motivational Testing Situations on an Endurance Test." Unpublished study, Northeast Louisiana University, Monroe, 1963.

———, "Practical Tests of Muscular Endurance." Unpublished study, Northeast Louisiana University, Monroe, 1967.

———, and M. J. Garcia, *Fitness and Performance for Everyone*. Portland, Tex.: Brown & Littleman, 1977, p. 16.

Johnson, W. R., and G. F. Kramer, "Effects of Different Types of Hypnotic Suggestions Upon Physical Performance." *Research Quarterly* 31:469–473, October 1960.

———, "Effects of Stereotyped Non-hypnotic, Hypnotic, and Post-hypnotic Suggestions Upon Strength, Power, and Endurance." *Research Quarterly* 32:522–529, December 1961.

Karpovich, P. V., "Studies of the AAF Physical Fitness Test: Selection of a Time Limit for Sit-ups." Project No. 245, Report No. 3, AAF School of Aviation Medicine, Randolph Field, Tex., July 1944.

———, et al., "Relation Between Leg-Lift and Sit-up." *Research Quarterly* 17:21–24, March 1946.

Kroll, W., "Analyses of Local Muscular Fatigue Patterns." (The 1981 C. H. McCloy Research Lecture.) *Research Quarterly for Exercise and Sport* 52:523–539, December 1981.

———, P. M. Clarkson, G. Kamen, and J. Lambert, "Muscle Fiber Type Composition and Knee Extension Isometric Strength Fatigue Patterns in Power- and Endurance-Trained Males." *Research Quarterly for Exercise and Sport* 51:323–333, May 1980.

Kusinitz, I., and C. E. Keeney, "Effects of Progressive Weight Training on Health and Physical Fitness of Adolescent Boys." *Research Quarterly* 29:294, October 1958.

Loveless, J. C., "Relationship of the Wartime Navy Physical Fitness Test to Age, Height, and Weight." *Research Quarterly* 23:347, October 1952.

Luttgens, K., and K. F. Wells, *Kinesiology.* 7th ed. Philadelphia: W. B. Saunders, 1982, pp. 558–559.

Martens, R., and B. J. Sharkey, "Relationship of Phasic and Static Strength and Endurance." *Research Quarterly* 37:435–436, October 1966.

Massey, B., et al., "Effect of Warm-up Exercise Upon Muscular Performance Using Hypnosis to Control the Psychological Variable." *Research Quarterly* 32:63–71, March 1961.

Mathews, D. K., et al., "Cross Transfer Effects of Training on Strength and Endurance." *Research Quarterly* 27:206–212, May 1956.

———, and R. Kruse, "Effects of Isometric and Isotonic Exercises on Elbow Flexor Muscle Groups." *Research Quarterly* 28:26–37, 1957.

McCloy, C. H., and N. D. Young, *Tests and Measurements in Health and Physical Education.* 3rd ed. New York: Appleton-Century-Crofts, 1954, p. 168.

McCraw, L. W., and S. Burnham, "Resistive Exercises in the Development of Muscular Strength and Endurance." *Research Quarterly* 37:79–88, March 1966.

Nelson, J. K., "An Analysis of the Effects of Applying Various Motivational Situations to College Men Subjected to a Stressful Physical Performance." Microcarded doctoral dissertation, University of Oregon, Eugene, 1962.

———, "Motivating Effects of the Use of Norms and Goals With Endurance Testing." *Research Quarterly* 49:317–321, October 1978.

Petersen, F. B., "Muscle Training by Static, Concentric, and Eccentric Contraction." *Acta Physiologica Scandinavica* 48:406–416, 1960.

Piscopo, J., "Assessment of Forearm Positions Upon Upper Arm and Shoulder Girdle Strength Performance." *Kinesiology* 4:53–57, 1974.

Rasch, P. J., "Effect of Position of Forearm on Strength of Elbow Flexion." *Research Quarterly* 27:333–337, October 1956.

Rich, G. Q., 3rd, "Muscular Fatigue Curves of Boys and Girls." *Research Quarterly* 31:485–498, October 1960.

Sedgwick, A. W., and H. R. Wahalen, "Effect of Passive Warm-up on Muscular Strength and Endurance." *Research Quarterly* 35:45–59, March 1964.

Sills, F. D., and W. Everett, "The Relationship of Extreme Somatotypes to Performance in Motor and Strength Test." *Research Quarterly* 24:223–228, May 1953.

Start, K. B., and J. S. Graham, "Relationship Between the Relative and Absolute Isometric Endurance of an Isolated Muscle Group." *Research Quarterly* 35:193–194, May 1964.

———, and R. Holmes, "Local Muscle Endurance With Open and Occluded Intramuscular Circulation." *Journal of Applied Physiology* 18:804–807, 1963.

Stull, G. A., and D. H. Clarke, "High-Resistance, Low-Repetition Training as a Determiner of Strength and Fatigability." *Research Quarterly* 41:189–193, 1970.

Stumiller, B., and B. L. Johnson, "Effect of Three Different Leg Positions on Flexed-Arm Hang Performance." Unpublished study, Corpus Christi State University, Corpus Christi, Tex., 1976.

Torranin, C., D. P. Smith, and R. J. Byrd, "The Effect of Acute Thermal Dehydration and Rapid Rehydration on Isometric and Isotonic Endurance." *Journal of Sports Medicine and Physical Fitness* 19:1–9, 1979.

Wallace, J., "The Development of Muscular Strength and Muscular Endurance Through Isotonic and Isometric Exercise." *New Zealand Journal of Physical Education* 14:3–9, 1958.

Walters, C. E., et al., "Effect of Short Bouts of Isometric and Isotonic Contractions on Muscular Strength and Endurance." *American Journal of Physical Medicine* 39:131–141, 1960.

CHAPTER 9

THE MEASUREMENT OF CARDIORESPIRATORY CONDITION

O B J E C T I V E S

After reading this chapter, the student should be able to:

1. Define cardiorespiratory endurance and list four measurable physiologic differences between high and low levels of cardiorespiratory fitness

2. Recognize the differences between laboratory

and field measures of cardiorespiratory endurance

3. Understand and anticipate some of the problems involved in measuring cardiorespiratory endurance

4. Follow the directions for administering step tests and distance runs in the assessment of cardiorespiratory endurance

---

To most people, being in *good shape* is exemplified by such feats as being able to climb several flights of stairs without becoming red in the face and breathing hard or to resume hiking, cycling, or jogging comfortably after a scant few minutes of rest. In slightly more technical language, being in good shape means having good cardiorespiratory function, that is, that the circulatory and respiratory systems are able to adjust to and recover from the effects of exercise or work. This ability is unquestionably one of the key components of physical fitness, and to some physical educators it is the single most indicative measure of physical condition. The most accurate measure of cardiorespiratory function is generally considered maximum oxygen uptake (VO_2 max), which is the amount of oxygen consumed per kilogram of body weight per minute of exercise. However, measurement of VO_2 max requires expensive equipment and is time consuming and rigorous, factors that make the technique out of reach of most schools and colleges.

A number of other tests have been devised to measure cardiorespiratory function. Some tests

simply require the subject to perform a task that calls for sustained total body movement. A common test of this type involves having the subject run a prescribed distance, cardiorespiratory endurance being measured by the time required to cover the distance. This pragmatic approach is often employed in physical fitness test batteries.

Other tests have sought to determine cardiorespiratory fitness through measures of pulse rate and blood pressure under various conditions involving changes in body position and before and after different amounts of work. Such tests are based on the accepted principle that a physically fit person has more efficient circulatory and respiratory systems than an untrained person. The conditioned individual has a greater stroke volume, which means more blood is pumped each stroke, which enables fewer strokes per minute to do the work. The trained person also has fuller oxygen–carbon dioxide exchange, resulting in more oxygen from the air being available to the body, a slower rate of breathing, and a lower rate of lactic acid formation.

Heart rate increases with exercise. The rate of

increase is proportional to the work load. Fitness is reflected by the rate of increase. In general, the physically fit individual has a lower heart rate for a specified work load. To view the relationship from another standpoint, at a given heart rate the trained individual is able to exercise at a higher work load than the untrained person.

Heart rate increases with oxygen consumption. Since the latter is considered the most valid measure of cardiorespiratory fitness, this relationship has been used in tests to predict oxygen consumption. Heart rate provides a great deal of information about the body's reaction to the stress of exercise, and its measurement is quick and easy. Hence, it can serve as a valuable tool to monitor the strenuousness of an exercise program and to provide a valid indicator of an individual's cardiorespiratory fitness.

The systolic blood pressure of the trained person is usually lower during strenuous exercise than that of the poorly trained person. The heart rate, blood pressure, and breathing rate return to preexercise levels after exercise more quickly in a person in good physical condition than in an individual in poor condition.

USES OF CARDIORESPIRATORY TESTS

Cardiorespiratory tests may be given for any of several purposes within the school setting. One purpose, and probably the most common, is as part of a physical fitness test battery in classifying and rating students for assessment of status and improvement. In this capacity, the test is generally in the form of a distance run or endurance exercise rather than of physiologic measurements.

Another purpose may be screening. A note of caution should be sounded here. Certainly a screening test should not be one that requires maximal effort. Furthermore, such a test should not be considered a substitute for a medical examination.

The physical educator may use cardiorespiratory tests for the purpose of research. Such research may be in the form of observation, in which measures are taken of status or for establishing norms, or of tests given before and after a training program to measure improvement.

Perhaps one of the most important uses of cardiorespiratory tests in which pulse rate and blood pressure are measured is as an educational device. The tests may be given in conjunction with a health unit or a biology class or as a special physical education activity. In any case, such tests can be effective for their motivational properties and for the information they provide concerning the circulatory and respiratory systems.

PROBLEMS ASSOCIATED WITH CARDIORESPIRATORY FITNESS TESTING

So many variables can affect the pulse rate and blood pressure that obtaining an *average* or *typical* measurement on any given day is difficult. Emotions, for example, have a noticeable effect on cardiorespiratory functions. Physicians often allow for this when they are taking a patient's pulse rate and blood pressure during a medical examination.

Besides nervousness, tension, and other emotional manifestations, it has been found that temperature, time of day, exercise, changes in body position, altitude, humidity, digestion, and current state of health also may influence cardiorespiratory measurements. Consequently, reliability and objectivity coefficients are often low.

The main influencing factors mentioned dictate that great care must be taken in the measurement of pulse rate and blood pressure. If a resting or normal pulse rate is desired, the subject should be allowed to rest for several minutes until the count has stabilized. Stabilization can be determined by the taking of consecutive readings until they are similar. It has been observed that a subject's pulse rate is sometimes lower after mild exercise than when he or she first entered the laboratory.

One of the foremost problems associated with cardiorespiratory fitness testing in physical education classes is the time required for testing. This problem, in turn, relates to the purpose of the tests. Group tests are not overly time consuming. Furthermore, these tests are generally most effective in differentiating between different levels of fitness in normal students.

PRACTICAL TESTS OF CARDIORESPIRATORY FITNESS

While tests of cardiorespiratory condition are numerous, only a few will be presented here. Most tests are too involved or too time consuming for use in physical education classes, or they require expensive equipment. The tests presented can all be administered to students in groups.

12-Minute (or 9-Minute) Run—Walk Test

Objective: To measure cardiorespiratory fitness.

Sex: Satisfactory for both boys and girls.

Age: Junior high school through college age.

Reliability: A test–retest reliability of .94 was reported by Doolittle and Bigbee.

Validity: Validity coefficients of .64 to .90 have been obtained when maximum oxygen intake was used as the criterion.

Facilities, Equipment, and Materials: If possible, a specific course measured in distance so that the number of laps completed can be counted and multiplied by the course distance; it is also helpful to have markers divide the course into quarters or eighths, which enables the tester to determine quickly the exact distance covered in 12 min; a stopwatch; a whistle; and distance markers.

Directions: Usually, the most efficient procedure is to assign a spotter to each runner. The runners start behind a line and, on the starting signal, run or walk or both as many laps as possible around the course within 12 min. The spotters maintain a count of each lap; when the signal to stop is given, they run to the spot at which their runner was at the instant the whistle or command to stop was given.

Scoring: The score in yards is determined by multiplying the number of completed laps times the distance of each lap (e.g., 440 yd), plus the number of segments (e.g., quarters, eighths, 10-yd intervals) of an incomplete lap, plus the number of yards stepped off between a particular segment.

For example, the 12-minute run is given on a 440-yd track sectioned off into eighths. A student completes 5 laps plus three one-eighth segments plus 11 yd. The student's score is 5 × 440 = 2200; plus 3 × 55 (each one-eighth segment is 55 yd) = 165; plus 11 yd (i.e., 2200 + 165 + 11 = 2376 yd covered in 12 min).

Additional Pointers:

1. The spotter should be strongly impressed with the necessity of maintaining an accurate count of the number of laps; it is most disconcerting for a runner to exert a great deal of effort and then be given an inaccurate score.

2. For added protection, the runner should also count the number of laps covered.

3. The tester should alert the spotters at least 30 sec before the end of the 12 min.

4. It usually is most efficient to have the spotters remain in the exact spot at which their runner was when the whistle sounded. The tester can then move to each spot and record the scores.

5. The spotter should tell the tester the number of laps and the tester can then record the number of segments of the incomplete lap and step off the extra yards. This may prove more accurate than reliance on the spotters to compute the scores. It is good experience for the spotters to calculate their runner's total yardage, but it is important that the tester be able to check the figures.

6. Although the test can be administered in a variety of settings, such as a 440-yd track, football fields, or streets, one should not expect comparable performance on each. It has been demonstrated that the more turns a runner has to make, the more time he or she needs. While working on the Texas Physical Fitness–Motor Ability Test, Coleman and Jackson recommended two test arrangements for the 9- or 12-minute run: the 440-yd track and the 110-yd straightaway, as shown in Figure 9.1. They found no meaningful difference between the two. The norms in Tables 9.1 and 9.2 are from the *AAHPERD Health Related Physical Fitness Test*.

7. Research has shown that if the 12-minute test is deemed too long for a particular age level or situation, a 9-minute test can be administered in the same way with apparently no significant loss in validity (Jackson and

Areas Suitable for Distance Run Tests

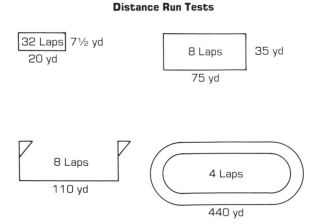

Figure 9.1. Test patterns for 9-minute and 12-minute and 1-mile and 1.5-mile runs (as suggested in the *AAHPERD Health Related Physical Fitness Test Manual*. Reston, Va.: AAHPERD, 1980)

Table 9.1.   Percentile Norms in Yards for 9-Minute Run

PERCENTILE	AGE												
	5	6	7	8	9	10	11	12	13	14	15	16	17+
						GIRLS							
95	1540	1700	1900	1860	2050	2067	2000	2175	2085	2123	2161	2199	2237
75	1300	1440	1540	1540	1650	1650	1723	1760	1785	1823	1861	1899	1937
50	1140	1208	1344	1358	1425	1460	1480	1590	1577	1615	1653	1691	1729
25	950	1017	1150	1225	1243	1250	1345	1356	1369	1407	1445	1483	1521
5	700	750	860	970	960	940	904	1000	1069	1107	1145	1183	1221
						BOYS							
95	1760	1750	2020	2200	2175	2250	2250	2400	2402	2473	2544	2615	2615
75	1320	1469	1683	1810	1835	1910	1925	1975	2096	2167	2238	2309	2380
50	1170	1280	1440	1595	1660	1690	1725	1760	1885	1956	2027	2098	2169
25	990	1090	1243	1380	1440	1487	1540	1500	1674	1745	1816	1887	1958
5	600	816	990	1053	1104	1110	1170	1000	1368	1439	1510	1581	1652

Source: Adapted from *AAHPERD Health Related Physical Fitness Test Manual*. Reston, Va.: AAHPERD, 1980. Used by permission.

Table 9.2.   Percentile Norms for 12-Minute (Yards) and 1.5-Mile (Minutes and Seconds) Run, Girls and Boys Aged 13 to 18 Years

PERCENTILE	SCORE			
	Girls		Boys	
	12-Minute	1.5 Mile	12-Minute	1.5 Mile
95	2448	12:17	3297	8:37
75	2100	15:03	2879	10:19
50	1861	16:57	2592	11:29
25	1622	18:50	2305	12:39
5	1274	21:36	1888	14:20

Source: Adapted from *AAHPERD Health Related Physical Fitness Test Manual*. Reston, Va.: AAHPERD, 1980. Used by permission.

Coleman 1976). For women, a 6-minute test has also been found to have validity comparable to that of the 12-minute test (Custer and Chaloupka 1977).

8. For the 9- or the 12-minute test on the 440-yd track or 110-yd straightaway, it has been recommended that markers be made with the appropriate distances on front and back. For example, on the 110-yd course, the first sign would have "start" on one side and "220" on the other; the second would have "10" on one side and "210" on the other, and so on, until the entire 110 yd has been marked off.

1-Mile and 1.5-Mile Distance Runs

Objective: To measure cardiorespiratory fitness.

Sex and Age: 1-Mile run: satisfactory for both sexes, ages 5 through adult. 1.5-Mile run: recommended for both sexes, ages 13 and older.

Validity: The validity of distance runs of 1 mi and over has been demonstrated in a number of studies, such as that by Disch, Frankiewicz, and Jackson, through factor analysis.

Equipment: A stopwatch and a track or some type of open area of known dimensions (Figure 9.1).

Directions: As many as a dozen people can run at a time. The subject is told that walking is permitted, but the objective is to cover the distance in the shortest possible time. Each runner is assigned a spotter. A tester gives the command, "Ready? Go!" The subject uses a standing start. The spotter is positioned near the finish line in order to clearly hear the timer, who calls aloud the time in seconds as the runners cross the finish line. The spotter must watch his or her runner and remember the announced time. Spotters must be impressed with the importance of paying close attention and not talking to other students until they give their runner's time to the recorder.

Scoring: The score is the time in minutes and seconds needed to complete the run. Norms are shown in Tables 9.2, 9.3, and 9.4.

Additional Pointers:

1. The same partners should not score each other.

2. Some practice in spotting should be given.

3. The timer must guard against the tendency to stop the watch as soon as the first runner finishes.

4. Each runner should be instructed to listen for his or her own time as a safeguard against the possibility of a spotter forgetting the time.

600-Yard Run—Walk Test

Objective: To measure cardiorespiratory efficiency.

Sex: Satisfactory for both boys and girls.

Age: 6 through 12.

Reliability: A coefficient of .92 was obtained for both boys and girls at the junior high school level (Willgoose and Askew 1961).

Objectivity: No objectivity coefficient has been reported.

Validity: Validity coefficients of .96, .88, and .76 were found by Biasiotto and Cotten for third, fifth, and seventh grade boys, respectively.

Equipment: A stopwatch and a track, football field, or similar open area. The *AAHPERD Youth Fitness Test Manual* shows diagrams of three suggested areas: (1) A football field on which four flags are placed at the end line of the end zone 30 yd apart. These markers make a rectangular course 120 × 30 yd; twice around equals 600 yd. (2) Any open area in the form of a square measuring 50 yd on each side. Three times around measures 600 yd. (3) The inside circumference of a 440-yd track. In this case the tester might start the runners and then walk 160 yd down the track to the finish line.

Directions: Same as for the 1- and 1.5-mile runs.

Scoring: The time to complete the run in minutes and seconds is recorded. Table 9.5 shows norms for boys and girls aged 10 to 12.

Additional Pointers: Same as for the 1- and 1.5-mile runs.

Modified OSU Step Test

The OSU (Ohio State University) Step Test (Kurucz 1967) was developed as a submaximal cardiorespiratory fitness test designed to overcome the adverse criticisms, such as fatigue, muscle soreness, and expensive equipment, associated with the methods then used for assessing cardiorespiratory fitness, such as maximum oxygen consumption, the Balke Treadmill Test, and the Harvard Step Test. The rationale for this test is that the exercise time required to reach a pulse rate of 150 beats/min is a valid indicator of the subject's capacity for more strenuous work. It employs a split-level bench with an adjustable hand bar. One level of the bench is 15 in. high; the other is 20 in. high.

Cotten reported a modification of the OSU Step Test that he believed would be applicable for high school physical education classes. He sought to

Table 9.3.   Percentile Norms in Minutes and Seconds for 1-Mile Run

PERCENTILE	AGE												
	5	6	7	8	9	10	11	12	13	14	15	16	17+
							GIRLS						
95	9:45	9:18	8:48	8:45	8:24	7:59	7:46	7:26	7:10	7:18	7:39	7:07	7:26
75	13:09	11:24	10:55	10:35	9:58	9:30	9:12	8:36	8:18	8:13	8:42	9:00	9:03
50	15:08	13:48	12:30	12:00	11:12	11:06	10:27	9:47	9:27	9:35	10:05	10:45	9:47
25	17:59	15:27	14:30	14:16	13:18	12:54	12:10	11:35	10:56	11:43	12:21	13:00	11:28
5	19:00	18:50	17:44	16:58	16:42	17:00	16:56	14:46	14:55	16:59	16:22	15:30	15:24
							BOYS						
95	9:02	9:06	8:06	7:58	7:17	6:56	6:50	6:27	6:11	5:51	6:01	5:48	6:01
75	11:32	10:55	9:37	9:14	8:36	8:10	8:00	7:24	6:52	6:36	6:35	6:28	6:36
50	13:46	12:29	11:25	11:00	9:56	9:19	9:06	8:20	7:27	7:10	7:14	7:11	7:25
25	16:05	15:10	14:02	13:29	12:00	11:05	11:31	10:00	8:35	8:02	8:04	8:07	8:26
5	18:25	17:38	17:17	16:19	15:44	14:28	15:25	13:41	10:23	10:32	10:37	10:40	10:56

Source: Adapted from *AAHPERD Health Related Physical Fitness Test Manual.* Reston, Va.: AAHPERD, 1980. Used by permission.

Table 9.4. Percentile Norms in Minutes and Seconds for 1.5-Mile Run Gathered From College Students at Midterm and at Completion of 16-Week Jogging–Conditioning Course[a]

PERCENTILE	SCORE			
	Women		Men	
	Midterm	Final	Midterm	Final
99	11:04	10:08	7:35	7:18
95	11:18	11:03	8:59	8:20
90	11:32	11:24	9:05	8:37
85	12:59	11:35	9:24	8:47
80	13:03	11:50	9:30	8:55
75	13:18	11:55	9:45	9:01
70	13:30	12:03	9:59	9:08
65	13:56	12:16	10:03	9:11
60	14:19	12:23	10:13	9:14
55	14:28	12:30	10:23	9:21
50	14:44	12:35	10:34	9:28
45	15:09	12:38	10:40	9:35
40	15:23	12:55	10:50	9:43
35	15:37	13:04	11:03	10:06
30	15:45	13:21	11:32	10:19
25	16:00	13:39	11:45	10:27
20	16:10	13:48	12:15	10:38
15	16:54	14:05	12:32	10:56
10	17:32	14:45	13:23	11:35
5	18:27	15:18	13:56	11:46
1	20:05	16:04	16:27	13:47

[a]Scores from 100 men and 100 women selected randomly from over 800 men and 800 women enrolled in jogging–conditioning courses at Louisiana State University, Baton Rouge.

Table 9.5. 600-Yard Run–Walk Scores in Minutes and Seconds, Boys and Girls

PERCENTILE	SCORE					
	Boys of Age:			Girls of Age:		
	10	11	12	10	11	12
95	1:58	1:59	1:52	2:05	2:13	2:14
75	2:18	2:14	2:09	2:30	2:32	2:31
50	2:33	2:27	2:21	2:48	2:49	2:49
25	2:49	2:42	2:39	3:08	3:15	3:11
5	3:23	3:30	3:32	3:45	3:59	4:00

Source: Adapted from *AAHPERD Youth Fitness Test Manual.* Reston, Va.: AAHPERD, 1976. Used by permission.

develop a procedure that would be suitable for mass testing, be economical in terms of time, require little special equipment, and also require a minimum of student motivation (motivation is necessary in cardiorespiratory measures that require strenuous effort to complete the test).

Sex: Recommended for boys only.

Age: Grades 9 to 12 and adult.

Validity and Reliability: The modified test had a correlation of .84 with the Balke Treadmill Test. Test–retest reliability was .95 with college men as subjects and was .75 with high school subjects. However, some counting errors may have been responsible for the lower reliability coefficient with the high school students.

Equipment and Materials: Bleacher steps 17 in. high (Cotten thought that the test would still be valid for bleacher heights that varied an inch or two from this height); a tape recorder; a stop-watch, a metronome; and score sheets.

Directions: The commands and cadences for the 18 innings should be prerecorded to ensure accuracy. The class is divided into pairs of partners. The exercising subjects are instructed to sit on the bottom bleacher step and the partner sits behind them on the second row.

The work loads for the three phases of the test are:

Phase I: Six innings—24 steps/min

Phase II: Six innings—30 steps/min

Phase III: Six innings—36 steps/min

At the command to begin, the subject steps up and down for 30 sec in cadence with the metronome. The stepping is performed as a four-count exercise of "up, up, down, down" in which the subject places one foot and then both feet on the platform (Figure 9.2), straightens the legs and back, and immediately steps down again, one foot at a time. It is normally easier for the subject to lead off with the same foot each time; however, alternating feet is permitted if one leg gets tired. No crouching is allowed.

At the command "stop," the subject immediately sits down and finds his pulse. After exactly 5 sec, the command "count" is given, and after another 15 sec, the commands "stop" and "prepare to exercise" are given. The subject records the number of beats counted in the 10-sec period. After 5 more sec, the subject is commanded to start stepping again for another 30-sec exercise bout. This procedure is continued for six innings in phase I, or until a pulse count of 25 (which

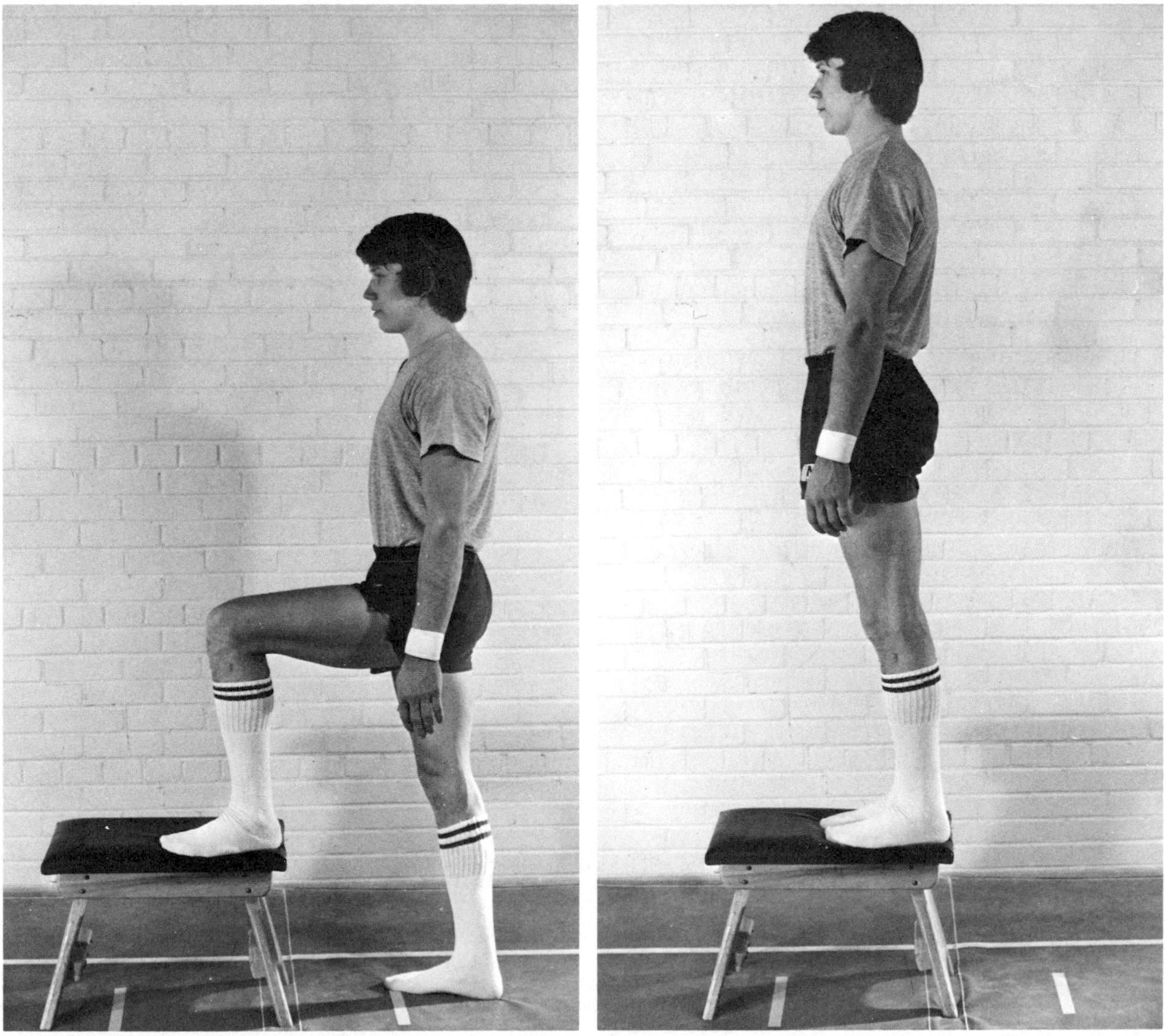

Figure 9.2.   Proper form for all step tests

corresponds to a heart rate of 150 beats/min) is reached. *Each inning consists of 30 sec of stepping and a 20-sec rest period, during which a 10-sec pulse count is taken from the 5th to 15th sec.*

Prior to the seventh inning, the subject is informed that the cadence will be increased, and to continue the same procedure. Prior to the 13th inning, the subject is again told that the cadence will be increased. The three phases are continuous.

Scoring: The score is the inning in which the pulse count is 25 for the 10-sec period (150 beats/min). If the subject completes the 18 innings, he is given a score of 19.

Additional Pointers:

1.   Half of the class can be tested simultaneously using the buddy system.

2.   Vigorous exercise should not precede the test.

3.   A 15-min rest period should be allowed prior to the test. During this time, instructions should be given and a complete inning demonstrated. Also during this time, students should practice finding and counting the pulse rate at the carotid artery.

4.   Having the nonexercising partner sit in the row above the exercising subject makes it convenient for them to immediately find the pulse at the carotid artery when their partner sits down each time after exercising.

5.   Local norms should be established, particularly if the bleacher heights are not 17 in.

6.   To facilitate the cadence, the number of steps should be multiplied by 4 so that the metronome is set at 96 for the 24-steps/min, 120 for the 30-steps/min, and 144 for the 36-steps/min cadence. Thus, each click of the metronome signifies a foot placement.

Queens College Step Test (McArdle et al. 1972)

Objective: To provide a practical, convenient means for assessing cardiorespiratory fitness.

Sex: Women and men.

Age: College age.

Reliability: A reliability coefficient of .92 was reported.

Validity: With use of maximal oxygen consumption as the criterion, a correlation of $-.75$ was obtained between the first heart rate recovery score (5-20 sec after exercise) and VO_2 max expressed in milliliters per kilogram per minute (ml/kg/min).

Equipment and Materials: Bleachers to serve as the stepping bench (16–17 in.); a metronome (amplification of the sound via loudspeakers is desirable); and a stopwatch.

Directions: Half of the class may be tested at one time, the other half serving as partners to count the pulse rate. Following the explanation of the testing and pulse-counting procedures, the counters are allowed several practices in counting their partner's pulse rate for 15-sec intervals. The cadence of 22 steps/min for women is established by setting the metronome at 88 beats/min. For men, the cadence is 24 steps/min (metronome setting 96). A demonstration is given and then subjects practice at the required cadence for 15 sec.

The test consists of stepping up and down on the bleacher step for 3 min. At the end of this period, the subjects remain standing while the partners count their pulse rate for a 15-sec interval beginning 5 sec after the cessation of exercise. The counters and steppers then exchange places and the test is repeated.

Scoring: The 15-sec pulse count is multiplied by 4 to express the score in beats per minute. McArdle and associates (1973) established norms for 300 women at Queens College (Table 9.6). Table 9.7 shows norms for 100 physical education majors at Louisiana State University. Equations for predicting maximal oxygen consumption have been developed for both women and men as follows:[1]

VO_2 max (ml/kg/min) (women) $= 65.81 - .185$ (pulse rate beats/min)

VO_2 max (ml/kg/min) (men) $= 111.33 - .42$ (pulse rate beats/min)

Additional Pointers:

1.   With practice, subjects can be trained to take their own pulse rate.

2.   Subjects should refrain from talking after exercise until the pulse counting is completed.

3.   The tester may elect to call out the cadence "up, up, down, down" rather than amplify the metronome, or the entire test procedure and instructions may be recorded on tape.

LSU Step Test (Nelson 1976)

Objective: To measure heart rate response to submaximal exercise; to provide students with a graphic illustration of heart rate adjustments to exercise and recovery.

---

1. Katch, F. I., and W. D. McArdle, *Nutrition, Weight Control and Exercise.* Boston: Houghton Mifflin, 1977, p. 289.

Table 9.6. Percentile Norms for Pulse Rate in Beats per Minute for Queens College Step Test From 300 College Women

PERCENTILE	PULSE RATE	PERCENTILE	PULSE RATE
100	128	45	168
95	140	40	170
90	148	35	171
85	152	30	172
80	156	25	176
75	158	20	180
70	160	15	182
65	162	10	184
60	163	5	196
55	164	0	216
50	166		

Source: Adapted from W. D. McArdle, G. S. Pechar, F. I. Katch, and J. R. Magel, "Percentile Norms for a Valid Step Test in College Women." *Research Quarterly* 44:498–500, December 1973, published by AAHPERD.

Table 9.7. Percentile Norms for Pulse Rate in Beats per Minute for Queens College Step Test From 100 Women Physical Education Majors[a]

PERCENTILE	PULSE RATE	PERCENTILE	PULSE RATE
100	110	45	149
95	119	40	152
90	126	35	154
85	131	30	156
80	134	25	160
75	137	20	163
70	139	15	166
65	141	10	170
60	144	5	177
55	146	0	188
50	148		

[a]Women from Louisiana State University, Baton Rouge, 1978.

Sex: Both males and females.

Age: Grades 9 to 12 and adults.

Validity and Reliability: Construct validity has been demonstrated through experimental research. The constructs were that resting heart rate, heart rate immediately after exercise, and heart rate during recovery are indicators of cardiorespiratory fitness and may be modified through conditioning. The sensitivity of the test in detecting changes resulting from a conditioning program was evidenced in a study involving university scuba diving classes in which the subjects trained by swimming a conditioning circuit (Patterson and Nelson 1976). Significant reductions in heart rate were found for each of the five pulse counts following a 6-week conditioning period. A leveling-off effect was also noted between the end of the circuit training and the end of a 7-week period of less strenuous activity.

Test–retest reliability coefficients for the five pulse counts have been reported as follows: before exercise, .86; 5 sec after exercise, .88; 1 min after exercise, .85; 2 min after exercise, .87; and 3 min after exercise, .80.

Equipment and Materials: Benches, chairs, or bleachers (the height may vary but most chairs and bleachers are approximately 17 or 18 in. high); a stopwatch; and a metronome (helpful in establishing cadence).

Directions: It is recommended that half of a class or group of subjects be tested at a time so the other half can serve as counters. Subjects should pair up, and practice should be allowed for finding the pulse and counting pulse rate. When bleachers or chairs are used, it is advisable that the counters sit or stand behind the steppers and that they use the carotid artery for the pulse counting. The steppers are also encouraged to count their own pulse using the radial artery.

After the students, while seated, have practiced finding the pulse and counting pulse rate for several minutes, the *before exercise* pulse rate is taken. This is done by taking at least three consecutive 10-sec counts until the pulse rate has stabilized and the tester is satisfied that the counters are competent in the pulse-counting procedure.

The steppers then stand in front of the bench and, on the command, begin stepping at the cadence of 24 steps/min for females and 30 steps/min for males. The cadence should be established with a metronome by multiplying the desired steps per minute by 4 (i.e., the metronome is set at 96 for 24 steps/min and at 120 for 30 steps/min). After the 2 min of stepping, the commands *"stop, sit down, find your pulse"* are given, and after 5 sec has elapsed, a 10-sec pulse count is taken.

Three recovery pulse counts are then taken (each for 10 sec) at 1 min, 2 min, and 3 min after exercise.

Following the third recovery pulse count, the steppers and counters change places and the test is given again to the new steppers.

The following are the directions to be read to students. (You may wish to modify the language in keeping with the level of your subjects.)

Today we are going to take a test that is designed to reflect your cardiorespiratory fitness. This refers to your body's ability to adjust to exercise and then recover. You know that when you exercise, such as when you run, play a sport, or dance vigorously, your heart beats faster and then it gradually slows down afterward. If you are in good shape—have good cardiorespiratory fitness—you can exercise longer and harder than someone who is not in as good shape, and also you can recover faster.

We will count our pulse rate before exercise, then step up and down on a bench for 2 (or 3) minutes, and then count our pulse immediately afterward, then again at 1, 2, and 3 minutes after exercise to see how quickly the pulse rate returns to normal. Talking, laughing, and moving about will cause the heart rate to fluctuate. Therefore, it is very important that you sit down right away after exercise and remain quiet for the 3 minutes during which the pulse counts are taken.

When counting pulse rate, if you feel a beat at the same instant that you are told to begin counting, count that beat as zero.

Later you will plot your pulse rates on a graph so you can see how your heart adjusts to exercise and recovers.

Scoring: The five 10-sec pulse counts are recorded on the score sheet. The 10-sec counts are then multiplied by 6 to express the scores in beats per minute (Table 9.8). The beats-per-minute scores

Table 9.8. Norms for Heart Rate in Beats per Minute for LSU Step Test for College Students Before and After 15-Week Conditioning Program

PERCENTILE		SCORE				
		Before Exercise	5-Sec After Exercise	1-Min After Exercise	2-Min After Exercise	3-Min After Exercise
		WOMEN (NO. = 121)				
75	Before conditioning	78	162	114	96	90
	After conditioning	72	150	102	84	78
50	Before conditioning	90	174	126	114	96
	After conditioning	78	162	114	96	90
25	Before conditioning	102	180	138	120	114
	After conditioning	90	174	126	108	102
		MEN (NO. = 105)				
75	Before conditioning	72	150	96	78	78
	After conditioning	66	138	90	72	72
50	Before conditioning	78	162	120	96	90
	After conditioning	72	150	102	84	78
25	Before conditioning	84	174	126	108	96
	After conditioning	78	162	114	96	90

are plotted on each student's graph to provide a picture of the pulse rate adjustments to exercise (Figure 9.3).

Conditioning effects can be dramatically demonstrated by plotting subsequent test results on the same graph following a conditioning program.

Additional Pointers:

1. As with most step tests, it is advisable to record the entire test on tape. This frees the tester to concentrate on supervisory functions rather than being enslaved by the stopwatch.

2. A 3-min test can be given if a longer test is deemed more appropriate. However, the correlations between the 2-min version and 3-min version have been found to be quite high and no significant differences have been evidenced between the two versions on the construct validity parameters.

3. For best results, one day should be allowed for students to practice and become familiar with the procedures, the test being given the next session.

4. The test and analysis of the scores on the graphs usually stimulate a number of questions. This is thus a "teachable moment" for discussion of basic exercise physiology.

5. Stress to subjects the critical importance of finding the pulse rate quickly, especially immediately after the exercise. Also stress the importance of keeping quiet and not talking, laughing, or getting up from their seat after the exercise. Explain that these will greatly affect the pulse rate and result in their having to take the test again.

Harvard Step Test (Brouha 1943)

Objective: To measure physical fitness for muscular work and the ability to recover from work.

Sex and Age Level: Originally designed for young men of college age.

Validity: Brouha tested 2200 men students at Harvard University in the original validation of the step test. Athletes were found to score considerably higher than nonathletes, and their scores improved during training and decreased after training. Taddonio and Karpovich also found evidence supporting its validity.

Equipment and Materials: A stable bench or platform 20 in. high and a watch with a second hand. A large wall clock with a second hand may be used effectively for group testing.

Directions: The cadence is 30 steps/min. The body should be erect when the subject steps onto

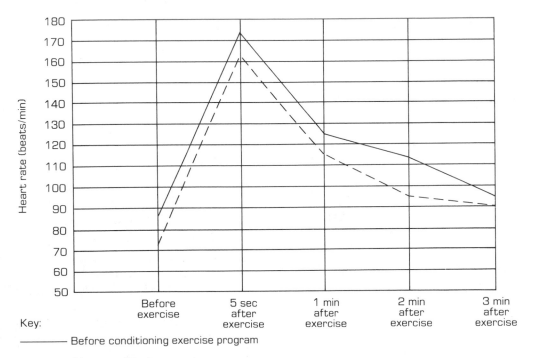

Key:

——————— Before conditioning exercise program

— — — — — After conditioning exercise program

Figure 9.3. Graph showing improvement in cardiorespiratory fitness in college women after a 15-week conditioning exercise program as reflected by the Louisiana State University Step Test. Data from Table 9.8, percentile 50

the bench. The subject continues to exercise at the prescribed cadence for 5 min unless he must stop earlier because of exhaustion. As soon as he stops exercising, he sits down and remains seated and quiet throughout the pulse counts.

There are two forms of the test, the long form and the short form. In the long form the pulse is counted 1 to 1½, 2 to 2½, and 3 to 3½ min after exercise. In the short form the pulse is taken only once, 1 to 1½ min after exercise.

Scoring: For the long form, a physical efficiency index (PEI) is computed with this formula:

$$PEI = \frac{\text{duration of exercise in seconds} \times 100}{2 \times \text{sum of pulse counts in recovery}}$$

Example: A subject exercises for the full 5 min (300 sec). His pulse counts are 83 for 1 to 1½ min; 67 for 2 to 2½ min; and 50 for 3 to 3½ min after exercise. His PEI score is

$$PEI = \frac{300 \times 100}{2 \times 200} = \frac{30,000}{400} = 75$$

The following standards of performance were established after the testing of approximately 8000 college students:

Below 55: Poor
55 to 64: Low average
65 to 79: High average
80 to 89: Good
Above 90: Excellent

For the short form, the scoring formula is as follows:

$$PEI = \frac{\text{duration of exercise in seconds} \times 100}{5.5 \times \text{pulse count for 1 to 1½ min after exercise}}$$

A table for scoring the short form of the Harvard Step Test has been developed (Table 9.9). The score in arbitrary units is based on duration of exercise and the rate of the recovery pulse. The following norms have been established for interpretation:

Below 50: Poor
50-80: Average
Above 80: Good

Additional Pointers:

1. The short form correlates highly with the long form and, in the interest of time, may be preferable to the long form.

2. During the exercise, the tester can help the subject to maintain the cadence by calling out "up, up, down, down." Even more effective is playing of a tape recording of the cadence. This allows the tester to supervise all aspects of the testing more closely.

3. When a subject is forced to stop prior to the end of the 5 min, it is imperative that the duration of exercise be recorded and that timing for the pulse taking after exercise be started. A large wall clock with a second hand is valuable in such a case. It is a simple matter for the counter to record the time at the start of the exercise and when the subject is forced to stop, to begin taking the pulse a minute afterward for 30 sec, and so on. Trained assistants may also serve in this capacity.

Safety Precautions:

1. The principal safety factor is inherent in the test itself—which is that the test is rather strenuous and might be dangerous for someone in poor health. This underlies the importance of medical examinations for all students and cautions against giving the step test to persons known to have some abnormalities.

2. About the only other safety precaution involves the possibility of the subject missing his footing and hitting his knee against the bench. Padding of some kind is recommended. Sometimes a mat folded over a bench or bleacher will provide the exact 20-in. height as well as serve as protective padding.

Cardiovascular Efficiency Test for Girls and Women (Hodgkins and Skubic 1963; Skubic 1964)

Skubic and Hodgkins conducted extensive research with junior and senior high school girls and college women throughout the United States. They established national norms for cardiorespiratory efficiency.

Sex and Age Level: Junior high school girls, senior high school girls, and college women.

Validity and Reliability: Norms were prepared from 686 junior high school girls and 1332 senior high school girls from 55 secondary schools, and from 2360 college women from 66 colleges. The test successfully differentiated among sedentary, active, and well-trained subjects. A reliability coefficient of .82 was reported using the test–retest method (Skubic and Hodgkins 1963).

Equipment and Materials: An 18-in. bench and a stopwatch or wall clock with second hand.

Directions: The same basic directions are followed as for the Harvard Step Test. The differences are that the cadence is 24 steps/min instead of 30, the bench is 18 in. high instead of 20, and the maximum duration of exercise is 3 min instead of 5. Only one pulse count is taken. The pulse rate is felt at the carotid artery and is counted from 1 to 1½ min after exercise. The same procedures apply for a subject who stops before the end of the 3 min as in the Harvard test: The time is noted and the pulse is counted for 30 sec, starting 1 min after cessation of stepping.

Scoring: The following formula is employed in computing the subject's cardiorespiratory efficiency score:

$$\frac{\text{number of seconds completed} \times 100}{\text{recovery pulse} \times 5.6}$$

Example: A junior high school girl exercises for the full 3 min (180 sec). Her recovery pulse count measured from 1 to 1½ min after exercise is 55. Her cardiorespiratory efficiency score is

$$\frac{180 \times 100}{5.6 \times 55} = \frac{18,000}{308} = 58.4 \text{ (round off to 58)}$$

Norms for junior high school girls, senior high school girls, and college women are presented in Table 9.10.

Additional Pointers: Essentially the same as for the Harvard Step Test.

Safety Precautions: Essentially the same as for the Harvard Step Test.

SOME POINTS ON PULSE COUNTING

The pulse for step tests is usually counted at the radial or carotid artery. In both cases, two or three fingers should be used to feel the pulse rather than the thumb, owing to possible confusion arising from the counter feeling his or her own pulse transmitted through the thumb. The carotid artery is located immediately below the angle of the jaw. The radial pulse can be counted in the hollow on the thumb side of the wrist about an inch from the base of the thumb.

It is important that the counter not press too hard on the carotid artery so that a reaction to pressure does not produce an alteration in the beat. A beat felt at the moment the signal to start counting is given should be designated zero. It should be pointed out that a mistake of one pulse count represents a 6-beat error in a 10-sec pulse count, 4 beats in a 15-sec count, and so on.

The person whose pulse is being counted must remain silent and refrain from laughing or talking, since this affects pulse rate. If two people count the same person's pulse, some criterion needs to be established for cases where the two counters disagree. A maximum allowable difference might be set (depending on the length of the counting interval). If the difference is more than that set, the subject must be retested. A practical exception would be when one of the counters admits that he or she simply lost count.

Obviously, the keys to accurate testing and pulse counting are orientation to the test and the counting procedures and practice.

Resting Heart Rate

Resting heart rate is difficult to determine, that is, many factors can influence heart rate at any given time. Such factors include temperature, humidity, previous activity, emotions, time since eating, smoking, fatigue, and infection. Resting heart rate is more variable than exercise or recovery heart rate. Therefore, caution must be used in evaluating pulse counts.

As mentioned previously, resting heart rate is indicative of physical fitness from the standpoint that resting heart rate is usually lowered as a result of aerobic conditioning. For example, distance runners tend to have low resting heart rates. Apparently, however, some individuals inherit relatively high or low heart rates that seem to resist changes.

With due recognition of the limitations of resting pulse counts, the following sitting pulse rate test is presented:

Example: A stopwatch or wristwatch with a second hand is the only equipment needed. The students rest in a sitting position for several minutes while the tester explains pulse-counting procedures. The students are allowed several minutes to practice counting their own and each other's pulse rates.

The students are divided into pairs of the same sex. On signal, they count each other's pulse for 1 min.

A reliability coefficient of .83 was found for college men and women. An objectivity coefficient of .94 was obtained when testers measured the same subjects and recorded the scores independently. Table 9.11 presents some norms for college men and women.

Table 9.9. Scoring for the Harvard Step Test

DURATION OF EFFORT (MIN)	TOTAL HEARTBEATS 1½ MIN IN RECOVERY											
	40–44	45–49	50–54	55–59	60–64	65–69	70–74	75–79	80–84	85–89	90–94	95–99
	Score (Arbitrary Units)											
Under ½	6	6	5	5	4	4	4	4	3	3	3	3
½ –1	19	17	16	14	13	12	11	11	10	9	9	8
1 –1½	32	29	26	24	22	20	19	18	17	16	15	14
1½–2	45	41	38	34	31	29	27	25	23	22	21	20
2 –2½	58	52	47	43	40	36	34	32	30	28	27	25
2½–3	71	64	58	53	48	45	42	39	37	34	33	31
3 –3½	84	75	68	62	57	53	49	46	43	41	39	37
3½–4	97	87	79	72	66	61	57	53	50	47	45	42
4 –4½	110	98	89	82	75	70	65	61	57	54	51	48
4½–5	123	110	100	91	84	77	72	68	63	60	57	54
Over 5	129	116	105	96	88	82	76	71	67	63	60	56

Source: C. F. Conzolazio, R. E. Johnson, and L. J. Pecora, *Physiological Measurements of Metabolic Function in Man.* New York: McGraw-Hill, 1963. Used by permission.

Table 9.10. Norms (Pulse Rate in Beats per Min) for Cardiovascular Efficiency Test, Girls and Women

RATING	JUNIOR H.S. AGE[a]		SENIOR H.S. AGE[a]		COLLEGE AGE[b]	
	Cardiovascular Efficiency Score	30-Sec Recovery Pulse	Cardiovascular Efficiency Score	30-Sec Recovery Pulse	Cardiovascular Efficiency Score	30-Sec Recovery Pulse
Excellent	72–100	44 and below	71–100	45 and below	71–100	43 and below
Very good	62– 71	45–52	60– 70	46–54	60– 70	44– 54
Good	51– 61	53–63	49– 59	55–66	49– 59	55– 66
Fair	41– 50	64–79	40– 48	67–80	39– 48	67– 83
Poor	31– 40	80–92	31– 39	81–96	28– 38	84–116
Very poor	0– 30	93 and above	0– 30	97 and above	0– 27	117–120

[a]Source: Reproduced from V. Skubic and J. Hodgkins, "Cardiovascular Efficiency Test Scores for Junior and Senior High School Girls in the United States." *Research Quarterly* 35:184–192, May 1964, published by AAHPERD. Used by permission.

[b]Source: Extracted from J. Hodgkins and V. Skubic, "Cardiovascular Efficiency Test Scores for College Women in the United States." *Research Quarterly* 34:454–461, December 1963, published by AAHPERD. Used by permission.

Table 9.11. Resting Heart Rate in Beats per Minute[a]

PERFORMANCE LEVEL	HEART RATE	
	Men	Women
Excellent	53 and below	56 and below
Good	60–54	64–57
Fair	65–61	71–65
Poor	75–66	79–72
Very poor	76 and above	80 and above

[a]Based on the scores of 200 college men and 200 college women, Corpus Christi State University, Corpus Christi, Tex., 1976.

BLOOD PRESSURE MEASUREMENT

The measurement of systolic and diastolic blood pressure is relatively simple; however, like most testing, considerable practice is required for proficiency. The cuff of the sphygmomanometer is wrapped around the subject's bare arm above the elbow. The earphones of the stethoscope are placed in the tester's ears and the bell of the stethoscope is placed on the subject's brachial artery just above the hollow of the elbow. The cuff is pumped up until the artery has been collapsed, that is, until no pulse can be heard. Pressure is then slowly released as the tester watches the gauge or mercury column. When the first sound of the pulse is heard, the reading in millimeters of mercury at that instant is recorded as the *systolic* pressure. The tester continues to slowly release pressure until a very dull, weak beat is noted. At that instant the pressure in millimeters of mercury is noted; this pressure represents the *diastolic* pressure. The measures are recorded with the systolic pressure first, then the diastolic pressure. A typical reading is 120/80 or 125/75.

Table 9.12 presents some norms for systolic and diastolic pressures based on a physician's records. It is recommended that pressures be taken after the subject has been sitting quietly for about 30 min and that the median of three trials be taken as the score.

FINDINGS AND CONCLUSIONS FROM CARDIORESPIRATORY FITNESS TEST RESEARCH

Differences of opinion have been expressed concerning the significance of pulse rate measurements before, during, and after exercise. Tuttle contended that it was necessary to obtain a ratio of resting pulse rate to pulse rate after exercise. Brouha, in developing the Harvard Step Test, stated that initial or preexercise pulse rate is relatively unimportant and only the recovery pulse rate need be considered. Henry concluded that a decrease in heart rate is an effective measure of change in athletic conditioning and that the resting pulse rate has validity as an indirect indication of condition. Conger and MacNab found the preexercise heart rate and the postexercise heart rate of women participants in intercollegiate sports were significantly lower than those of nonparticipants. Pollock, Broida, and Kendrick concluded that the palpation technique for estimating heart rate can be used with acceptable accuracy.

In general, correlations among various tests of cardiorespiratory condition have been quite low. Several explanations have been suggested, such as the fact that the scoring systems are different. In addition, some use preexercise pulse rates, some use postexercise rates, and some employ both. The differing relationships between preexercise and postexercise pulse rate following different degrees of work also have been suggested as possible cause for the lack of relationship among tests. Clark found that recovery pulse rate increased in proportion to the duration of exercise up to 2 min of exercise. After that point the increase in recovery pulse rate diminished markedly in magnitude.

Farrell, Wilmore, and Coyle reported that heart rate corresponding to a standardized treadmill velocity is only a moderately good predictor of running performance.

Franklin, Hodgson, and Buskirk determined the regression line for percent relative oxygen uptake on relative heart rate among women of various ages, body fatness, and maximum oxygen consumption. The linear relationship was similar for men and women; thus, a common regression equation can be employed for exercise prescription. The large individual variability suggests that the relative metabolic work load and the conditioning response may differ considerably among individuals trained at a given percent of maximum heart rate.

Table 9.12. Systolic–Diastolic Blood Pressure Scale

RATING	SYSTOLIC	DIASTOLIC
Excellent	112 and below	77 and below
Good	120–113	80–78
Fair	129–121	86–81
Poor	140–130	96–87
Very poor	141 and above	97 and above

Katch, Sady, and Freedson assessed the biological variability in maximum aerobic power and pointed out the necessity for securing control data when attempting to study training effects.

Freedson and associates found that younger children attained steady-state oxygen consumption on a constant-load submaximum bicycle ergometer test more quickly than older children.

Eisenman and Golding found that the magnitude and rate of improvement in aerobic capacity resulting from a 14-week training program were similar for girls 12 to 13 years of age and for young women 18 to 21 years of age.

Burke (1977) compared males and females after an 8-week training program in which all subjects exercised at a heart rate 75% to 85% of maximum with total distance run held equal. It was concluded that while hereditary factors may limit the potential of females in relation to males, the average female can expect relative improvement in aerobic power similar to that of the male.

Conley and colleagues reported that trained, experienced female runners operate at a percentage of their VO_2 max similar to that of trained male runners.

Powers, Riley, and Howley found no differences in fat metabolism between sexes during prolonged aerobic running at moderate intensity when subjects were matched according to VO_2 max and amount of endurance running. Both men and women show a progressive increase in the percent of energy metabolism derived from fat oxidation as the duration of the run increases.

Cooper did extensive research in an attempt to establish a rating scale for measuring relative values of activities in terms of cardiorespiratory conditioning. His research showed the importance of such activities as running, swimming, cycling, walking, handball, basketball, and squash in the development of cardiorespiratory endurance. Cooper advocated a simple 12-minute run–walk scoring scale for people to evaluate their own condition. Doolittle and Bigbee reported that the 12-minute run–walk had a high correlation ($r = .90$) with maximum oxygen intake and was thus a highly valid and reliable indicator of cardiorespiratory fitness.

The validity of distance runs has been tested in several studies. With college men, Disch, Frankiewicz, and Jackson found through factor analysis that tests of distance longer than 1 mi tended to be loaded almost exclusively on the distance run factor, while shorter distance tests yielded complex factor structures. Jackson and

Coleman administered distance runs of 3, 6, 9, and 12 min duration to 866 boys and 803 girls. Factor analysis supported the construct validity of distance runs, with the 9- and 12-minute runs deemed most suitable. Both runs were significantly related to maximum oxygen uptake, with no appreciable difference between the 9- and 12-minute runs.

With maximal oxygen consumption as the criterion, the validity of timed distance runs of 600 yd, three-quarters of a mile, and a mile for 8-year-olds was investigated by Krahenbuhl and colleagues. Boys exceeded girls in maximal oxygen consumption and had faster times in the two longer runs. The mile run was found to be the best predictor of maximal oxygen consumption in the boys, but none of the three distances was suitable for the girls.

Researchers have found a wide range of validity coefficients between various distance runs and maximal oxygen consumption (Burke 1976; Katch et al. 1973a; Mayhew and Andrew 1975; Shaver 1972). Although exercise physiologists maintain that longer distance runs are more valid than shorter runs, pacing and practice have a vast influence on the validity and reliability of the longer runs (Katch et al. 1973b). Dorociak and Nelson found that when body weight is accounted for, the validity of the 1- and 2-mile runs is too low for predictive values for college women when VO_2 max is the criterion. These results were in agreement with those of Katch and associates (1973a). Conversely, Getchell and Cleary studied lean, well-conditioned female subjects and obtained a correlation of .91 between VO_2 max and the 1.5-mile run.

Numerous studies have shown that conditioning programs improve scores on cardiorespiratory fitness tests. This improvement has been in the form of lowered pulse rates, higher resting stroke volumes, and increased resting cardiac output.

The intensity, frequency, and duration of exercise are important variables in bringing about improvements in cardiorespiratory condition. A number of studies have been devoted to the manipulation of these variables. Karvonen concluded that an intensity threshold level of at least 60% of the difference between resting and maximum heart rates was necessary for significant improvement in cardiorespiratory condition. Davis and Convertino compared different indices of predicting endurance training intensity. They found that the Karvonen method yielded more accurate prediction of exercise intensities than did use of a percentage of maximal heart rate, which tended to overpredict intensities.

Gettman and associates (1976) compared the physiologic responses of adult men in 1-, 3-, and 5-days/week training programs. Significant improvements were realized in resting and recovery heart rates, treadmill performance time, VO_2 max, maximum O_2 pulse, and V_E max. The degree of improvement was in direct proportion to frequency of training. Moffatt, Stamford, and Neill found significant improvement in aerobic capacity in college men who trained 3 days/week for 10 weeks. The amount of improvement did not differ whether the subjects exercised 3 consecutive days each week or skipped a day between exercise days.

Milesis and colleagues measured the effects of 15, 30, and 45 min of conditioning on cardiorespiratory fitness variables, body composition, pulmonary function, and serum lipids. Improvements in treadmill performance time, VO_2 max, maximum O_2 pulse, and diastolic blood pressure were in proportion to duration of the training sessions. Crews and Roberts studied the interaction of frequency and intensity of training on the physical work capacity and cardiorespiratory function of men. They found no interaction effect. However, subjects who trained at a heart rate of 150 beats/min showed greater training effects than those who trained at a heart rate of 120 beats/min, and both 5- and 3-days/week groups had significantly greater gains in work capacity scores than the 1-day/week group. No difference was found between 5- and 3-days/week groups.

A study by Cunningham and Hill supported the contention that the more sedentary the subjects, the greater the gains in aerobic power. The gains occurred rapidly and were most notable after the initial 9 weeks of training. These investigators concluded that short-term gains in aerobic power reflect changes in stroke volume, whereas long-term training programs may result in both increased stroke volume and peripheral adaptation.

The results of a study by Hickson and associates indicated that unless the training stimulus is progressively increased, a daily high-intensity exercise program becomes a maintenance program without any further increase in VO_2 max after 3 weeks.

Hickson and Rosenkoetter reported that the VO_2 max values produced by a 10-week endurance training program could be maintained for 15 weeks when the frequency of training was reduced from 6 days/week to 4 or 2 days/week. The authors concluded that more exercise is required to increase cardiorespiratory fitness than is required to maintain it at the training level.

A bench-stepping exercise was given female subjects by Andzel and Gutin until a heart rate of 140 beats/min was achieved. After the exercise the subjects were given no rest, 30 sec rest, or 60 sec rest before starting a 10-min stepping task. Performances following the 30- and 60-sec rest periods were significantly better than those of controls who had no prior exercise or of those who had no rest following prior exercise. The improvement in performance was attributed to the mobilization of the oxygen transport system.

Siebers and McMurray compared the effects of swimming or walking during recovery following 2 min of exercise at 90% VO_2 max on a subsequent 200-yd swim for time. Neither mode of recovery significantly influenced the swimming performance. The authors concluded that 15 min of recovery may be adequate between high-intensity exercise bouts lasting 3 min or less.

Many studies also have been undertaken to investigate the comparative contributions of different activities in improving cardiorespiratory fitness. Kozar and Hunsicker studied the relative strenuousness of six sports as measured by telemetered heart rates. They found that while there were no differences among handball, paddleball, tennis, and badminton, these four activities were superior to volleyball and bowling. Volleyball, in turn, produced higher heart rates than bowling.

Wilmore and colleagues compared bicycling, tennis, and jogging on increases in VO_2 max. Bicycling and jogging provided comparable physiologic benefits. Tennis produced only modest increases in endurance capacity.

Pollock and associates (1975) compared the training effects of running, walking, and bicycling on cardiovascular function. All three programs produced significant improvement. Training effects were independent of mode of training when frequency, duration, and intensity were held constant.

Pollock, Jackson, and Pate (1980) used discriminant analysis of the physiologic differences between good and elite distance runners. The elite runners significantly differed from the good runners in general physiologic efficiency. The marathon runners had lower lactic acid submaximal values and the middle-long distance runners had the highest VO_2 max values.

Cardiorespiratory responses of elite ballet

dancers were studied by Cohen and associates. The authors concluded that the static nature of ballet exercise in conjunction with the sprint, or burstlike, nonendurance component of ballet tends to stimulate aerobic capacity only modestly. Hence, the VO_2 max values of elite ballet dancers are within the range of nonendurance athletes.

Sinning and Adrian reported that the training program during a women's basketball season was not strenuous enough for the subjects to reach maximum physical work capacity. McArdle, Magel, and Kyvallos also reported nonsignificant changes in body weight, heart rate, and VO_2 max during a season for a women's college basketball team.

Several studies have measured the physiologic effects of rope skipping. Jette, Mongeon, and Routhier; Getchell and Cleary; and Quirk and Sinning concluded that rope skipping is too strenuous to be recommended for sedentary subjects. Myles, Dick, and Jantti compared the effects of different rope skipping styles and rates on heart rate. Their results suggested that a training program using the rhythm hop and rhythm leap can be recommended for individuals up to middle age. All subjects were able to skip continuously for at least 10 min.

Seals and Mullin reported that athletes in sports demanding heavy upper body conditioning were able to attain higher VO_2 max values than untrained individuals in exercise involving upper body musculature.

Hickson, Rosenkoetter, and Brown studied the effects of leg strength training on aerobic power and short-term endurance. Time to exhaustion was significantly increased, but nonsignificant increases in VO_2 were reported.

Gettman, Ward, and Hagan reported significant gains in VO_2 max and other parameters of fitness following a 12-week conditioning program in which males and females participated in one of two training groups: a combined weight-training and running program or a circuit weight-training program. No differences were found between the two groups.

Shvartz compared the effects of isotonic and isometric exercises on heart rate. He found that isometric exercise performed for 45 sec at one-half maximum resistance stimulated the heart rate to the same extent as isotonic exercise of similar intensity and duration. He also reported that maximum isometric tension resulted in nearly a two-fold increase in heart rate.

Crowder found that regular sauna treatments resulted in significant improvement in cardiovas-cular efficiency as measured by the Harvard Step Test. Spears reported that exposure to sauna treatments significantly lowered resting pulse rate, blood pressure, body temperature, and metabolism but that these changes quickly disappeared when the training program was interrupted. Falls determined that cold showers taken as long as 20 min before exercise significantly reduced exercise and recovery heart rates associated with submaximal exercise.

BIBLIOGRAPHY

AAHPERD Health Related Physical Fitness Test Manual. Reston, Va.: AAHPERD, 1980.

AAHPERD Youth Fitness Test Manual. Reston, Va.: AAHPERD, 1976.

Andzel, W. D., and B. Gutin, "Prior Exercise and Endurance Performance: A Test of the Mobilization Hypothesis." *Research Quarterly* 47:269–276, May 1976.

Biasiotto, J., and D. Cotten, "Validity of 600-Yard Run-Walk for Elementary School Males." Unpublished study, Georgia Southern College, Statesboro, 1972.

Brouha, L., "The Step Test: A Simple Method of Measuring Physical Fitness for Muscular Work in Young Men." *Research Quarterly* 14:31–36, March 1943.

Burke, E. J., "Validity of Selected Laboratory and Field Tests of Physical Working Capacity." *Research Quarterly* 47:95–104, March 1976.

———, "Physiological Effects of Similar Training Programs on Males and Females." *Research Quarterly* 48:510–517, October 1977.

Clark, J. W., "The Relationship of Initial Pulse Rate, Recovery Pulse Rate, Recovery Index and Subjective Appraisal of Physical Condition After Various Deviations of Work." Unpublished master's thesis, Louisiana State University, Baton Rouge, 1966.

Cohen, J. L., K. R. Segal, I. Witriol, and W. D. McArdle, "Cardiorespiratory Responses to Ballet Exercise and the VO_2 max of Elite Ballet Dancers." *Medicine and Science in Sports and Exercise* 14:213–217, 1982.

Coleman, A. E., and A. S. Jackson, "Two Procedures for Administering the 12-Minute Run." *JOHPER* 45:60–62, February 1974.

Conger, P. R., and R. B. J. MacNab, "Strength, Body Composition, and Work Capacity of Participants and Non-participants in Women's Intercollegiate Sports." *Research Quarterly* 38:184–192, May 1967.

Conley, D. L., G. S. Krahenbuhl, L. N. Burkett, and A. L. Millar, "Physiological Correlates of Female Road Racing Performance." *Research Quarterly for Exercise and Sport* 52:441–448, December 1981.

Cooper, K. H., *Aerobics*. New York: Bantam Books, 1968.

Cotten, D. J., "A Modified Step Test for Group Cardiovascular Testing." *Research Quarterly* 42:91–95, March 1971.

Crews, T. R., and J. A. Roberts, "Effects of Interaction of Frequency and Intensity of Training." *Research Quarterly* 47:48–55, March 1976.

Crowder, V. R., "A Study to Determine the Effects of the Sauna Bath on Cardiovascular Efficiency." Unpublished doctoral dissertation, Louisiana State University, Baton Rouge, 1969.

Cunningham, D. A., and J. S. Hill, "Effect of Training on Cardiovascular Response to Exercise in Women." *Journal of Applied Physiology* 39:891–895, December 1975.

Custer, S. J., and E. C. Chaloupka, "Relationship Between Predicted Maximal Oxygen Consumption and Running Performance of College Females." *Research Quarterly* 48:47–50, March 1977.

Davis, J. A., and V. A. Convertino, "A Comparison of Heart Rate Methods for Predicting Endurance Training Intensity." *Medicine and Science in Sports* 7:295–298, Winter 1975.

Disch, J., R. Frankiewicz, and A. Jackson, "Construct Validity of Distance Run Tests." *Research Quarterly* 46:169–176, May 1975.

Doolittle, T. L., and R. Bigbee, "The Twelve-Minute Run-Walk: A Test of Cardiorespiratory Fitness of Adolescent Boys." *Research Quarterly* 39:491–495, October 1968.

Dorociak, J. J., and J. K. Nelson, "The 1 Mile and 2 Mile Runs as Measures of Cardiovascular Fitness in College Women." *Journal of Sports Medicine and Physical Fitness* 23:322–325, September 1983.

Eisenman, P. A., and L. A. Golding, "Comparison of Effects of Training on VO_2 max in Girls and Young Women." *Medicine and Science in Sports* 7:136–138, Summer 1975.

Falls, H. B., "Circulatory Response to Cold Showers: Effect of Varied Time Lapses Before Exercise." *Research Quarterly* 40:45–49, March 1969.

Farrell, P. A., J. H. Wilmore, and E. F. Coyle, "Exercise Heart Rate as a Predictor of Running Performance." *Research Quarterly for Exercise and Sport* 51:417–421, May 1980.

Franklin, B. A., J. Hodgson, and E. R. Buskirk, "Relationship Between Percent Maximal O_2 Uptake and Percent Maximal Heart Rate in Women." *Research Quarterly for Exercise and Sport* 51:616–624, December 1980.

Freedson, P. S., T. B. Gilliam, S. P. Sady, and V. L. Katch, "Transient VO_2 Characteristics in Children at the Onset of Steady-Rate Exercise." *Research Quarterly for Exercise and Sport* 52:167–173, May 1981.

Getchell, B., and P. Cleary, "The Caloric Costs of Rope Skipping and Running." *Physician and Sportsmedicine* 8:56–60, February 1980.

Gettman, L. R., et al., "Physiological Responses of Men to 1-, 3-, and 5-Day-per-Week Training Programs." *Research Quarterly* 47:638–646, December 1976.

———, P. Ward, and R. D. Hagan, "A Comparison of Combined Running and Weight Training With Circuit Weight Training." *Medicine and Science in Sports and Exercise* 14:229–234, 1982.

Henry, F. M., "Influence of Athletic Training on the Resting Cardiovascular System." *Research Quarterly* 25:28–41, March 1954.

Hickson, R. C., J. M. Hagberg, A. A. Ehsani, and J. O. Holloszy, "Time Course of the Adaptive Responses of Aerobic Power and Heart Rate to Training." *Medicine and Science in Sports and Exercise* 13:17–20, 1981.

———, and M. A. Rosenkoetter, "Reduced Training Frequencies and Maintenance of Increased Aerobic Power." *Medicine and Science in Sports and Exercise* 13:13–16, 1981.

———, ———, and M. M. Brown, "Strength Training Effects on Aerobic Power and Short-Term Endurance." *Medicine and Science in Sports and Exercise* 12:336–339, 1980.

Hodgkins, J., and V. Skubic, "Cardiovascular Efficiency Scores for College Women in the United States." *Research Quarterly* 34:454–461, December 1963.

Jackson, A. S., and E. Coleman, "Validation of Distance Run Tests for Elementary School Children." *Research Quarterly* 47:86–94, March 1976.

Jette, M., J. Mongeon, and R. Routhier, "The Energy Cost of Rope Skipping." *Journal of Sports Medicine and Physical Fitness* 19:33–37, 1979.

Karvonen, M. J., "Effects of Vigorous Exercise on the Heart." In F. F. Rosenbaum and E. L. Belknap, Eds., *Work and the Heart*. New York: Paul B. Hoeber, 1959.

Katch, F. I., W. D. McArdle, R. Czula, and G. Pechar, "Maximal Oxygen Intake, Endurance

Running Performance, and Body Composition of College Women." *Research Quarterly* 44:301–312, October 1973a.

————, G. S. Pechar, W. D. McArdle, and A. L. Weltman, "Relationship Between Individual Differences in a Steady Pace Endurance Running Performance and Maximal Oxygen Intake." *Research Quarterly* 44:206–215, May 1973b.

Katch, V. L., S. P. Sady, and P. Freedson, "Biological Variability in Maximum Aerobic Power." *Medicine and Science in Sports and Exercise* 14:21–25, 1982.

Kozar, A. J., and P. Hunsicker, "A Study of Telemetered Heart Rate During Sports Participation of Young Adult Men." *Journal of Sports Medicine and Physical Fitness* 3:1–5, March 1963.

Krahenbuhl, G. S., et al., "Field Estimation of VO_2 max in Children Eight Years of Age." *Medicine and Science in Sports* 9:37–40, Spring 1977.

Kurucz, R. L., "Construction of the Ohio State University Cardiovascular Fitness Test." Unpublished doctoral dissertation, Ohio State University, Columbus, 1967.

Mayhew, J. L., and J. Andrew, "Assessment of Running Performance in College Males for Aerobic Capacity Percentage Utilization Coefficients." *Journal of Sports Medicine and Physical Fitness* 15:342–346, 1975.

McArdle, W. D., J. R. Magel Jr., and L. C. Kyvallos, "Aerobic Capacity, Heart Rate, and Estimated Energy Cost During Women's Competitive Basketball." *Research Quarterly* 42:178–186, May 1971.

————, et al., "Reliability and Interrelationships Between Maximal Oxygen Intake, Physical Work Capacity, and Step Test Scores in College Women." *Medicine and Science in Sports* 4:182–186, Winter 1972.

————, et al., "Percentile Norms for a Valid Step Test in College Women." *Research Quarterly* 44:498–500, December 1973.

Milesis, C. A., et al., "Effects of Different Durations of Physical Training on Cardio-respiratory Function, Body Composition, and Serum Lipids." *Research Quarterly* 47:716–725, December 1976.

Moffatt, R. J., B. A. Stamford, and R. D. Neill, "Placement of Tri-weekly Training Sessions: Importance Regarding Enhancement of Aerobic Capacity." *Research Quarterly* 48:583–591, October 1977.

Myles, W. S., M. R. Dick, and R. Jantti, "Heart Rate and Rope Skipping Intensity." *Research Quarterly for Exercise and Sport* 52:76–79, March 1981.

Nelson, J. K., "Fitness Testing as an Educational Process." In Jan Broekhoff, Ed., *Physical Education, Sports and the Sciences*. Eugene, Ore.: Microform Publications, 1976, pp. 65–74.

Patterson, M. L., and J. K. Nelson, "Influence of an Aquatic Conditioning Program on Selected Heart Rate Responses," *Proceedings of the International Conference on Underwater Education, San Diego, 1976*. Montclair, Calif.: National Association of Underwater Instructors.

Pollock, M. L., J. Broida, and Z. Kendrick, "Validity of the Palpation Technique of Heart Rate Determination and its Estimation of Training Heart Rate." *Research Quarterly* 43:77–81, March 1972.

————, et al., "Effects of Mode of Training on Cardiovascular Function and Body Composition of Adult Men." *Medicine and Science in Sports* 7:139–145, Summer 1975.

————, A. S. Jackson, and R. R. Pate, "Discriminant Analysis of Physiological Differences Between Good and Elite Distance Runners." *Research Quarterly for Exercise and Sport* 51:521–532, October 1980.

Powers, S. K., W. Riley, and E. T. Howley, "Comparison of Fat Metabolism Between Trained Men and Women During Prolonged Aerobic Work." *Research Quarterly for Exercise and Sport* 51:427–431, May 1980.

Quirk, J. E., and W. E. Sinning, "Anaerobic and Aerobic Responses of Males and Females to Rope Skipping." *Medicine and Science in Sports and Exercise* 14:26–29, 1982.

Seals, D. R., and J. P. Mullin, "VO_2 max in Variable Type Exercise Among Well-Trained Upper Body Athletes." *Research Quarterly for Exercise and Sport* 53:58–63, March 1982.

Shaver, L. G., "Maximum Aerobic Power and Anaerobic Work Capacity Prediction From Various Running Performances of Untrained College Men." *Research Quarterly* 43:89–93, March 1972.

Shvartz, E., "Effect of Isotonic and Isometric Exercises on Heart Rate." *Research Quarterly* 37:121–125, March 1966.

Siebers, L. S., and R. G. McMurray, "Effects of Swimming and Walking on Exercise Recovery and Subsequent Swim Performance." *Research Quarterly for Exercise and Sport* 52:68–75, March 1981.

Sinning, W. E., and M. J. Adrian, "Cardiorespiratory Changes in College Women Due to a Season of Competitive Basketball." *Journal of Applied Physiology* 25:720–724, 1968.

Skubic, V., "Cardiovascular Efficiency Test Scores for Junior and Senior High School Girls in the

United States." *Research Quarterly* 35:184–192, May 1964.

———, and J. Hodgkins, "Cardiovascular Efficiency Test for Girls and Women." *Research Quarterly* 34:191–198, May 1963.

Spears, C. D., "Analysis of Physiological Effects on College Women of Two Programs of Regular Exposures to Extreme Heat." Unpublished doctoral dissertation, Louisiana State University, Baton Rouge, 1969.

Taddonio, D. A., and P. V. Karpovich, "Endurance as Measured by the Harvard Step Test." *Research Quarterly* 22:381–384, October 1951.

Tuttle, W. W., "The Use of the Pulse-Ratio Test for Rating Physical Efficiency." *Research Quarterly* 2:5–17, May 1931.

Willgoose, C. E., and N. R. Askew, "Reliability of the 600-Yard Run-Walk Test at the Junior High School Level." *Research Quarterly* 32:264, May 1961.

Wilmore, J. H., J. A. Davis, R. S. O'Brien, P. A. Vodak, G. R. Walder, and E. A. Amsterdam, "Physiological Alterations Consequent to 20-Week Conditioning Programs of Bicycling, Tennis, and Jogging." *Medicine and Science in Sports and Exercise* 12:1–8, 1980.

CHAPTER 10

ANTHROPOMETRIC MEASUREMENT, BODY BUILD, AND BODY COMPOSITION

Anthropometric measurements have been a part of physical education since its inception in this country. The earliest research in physical education was in anthropometry, with emphasis on changes in muscle size brought about through exercise. The modern physical educator is often assigned the task of measuring height and weight of students. These measures, like any of the other measures taken in school, should be used and not merely recorded and then ignored.

The question is frequently raised, "What do you do with such measures?" "You certainly can't grade on whether a student grows or not." It is indeed true that growth does not constitute a valid criterion for grading a student. However, height, weight, and certain anthropometric measures, used in conjunction with other pertinent data, do represent potentially valuable information. The first portion of this chapter will consider the use of these measures under three general headings: classification indexes, assessment of normal growth and nutrition, and body build classifica-

tion, otherwise called somatotyping. The remainder of the chapter is devoted to the assessment of body composition through the use of underwater weighing, skin fold measurements, circumferences, and body diameters.

PROBLEMS ASSOCIATED WITH ANTHROPOMETRIC, BODY BUILD, AND BODY COMPOSITION MEASUREMENT

Undoubtedly, the major problem in the area of height and weight, body type, and body composition assessment is not in the use to which this information is put but rather in its misuse. Obviously, people come in all shapes and sizes. Some individuals seem to be all legs with a very small trunk and shoulders. Others have massive shoulders, arms, and chest and almost puny legs. Still others appear to be evenly proportioned. To judge everyone on the same standard, for example, to decide whether someone is overweight or underweight on the basis of a single factor such as height, is indeed ludicrous.

The basic purpose of classification indexes is to allow for more equal competition. These indexes are founded on the premise that older, taller, and heavier children should be stronger and more physically mature than children who are smaller and younger. This premise is not infallible, however, and body build is an important factor. An endomorph would surely not be an *equal* competitor to a mesomorph of the same age, height, and weight. Wear and Miller suggested that students with excess weight usually are doubly penalized in physical performance tests: They must perform while carrying the excess weight, and their classification index is higher than that of a lighter student of comparable age and height, which means they have to do more to achieve a similar percentile rank. Perhaps these limitations help motivate the students to shed excess pounds. On the other hand, they may have negative motivational effects by making the task seem almost hopeless.

Growth charts such as the Wetzel Grid and the Meredith graphs can be valuable tools if employed wisely. Obviously, one must recognize that there are wide differences among individuals in height, weight, and body build that are still within the limits of normal growth and maturation. The real value of these devices lies in their potential for detecting changes in growth patterns, as shown by successive plottings. Another important feature of these charts is that they allow the child to be evaluated in relation to his or her own growth pattern, rather than being compared favorably or unfavorably with someone else or by some arbitrary standard.

Among the various measures that have been used to indicate nutritional status are chest width, chest depth, chest circumference, bi-iliac hip width, trochanteric hip width, shoulder width, knee width, thigh girth, upper and lower arm girths, wrist girth, and ankle and calf girths. Fat measures are frequently taken at the abdomen, the side, the chest, the back, the arm, and the thigh. The length of the body and body segments has been measured to determine standing height, lying height, sitting height, arm length, arm span, leg length, forearm length, hand width, and finger span. Numerous other anthropometric measurements have been studied. Sargent's profile chart for appraising the physical development of college men contained 44 anthropometric measurements.

The science of somatotyping requires extensive preparation and experience. In the method devised by Sheldon, somatotyping requires exacting photography and analysis. In the more practical methods such as the Heath–Carter technique, careful anthropometric measurements are needed.

A major criticism of age–height–weight tables is that even though some allow for basic differences in body framework, they do not account for differences in proportion of muscle and fat. In the past decade or so, a great deal of attention has been directed toward the measurement of body density. From body density, percent fat and lean body weight can then be estimated. This approach is undoubtedly more sound than one that uses just height and weight. However, underwater weighing and other laboratory techniques are impractical for field tests, so estimates of body density are made with skin folds, circumferences, and diameters. As with all forms of anthropometry, such measurements require knowledge, skill, and a great deal of practice for results to be reliable. Unfortunately, there are no universal standards for the location of the various body sites, and relatively small differences in location can result in large differences in body density and percent fat predictions.

Measurement of Height

In measuring height, the only equipment and materials necessary are a flat surface against which the subject stands, a measuring tape or marked surface, and an object to place on the subject's head that forms a right angle to the wall or a backboard. If a wall is used, it should not have quarter round or wainscoting so that the subject can stand against it with heels, buttocks, upper back, and back of the head making firm contact.

For permanent mounting, the markings can be painted on the wall or backboard. Most classification devices and nutritional status instruments call for height measured to the nearest one fourth of an inch. Therefore, the scale should be marked in these units. For greater versatility and application, however, it is recommended that a parallel scale be prepared that reads in centimeters.

Frequently, weight scales have stadiometers attached consisting of a sliding calibrated rod with a hinged top piece. These sometimes are found to be unsatisfactory in cases where the top piece is loose and fails to make a right angle or when the rod sticks or perhaps is too loose.

The subject should be measured without shoes. Standing with the back against a support helps the subject to stretch to full height. The chin is tucked in slightly and the head is held erect. The object used to form a right angle to the backboard is pressed firmly on the subject's head. It must be horizontal and not tilted and the pressure must not cause the subject to slump or alter position. Finally, the subject bends the knees slightly when he or she steps away so as to not disturb the angle before the height is recorded.

Measurement of Weight

Generally speaking, scales based on the lever system are more reliable than spring scales. Both types, however, require periodic inspection and rather delicate handling.

The subject to be weighed should wear a minimum of clothing, such as only gym shorts. While more accurate results are obtained when subjects are weighed in the nude, this often is not practical or desirable. Actually, no appreciable accuracy is lost if the amount of clothing is kept consistent. Consistency is the key to all measurements. The subject should be weighed at the same time of day and to the same degree of accuracy, usually the nearest half pound (or tenth of a kilogram).

The teacher should attempt to control the weighing situation so there is minimal embarrassment on the part of students. With experience the teacher can predict the approximate body weight of students as they step to the scale. This eliminates having to jiggle the scale's sliding weights back and forth.

CLASSIFICATION INDEXES

Physical educators have long realized that the performance of boys and girls is greatly influenced by such factors as age, height, weight, and body structure. They also know that persons of the same age vary considerably in body size and shape, that individuals of the same height differ greatly in body weight, and that persons of the same weight have different proportions of muscle, fat, and bone. Thus, no single measure is satisfactory for the purpose of classifying students into homogeneous groups.

The U.S. school system is based primarily on a single classification—age. Children start to school at a specified age and if they make satisfactory progress they advance a grade each year. The main objection to this system lies in the known differences in maturity within a given chronologic age. Clarke (1967) tested boys within 2 months of their tenth birthday and reported differences in skeletal maturity ranging from 8 years and less to 12 years and more. Certainly it is unfair to expect a boy who is at a maturation level of 8 years to compete equally with a boy of 12 years. Yet we continually do this as long as our only classification index is chronologic age.

The assessment of skeletal age or physical maturity by roentgenography is not practical for the school situation. Therefore, physical educators must use other devices if they wish to classify students into homogeneous groupings.

Examples of some earlier, commonly used classification formulas are the McCloy and the Neilson–Cozens classification indexes which use combinations of age, height, and weight.

McCloy and Neilson–Cozens Classification Indexes

The renowned pioneer in measurement, C. H. McCloy, found that age, height, and weight correlated highly with valid criteria of competition, and because of their convenience they should be used for classification purposes. He developed three indexes for elementary, high school, and college levels. His elementary grade index (CI) is:

$$CI = 10 \text{ (age in years)} + \text{weight (lb)}$$

According to McCloy, height is not an important factor at the elementary level.

The Neilson–Cozens Classification Index (CI) has been employed rather extensively and is as follows:

$$CI = 20 \text{ (age in years)} \\ + 5.55 \text{ (height in inches)} + \text{weight (lb)}$$

The Neilson–Cozens Classification Index can be quickly and easily determined by consulting a table. The teacher simply finds the exponent value for each of the variables of height, age, and weight. After addition of the three exponents, the class, in the form of a letter A, B, C, and so on, is established. For elementary and junior high school students, eight classes (A through H) are given. For high school only three classes (A, B, and C) are determined. The *AAHPERD Youth Fitness Test Manual* presents norms based on the Neilson–Cozens Classification Index as well as norms based on age only.

Other Height–Weight Indexes

A number of height–weight ratios have been used as rough indicators of body build. Height–weight indexes have been used for a variety of purposes such as determination of nutritional status and study of physique with regard to heat tolerance.

Ponderal Index

The ponderal index (PI) is the height divided by the cube root of weight:

$$\frac{\text{height}}{\sqrt[3]{\text{weight}}}$$

A nomogram can be used to calculate PI (Figure 10.1). The ponderal index is the maximal achieved mass over surface area. It is used in the somatotyping process. The higher the PI, the thinner, or more ectomorphic, the individual.

Body Mass Index

The body mass index (BMI) has been used in body composition studies as an index of weight in relation to height. The formula is:

$$\text{BMI} = \frac{\text{weight (kg)}}{\text{height}^2 \text{ (m)}}$$

The BMI is considered a measure of obesity because of its rather close relationship to body fat as measured by body density. It has a relatively low correlation with height, and therefore it correlates highly but negatively with the ponderal index.

Surface Area/Weight Ratio

The surface area/weight ratio (SA/w) has been used in studies comparing people of different cultures on heat and cold tolerance, because of the importance of body surface area in heat exchange. Leaner individuals have higher SA/w ratios. The formula is:

$$\text{SA/w} = \text{surface area (m}^2) \times \left(\frac{100}{\text{weight (kg)}}\right)$$

Surface area can be obtained from the Dubois Body Surface Chart (W. M. Boothby and J. Berkson, Mayo Clinic, Rochester, Minn.). Surface area also can be calculated by the formula (Katch, Behnke, and Katch 1979):

$$\text{SA(m}^2) = \sqrt{\frac{\text{weight (kg)}}{\text{height (cm)}} \times 3} \times \text{height (cm)} \times 0.01762$$

The SA/w ratio correlates rather highly with the ponderal index and highly negatively with the body mass index.

GROWTH AND NUTRITIONAL STATUS MEASUREMENT

Many attempts have been made to establish standards for assessing normal growth, desirable body weight, and nutritional status. Tables are available for both sexes at different age levels. Of course, those tables that attempt to take into account differences in body structure are generally more reliable than tables based only on height. Even so, one should exercise reasonable judgment in using such tables because of their inherent limitations.

The Wetzel Grid

One of the most extensively used devices for plotting and evaluating growth in the last quarter century has been the Wetzel Grid (Figure 10.2). This chart and record form was developed by Wetzel on the principle that normal, healthy development proceeds in an orderly manner in keeping with an individual's natural physique. Therefore, the child serves as his or her own standard of comparison.

Although on first appearance the grid gives the impression of being complicated, it is quite easy to use. The validity of the grid in detecting growth failure and nutritional disturbance has been well documented.[1]

Nine general body types were designated by Wetzel. These are identified on the chart by channels A_4, A_3, A_2, A_1, M, B_1, B_2, B_3, B_4. The M channel represents the average or medium build; along with A_1 and B_1 it forms a central grouping of *good physical status*. Channels A_2 and A_3 represent stocky builds. The majority of A_4s are obese. Channels B_2, B_3, and B_4 reflect increasing degrees of thinness, respectively. The procedures for using the grid are as follows:

1. The child's height and weight are recorded on the left side of the chart and then plotted,

---

1. For references see R. M. Grueninger, *Don't Take Growth for Granted*. Cleveland: N.E.A. Service, 1961.

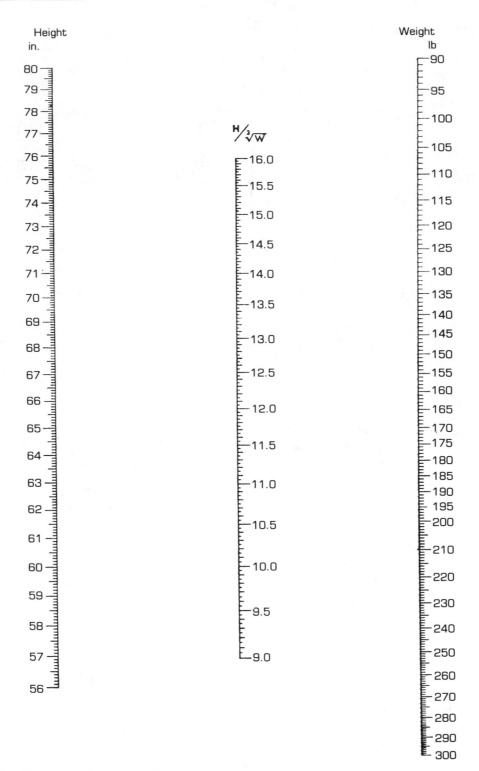

Figure 10.1.   Nomogram for ponderal index

which places the child in a particular physique channel in the middle of the chart (panel A). The corresponding developmental level is read from the horizontal lines crossing the physique channels and entered

on the left side of the chart. In the example shown in Figure 10.2, the boy's height is 52½ in. and his weight is 61 lb, yielding a point on the border of B_1 and B_2 at developmental level 76.

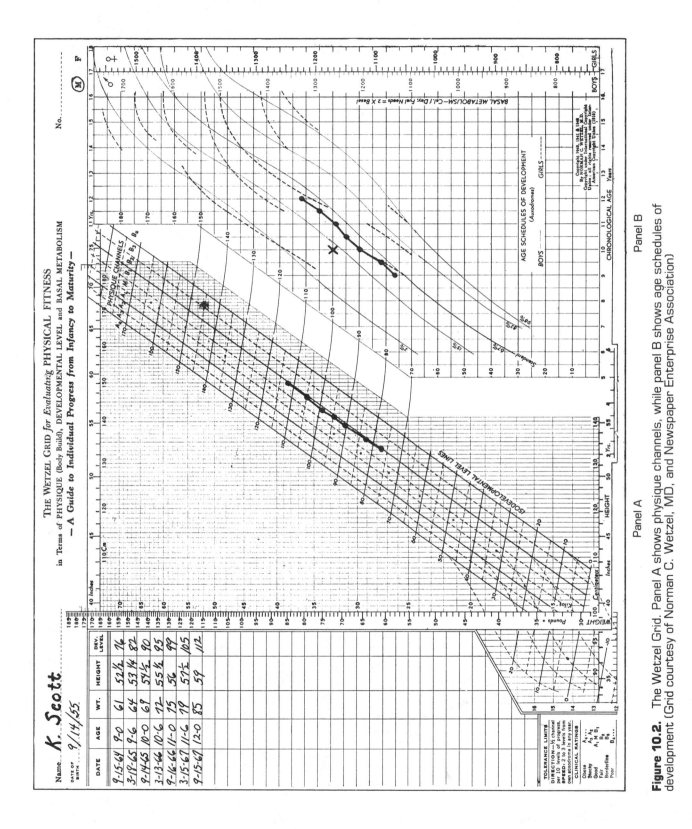

Figure 10.2.   The Wetzel Grid. Panel A shows physique channels, while panel B shows age schedules of development (Grid courtesy of Norman C. Wetzel, MD, and Newspaper Enterprise Association)

It should be emphasized that the first plotting reveals very little in terms of *quality of growth*. The successive plottings are of primary importance in indicating the character of growth progress. All plots should be checked for accuracy; in case of notable irregularity, weight and height should be remeasured.

2. The child's developmental level is plotted against age on the right side of the chart (panel B) (e.g., level 76 at age 9).

3. The next measurement in this instance is made 6 months later. Height and weight are again plotted in the physique channel and the developmental level at age 9 years 6 months in panel B.

4. Subsequent plottings build up the channel and auxodrome trends. The plots are interpreted in relation to the standards shown on the grid of direction and speed of physical development, thereby revealing the *quality of individual growth*.

5. A child's advancement in panel B is interpreted by referring to the curved age schedules, or *auxodromes*. The standard of reference for determining whether a child is normal, advanced, or retarded in development is the 67% auxodrome. To illustrate how this may be used, the X in panel B shows a child, aged 10 years, at developmental level 100. This child would be considered advanced 1½ years in development, since the standard auxodrome does not cross the 100 level until the age of 11½ years.

The dotted-line curves in panel B (for girls) level off sooner than the solid line (for boys). This is because girls ordinarily mature at an earlier age.

Although one should not expect the plotted lines to stay exactly in a particular channel or along an auxodrome, experience has shown that healthy growth and development are remarkably precise in these respects. In the example in Figure 10.2, the boy's growth and development are progressing very satisfactorily.

6. Any marked deviation of a child's growth from a previously well-followed channel or auxodrome should be investigated. Children in channel A$_4$ (obese) should be observed closely, and children in channel B$_2$ and to the right of the 67% auxodrome

also should be carefully watched. In his early work with the grid, Wetzel was able to identify 95% of children that had been rated as poor or borderline by physicians.

7. The last two columns on the chart are for estimating basal metabolism and daily caloric requirements. Although these standards were announced almost 30 years ago, they nonetheless correspond with current National Research Council recommended allowances.

Meredith Height–Weight Chart

After much study of growth records of children at various age levels, Meredith was able to construct a zone classification system for height and weight for boys and girls 4 to 18 years of age. The charts that were prepared for convenient use by the classroom teacher contain curved zones for height and weight on which the child's growth progress can be plotted. There are five zones for height: tall, moderately tall, average, moderately short, and short. Similarly, there are five zones for weight: heavy, moderately heavy, average, moderately light, and light. The height zones are at the top of the chart and the weight zones are at the bottom.

When the height and the weight of the child are plotted at the appropriate age column, an immediate check is available to see whether the child's height and weight are in similar zones. Normally, a child who is moderately short is expected to be light, and a child who is tall is expected to be heavy, and so on. When the zones are dissimilar, it should be determined whether the child's physique accounts for the dissimilarity, for example, whether the child is naturally tall and slender or short and stocky, and so on. If this is not the case, further examination is made for possible health problems such as malnutrition, obesity, and illness. Moreover, as successive plottings are made, growth patterns can be observed. A child's height and weight are expected essentially to parallel one another in their zones. Any marked deviation from one zone to another is usually cause for referral.

BODY BUILD CLASSIFICATION (SOMATOTYPING)

The association of certain body builds with personality and behavior patterns, health problems, and physical performance has long been recognized. Most of us have rather stereotyped notions of what the typical fat person is like, the skinny person, and the person who is "all muscle." This concept that people behave as they do because of what they are represents the foundation of somatotyping (Willgoose 1961).

William H. Sheldon is without doubt the foremost name in the field of somatotyping. He, in turn, was influenced by the work of Kretschmer and others before him. Sheldon and his co-workers (1940) concluded that while there are three basic body types, people have varying amounts or degrees of all three. The three primary components are called *endomorphy, mesomorphy,* and *ectomorphy.*

Endomorphy is characterized by roundness of body parts with concentration in the center. This is the pear-shaped individual with a large abdomen, round head, short neck, narrow shoulders, fatty breasts, short arms, wide hips, heavy buttocks, and short, heavy legs.

Mesomorphy is evidenced by rugged musculature and large bones. The mesomorph has prominent facial bones, a rather long but muscular neck, wide sloping shoulders, muscular arms and forearms, broad chest, heavily muscled abdomen, low waist, narrow hips, muscular buttocks, and powerful legs.

Ectomorphy is characterized by small bones, with linearity and fragility predominating. The ectomorph has a large forehead, small facial bones, a long skinny neck, narrow chest, round shoulders with winged scapulae, long slender arms, flat abdomen, inconspicuous buttocks, and long, thin legs.

In determining the body build classification, or somatotype, the individual is scaled from 1 to 7 in each component. The somatotype is thus given in a three-number sequence in which the first number represents the endomorphic component; the second, mesomorphy; and the third, ectomorphy. An extreme endomorph is classified as a 7-1-1, an extreme mesomorph is a 1-7-1, and an extreme ectomorph is a 1-1-7.

Most people are dominated by two components. The lesser of the two is usually employed as the adjective in describing the somatotype. For example, a 2-6-4 would be an ectomorphic mesomorph.

Accurate somatotyping for research purposes requires a great amount of training and practice. The specifications and instructions for taking the photographs and the steps and procedures in the somatotyping process are given in detail in Sheldon's *Atlas of Men.* Briefly, they are as follows: The subject is photographed, preferably in the nude, from three views—front, side, and back. To minimize any changes in body position, a revolving pedestal is used. The subject's height and weight are carefully measured and the ponderal index is then determined. (The ponderal index is the height divided by the cube root of weight, $height/\sqrt[3]{weight}$.) It is the maximal achieved mass over surface area; in other words, it indicates the person's position in relation to ectomorphy. The higher the ponderal index, the more the subject tends toward ectomorphy. A table is consulted showing the possible somatotypes for the obtained ponderal index, and photographs are used for comparative reference.

Sheldon refined the somatotyping process by making it more objective through the computation of a trunk index. A planimeter is used to measure the abdominal and thoracic trunk areas on the photograph. Tables have been developed in which the combination of ponderal index, trunk index, and height enable the researcher to accurately identify the subject's somatotype. These tables have not yet been incorporated into the *Atlas.*

Heath–Carter Somatotype Rating Form

One of the most widely used laboratory methods for determining somatotype without the use of photography is the Heath–Carter system. It involves the anthropometric measurements of height, weight, skin folds, circumferences, and diameters. The rating form (Figure 10.3) comprises three sections, one for each somatotype component. Endomorphy is determined by skin folds, mesomorphy by diameters and girths, and ectomorphy by a height/weight ratio, the ponderal index. Mathews provided a very detailed explanation of the entire somatotyping procedure using the Heath–Carter method.

1. In the first section, the sum of the triceps, subscapular, and suprailiac skin folds (in millimeters) is entered on the chart by circling the closest value. (The latter part of this chapter has instructions for taking skin fold measurements.) The first component (endomorphy) is then determined by circling the number directly under the column of numbers with the total skin fold entry.

2. In the second section, the height (in inches) is marked by an arrow at the appropriate spot on the continuous scale. Then diameters of the humerus and the femur are entered by circling the closest value in the appropriate row.

HEATH-CARTER SOMATOTYPE RATING FORM

NAME .... KARYN L. .... AGE 27-0 SEX: M (F) NO: 19

OCCUPATION .. Teacher .... ETHNIC GROUP Caucasian .... DATE 21 Nov 1981

PROJECT.. P.M. .... MEASURED BY: J.P.

TOTAL SKINFOLDS (mm)

Skinfolds (mm):

Triceps = 18

Subcapular = 7

Supraliac = 11

TOTAL SKINFOLDS = 36

Calf = 16

	½	1	1½	2	2½	3	3½	4	4½	5	5½	6	6½	7	7½	8	8½	9	9½	10	10½	11	11½	12
Upper Limit	10.9	14.9	18.9	22.9	26.9	31.2	35.8	40.7	46.2	52.2	58.7	65.7	73.2	81.2	89.7	98.9	108.9	119.7	131.2	143.7	157.2	171.9	187.9	204.0
Mid-point	9.0	13.0	17.0	21.0	25.0	29.0	33.5	38.0	43.5	49.0	55.5	62.0	69.5	77.0	85.5	94.0	104.0	114.0	125.5	137.0	150.5	164.0	180.0	196.0
Lower Limit	7.0	11.0	15.0	19.0	23.0	27.0	31.3	35.9	40.8	46.3	52.3	58.8	65.8	73.3	81.3	89.8	99.0	109.0	119.8	131.3	143.8	157.3	172.0	188.0

FIRST COMPONENT

	½	1	1½	2	2½	3	3½	4	4½	5	5½	6	6½	7	7½	8	8½	9	9½	10	10½	11	11½	12
Height (in.) = 67.1	55.0	56.5	58.0	59.5	61.0	62.5	64.0	65.5	67.0	68.5	70.0	71.5	73.0	74.5	76.0	77.5	79.0	80.5	82.0	83.5	85.0	86.5	88.0	89.5
Bone: Humerus = 6.1	5.19	5.34	5.49	5.64	5.78	5.93	6.07	6.22	6.37	6.51	6.65	6.80	6.95	7.09	7.24	7.38	7.53	7.67	7.82	7.97	8.11	8.25	8.40	8.55
(cm) Femur = 9.3	7.41	7.62	7.83	8.04	8.24	8.45	8.66	8.87	9.08	9.28	9.49	9.70	9.91	10.12	10.33	10.53	10.74	10.95	11.16	11.37	11.58	11.79	12.00	12.21
Muscle: Biceps 27 (cm) − 1.8 = 25.2	23.7	24.4	25.0	25.7	26.3	27.0	27.7	28.3	29.0	29.7	30.3	31.0	31.6	32.2	33.0	33.6	34.3	35.0	35.6	36.3	37.1	37.8	38.5	39.3
−(triceps skinfold) Calf 34.6 = 33.0 −(calf skinfold) 1.6	27.7	28.5	29.3	30.1	30.8	31.6	32.4	33.2	33.9	34.7	35.5	36.3	37.1	37.8	38.6	39.4	40.2	41.0	41.8	42.6	43.4	44.2	45.0	45.8

SECOND COMPONENT

	½	1	1½	2	2½	3	3½	4	4½	5	5½	6	6½	7	7½	8	8½	9
Upper limit	11.99	12.32	12.53	12.74	12.95	13.15	13.36	13.56	13.77	13.98	14.19	14.39	14.59	14.80	15.01	15.22	15.42	15.63
Mid-point	and	12.16	12.43	12.64	12.85	13.05	13.26	13.46	13.67	13.88	14.01	14.29	14.50	14.70	14.91	15.12	15.33	15.53
Lower limit	below	12.00	12.33	12.54	12.75	12.96	13.16	13.37	13.56	13.78	13.99	14.20	14.40	14.60	14.81	15.02	15.23	15.43

THIRD COMPONENT

Weight (lb.) = 120

Ht. / ³√Wt. = 13.6

	FIRST COMPONENT	SECOND COMPONENT	THIRD COMPONENT
Anthropometric Somatotype	4	3	4.5
Anthropometric plus Photoscopic Somatotype			

BY: ....

RATER: .. J.P.

Source of form: B. H. Heath and J. E. L. Carter, A Modified Somatotype Method. *American Journal of Physical Anthropology* 27:64, July 1967.

Figure 10.3. Heath–Carter Somatotype Rating Form

a. The diameters are taken with a sliding steel caliper. The biepicondylar diameters are measured for the humerus and femur. For the humerus, the arm is raised to shoulder level with the forearm flexed 90 degrees. Firm pressure is applied. The femur diameter is taken with the subject sitting in a chair with the foot on the floor and the leg vertical.

b. The biceps girth is measured with a flexible steel or linen tape. The subject flexes the biceps as strongly as possible with fist clenched. The tape is placed around the biceps at a right angle to the long axis of the bone at the point of maximum girth (in centimeters). The triceps skin fold (in centimeters) is then subtracted from the biceps girth and the closest value is circled.

c. The calf girth is taken with the subject standing with feet 6 to 9 in. apart and the weight equally distributed. The point of greatest girth is located. The calf skin fold is taken with the subject seated in the same position as for the femur diameter. The skin fold is lifted on the medial side of the right calf just above the point of maximum girth. The calf skin fold (in centimeters) is subtracted from the calf girth and the entry is circled.

3. To obtain the second component (mesomorphy), the procedure is as follows:

a. Disregarding the height row, the starting point is the circled value in this section that is farthest to the left. The number of columns by which each other circled value deviates from this starting point is counted and the sum of the deviations is divided by 4.

b. The number of columns that the average deviation in (a) is to the right of the original starting point column is counted and an asterisk is placed at that point.

c. The number of columns that the asterisk deviates from the height column, indicated by the arrow, is counted.

d. Starting at the number 4 in the row entitled "Second Component," the number of columns that the asterisk deviates left or right from the height column is counted. This point is circled as the second component.

4. The third component (ectomorphy) is found by calculating the ponderal index (height/$\sqrt[3]{\text{weight}}$). One can use the nomogram in Figure 10.1. The closest value is circled, and the third component is thus located directly below this column.

Simplified Somatotype Assessment

Willgoose presented a rather comprehensive discussion of somatotyping, its implications, and its applications. In his discussion he suggested a method of somatotyping that, while not meant to be as accurate as Sheldon's process, has more practical application for the physical education teacher.

The teacher rates the subject on the primary component on the 1 to 7 scale. He or she then rates the second and third components in the same manner. The ponderal index is calculated by using the nomogram shown in Figure 10.1. In using the nomogram, the teacher places a ruler on the scale so that it connects the subject's height and weight. The point at which the ruler intersects the middle column is the ponderal index.

The teacher may then consult Sheldon's *Atlas of Men* and study the charts of possible somatotypes to confirm the somatotype classification. Willgoose maintained that even without the *Atlas* or the ponderal index, one can estimate somatotypes accurately enough for use in the school situation.

Cureton's Subjective Somatotype Form

Cureton employed a subjective method of estimating somatotype in his research. It consisted of studying the five major regions of the body and rating the degree of endomorphy, mesomorphy, and ectomorphy of each region. Then the components were averaged and the somatotype thus estimated. The rating can be done using either the subject or posed pictures including front, back, and side views. A summary of the steps is as follows:

1. With use of the form in Figure 10.4, the amount of each somatotype component is rated on a 1 to 7 scale for region I (head, face, and neck). The number representing the amount of endomorphy is circled, the number for mesomorphy is circled, and the rating for ectomorphy is circled, for example, 1 for endomorphy, 3 for mesomorphy, and 5 for ectomorphy.

Region of the Body	Endomorphy	Mesomorphy	Ectomorphy
I Head, face, and neck notations	1 2 3 4 5 6 7	1 2 3 4 5 6 7	1 2 3 4 5 6 7
II Thoracic trunk notations	1 2 3 4 5 6 7	1 2 3 4 5 6 7	1 2 3 4 5 6 7
III Arms, hands, and shoulders notations	1 2 3 4 5 6 7	1 2 3 4 5 6 7	1 2 3 4 5 6 7
IV Abdominal trunk notations	1 2 3 4 5 6 7	1 2 3 4 5 6 7	1 2 3 4 5 6 7
V Legs and feet notations	1 2 3 4 5 6 7	1 2 3 4 5 6 7	1 2 3 4 5 6 7
VI Average rating	_____	_____	_____

Subject's name_____ Age _____ Ht _____ Wt _____

Ponderal index (height/$\sqrt[3]{\text{weight}}$ "t") _____ _____ _____

Estimated somatotype number (from VI above) _____

Somatotype name _____

Figure 10.4. Cureton's subjective classification of body type (Excerpted from T. K. Cureton, "Body Build as a Framework of Reference for Interpreting Physical Fitness and Athletic Performance." *Supplement to Research Quarterly* 12:301–330, May, 1941, published by AAHPERD, Reston, Va., used by permission)

2. The same procedure is followed for regions II, III, IV, and V.

3. The average endomorphy rating for the five regions is computed. The average mesomorphy and ectomorphy values are also computed. As a further check, it is recommended that the teacher consult Sheldon's table in which the ponderal index values for possible somatotypes for corresponding numbers are indicated.

4. The average scores for the three components are placed in the order just given, for example, 2-4-5. The somatotype is then named: in this case, mesomorphic ectomorph.

A question often raised is, "Of what value is somatotyping to the physical education teacher?" It certainly would not be practical to consume large blocks of class time for the sole purpose of somatotyping students. On the other hand, somatotyping can be done quite efficiently (with practice) on a scheduled individual observation basis. That is, the teacher can make a point of observing one or more particular students each day. Through careful observation, the teacher is able to gain valuable information about each student not only about posture and somatotype but also about motor performance, strengths and weaknesses, and social adjustment and personality. This is not meant to sound like a one-shot proposition. Observation should be continuous throughout the year, the teacher thus having the opportunity to observe each student in various situations. The main advantage of this plan is that it ensures that the teacher will consciously study every person in the class rather than just notice loud students, those who misbehave, and good and bad performers.

Thus, the real value of somatotyping lies in its contribution toward a better understanding of the individual. Better understanding in turn enables the teacher to better meet the needs of each student. The mesomorph's energetic need for physical exercise, excitement, and adventure; the endomorph's inclination toward social activities and relaxing recreational games; and the ectomorph's tendency to shy away from team sports and group activities all present a challenge to the physical educator. The discerning teacher who is able to anticipate the sensitivity of the ectomorph and the endomorph in situations in which their physique and poor physical abilities are apt to evoke ridicule can contribute a great deal to making friends instead of enemies for physical education.

The physical educator and the coach can use knowledge of somatotyping along with physical performance measures in predicting potential athletic ability. Since most people are mixtures rather than extremes of a single component, the teacher and coach who are skilled in identifying body structure characteristics will most likely be successful in predicting abilities and channeling students into activities best suited for their needs, interests, and capabilities.

BODY COMPOSITION

It has been well documented that obesity is a critical health problem in the United States. Obesity has been shown to be associated with high blood pressure, coronary heart disease, diabetes, respiratory problems, hernias, orthopedic disorders, and various other health problems and also creates a surgical risk. Understandably, the medical professions are concerned about preventing obesity.

Until rather recently, the bulk of the attention accorded to weight control focused on the adult population. So-called "creeping obesity" refers to the gradual accumulation of fat over a period of years. To gain 1 or 2 lb of weight in a year seems inconsequential, but if projected over a 20-yr time span it represents a very significant amount of excess fat. Unfortunately, the individual wants to lose the slowly acquired weight overnight. This leads to crash diets until a target amount of weight is lost, then immediate resumption of the regular life-style and the resultant gain of weight and then another crash diet: the yo-yo phenomenon. Statistics reporting that 30% to 40% of the adult population is obese indicate that the United States is losing the battle of the bulge. Moreover, data gathered through case studies and extensive observations point heavily to the need for more efforts devoted to obesity in children and the preventive role that exercise can play in weight control and fat reduction.

Some of the findings are as follows:

1. Approximately 25% of the children in the United States are overfat (Corbin et al. 1974; Wilmore 1977).

2. Evidence is increasing that fat children are not the prototypes of healthy adults; fat children become fat adults (Mayer 1968).

3. Inactivity appears more and more to be the most common denominator in obesity, rather than overeating or glandular disturbances (Corbin and Pletcher 1968).

4. Case studies have revealed that a large percentage of fat adults trace the beginning of their weight problems to the point in their life when they stopped regular activity (Corbin et al. 1974).

5. Exercise is of value in the loss of fat and in weight control. Severe dieting alone causes loss of lean body tissue in addition to loss of fat. Exercise programs and exercise plus dieting bring about greater fat reduction without loss of muscle mass (Zuti 1972).

6. Muscle uses more energy than fat. Thus, the maintenance of adequate muscle mass through regular exercise can help prevent the accumulation of fat, by burning more calories even while the body is at rest. This is one of the primary reasons for weight problems as a person grows older. Owing to inactivity and the subsequent reduction of muscle mass, the individual uses fewer calories than before. A paradox develops in that a person with reduced muscle mass and a higher percentage of fat actually has to exercise more and more just to avoid gaining more weight (Lamb 1975).

The problem of obesity and its causes is complex. There are no simple solutions. Researchers in health, medicine, and exercise physiology have done much to dispel some of the fallacies concerning obesity and the role of exercise. In light of the seriousness of obesity—its medical, psychologic, and social implications—and the acknowledged value of exercise in its prevention and treatment, physical educators now generally list weight control and the avoidance of obesity as one of the components of physical fitness.

MEASUREMENT OF BODY COMPOSITION

The inclusion of weight control as a component of physical fitness carries with it the obligation of measurement. For years, health educators and physical educators have recognized and sporadically attempted to determine and predict proper or ideal body weight. Differences in body size have long been recognized as important variables in the interpretation of fitness test scores.

Because of the medical risk factors associated with obesity, insurance companies have been concerned with "proper" weight for many years. Their age–height–weight tables with rough classifications of body frame have been widely used as standards for normal weight. The Armed Services have developed similar scales.

The major flaw in the age–height–weight scales is their inability to account for differences in percentage of lean body weight and fat. Numerous demonstrations of the tables' limitations have been reported. Wilmore (1974) cited the case of a 265-lb professional football player who was classified by the insurance tables as being 75 lb overweight. However, according to body composition measurements, his lean body weight was 225 lb. Thus, for him to meet the insurance table's specifications he would have had to lose 33 lb of muscle, or the equivalent of an arm or a leg! Another frequently cited study involved the comparison of weight classification by U.S. Air Force standards and actual percentage of body fat and lean body weight determined through laboratory methods. It was shown that over 40% of the subjects were incorrectly classified by the tables (Wamsley and Roberts 1963).

The only true determination of body composition would be through dissection of a cadaver. One method of assessment that is currently employed to estimate body composition is radiography in which bone, muscle, fat, and skin are quantified by x-ray analysis. Another is the potassium-40 method, which employs the measurement of gamma radiation from the body. This method requires a chamber and elaborate equipment. Still another is the helium dilution method, in which volume differences between volume in a special chamber and subject volume are analyzed.

The most frequently used method of assessing body composition is the underwater weighing technique, in which body density is determined indirectly by the body's loss of weight in water and the application of Archimedes' principle, which states that the loss of weight of the body in water is equal to the weight of the water displaced by the body. A body's density is weight divided by volume. While this may sound rather simple, the method requires equipment, very careful preparatory procedures, and repeated weighings and correction for the volume of the air in the lungs. Another method using the same principle involves measurement of the actual displacement of water caused by the submersion of a body in a water-filled container.

Once density has been estimated, the percentage of fat is calculated on the basis of known differences in density of fat and lean tissue. Siri's equation is most often used for converting body density to percentage of fat:

$$\% \text{ fat} = \left(\frac{4.950}{\text{density}} - 4.500 \right) \times 100$$

Although the underwater weighing technique is employed rather widely in college and university laboratories, obviously it is not applicable for widespread use in physical education programs. Simpler measurements such as body girths, diameters, and skin fold thicknesses have been employed, and regression equations have been calculated to predict density and relative body fat.

Anthropometric Instruments

Several instruments have been devised to measure various parts of the body or skin fold thickness. A partial list is as follows:

1. Shoulder breadth, length caliper (Figure 10.5). This instrument measures shoulder width and thigh length.

2. Chest depth caliper (Figure 10.6). This measures minimum chest expansion.

3. Compact indicating caliper (Figure 10.7). This caliper allows a direct reading of inside or outside linear measurements to a length of 6 in.

4. Gulick tape (Figure 10.8). This includes a spring attachment that permits a slight amount of constant tension on the tape.

5. Lange skin fold caliper (Figure 10.9). This measures subcutaneous and adipose (fat) tissue with constant tension.

6. Harpenden skin fold caliper (Figure 10.10). This measures skin folds to an accuracy of 0.2 mm. It provides constant pressure across the full range of the jaw openings.

7. Fat-O-Meter (Figure 10.11). This inexpensive plastic skin fold caliper is affordable by any school or organization.

Practical Method of Underwater Weighing (Wilmore 1977)

Underwater, or hydrostatic, weighing is usually performed in a laboratory setting with a specially constructed tank and expensive equipment for measuring residual volume by nitrogen washout or helium dilution.

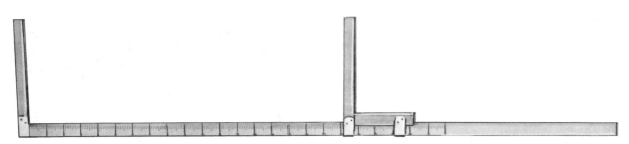

Figure 10.5.   Shoulder breadth, length caliper (reprinted by permission of J. A. Preston Corporation, 1973)

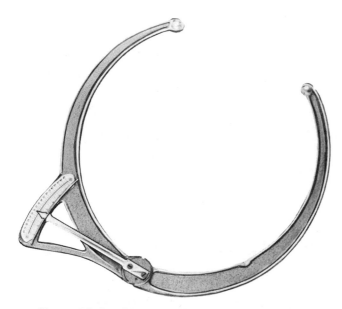

Figure 10.6.   Chest depth caliper (reprinted by permission of J. A. Preston Corporation, 1973)

Figure 10.8.   Gulick tape (reprinted by permission of J. A. Preston Corporation, 1973)

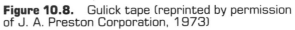

Figure 10.7.   Compact indicating caliper (reprinted by permission of J. A. Preston Corporation, 1973)

Figure 10.9.   Lange skin fold caliper (reprinted by permission of J. A. Preston Corporation, 1973)

Figure 10.10. Harpenden skin fold caliper (Courtesy of Quinton Instruments, Seattle)

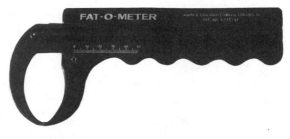

Figure Figure 10.11 Fat-O-Meter (B & L Products, Portland, Texas 78374)

Wilmore described a field test for underwater weighing that can be used by physical educators who have access to a swimming pool and an accurate scale that can be hung from a diving board or some other support. The scale must initially be calibrated by hanging known weights from it.

The water should be at least 3 ft deep. If the scale is hung from the diving board, this of course means deep water and the subject should be able to swim and be comfortable in the water.

1. The subject sits in a chair or simply hangs from a rope or chain that is attached to the scale. The subject then totally submerges, exhaling "all" of the air in the lungs beforehand. Several trials need to be given (five to ten), since considerable practice is needed to exhale air completely. The average of the two or three heaviest trials is recorded as the underwater weight.

    Some weights often need to be attached to the subject by a weight belt or to the chair to allow complete submersion. This weight and the weight of the chair, supporting chain, and any other equipment must be subtracted from the subject's underwater weight to obtain the net weight.

2. The subject is weighed on land (weight in air) as accurately as possible. The measurements used in underwater weighing are in metric units, so the subject's body weight in air is converted to kilograms (lb/2.2).

3. In the basic equation for computing body density (body weight/volume), the calculations for estimating volume must take into consideration the density of the water, corrected for temperature, and the residual volume in the lungs. The density of water at various water temperatures can be obtained from tables or, as suggested by Wilmore, one can use a density of 0.997, since most pools are heated to about 76 to 78 °F.

4. Residual lung volume can be estimated using Table 10.1.

The formula for body density (BD) in grams per cubic centimeter is

$$\dfrac{\text{weight in air (kg)}}{\left(\dfrac{\dfrac{\text{weight}}{\text{in air}} - \dfrac{\text{net underwater}}{\text{weight}}}{\text{density of water } 0.977}\right) - \dfrac{\text{residual volume}}{\text{(from Table 10.1)}}}$$

For example, a 17-year-old boy weighs 165 lb (75 kg) in air. When submerged in water seated in a chair to which a 5-lb (2.3-kg) weight plate is attached, the subject weighs 15 lb (6.8 kg). After subtraction of the weight of the chair, the chain attaching the chair to the scale, and the added weight plate, a total of 8 lb (3.6 kg), his net underwater weight is 7 lb (3.2 kg).

Using 0.997 as the density of water and 1.3 liters for residual lung volume (from Table 10.1), body density can be calculated as follows:

$$BD(gm/cc) = \dfrac{75 \text{ kg}}{\left(\dfrac{75 - 3.2}{0.997}\right) - 1.3}$$

$$= \dfrac{75}{70.7} = 1.061$$

Then, inserting the BD in the formula to convert density to percent fat

$$\% \text{ fat} = \left(\dfrac{4.95}{BD} - 4.50\right) \times 100$$

$$= \left(\dfrac{4.95}{1.061} - 4.50\right) \times 100 = 16.5\%$$

Table 10.1. Estimated Residual Lung Volume by Sex and Age

AGE (YR)	FEMALE	MALE
6–10	0.60	0.90
11–15	0.80	1.10
16–20	1.00	1.30
21–25	1.20	1.50
26–30	1.40	1.70

From Jack H. Wilmore, *Athletic Training and Physical Fitness: Physiological Principles and Practices of the Conditioning Process.* Allyn & Bacon, Inc., 1977, pp. 245–246. Reprinted with permission.

Lean body weight equals body weight minus fat weight. Fat weight equals body weight times percent fat. Thus,

$$\text{fat weight} = 165 \text{ lb} \times 16.5\% = 27 \text{ lb}$$

and lean body weight is $165 - 27 = 138$ lb. If we should wish to calculate this person's desired weight on the basis of a certain desired percent fat, we can do so with the formula

$$\text{desired weight} = \frac{\text{lean body weight}}{100\% - \text{desired \% fat}} \times 100$$

Consequently, if the subject in the example wished to lose weight to achieve a desired 12% fat, his desired weight (or target weight) would be 157 lb.

$$\text{desired weight} = \frac{138}{100\% - 12\%}$$
$$= \frac{138}{88} \times 100 = 157$$

CIRCUMFERENCE (GIRTH) MEASUREMENTS

Circumferences at numerous body sites have been measured and evaluated. From a common-sense standpoint, we tend to incorporate the girth of various body segments in our appraisal of a person's body build. Obesity is characterized by large abdominal and hip girths in relation to chest circumference.

The measurement of circumference requires great care. One of the main difficulties is locating the exact body site to measure. The circumferences must be at right angles to the long axis of the body or body segment and not be tilted. Another potential source of error is the compression of the skin by the tape. The Gulick tape (Figure 10.8) is used widely in research because it has a spring attached to the handle that permits a constant amount of tension to be applied during measurement. A steel or cloth tape may be used.

Some of the body sites most frequently measured are:

Neck. Immediately below the larynx (Figure 10.12).

Chest. In males, at nipple level (Figure 10.13). In females, chest measurements are sometimes taken at the level of the breasts (maximum circumference), just above the breasts, or just below the breasts. All chest measurements should be taken at the end of normal expiration.

Hips. At a level from the maximal protrusion of the buttocks to the symphysis pubis (Figure 10.12).

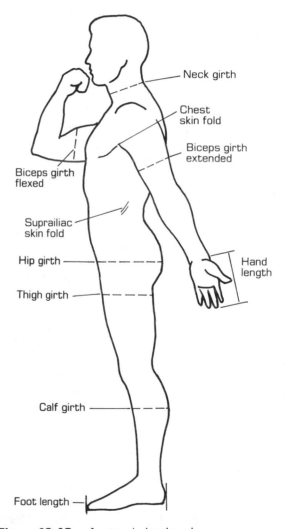

Figure 10.12. Anatomic landmarks

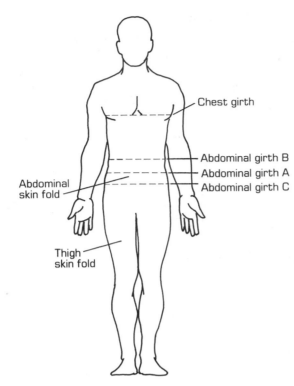
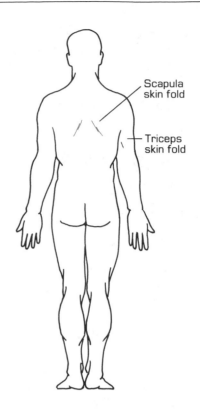

Figure 10.13. Anatomic landmarks

Thigh. The point of maximal thigh circumference (Figure 10.12).

Calf. The point of maximal calf circumference (Figure 10.12).

Biceps. Greatest girth when arm is (1) maximally flexed and muscles are fully contracted (Figure 10.12) and (2) fully extended and muscles are contracted (Figure 10.12).

Abdomen. Abdominal girths have been taken at different locations. Three are:

1. At the level of the umbilicus and iliac crests (Figure 10.13, abdominal girth A).
2. At the point of minimal circumference, halfway between the umbilicus and xiphoid process of the sternum between the bottom of the rib cage and iliac crests (Figure 10.13, abdominal girth B).
3. At the maximal abdominal girth in women about 2 in. below the umbilicus (Figure 10.13, abdominal girth C).

BODY DIAMETER MEASUREMENTS

Calipers and anthropometers are employed in diameter measurements. For most measurements the anthropometer is used; it consists of a metric scale with a fixed blade and a movable blade. An anthropometer can be easily made with a meter stick and some type of blades.

The tester should locate the body landmarks with his or her fingers before applying the anthropometer. The blades should be applied with sufficient pressure to compress as much of the soft tissue as possible. This makes for greater bone contact and therefore more accurate and reliable measurements.

Anatomic landmarks for diameter measurements include the following:

Head width. Above the ears at the widest point of the head (Figure 10.14).

Biacromial diameter. The most lateral margins of the acromial processes with shoulders relaxed and elbows close to the body. Measured from behind the subject (Figure 10.14).

Chest width. At the nipple line, at the level of the fifth and sixth rib with arms at the side of the body (Figure 10.14).

Bi-iliac diameter. Greatest width of the pelvic girdle at the lateral margins of the iliac crests, taken from in front of the subject (Figure 10.14).

Bitrochanteric diameter. The lateral margins of the greater trochanters (Figure 10.14).

Knee diameter. With knee flexed to 90 degrees, the widest margins between the lateral and medial epicondyles of the femur (Figure 10.14).

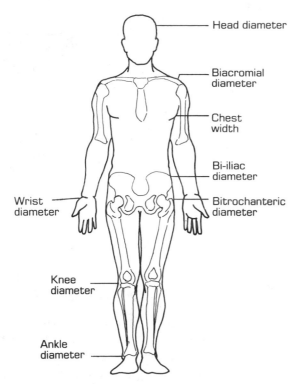

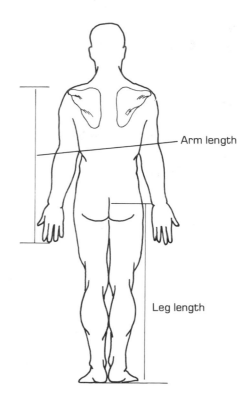

Figure 10.14.   Anatomic landmarks

Ankle diameter. Anthropometer is tilted upward at a 45-degree angle with blades touching the malleoli (Figure 10.14).

Wrist diameter. The styloid processes of the radius and ulna (Figure 10.14).

LENGTH MEASUREMENTS

Standing height. See page 175.

Sitting height. The subject is on a bench or table, sitting as erect as possible with the legs hanging down and the arms resting on the thighs. Distance is measured from the bench to the vertex (highest point on top of the head).

Leg length. Measured from the end of the spinal column to the floor. Also taken from greater trochanter to floor (Figure 10.14). Sometimes the difference between sitting and standing heights is used.

Trunk length. This is the standing height minus the leg length.

Arm length. Measured from the acromion process to the tip of the third finger (Figure 10.14). It is sometimes measured while the subject is holding a wand; measurement is from the acromion process to the upper surface of the wand.

Arm span. Distance from the outstretched fin-gertips of one hand to the fingertips of the other, while the subject stands with the back against a wall, arms extended horizontally.

Hand length. Measured from the tip of the third finger to the base of the thumb (most proximal carpal bone) (Figure 10.12).

Foot length. Measured from the tip of the most distal toe to the most posterior portion of the heel (Figure 10.12).

SKIN FOLD MEASUREMENTS

Skin fold measurements require precise calipers designed to apply the same tension throughout their range of motion. The tester grasps the skin fold between thumb and index finger and attaches the jaws of the calipers about 1 cm from the thumb and finger. The measurements are in millimeters.

Skin folds provide an indication of subcutaneous fat, since the tester's pinch includes the fat contained between the double thickness of skin and excludes the muscle tissue. If there is ever a question as to whether the pinch encompasses muscle, the tester should ask the subject to contract the underlying muscle. Measurements are usually taken on the right side of the body with the subject standing.

Some anatomic sites that are frequently used for skin fold measurements are:

Scapula. The inferior angle of the scapula. The skin fold is lifted on a 45-degree diagonal plane parallel to the axillary border (Figure 10.13).

Chest. Midway between the anterior fold of the axilla and the nipple (Figure 10.12).

Triceps. On the back of the arm midway between the acromion process and the olecranon process. The skin fold is taken parallel to the long axis of the arm (Figure 10.13).

Abdomen. A vertical fold about 1 cm to the right of the umbilicus (Figure 10.13).

Suprailium. Just above the crest of the ilium at the midaxillary line. The fold is lifted diagonally, following the natural line of the iliac crest (Figure 10.12).

Thigh. With the subject's weight on the left foot, a vertical fold on the front of the right thigh halfway between the hip and the knee (Figure 10.13).

REGRESSION EQUATIONS

A brief word of caution is warranted concerning regression equations that employ various anthropometric measures such as skin folds, diameters, and circumferences for the prediction of percentage of fat and lean body weight. Usually, the criterion is body density or fat percentage derived from underwater weighing. There have been quite a number of studies in which predictive equations have been derived. Many of these equations are quite accurate in terms of small standard errors. They are mostly population specific, however, which means that they are most accurate when applied to samples very similar to the original samples. Behnke and Wilmore derived several regression equations using hydrostatic weighing determinations of body density and lean body weight as criteria. Equations are presented involving skin folds, body diameters, and circumferences alone and all three variables together. For example, with only one skin fold measure and body weight, an R of .931 was found for the equation for young men:

$$\text{lean body weight} = 10.260 \\ + 0.7927 \text{ (weight, kg)} \\ - 0.3676 \text{ (abdominal skin fold)}$$

With all three types of measures, an R of .958 was reported for the equation for young men:

$$\text{lean body weight} = 10.138 + 0.9259 \text{ (weight, kg)} \\ - 0.1881 \text{ (thigh skin fold)} \\ + .6370 \text{ (bi-iliac diameter)} \\ + 0.4888 \text{ (neck circumference)} \\ - 0.5951 \text{ (abdomen circumference taken laterally,}$$
at level of the iliac crests, and anteriorly, at umbilicus)

Behnke and Wilmore also developed several equations for young women, such as the following, which uses only skin folds:

$$\text{lean body weight} = 8.629 + 0.680 \text{ (weight, kg)} \\ - 0.163 \text{ (scapula skin fold)} \\ - 0.100 \text{ (triceps skin fold)} \\ - 0.054 \text{ (thigh skin fold)}$$

For this equation, $R = .916$.

Using all three measures, the following equation has an R of .929:

$$\text{lean body weight} = 1.661 + 0.668 \text{ (weight, kg)} \\ - 0.158 \text{ (scapula skin fold)} \\ - 0.081 \text{ (triceps skin fold)} \\ + 0.555 \text{ (neck circumference, cm)} \\ - 0.141 \text{ (maximum abdominal circumference, cm)}$$

Jackson and Pollock and Jackson, Pollock, and Ward developed "generalized" equations for predicting body density of men and women, respectively. They maintained that a large part of the problem of population specificity stems from the fact that the relationship between skin fold fat and body density is curvilinear rather than linear, as assumed in most previous prediction equations. They generated equations using skin folds, circumferences, and age. The following equations for men and women each use the sum of three skin folds.

Men: body density $= 1.1093800 - 0.0008267$ (sum of chest, abdomen, and thigh skin folds) $+ 0.0000016$ (sum of same 3 skin folds)^2 $- 0.0002574$ (age in years)

Women: body density $= 1.0994921 - 0.0009929$ (sum of triceps, suprailium, and thigh skin folds) $+ 0.0000023$ (sum of same 3 skinfolds)^2 $- 0.0001392$ (age in years)

The multiple Rs for the equations were $R = .905$, $SE = 0.0077$ for the formula for men and $R = .842$, $SE = 0.0086$ for that for women.

Baun, Baun, and Raven devised a nomogram for using the generalized equations of Jackson and Pollock and Jackson, Pollock, and Ward. The nomogram greatly simplifies the estimation of percent body fat. One simply places a straightedge on the nomogram (Figure 10.15) so as to connect the subject's age (left axis) to the sum of the three skin folds on the right axis. The point at which it crosses the appropriate middle scale is the individual's estimated percent body fat.

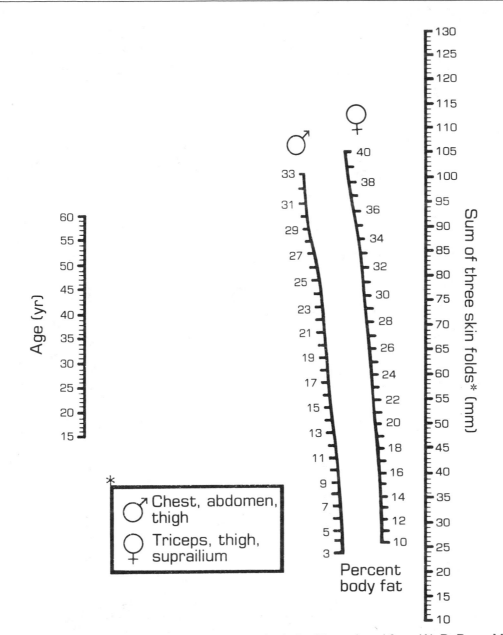

Figure 10.15. Nomogram for the estimate of percent body fat (Reproduced from W. B. Baun, M. R. Baun, and P. B. Raven, "A Nomogram for the Estimate of Percent Body Fat From Generalized Equations." *Research Quarterly for Exercise and Sport* 52:380–384, October 1981 published by AAHPERD, Reston, Va., used by permission)

For example, a 21-year-old woman has the following skin fold measures: triceps, 15 mm; suprailium, 18 mm; and thigh, 22 mm; for a total of 55 mm. By connecting her age (21) with the sum of the skin folds (55) on the nomogram, the estimated percent fat is 22%. If we were to calculate the percent fat by the Jackson, Pollock, and Ward and the Siri formulas, the procedure would be as follows:

$$density = 1.0994921 - 0.0009929(55)$$
$$+ 0.0000023(55)^2 - 0.0001392(21)$$
$$= 1.0489 \text{ gm/cc}$$

$$\% \text{ fat (Siri formula)} = \left(\frac{4.95}{1.0489} - 4.50\right) \times 100$$
$$= 21.9, \text{ or } 22\%$$

Some researchers have simply used the total of several skin fold measures as the criterion of amount of fat and as the dependent variable in studies to assess the amount of fat lost through different exercise programs. This approach is particularly appropriate with children, since the exact relationship between density and fat content in adolescence is not known, and the validity of equations for adults in predicting percent fat in children has not been tested (Durnin and Rahaman 1967).

AAHPERD HEALTH RELATED PHYSICAL FITNESS TEST

Body composition is assessed in the AAHPERD Health Related Physical Fitness Test by two skin fold measures: the triceps and the subscapular. No attempt is made to predict percent body fat. The score is the sum of the two skin folds, and percentile norms for ages 6 to 17 are provided. Norms are also given for the triceps measure only (Tables 10.2 and 10.3).

Rich and Vincent studied the validity and reliability of an inexpensive skin fold caliper (the Fat-O-Meter) for use with the AAHPERD Health Related Physical Fitness Test. Their results indicated the instrument is both valid and reliable. Thus, any school can afford an accurate instrument for measuring body composition as described on the AAHPERD Test.

Johnson, Nelson, and Garcia presented scoring scales for rating weight on the basis of a

Table 10.2. Percentile Norms in Millimeters for Sum of Triceps and Subscapular Skin Folds, Boys and Girls[a]

PERCENTILE	AGE											
	6	7	8	9	10	11	12	13	14	15	16	17
					BOYS							
95	8	9	9	9	9	9	9	9	9	9	9	9
75	11	11	11	11	12	12	11	12	11	12	12	12
50	12	12	13	14	14	16	15	15	14	14	14	15
25	14	15	17	18	19	22	21	22	20	20	20	21
5	20	24	28	34	33	38	44	46	37	40	37	38
					GIRLS							
95	9	10	10	10	10	11	11	12	13	14	14	15
75	12	12	13	14	14	15	15	16	18	20	20	20
50	14	15	16	17	18	19	19	20	24	25	25	27
25	17	19	21	24	25	25	27	30	32	34	34	36
5	26	28	36	40	41	42	48	51	52	56	57	58

[a]The norms for age 17 can be used for age 18.
Source: Adapted from *AAHPERD Health Related Physical Fitness Test Manual.* Reston, Va.: AAHPERD, 1980. Used by permission.

Table 10.3. Percentile Norms in Millimeters for Tricep Skin Fold, Boys and Girls[a]

PERCENTILE	AGE											
	6	7	8	9	10	11	12	13	14	15	16	17
					BOYS							
95	5	4	4	5	5	5	5	4	4	4	4	4
75	6	6	6	7	7	7	7	7	6	6	6	6
50	8	8	8	8	9	10	9	9	8	8	8	8
25	9	10	11	12	12	14	13	13	12	11	11	11
5	13	14	17	20	20	22	23	23	21	21	20	20
					GIRLS							
95	6	6	6	6	6	6	6	6	7	7	8	8
75	7	8	8	9	9	9	9	9	11	12	12	12
50	9	10	10	11	12	12	12	12	14	15	16	16
25	11	12	14	14	15	15	16	17	18	20	21	20
5	16	17	20	22	23	23	25	26	27	29	30	29

[a]The norms for age 17 can be used for age 18.
Source: Adapted from *AAHPERD Health Related Physical Fitness Test Manual.* Reston, Va.: AAHPERD, 1980. Used by permission.

height–weight scale (Table 10.4). While these scoring scales are simple and practical for widespread use, the height–weight rating scale on which they are based is only a rough estimation of a desirable relationship between height and weight.

Height–Weight Rating

The student's height and weight are measured with the student wearing regular street clothes. Shoes should have the standard 1-in. heel. The student's body frame size (small, medium, or large) is then estimated and the difference between the student's weight and the recommended upper or lower limits (depending on whether the student is overweight or underweight) shown in Table 10.5 is computed.

Example: Jane Doe is 5 ft 2 in. tall and has a medium frame. She weighs 135 lb.

Table 10.4. Height–Weight Rating Scale

LEVEL	DIFFERENCE STANDARD
Optimal	0 to ±4 lb
Acceptable	± 5 lb to ±9 lb
Minimal	±10 lb to ±14 lb
Poor	±15 lb to ±19 lb
Very poor	±20 lb to higher

Source: B. L. Johnson, J. K. Nelson, and M. J. Garcia, *Conditioning: Fitness and Performance for Everyone.* Portland, Tex.: Brown and Littleman, 1982, p. 54.

According to a Metropolitan height–weight table, the upper weight limit for her height and frame is 132 lb. Thus she subtracts 132 from 135 for an excess of 3 lb. On the basis of the ratings in Table 10.4, she determines that her weight is in the optimal level.

Body Fat Rating

Johnson, Nelson, and Garcia also devised a simplified rating scale for body fat based on the triceps and suprailiac skin fold measurements. These skin folds are each measured three times and the average is computed. The two averages are then added together and compared with values in the scale in Table 10.6.

FINDINGS AND CONCLUSIONS FROM ANTHROPOMETRIC, BODY BUILD, AND BODY COMPOSITION MEASUREMENT AND RESEARCH

Kistler reported a correlation of .81 between McCloy's Classification Index and selected track and field events. A lower relationship ($r = .57$) was obtained between certain sports skills and the McCloy Index. In separate studies, Miller found both the Wetzel Grid and the Neilson and Cozens Index effectively to equate college men according to body size.

Table 10.5. Height–Weight Table[a]

MEN					WOMEN			
Height		Weight (lb) for Frame Size:			Height		Weight (lb) for Frame Size:		
ft	in.	Small	Medium	Large	ft	in.	Small	Medium	Large
5	2	128–134	131–141	138–150	4	10	102–111	109–121	118–131
5	3	130–136	133–143	140–153	4	11	103–113	111–123	120–134
5	4	132–138	135–145	142–156	5	0	104–115	113–126	122–137
5	5	134–140	137–148	144–160	5	1	106–118	115–129	125–140
5	6	136–142	139–151	146–164	5	2	108–121	118–132	128–143
5	7	138–145	142–154	149–168	5	3	111–124	121–135	131–147
5	8	140–148	145–157	152–172	5	4	114–127	124–138	134–151
5	9	142–151	148–160	155–176	5	5	117–130	127–141	137–155
5	10	144–154	151–163	158–180	5	6	120–133	130–144	140–159
5	11	146–157	154–166	161–184	5	7	123–136	133–147	143–163
6	0	149–160	157–170	164–188	5	8	126–139	136–150	146–167
6	1	152–164	160–174	168–192	5	9	129–142	139–153	149–170
6	2	155–168	164–178	172–197	5	10	132–145	142–156	152–173
6	3	158–172	167–182	176–202	5	11	135–148	145–159	155–176
6	4	162–176	171–187	181–207	6	0	138–151	148–162	158–179

[a]Weights at ages 25 to 59. Based on lowest mortality weight in pounds according to frame (in indoor clothing weighing 5 lb (men) or 3 lb (women), shoes with 1-in. heels).

Source: Joan Parks, Managing Editor, Metropolitan Life Insurance Co., 1 Madison Ave., New York, NY 10010. Used by permission.

Table 10.6. Percent of Body Fat Scale

RATING	MEN		WOMEN	
	Skin Fold Thickness[a] (mm)	% Fat	Skin Fold Thickness[a] (mm)	% Fat
Excellent	14 and below	15 and below	26 and below	19 and below
Good	24–18	18–16	38–30	23–20
Average	32–26	21–19	44–40	26–24
Poor	42–34	25–22	56–48	30–27
Very poor	44 and above	26 and above	58 and above	31 and above

[a]Average of three measurements each of triceps and suprailiac skin folds.
Source: From B. L. Johnson, J. K. Nelson, and M. J. Garcia, *Conditioning: Fitness and Performance for Everyone.* 3rd ed. Portland, Tex.: Brown and Littleman, 1982, p. 54. Reprinted by permission.

Wear and Miller studied the relationship of physique and developmental level, as determined by the Wetzel Grid, to performance in fitness tests of junior high school boys. Subjects of medium physique and normal development were the best performers, while subjects of heavy physique were the poorest. Clarke and Petersen compared boy athletes with nonathletes in elementary and junior high school as to Wetzel physique channel ratings, and found no significant differences. Weinberg obtained significant correlations between Wetzel physique channels and results of anthropometric and strength tests. He also found a high relationship between Wetzel's developmental level and weight.

Gross and Casciani used data from over 13,000 students to determine the value of age, height, and weight as a classification device for the AAHPERD Youth Fitness Test. They reported that in all four groups of junior and senior high school boys and girls, the factors of age, height, and weight had practically no value, singly or in combination, as classifiers for the seven test items. Similarly, Espenschade found low correlations between performances and height and weight when age was held constant, and recommended the use of age alone for test norms.

Somatotype ratings and anthropometric measurements were studied by Hebbelinck and Postma as to their relationship to performance on motor fitness tests. Generally, the correlations between body measurements and motor performance were low. The subjects classified as mesomorphs were superior in all motor fitness tests, and the ecto-mesomorphs outperformed the endo-mesomorphs except in the shot put. In a study involving college women, Garrity found a general tendency for mesomorphic-ectomorphs to perform in a more efficient manner on physical fitness tests than other

groups. The ecto-endomorph group was consistently low in all test items.

Studies employing radiography to determine skeletal maturity have been reported in the literature. Especially prominent have been those conducted as a part of the Medford Growth Study. Clarke and Harrison found that the more physically mature group had a higher mean in all cases where differences in physical and motor traits were significant. Clarke and Degutis compared skeletal ages and selected physical and motor measures with the pubescent development of 10-, 13-, and 16-year-old boys. Physical maturation was effectively differentiated by pubescence assessment at 13 years of age, but pubescence was not as sensitive as skeletal age. Rarick and Oyster found skeletal maturity to be of little consequence in explaining individual differences in strength and motor proficiency of second-grade boys. Of the four physical maturity indicators used, chronologic age was the most important.

Mayer provided a cogent summary of the health problems associated with obesity. Clarke (1975) presented an excellent review of the disadvantages, causes, and determination of obesity, as well as a synopsis of research with regard to the effects of exercise on obesity. Behnke and Wilmore have made a significant contribution to the literature with their monograph, *Evaluation and Regulation of Body Build and Composition.* Lohman (1981) presented an excellent review of the relationship of skin folds and body density to body fatness.

Different techniques for estimating body density, percent fat, and lean body weight have been compared by several researchers and found to be relatively comparable (Cureton, Boileau, and Lohman 1975; Krzywicki et al. 1974). Skin fold measurements have been employed extensively as field tests of body fatness assessment. The use of skin folds rests on the assumption that subcutaneous fat constitutes a constant or at least a predictable proportion of total body fat (Womersley and Durnin 1977). Furthermore, it is generally assumed that individuals with considerable thickness of subcutaneous fat at one site tend to be correspondingly fat at other sites regardless of age, sex, or race (Johnston, Hamill, and Lemeshow 1972, 1974).

One of the largest normative surveys on skin fold thicknesses in children in the United States was the Health Examination Survey (Johnston, Hamill, and Lemeshow 1972, 1974). The data gathered from over 13,000 children were used for norms in the AAHPERD Health Related Physical Fitness Test. Over 100 equations have been developed in the last 30 years using skin folds or skin folds in combination with other anthropometric measurements for predicting body fat. Weltman and Katch presented theoretical justification for the use of circumference measurements for estimating total body volume and body density. They concluded that total body volume can be accurately predicted with use of appropriate circumference measurements. Furthermore, the derived equations for predicting total body volume, when used for calculating percentage of body fat, did not appear to be population specific.

The problem of population specificity has been investigated in different ways. Durnin and Womersley used the log of several skin folds for prediction. Jackson and Pollock and Jackson, Pollock, and Ward developed what they called generalized equations for men and women based on a curvilinear relationship between body density and skin folds. Most studies that have analyzed the validity of skin fold measurements have concluded that the sum of several skin folds is more valid than combinations of two or three.

Much has been written about anthropometric differences in black and white populations such as in body build, body segment lengths, trunk–leg–height indexes, and body composition. Blacks have been found to have heavier skeletons than whites (Malina 1969; Trotter and Peterson 1970). Body composition differences between blacks and whites have been found in density (Harsha, Frerichs, and Berenson 1978) and in total body water (Schutte 1980). Racial differences in body density have been ascribed to the larger bone density of blacks (Adams et al. 1981). Racial differences in skin fold thicknesses have been reported in several studies (Harsha,

Frerichs, and Berenson 1978; Johnston, Hamill, and Lemeshow 1972, 1974; Piscopo 1962). Cronk and Roche reported large differences between the races in triceps and subscapular skin fold measurements and expressed the need for separate sets of reference charts for blacks and whites.

Differences in body fat between males and females have long been recognized. Generally, males have lower skin fold scores than females. However, the differences in young boys and girls are not as pronounced. Hensley, East, and Stillwell found no sex difference in the sum of skin folds in 563 prepubescent children. Developmentally, girls tend to acquire progressively more fat over time, while the increase in fat in boys in early adolescence is temporary and is followed by an actual reduction in fat (Forbes and Amirhakimi 1970). Correlations among skin folds are higher among boys than among girls, which may indicate greater independence of fat patterning in girls, especially after age 12 (Johnston, Hamill, and Lemeshow 1972, 1974).

Physical training is effective in reducing body fat. A number of studies have shown relative fatness to vary inversely with training (Bale 1980; Hebbelinck et al. 1980; Helmuth 1980). The measurement and monitoring of relative fatness has become popular in athletics. Morrow and colleagues found that intercollegiate women volleyball players on the more successful teams were stronger, faster, and leaner than players on less successful teams. Katch and Katch reported no differences among power weight lifters, body builders, and Olympic weight lifters in percent fat, lean body weight, skin folds, and diameters. Ward, Groppel, and Stone found similar anthropometric profiles between Olympic and master weight lifters except in weight. Studies of runners have clearly demonstrated that low percent body fat is an important characteristic for success (Burke and Brush 1979; Flack and Hagarman 1980). Comparisons of body composition in football players have consistently shown differences among positions, with backs having less fat than linemen (Burke, Winslow, and Strube 1980; White, Mayhew, and Piper 1980).

Several studies have investigated the effects of exercise programs on body composition changes. Pollock and colleagues found reductions in weight and fatness to be similar in running, walking, and bicycling training regimens. The training effects were independent of the method of training when the frequency, duration, and intensity were similar. Gettman and associates reported a greater loss in fat for a 5-days/week exercise program than when subjects exercised only 3 or 1 days/week. Milesis and colleagues compared the effects of 15-, 30-, and 45-min exercise sessions on body composition and found that total skin fold measures were reduced in proportion to the duration of the training sessions.

BIBLIOGRAPHY

AAHPERD Health Related Physical Fitness Test Manual. Reston, Va.: AAHPERD, 1980.

Adams, J., K. Bagnall, K. McFadden, and M. Mottola, "Body Density Differences Between Negro and Caucasian Professional Football Players." *British Journal of Sports Medicine* 15:257–260, 1981.

Bale, P., "The Relationship of Physique and Body Composition to Strength in a Group of Physical Education Students." *British Journal of Sports Medicine* 14:193–198, 1980.

Barnes, W., "Selected Physiological Characteristics of Elite Male Sprint Athletes." *Journal of Sports Medicine and Physical Fitness* 21:49–52, 1981.

Baun, W. B., M. R. Baun, and P. B. Raven, "A Nomogram for the Estimate of Percent Body Fat From Generalized Equations." *Research Quarterly for Exercise and Sport* 52:380–384, October 1981.

Behnke, A. R., and J. H. Wilmore, *Evaluation and Regulation of Body Build and Composition*. Englewood Cliffs, N.J.: Prentice-Hall, 1974, pp. 66–67.

Burke, E., and F. C. Brush, "Physiological and Anthropometric Assessment of Successful Teenage Female Distance Runners." *Research Quarterly* 50:180–187, May 1979.

——— , E. Winslow, and W. Strube, "Measures of Body Composition and Performance in Major College Football Players." *Journal of Sports Medicine and Physical Fitness* 20:173–180, 1980.

Clarke, H. H., *Application of Measurement to Health and Physical Education*. 4th ed. Englewood Cliffs, N.J.: Prentice-Hall, 1967, p. 79.

——— , Ed., *Physical Fitness Research Digest*. Series 5, No. 2, April 1975.

——— , and E. W. Degutis, "Comparison of Skeletal Age and Various Physical and Motor Factors With the Pubescent Development of 10, 13, and 16 Year Old Boys." *Research Quarterly* 33:356–368, October 1962.

——— , and J. C. E. Harrison, "Differences in Physical and Motor Traits Between Boys of Advanced, Normal, and Retarded Maturity." *Research Quarterly* 33:13–25, March 1962.

——— , and K. H. Petersen, "Contrast of Maturational, Structural, and Strength Characteristics of Athletes and Nonathletes 10 to 15 Years of Age." *Research Quarterly* 32:163–176, May 1961.

Corbin, C. B., and P. Pletcher, "Diet and Physical Activity Patterns of Obese and Non-obese Elementary School Children." *Research Quarterly* 39:922–928, December 1968.

——— , L. J. Dowell, R. Lindsey, and H. Tolson, *Concepts in Physical Education*. 2nd ed. Dubuque, Iowa: William C. Brown, 1974, pp. 43–46.

Cronk, C. E., and A. F. Roche, "Race- and Sex-Specific Reference Data for Triceps and Subscapular Skinfolds and Weight/Stature^2." *American Journal of Clinical Nutrition* 35:347–354, 1982.

Cureton, T. K., "Body Build as a Framework of Reference for Interpreting Physical Fitness and Athletic Performance." *Research Quarterly Supplement* 12:301–330, May 1941.

——— , R. A. Boileau, and T. G. Lohman, "A Comparison of Densitometric, Potassium-40 and Skinfold Estimates of Body Composition in Prepubescent Boys." *Human Biology* 47:321–336, 1975.

Durnin, J. V. G. A., and M. M. Rahaman, "The Assessment of the Amount of Fat in the Human Body From Measurements of Skinfold Thickness." *British Journal of Nutrition* 21:681–689, 1967.

——— , and J. Womersley, "Body Fat Assessed From Total Body Density and its Estimation From Skinfold Thickness: Measurements on 481 Men and Women Aged 16 to 72 Years." *British Journal of Nutrition* 32:77–97, 1974.

Espenschade, A. S., "Restudy of Relationships Between Physical Performances of School Children and Age, Height, and Weight." *Research Quarterly* 34:144–153, May 1963.

Flack, S., and G. Hagarman, "Athletes' Body-Fat Charts Show Interesting Modern Trends." *Olympian* 7:14–16, 1980.

Forbes, G. B., and G. H. Amirhakimi, "Skinfold Thickness and Body Fat in Children." *Human Biology* 42:401–418, 1970.

Garrity, H. M., "Relationship of Somatotypes of College Women to Physical Fitness Performance." *Research Quarterly* 37:340–352, October 1966.

Gettman, L. R., et al., "Physiological Responses of Men to 1-, 3-, and 5-Day-per-Week Training Programs." *Research Quarterly* 47:638–646, December 1976.

Gross, E. A., and J. A. Casciani, "Value of Age, Height, and Weight as a Classification Device for Secondary School Students in the Seven AAHPER Youth Fitness Tests." *Research Quarterly* 33:51–58, March 1962.

Harsha, D. W., R. R. Frerichs, and G. S. Berenson, "Densitometry and Anthropometry of Black and White Children." *Human Biology* 50:261–280, 1978.

Heath, B. H., and J. E. L. Carter, "A Modified Somatotype Method." *American Journal of Physical Anthropology* 27:57–74, July 1967.

Hebbelinck, M., and J. W. Postma, "Anthropometric Measurements, Somatotype Ratings, and Certain Motor Fitness Tests of Physical Education Majors in South Africa." *Research Quarterly* 34:327–334, October 1963.

———, W. D. Ross, J. E. Carter, and J. Borms, "Anthropometric Characteristics of Female Olympic Rowers." *Canadian Journal of Sports Science* 5:255–262, 1980.

Helmuth, H. S, "Anthropometric Survey of Young Swimmers." *Anthropologischer Anzeiger* 38:17–34, 1980.

Hensley, L. D., W. B. East, and J. L. Stillwell, "Body Fatness and Motor Performance During Preadolescence." *Research Quarterly for Exercise and Sport* 53:133–140, June 1982.

Jackson, A. S., and M. L. Pollock, "Generalized Equations for Predicting Body Density of Men." *British Journal of Nutrition* 40:497–504, 1978.

———, ———, and A. Ward, "Generalized Equations for Predicting Body Density of Women." *Medicine and Science in Sports and Exercise* 12:175–182, 1980.

Johnson, B. L., J. K. Nelson, and M. J. Garcia, *Conditioning: Fitness and Performance for Everyone.* 3rd ed. Portland, Tex.: Brown and Littleman, 1982.

Johnston, F. E., P. V. Hamill, and S. Lemeshow, *Skinfold Thickness of Children 6-11 Years* (Series 11, No. 120, 1972) and *Skinfold Thickness of Youth 12-17 Years* (Series 11, No. 132, 1974). Washington, D.C.: U.S. National Center for Health Statistics, U.S. Department of Health, Education, and Welfare.

Katch, F. I., A. R. Behnke, and V. L. Katch, "Estimation of Body Fat From Skinfolds and Surface Area." *Human Biology* 51:411–424, 1979.

Katch, V. L., and F. I. Katch, "Muscular Development and Lean Body Weight in Body Builders and Weightlifters." *Medicine and Science in Sports and Exercise* 12:168–171, 1980.

Kistler, J. W., "A Comparative Study of Methods for Classifying Pupils." *Research Quarterly* 5:42–48, March 1934.

Krzywicki, H. J., et al., "A Comparison of Methods for Estimating Human Body Composition." *American Journal of Clinical Nutrition* 27:1380–1385, December 1974.

Lamb, L. E., Ed., *The Health Letter,* Vol. 5, No. 4, February 28, 1975.

Lohman, T. G., "Skinfold and Body Density and Their Relation to Body Fatness: A Review." *Human Biology* 52:181–225, 1981.

———, "Measurement of Body Composition in Children." *JOPERD* 53:67–70, October 1982.

Malina, R. M., "Quantification of Fat, Muscle, and Bone in Man." *Clinical Orthopaedics and Related Research* 65:9–38, 1969.

Mathews, D. K., *Measurement in Physical Education.* 5th ed. Philadelphia: W. B. Saunders, 1978, pp. 313–325.

Mayer, J., *Overweight Causes, Cost and Control.* Englewood Cliffs, N.J.: Prentice-Hall, 1968.

McCloy, C. H., *The Measurement of Athletic Power.* New York: A. S. Barnes, 1932.

Meredith, H. V., "A Physical Growth Record for Use in Elementary and High Schools." *American Journal of Public Health* 39:878–885, July 1949.

Milesis, C. A., et al., "Effects of Different Durations of Physical Training on Cardiorespiratory Function, Body Composition, and Serum Lipids." *Research Quarterly* 47:716–725, December 1976.

Miller, K. D., "The Wetzel Grid as a Performance Classifier With College Men." *Research Quarterly* 22:63–70, March 1951.

Morrow, J. R., A. S. Jackson, W. W. Hosler, and J. K. Kachurik, "The Importance of Strength, Speed, and Body Size for Team Success in Women's Intercollegiate Volleyball." *Research Quarterly* 50:429–437, October 1979.

Neilson, N. P., and F. W. Cozens, *Achievement Scales in Activities for Boys and Girls in Elementary and Junior High Schools.* New York: A. S. Barnes, 1934.

Piscopo, J., "Skinfold and Other Anthropometric Measurements of Pre-adolescent Boys From Three Ethnic Groups." *Research Quarterly* 33:255–264, May 1962.

Pollock, M. L., et al., "Effects of Mode of Training on Cardiovascular Function and Body Composition of Adult Men." *Medicine and Science in Sports* 7:139–145, Summer 1975.

Rarick, G. L., and N. Oyster, "Physical Maturity, Muscular Strength, and Motor Performance of Young School-Age Boys." *Research Quarterly* 35:522–531, December 1964.

Rich, G. Q., and J. Vincent, "Validity and Reliability of an Inexpensive Skinfold Caliper." Unpublished study, California State University, Northridge, Calif., 1981.

Schutte, J. E., "Prediction of Total Body Water in Adolescent Males." *Human Biology* 52:381–394, 1980.

Sheldon, W. H., *Atlas of Men*. New York: Harper and Brothers, 1954.

——— , S. S. Stevens, and W. B. Tucker, *The Varieties of Human Physique*. New York: Harper and Brothers, 1940.

Siri, W. E., "Gross Composition of the Body." In J. H. Lawrence and C. A. Tobias, Eds., *Advances in Biological and Medical Physics*. New York: Academic Press, 1956.

Trotter, M., and R. P. Peterson, "Weight of the Skeleton During Postnatal Development." *American Journal of Physical Anthropology* 33:313–324, 1970.

Wamsley, J. R., and J. E. Roberts, "Body Composition of USAF Flying Personnel." *Aerospace Medicine* 34:403–405, 1963.

Ward, T., J. L. Groppel, and M. Stone, "Anthropometry and Performance in Master and First Class Olympic Weightlifters." *Journal of Sports Medicine and Physical Fitness* 19:205–212, 1979.

Wear, C. L., and K. Miller, "Relationship of Physique and Developmental Level to Physical Performance." *Research Quarterly* 33:615–631, December 1962.

Weinberg, H. A., "Structural, Strength, and Maturity Characteristics as Related to Aspects of the Wetzel Grid for Boys Nine Through Fifteen Years of Age." Microcarded doctoral dissertation, University of Oregon, Eugene, 1964.

Weltman, A., and V. Katch, "Preferential Use of Casing (Girth) Measures for Estimating Body Volume and Density." *Journal of Applied Physiology* 38:560–563, March 1975.

Wetzel, N. C., *The Treatment of Growth Failure in Children*. Cleveland: National Education Association Service, 1948.

White, J., J. Mayhew, and F. Piper, "Prediction of Body Composition in College Football Players." *Journal of Sports Medicine and Physical Fitness* 20:317–322, 1980.

Willgoose, C. E., *Evaluation in Health Education and Physical Education*. New York: McGraw-Hill, 1961, Chapter 13.

Wilmore, J. H., "The Role of Health and Physical Education." Symposium on Overweight and Obesity, AAHPERD Convention, Anaheim, Calif., 1974.

——— , *Athletic Training and Physical Fitness*. Boston: Allyn and Bacon, 1977, p. 202.

Womersley, J., and J. V. G. A. Durnin, "A Comparison of the Skinfold Method With Extent of 'Overweight' and Various Weight-Height Relationships in the Assessment of Obesity." *British Journal of Nutrition* 38:271–284, 1977.

Zuti, W. B., "Effects of Diet and Exercise on Body Composition of Adult Women During Weight Reduction." Doctoral dissertation, Kent State University, Kent, Ohio, 1972.

CHAPTER 11

PHYSICAL FITNESS TEST BATTERIES

OBJECTIVES

After reading this chapter, the student should be able to:

1. Identify the components that should be represented by test items in a health-related physical fitness test battery

2. Differentiate between motor performance components and health-related fitness components in selecting test items for a physical fitness test battery

3. Administer one or more physical fitness test items in a practical testing situation

The preceding five chapters, Chapters 6 through 10, have presented a variety of test items dealing with each aspect of physical fitness. Now we are ready to look at some possible combinations of test items to make up physical fitness test batteries. Two primary criteria have been used in suggesting the following batteries: that test items not require expensive equipment and that each test battery be composed of at least one item from each of the five areas of physical fitness. This second criterion means that there will be at least one test item from each of the components of *strength, muscular endurance, flexibility, cardiorespiratory endurance,* and height–weight or *body composition.*

No physical fitness battery has heretofore included test items for all five of the areas of physical fitness, although the new AAHPERD Health Related Physical Fitness Test comes close. We will present this new test and also several suggested school-level batteries that do include all five fitness areas.

Anyone who attempts to establish a single test battery that purports to encompass several specific abilities is vulnerable to criticism. Such a person is immediately accused of making value judgments and certain assumptions that are virtually impossible to defend on a strict scientific basis. A very hazardous assumption concerns the generality of abilities or performances, which is not supported by research. For example, the inclusion of only one strength or endurance item in the battery would seem to indicate that the item tests "total" body strength or endurance. Furthermore, every test that is offered in the battery can spark debate over its merits and weaknesses relative to other tests that could equally well be offered. Certainly any selection is a reflection of the individual's philosophy and bias. (We by no means agree with each other on all the items we include!)

The test batteries we propose here have not been developed through any statistical selection process. Our primary assumption is that each test is a valid and reliable *indicator* of the desired quality, but is certainly not the only one. Furthermore, the components themselves are not mutually exclusive. Muscular endurance, for example, enters into cardiorespiratory testing, and vice versa; and strength is involved in any measure of fitness, whether it be muscular endurance, flexibility, or cardiorespiratory endurance. We have tried to remain mindful of the criterion of practical application as well as the other criteria of test evaluation and selection.

The tests selected have been described in preceding chapters. The equipment needed is inexpensive and easily acquired regardless of budget. Furthermore, we suggest alternatives for each test. This exemplifies our philosophy of measurement and evaluation. We believe teachers should not feel bound to use only those tests that are recommended by their department, the school system, the state, a particular textbook, or whatever the source might be. *No single test is that good.* Effective evaluation of specific qualities or of a general concept such as physical fitness is dependent on a number of measurements and judgments, not on any one test.

COMBINATIONS OF TESTS

Recommended Elementary School Physical Fitness Test

The objective of this test battery is to determine the physical fitness level of elementary school students. It is satisfactory for boys and girls of 6 to 11 years. The test items covered are:

Strength. Pull-ups, presented in Chapter 7.

Muscular endurance. Modified push-ups, presented in Chapter 8; bent-knee sit-ups, presented in Chapter 8.

Flexibility. Modified sit-and-reach or trunk-and-neck extension, both presented in Chapter 6.

Cardiorespiratory endurance. 1-Mile or 9-minute run, both presented in Chapter 9.

Height–weight rating or body composition. Students' height and weight are compared with the averages in Table A.1 in Appendix A and the deviations are rated according to the rating scale shown in Table 11.1. The

triceps and subscapular skin fold measurements may also be used. Norms were presented in Chapter 10.

The reliability, objectivity, and validity for the battery, as well as needed equipment and materials, are found under the individual test items. It is recommended that local norms be established and that scoring be patterned in a fashion similar to the scoring suggested for high school and collegiate tests (Table 11.5). Limited elementary school norms appear in Table 11.2. These norms reflect only average scores for each age listed. Furthermore, the scores were gathered from students who, in some cases, were not in a high state of physical fitness. The norms should be used to determine weak performance areas and to encourage children to train to far exceed the scores listed.

Recommended Junior High School Physical Fitness Test

The objective of this battery is to determine the physical fitness level of junior high school students. It is satisfactory for boys and girls of 12 to 14 years. The test items covered are:

Strength. Boys—spring scale press test, presented in Chapter 7; girls—two-hand push test (spring scale), presented in Chapter 7.

Muscular endurance. Boys—pull-up or spring scale repetitive press test, presented in Chapter 8; girls—flexed-arm hang or spring scale repetitive press test, presented in Chapter 8; boys and girls—bent-knee sit-ups, presented in Chapter 8.

Flexibility. Modified sit-and-reach or trunk-and-neck extension, presented in Chapter 6.

Cardiorespiratory endurance. 1-Mile or 9-minute run-walk test, presented in Chapter 9.

Table 11.1. Height–Weight Rating Scale for Elementary School, Junior High School, High School, and College Level

RATING	DEVIATION FROM AVERAGE (lb)			
	Elementary	Junior High	High	College
Excellent	0 to ± 2	0 to ± 3	0 to ± 4	0 to ± 4
Good	± 3 to ± 4	± 4 to ± 5	± 5 to ± 7	± 5 to ± 9
Average	± 5 to ± 7	± 6 to ± 8	± 8 to ±12	±10 to ±14
Poor	± 8 to ±12	± 9 to ±13	±13 to ±16	±15 to ±19
Very poor	±13 and above	±14 and above	±17 and above	±20 and above

ᵃCompare with norms in Appendix A.

Table 11.2. Average Score for Fitness Performance for Elementary School Students

TEST ITEM[a] (UNIT)	AGE				
	7	8	9	10	11
	BOYS				
Pull-ups (no.)[b]	1	1	2	3	4
Sit-and-reach (in.)	15½	15½	15½	15½	15½
Bent-knee sit-ups (no.)	30	34	37	39	43
1-Mile run (min)	10:15	9:54	9:32	9:07	8:45
	GIRLS				
Flexed-arm hang (sec)	7.30	6.70	6.26	6.86	6.60
Sit-and-reach (in.)	17¾	18	18¼	18½	18¾
Bent-knee sit-ups (no.)	24	26	28	29	32
1-Mile run (min)	12:05	11:38	11:03	10:30	9:59

[a]All data from M. C. Gomez, Corpus Christi, Tex., 1974, except boys sit-and-reach, from M. J. Garcia, Corpus Christi, Tex., 1974, and girls flexed-arm hang, from J. DiNucci, Stephen F. Austin State University, Nacogdoches, Tex., 1974.
[b]Reverse grip.
Source: Adapted from B. L. Johnson, J. K. Nelson, and M. J. Garcia, *Conditioning: Fitness and Performance for Everyone.* 3rd ed. Portland, Tex.: Brown and Littleman, 1982. Used by permission.

Height–weight rating or body composition. Students' height and weight are compared with the averages shown in Tables A.1 and A.2 in Appendix A and the deviations are rated according to the rating scale shown in Table 11.1. Measurements of triceps and subscapular skin folds may also be used. Norms were presented in Chapter 10.

The reliability, objectivity, and validity for the battery, as well as needed equipment and materials, are found under the individual test items. It is recommended that local norms be established and that scoring be patterned after the scores appearing in Table 11.5. Limited junior high norms appear in Table 11.3. These norms reflect only average scores for each age listed. Furthermore, the scores were gathered from students who, in some cases, were not in a high state of physical fitness. These norms should be used to determine weak performance areas and to encourage students to train to far exceed the scores listed.

Table 11.3. Average Scores for Fitness Performance for Junior High School Students

TEST ITEM[a] (UNIT)	AGE		
	12	13	14
	BOYS		
Pull-ups (no.)	4	5	6
Sit-and-reach (in.)	16	16½	17
Bent-knee sit-ups (no.)	46	46	48
12-Minute run (mi)	1.25	1.28	1.30
	GIRLS		
Flexed-arm hang (sec)	6.25	13.89	7.74
Sit-and-reach (in.)	18¾	19	19¼
Bent-knee sit-ups (no.)	33	35	36
12-Minute run (mi)	1.15	1.18	1.24

[a]All data from M. C. Gomez, Corpus Christi, Tex., 1974, except boys sit-and-reach, from R. Stumiller and L. Mangum, Corpus Christi, Tex., 1974, and girls flexed-arm hang, from J. DiNucci, Stephen F. Austin State University, Nacogdoches, Tex., 1974.
Source: Adapted from B. L. Johnson, J. K. Nelson, and M. J. Garcia, *Conditioning: Fitness and Performance for Everyone.* 3rd ed. Portland, Tex.: Brown and Littleman, 1982. Used by permission.

Recommended High School and Collegiate Physical Fitness Test

The objective of this battery is to determine the overall physical fitness level of high school and college students. It is recommended for boys and girls of the tenth grade through college. The test items are:

Strength. Two-hand push test, presented in Chapter 7.

Flexibility. Modified sit-and-reach test, presented in Chapter 6.

Muscular endurance. Men—chin-up test, presented in Chapter 8; women—flexed-arm hang test, presented in Chapter 8.

Cardiorespiratory endurance. 12-Minute run-walk test, presented in Chapter 9.

Height–weight rating or body composition. Students' height and weight are compared with the averages shown in Table A.2 in Appendix A (college students use averages shown for age 18) and the deviations are rated according to the rating scale shown in Table 11.1. Measurements of triceps and subscapular skin folds may also be used. Norms were presented in Chapter 10.

The reliability, objectivity, and validity for the battery, as well as needed equipment and materials, are found under the individual test items.

Limited norms for high school students are shown in Table 11.4 and for college students in Table 11.5. In the case of high school students, the norms reflect only average scores for each age listed. Furthermore, the scores were gathered from students who, in some cases, were not in a high state of physical fitness. The norms should be used to determine weak performance areas and to encourage students to train to far exceed the scores listed.

OTHER PHYSICAL FITNESS TEST BATTERIES

Although the following test batteries do not include all components of physical fitness, the items in them represent two or more of the five components of physical fitness. The batteries do not include motor performance items.

AAHPERD Health Related Physical Fitness Test (1980)

After several years of deliberation and study, the AAHPERD charged a task force with the responsibility of developing a health-related physical fitness test. The task force selected test items on the basis of the following criteria:

1. The test should measure a range of fitness

Table 11.4. Average Scores for Fitness Performance for High School Students

TEST ITEM[a] (UNIT)	AGE		
	15	16	17
BOYS			
Pull-ups (no.)	6	7	8
Sit-and-reach (in.)	17	17¼	17½
Bent-knee sit-ups (no.)	48	49	51
12-Minute run (mi)	1.30	1.32	1.35
GIRLS			
Flexed-arm hang (sec)	7.55	7.65	11.02
Sit-and-reach (in.)	19¼	19	19
Bent-knee sit-ups (no.)	26	24	28
12-Minute run (mi)	1.18	1.20	1.16

[a]All data from M. C. Gomez, Corpus Christi, Tex., 1974, except boys sit-and-reach, from Ed Livsey, Corpus Christi, Tex., 1974, and girls flexed-arm hang, from J. DiNucci, Stephen F. Austin State University, Nacogdoches, Tex., 1974.

Source: B. L. Johnson, J. K. Nelson, and M. J. Garcia, *Conditioning: Fitness and Performance for Everyone.* 3rd ed. Portland, Tex.: Brown and Littleman, 1982. Used by permission.

Table 11.5. Norms for Collegiate Physical Fitness Test[a]

PERFORMANCE LEVEL	TWO-HAND PUSH[b]	PULL-UPS (NO.)	SIT-AND-REACH (IN.)	12-MINUTE (MI)	RUN-WALK (GYM LAPS)
			MEN		
Excellent	1.16 and above	15 and above	23¾ and above	1.75 and above	32.2 and above
Good	1.07–1.15	12–14	21¼–23½	1.50–1.74	27.4–32.1
Average	.90–1.06	8–11	18¾–21.0	1.25–1.49	24.0–27.3
Poor	.81– .89	5– 7	17.0–18½	1.01–1.24	20.4–23.9
Very poor	.00– .80	0– 4	0 –16¾	0 –1.0	0 –20.3
			WOMEN		
Excellent	.99 and above	37 and above	25¾ and above	1.65 and above	29.2 and above
Good	.92–.98	25–36	22½–25½	1.35–1.64	25.2–29.1
Average	.64–.91	10–24	20 –22¼	1.15–1.34	20.4–25.1
Poor	.52–.63	5– 9	18 –19¾	.96–1.14	18.0–20.3
Very poor	.00–.51	0– 4	0 –17¾	0 – .95	0 –17.9

EXAMPLE	RATING FOR JOE DOE	OVERALL RATING
Each excellent = 5 pts	Height–weight Good = 4	23–25 Excellent
Each good = 4 pts	Two-hand push: Excellent = 5	18–22 Good
Each average = 3 pts	Pull-up: Average = 3	13–17 Average
Each poor = 2 pts	Sit-and-reach: Poor = 2	8–12 Poor
Each very poor = 1 pt	12-Minute run-walk Good = 4	0– 7 Very poor
	18 pts = Good	

[a]Based on the socres of 250 men and 200 women at Corpus Christi State University, Corpus Christi, Tex., 1975.
[b]Score obtained by dividing body weight into weight lifted.

from severely limited dysfunction to high levels of function.

2. The test should encompass capacities that can be improved with physical activity.

3. The test should accurately reflect physical fitness status and changes in functional capacity in its scores.

Three areas of physiologic function that were deemed to be related to positive health, were of national concern, and which met these criteria were cardiorespiratory function, body composition (leanness–fatness), and abdominal and low back–hamstring musculoskeletal function. The components and test items for the AAHPERD Health Related Physical Fitness Test are as follows:

Cardiorespiratory function. 1-Mile run or 9-minute run, presented in Chapter 9 (1.5-mile or 12-minute runs are optional for students 13 years of age or older; see Chapter 9).

Body composition (leanness–fatness). Sum of triceps and subscapular skin folds, presented in Chapter 10 (triceps skin fold is optional if only one site is selected).

Abdominal and low back–hamstring musculoskeletal function. Modified, timed sit-ups, presented in Chapter 8; sit-and-reach, presented in Chapter 6.

U.S. Army Physical Fitness Test (Department of the Army 1957)

Objective: To measure physical fitness through measurement of endurance.

Sex and Age Level: Recommended for men 18 years and older.

Reliability: None indicated in the Army guide (see individual test items in Chapter 8).

Objectivity: None indicated in the Army guide (see individual test items in Chapter 8).

Validity: According to Field Manual 21–20 (October 1957), groups previously deemed to be in excellent condition scored high on this test, while groups previously deemed to be in poor physical condition scored low on the test. Moreover, the directions and test items meet the criteria for certain components of physical fitness. Basically, this test battery is one of muscular endurance with one item (300-yard run) intended for circulorespiratory endurance. However, the 300-yard run is of doubtful validity as a circulorespiratory test for adult men, and the 60-second squat-thrust test may be substituted.

Test Equipment and Materials: Listed under individual test items in Chapter 8 and under distance runs in Chapter 9.

Test Items:

Pull-ups. Presented in Chapter 8.

Push-ups. Presented in Chapter 8.

300-Yard run or longer distance runs. Presented in Chapter 9.

Squat-thrust. Presented in Chapter 8.

Scoring: Five of the six events are totaled for the individual total test score. The 300-yard run and the 60-second squat-thrust (Burpee) test are offered as a choice of one test item to be included with the other four items. Raw scores are converted to point scores by use of the scoring tables. For example, 12 pull-ups equal 78 points. Table 11.6 shows a rating scale.

U.S. Navy Physical Fitness Test (Department of the Navy 1957)

Objective: To measure physical fitness through measurement of muscular endurance.

Sex and Age Level: Recommended for men 18 years of age and older.

Reliability: None indicated (see individual test items in Chapter 8).

Objectivity: None indicated (see individual test items in Chapter 8).

Validity: None reported; however, the test items are acceptable on the basis of face validity as muscular endurance items, one of the components of physical fitness.

Test Equipment and Materials: Listed under individual test items in Chapter 8.

Test Items:

Squat thrusts. Presented in Chapter 8.

Sit-ups. Presented in Chapter 8.

Push-ups. Presented in Chapter 8.

Pull-ups (chin-ups). Presented in Chapter 8.

Scoring: The number of repetitions for each test item is recorded and the result compared with a

T-score scale. *T* scores for the five items may be added and averaged for a total test score. Table 11.7 shows *T*-score norms.

OTHER FITNESS TESTS THAT INCLUDE MOTOR PERFORMANCE ITEMS

Texas Physical Fitness—Motor Ability Test (Texas Governor's Commission, N.D.)

The Texas Governor's Commission on Physical Fitness designed a test that separated fitness components from motor components. The physical fitness section of the test includes the following items:

Muscular endurance items
Pull-ups (for boys)
Flexed-arm hang (for girls)
Dips
Bent-knee sit-ups

Cardiorespiratory endurance items
12-Minute run–walk
1.5-Mile run–walk
9-Minute run or 1-mile run (for grades 4–6)

No items specifically measure flexibility, strength, or body composition (height–weight rating). A frequent criticism of the test by public school teachers of Texas is that the norm tables are confusing and difficult to understand. A strong point of the test, however, is the fact that it does separate fitness components from motor performance components.

AAHPERD Youth Fitness Test (1976 Revision)

The latest revision of the AAHPERD Youth Fitness Test has improved the test battery considerably. The softball throw for distance (strictly a specific sports skill item) was eliminated. The sit-up test was changed from straight leg to bent knee, and is now timed (1 min). The distance run item provides for optional distances. The 1-mile or 9-minute run is suggested for ages 10 to 12 and the 1.5-mile or 12-minute run for ages 13 and over. Norms for these longer distance runs are taken from the Texas Physical Fitness Test.

The classification of the test items as physical fitness or motor performance items is shown in Table 11.8.

Table 11.6.   U.S. Army Physical Fitness Scale[a]

PERFORMANCE LEVEL	PULL-UPS (NO.)	SQUAT JUMPS (NO.)	PUSH-UPS (NO.)	SIT-UPS (NO.)	300-YARD RUN (SEC)	60-SECOND SQUAT THRUSTS (NO.)
Excellent	12–18	77–95	48–60	72–85	50–44	35–41
Good	7–11	53–76	28–47	48–71	58–50.5	30–34
Average	6	52	27	47	58.5	29
Poor	3–5	27–51	10–26	22–46	67–59	22–28
Very poor	1–2	3–26	1–9	1–21	73.5–67.5	14–21

[a]Modified from the Department of the Army, *Physical Training,* Washington, D.C.: Headquarters, Dept. of Army, Oct. 1957, pp. 197–201.

Table 11.7.   *T* Scores for Navy Standard Physical Fitness Test[a]

T SCORES	SQUAT THRUSTS (NO.)	SIT-UPS (NO.)	PUSH-UPS (NO.)	SQUAT JUMPS (NO.)	PULL-UPS (NO.)
80–100	41–48	100–205	54–89	75–127	23–37
60–79	33–40	51– 99	35–53	45– 74	13–22
40–59	25–32	25– 50	22–34	27– 44	6–12
20–39	15–24	13– 24	13–21	16– 26	2– 5
0–19	0–14	0– 12	0–12	0– 15	0– 1

[a]Modified from the Department of the Navy, *Physical Fitness Manual for the U.S. Navy,* Washington, D.C.: Bureau of Navy Personnel, Training Division, Physical Section, 1943, Ch. IV.

Table 11.8. Classification of AAHPERD Youth Fitness Test Items Into Physical or Motor Fitness Measures

TEST ITEMS	COMPONENT	SEX
PHYSICAL FITNESS ITEMS		
Pull-up test	Muscular endurance	Male
Flexed-arm hang	Muscular endurance	Female
Sit-up (bent knees)	Muscular endurance	Both
600-Yard run[a]	Cardiorespiratory endurance	Both
MOTOR PERFORMANCE ITEMS		
Shuttle run	Agility	Both
Standing long jump	Power	Both
50-Yard dash	Speed	Both

[a]Options offered to the 600-yard run test include the 1-mile or 9-minute run for ages 10–12 and the 1.5-mile or 12-minute run for ages 13 and older.

BIBLIOGRAPHY

AAHPERD Youth Fitness Test Manual. Reston, Va.: AAHPERD, 1976.

AAHPERD Health Related Physical Fitness Test Manual. Reston, Va.: AAHPERD, 1980.

Clarke, H. H., *Application of Measurement to Health and Physical Education*. New York: Prentice-Hall, 1950, pp. 155–185.

Department of Army, *Physical Training*. Washington, D.C.: Headquarters, Department of Army, October 1957, pp. 197–201.

Department of Navy, *Physical Fitness Manual for the U.S. Navy*. Washington, D.C.: Bureau of Navy Personnel, Training Division, Physical Section, 1943, Chapter IV.

Johnson, B. L., J. K. Nelson, and M. J. Garcia, *Conditioning: Fitness and Performance for Everyone*. 3rd ed. Portland, Tex.: Brown and Littleman, 1982.

McCloy, C. H., and N. D. Young, *Tests and Measurements in Health and Physical Education*. New York: Appleton-Century-Crofts, 1954, pp. 129–141.

Texas Governor's Commission on Physical Fitness, *Texas Physical Fitness–Motor Ability Test*. Austin: Texas Governor's Commission on Physical Fitness (N.D.).

CHAPTER 12

THE MEASUREMENT OF POWER

OBJECTIVES

After reading this chapter, the student should be able to:

1. Define power and differentiate it from the components of speed and strength
2. Distinguish between athletic-power and work-power tests
3. Understand and anticipate some of the administrative problems in measuring power in physical education
4. Follow the directions for administering practical tests of power

Power may be defined as the ability to release maximum force in the fastest possible time. It is exemplified in the vertical jump, the long jump, the shot put, and other movements involving rapid muscular contractions.

The measurement of power in physical education has recently become controversial enough to warrant recognition of two types of such measurement. They are:

Athletic-power measurement. This type of measurement is expressed in terms of the distance through which the body or an object is propelled through space. Such tests as the vertical jump, long jump, and vertical arm-pull test (distance) are practical and common tests of athletic power. While such tests involve both force and velocity, their results are also influenced by other factors. The factors of force and velocity are not measured as such; only the resultant distance (inches or feet) is recorded in athletic-power measurement.

Work-power measurement. In measuring power for research purposes, special efforts are usually made to eliminate extraneous movements, so that maximum effort is expended by the specific muscle group to be studied. The result is usually expressed as work (force × distance) or power (work/time). Examples of this type of measurement are the vertical power jump (Glencross 1960), the power lever (Glencross 1966b), the modified vertical power jump (work) (Glencross 1960), and the vertical arm pull (work) (Johnson 1969).

Athletic-power tests are quite practical for the majority of schools and have been widely used in athletics and motor-testing programs. New tests, the modified vertical power jump (work) and the vertical arm pull (work), also have been developed for practical use in physical education programs and for research. Because power includes the important factors of strength and speed of movement, it may become confused with these types of tests. However, strength tests are concerned only with the force exerted or the number of pounds successfully lifted, and speed tests are concerned with the amount of time taken to cover a specified distance or the distance covered in a specified amount of time. In power tests, the distance, force, and time factors should be specified, while the resistance is usually either body weight or an object weighing a certain number of pounds. The Margaria Test of Anaerobic Power (Margaria, Aghemo, and Rovelli 1966) has been used in a number of research studies as a criterion of power. The 40-, 50-, and 60-yard dashes and some agility runs have been used as tests of power, and this has caused some confusion in power measurement. Since these tests are more characteristic of speed and agility, however, they should not be considered power tests.

USES OF POWER TESTS

Power tests can be used in physical education in several ways:

1. As a factor in motor ability tests
2. As a means to motivate students to improve their status within the class
3. As a measure for determining achievement and grades when improvement in athletic power is a specific objective in a physical activity class
4. As a means to indicate an individual's potential for varsity athletics

PROBLEMS ASSOCIATED WITH POWER TESTING

Several of the problems associated with power testing are listed as follows:

1. Vigorous activity prior to jumping performance tests seems to have a significantly negative effect on performance. Therefore, more consideration should be given to rest for participants prior to testing of jumping performance (Nelson 1961, 1962).
2. Practice and coaching tips seem to affect the reliability and validity of athletic power tests, owing to improved use of extraneous movements rather than to actual increase in power itself. Thus, it seems necessary to either eliminate the extraneous movements or practice the test movements until all are executed correctly, before scores are recorded.
3. The level of motivation must be controlled so that all students are tested under the same conditions. Conditions that are usually considered standard are knowledge of results, testing in the presence of peers, and avoidance of cheering and other unusual circumstances.

4. The common tests of athletic power (e.g., vertical jump, long jump, medicine ball put) are inadequate for use in experimental research, since the effects of learning could be misinterpreted as an increase in power. Therefore, such tests as the vertical power jump and the power lever may be appropriate, since extraneous movements are controlled to a greater extent in these tests than in athletic-power tests.
5. Norms are needed at all grade levels for both boys and girls on certain power tests. The norms for several tests presented in this chapter are based on the scores of local high school and college students.

PRACTICAL TESTS OF ATHLETIC POWER

Several tests of athletic power that are practical in terms of time, equipment, and cost are presented here.

Vertical Jump (Sargent Chalk Jump) (Sargent 1921)

Objective: To measure the power of the legs in jumping vertically upward.

Age Level: Satisfactory for age 9 through adulthood.

Sex: Satisfactory for both boys and girls.

Reliability: An r as high as .93 has been reported.

Objectivity: An objectivity coefficient of .93 was obtained by Jack Clayton, Northeast Louisiana University, Monroe, 1969.

Validity: A validity of .78 has been reported with the criterion of a sum of four track and field event scores.

Equipment and Materials: A yardstick; several pieces of chalk; and a smooth wall at least 12 ft high.

Directions: The performer stands with one side toward a wall, heels together, and holds a 1-in. piece of chalk in the hand nearest the wall. Keeping the heels on the floor, the student reaches upward as high as possible and makes a mark on the wall. The performer then jumps as high as possible and makes another mark at the height of the jump (Figure 12.1). Three to five trials are allowed.

Scoring: The number of inches (or centimeters) between the reach and the jump marks in the best

Figure 12.1.   Vertical jump test

trial, measured to the nearest half inch, is the score. Table 12.1 shows norms for this test.

Additional Pointers:

1. A double jump or a "crow hop" is not permitted on takeoff.

2. The chalk should be extended no further than necessary beyond the fingertips to make the standing and jumping marks.

3. The reliability and validity of the test can be slightly improved if the performer prac-

Table 12.1.   Vertical Jump Scoring Table

AGE	SEX	SCORE										
		100	90	80	70	60	50	40	30	20	10	0
9–11	Boys and girls	16	15	14	12	11	10	9	7	4	2	0
12–14	Boys	20	18	17	16	14	13	11	9	5	2	0
	Girls	16	15	14	13	12	11	10	8	4	2	0
15–17	Boys	25	24	23	21	19	16	12	8	5	2	0
	Girls	17	16	15	14	13	11	8	6	3	2	0
18–34	Men	26	25	24	23	19	16	13	9	8	2	0
	Women	14	13	13	12	10	8	6	4	2	1	0

Source: Harold T. Friermood, "Volleyball Skills Contest for Olympic Development." In United States Volleyball Association, *Annual Official Volleyball Rules and Reference Guide of the U.S. Volleyball Association.* Berne, Ind.: USVBA Printer, 1967, pp. 134–135.

tices the jump until it is correctly executed before being tested.

4. Body weight may be included in the score, which is then in terms of foot-pounds.

Standing Broad or Long Jump (AAHPERD 1976)

Objective: To measure the athletic power of the legs in jumping forward.

Age Level: Age 6 through college age.

Sex: Satisfactory for both boys and girls.

Reliability: An *r* as high as .963 has been reported.

Objectivity: An objectivity coefficient of .96 was obtained by Jack Clayton, Northeast Louisiana University, Monroe, 1969.

Validity: A validity of .607 has been reported for this test when a pure power test was used as the criterion.

Equipment and Materials: Either a mat or the floor; marking material (tape or chalk) (to mark the starting line); and a tape measure (to mark off increments of distance along the landing area).

Directions: With the feet parallel to each other and behind the starting mark, the performer bends the knees, swings the arms, and jumps as far forward as possible (Figure 12.2). Three trials are permitted.

Scoring: The number of inches between the starting line and the nearest heel on landing in the best of three trials is the score. Tables 12.2 and 12.3 show norms.

Additional Pointers:

1. If the performer falls backward on landing, the measurement is made between the starting line and the nearest part of the body touching the landing surface.

2. The student should practice the jump until the movement can be executed correctly, since practice improves the test's validity and reliability.

Vertical Arm-Pull Test (Distance) (Johnson 1973)

Objective: To measure the power of the arms and shoulder girdle in pulling the body upward. This test may be used to indicate potential in pole vaulting and gymnastics.

Age Level: Age 14 through college age.

Figure 12.2. Standing broad (or long) jump

Table 12.2. Percentile Scores for Standing Long Jump, Boys and Girls

PERCENTILE	AGE							
	9–10	11	12	13	14	15	16	17+
				GIRLS				
95	5'10"	6'0"	6'2"	6'5"	6'8"	6'7"	6'6"	6'9"
75	5'2"	5'4"	5'6"	5'9"	5'11"	5'10"	5'9"	6'0"
50	4'8"	4'11"	5'0"	5'3"	5'4"	5'5"	5'3"	5'5"
25	4'1"	4'4"	4'6"	4'9"	4'10"	4'11"	4'9"	4'11"
5	3'5"	3'8"	3'10"	4'0"	4'0"	4'2"	4'0"	4'1"
				BOYS				
95	6'0"	6'2"	6'6"	7'1"	7'6"	8'0"	8'2"	8'5"
75	5'4"	5'7"	5'11"	6'3"	6'8"	7'2"	7'6"	7'9"
50	4'11"	5'2"	5'5"	5'9"	6'2"	6'8"	7'0"	7'2"
25	4'6"	4'8"	5'0"	5'2"	5'6"	6'1"	6'6"	6'6"
5	3'10"	4'0"	4'2"	4'4"	4'8"	5'2"	5'5"	5'3"

Source: Adapted from *AAHPERD Youth Fitness Test Manual.* Reston, Va.: AAHPERD, 1976. Used by permission.

Table 12.3. Percentile Scores for Standing Long Jump, Elementary School Children[a]

PERCENTILE	SEX	AGE					
		6	7	8	9	10	11
99	Boys	56	57	68	67	69	66
	Girls	49	54	58	61	67	62
90	Boys	47	50	56	60	61	64
	Girls	44	48	52	56	57	61
80	Boys	44	47	54	56	58	61
	Girls	40	43	48	52	55	59
70	Boys	42	44	52	54	56	59
	Girls	39	41	47	50	52	55
60	Boys	41	43	50	53	55	57
	Girls	37	39	44	49	50	53
50	Boys	40	42	49	51	54	55
	Girls	34	38	42	47	49	50
40	Boys	40	40	47	50	52	52
	Girls	32	37	41	43	48	49
30	Boys	39	39	44	48	50	50
	Girls	30	36	40	42	46	48
20	Boys	38	37	42	46	48	49
	Girls	25	33	38	40	43	47
10	Boys	35	34	39	43	46	45
	Girls	24	30	37	37	40	46
N	Boys	27	116	126	203	149	50
	Girls	31	101	113	100	82	32

[a]Measurements were taken to the nearest inch, and the best score of two trials was recorded.

Source: D. H. Hardin and J. Ramirez, "Elementary School Performance Norms." *TAHPER Journal*, February 1972, pp. 8–9.

Sex: Satisfactory for boys only.

Reliability: An *r* of .97 was found for this test.

Objectivity: An *r* of .99 indicated a high degree of objectivity.

Validity: An *r* of .80 was found when the distance score test was correlated with the vertical power pull test (work/time).

Equipment and Materials: A climbing rope; marking tape; a tape measure; and a chair. Required dress is shorts, light shirt, and no shoes.

Directions: The performer's name is recorded and he then assumes a sitting position on a chair or bench (seat level at least 15 in. off the floor) and with both hands grasps as high up the rope as possible without raising the buttocks from the chair or bench seat. The hand of the preferred arm should be just above the other hand. The tester places a piece of marking tape around the rope just above the uppermost hand (Figure 12.3a). The performer then pulls himself up (without letting the feet touch the floor) and reaches as high up the rope as possible, holding the rope until the tester can again place a piece of marking tape above the uppermost hand (Figure 12.3c). Three trials are allowed; any trial in which the feet touch the floor during the pull is disregarded. On the third trial, the tester says, "This is your last pull. Try to beat your last two pulls."

Scoring: The distance between the two tape marks in the best pull, measured to the nearest quarter inch, is the score. Table 12.4 shows norms for males of different ages.

Additional Pointers:

1. The tester must have marking tape ready to immediately place above the uppermost hand as it grasps the rope.

2. The performer should be instructed to vigorously pike (flex) the hips as he makes the pull.

3. The performer may close his legs in around the rope following his pull and grasp (but not before the uppermost hand makes its grasp).

4. The rope should hang directly downward so that it touches the front edge of the chair between the legs of the performer.

5. As the performer's buttocks leave the chair, the tester may step on the chair to mark the height of the performer's reach.

6. From the starting position, the uppermost hand will be the pulling hand; the lower hand will become the reaching hand during the pull. (This is a one-pull-and-grasp test, not a climbing-sequence test.)

Two-Hand Medicine Ball Put (6 lb)

Objective: To measure the power of the arms and shoulder girdle.

Age Level: Age 12 through college age.

Sex: Satisfactory for boys and girls.

Reliability: An *r* of .81 was found for college girls, while an *r* of .84 was found for college men.

Objectivity: An *r* of .99 was reported by Gene Ford, Northeast Louisiana University, Monroe, 1969.

Validity: An *r* of .77 was obtained by correlating distance scores with scores computed by the power formula. The angle of release was not analyzed, however, although this is a definite limiting factor affecting validity.

Equipment and Materials: A 6-lb medicine ball; marking material (chalk or tape); a small rope; a chair; and a tape measure.

Directions: From a sitting position in a straight-back chair, the performer holds the ball in both hands with the ball drawn back against the chest and just under the chin. He or she then pushes the ball upward and outward for maximum distance. The rope is placed around the performer's chest and held taut to the rear by a partner, to eliminate rocking action during the push (Figure 12.4). The performer's effort should be primarily with the arms. Three trials are allowed.

Scoring: The distance the ball is thrown in the best of three trials, measured to the nearest foot, is recorded as the score. One or more practice trials may be taken before scoring. Table 12.5 shows norms for college students.

Additional Pointers:

1. The three trials should be taken in succession.

2. Distance is measured from the forward edge of the chair to the point of contact of the ball with the floor.

Shot-Put Test (With Softball)

Objective: To measure general body power in putting a softball as far as possible.

Age Level: Age 10 through college age.

Sex: Satisfactory for both boys and girls.

Reliability: An *r* of .83 was found when the best of three trials of one test date was correlated with

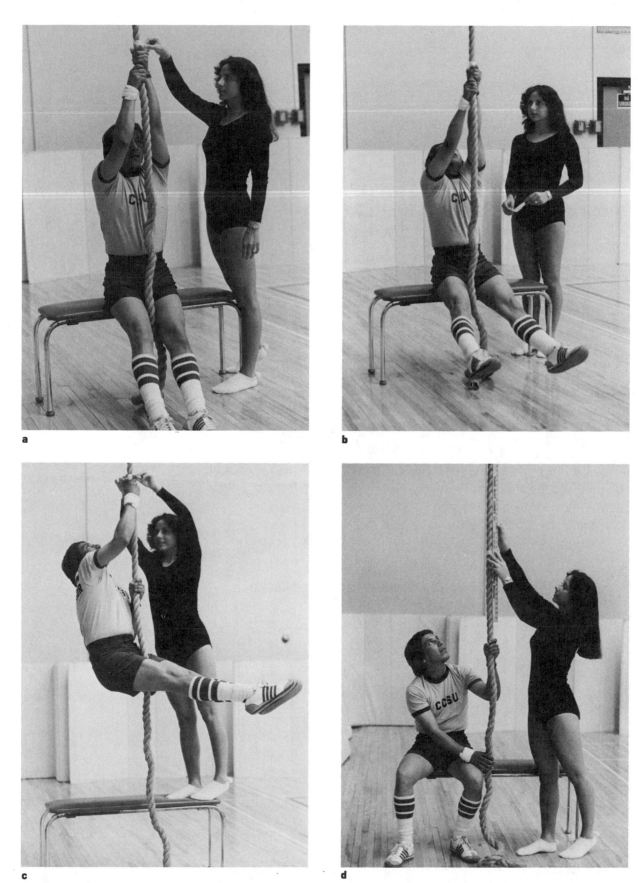

Figure 12.3.   Vertical arm-pull test for distance

Table 12.4. Norms for Vertical Arm-Pull Test (Distance)

PERFORMANCE LEVEL	HIGH SCHOOL AND COLLEGE POLE VAULTERS AND GYMNASTS[a]		COLLEGE MEN[b]	
	Inches	Centimeters	Inches	Centimeters
Advanced	31 –33¾	78.7–85.7	28¾–30¼	73.0–76.8
Advanced intermediate	29 –30¾	73.7–78.1	26¼–28½	66.7–72.4
Intermediate	25 –28¾	63.5–73.0	19¼–26	48.9–66.0
Advanced beginner	20½–24¾	52.1–62.9	15½–19	39.4–48.3
Beginner	0 –20¼	0 –51.4	0 –15¼	0 –38.7

PERFORMANCE LEVEL	HIGH SCHOOL BOYS[c]		JUNIOR HIGH SCHOOL BOYS[d]	
	Inches	Centimeters	Inches	Centimeters
Advanced	26 –29½	66.0–74.9	24¼–26¼	61.6–66.7
Advanced intermediate	24½–25¾	62.2–65.4	22½–23¾	57.2–60.3
Intermediate	19 –24¼	48.3–61.6	15 –22¼	38.1–56.5
Advanced beginner	15¼–18¾	38.7–47.6	12 –14¾	30.5–37.5
Beginner	0 –15	0 –38.1	0 –11¾	0 –29.8

[a]Based on the scores of 25 pole vaulters and gymnasts in Louisiana.
[b]Based on the scores of 150 college men in Texas and Louisiana.
[c]Based on the scores of 125 high school boys in Texas and Louisiana.
[d]Based on the scores of 65 junior high school students in Texas and Louisiana.

Figure 12.4. Position for two-hand medicine ball put

the best of three trials on a second test date, as reported by Robert Martinez, Corpus Christi State University, Corpus Christi, Tex., 1982.

Objectivity: An *r* of .97 was reported by George Adkison and Robert Martinez, Corpus Christi, Tex., when the two testers independently recorded a group of performers.

Validity: Face validity is accepted for this test when it is scored as an athletic power test.

Equipment: Several regulation softballs; marking tape or chalk; and a field tape.

Directions: The tester marks off two limit lines 7 ft apart. The performer holds the ball on four fingers and a thumb with the hand near the upper front of the shoulder (Figure 12.5). Starting near the back limit line, the performer advances to the front limit line in a typical shot-put style and thrusts the ball as far as possible without stepping over the front line. Movement of the ball must be the result of a thrust, not a throw. Three trials are allowed.

Scoring: The distance from the inside front line to the point of landing in the best of three trials, measured to the nearest foot, is the score. Table 12.6 shows norms for young adults.

PRACTICAL TESTS OF WORK POWER

Vertical Arm-Pull Test (Work) (Johnson 1969)

Objective: To measure the power of the arms and shoulder girdle in pulling the body upward.

Age Level: Age 14 through college age.

Sex: Satisfactory for boys only.

Reliability: An *r* of .94 was found for this test.

Objectivity: An *r* of .99 was obtained by two testers.

Validity: An *r* of .76 was found when the work score (foot-pounds) was correlated with the vertical power pull (work/time).

Equipment and Materials: A climbing rope; marking tape; a tape measure; and weight scales. Required dress is shorts, light shirt, and no shoes.

Directions: Same as for vertical arm-pull test (distance) (p. 214).

Scoring: The score of the best pull (distance between the two tape marks) is used in the following formula:

$$\frac{\text{distance of pull} \times \text{body weight}}{12} = \text{foot-pounds}$$

Table 12.5. Norms in Feet for Two-Hand Medicine Ball Put, College Students[a]

PERFORMANCE LEVEL	SCORE	
	Men	Women
Advanced	26 and above	15 and above
Advanced intermediate	22–25	13–14
Intermediate	14–20	8–12
Advanced beginner	10–12	5–7
Beginner	0–9	0–4

[a]Based on 100 scores for men and 65 scores for women secured from physical education classes at Corpus Christi State University, Corpus Christi, Tex., 1976.

Figure 12.5. Position for shot-put test with softball

Table 12.7 shows norms for high school boys and college men.

Additional Pointers: Same as for vertical arm-pull test (distance).

Vertical Power Jump (Work) (Glencross 1960)

Objective: To measure power of the legs in jumping vertically upward.

Age Level: Age 10 through college age.

Sex: Satisfactory for both boys and girls.

Reliability: An r as high as .977 has been reported for college men.

Objectivity: An r of .99 was reported by Steve Long, Northeast Louisiana University, Monroe, 1972.

Validity: An r as high as .989 has been reported for college men with the vertical power jump (horse power) as the criterion.

Equipment and Materials: A jump board marked off in half inches; chalk dust; and weight scales. Required dress is shorts, light shirt, and no shoes.

Directions: The performer's weight is recorded and he then assumes a standing position facing sideways to the jump board, the preferred arm behind the back (hand grasping top of shorts at the back), the other arm raised vertically with the hand turned outward and fingers extended (Figure 12.6a). Holding this position, the performer stands as tall as possible on the toes so that the height of the extended middle finger of the raised arm can be recorded. Chalk dust is then placed on the middle finger and the performer adopts a full squat position with head and back erect and body in balance (Figure 12.6b). The performer then jumps as high as possible (using only the legs) and touches the board at the top of the jump (Figure 12.6c). The tester must watch and disregard any jump in which balance or position is lost. The tester rec-

Table 12.6. Norms in Feet for Shot-Put Test With Softball, Young Adults[a]

PERFORMANCE LEVEL	SCORE	
	Men	Women
Advanced	97 and above	50 and above
Advanced intermediate	78–96	44–49
Intermediate	60–77	37–43
Advanced beginner	56–59	32–36
Beginner	0–55	0–31

[a]Based on the scores of 30 men and 20 women as reported by George Adkison, Robert Martinez, Gracie Sosa, and Irene Waak, Corpus Christi, Tex., 1982.

Table 12.7. Norms in Foot-Pounds[a] for Vertical Arm-Pull Test (Work)[b]

PERFORMANCE LEVEL	SCORE	
	High School Boys	College Men
Advanced	431 and above	491 and above
Advanced intermediate	344–430	392–490
Intermediate	166–343	190–391
Advanced beginner	79–165	91–189
Beginner	0–78	0–90

[a](Distance of pull × body weight)/12 = score in foot-pounds.
[b]Based on the scores of 150 college men and 200 high school boys.

ords the height of the chalk mark on the jump board. Each performer is allowed three trials. On the last trial the tester should say, "This is your last jump. Try to beat your last two jumps."

Scoring: The measure of the best jump (difference between the reaching height and jumping height) is used in the following formula to compute the score:

$$\frac{distance \times body\ weight}{12} = foot\text{-}pounds$$

Table 12.8 shows norms for various groups.

Margaria Anaerobic Power Test (Margaria, Aghemo, and Rovelli 1966)

Objective: To measure maximal anaerobic power.

Age and Sex: Suitable for high school and col-

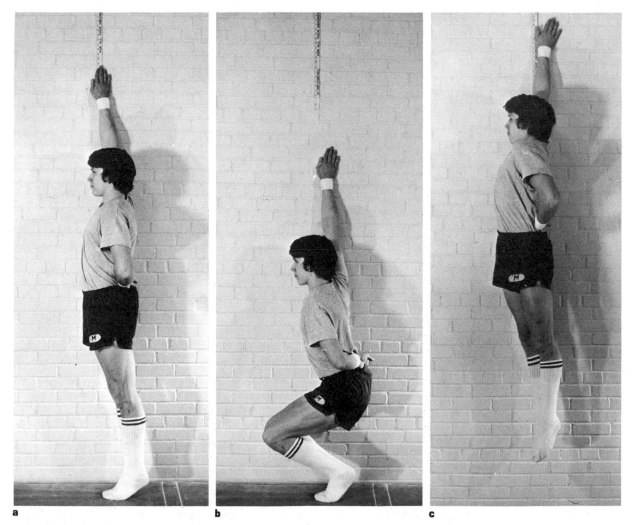

a   b   c

Figure 12.6.   Vertical power jump (work)

Table 12.8. Norms in Foot-Pounds[a] for Vertical Power Jump (Work)[b]

PERFORMANCE LEVEL	SCORE		
	College Men	College Women	High School Girls
Advanced	301 and above	134 and above	119 and above
Advanced intermediate	240–300	108–133	98–118
Intermediate	115–239	55–107	51–97
Advanced beginner	54–114	30–54	29–50
Beginner	0–53	0–29	0–28

[a](Distance jumped × body weight)/12 = score in foot-pounds.
[b]Based on the scores of 125 college men, 100 college women, and 100 high school girls.

lege age men and women. It can be given to elementary school children with appropriate modification, such as was done by Chaloupka (Mathews 1973).

Validity: The test has face validity in that it includes the components of mechanical power: work per unit of time. Margaria computed anaerobic power output in kilocalories per kilogram of body weight per hour by the stair-climb test and had results comparable to those of another method in which measurements were taken with the subject running on a treadmill. In terms of construct validity, sprinters have been found to have higher scores than distance runners, and athletes higher scores than nonathletes.

Equipment and Materials: A timer sensitive to 0.01 sec (an electric timer with switch mats to start and stop the timer at the desired steps is preferable. Although not advisable for research purposes, a 0.01-sec stopwatch provides quite consistent results); a staircase of preferably 12 to 16 stairs of normal incline, with steps measuring between 6 and 8 in. (15–20 cm); a weight scale.

Directions: There are several versions of the test. For example, Margaria computed power by measuring the vertical component of the speed between the second and fourth seconds of the stair climb. The test is usually measured, however, by allowing a short sprint on the floor and then timing the speed of climb between certain steps.

A short sprint of about 6 ft (2 m) is recommended so that the subject can begin the stair climb at near maximal forward velocity. The timing should encompass about four to eight steps, that is, somewhere between 0.5 and 1.0 sec.

DeVries described a method employing a flight of stairs of at least 16 steps with the subject starting 6 ft in front of the first step and running up the stairs as fast as possible, taking two steps at a time. The timing interval is between the fourth and twelfth steps. Kalamen revised the Margaria test as follows: The subject starts 6 m from the stairs and runs up the stairs three steps at a time; the switch mats are located on the third and ninth steps. Kalamen found that this procedure produced maximum power scores. Chaloupka's adaptation for elementary school boys involves the timed vertical distance speed between the second and sixth steps (Mathews 1973).

The deVries test arrangement (Figure 12.7) will be described here because it may be applicable to a more general population, since it requires running up two steps at a time instead of three and necessitates only 6 ft of running space before the first step instead of about 20, as in the Kalamen version.

In the deVries test, the subject is first weighed wearing the clothing and shoes in which he or she will run. The weight is recorded to the nearest pound (or converted to kilograms by dividing by 2.2). The subject begins from a line 6 ft (or 2 m) from the first step. The timer (with a stopwatch) is positioned to be able to observe the subject's foot when it strikes the fourth and the twelfth steps.

The subject is instructed to run up the stairs as fast as possible taking two steps at a time. The subject should continue past the twelfth step and not try to stop at that step.

Three trials are given. The timer starts the watch when the subject's foot strikes the fourth step and stops the watch when the subject's foot hits the twelfth step. The vertical height of each step is determined in inches (or millimeters) and multiplied by 8. For example, if each step is 7.5 in., the total vertical distance the subject lifts his or her body weight is 7.5 in. × 8 steps = 60 in., or 5 ft.

Scoring: The average of three trials to the nearest 0.01 sec is used as the time score. The subject's

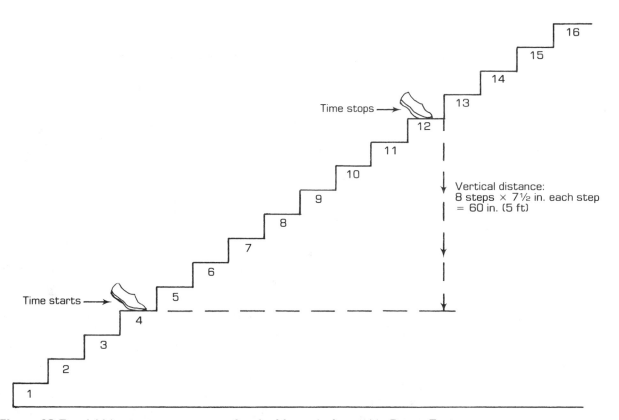

Figure 12.7.   deVries test arrangement for the Margaria Anaerobic Power Test

body weight is multiplied by the total vertical distance and the product is divided by the average time in seconds:

$$power = \frac{work}{time} = \frac{body\ weight \times distance}{time\ (sec)}$$

Example: A person weighing 140 lb runs up the eight steps (5 ft) in 0.8 sec.

$$power = \frac{140\ lb \times 5\ ft}{0.8\ sec} = \frac{700\ ft\ lb}{0.8}$$
$$= 875\ ft\ lb/sec$$

In metric units:

140 lb = 63.6 kg; 5 ft = 1.5 m
$$power = \frac{63.6 \times 1.5}{0.8}$$
$$= \frac{95.4\ kilogram\text{-}meters\ (kgm)}{0.8\ sec}$$
$$= 119.25\ kgm/sec$$

The power scores can be expressed in horsepower by dividing foot-pounds/second by 550 and kilogram-meters/second by 76.07. In the preceding example, 875 ft lb/sec ÷ 550 = 1.59 hp. Table 12.9 shows norms for high school and college age men.

Additional Pointers:

1. Mechanical work is expressed in foot-pounds or kilogram-meters. Therefore, the distance must be converted to feet or meters. If, for example, the step is 7.25 in. and the number of steps is six, the vertical distance in feet would be

$$7.25\ in. \times 6 = \frac{43.5\ in.}{12} = 3.6\ ft$$

The tester may first wish to multiply body weight times the distance in inches and divide the product by 12. For example, a 150-lb person × 7.25 in. × 6 = 6525 ÷ 12 = 543.75 ft lb. In metric units, if the step measures 180 mm, this must be converted to meters. In this example, 180 mm is 0.18 m (180 ÷ 1000), so 6 × 0.18 m = 1.08 m. Thus, a 150-lb person represents 68.2 kg × 1.08 m = 73.7 kgm.

2. One of the advantages of the Margaria test is that it does not require skill or training. However, as with nearly any test item, familiarization is important. Several practice trials are advisable.

Table 12.9. Margaria Stair Climb Performances in Horsepower, High School Boys and College Men[a]

PERFORMANCE LEVEL	SCORE		
	16-Year-Olds	17-Year-Olds	College Age
Advanced	1.74 and above	1.91 and above	2.16 and above
Advanced intermediate	1.45–1.73	1.60–1.90	1.80–2.15
Intermediate	1.16–1.44	1.27–1.59	1.43–1.79
Advanced beginner	0.87–1.15	0.96–1.26	1.07–1.42
Beginner	0.86 and below	0.95 and below	1.06 and below

[a]Test was with eight stairs, 4.33 ft total vertical distance. See text for computation of horsepower. Norms gathered on 200 16- and 17-year-old boys and 300 college men (adapted Carter 1979).

3. The mechanical power output can be expressed in terms of energy consumption (kilocalories per minute per kilogram) if the work efficiency value is assumed to be 25%.

4. A word of caution is necessary. Owing to the nature of the test, injuries can occur, such as stubbing of a toe or falling. With some practice and reasonable precautions, however, the test can be administered safely. It sometimes helps to place tape or cardboard markers on the stairs on which the students are to step.

FINDINGS AND CONCLUSIONS FROM POWER MEASUREMENT RESEARCH

Power has been measured and analyzed in a number of ways since Sargent first proposed the "physical test of a man," which consisted of the vertical jump. Most of the studies have measured power by jumps or throws, such as the vertical jump, standing long jump, or medicine ball throw. Some of the studies have attempted to analyze power performance of certain muscle groups while controlling other body action, such as measuring leg power while arm and trunk action is minimized (Glencross 1966a, 1966b; Gray, Start, and Glencross 1962a; Gray et al. 1962b).

The importance of power in athletics has prompted a number of studies that have investigated power and performance and the relationship of strength, speed, and power. The renowned swimming coach, James Counsilman of Indiana University, has long used the vertical jump as a means of classifying swimmers as to being best suited for the sprints, the mid-distance races, or the long distance events (Counsilman 1980).

Dyer found correlations ranging from .69 to .95 between anaerobic power, as measured by a timed vertical jump, and coaches' ratings of basketball-playing ability. Team success, indicated by winning percentages, correlated .70 with average anaerobic power scores.

Considine and Sullivan correlated several power tests, including the vertical jump, standing long jump, and short sprints with leg strength tests. All of the correlations were low to moderate. The authors concluded that strength's contribution to power is minor and that power is a complex unity. On the other hand, studies have shown that strength development through weight training can improve power performance (Capen 1950; Chui 1950). Stone and co-workers reported that strength training improved power as measured by the vertical jump. Moreover, the vertical jump is considered a significant indicator of weight-lifting ability. In a series of weight-lifting experiments, O'Bryant found vertical jump performance to be significantly improved by weight lifting.

Significant (moderate) correlations are obtained between jumps and short dashes; these tests presumably have a common feature in the push-off type motion required (Fleishman 1964). Costill and colleagues correlated power of the legs as measured by the Margaria test with selected explosive leg strength tests. They concluded that anaerobic power is related to dynamic leg strength and body weight (Costill et al. 1968; McClements 1966). Lawson found significant correlations between 100-yd running performance and the Margaria-Kalamen Index, maximal oxygen deficit, and the cross-sectional area of fast twitch fibers of the vastus lateralis muscle. Constable, Collins, and Krahenbuhl reported that endurance training produced no significant improvement in leg power or individual muscle fiber size.

The advent of isokinetic strength training has spawned a number of studies that have attempted to assess the effectiveness of isokinetic training on the development of power. Van Oteghen reported that both slow-speed and fast-speed isokinetic training programs brought about improved vertical jump performance in college volleyball players. Comparisons among isotonic, isometric, and isokinetic training in developing athletic power have generally resulted in no differences. All three methods have been shown to be effective in improving power (Ruley 1979; Spielman 1978). The effectiveness of isometric training has been masked somewhat by the training techniques and testing procedures. The measurement of force is essential in isometric training so students will know how much effort they are exerting, in order for significant gains to be made. It is important for subjects to train at the angles where the greatest force is needed in power performance, whether it be by isometric, isotonic, or isokinetic methods. Specificity of practice is always a factor. Coyle and colleagues found improvement in maximal power, as measured by peak torque of the quadriceps, to result from velocity-specific and muscle action-specific training. Genuario and Dolgener studied the relationship between vertical jumping ability and the ability of female athletes to develop peak isokinetic torque in leg flexion and extension and in foot plantar flexion. The authors concluded that there was little if any relationship between torque at a fast or slow angular velocity and vertical jumping ability.

Wilt coined the term *plyometrics* for methods used in developing power that involve depth jumps, whereby the person jumps from a certain-height bench or box and on landing on the floor immediately jumps upward with maximal effort. Researchers have studied the effectiveness of plyometric training on power development. Blattner and Noble found no differences between plyometric training and isokinetic training. Both methods increased vertical jumping performance. Steben and Steben compared different forms of plyometric training (depth jump and box drill) and flexibility-agility exercise in producing improvements in the high jump, triple jump, and long jump with junior high school boys and girls. They found all methods brought about improvements, with the greatest gains being caused by those exercises that were most specific to the event.

Several studies have shown that previous activity such as basketball and swimming (Nelson 1961, 1962; Ruley 1979; Sargent 1921) have a negative effect on jumping tests. Therefore, rest prior to athletic power jump tests should be considered if optimum results are to be achieved.

Concerning physical activities, McCloy found the Sargent jump significantly related to the total point score of select track and field events, and Bushey found a significant relationship between vertical jump scores and modern dance performance.

In studying the effects of various positions on vertical jump performance, Martin and Stull found that the most effective knee angle is approximately 115 degrees, while foot spacings should range between 5 to 10 in. laterally and slightly better than 5 in. anteriorly posteriorly.

BIBLIOGRAPHY

AAHPERD Youth Fitness Test Manual. Reston, Va.: AAHPERD, 1976.

Blattner, S. E., and L. Noble, "Relative Effects of Isokinetic and Plyometric Training on Vertical Jumping Performance." *Research Quarterly* 50:583–588, December 1979.

Bushey, S. R., "Relationship of Modern Dance Performance to Agility, Balance, Flexibility, Power, and Strength." *Research Quarterly* 37:313, October 1966.

Capen, E. K., "The Effect of Systematic Weight Training on Power, Strength, and Endurance." *Research Quarterly* 21:83–93, May 1950.

Carter, D. R., "Measurement of Anaerobic Power in High School and College Males." Unpublished study, Louisiana State University, 1979.

Chui, E. F., "The Effect of Systematic Weight Training on Athletic Power." *Research Quarterly* 21:188–194, October 1950.

Considine, W. J., and W. J. Sullivan, "Relationship of Selected Tests of Leg Strength and Leg Power on College Men." *Research Quarterly* 44:404–416, December 1973.

Constable, S. H., R. L. Collins, and G. S. Krahenbuhl, "The Specificity of Endurance Training on Muscular Power and Muscle Fibre Size." *Ergonomics* 23:667–678, 1980.

Costill, D. L., S. J. Miller, W. C. Myers, F. M. Kehoe, and W. M. Hoffman, "Relationship Among Selected Tests of Explosive Leg Strength and Power." *Research Quarterly* 39:785–787, October 1968.

Counsilman, J. E., "The Importance of Speed in Exercise." In E. J. Burke, Ed., *Toward an Understanding of Human Performance.* 2nd ed. Ithaca, N.Y.: Mouvement Publications, 1980.

Coyle, E. F., D. C. Feiring, T. C. Rotkis, R. W. Cote, F. B. Roby, W. Lee, and J. H. Wilmore, "Specificity of Power Improvements Through Slow and Fast Isokinetic Training." *Journal of Applied Physiology* 51:1437–1442, 1981.

deVries, H. A., *Laboratory Experiments in Physiology of Exercise*. Dubuque, Iowa: William C. Brown, 1971, pp. 101–104.

Dyer, G. A., "Measurement of the Anaerobic Power of High School Basketball Players." Unpublished master's thesis, Louisiana State University, Baton Rouge, 1978.

Fleishman, E. A., *The Structure and Measurement of Physical Fitness*. Englewood Cliffs, N.J.: Prentice-Hall, 1964.

Genuario, S. E., and F. A. Dolgener, "The Relationship of Isokinetic Torque at Two Speeds to the Vertical Jump." *Research Quarterly for Exercise and Sport* 51:593–598, December 1980.

Glencross, D. J., "The Measurement of Muscular Power: A Test of Leg Power and a Modification for General Use." Microcarded doctoral dissertation, University of Western Australia, Nedlands, 1960.

———, "The Nature of the Vertical Jump Test and the Standing Broad Jump." *Research Quarterly* 37:353–359, October 1966a.

———, "The Power Lever: An Instrument for Measuring Muscle Power." *Research Quarterly* 37:202, May 1966b.

Gray, R. K., K. B. Start, and D. J. Glencross, "A Test of Leg Power." *Research Quarterly* 33:44–50, March 1962a.

———, et al., "A Useful Modification of the Vertical Power Jump." *Research Quarterly* 33:230–235, May 1962b.

———, K. A. Start, and A. Walsh, "Relationship Between Leg Speed and Leg Power." *Research Quarterly* 33:395–400, October 1962c.

Johnson, B. L., "A Comparison of Isometric and Isotonic Exercises Upon the Improvement of Velocity and Distance as Measured by a Vertical Rope Climb Test." Unpublished master's thesis, Louisiana State University, Baton Rouge, 1964.

———, "The Establishment of a Vertical Arm Pull Test (Work)." *Research Quarterly* 40:237–239, March 1969.

———, "A Screening Test for Pole Vaulting and Selected Gymnastic Events." *JOHPER* 44:71–72, May 1973.

Kalamen, J., "Measurement of Maximum Muscular Power in Man." Doctoral dissertation, Ohio State University, Columbus, 1968.

Lawson, D. L., "Physiological Parameters Limiting Performance in Middle Distance and Sprint Running." Doctoral dissertation, Kent State University, Kent, Ohio, 1975.

Margaria, R., P. Aghemo, and E. Rovelli, "Measurement of Muscular Power (Anaerobic) in Man." *Journal of Applied Physiology* 21:1662–1664, September 1966.

Martin, T. P., and G. A. Stull, "Effects of Various Knee Angle and Foot Spacing Combinations on Performance in the Vertical Jump." *Research Quarterly* 40:324–331, May 1969.

Mathews, D. K., *Measurement in Physical Education*. 4th ed. Philadelphia: W. B. Saunders, 1973.

———, and E. L. Fox, *The Physiological Basis of Physical Education and Athletics*. 2nd ed. Philadelphia: W. B. Saunders, 1976.

McClements, L. C., "Power Relative to Strength of Leg and Thigh Muscles." *Research Quarterly* 37:71, March 1966.

McCloy, C. H., "Recent Studies in the Sargent Jump." *Research Quarterly* 3:35, May 1932.

Nelson, D. O., "Effect of a Single Day's Swimming on Selected Components of Athletic Performance." *Research Quarterly* 32:389–393, October 1961.

———, "Effects of Swimming and Basketball on Various Tests of Explosive Power." *Research Quarterly* 33:586, December 1962.

O'Bryant, H. S., "Periodization: A Hypothetical Training Model for Strength and Power." Unpublished doctoral dissertation, Louisiana State University, Baton Rouge, 1982.

Ruley, A. J., "The Effects of Isotonic and Isokinetic Training in the Vertical Jump Performance of Female Intercollegiate Basketball Players." Master's thesis, Western Illinois University, Macomb, 1979; HPER Microform Publication, No. PE 2316f.

Sargent, D. A., "The Physical Test of a Man." *American Physical Education Review* 25:188–194, April 1921.

Spielman, J. T., "The Influence of Isotonic and Isometric Weight Training on Vertical Jumping Proficiency." Master's thesis, South Dakota State University, Brookings, 1978; HPER Microform Publication, No. PE 2144f.

Start, K. B., et al., "A Factorial Investigation of Power, Speed, Isometric Strength, and Anthropometric Measures in the Lower Limb." *Research Quarterly* 37:554–558, December 1966.

Steben, R. E., and A. H. Steben, "The Validity of the Stretch Shortening Cycle in Selected Jumping Events." *Journal of Sports Medicine and Physical Fitness* 21:28–37, March 1981.

Stone, M. H., R. L. Johnson, and D. R. Carter. "A Short Term Comparison of Two Different Methods of Resistance Training on Leg Strength and Power." *Athletic Training* 14:158–160, 1979.

United States Volleyball Association, *1967 Annual Official Volleyball Rules and Reference Guide of the U.S. Volleyball Association*. San Francisco: Berne, Inc., U.S. Volleyball Association Printer, 1967, pp. 134–135.

Van Oteghen, S. L., "Two Speeds of Isokinetic Exercise as Related to the Vertical Jump Performance of Women." *Research Quarterly* 46:78–84, March 1975.

Wilt, F., "Plyometrics: What It Is—How It Works." *Athletic Journal* 55:76, 89–90, 1975.

CHAPTER 13

THE MEASUREMENT OF AGILITY

OBJECTIVES

After reading this chapter, the student should be able to:

1. Define agility and distinguish between the terms *agility* and *speed*

2. Recognize the specificity of agility and the diverse ways by which agility is measured

3. Understand and anticipate some of the administrative problems in measuring agility

4. Follow the directions for administering practical tests of agility

Agility may be defined as the physical ability that enables rapid and precise change of body position and direction. Agility is an important ability in many sports activities, as exemplified by two experienced players playing badminton or by the trampolinist executing a triple twisting back somersault. By the proper use of testing, the physical education teacher can determine which individuals in a class are most agile and which ones need work in agility to better perform the particular activity.

USES OF AGILITY TESTS

Agility tests can be used in physical education in several ways:

1. As an element for predicting potential in different sports activities

2. As a measure for determining achievement, progress, and grades when agility is a specific objective in the teaching unit

3. As a factor in motor ability tests

4. As a means to evaluate the effectiveness of a specific unit of instruction on improve-

ment in agility. For example, if agility is measured before and after a unit of instruction in weight training, the weight training can be evaluated as to its efficacy in improving agility.

PROBLEMS ASSOCIATED WITH AGILITY TESTING

There are several problems and limitations in agility testing, as follows:

1. The surface area and the type of footwear seem to have a definite bearing on the scoring ability of students in certain tests such as the side step test. Perhaps this problem could be overcome by use of a nonslip surface and the requirement that all students either go barefooted or wear the same type of shoes.

2. Considerable time is needed to administer certain agility tests to large groups. Two or more test stations are advised.

3. Too many tests of agility involve running ability or the ability to change body position rapidly as initiated by the legs. In our opin-

ion, there is need for more tests that make use of various body parts.

4. Several agility tests do not have sufficient spread of scores to discriminate between good and poor performance.

5. Agility is quite specific. In other words, one type of agility, such as the shuttle run, does not correlate highly with another, such as the squat thrust.

PRACTICAL TESTS OF AGILITY

Tests of agility that are practical in terms of time, equipment, and cost are presented in the following pages.

Burpee Test (or Squat Thrust)[1]

Objective: To measure the rapidity with which body position can be changed.

Age Level: Age 10 through college age.

Sex: Satisfactory for both girls and boys.

Reliability: An r of .921 has been reported.

Objectivity: An r of .99 was obtained by Doyle Hammons, Northeast Louisiana University, Monroe, 1969.

Validity: With the criterion of general athletic ability, an r of .553 has been reported for boys and .341 for girls.

Equipment and Materials: Stopwatch or wristwatch with a second hand.

Directions: From a standing position, the student squats and places the hands on the floor in front

_____
1. To the best of our knowledge, this test was first presented by Royal H. Burpee and was first checked for reliability and validity by C. H. McCloy.

of the feet, thrusts the legs backward to a front-leaning rest position, returns to the squat-rest position, and rises to a standing position. From the signal "Go," this movement is repeated as rapidly as possible until the command "Stop" is given (see Figure 8.11).

Scoring: The test is scored in terms of the number of parts of the test executed in 10 sec. For example, squatting and placing the hands on the floor is one part, thrusting the legs to the rear is two, returning to the squat-rest position is three, and returning to the standing position is four. Table 13.1 shows norms for various groups.

Penalty: There is a 1-point penalty for any of the following faults: (1) if the feet move to the rear before the hands touch the floor, (2) if there is excessive sway or pike of the hips in the rearward position, (3) if the hands leave the floor before the feet are drawn up in position number three, and (4) if the stand is not erect with the head up.

AAHPERD Shuttle Run (AAHPERD 1976)

Objective: To measure the agility of the performer in running and changing direction.

Age Level: Age 9 through college age.

Sex: Satisfactory for both boys and girls.

Reliability: Not reported in AAHPERD test booklet.

Objectivity: Not reported in AAHPERD test booklet.

Validity: Not reported in AAHPERD test booklet.

Equipment and Materials: Marking tape; a stopwatch; and two blocks of wood 2 in. × 2 in. × 4 in.

Table 13.1. Raw Score Norms for Burpee (Squat Thrust) Test, Various Groups[a]

PERFORMANCE LEVEL	SCORE		
	College Men	High School and College Girls and Women	High School Boys
Advanced	34 and above	30 and above	32 and above
Advanced intermediate	29–33	26–29	28–31
Intermediate	17–28	14–25	16–27
Advanced beginner	12–16	10–13	12–15
Beginner	0–11	0–9	0–11

[a]Based on the scores of 125 college men, 150 high school girls and college women, and 125 high school boys from Texas and Louisiana, 1976. Each part of test counts 1 point. Total score is number of parts completed in 10 sec.

Directions: The performer stands behind the starting line and on the signal "Go" runs to the blocks, picks up one, returns to the starting line, and places the block behind the line; the student then repeats the process with the second block (Figure 13.1). Two trials are given, with rest allowed between them.

Scoring: The score for each performer is the length of time required (to the nearest tenth of a second) to complete the course in the better of the two trials. Table 13.2 shows norms for boys and girls.

Additional Pointers:

1. The importance of running as hard as possible across the finish line with the second block should be stressed.

2. Marking tape should be used to designate the starting and finishing line.

3. The performer may touch behind the line and not use blocks, since blocks may be tumbled, dropped, kicked, or thrown and thus necessitate additional testing or cause problems in standardization.

Quadrant Jump[2]

Objective: To measure the agility of the performer in changing body position rapidly by jumping in different directions.

Age Level: Age 10 through college age.

Sex: Satisfactory for both boys and girls.

Reliability: An r of .89 was found for this test when the best of two trials administered on different days was correlated.

Objectivity: An r of .96 was obtained by Larry Malone, Northeast Louisiana University, Monroe, 1969.

Validity: Face validity is accepted.

Equipment and Materials: Marking tape and a stopwatch or wristwatch with a second hand.

---

2. This test is a modification of a test once demonstrated by a colleague in a measurements class.

Figure 13.1. Shuttle run

Table 13.2. Norms in Seconds for Shuttle Run, Boys and Girls

PERCENTILE	AGE							
	9–10	11	12	13	14	15	16	17+
	TIME (SEC) FOR GIRLS							
95	10.2	10.0	9.9	9.9	9.7	9.9	10.0	9.6
75	11.1	10.8	10.8	10.5	10.3	10.4	10.6	10.4
50	11.8	11.5	11.4	11.2	11.0	11.0	11.2	11.1
25	12.5	12.1	12.0	12.0	12.0	11.8	12.0	12.0
5	14.3	14.0	13.3	13.2	13.1	13.3	13.7	14.0
	TIME (SEC) FOR BOYS							
95	10.0	9.7	9.6	9.3	8.9	8.9	8.6	8.6
75	10.6	10.4	10.2	10.0	9.6	9.4	9.3	9.2
50	11.2	10.9	10.7	10.4	10.1	9.9	9.9	9.8
25	12.0	11.5	11.4	11.0	10.7	10.4	10.5	10.4
5	13.1	12.9	12.4	12.4	11.9	11.7	11.9	11.7

Source: Adapted from *AAHPERD Youth Fitness Test Manual.* Reston, Va.: AAHPERD, 1976. Used by permission.

Directions: The performer begins behind the small starting tick mark (Figure 13.2) and jumps with both feet into quadrant 1, then into quadrant 2, into 3, into 4, and back to 1. The pattern is continued until the signal "Stop" is given. Two trials are allowed, with a rest between trials.

Scoring: The score is the number of times the feet land in correct quadrants in 10 sec. The better score of the two trials is the test score. Table 13.3 shows norms for college students.

Penalty: There is a half-point penalty for each time the feet land on a line or in an improper zone.

Additional Pointers:

1. The two cross lines should each be 3 ft long.

2. One assistant should count the number of errors. The half-point errors should then be totaled and subtracted from the number of jumps.

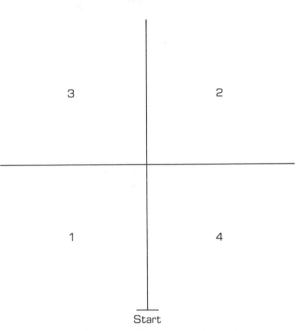

Figure 13.2. Diagram for the quadrant jump

Table 13.3. Raw Score Norms for Quadrant Jump, College Students[a]

PERFORMANCE LEVEL	SCORE	
	Men	Women
Advanced	31 and above	33 and above
Advanced intermediate	25–30	27–32
Intermediate	13–24	14–26
Advanced beginner	7–12	8–13
Beginner	0–6	0–7

[a]Based on the scores of 75 men and 75 women at Corpus Christi State University, Corpus Christi, Tex., 1976. The raw score is the number of times the feet land in the correct quadrant in 10 sec.

3. A performer who stops or who could obviously do better should be retested.

4. Each zone may be identified by marking tape.

SEMO Agility Test (Kirby 1971)

Objective: To measure the general agility of the body in maneuvering forward, backward, and sideward.

Age Level: High school and college age.

Sex: Satisfactory for both boys and girls.

Reliability: Using trials one and two, an *r* of .88 was found for high school boys and college men.

Objectivity: An *r* of .97 was found when the scores from two test administrators were correlated.

Validity: An *r* of .63 was found when the SEMO test was correlated with the AAHPERD shuttle run test.

Equipment and Materials: The free-throw lane of a basketball court or any smooth area 12 × 19 ft with adequate running space around it; four plastic cones (9- × 9-in. base with 12-in. height) or suitable substitute objects; and a stopwatch.

Directions: The cones are placed squarely in each corner of the free-throw lane, as seen in Figure 13.3. The student lines up outside the free-throw lane (at A) with the back to the free-throw line. At the signals "Ready," "Go," the student side steps from A to B and passes outside the corner cone; then backpedals from B to D and passes to the inside of the corner cone; then sprints forward from D to A and passes outside the corner cone; then backpedals from A to C and passes to the inside of the corner cone; then sprints forward from C to B and passes outside of the corner cone; and finally side steps from B to the finish line at A. The diagram is shown in Figure 13.3. Two trials are allowed.

Scoring: The better of two trials (recorded to the nearest 1/10 sec) is recorded as the score. Table 13.4 shows norms for college students.

Additional Pointers:

1. In performing the side step, the crossover step cannot be used.

2. In performing the back pedal, the student must keep his or her back perpendicular to an imaginary line connecting the corner cones.

3. Incorrect procedure makes the trial invalid, and the student should be tested until one correct trial is completed.

4. At least one practice trial should be given.

Right-Boomerang Run (Gates and Sheffield 1940)

Objective: To measure agility in running and changing direction.

Age Level: Age 10 through college age.

Sex: Satisfactory for both boys and girls.

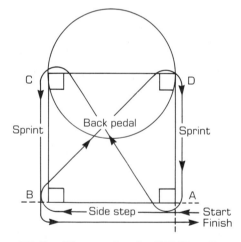

Figure 13.3. Diagram for the SEMO agility test

Table 13.4. Norms in Seconds for SEMO Agility Test, College Students[a]

PERFORMANCE LEVEL	SCORE	
	Men	Women
Advanced	10.72 and below	12.19 and below
Advanced intermediate	11.49–10.73	12.99–12.20
Intermediate	13.02–11.50	13.90–13.00
Advanced beginner	13.79–13.03	14.49–13.91
Beginner	13.80 and above	14.50 and above

[a]Scores for men were obtained by Dr. Ronald Kirby, Southeast Missouri State University, Cape Girardeau, Mo., 1971. Scores for women were from a small group of subjects from Corpus Christi State University, Corpus Christi, Tex., 1976.

Reliability: An *r* of .93 has been reported for boys and .92 for girls.

Objectivity: An *r* of .98 was obtained by Steve Long, Northeast Louisiana University, Monroe, 1972.

Validity: An *r* of .82 for boys and an *r* of .72 for girls using the sum of *T* scores for 16 and 15 tests of agility, respectively, as the criterion have been reported.

Equipment and Materials: A jumping standard or chair for the center station; four Indian clubs or small similar objects for the outside stations; a stopwatch; and marking tape.

Directions: The objects are placed in each corner of the course (Figure 13.4). On hearing the signal "Go," the performer runs to the center station, makes a quarter right turn, runs to and around the first outside station, returns to the center, makes another quarter right turn, and continues through the course (Figure 13.4).

Scoring: The score is the time taken to complete the course to the nearest tenth of a second. Tables 13.5 and 13.6 show norms for junior high school boys and for college students, respectively.

Penalty: There is a 0.1-sec penalty for each object touched at the various stations.

Additional Pointers:

1. Running as hard as possible across the finish line should be stressed.

2. The importance of not touching the object at each station should be stressed.

3. The performer should be retested when he or she obviously could have done better.

4. The student is allowed to jog through the course once to become familiar with the pattern.

LSU Agility Obstacle Course

Objective: To measure various kinds of agility in one test involving zigzagging, dodging, shuttle running, and squat thrusts. (Owing to the specificity of agility, the inclusion of several different

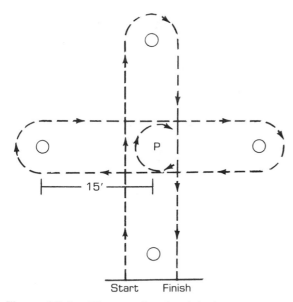

Figure 13.4. Diagram for the right-boomerang run

Table 13.5. *T*-Score Norms to the Nearest One Tenth of a Second for Right-Boomerang Run, Boys in the Seventh and Eighth Grades[a]

RAW SCORE	*T* SCORE	RAW SCORE	*T* SCORE	RAW SCORE	*T* SCORE
10.9	72	13.0	55	15.2	38
11.0	71	13.1	54	15.3	37
11.1	70	13.3	53	15.5	36
11.2	69	13.4	52	15.6	35
11.3	68	13.5	51	15.7	34
11.4	67	13.7	50	15.9	33
11.6	66	13.8	49	16.0	32
11.7	65	13.9	48	16.1	31
11.8	64	14.0	47	16.3	30
12.0	63	14.2	46	16.4	29
12.1	62	14.3	45	16.5	28
12.2	61	14.4	44	16.6	27
12.4	60	14.6	43	16.8	26
12.5	59	14.7	42	16.9	25
12.6	58	14.8	41	17.0	24
12.7	57	14.9	40	17.2	23
12.9	56	15.1	39	17.3	22

[a]Based on the scores of 100 students from East Baton Rouge Parish Schools, Baton Rouge, La., 1968.

Table 13.6. Norms in Seconds for Right-Boomerang Run, College Students[a]

PERFORMANCE LEVEL	SCORE	
	Men	Women
Advanced	10.79 and below	12.60 and below
Advanced intermediate	11.49–10.80	12.99–12.61
Intermediate	12.60–11.50	14.59–13.00
Advanced beginner	13.90–12.61	15.99–14.60
Beginner	13.91 and above	16.00 and above

[a]Based on the scores of a limited number of men and women at Corpus Christi State University, Corpus Christi, Tex., 1977.

types of agility in one test is believed to provide a more accurate assessment of overall agility performance.)

Age Level: Age 10 through college age.

Sex: Satisfactory for both boys and girls.

Reliability: Through intraclass correlation the reliability of two trials was .91.

Objectivity: An intraclass correlation of .98 was obtained by two testers with college men and women.

Validity: Face validity and construct validity are assumed.

Equipment and Materials: A badminton court without the net; seven traffic cones; and a stopwatch. (No markings are needed.)

Directions: The traffic cones are placed as shown in Figure 13.5. The subject lies on his or her back with feet behind the end line. When ready, the subject scrambles to the feet and runs to the left and all the way around cone 1. The subject performs one squat thrust, then runs to the left of cone 2, to the right of cone 3, and so on, as shown in the figure. After passing cone 7, the runner performs two squat thrusts, then races to the opposite sideline and touches the hand to the floor just over the line. The subject shuttles back and forth, touching the floor twice more (three hand touches in all); the subject then races across the finish line (Figure 13.5).

Scoring: The tester starts the stopwatch when the performer begins to scramble to his or her feet. The stopwatch is stopped when the subject crosses the finish line. The score is the time to the nearest tenth of a second. Table 13.7 shows norms for college students.

Penalty: A penalty of 0.5 seconds is added to the score each time a subject fails to perform the squat thrust in the correct four count sequence.

Additional Pointers:

1. Students should practice the test several times for familiarization prior to testing, as scores tend to improve over the first three trials.

2. The tester should stress the point that students must not "short cut the squat thrusts."

3. No penalty is assessed if a cone is hit accidentally.

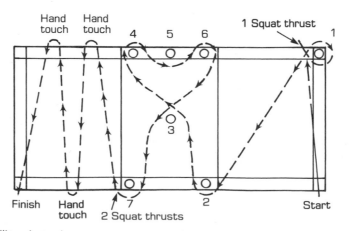

Figure 13.5. LSU agility obstacle course

Table 13.7. Norms in Seconds for LSU Agility Obstacle Course, College Students[a]

PERFORMANCE LEVEL	SCORE	
	Men	Women
Advanced	21.1 and below	23.0 and below
Advanced intermediate	22.3–21.2	25.1–23.1
Intermediate	23.6–22.4	27.4–25.2
Advanced beginner	24.8–23.7	29.5–27.5
Beginner	24.9 and above	29.6 and above

[a]Scores from 65 men and 84 women physical education majors at Louisiana State University, Baton Rouge, La., 1972.

Cozens' Dodging Run Test (Cozens 1929)

Objective: To measure agility in covering the prescribed course.

Age Level: Age 10 through college age.

Sex: Satisfactory for both boys and girls.

Reliability: Reportedly as high as .93.

Objectivity: Reportedly as high as .99.

Validity: Reportedly as high as .82 when correlated with other agility tests.

Equipment and Materials: Marking tape; a stopwatch; and either 5 hurdle standards or 10 rubber cones.

Directions: One hurdle or two cones are placed at each position shown in Figure 13.6. The performer starts from behind the line to the right of the first hurdle (or cones), which is the starting line. On the signal "Go," the performer runs to the left of the second hurdle and follows the course as shown in the figure. Two complete round trips constitute a run, and two runs are made.

Scoring: The better of the two runs recorded to the nearest tenth of a second is the score. Table 13.8 shows norms for college students.

FINDINGS AND CONCLUSIONS FROM AGILITY MEASUREMENT RESEARCH

A glance at the bibliography that follows this chapter shows that relatively little research has been done on agility in recent years. Chelladurai examined agility tests with regard to spatial, temporal, or universal stimuli and concluded that all agility tests measure only simple or temporal agility or both. He recommended that spatial agility

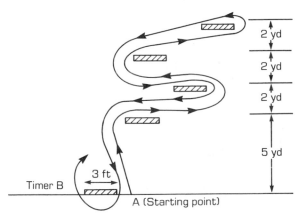

Figure 13.6. Diagram for Cozens' dodging run test

Table 13.8. Norms in Seconds for Cozens' Dodging Run Test, College Students[a]

PERFORMANCE LEVEL	SCORE	
	Men	Women
Advanced	23.0 and below	24.7 and below
Advanced intermediate	24.2–23.1	25.8–24.8
Intermediate	26.7–24.3	28.6–25.9
Advanced beginner	28.5–26.8	31.2–28.7
Beginner	28.6 and above	31.3 and above

[a]Scores from 35 men and 40 women physical education majors at Corpus Christi State University, Corpus Christi, Tex., 1982.

and universal agility, which is a combination of temporal and spatial agility, should be measured if agility scores are to relate to athletics. Chelladurai and associates developed an agility test that incorporated simple, temporal, spatial, and universal agility components. The test involves reaction time and movement time test apparatus. Mean scores progressively increased over simple, spatial, temporal, and universal uncertainty conditions, suggesting a grading of task difficulty. Performances were highly reliable.

In the past it was generally believed that agility was almost entirely dependent on heredity; however, measurement and research revealed that it could be improved through practice, training, and instruction (Bennett 1956; Calvin 1958; Lafuze 1951; Masley, Hairabedian, and Donaldson 1953).

Seils, in testing primary-grade children, found a moderately high positive correlation between physical growth and agility performance in boys and girls. Espenschade noted that both boys and girls increase in agility performance up to 14 years of age, after which girls seem to decline while boys rapidly gain in agility performance.

Concerning body types, there is general agreement among investigators that endomorphs (fatty types) have the least potential of the somatotypes concerning performance in agility (Bookwalter et al. 1952; Cureton 1941; Perbis 1954; Sills 1953). However, some disagreement exists concerning whether mesomorphs (muscular types) are superior to ectomorphs (thin types). While Sills found the mesomorphs superior, Bookwalter and associates noted that thin boys of average size perform better than medium physique boys of average size. Klinzing used an agility test in assessing the fitness of police officers. The officers did more poorly on the fitness battery than did a control group of college students. Body fat was deemed detrimental to agility in this study.

Solley found no significant evidence to support the claim that boys who are big for their age or small for their age may be expected to perform better or worse on agility items.

Numerous investigators have indicated the importance of agility as a factor in the prediction of motor ability or sports ability or both (Carruth, 1952; Gates and Sheffield 1940; Hoskins 1934; Johnson 1934; Larson 1941; Lehsten 1948; McCloy 1942). Agility seems to be fundamental to skill in certain sports activities (Beise and Peasely 1947; Mohr and Haverstick 1956; Rarick 1937). Mohr and Haverstick found significant associations between volleying skill in volleyball and agility, while Hoskins, Lehsten, and Johnson

found agility important to basketball performance. Rope-jumping routines were advocated by Hipscher in developing agility skills needed in sports.

For many years, physical educators and coaches generally believed that muscular development associated with weight training was harmful to skill coordination. However, in recent years investigators have elicited results that indicate that progressive resistance exercises tend to affect favorably the coordination of performers (Calvin 1959; Kurt 1956; Masley, Hairabedian, and Donaldson 1953).

BIBLIOGRAPHY

AAHPERD Youth Fitness Test Manual. Reston, Va.: AAHPERD, 1976.

Beise, D., and V. Peasely, "The Relation of Reaction Time, Speed, and Agility of Big Muscle Groups to Certain Sports Skills." Research Quarterly 18:133–142, March 1947.

Bennett, C. L., "Relative Contributions of Modern Dance, Folk Dance, Basketball, and Swimming to Motor Abilities of College Women." Research Quarterly 27:256–257, October 1956.

Bookwalter, K. W., et al., "The Relationship of Body Size and Shape to Physical Performance." Research Quarterly 23:279, October 1952.

Calvin, S., "Effects of Progressive Resistive Exercises on the Motor Coordination of Boys." Research Quarterly 30:387, December 1959.

Carruth, W. A., "An Analysis of Motor Ability and Its Relationship to Constitutional Body Patterns of College Women." Unpublished doctoral dissertation, New York University, New York, 1952.

Chelladurai, P., "Manifestations of Agility." Journal of the Canadian AAHPERD 42:36–41, 1976.

————, M. S. Yuhasz, and R. Sipura, "The Reactive Agility Test." Perceptual and Motor Skills 44:1319–1324, 1977.

Cozens, F. W., The Measurement of General Athletic Ability in College Men. Eugene, Ore.: University of Oregon Press, 1929.

Cureton, T. K., "Body Build as a Framework of Reference for Interpreting Physical Fitness and Athletic Performance." Research Quarterly Supplement, 12:301–330, May 1941.

Espenschade, A., "Development of Motor Coordination in Boys and Girls." Research Quarterly 18:30–43, March 1947.

Gates, D. P., and R. P. Sheffield, "Tests of Change of Direction as Measurement of Different Kinds of Motor Ability in Boys of the 7th, 8th, and 9th

Grades." *Research Quarterly* 11:136–147, October 1940.

Hipscher, D., "For Agility, Quickness, and Conditioning, Incorporate the Jump Rope." *Athletic Journal,* 59:64–65, October 1978.

Hoskins, R. N., "The Relationships of Measurements of General Motor Capacity to the Learning of Specific Psycho-Motor Skills." *Research Quarterly* 5:63–72, March 1934.

Johnson, L. W., "Objective Basketball Tests for High School Boys." Unpublished master's thesis, University of Iowa, Iowa City, 1934.

Kirby, R. F., "A Simple Test of Agility." *Coach and Athlete,* June 1971, pp. 30–31.

Klinzing, J. E., "The Physical Fitness Status of Police Officers." *Journal of Sports Medicine and Physical Fitness* 20:291–296, 1980.

Kurt, C. P., "The Effect of Weight Training on Hand-Eye Coordination, Balance, and Response Time." Microcarded master's thesis, State University of Iowa, Iowa City, 1956, p. 26.

Lafuze, M., "A Study of the Learning of Fundamental Skills by College Freshmen Women of Low Motor Ability." *Research Quarterly* 22:149–157, May 1951.

Larson, L., "A Factor Analysis of Motor Ability Variables and Tests, With Tests for College Men." *Research Quarterly* 12:499–517, October 1941.

Lehsten, N., "A Measure of Basketball Skills for High School Boys." *Physical Educator* 5:103–109, December 1948.

Masley, J. W., A. Hairabedian, and D. N. Donaldson, "Weight Training in Relation to Strength, Speed, and Coordination." *Research Quarterly* 24:308–315, October 1953.

McCloy, C. H., "Blocks Test of Multiple Response." *Psychometrika* 7:165–169, September 1942.

———, and N. D. Young, *Tests and Measurements in Health and Physical Education.* New York: Appleton-Century-Crofts, 1954, p. 78.

Mohr, D. R., and M. L. Haverstick, "Relationship Between Height, Jumping Ability and Agility to Volleyball Skill." *Research Quarterly* 27:74, March 1956.

Perbis, J. A., "Relationships Between Somatotype and Motor Fitness in Women." *Research Quarterly* 25:84, March 1954.

Rarick, L., "An Analysis of the Speed Factor in Simple Athletic Events." *Research Quarterly* 8:89, December 1937.

Scott, M. G., and E. French, *Measurement and Evaluation in Physical Education.* Dubuque, Iowa: William C. Brown, 1959.

Seils, L. G., "Agility-Performance and Physical Growth." *Research Quarterly* 22:244, May 1951.

Sills, F., "The Relationship of Extreme Somatotypes to Performance in Motor and Strength Tests." *Research Quarterly* 24:223–228, May 1953.

Solley, W. H., "Ratio of Physical Development as a Factor in Motor Coordination of Boys Ages 10-14." *Research Quarterly* 28:295–303, October 1957.

CHAPTER 14

THE MEASUREMENT OF BALANCE

OBJECTIVES

After reading this chapter, the student should be able to:

1. Define balance and identify the physiologic factors that contribute to balance performance

2. Differentiate between static balance tests and dynamic balance tests

3. Understand the problems associated with the measurement of balance

4. Follow the directions for administering practical tests of static and dynamic balance

The two types of balance tests in common use in physical education are tests of static balance and of dynamic balance. Static balance may be defined as the physical ability that enables holding of a stationary position, while dynamic balance is the ability to maintain balance during movement, as in walking a fence or leaping from stone to stone while crossing a brook. Evidence indicates that the ability to balance easily, whether statically or dynamically, depends on the function of the mechanisms in the semicircular canals; kinesthetic sensations in the muscles, tendons, and joints; visual perception while the body is in motion; and the ability to coordinate these three sources of stimuli (Bass 1939). Balance is an important ability that is used in everyday activities, such as walking and standing, as well as in most games and sports.

USES OF BALANCE TESTS

Balance tests may be used in physical education as follows:

1. As a measure for determining achievement when balance is a specific objective in the teaching unit

2. As an element for assessing potential in gymnastics, diving, and other individual and team activities

3. As a means to determine whether there has been injury or damage to one or more of the kinesthetic receptors in the body or its parts

4. As a factor in motor fitness evaluation

PROBLEMS ASSOCIATED WITH BALANCE TESTING

Several of the problems and limitations associated with the testing of balance are listed and discussed as follows:

1. Strength seems to have a considerable influence on certain tests of balance. This is especially noticeable in the Bass stick tests and the progressive inverted balance test.

2. Although research reveals controversy on this point, it seems logical to us that moderate to severe fatigue affects the balance scores of a student. Thus, it would seem logical to conduct balance skills prior to the more strenuous tests that may be given dur-

ing a testing program (Nelson and Johnson 1973).

3. Because of the exact position required (and display of force to get in that position), students may need as many as three trials on certain tests to get their best score. This, of course, requires more time.

4. Norms in balance testing are primarily for the college age level. There is need for norms to be constructed at the elementary, junior high, and high school levels for both boys and girls.

5. Since static balance is positional or specific in nature, a student may score poorly in one aspect of balance and yet be quite proficient in other aspects. Perhaps motor ability tests that include static balance items should have several balance items of similar difficulty from which students can choose.

6. Certain balance tests require not only expensive equipment but also excessive amounts of time to administer. Therefore, the tests presented in this chapter are of practical value when several stations are set up and students are rotated between stations. Further attempts should be made to devise inexpensive balance tests for the average school situation.

PRACTICAL TESTS OF BALANCE

Several practical tests of balance in terms of time, equipment, and cost are presented on the following pages.

Static Balance Tests

Stork Stand

Objective: To measure static balance of the performer supported on the ball of the foot of the dominant leg.

Age Level: Age 10 through college age.

Sex: Satisfactory for both boys and girls.

Reliability: An *r* of .87 was found for this test when the best trial of the initial test was correlated with the best trial of the second test, which was given on a different day.

Objectivity: Reportedly as high as .99, as determined by Jim Knox, Northeast Louisiana University, Monroe 1969.

Validity: Face validity is accepted for this test.

Equipment and Materials: A stopwatch or a wristwatch with a second hand.

Directions: The student stands on the foot of the dominant leg and places the other foot on the inside of the supporting knee and the hands on the hips. On a given signal, he or she raises the heel from the floor and maintains the balance as long as possible without moving the ball of the foot from its initial position or letting the heel touch the floor (Figure 14.1). Three trials are given.

Scoring: The score is the longest time in seconds between when the heel is raised and the balance

Figure 14.1.   Stork stand

is lost on the best of three trials. Table 14.1 shows norms for college students.

Additional Pointers:

1. Students may be tested in pairs, with one performing while the other notes how long the performer balances as the number of seconds are counted off (aloud) by the timer.

2. Students who fail to get started on time are retested.

3. The performer cannot remove the hands from the hips during the test.

Bass Stick Test (Crosswise) (Bass 1939)

Objective: To measure static balance of the performer supported on a narrow surface on the ball of the foot.

Age Level: Age 10 through college age.

Sex: Satisfactory for both boys and girls.

Reliability: Reportedly as high as .90.

Validity: Accepted for its obvious face validity.

Equipment and Materials: Several sticks 1 in. wide, 1 in. high, and 12 in. long; a stopwatch or wristwatch with a second hand; and adhesive tape.

Directions: Several performers stand in one line and an observer for each performer stands in an opposite line. Each performer places the ball of the foot crosswise on the stick and (on a given signal) lifts the opposite foot from the floor, holding the balance for as long as possible up to a maximum of 60 sec (Figure 14.2). As the timer counts aloud, each observer takes note of how long his or her performer maintains balance. Each performer executes the test six times, three times on the right leg and three times on the left.

Scoring: The score is the sum of the times in seconds for all six trials. Table 14.2 shows norms for college students.

Figure 14.2. Bass crosswise stick test

Additional Pointers:

1. The sticks are taped to the floor.

2. If either the heel or the toe of the performer's supporting foot touches the floor, the observer terminates the count for that trial.

Table 14.1. Norms in Seconds for Stork Stand, College Students[a]

PERFORMANCE LEVEL	SCORE	
	Men	Women
Advanced	51 and above	28 and above
Advanced intermediate	37–50	23–27
Intermediate	15–36	8–22
Advanced beginner	5–14	3–7
Beginner	0–4	0–2

[a]Based on the scores of 50 men and 50 women, Corpus Christi State University, Corpus Christi, Tex., 1976.

Table 14.2. Norms in Seconds for Bass Crosswise Stick Test, College Students[a]

PERFORMANCE LEVEL	SCORE	
	Men	Women
Advanced	225 and above	180 and above
Advanced intermediate	165–224	140–179
Intermediate	65–164	60–139
Advanced beginner	15–64	15–59
Beginner	0–14	0–14

[a]Based on the scores of 50 men and 50 women, Corpus Christi State University, Corpus Christi, Tex., 1976. Scores are the total time for six trials, three on each foot.

3. Performers who lose their balance within the first 3 sec of a trial should be retested.

4. Although a large number of trials increases reliability, we have found that little reliability is lost when subjects are given only three trials on the preferred leg. In the interest of time and application of test results, the instructor might consider shortening this test.

Bass Stick Test (Lengthwise) (Bass 1939)

This test is the same as the previous test except that the foot rests on the stick lengthwise (Figure 14.3). Table 14.3 shows norms for college students.

Progressive Inverted Balance Test (Long Form and Short Form) (Johnson 1966)

Objective: To measure the ability to balance in an inverted position. These tests are probably most appropriate for a gymnastics unit or self-testing activities unit.

Age Level: Age 9 through college age.

Sex: Satisfactory for both boys and girls.

Reliability: An *r* of .82 was found for this test when subjects were tested on separate days.

Validity: Face validity is accepted for this test.

Equipment and Materials: A stopwatch and a tumbling mat.

Directions: The inverted balance test consists of five inverted balance stunts:

1. *Tripod Balance.* From a squatting position, the student places the hands shoulder-width apart, with the fingers pointing straight ahead. He or she leans forward, bending at the elbows, and places the inside of the knees against and slightly above the outside of the

Figure 14.3. Bass lengthwise stick test

Table 14.3.   Norms in Seconds for Bass Lengthwise Stick Test, College Students[a]

PERFORMANCE LEVEL	SCORE	
	Men	Women
Advanced	346 and above	336 and above
Advanced intermediate	306–345	301–335
Intermediate	221–305	206–300
Advanced beginner	181–220	166–205
Beginner	0–180	0–165

[a]Based on the scores of 50 men and 50 women, Corpus Christi State University, Corpus Christi, Tex., 1976. Scores are the total time for six trials, three on each foot.

elbows. The student continues to lean forward until the feet come off the floor and the forehead rests on the mat. He or she balances in this position for as many counts as possible up to a maximum of 5 sec (Figure 14.4a).

2. *Tip-up Balance.* Same as for the tripod balance except the head does not rest on the mat but balances with the face several inches from the floor (Figure 14.4b).

3. *Head Balance.* The student places the forehead on the mat several inches ahead of the hands and kicks upward, one foot at a time, and maintains the balance with the back slightly arched, legs straight and together, and toes pointed. Body weight should be primarily on the hands, with some weight on the forehead. The student balances in this position for as many counts as possible up to a maximum of 5 sec (Figure 14.4c). To recover from this position, the student pushes with the hands, ducks the head, and rolls forward, or steps down one foot at a time.

Safety Tip: A partner may grasp the performer's legs and assist him or her to the proper position before the balance begins.

4. *Head and Forearm Balance.* The student places the forearms on the mat and brings the hands close enough together for the thumbs and forefingers to form a cup for the head to fit into. He or she places the back of the head in the cup formed by the thumbs and fingers and kicks upward, one foot at a time, and balances between the tripod support formed by the head and forearms (Figure 14.4d). Balance is held

for as many counts as possible up to a maximum of 5 sec.

Safety Tip: Same as for the head balance.

5. *Handstand.* The student bends forward and places the hands on the mat about shoulder-width apart. He or she leans the shoulders over the hands and separates the feet so that one foot is ahead of the other. With the eyes looking forward of the fingertips, the student swings the rear foot upward as the front foot pushes from the mat, and maintains a balanced position with the feet overhead for as many counts as possible up to a maximum of 5 sec (Figure 14.4e).

Safety Tip: Same as for the head balance.

Scoring:

Long Form: The balances described carry the following weights:
Tripod—weight of 1.
Tip-up—weight of 2.
Head balance—weight of 3.
Head and forearm—weight of 4.
Handstand—weight of 5.

Each balance may be held for a maximum of 5 points (1 point for each second). The total score is figured by multiplying the weight of the balance by the number of seconds it was held and then adding the five scores together for the final score. The maximum raw score possible is 75 points. If a student cannot balance or fails to try a particular balance, his or her score is zero for that balance. Table 14.4 shows norms for college students.

Short Form: Same as for the long form except that the student chooses any one of the five balances to perform. For example, if a student

Figure 14.4   Parts of the inverted balance test: (a) Tripod balance, (b) tip-up balance, (c) head balance, (d) head and forearm balance, and (e) handstand

Table 14.4. *T*-Score Norms for Progressive Inverted Balance Test (Long Form), College Students[a]

PERFORMANCE LEVEL	SCORE	
	Men	Women
Advanced	70 and above	64 and above
Advanced intermediate	59–69	49–63
Intermediate	28–58	22–48
Advanced beginner	17–27	7–21
Beginner	0–16	0–6

[a]Based on the scores of 50 men and 50 women, Corpus Christi State University, Corpus Christi, Tex., 1976. See text for description of scoring system.

chose the head balance with a weight of 3 and held the position for 5 sec, the score would be 15 points. The maximum score possible for the short form test is 25 points.

SHORT FORM SCORING SCALE	
SCORE	PERFORMANCE LEVEL
25	Advanced
20	Advanced intermediate
15	Intermediate
10	Advanced beginner
5	Beginner

Dynamic Balance Test

Modified Bass Test of Dynamic Balance (Bass 1939; Johnson and Leach 1968)

Objective: To measure the ability to jump accurately and maintain balance during movement and after movement.

Age Level: High school and college age.

Sex: Appropriate for both boys and girls.

Reliability: An *r* of .75 was found for this test when subjects were tested on separate days.

Objectivity: An *r* of .97 was found when two testers scored 25 subjects independently on the test.

Validity: An *r* of .46 was found when this test was correlated with the Bass test of dynamic balance.

Equipment and Materials: Stopwatches; ¾-in. marking tape; and yardsticks.

Directions: The tester cuts 11 1- × ¾-in. pieces of marking tape and tapes them in the proper pattern (Figure 14.5) to the floor. Standing with the right foot on the starting mark, the performer leaps to the first tape mark with the left foot and

tries to hold a steady position on the ball of the left foot for as many seconds as possible up to 5 sec. He or she then leaps to the second tape with the right foot, and so on, alternating the feet from tape to tape. The performer should remain on

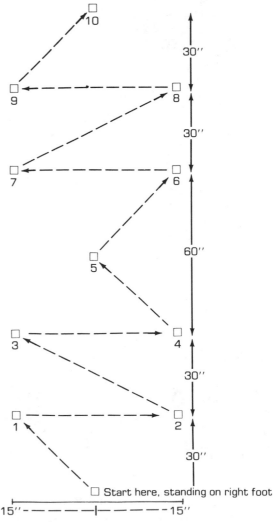

Figure 14.5. Floor pattern for modified Bass dynamic balance test

each tape mark for as many seconds as possible up to a maximum of 5 sec, and the foot must completely cover the tape so that the tape cannot be seen.

Scoring: Each mark successfully landed on scores 5 points; in addition, 1 point is awarded for each second the balance is held up to 5 sec per mark. Thus, a performer may earn a maximum of 10 points per marker and a total of 100 points for the test. Table 14.5 shows norms for college women.

Penalties: The penalties for this test may be classified into landing errors and balance errors.

Landing errors: The performer sacrifices 5 points for improper landing if he or she commits any of the following errors: (1) failing to stop on landing from the leap, (2) touching the heel or any other part of the body to the floor other than the ball of the supporting foot on landing, or (3) failing to completely cover the marker with the ball of the foot. The performer is allowed to reposition the body for the 5-sec balance on the ball of the foot after making a landing error.

Balance errors: The performer sacrifices remaining points at the rate of 1 point per second if he or she commits either of the balance errors described here before completion of the 5 sec: (1) touching any part of the body to the floor other than the ball of the supporting foot or (2) moving the foot while in the balance position. When the performer loses balance, he or she must step back on the proper marker and then leap to the next marker.

Additional Pointers:

1. The seconds of each balance attempt should be counted aloud for the performer.

2. The landing score and the balance score should be recorded for each marker.

Balance Challenger Tests (Johnson 1979)

The objective of the Balance Challenger tests is to measure balance in various positions with the Balance Challenger (or Levelometer Board), a simple device that enables the execution of certain balance skills related to various sports skills.

Table 14.5. *T*-Score Norms for Modified Bass Dynamic Balance Test, College Women[a]

T SCORE	RAW SCORE	*T* SCORE	RAW SCORE
67	100	40	60
66	98	39	59
65	97	38	57
64	95	37	56
63	94	36	54
62	93	35	53
61	91	34	51
60	90	33	50
59	88	32	48
57	85	31	47
56	84	30	45
55	82	29	44
54	81	28	42
53	79	27	41
52	78	26	39
51	76	25	38
50	75	24	36
49	73	23	35
48	72	22	34
47	70	20	32
46	69	19	30
45	67	18	29
44	66	17	27
43	64	16	26
42	63	15	24
41	62	14	23

[a]Based on the scores of 100 women at East Texas State University, Commerce, Tex., 1968. See text for description of how scores are computed.

The Balance Challenger (or Levelometer Board) is relatively inexpensive and may be purchased from B. & L. Products, P.O. Box 473, Portland, TX 78374. The order consists of the Levelometer Board, one brake block and cord, one carpet square (for indoor testing), four training blocks (for optional beginner training), and a test booklet with multilevel performance scales for eight test items. Figure 14.6 shows the equipment.

Students should be allowed to become familiar with the balance test items at least several days before being tested. They should warm up before testing and should be allowed three trials to gain the best possible score. They may take the test barefooted or in gym shoes (they can experiment beforehand to see which gives the best foot grip).

Two-Foot Standing Balance Test

Objective: To measure the performer's standing balance while on an unsteady base.

Age Level: All school ages.

Sex: Recommended for both boys and girls.

Reliability: An *r* of .83 was found in a correlation of the best score of three trials from two separate test dates, as reported by Arturo Rodriguez, Corpus Christi, Tex., in 1979.

Objectivity: An *r* of .98 was found in a correlation of the scores of an experienced tester with those of an inexperienced tester.

Validity: Face validity is accepted for this test as a measure of balance.

Equipment: Balance board; a carpet square; a brake block and cord; safety mats; and a timer.

Directions: The performer sets the balance board cross supports in the center of the carpet square, with the carpet square on a firm surface, and sets the brake block under the *right*-foot side of the balance board. Grasping the cord with only one hand, the performer steps up on the board, *right* foot first. When ready, he or she gently pulls the block or stick out from under the board, drops it to the floor, and then balances on the board for as long as possible (Figure 14.7). The timer starts timing at the moment the block or stick disengages from the board. Three trials are allowed.

Scoring: The best time of three trials, measured to the nearest second, is the score. Sixty seconds should normally be considered a maximum score. Table 14.6 shows average scores.

Additional Pointer: Any recontact of the brake block or stick with the board once it is disengaged from the board terminates the trial.

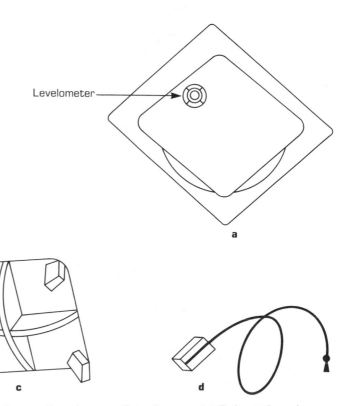

Figure 14.6. Equipment needed for Balance Challenger (Levelometer Board) tests: (a) Balance board centered on carpet square. (b) Lower assembly cross supports. (c) Lower assembly with training blocks installed. (d) Brake block cord

Figure 14.7. Two-foot standing balance test

One-Foot Standing Balance Test

Objective: To measure the performer's standing balance on one foot while standing on an unsteady base.

Age Level: All school ages.

Sex: Recommended for both boys and girls.

Reliability: An *r* of .78 was found in a correlation of the best score of three trials from two separate test dates, as reported by Arturo Rodriguez, Corpus Christi, Tex., in 1979.

Objectivity: An *r* of .98 was found in a correlation of the scores of an experienced tester with those of an inexperienced tester.

Validity: Face validity is accepted for this test as a measure of balance.

Equipment: Balance board; a carpet square; safety mats; and a wristwatch with second hand.

Directions: The performer sets the balance board cross supports in the center of the carpet square, with the carpet square on a firm surface. He or she then places the preferred foot in the center of the balance board, gently lifts the other foot from the floor, and balances as long as possible (Figure 14.8). The timer starts timing at the moment the foot leaves the floor.

Figure 14.8. One-foot standing balance test

Table 14.6. Scoring Scale in Seconds for Two-Foot Standing Balance Test, College Students

PERFORMANCE LEVEL	SCORE	
	Men	Women
Advanced	45 and above	42 and above
Advanced intermediate	33–44	30–41
Intermediate	15–32	13–29
Advanced beginner	5–14	4–12
Beginner	0–4	0–3

Scoring: The best time of three trials, measured to the nearest second, is the test score. Table 14.7 shows average scores.

Additional Pointer: Once the nonsupporting foot leaves the floor, it may not be used again without terminating the time trial.

Four Corner Touch Test

Objective: To measure dynamic balance through weight shifting from corner to corner of the balance board.

Age Level: Age 10 through college age.

Sex: Recommended for both boys and girls.

Reliability: An *r* of .77 was found in a correlation of the best score of three trials from two separate test dates, as reported by Arturo Rodriguez, Corpus Christi, Tex., in 1979.

Objectivity: An *r* of .94 was found in a correlation of the scores of an experienced tester with those of an inexperienced tester.

Validity: Face validity is accepted for this test as a measure of dynamic balance.

Equipment: Balance board; a carpet square; a brake block; and safety mats. Athletic footwear with good gripping action is recommended.

Directions: Same as for the two-foot standing balance test except that when timing starts the performer shifts the weight so that the front left corner of the board touches the floor, then the front right corner, the back left corner, and finally the back right corner (Figure 14.9). The performer does this as many sequences as possible in 2 min without falling off the board. The sequence front left corner, front right corner, back left corner, back right corner should be stressed.

Scoring: The number of touches made in proper sequence within 2 min is the score, 1 point being awarded per touch. The best of three trials is recorded. Table 14.8 shows average scores.

Figure 14.9. Four-corner touch test

Additional Pointers:

1. Same as for the two-foot standing balance test.

2. If a corner is touched out of sequence, the touch does not count. The performer may return to the proper sequence and continue to score points.

3. Each performer should have adequate practice prior to testing.

Table 14.7. Scoring Scale in Seconds for One-Foot Standing Balance Test, College Students

PERFORMANCE LEVEL	SCORE	
	Men	Women
Advanced	17 and above	15 and above
Advanced intermediate	11–16	9–14
Intermediate	5–10	5–8
Advanced beginner	3–4	3–4
Beginner	1–2	1–2

Table 14.8. Scoring Scale for Four-Corner Touch Test, College Students[a]

PERFORMANCE LEVEL	SCORE	
	Men	Women
Advanced	18 and above	16 and above
Advanced intermediate	12–17	10–15
Intermediate	7–11	5–9
Advanced beginner	4–6	3–4
Beginner	0–3	0–2

[a]Score is number of touches made in proper sequence in 2 min.

Combination Static and Dynamic Balance Test

Nelson Balance Test (Nelson 1968)

Objective: To measure both static and dynamic balance in a single test.

Age Level: Age 9 through college age.

Sex: Satisfactory for both boys and girls.

Reliability: Test–retest coefficients of .91, .90, and .68 were obtained for fourth, fifth, and sixth grade boys, respectively.

Validity: The test has face validity as a measure of balance. Moreover, a coefficient of .77 was found when the test was correlated with the combined score of several standard balance measures.

Equipment and Materials: Seven small wooden blocks, 2 in. × 4 in. × 8 in., four of them painted red or otherwise distinguished; a 10-ft wooden balance beam, 2 in. × 4 in.; three triangular-shaped supports to hold the beam edgewise (Figure 14.10a); pieces of rubber to be glued to the bottom of each block, to prevent the blocks from sliding or tipping and to protect the gymnasium floor; a stopwatch; a tape measure; and possibly chalk or tape to mark the position of the blocks on the floor.

Directions: Two lines may be drawn 24 in. apart and 20 ft long. The blocks are placed crosswise; the blocks and balance beam are positioned as shown in Figure 14.10b.

Phase 1: When ready, the subject steps onto the first block (a red block) on the ball of the left foot. He or she balances on the block while the tester counts out the seconds, "1-2-3-4-5." The tester counts each time the subject mounts a red block but not when he or she mounts others. The performer proceeds along the route indicated in Figure 14.10b, leaping from one block to the next, alternating feet each time.

He or she tries to go as fast as possible without making mistakes. There are four red 5-sec-hold blocks on which the subject must balance on one foot while the tester calls out the 5 sec. When crossing the balance beam in the first phase of the test, the performer walks heel to toe the first half of the beam and then turns sideways and sidesteps to the *right* the remainder of the distance. He or she steps *off* the beam on the *right* foot and completes the first phase of the test.

Phase 2: As soon as the subject steps off the last block, he or she turns and steps back on the block on the ball of the left foot, holds for 5 sec, leaps to the next block onto the right foot, and proceeds according to the diagram in Figure 14.10c. The subject walks across the first half of the balance beam heel to toe and then turns sideways and sidesteps to the *left* the last half of the beam. He or she steps off with the *left* foot and completes the remainder of the course.

Scoring: The score is entirely based on cumulative time to the nearest $\frac{1}{10}$ sec for the completion of both phases of the test. The stopwatch is started when the subject steps on the first block and stops when he or she steps off the seventh block at the end of the first phase. *The watch is not reset.* It is then started again as soon as the subject steps back on the block and is stopped at the completion of the second phase. Score is based on one complete trial. Table 14.9 shows norms for grade-school boys.

Penalties: Any time the foot touches the floor, the performer must get back on the block at the place where he or she fell off and proceed from that point. If the subject should leave one of the "hold" blocks before the 5 sec has elapsed, he or she must return and "hold" for the remaining seconds (i.e., if the subject should leave a red block

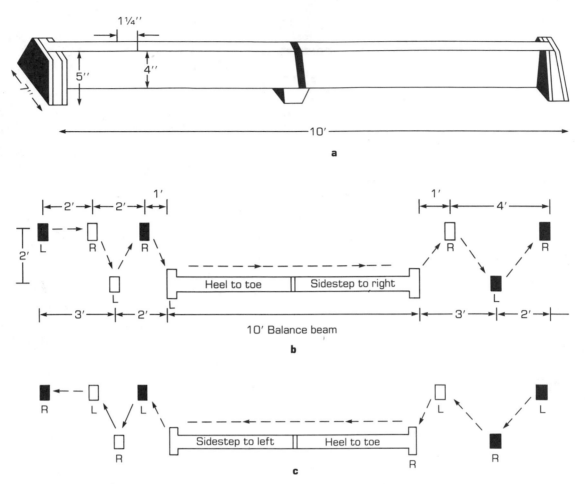

Figure 14.10. Nelson balance test. (a) Balance beam. (b) Sequence for test phase 1. Dark blocks are those on which subject must balance for 5 sec. (c) Sequence for test phase 2

Table 14.9. *T*-Score Norms in Seconds for Nelson Balance Test, Fourth, Fifth, and Sixth Grade Boys[a]

T SCORE	SCORE		
	Grade 4	Grade 5	Grade 6
80	48.7 and above	45.0 and above	45.7 and above
75	53.2–48.8	48.5–45.1	48.2–45.8
70	57.7–53.3	52.0–48.6	50.7–48.3
65	62.2–57.8	55.5–52.1	53.2–50.8
60	66.7–62.3	59.0–55.6	55.7–53.3
55	71.2–66.8	62.5–59.1	58.2–55.8
50	75.7–71.3	66.0–62.6	60.7–58.3
45	80.2–75.8	69.5–66.1	63.2–60.8
40	84.7–80.3	73.0–69.6	65.7–63.3
35	89.2–84.8	76.5–73.1	68.2–65.8
30	93.7–89.3	80.0–76.6	70.7–68.3
25	98.2–93.8	83.5–80.1	73.2–70.8
20	102.7–98.3	87.0–83.6	75.7–73.3

[a]See text for description of the test and scoring.

after 3 sec, he would have to return and hold for 2 sec to satisfy the 5-sec requirement for the red blocks). Subjects are allowed to practice by going through both phases of the test prior to actual testing.

Similarly, if the subject should fall off, or deviate from the heel-toe or sidestep walk across the balance board, she must return to the point at which the fault occurred and resume the walk across the board.

In all cases the watch continues to run until the end of the last 5-sec-hold count at the end of the course.

Broadhead Dynamic Balance Test (Broadhead 1974)

See Chapter 18 for the test description.

FINDINGS AND CONCLUSIONS FROM BALANCE MEASUREMENT AND RESEARCH

It is frequently heard, and inaccurately so, that girls have better balance than boys because of their lower center of gravity. In an upright position, however, a female's center of gravity is not enough lower than the male's to overcome the greater strength factor that rests in favor of the male. Moreover, in the inverted position the male assumes the lower center of gravity, while still having the strength factor in his favor. Therefore, the findings of Smith and Hoffman that boys are superior to girls of compatible ages in balance activities seem most logical and valid.

Eckert studied the theorized inverse relationship of balance and stability. Females, who were encouraged to use associated sensorimotor systems plus structural stability, outperformed the males on the stabilometer. Males performed better than females on the ladder climb owing to greater sensorimotor development.

Broadhead found no sex differences in performance on a beam walking test with minimally brain-injured and educable mentally retarded children.

Another fallacy frequently heard is that balance is inherited and that there is very little the average person can do to improve balance. While the ability to balance may be inherited to a certain extent, it can be significantly improved as determined in studies by Espenschade and associates, Lafuze, Smith, Gunden, and Garrison. Furthermore, Espenschade and associates found that balance improved with an increase in chronologic age between the ages of 11 and 16 years, but the rate of gain for boys between the ages of 13 and 15 was noticeably slowed.

Vanfraechem and Vanfraechem reported that the balancing ability of elderly, sedentary people can be significantly improved with training. Similarly, young children can learn balancing tasks more easily if they are shown a model before they attempt the task (Thomas, Pierce, and Ridsdale 1977).

Concerning mental ability, Hoffman has stated that fast-learning groups for each sex and grade tend to be superior to slow-learning groups on balance tests.

The balancing abilities of educable mentally retarded children are not as well developed as in nonhandicapped children (Horgan 1977).

Scott (1955) advised that specific balance tests should be a part of any kinesthesis battery, since the balance leap and the balance stick tests were consistently reliable and valid in her study.

In identifying factors of balance, Whelan found four factors that corresponded with the findings of Bass. They were general static balance kinesthetic response, vertical semicircular canal function, general ampular sensitivity, and convergence of the eyes. Whelan also found that little difference existed between the blind and the sighted in balance ability, and that balance ability in the blind probably does not overcompensate for the loss of sight, as do other factors such as hearing and touch.

Padden found that poor balance groups among deaf students made significantly poorer showings in the ability to orient themselves under water than better balance groups among such students when the eyes were blindfolded. However, in Padden's study the groups were not equated in swimming ability, and there is a possibility that lack of experience, and not poor balance, brought about the results.

Deaf children were found to have poorer static and dynamic balance than hearing children by Lindsey and O'Neal. Effgen reported significant improvement in static balance of deaf children as a result of an exercise program, when balance was measured by time.

Some controversy exists among physical educators concerning whether fatigue reduces balance control. Although Scott and French maintained that excessive fatigue reduces balance control, Culane reported that fatigue has no noticeable effect on balance. However, in our opinion, Culane should have used the terms *slight fatigue* or *warm-up* to specify the degree of fatigue, since the exercises she used were not severe enough to cause "moderate" or "severe" fatigue to the average student. It has been noted by gymnastic coaches and performers that moderate to severe fatigue usually has an adverse effect on static balance. Moreover, Johnson and colleagues found that squat thrusts performed for maximum repetition significantly decreased static balance performance as measured by the stork stand (heel-up) test.

Nelson and Johnson reported that both local and general body fatigue impaired static balance performance, with general body fatigue producing significantly greater decrement than local fatigue.

If balance is of importance in athletic activities, it is logical to assume that athletes will perform better than nonathletes on tests of balance. Lessl found evidence to this effect when he compared college athletes with average college students. Other investigators have found similar results. Slater-Hammel found varsity athletes significantly better than physical education majors, and the Reynolds' balance test showed that physical education majors were significantly better than liberal arts majors. Mumby found that good wrestlers were somewhat better than poor wrestlers in the ability to balance and to learn to balance. Gross and Thompson concluded that good swimmers have better dynamic balance than poor swimmers.

Several investigators have attempted to determine the contribution of physical education activities to improvement in balance. Greenlee conducted a study in which a significant relationship was found between dynamic balance and bowling performance. Bennett concluded at the end of 16 weeks of participation that there were no significant differences in balance among those participating in modern dance, swimming, folk dance, or basketball, as measured by the Bass leap test. It should be pointed out, however, that since an initial test was not given before participation, the author was unable to assess the amount of improvement that was made. Consequently, it was not known whether initial differences among groups might have masked any differences in improvement in balance brought about by the activities. Gunden found that participation in basketball, tumbling, tennis, and volleyball resulted in improvement in the balance ability of college women.

A number of researchers have reported a positive relationship between static balance and ability in gross motor activity (Carruth 1952; Cumbee 1954; Cumbee et al. 1957; Espenschade et al. 1953; Estep 1957; Scott 1955; Wiebe 1951). However, Drowatzky and Zuccato found low intercorrelations among balance tests, which suggested that each balance test measured a different type of balance. Sandborn and Wyrick also found little relationship among balance tests used in their study. However, they did find that the most effective combination of predictors of balance beam skill were two tests of dynamic balance, the sideward leap and the modified sideward leap. Wyrick further found that balance performance was a general ability and not specific to task height.

BIBLIOGRAPHY

Bass, R. I., "An Analysis of the Components of Tests of Semi-circular Canal Function and of Static and Dynamic Balance." *Research Quarterly* 10:33, May 1939.

Bennett, C. L., "Relative Contributions of Modern Dance, Folk Dance, Basketball, and Swimming to Motor Abilities of College Women." *Research Quarterly* 27:261, October 1956.

Broadhead, G. D., "Beam Walking in Special Education." *Rehabilitation Literature* 35:145–151, May 1974.

Carruth, W. A., "An Analysis of Motor Ability and Its Relationship to Constitutional Body Patterns of College Women." Unpublished doctoral dissertation, New York University, New York, 1952.

Culane, M. J., "The Effect of Leg Fatigue Upon Balance." Microcarded master's thesis, State University of Iowa, Iowa City, 1956.

Cumbee, F. J., "A Factorial Analysis of Motor Coordination." *Research Quarterly* 25:420, December 1954.

————, et al., "Factorial Analysis of Motor Coordination Variables for Third and Fourth Grade Girls." *Research Quarterly* 28:107–108, May 1957.

Drowatzky, J. N., and J. C. Zuccato, "Inter-relationships Between Selected Measures of Static and Dynamic Balance." *Research Quarterly* 38:509, October 1967.

Eckert, H. M., "Balance and Stability." *Perceptual and Motor Skills* 49:149–150, 1979.

Effgen, S. K., "Effect of an Exercise Program on the Static Balance of Deaf Children." *Physical Therapy* 61:873–877, 1981.

Espenschade, A., et al., "Dynamic Balance in Adolescent Boys." *Research Quarterly* 24:270, October 1953.

Estep, D. P., "Relationship of Static Equilibrium to Ability in Motor Activities." *Research Quarterly* 28:5, March 1957.

Garrison, L. E., "An Experiment in Improving Balance Ability Through Teaching Selected Exercises." Unpublished master's thesis, State University of Iowa, Iowa City, 1943.

Greenlee, G. A., "The Relationship of Selected Measures of Strength, Balance, and Kinesthesis to Bowling Performance." Unpublished master's thesis, State University of Iowa, Iowa City, 1958.

Gross, E. A., and H. L. Thompson, "Relationship of Dynamic Balance to Speed and Ability in Swimming." *Research Quarterly* 28:346, December 1957.

Gunden, R. E., "The Effect of Selected Sports Activities Upon the Balance Ability of College Women. Microcarded master's thesis, State University of Iowa, Iowa City, 1956.

Hoffman, V., "Relation of Selected Traits and Abilities to Motor Learning." Microcarded doctoral dissertation, Indiana University, Bloomington, 1955.

Horgan, J. S., "Stabilometer Performance of Educable Mentally Retarded Children Under Differential Feedback Conditions." *Research Quarterly* 48:711–716, December 1977.

Johnson, B. L., "A Progressive Inverted Balance Test." Unpublished study, Northeast Louisiana University, Monroe, 1966.

———, *Balance Challenger Test Booklet*. Portland, Tex.: Brown and Littleman, 1979.

———, and J. Leach, "A Modification of the Bass Test of Dynamic Balance." Unpublished study, East Texas State University, Commerce, Tex., 1968.

———, et al., "The Effect of Fatigue Upon Balance." *Abstracts of Research Papers 1968 AAHPERD Convention*. Reston, Va.: AAHPERD, 1968, p. 118.

Lafuze, M., "A Study of the Learning of Fundamental Skills by College Freshmen Women of Low Motor Ability." *Research Quarterly* 22:156, May 1951.

Lessl, R. F., "The Development of a New Test of Balance and Its Use in Comparing College Athletes and Average College Students in Their Ability to Balance." Microcarded master's thesis, University of Wisconsin, 1954.

Lindsey, D., and J. O'Neal, "Static and Dynamic Balance Skills of Eight Year Old Deaf and Hearing Children." *American Annals of the Deaf* 121:49–55, 1976.

Mumby, H. H., "Kinesthetic Acuity and Balance Related to Wrestling Ability." *Research Quarterly* 24:334, October 1953.

Nelson, J. K., "The Nelson Balance Test." Unpublished study, Louisiana State University, Baton Rouge, 1968.

———, and B. L. Johnson, "Effects of Local and General Fatigue on Static Balance." *Perceptual and Motor Skills* 37:615–618, 1973.

Padden, D. A., "Ability of Deaf Swimmers to Orient Themselves When Submerged in Water." *Research Quarterly* 30:225, May 1959.

Reagh, H. C., Jr., "Construction of Norms for the Revised Nelson Balance Test." Unpublished study, Louisiana State University, Baton Rouge, 1971.

Russell, C., "A Study of the Relationship Between the Bass Test of Dynamic Balance and the Modified Bass Test of Dynamic Balance." Unpublished study, Northeast Louisiana University, Monroe, 1970.

Sandborn, C., and W. Wyrick, "Prediction of Olympic Balance Beam Performance From Standardized and Modified Tests of Balance." *Research Quarterly* 40:174–184, March 1969.

Scott, M. G., "Motor Ability Tests for College Women." *Research Quarterly* 14:402, December 1943.

———, "Measurement of Kinesthesis." *Research Quarterly* 26:337, October 1955.

———, and E. French, *Measurement and Evaluation in Physical Education*. Dubuque, Iowa: William C. Brown, 1959.

Slater-Hammel, A. T., "Performance of Selected Groups of Male College Students on the Reynold's Balance Test." *Research Quarterly* 27:351, October 1956.

Smith, J. A., "Relation of Certain Physical Traits and Abilities to Motor Learning in Elementary School Children." *Research Quarterly* 27:228, May 1956.

Thomas, J. R., C. Pierce, and S. Ridsdale, "Age Differences in Children's Ability to Model Motor Behavior." *Research Quarterly* 48:592–597, December 1977.

Vanfraechem, J., and R. Vanfraechem, "Studies of the Effect of a Short Training Period on Aged Subjects." *Journal of Sports Medicine and Physical Fitness* 17:373–380, 1977.

Whelan, T. P., "A Factor Analysis of Tests of Balance and Semicircular-Canal Function."

Microcarded doctoral dissertation, State University of Iowa, Iowa City, 1955.

Wiebe, V. R., "A Study of Tests of Kinesthesis." Unpublished master's thesis, State University of Iowa, Iowa City, 1951.

Witte, F., "A Factorial Analysis of Measures of Kinesthesis." Doctoral dissertation, Indiana University, Bloomington, 1953.

Wyrick, W., "Effect of Task Height and Practice on Static Balance." *Research Quarterly* 40:215–221, March 1969.

CHAPTER 15

THE MEASUREMENT OF SPEED AND REACTION TIME

OBJECTIVES

After reading this chapter, the student should be able to:

1. Define and distinguish among the terms *speed of movement, reaction time,* and *response time*

2. List at least five physiologic and motivational influences on reaction time performance

3. Understand and anticipate some of the administrative problems in the measurement of speed and reaction time

4. Follow the directions for administering practical tests of speed of movement and reaction time

---

Fast movement and quick reactions are prized qualities in athletics. Coaches frequently praise certain players or an entire team for their *quickness*. In football a player who is extremely fast poses a constant threat to break away for the long run; in baseball the fast runner causes hurried throws and adjustments in pitching and defensive strategy; the full-court press is a potent weapon in basketball if a team has the speed to make it effective; and in track speed is the essence of the sport.

Despite these commonplace observations, the study of speed of movement and speed of reaction is much more complex than it might appear. Speed of movement, for example, entails much more than mere running speed. The speed with which a wrestler executes a reversal, the lightning flash of a boxer's jab, the explosive spring of the shot putter's move across the throwing circle, and the graceful swiftness of the swimmer and skater are but a few of the many different kinds of movement speeds that are involved in physical performance. *Speed of movement shall thus be defined as the rate at which a person can propel the body, or parts of the body, between two points.*

Reaction time is the interval between the presentation of a stimulus and the initiation of the response. While reaction time was initially thought to be a rather simple and easily measured phenomenon, it has been shown to be influenced by a number of variables. An individual cannot be described as having a single reaction time without specifying the conditions under which testing occurs. Some of the factors that have been found to influence reaction time are the following: the sense organ involved, the intensity of the stimulus, the preparatory set, general muscular tension, motivation, practice, the response required, fatigue, and general state of health.

Analysis of speed of movement and reaction time when the two are combined is even more complex. It has been fairly well established that some individuals react quickly but move slowly, and some react slowly but are able to run or move very rapidly once they start. Even though speed of movement and speed of reaction may not show a significant positive relationship when measured separately and then correlated with each other, it is difficult to separate them in actual performance. A linebacker in football, for instance, might react quickly in diagnosing the play but still has to move fast enough to be able to make the tackle, if he is to be a successful performer.

Therefore, while measurement of each factor separately may be highly desirable for diagnostic purposes and for research, it would seem more practical for the coach and physical educator to measure them together in test situations that duplicate response movements that are required in the activity in question. Speed and reaction time are considered largely innate abilities; however, both can be improved through practice and training. Consequently, it seems only logical that practice and training would combine the two in a *gamelike* sequence of movements.

Generally, speed has been measured by short dashes. A distance over 100 yd is usually not recommended, because endurance then becomes a factor. Naturally, the age, sex, and characteristics of the subjects should be the major consideration in selecting tests of speed.

Reaction time has usually been more complicated and more expensive to measure because of the timing device that has been employed. The device usually has a stimulus-presenting mechanism, such as a light or buzzer, and a switch that the subject presses or releases in response to the stimulus. A precise timer is needed to measure the interval of time from the stimulus to the response.

USES OF SPEED AND REACTION TIME TESTS

Speed of movement and reaction time measures may be used by physical educators in a number of ways, some of which are suggested here:

1. As a factor in motor ability tests, motor fitness tests, and sports skills tests

2. For diagnosis prior to specific practice and conditioning work

3. For classification of individuals into homogeneous groups for certain activities

4. For motivation and information purposes in conjunction with health, safety, and driver education units

PROBLEMS ASSOCIATED WITH SPEED AND REACTION TIME TESTING

Some of the problems and limitations that are associated with speed and reaction time measurement were mentioned in the first part of this chapter. We pointed out that equipment would be a major obstacle if the physical educator wished to secure very precise measures for a variety of response movements. The need for elaborate equipment, however, depends on the purposes for which the measures are to be used.

When speed of movement and reaction time are to be studied separately, the specificity of each must be considered, as well as how each may operate in relation to the movements involved and the task. In other words, it would not make much sense to measure reaction time by having the subject release a telegraph key device on hearing a buzzer and to measure speed of movement by the 100-yard dash, and then attempt to make conclusions regarding the reaction and movement speed of a defensive lineman in football. The tasks are too unrelated. It would be much more meaningful and accurate to have the subject react to the movement of the ball on an actual pass from the center and to have the subject then move to hit a dummy some distance away. To get both reaction time and speed of movement in the same trial would require a timing device with two clocks. One clock would start when the ball was moved and would stop when the subject started to move (such as if he or she lifted the hand from a switch on the ground). This would measure reaction time. A second clock would start when the subject started to move and would stop when contact was made with the dummy, which would measure movement time.

The meaningfulness and challenge of the test, the testing position, and the skill and past experience of the subject are all important points to be considered. The reaction of a football player may be much faster in the situation just described than in an artificial setting such as the telegraph key and buzzer described earlier. As in all tests, the tester must carefully evaluate the nature of the performance that is being measured. In a great many sports, for example, the crucial speed that the sport requires is needed for only a very few yards. The abilities to perceive the meaning of the stimulus, react correctly, and move to the required spot just a few feet away are of vital importance in tennis, badminton, handball, football, basketball, baseball, softball, and many other sports. The speed at which a person can run 100 yd is not nearly so important in those activities.

The use of a standing start as opposed to the crouched sprinter's stance is ordinarily recommended in physical education class testing. This is due to the fact that persons who have not practiced crouched starts would be at a definite disadvantage. This disadvantage would be even more pronounced if such individuals were given their choice and elected to start from the crouched position without any training. The untrained individual's first move from the sprinter's stance is usually to stand up rather than to start running, which is wasted motion.

Concentration and the state of readiness to react are essential for speed and reaction measurement, and therefore the testing situation should be conducive for optimum performance. The importance of the proper interval between the preparatory command and the signal to respond will be discussed in the descriptions of the tests. The tester must be ever conscious of this foreperiod and guard against the tendency to give the same interval each time. In test situations it is best to have a definite sequence established.

The consumption of class time is not a limiting factor if the measures employed consist only of dashes. If the physical educator wishes, however, to measure functional response movements, then considerable time is needed for a sufficient number of trials.

PRACTICAL TESTS OF SPEED AND REACTION TIME

The physical educator is ordinarily not able to justify the purchase of an expensive timing device and is therefore somewhat limited in the measurement of speed of movement and, particularly, in the measurement of reaction time. Nevertheless, armed with only a stopwatch and imagination, the physical educator can obtain valuable measures of both of these traits, which are both meaningful and sufficiently accurate.

The tests presented here include a hand reaction test, a foot reaction test, several dashes, and a choice–response accuracy test. None of the tests requires expensive timing devices or elaborate equipment.

Nelson Reaction Tests

In the 1960s F. B. Nelson developed a measuring device that is both simple and inexpensive. The Nelson Reaction Timer[1] is based on the law of constant acceleration of free-falling bodies and

consists of a stick scaled to read in time as computed from the following formula:

$$\text{time} = \sqrt{\frac{2 \times \text{distance stick falls}}{\text{acceleration due to gravity}}}$$

This device is used to measure reaction time of the hand and the foot and the speed of movement of the hands. It comes with an instructional leaflet.

Nelson Hand Reaction Test

Objective: To measure the speed of reaction of the hand in response to a visual stimulus.

Age Level: Any age from kindergarten upward. The only limiting factor is the subject's ability to catch the falling stick with the fingers.

Sex: Satisfactory for both boys and girls.

Validity: The validity of the timing device is inherent, since the earth's gravitational pull is consistent; therefore, the timer falls at the same rate of acceleration each time.

Reliability: A reliability coefficient of .89 was obtained using average scores taken on two separate test administrations.

Test Equipment and Materials: Nelson Reaction Timer; a table and chair or a desk chair.

Directions: The subject sits with the forearm and hand resting comfortably on the table or desk chair. The tips of the thumb and index finger are held in a *ready-to-pinch* position about 3 or 4 in. beyond the edge of the table (Figure 15.1a). The upper edges of the thumb and index finger should be in a horizontal position. The tester holds the stick-timer near the top, letting it hang between the subject's thumb and index finger. The baseline on the stick should be even with the upper surface of the subject's thumb (Figure 15.1b).

The subject is directed to look at the *concentration zone* (which is a black shaded zone between the 0.120 and 0.130 sec lines on the stick) and to react by catching the stick (by pinching the thumb and index finger together) when it is released. The subject should not look at the tester's hand nor move the hand up or down while attempting to catch the falling stick. Twenty trials are given. Each drop is preceded by a preparatory command of "ready."

Scoring: When the subject catches the stick, the score is read just above the upper edge of the thumb (Figure 15.1c). The five slowest and the five fastest trials are discarded, and an average of the middle ten is recorded as the score. Numbers

1. Nelson Reaction Timer, Model RT-2, Copyright 1965 by F. B. Nelson, P.O. Box 51987, Lafayette, LA 70505.

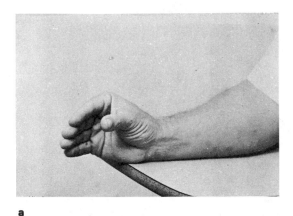

a

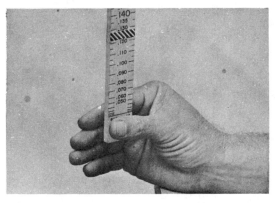

b

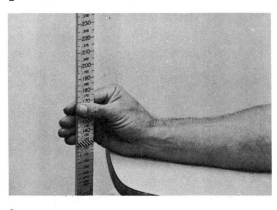

c

Figure 15.1. Nelson hand reaction test.
(a) Position of hand and fingers for the test.
(b) Position of baseline of the stick-timer for the
test. (c) Example of scoring the test (0.170 sec in
this example)

on the timer represent thousandths of a second.
Scores may be recorded to the nearest 5/1000 of
a second.

Norms for this test are not complete at this
time. For college men, the average reaction time
is around 0.16 sec with a range of 0.13 to 0.22.
For small children (first graders), the average is
about 0.26 sec.

Additional Pointers:

1. The testing environment should be such that
    the subject is able to concentrate.

2. The subject should be allowed three or four
    practice trials to make sure he or she under-
    stands the procedures and becomes familiar
    with the task.

3. The interval of time between the prepara-
    tory command of "ready" and the release
    is extremely important. It should be varied,
    to prevent the subject from becoming
    accustomed to a constant pattern. On the
    other hand, this interval should remain within
    a range of not less than 0.5 sec or longer
    than approximately 2 sec. If too short, it
    catches the subject unprepared, and if too
    long, the subject loses the optimal state of
    readiness. For standardization, the tester
    could have a specific order of these inter-
    vals. For example, on the first trial he or
    she could say "ready," then silently count
    "1001," then release; on the second trial,
    after "ready" the count might be just "1,"
    then release, and so on.

4. Obvious anticipations should be discarded
    and not be counted as one of the 20 trials.

5. The tester must be careful that the subject's
    thumb or index finger is not touching the
    timer.

6. If the subjects are young children, the test
    should be conducted like a challenging game.

7. The subjects should use the dominant hand
    if only one hand is to be tested.

8. The thumb and index finger should not be
    more than 1 in. apart at the start.

Nelson Foot Reaction Test

Objective: To measure the speed of reaction by
the foot in response to a visual stimulus.

Age and Sex: Same as for the Nelson hand reaction test.

Validity: Same as for the hand reaction test.

Reliability: A reliability coefficient of .85 was
obtained with college men as subjects.

Test Equipment and Materials: Nelson Reaction Timer; a table or bench; wall space.

Directions: The subject sits on a table or bench
that is about 1 in. from the wall. With the shoe
off, the subject positions the foot so that the ball
of the foot is about 1 in. from the wall, with the
heel resting on the table about 2 in. from the edge.

The tester holds the reaction timer next to the wall so that it hangs between the wall and the subject's foot with the baseline opposite the end of the big toe (Figure 15.2). The subject looks at the concentration zone and is told to react, when the stick-timer is dropped, by pressing the stick against the wall with the ball of the foot. Twenty trials are given.

Scoring: The reaction time for each trial is the line just above the end of the big toe when the foot is pressing the stick to the wall. The slowest five trials and the fastest five trials are discarded and the average of the middle ten trials is the score.

Norms are incomplete. The average reaction time for college men is approximately 0.21 sec.

Additional Pointers: Same as for the Nelson hand reaction test.

Nelson Speed of Movement Test

Objective: To measure combined reaction and speed of movement of the hands.

Age and Sex: Same as for the Nelson hand reaction test.

Validity: Face validity is accepted as long as no attempt is made to separate reaction time and speed of movement.

Reliability: A reliability coefficient of .75 was found for college men.

Test Equipment and Materials: Nelson Reaction Timer; a table and chair; chalk or a tape and ruler.

Directions: The subject sits at a table with the hands resting on the edge. The palms face one another with the inside border of the little fingers along two lines marked on the edge of the table

12 in. apart. The tester holds the timer near its top so that it hangs midway between the subject's palms. The baseline is positioned so it is level with the upper borders of the subject's hands (Figure 15.3a).

The preparatory command "ready" is given, the timer is released, and the subject attempts to stop it as quickly as possible by clapping the hands together. The subject must be careful not to allow the hands to move up or down when clapping the hands together. Twenty trials are given.

Scoring: The score for the combined response-movement is read from the timer at the point just above the upper edge of the hand after the catch (Figure 15.3b). The average of the middle ten trials, after the slowest and fastest five trials have been discarded, is recorded.

Norms for this test are incomplete at this time. The average time has been found to be about 0.24 sec for college men.

Additional Pointers:

1. The pointers listed for the Nelson hand reaction test are applicable for this test.

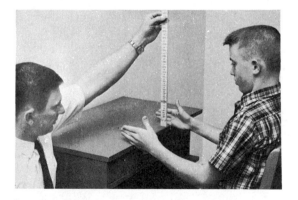

a

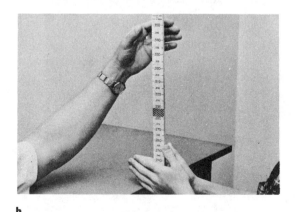

b

Figure 15.3.   Nelson speed of movement test (a) Ready position with the hands 12 in. apart. (b) Scoring the test (0.240 sec in this example)

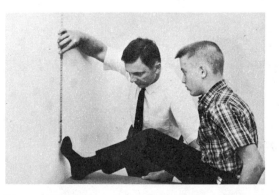

Figure 15.2.   Ready position with the end of big toe at the baseline for the Nelson foot reaction test

2. After the subject has the hands in the ready position, a 12-in. ruler should be used to make sure the hands are the correct distance apart.

3. A small mark exactly between the two marks should be made to facilitate the positioning of the timer prior to release.

4. The subject should remove any rings to prevent the denting or marring of the timer's surface.

Running Speed, Endurance Tests

Four-Second Dash

This test is described in Chapter 19 (Scott Motor Ability Test). The test could be used for junior high school, high school, and college-age individuals. Norms for college students are shown in Table 15.1.

Six-Second Dash (McCloy and Young 1954)

Objective: To measure speed of movement. (Although this event has been used as a measure of running endurance, it would seem to be appropriate as a test of speed, at least for older students. Except for the extremely fast high school or college student, the distance covered would rarely be over 50 yd, and endurance should not be a factor.)

Age Level: Junior high school, high school, and college age.

Sex: Satisfactory for both boys and girls.

Validity: Face validity is accepted.

Reliability: No figures given.

Test Equipment and Materials: A stopwatch; a whistle; a running space at least 70 yd to allow for a gradual stop; approximately 14 markers placed at 2-yd intervals from 34 to 60 yd.

Directions: The subject starts from a standing position with both feet behind the end line. The starter uses the preparatory commands of "get set" and "go." On the command to go, the subject runs in a straight line as fast as possible until the whistle is blown at the end of 6 sec. The subject does not have to come to a sudden stop at the sound of the whistle, he or she merely begins to slow down. Two trials are given 5 min apart.

Scoring: A spotter is assigned to each runner and is positioned about 45 yd from the starting line. At the sound of the whistle, the spotter immediately runs to the place where the runner was at the time the whistle was blown. This point is then measured from the nearest marker (or line, if lines are drawn across the running lane). The score is recorded to the nearest yard, and the better of the two trials is used. Table 15.2 shows norms for high school and college students.

Safety Precautions: Students should be allowed sufficient warm-up time to avoid strained muscles. Adequate space should be provided along the sides of the running lanes and at the end of the lanes. Proper footwear should be insisted on.

Additional Pointers:

1. The main advantage of this type of run is that several subjects can be tested with one stopwatch, and therefore, more than one runner should be tested at a time. Otherwise, running a specific distance for time is a more precise measure.

2. Each spotter must be impressed with the necessity of watching only his or her runner and not looking to see who is winning.

3. In judging the exact spot at which the run-

Table 15.1. Norms in Feet for Four-Second Dash, College Students[a]

PERFORMANCE LEVEL	SCORE	
	Men	Women
Advanced	93 and above	76 and above
Advanced intermediate	88–92	72–75
Intermediate	82–87	65–71
Advanced beginner	70–81	59–64
Beginner	0–69	0–58

[a]Based on the scores of 43 men and 43 women, Corpus Christi State University, Corpus Christi, Tex., 1977. Test was conducted indoors on gym floor.

ner was when the whistle sounded, the spotter should use the subject's chest as the point of reference.

4. The tester (or timer) should focus on the watch and not on the runners. The timer should count loudly the seconds 3, 4, and 5 to alert the spotters as to the approximate point at which their runners will be.

5. Chalk or painted lines across the running lanes at 2-yd intervals facilitates scoring.

6. Although 5 min is suggested as the interval between trials, more time should be allowed if fatigue is adjudged to be a possible influence on the second trial.

50-Yard Dash (AAHPERD 1976)

Objective: To measure speed.

Age Level: Age 6 through 17.

Sex: Satisfactory for both boys and girls.

Reliability: None reported.

Objectivity: None reported.

Validity: Face validity is accepted.

Equipment: Two stopwatches or a watch with a split-second timer; a suitable running area to allow the 50-yard run plus extension for stopping.

Directions: It is advised that two subjects run at the same time. Both start from a standing position. The commands, "are you ready?" and "go!" are given. At the command to go, the starter drops his or her arm so that the timer at the finish line can start the timing. The subjects run as fast as possible across the finish line.

Scoring: The elapsed time from the starting signal until the runner crosses the finish line is measured to the nearest tenth of a second. Tables 15.3 and 15.4 show norms for children.

Choice—Response Test

Nelson Choice—Response Movement Test (Nelson 1967)

Objective: To measure ability to react and move quickly and accurately in accordance with a choice stimulus. (This type of test was believed to simulate movement patterns found in a number of sports.)

Age Level: Age 10 through college age.

Sex: Satisfactory for both boys and girls.

Validity: Face validity is accepted.

Reliability: A reliability coefficient of .87 was found for college men, using the test–retest method.

Objectivity: An objectivity coefficient of .83 was obtained with two testers scoring the same individuals. However, much of the difference was believed to be due to the difficulty of synchronizing the start with two watches.

Test Equipment and Materials: Stopwatch; measuring tape; marking equipment.

Directions: Two side lines are marked 14 yd apart, as shown in Figure 15.4. The subject faces the tester while crouching in an on-guard position at a spot exactly between the two side lines. The tester holds the stopwatch in an upraised hand. The tester then abruptly waves an arm to either the left or right and simultaneously starts the watch. The subject responds to the hand signal by running as quickly as possible in the indicated direction to the boundary line. The watch is stopped when the subject crosses the correct line. If the subject starts to move in the wrong direction, the watch continues to run until the subject reverses direction and reaches the correct side line. Ten trials are given, five to each side, but in a random sequence. A rest interval of at least 20 sec is provided between each trial.

Table 15.2.   Norms in Yards for Six-Second Run, High School and College Students[a]

PERFORMANCE LEVEL	SCORE			
	College Men	College Women	High School Boys	High School Girls
Excellent	54 and above	45 and above	51 and above	43 and above
Good	51–53	42–44	48–50	40–42
Average	42–50	35–41	43–47	35–39
Poor	37–41	29–34	40–42	32–34
Very poor	0–36	0–28	0–39	0–31

[a]Based on the scores of 50 students for each group as reported by Leroy Scott, Northeast Louisiana University, Monroe, La., 1973.

Table 15.3. Norms in Seconds for Fifty-Yard Dash, Elementary School Children

PERCENTILE	SEX	AGE					
		6	7	8	9	10	11
99	Boys	8.3	8.4	7.6	7.5	7.3	7.4
	Girls	9.2	8.6	8.0	7.7	7.7	7.5
90	Boys	8.8	8.6	7.9	7.8	7.6	7.7
	Girls	9.4	8.9	8.4	8.0	7.8	7.6
80	Boys	9.0	8.8	8.1	8.0	7.8	7.9
	Girls	9.7	9.1	8.7	8.2	8.0	7.8
70	Boys	9.3	9.1	8.4	8.1	8.0	8.1
	Girls	9.9	9.4	8.9	8.5	8.4	8.0
60	Boys	9.4	9.2	8.6	8.3	8.2	8.3
	Girls	10.1	9.5	9.1	8.7	8.6	8.1
50	Boys	9.5	9.5	8.7	8.4	8.3	8.4
	Girls	10.2	9.9	9.3	9.0	8.8	8.5
40	Boys	9.5	9.7	9.0	8.7	8.5	8.6
	Girls	10.5	10.0	9.5	9.2	9.1	9.0
30	Boys	9.9	10.1	9.2	8.9	8.7	8.8
	Girls	10.9	10.2	9.9	9.5	9.4	9.4
20	Boys	10.6	10.5	9.7	9.4	9.0	9.4
	Girls	11.5	10.8	10.5	10.0	9.8	9.7
10	Boys	12.5	12.3	12.6	11.4	10.5	9.8
	Girls	13.4	14.8	17.5	12.5	11.4	10.8
N	Boys	27	116	126	203	149	50
	Girls	31	101	113	100	82	32

Source: D. H. Hardin and J. Ramirez, "Elementary School Performance Norms." *TAHPER Journal*, February 1972, pp. 8–9.

Table 15.4. Norms in Seconds for AAHPERD 50-Yard Dash[a]

PERCENTILE	AGE							
	10	11	12	13	14	15	16	17
				GIRLS				
95	7.0	7.0	7.0	7.0	7.0	7.1	7.0	7.1
75	7.9	7.9	7.8	7.7	7.6	7.7	7.7	7.8
50	8.5	8.4	8.2	8.1	8.0	8.1	8.3	8.2
25	9.0	9.0	8.9	8.8	8.9	8.8	9.0	9.0
5	10.0	10.0	10.0	10.2	10.4	10.0	10.5	10.4
				BOYS				
95	7.0	7.0	6.8	6.5	6.3	6.1	6.0	6.0
75	7.6	7.6	7.3	7.0	6.8	6.5	6.3	6.3
50	8.2	8.0	7.8	7.5	7.1	6.9	6.7	6.6
25	8.8	8.5	8.3	8.0	7.6	7.2	7.0	7.0
5	10.0	9.5	9.2	8.9	8.6	8.1	7.8	7.7

[a]Percentile scores based on age.

Source: *AAHPERD Youth Fitness Test Manual*. Reston, Va.: AAHPERD, 1976. Used by permission.

Scoring: The time for each trial is read to the nearest tenth of a second. The average score is then recorded. Table 15.5 shows norms for college students.

Safety Precautions: The teacher should insist that students have adequate footwear and should provide warm-up exercises. The testing area must be kept free from obstructions.

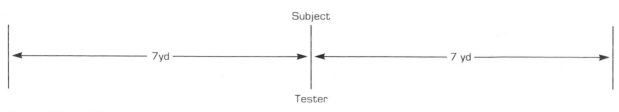

Figure 15.4.   Diagram for Nelson choice—response movement test

Additional Pointers:

1. Several practice trials should be given to acquaint subjects with the test procedure.

2. The tester should practice the starting signals to attain proficiency in synchronizing the hand signal with the start of the watch.

3. In selecting the sequence of direction, the tester can simply put five slips with *right* on them and five slips with *left* on them in a box for a random draw. This procedure prevents the subject from anticipating the direction from one trial to the next. The *subject should not be told* that there will be five trials in each direction. In fact, the subject should probably be told that this is not the case—that the distribution of trials is entirely based on random selection and that there may be more in one direction than another. Several sequences should be prepared beforehand so that students waiting to be tested cannot memorize the order of directions.

4. This test could be adapted to be more applicable to a specific activity. For example, tackling dummies could be placed at each sideline and the subject must hit these to stop the clock.

5. As in all speed and reaction tests, the interval between the command "ready" and the starting signal should be within a range of approximately 0.5 to 2 sec.

Speed of Vertical Movement Test

20-Foot Rope Climb Test

Objective: To measure speed of movement in climbing vertically upward.

Age Level: Age 12 through college age.

Sex: Recommended for males; however, some females may enjoy this test.

Reliability: An *r* of .91 was found when the best score of three trials was correlated with the best score of three trials on a second day of testing with an advanced gymnastics class.

Objectivity: An *r* of .97 was found when an experienced tester's scores were correlated with an inexperienced tester's scores.

Validity: Face validity is accepted for this test when the performers have trained for the test and are in good physical condition for climbing. Otherwise, a lack of muscular endurance may severely diminish this test's validity for speed of movement.

Equipment: A 20-ft climbing rope with a tambourine; a mat; standard chair or bench; and a stopwatch.

Directions: The performer sits on a chair or bench (seat level at least 15 in. off the floor) and grasps as high up the rope as possible without raising the buttocks from the seat. With the feet held out (not touching the floor), the performer climbs hand

Table 15.5.   Norms in Seconds for Nelson Choice-Response Movement Test, College Students[a]

PERFORMANCE LEVEL	SCORE	
	Men	Women
Advanced	1.30 and below	1.60 and below
Advanced intermediate	1.60–1.35	1.90–1.65
Intermediate	2.40–1.65	2.55–1.95
Advanced beginner	2.70–2.45	2.85–2.60
Beginner	2.75 and above	2.90 and above

[a]Data gathered from 200 men, Louisiana State University, Baton Rouge, La., 1968, and 45 women, Corpus Christi State University, Corpus Christi, Tex., 1976.

over hand upward until he touches the tambourine at the top of the rope (20-ft mark) with his fingertip. The feet and legs may be used to assist the hands and arms in climbing the rope (Figure 15.5).

Scoring: The performer is timed from the lift of the buttocks from the seat level to the touch of the tambourine overhead. Table 15.6 shows norms for college men.

Additional Pointers:

1. The performer should climb back down the rope, not slide or drop to the mat.

2. The chair or bench should be moved away as soon as the performer lifts off.

3. The mat should be centered under the rope in the event of a fall.

FINDINGS AND CONCLUSIONS FROM SPEED AND REACTION TIME MEASUREMENT AND RESEARCH

A vast amount of reseach has been done in psychology, physiology, and physical education on speed of movement and reaction time. Despite the voluminous literature, however, much research is still needed.

A misconception held for years by many coaches and physical educators was that strength-building exercises would be detrimental to speed of movement. Research has shown quite convincingly that just the opposite is true (Chui 1950; Masley, Hairabedian, and Donaldson 1953; Wilkin 1952; Zorbas and Karpovich 1951).

Meadows and Johnson further found that both isotonic and isometric exercises improved speed of movement, while Crowder reported isotonic and isometric exercises produced significant improvement in reaction time.

Several studies have reported low correlations between reaction time and movement time. Representative of such studies are those by Henry (1961), Clarke, and Owens.

Magill and Powell investigated the often-reported finding that reaction time and movement time are totally unrelated. They concluded that the significance of the relationship is highly dependent on the experimental situation. In other words, by manipulation of certain variables such as age, sex, set, and amount of practice, significant or nonsignificant relationships between reaction time and movement time may be attained.

Smith (1964) found that reaction time and velocity of the arm when in a state of stretch were not significantly faster than when the arm was relaxed or tensed. But when the prime movers of the limb were stretched, significantly faster performances resulted. The results of another study by Smith (1969) gave further support to the theory of specificity, in that differences in movement time of a limb involving a single joint are largely independent of strength measures of that limb and joint.

Motivation has been shown to be quite effective in bringing about faster speed of movement and reaction.

Figure 15.5. Twenty-foot rope climb test

Table 15.6. Norms in Seconds for 20-Foot Rope Climb Test, College Men[a]

PERFORMANCE LEVEL	SCORE
Advanced	5.9 and below
Advanced intermediate	7.3–6.0
Intermediate	10.3–7.4
Advanced beginner	13.0–10.4
Beginner	13.1 and above

[a]Based on the scores of 30 men at Corpus Christi State University, Corpus Christi, Tex., 1975.

The intensity of the stimulus is a factor, as was revealed in Vallerga's study in which a loud sound was found to produce faster speed of movement and more forceful contraction than soft or medium sounds. Several studies (Henry 1951; Hipple 1954; Howell 1953) have shown that devices such as electric shock, suggested failure, and others result in increased tension and thus increased speed of response.

Henry (1951) found that a motivated simple response transferred its increase in speed to a more complex response. Fairclough reported that motivated improvement in speed in one part of the body could be transferred to another body part. Wilson and Thompson, Nagle, and Dobias reported that rhythmic starting signals improved reaction time performance. Reaction time has been partitioned into premotor time (PMT), the central component, and motor time (MT), the peripheral component. The PMT is the time interval between stimulus presentation until the first action potential is manifested, whereas MT is the interval between the first muscle action potential and the initiation of the movement. The two are not related (Stull and Kearney 1978).

Goggin and Christina analyzed reaction time, fractionated reaction time (PMT and MT), and movement time during performance of a rapid aiming movement to a circular target. Reaction time correlated highly with PMT but not with MT. Choice reaction time and its PMT component were dependent on target diameter, but simple reaction time and its PMT component were not. In all, slower choice reaction time for rapid movements to a small target is attributed to increased time needed for programming the response. Apparently, PMT is more negatively affected by fatigue than MT (Hanson and Lofthus 1978; Kroll 1974). Lofthus and Hanson investigated the influence of fatigue and laterality on reaction time performance. They found that the PMT component increased after fatiguing exercises for both preferred and nonpreferred limbs, while differential effects occurred between limbs for MT and total reaction time.

Levitt and Gutin administered five-choice reaction time and movement time tests while subjects walked on a treadmill at heart rates of 80, 115, 145, and 175 beats/min. The choice reaction time performance was best at 115 and poorest at 175 beats/min, whereas the movement time improved linearly with increases in heart rate. They concluded that reaction time and movement time are affected differently by physical exertion.

Reynolds tested physically conditioned and unconditioned subjects on reaction time while they were exposed to stress. Reaction time was not significantly affected by stress.

Christina tested the hypothesis advanced by Henry in conjunction with his memory drum theory that a sensory set would evoke faster reaction times than a motor set. The sensory set concentrates on the stimulus, while the motor set concentrates on the movement to be performed. Henry had hypothesized that concentration on the movement would interfere with the memory mechanism, resulting in slower reaction and movement. Christina's study found support for the sensory set with reaction time performance, but no significant differences were found for the movement time scores.

Norrie found support for the memory drum theory in that the decision-making process in simple movement tasks takes place before the start of the movement. She also found that as the number of choice conditions increased, the reaction time effect of increased complexity of movement lessened.

Thomas, Gallagher, and Purvis studied developmental effects on reaction time and anticipation time. As age increased, reaction speed increased, with boys having more rapid reaction times than girls. Reaction times and movement times of boys and girls aged 9 to 17 were analyzed by Fulton and Hubbard. Speed of reaction improved significantly with age, with girls showing consistently faster times. Movement times also improved markedly with age, and boys were faster.

A number of studies on aging and reaction time have been done on institutionalized individuals with various disabling illnesses, which could influence the results. Spirduso's work indicates that slowed reaction time may not be due to age alone (Spirduso and Clifford 1978). Piscopo and Baley reported that physical condition is highly important.

Spirduso found support for the association of activity and reaction time, concluding that reaction time and movement time are functions of both age and physical activity level. She reported that men 50 to 70 years of age who were highly active had faster central nervous system processing times and faster muscular movements than less active men.

Botwinick and Thompson found that elderly subjects were significantly slower in reaction time than young athletes, but they were not significantly slower than young nonathletes.

Chema investigated the response time of elderly subjects. Response times were fractionated into premotor reaction time, motor reaction time, and movement time. Elderly subjects evidenced slower premotor reaction times under all conditions of the study. Chema concluded that a central nervous system deficit was the most plausible premise regarding slowed response times in elderly individuals.

A number of studies have found faster reaction time in athletes than in nonathletes (Olsen 1956; Sigerseth and York 1954; Smith 1968). Smith (1968) found athletes to be faster than nonparticipants at three different ages in total-body and arm reaction time. Total-body completion time was shown to be the most signficant differentiator for successful athletic performance. In the study of fractionated reaction time of athletes and nonathletes, it has been theorized that the central processing component (PMT) may be improved through conditioning, which could explain the difference between athletes and nonathletes (Hanson and Lofthus 1978). Kamen and associates compared weight lifters and long-distance runners on fractionated knee extensor and plantar-flexor reaction time components to investigate specificity of training on reaction time. The weight lifters were found to have faster PMTs than the runners in knee extensor movements, but slower PMTs in plantar-flexor reaction. These authors concluded that power-trained and endurance-trained athletes exhibit differences in response to a fractionated reaction time task, under both baseline and fatiguing exercise conditions. Specific training in sprint starting was found to improve reaction performance in studies by Gibson and Gottshall. A conditioning exercise program was also found to result in improved reaction time in Gottshall's study.

In comparing four variations of the upright stance with knees straight or bent and weight on the balls of the feet or feet flat, Cotten and Denning concluded that optimum reaction-movement time results from a knees-bent, feet-flat stance.

Israel and Brown compared the crossover step, jab step, standing sprinter's start, and momentum start to determine the fastest start for optimum speed in base running in slow-pitch softball. The momentum start was found to be the fastest starting technique, with no differences among the other three. In an earlier study, Israel had concluded that the jab step was superior to the crossover step for base stealing in baseball.

Cox compared response times of the slide and crossover steps used by volleyball players. The slide step elicited the fastest times. However, in a follow-up study, Cox and colleagues determined that the jab crossover step is best for the generation of leg power in terms of actual jumping and blocking efficiency.

Krahenbuhl compared speed of movement on synthetic turf versus natural grass and also the relative effects of three types of footwear on movement speed on the two surfaces. Movement times were faster on synthetic turf regardless of the footwear employed. Tennis shoes or soccer-style shoes on synthetic turf produced the fastest movement times.

Nakamura studied the foreperiod between the preparatory command and the signal to go and found the optimum time interval to be 1.5 sec. Bresnahan, Tuttle, and Cretzmeyer found that a foreperiod of 1.4 to 1.6 sec yields the fastest reaction times.

Wrisberg analyzed the effects of manipulating both the length of the preresponse intervals within blocks of trials and the intersignal intervals on reaction time and movement time. He concluded that the most important time interval affecting reaction time is the interval separating the signal to respond from the one immediately preceding it.

Haywood and Teeple analyzed reaction time and movement time scores over 35 trials. They concluded that a minimum of eight trials, using the first two trials as practice, yields a representative score of performance for the 35 trials with little deviation in mean scores, reliability, or standard error.

BIBLIOGRAPHY

AAHPERD Youth Fitness Test Manual. Reston, Va.: AAHPERD, 1976.

Botwinick, J., and L. Thompson, "Age Difference in Reaction Time: An Artifact?" *Gerontologist* 8:25–28, 1968.

Bresnahan, G. T., W. W. Tuttle, and F. X. Cretzmeyer, *Track and Field Athletics.* 6th ed. St. Louis: C. V. Mosby, 1964.

Chema, H. M., "Reaction and Movement Times of the Elderly in Relation to Peripheral Nerve Conduction and the Central Nervous System." Master's thesis, Florida State University, Tallahassee, 1977.

Christina, R. W., "Influence of Enforced Motor and Sensory Sets on Reaction Latency and Movement Speed." *Research Quarterly* 44:483–487, December 1973.

Chui, E., "The Effect of Systematic Weight Training on Athletic Power." *Research Quarterly* 21:188–194, October 1950.

Clarke, D. H., "Correlation Between the Strength/ Mass Ratio and the Speed of an Arm Movement," *Research Quarterly* 31:570–574, December 1960.

Cotten, D. J., and D. Denning, "Comparison of Reaction-Movement Times From Four Variations of the Upright Stance." *Research Quarterly* 41:196–199, May 1970.

Cox, R. H., "Response Times of Slide and Cross-Over Steps as Used by Volleyball Players." *Research Quarterly for Exercise and Sport* 51:562–567, October 1980.

_____, L. Noble, and R. E. Johnson, "Effectiveness of the Slide and Cross-Over Steps in Volleyball Blocking—A Temporal Analysis." *Research Quarterly for Exercise and Sport* 53:101–107, June 1982.

Crowder, V. R., "A Comparison of the Effects of Two Methods of Strength Training on Reaction Time." Unpublished master's thesis, Louisiana State University, Baton Rouge, 1966.

Fairclough, R. H., "Transfer of Motivated Improvement in Speed of Reaction and Movement." *Research Quarterly* 23:20–27, March 1952.

Fulton, C. D., and A. W. Hubbard, "Effects of Puberty on Reaction and Movement Times." *Research Quarterly* 46:335–344, October 1975.

Gibson, D. A., "Effect of a Special Training Program for Sprint Starting on Reflex Time, Reaction Time and Sargent Jump." Microcarded master's thesis, Springfield College, Springfield, Mass., 1961.

Goggin, N. L., and R. W. Christina, "Reaction Time Analysis of Programmed Control of Short, Rapid Aiming Movements." *Research Quarterly* 50:360–368, October 1979.

Gottshall, D. R., "The Effects of Two Training Programs on Reflex Time, Reaction Time and the Level of Physical Fitness." Microcarded master's thesis, Springfield College, Springfield, Mass., 1962.

Hanson, C., and G. K. Lofthus, "Effects of Fatigue and Laterality on Fractionated Reaction Time." *Journal of Motor Behavior* 10:177–184, 1978.

Haywood, K. M., and J. B. Teeple, "Representative Simple Reaction and Movement Time Scores." *Research Quarterly* 47:855–856, December 1976.

Henry, F. M., "Increase in Speed of Movement by Motivation and by Transfer of Motivated Improvement." *Research Quarterly* 22:219–228, May 1951.

_____, "Independence of Reaction and Movement Times and Equivalence of Sensory Motivators of Faster Response." *Research Quarterly* 23:43–53, March 1952.

_____, "Reaction Time-Movement Time Correlations." *Perceptual and Motor Skills* 12:63–66, February 1961.

_____, and D. E. Rogers, "Increased Response Latency for Complicated Movements and a 'Memory Drum' Theory of Neuromotor Reaction." *Research Quarterly* 31:448–458, 1960.

Hipple, J. E., "Racial Differences in the Influence of Motivation on Muscular Tension, Reaction Time, and Speed of Movement." *Research Quarterly* 25:297–306, October 1954.

Howell, M. L., "Influence of Emotional Tension of Speed on Reaction and Movement." *Research Quarterly* 24:22–32, March 1953.

Israel, R. G., "Time Comparison Between the Cross-Over and Jab-Step Starts." *Research Quarterly* 50:521–523, October 1979.

_____, and R. L. Brown, "Response Time Comparisons Among Four Base Running Starting Techniques in Slow Pitch Softball." *Research Quarterly for Exercise and Sport* 52:324–329, October 1981.

Johnson, B. L., "A Comparison of Isometric and Isotonic Exercises Upon the Improvement of Velocity and Distance as Measured by the Rope Climb Test." Unpublished study, Louisiana State University, Baton Rouge, January 1964.

Kamen, G., W. Kroll, P. M. Clarkson, and S. T. Zigon, "Fractionated Reaction Time in Power-Trained and Endurance-Trained Athletes Under Conditions of Fatiguing Isometric Exercise." *Journal of Motor Behavior* 13:117–129, 1981.

Krahenbuhl, G. S., "Speed of Movement With Varying Footwear Conditions on Synthetic Turf and Natural Grass." *Research Quarterly* 45:28–33, March 1974.

Kroll, W., "Fractionated Reaction and Reflex Time Before and After Fatiguing Isotonic Exercise." *Medicine and Science in Sports* 6:260–266, 1974.

Levitt, S., and B. Gutin, "Multiple Choice Reaction Time and Movement Time During Physical Exertion." *Research Quarterly* 42:405–410, December 1971.

Lofthus, G. K., and C. Hanson, "The Influence of Laterality and Fatigue Upon the Performance of a Two-Handed Reaction Task." *Research Quarterly for Exercise and Sport* 51:501–508, October 1980.

Magill, R. A., and F. M. Powell, "Is the Reaction Time–Movement Time Relationship 'Essentially Zero'?" *Perceptual and Motor Skills* 41:720–722, December 1975.

Masley, J. W., A. Hairabedian, and D. N. Donaldson, "Weight Training in Relation to Strength, Speed, and Coordination." *Research Quarterly* 24:308–315, October 1953.

McCloy, C. H., and N. D. Young, *Tests and Measurements in Health and Physical Education.* 3rd ed. New York: Appleton-Century-Crofts, 1954, p. 186.

Meadows, P. E., "The Effect of Isotonic and Isometric Muscle Contraction Training on Speed, Force, and Strength." Microcarded doctoral dissertation, University of Illinois, Urbana-Champaign, 1959.

Nakamura, H., "An Experimental Study of Reaction Time of the Start in Running a Race." *Research Quarterly Supplement* 5:33–45, March 1934.

Nelson, J. K., "Development of a Practical Performance Test Combining Reaction Time, Speed of Movement and Choice of Response." Unpublished study, Louisiana State University, Baton Rouge, 1967.

Norrie, M. L., "Effects of Movement Complexity on Choice Reaction and Movement Times." *Research Quarterly* 45:154–161, May 1974.

Olsen, E. A., "Relationship Between Psychological Capacities and Success in College Athletics." *Research Quarterly* 27:79–89, March 1956.

Owens, J. A., "Effect of Variations in Hand and Foot Spacing on Movement Time and on Force of Charge." *Research Quarterly* 31:75, March 1960.

Piscopo, J., and J. A. Baley, *Kinesiology: The Science of Movement.* New York: John Wiley, 1981, p. 526.

Reynolds, H. L., "The Effects of Augmented Levels of Stress on Reaction Time in the Peripheral Visual Field." *Research Quarterly* 47:768–775, December 1976.

Sigerseth, P. O., and N. N. York, "A Comparison of Certain Reaction Times of Basketball Players and Non-athletes." *Physical Educator* 11:51–53, May 1954.

Smith, L. E., "Effect of Muscular Stretch, Tension, and Relaxation Upon the Reaction Time and Speed of Movement of a Supported Limb." *Research Quarterly* 35:546–553, December 1964.

_____, "Specificity of Individual Differences of Relationship Between Forearm 'Strengths' and Speed of Forearm Flexion." *Research Quarterly* 40:191–197, March 1969.

Smith, P. E., "Investigation of Total-Body and Arm Measures of Reaction Time, Movement Time, and Completion Time for Twelve, Fourteen, and Seventeen Year Old Athletes and Nonparticipants." Unpublished master's thesis, University of Oregon, Eugene, 1968.

Spirduso, W., "Reaction and Movement Time as a Function of Age and Physical Activity Level." *Journal of Gerontology* 30:435–440, 1975.

_____, and P. Clifford, "Replication of Age and Physical Activity Effects on Reaction and Movement Time." *Journal of Gerontology* 33:26–30, 1978.

Stull, G. A., and J. T. Kearney, "Effects of Variable Fatigue Levels on Reaction-Time Components." *Journal of Motor Behavior* 10:223–231, 1978.

Thomas, J. R., J. D. Gallagher, and G. J. Purvis, "Reaction Time and Anticipation Time: Effects of Development." *Research Quarterly for Exercise and Sport* 52:348–358, October 1981.

Thompson, C. W., F. J. Nagle, and R. Dobias, "Football Starting Signals and Movement Times of High School and College Football Players." *Research Quarterly* 29:222–230, May 1958.

Vallerga, J. M., "Influence of Perceptual Stimulus Intensity on Speed of Movement and Force of Muscular Contraction." *Research Quarterly* 29:92–101, March 1958.

Wilkin, B. M., "The Effect of Weight Training on Speed of Movement." *Research Quarterly* 23:361–369, October 1952.

Wilson, D. J., "Quickness of Reaction and Movement Related to Rhythmicity or Non-rhythmicity of Signal Presentation." *Research Quarterly* 30:101–109, March 1959.

Wrisberg, C. A., "The Effects of Temporal Variability Within and Between Series of Stimuli on Reaction Time and Movement Time." *Research Quarterly for Exercise and Sport* 52:518–522, December 1981.

Zorbas, W. S., and P. V. Karpovich, "The Effect of Weight Lifting Upon the Speed of Muscular Contraction." *Research Quarterly* 22:145–148, May 1951.

CHAPTER 16

THE MEASUREMENT OF SPORTS SKILLS

OBJECTIVES

After reading this chapter, the student should be able to:

1. List the uses of sports skills tests in physical education

2. Identify basic skill components of different

sports as indicated by the tests presented in this chapter

3. Understand and anticipate some of the problems in the measurement of sports skills

4. Follow directions for administering practical sports skills tests

One of the major objectives of physical education is the development of neuromuscular skills. It naturally follows that physical educators should strive to construct precise and meaningful measuring devices to help evaluate the extent to which this objective is being met. Much of the total physical education program is devoted to the acquisition of sports skills. Thus, it is doubly important that continued efforts be made to scientifically construct valid, reliable, and objective tests in the various sports activities.

USES OF SPORTS SKILLS TESTS

The teacher and the student may use skills tests in many ways. Some are the same as for tests in other areas. But again, because sports activities represent such a major part of the physical education program, sports skills tests are especially applicable to the instructional phase. Some specific uses of these tests are as follows:

1. As a measure of achievement in the particular sport activity:

   a. To help evaluate the instructional program in terms of the effectiveness of the teaching methods and the strengths and weaknesses of the course content

   b. To help determine the grade in conjunction with other information

2. As a teaching aid to supplement instruction and to be used for practice (individual progress records would be beneficial to the coach as well as to the teacher)

3. As a diagnostic tool to point out needs for special emphasis at each particular grade level in which a sport is taught (one way to avoid the needless repetition and lack of progression that characterize many physical education programs)

4. For competition in intramural programs and for rainy day activities

5. As one means of interpreting the program to the administration, the parents, and the public

6. As an excellent motivational device

PROBLEMS IN SPORTS SKILLS MEASUREMENT

In any sport, a number of skills and abilities are involved in a successful performance. Even though the fundamental components can be identified, their individual measurement does not adequately represent actual performance.

The basic concepts and criteria of test construction and selection discussed in Chapter 4 are especially pertinent in the area of sports skills measurement. Criteria such as ease of administration, needed equipment, time required to administer the tests, need for trained testers, meaningfulness of the test items, and ease and objectivity of scoring are all applicable. They also greatly contribute to or detract from the basic concepts of validity, reliability, and objectivity. Much of the discussion in Chapter 4 used skills tests in the examples; therefore, it would be redundant to discuss these problems again. There are, however, a few crucial points that deserve reiteration. One concerns objective scoring versus realism and validity. Test makers frequently attempt to eliminate the influence of a second person on the performance of the subject being measured. Consequently, in tennis, for example, one test might require the subject to drop the ball and then stroke it, rather than to stroke a ball that has first been hit by another person. Similarly, in softball tests the subject throws at a target instead of a person, or bats the ball from a batting tee, or tosses the ball and hits it instead of hitting a pitched ball. Furthermore, when a second person is involved in testing, that person's role is often out of context with regard to actual performance. Using tennis and softball again as examples, the second person in some tests may stand at the net and throw tennis balls to the subject; in softball, the second person sometimes throws ground balls or fly balls or both to the subject being tested.

Obviously, the reasons for using test items involving some other person throwing the ball rather than hitting it relate to the objectivity of scoring and presumably greater consistency in the test administration. But let us examine these practices with regard to the performance they are supposed to measure.

In some tennis tests, a definite skill is involved in the dropping of the ball and then successfully hitting it with a forehand (and particularly a backhand) stroke that is different from that used in the game. The perception, timing, and footwork necessary to execute a forehand or backhand drive during actual play are not involved in such a test.

In softball and similar sports, throwing at a target may be viewed as a violation of the well-established teaching and coaching point that the player should not *aim* the throw. The height of the target also should be examined. The softball and baseball player usually throws to a relatively low target, such as to the first baseman, who stretches to meet the throw, or to the catcher, who must make the tag low on the sliding runner. In batting, hitting from a tee is quite different from hitting a pitched ball. A batting tee is usually employed just in practice to help correct *hitches* in the swing and other fundamental faults in the stance and swing. The validity of fungo hitting as a measure of batting skill may also be questioned. During practice sessions the pitchers spend a large amount of time hitting fly balls to other players, but as a group they are notoriously poor hitters. Continuing to question other test items, such as whether the skills involved in fielding ground balls or catching fly balls are different when the ball is thrown or batted, seems pointless. The question essentially becomes that of *how much* deviation from the actual skill the teacher is willing to sacrifice to increase the objectivity of the test item.

To justify their use in terms of the time spent for testing, tests should optionally serve several functions, such as be usable for practice drills, serve as motivation, and provide indications of progress for the student. Permanent testing stations and mobile test equipment are extremely valuable in this respect.

The scoring of the test should be such that the test is able to distinguish among persons of different levels of ability. Decisions must be made as to target size, whether to give a score for hitting just behind the boundary lines, and whether the nature of the test encourages poor form. While it is of considerable value and interest for a test to have national norms, the physical education teacher is urged to construct and utilize local norms.

Finally, the teacher should exercise great care in regard to the proportion of a student's grade that is determined by performance in objective skills tests. The teacher must continually evaluate the degree to which performance on a specific test reflects the ability to play the game. Certain activities, of course, lend themselves to more precise evaluation than others. The performance in some sports like golf and bowling is measured by the scores themselves. Relative ability in certain activities like handball, badminton, and others can be assessed quite accurately through round-robin tournaments. In still others, such as swimming, diving, and gymnastics, the performance usually invokes subjective judgment. Performance in team sports like touch football, basketball, volleyball, and others is sometimes more difficult to determine. Here, as in all sports, skills tests can be used to good advantage for grading, provided that they are combined with careful subjective evaluation of the subject's actual performance in that sport.

SOME PRACTICAL SPORTS SKILLS TESTS

In this section some practical tests for measuring sports skills are presented. The reader is cautioned to not rely too heavily on one test or any battery of tests. Skills tests can only measure certain aspects of performance in a particular sport. Furthermore, even in the sports already mentioned, many factors such as environmental conditions, emotional pressure, and daily variations in performance greatly influence score. It is suggested that the teacher think of skills tests more as instructional aids and motivational devices for students than as valid measures of students' ability to play a particular sport. In addition, the teacher should be especially alert to use these tests in developing local norms that are applicable and meaningful to the individual situation with regard to age, sex, interests, and socioeconomic setting.

Sound tests have not been constructed for all sports. We have selected the tests presented here on the basis of their practicability in terms of the time required to administer them, the limited equipment needed, the ease of scoring, and their ability to measure at least certain aspects of performance in the sport. In some cases only one or two items have been taken from a particular battery; in other cases the entire battery is briefly described. The reader should consult the original reference if a more complete description of a specific test is desired.

Archery

AAHPERD Archery Test (Archery: AAHPERD 1967)

As a part of the Sports Skills Tests Project of AAHPERD, an archery test is available that is designed to measure skill in shooting at the standard 48-in. target from different distances for boys and girls aged 12 through 18.

Directions: It is recommended that the class be organized into squads of four, with one squad shooting at one target. Each archer shoots two ends of six arrows each (total of 12 arrows) at each distance, except that archers who do not score at least 10 points at one distance may not advance to the farther distance.

As each subject finishes shooting, an assistant withdraws the arrows and records the score for each arrow. Each subject is given four practice shots at each distance. Distances are 10, 20, and 30 yd for boys and 10 and 20 yd for girls.

Scoring: The standard 48-in. archery target is used with the point values 9, 7, 5, 3, and 1 for the respective circles from the center outward. The total point value of the 12 arrows (two ends) is the score for each distance. Norms are presented for boys and girls in Tables 16.1 and 16.2.

Badminton

The badminton set-up machine[1] is an inexpensive device used for testing and training in the sport of badminton. It provides for overhead stroke practice and has pitch-out capabilities. Models may be either automatic (Figure 16.1) or manual. Appendix J contains plans for construction of such a machine.

Badminton Smash Test

Objective: To measure skill in the overhead smash in badminton using the Johnson badminton set-up machine.

Age Level: Junior high school through college age.

Sex: Satisfactory for both boys and girls.

Reliability: An *r* of .77 was reported by Bill Parker, Northeast Louisiana University, Monroe, 1973.

Objectivity: An *r* of .94 was obtained between the scoring of an experienced tester and that of an inexperienced tester.

Validity: Face validity is accepted for this test.

Equipment: A Johnson badminton set-up machine (automatic or manual); a tightly strung badminton racket; and several shuttlecocks.

Directions: Figure 16.2 shows lines and points that should be marked with chalk or tape on the court. The machine should be placed 13 ft from

1. Badminton set-up machine, Model A-1, patent pending 1972, by B. L. Johnson, Corpus Christi State University, Corpus Christi, TX 78412.

Table 16.1. Norms in Total Points for AAHPERD Archery Test, Boys[a]

PERCENTILE	AGE																			
	12–13				14				15				16				17–18			
	10[b]	20	30	Total	10	20	30	Total	10	20	30	Total	10	20	30	Total	10	20	30	Total
95	83	53	28	156	88	61	34	179	97	77	50	215	99	78	56	220	98	78	64	222
75	67	31	16	112	72	38	18	143	84	58	28	167	90	59	36	181	88	59	39	184
50	54	22	8	81	63	26	10	119	69	39	15	120	79	46	23	148	77	43	26	144
25	38	12	0	47	45	16	0	87	51	24	10	87	67	33	13	117	59	29	16	112
5	16	3	0	15	25	6	0	43	25	9	2	43	40	14	2	61	27	11	3	65

[a]Percentile scores based on age.
[b]Distance in yards from target.
Source: *AAHPERD Archery Skills Test Manual for Boys and Girls.* Reston, Va.: AAHPERD, 1967. Complete norms are in manual. Reprinted by permission.

Table 16.2. Norms in Total Points for AAHPERD Archery Test, Girls[a]

PERCENTILE	AGE														
	12–13			14			15			16			17–18		
	10[b]	20	Total	10	20	Total	10	20	Total	10	20	Total	10	20	Total
95	69	40	100	74	47	109	82	55	130	87	58	134	87	71	149
75	41	17	64	54	28	79	63	34	89	64	36	96	66	42	109
50	30	9	42	41	18	58	49	23	70	46	22	72	48	26	85
25	16	0	25	28	8	42	34	13	51	31	12	52	35	16	60
5	6	0	5	12	0	22	13	0	25	16	0	26	19	0	30

[a]Percentile scores based on age.
[b]Distance in yards from target.
Source: *AAHPERD Archery Skills Test Manual for Boys and Girls.* Reston, Va.: AAHPERD, 1967. Complete norms are in manual. Reprinted by permission.

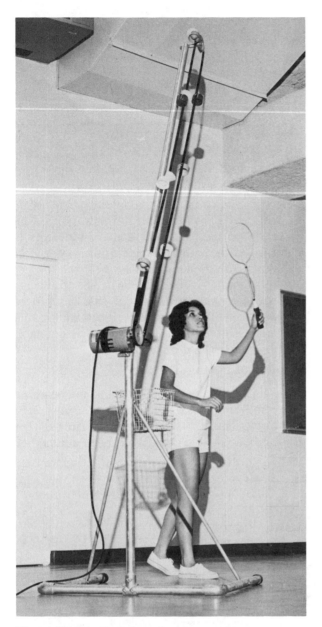

Figure 16.1. Badminton set-up machine (automatic model) shown in use with overhead smash test. The machine was invented by B. L. Johnson of Corpus Christi State University, Corpus Christi, Tex. Appendix J has plans for such a machine

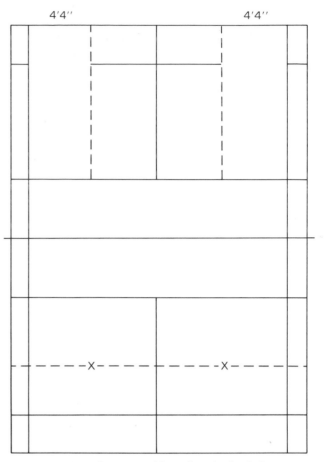

Figure 16.2. Court markings for the badminton smash test. The subject stands at "X." The target area is between the dotted line at the top and the singles side line. The subject may use either target area (left or right)

the net, with the arm rotating belt parallel to the net. The subject stands below the dropping point of the machine, facing the net. After seven practice trials, the student smashes the shuttlecock into the scoring areas along either side line. Ten trials are allowed. Trials done without reasonable speed and force are incorrect and must be repeated for scoring purposes.

Scoring: Each successful trial scores 1 point; the maximum score possible is 10 points. Norms are presented in Table 16.3.

Table 16.3. Norms in Points for Badminton Smash Test[a]

PERCENTILE	SEX	
	Boys	Girls
100	10	10
95	7	8
90	6	7
80	5.	6
70	4	5
60	4	5
50	3	4
40	2	4
30	2	3
20	1	2
10	1	1
0	0	0

[a]Percentile scores based on sex. See text for description of scoring.

Additional Pointers:

1. The student should be informed immediately when an incorrect stroke is to be repeated.

2. If a repeat trial is also incorrect, the trial is scored as zero.

3. The shuttle skirt should be placed skirt down in the cups of the machine so as to allow the bird a quick rotation to the tip-down position for the smash shot.

French Short-Serve Test (Badminton: Scott 1941)

Objective: To measure accuracy of placement and ability in the low, short serve in badminton.

Age and Sex: College women (but can be used equally well with men).

Reliability: Reliability coefficients from .51 to .89 have been obtained by using the odd-even method and the Spearman–Brown prophecy formula. The amount of playing experience apparently inversely influences the size of the reliability coefficient.

Validity: With tournament rankings as a criterion, coefficients from .41 to .66 have been reported.

Equipment: A clothesline rope stretched on the same standards as the net at a distance of 20 in. from the top of the net; a tightly strung badminton racket; and at least five serviceable shuttles for each player.

Directions: Markings 2 in. wide in the form of arcs are drawn on the floor at distances of 22, 30, 38, and 46 in. from the midpoint of the intersection of the center line and the short-service line of the right service court (Figure 16.3). The distances include the width of the 2-in. lines. The subject stands in the service court diagonally opposite the target. Twenty serves are attempted, either consecutively or in groups of ten. The subject tries to send the shuttle *between* the net and the rope. The scorer stands nearer the center of the left service court, facing the target (designated B in Figure 16.3). The subject tries to hit the target area nearest the intersection of the center line and short-service line. Shuttles that hit on a line are given the higher point value.

Scoring: The zones are given point values of 5, 4, 3, 2, and 1, as indicated in Figure 16.3. The value of the area in which each shuttle hits is recorded as the score for each trial. Any trial in which the shuttle does not pass between the net and rope counts as zero; similarly, any trial landing out of bounds, either to the side or short of the short-service line, is zero. If the shuttle hits the rope, it is re-served and no trial is counted. Norms are provided in Table 16.4.

Additional Pointers:

1. It is recommended that the test not be given until the students have had adequate practice. The test tends to be unreliable until a certain degree of skill has been attained.

2. The test is time consuming to administer unless there are several courts so that testing does not interfere with regular play.

Table 16.4. Norms for the French Short-Serve Test, College Women[a]

SCORE		CORRESPONDING T SCORE
Group 1[b]	Group 2[c]	
68	86	80
66	79	75
59	73	70
53	66	65
44	59	60
37	52	55
29	46	50
22	39	45
13	32	40
8	26	35
4	19	30
1	12	25
0	6	20

[a]See text for a discussion of scoring.
[b]Based on the performance of 385 women after a 25-lesson beginning course in badminton.
[c]Based on the performance of 46 women after a 30-lesson beginning course in badminton.

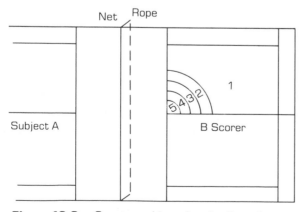

Figure 16.3. Court markings for the French short-serve test

3. In keeping with a realistic game situation, the subject should probably be instructed to serve from a point no closer than 2 or 3 ft from the short-service line in his or her court.

Poole Long-Serve Test (Badminton: Poole and Nelson 1970)

Objective: To measure ability to serve high and deep to the rear of the court.

Sex and Age Level: May be used with high school and college students of both sexes.

Reliability: The test–retest reliability coefficient was .81.

Validity: The test correlated .51 with the results of tournament play.

Equipment: Two rackets and preferably 12 shuttles in good condition.

Directions: The court is marked as shown in Figure 16.4. Four lines have to be drawn, which are indicated by the dashed lines in the figure. One line is drawn 2 in. behind and parallel to the back boundary line. A second line is drawn parallel to and 16 in. closer to the net than the first *drawn* line. This places the second drawn line 14 in.

from the back boundary line and 16 in. in back of the doubles long-service line. The third line is drawn 16 in. closer to the net and parallel to the doubles long-service line. The fourth line is drawn 16 in. closer to the net than the previous line, as indicated in Figure 16.4. It should be noted that the 5-point zone extends 2 in. beyond the back boundary line. A 15- $\times$ 15-in. square is drawn 11 ft from the net in the middle of the service court (O in Figure 16.4).

The subject stands anywhere in the right service court (X) and serves 12 shuttles over the extended racket of a student who stands in the square (O) in the target court. This student acts as the "opponent" and assists in the scoring by yelling "low" for any shuttle that does not go over his or her racket.

Scoring: The scorer stands at point Z in the figure. Each serve is scored according to the zone in which the shuttle hits. The best 10 of 12 serves are totaled. A perfect score would be 50. Shuttles hitting on the line are given the higher point value. One point is deducted for any shuttle that fails to clear the upheld racket of the player at O. Table 16.5 provides a scoring scale.

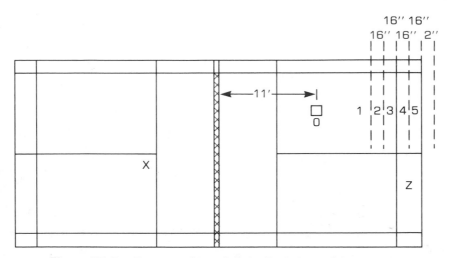

Figure 16.4.   Court markings for the Poole long-serve test

Table 16.5.   Poole Long-Serve Test Scoring Scale[a]

PERFORMANCE LEVEL	PRELIMINARY SKILL TEST	FINAL SKILL TEST
Advanced	26 and above	30 and above
Intermediate	17–25	20–29
Beginner	0–16	0–19

[a]Based on a limited number of beginner course students. See text for scoring method.

Additional Pointers:

1. Only legal serves are scored.

2. The height of the player O who extends the racket over the head is of little consequence. Naturally, extremes should be avoided.

3. Poole believed that this test represents a more gamelike situation than the use of a rope and that it sacrifices very little objectivity. In addition, it facilitates the test administration in terms of equipment and economy of time. If the tester wishes to use a rope, Poole recommended that it be 9 ft high and placed 11 ft from the net.

4. The 2-in. zone beyond the back boundary line is included in the maximum point zone because it was believed that an opponent would ordinarily play any shot that close to the baseline.

5. To expedite administration, the test could be shortened to the best six of eight trials. The score for this method has correlated .95 with the 10-of-12 score.

Poole Forehand Clear Test (Badminton: Poole and Nelson 1970)

Objective: To measure ability to hit the forehand clear from the back court high and deep into the opponent's court.

Sex and Age Level: May be used with high school and college age students of both sexes.

Reliability: The test–retest reliability coefficient was .90.

Validity: The test correlated .70 with the results of tournament play.

Equipment: Two rackets and preferably 12 shuttles in good condition.

Directions: The court with scoring zones is marked as shown in Figure 16.5. One line is drawn parallel to and halfway (6½ ft) between the short-service line and the doubles long-service line. Another line is marked 6 in. beyond the back boundary line. A 15- × 15-in. square is drawn 11 ft from the net astride the center line (O in Figure 16.5). On the other side of the court, a 15- × 15-in. square is drawn at the intersection of the doubles long-service line and the center line (X in Figure 16.5).

The subject stands with the right foot in the X square (assuming he or she is right-handed), holding the racket face up. The shuttle is placed feathers down on the forehand side of the racket. It is then tossed into the air and hit with an overhead forehand clear over the opponent's racket and deep into the opponent's court. The subject's right foot should stay in contact with the X square until the shuttle has been struck. A player stands at point O with racket extended overhead. He or she calls out "low" if any shuttle does not go over the racket. Twelve clears are attempted.

Scoring: The point value of the zone in which the shuttle hits is recorded as the score for each attempt. The best 10 of 12 shots are totaled. A perfect score is 40. Shuttles hitting on the line are given the higher point value. One point is deducted for any shuttle that fails to clear the racket of player O. Table 16.6 presents a scoring scale.

Additional Pointers:

1. Most of the pointers listed for the long-service test apply also for this test.

2. The tossing of the shuttle by the subject is

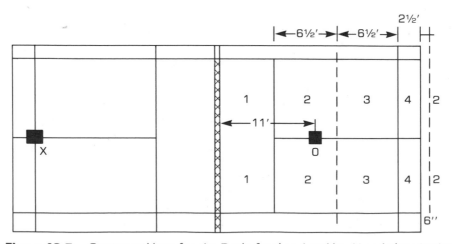

Figure 16.5. Court markings for the Poole forehand and backhand clear tests

Table 16.6. Poole Forehand Clear Test Scoring Scale[a]

PERFORMANCE LEVEL	PRELIMINARY SKILL TEST	FINAL SKILL TEST
Advanced	20 and above	24 and above
Intermediate	13–19	16–23
Beginner	0–12	0–15

[a]Based on a limited number of beginner course students. See text for scoring method.

a skill that needs some practice; however, it has been demonstrated that any beginner can quickly acquire this skill. This feature of the test (not having a second person serve shuttles to the subject) is thought to increase the objectivity of the test considerably and also to facilitate test administration.

3. The tossing and hitting of the shuttle serves as a drill that the student can practice alone on or off the court from the first day of class.

4. If desired, the test can be shortened to the best six of eight trials. This score has correlated .96 with the best 10-of-12 score.

Poole Backhand Clear Test (Badminton: Poole and Nelson 1970)

Objective: To measure ability to hit a backhand clear from the back court high and deep into the opponent's court.

Sex and Age Level: High school and college age students of both sexes.

Reliability: The test–retest reliability coefficient was .78.

Validity: The test correlated .56 with the results of tournament play.

Equipment: Same as for the Poole forehand clear test.

Directions: Same as for the Poole forehand clear test (Figure 16.5) with the following exception: The (right-handed) subject stands with the left foot in the X square. He or she places the shuttle

on the forehand side of the racket, tosses it into the air, and then executes a backhand clear shot deep into the opponent's court. Twelve trials are given.

Scoring: Same as for the Poole forehand clear test. Table 16.7 presents a scoring scale.

Additional Pointers:

1. Same as for the forehand clear test. The tossing skill needs practice. Placing the shuttle on the forehand side of the racket makes the test easier to perform than placing it on the backhand side of the racket.

2. If desired, the test can be shortened to the best six of eight trials. This score correlated .94 with the best 10-of-12 score.

Basketball

AAHPERD Basketball Skills Test[2] (Basketball: AAHPERD 1984)

Speed Spot Shooting

Objective: To measure skill in shooting rapidly from different positions, and to some extent to measure agility and ball handling.

Age Level: Age 10 through college age.

2. Validity estimates using judges' ratings were established for the entire test battery. They ranged from .65 to .95 for males and from .69 to .94 for females at elementary, junior high, senior high school, and college levels. Construct validity was demonstrated using comparisons between varsity and nonvarsity players.

Table 16.7. Poole Backhand Clear Test Scoring Scale[a]

PERFORMANCE LEVEL	PRELIMINARY SKILL TEST	FINAL SKILL TEST
Advanced	16 and above	22 and above
Intermediate	9–15	11–21
Beginner	0–8	0–10

[a]Based on a limited number of beginner course students. See text for a discussion of the scoring method.

Sex: Both sexes.

Reliability: Intraclass stability reliability estimates ranged from .87 to .95 for females and from .84 to .95 for males at the four school levels.

Equipment and Materials: Five floor markers 2 ft × 1 in.; a basketball; and a basketball goal and backboard.

Directions: The floor markers are placed on the floor at the different spots from which the students must shoot. The distance of the spots (Figure 16.6) from the basket varies according to grade level as follows:

Grades	Distance
5 and 6	9 ft
7 through 9	12 ft
10 through college	15 ft

The distances for spots B, C, and D (Figure 16.6) are measured from the center of the backboard; those for spots A and E are measured from the center of the basket.

The student starts from behind any of the five markers for his or her age level. On the signal, "Ready, go," the person shoots, retrieves the ball, and dribbles to and shoots from another spot. One foot must be behind the marker on each shot. A maximum of four lay-up shots may be tried, but no two may be in succession. The student must attempt one shot from each of the five spots. Three trials of 60 sec are given; the first is a practice trial, and the next two are recorded.

Scoring: The tester records the spots at which the shots are taken as well as the number of lay-ups attempted. It is recommended that a card be prepared such as

A B C D E 1 2 3 4

whereby a line can be drawn through each letter designating the spot on the floor and the number indicating a lay-up. Two points are given for each shot made. One point is given for any unsuccessful shot that hits the rim (from above) either initially or after bouncing from the backboard. The total points for each legal shot for each of the two trials is the score. Percentile norms are given in Table 16.8. *T*-score norms are provided in the AAHPERD manual.

Penalties: Penalties include ball-handling infractions such as traveling and double dribbling (the shot following the violation is scored as zero); two lay-ups in succession (the second lay-up is scored as zero); more than four attempts at lay-ups (all attempts over four are scored as zero); and failure to shoot from each of the five spots (the trial is repeated).

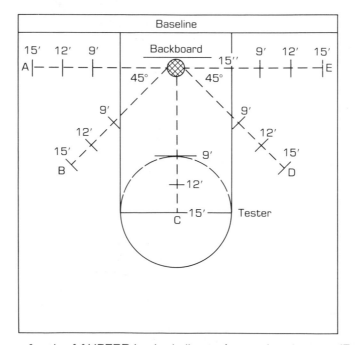

Figure 16.6. Diagram for the AAHPERD basketball speed spot shooting test (Reproduced from the *AAHPERD Basketball Skills Test Manual for Boys and Girls.* Reston, Va.: AAHPERD, 1984. Used by permission)

Table 16.8. Percentile Norms for Speed Spot Shooting

PERCENTILE	AGE							
	10	11	12	13	14	15	16–17	College
				GIRLS				
95	18	19	22	22	25	23	23	35
75	11	11	13	13	15	15	14	21
50	8	8	10	10	11	11	11	17
25	5	5	7	8	9	8	7	13
5	2	2	3	4	4	4	3	8
				BOYS				
95	23	25	27	28	30	27	28	30
75	17	18	19	19	23	20	22	25
50	13	14	15	15	18	16	16	22
25	10	10	11	12	13	11	12	19
5	7	6	7	7	9	6	7	14

Source: *AAHPERD Basketball Skills Test Manual for Boys and Girls.* Reston, Va.: AAHPERD, 1984. Used by permission.

Passing

Objective: To measure skill in passing and recovering the ball while moving.

Age Level: Age 10 through college age.

Sex: Both sexes.

Reliability: Intraclass stability reliability estimates ranged from .82 to .91 for females and from .88 to .96 for males at the elementary, junior high school, senior high school, and college levels.

Equipment and Materials: Basketball and marking materials.

Directions: Six 2-ft squares are marked on the wall so the squares are either 3 or 5 ft from the floor (Figure 16.7). The squares are 2 ft apart. A restraining line is marked 8 ft from the wall.

The performer stands facing the target on the left (A in Figure 16.7) from behind the restraining line, holding a ball. On the signal "Ready, go," the student chest passes to the first target, recovers

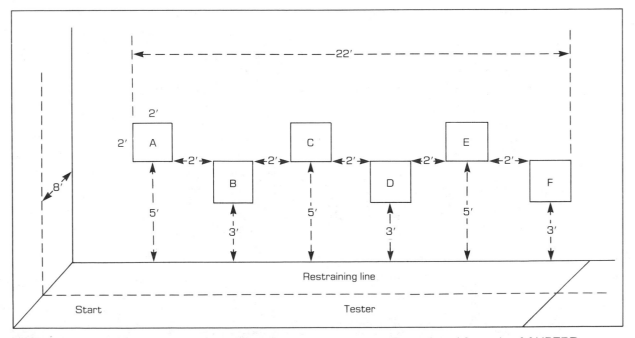

Figure 16.7. Diagram for the AAHPERD basketball passing test (Reproduced from the *AAHPERD Basketball Skills Test Manual for Boys and Girls.* Reston, Va.: AAHPERD, 1984. Used by permission)

the rebound while moving to a spot facing the second target, and chest passes to target B. The person continues this pattern until target F is reached, where two chest passes are performed. The subject then passes to E, repeating the pattern while moving to the left. Three 30-sec trials are given. The first is practice; the last two are recorded.

Scoring: Each pass that hits the target or the boundary lines counts 2 points. Each pass hitting the spaces between targets counts 1 point. The score is the total points of the two trials. Percentile norms are shown in Table 16.9. *T*-score norms are provided in the AAHPERD manual.

Penalties: Penalties include passing from in front of the restraining line (no points are awarded for the pass); passing twice in succession at targets B, C, D, or E (no points are awarded for the second pass); and failure to use the chest pass (no points are awarded for the pass).

Control Dribble

Objective: To measure ball-handling skill while moving.

Age Level: Age 10 through college age.

Sex: Both sexes.

Reliability: Intraclass stability reliability estimates ranged from .93 to .98 for females and from .88 to .95 for males at the elementary school, junior high school, senior high school, and college levels.

Equipment and Materials: A basketball and six cones.

Directions: The six cones are set up in the free-throw lane of a basketball court (Figure 16.8) to provide obstacles. On the signal "Ready, go," the performer starts dribbling with the nondominant hand from the nondominant side of cone A to the nondominant hand side of cone B. The student then follows the course using the preferred hand, changing hands as considered appropriate until both feet cross the finish line. Three timed trials are given. The first is practice; the last two are recorded.

Scoring: The score is the elapsed time in seconds (to the nearest tenth) for each trial. The final score is the sum of the two trials. Percentile norms are provided in Table 16.10. *T*-score norms are provided in the AAHPERD manual.

Penalties: Penalties include ball-handling infractions such as traveling and double-dribbling (the trial is stopped, the subject returns to the start and begins the test again); failure of either the student or the ball to remain outside the cone, including dribbling the ball either inside or over the cone (the trial is stopped, the subject returns to the start and begins the test again); and failure to begin at the point in the course where the subject lost control (the trial is stopped, the subject returns to the start and begins the test again).

Defensive Movement

Objective: To measure basic defensive movements.

Age Level: Age 10 through college age.

Sex: Both sexes.

Table 16.9. Percentile Norms for Passing Test

PERCENTILE	AGE							
	10	11	12	13	14	15	16–17	College
				GIRLS				
95	36	38	43	44	46	47	48	54
75	30	31	35	37	39	40	39	47
50	25	27	31	32	34	35	34	42
25	21	23	26	29	29	28	24	37
5	7	13	20	23	24	19	18	21
				BOYS				
95	41	43	48	54	55	55	57	70
75	35	36	40	43	45	48	49	58
50	31	32	35	39	40	39	41	53
25	25	28	30	35	35	23	25	47
5	8	18	22	23	23	18	21	35

Source: *AAHPERD Basketball Skills Test Manual for Boys and Girls.* Reston, Va.: AAHPERD, 1984. Used by permission.

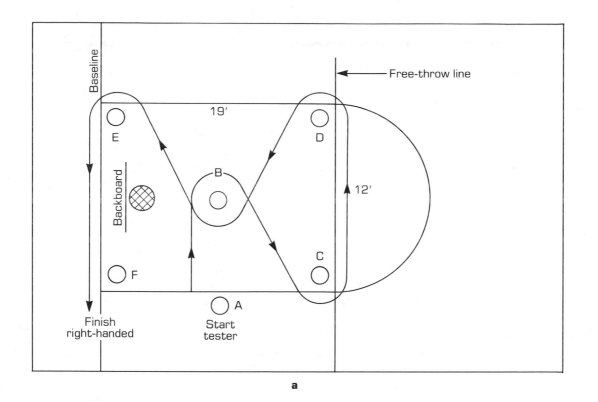

a

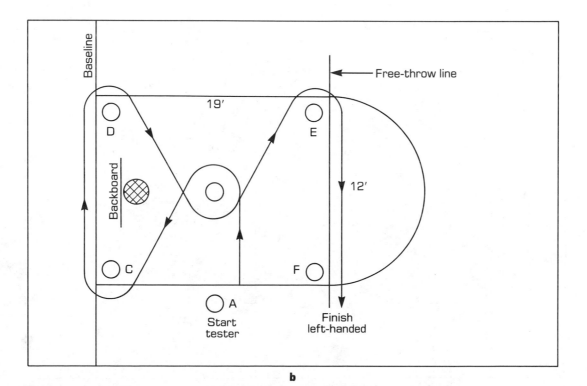

b

Figure 16.8.   Diagram for the AAHPERD basketball control dribble test. (a) Right-handed dribble. (b) Left-handed dribble (Reproduced from the *AAHPERD Basketball Skills Test Manual for Boys and Girls*. Reston, Va.: AAHPERD, 1984. Used by permission)

Table 16.10. Percentile Norms for Control Dribble

PERCENTILE	AGE							
	10	11	12	13	14	15	16–17	College
				GIRLS				
95	10.8	10.3	8.8	8.7	8.4	8.2	8.2	7.6
75	12.3	11.8	10.6	10.0	9.6	9.7	9.8	8.5
50	14.3	13.2	11.9	11.0	10.7	10.7	10.7	9.3
25	16.6	15.0	13.3	12.4	12.0	12.0	12.2	10.4
5	21.7	20.5	19.0	17.8	18.1	15.8	15.0	13.8
				BOYS				
95	9.2	9.0	8.7	7.8	7.5	7.0	7.0	6.7
75	10.4	10.1	9.5	9.0	8.5	8.1	8.1	7.3
50	11.7	11.1	10.5	9.8	9.3	8.9	9.0	7.8
25	13.7	12.6	11.7	10.7	10.3	10.0	10.0	8.5
5	23.0	16.8	16.0	14.4	13.5	12.0	12.4	10.0

Source: *AAHPERD Basketball Skills Test Manual for Boys and Girls.* Reston, Va.: AAHPERD, 1984. Used by permission.

Reliability: Intraclass stability reliability estimates ranged from .95 to .96 for females and from .90 to .97 for males at the elementary school, junior high school, senior high school, and college levels.

Equipment and Materials: Marking material such as adhesive tape.

Directions: The test boundaries are the free-throw line, the boundary line behind the basket, and the rebound lane lines. The middle rebound lane markers serve as targets C and F for the test (Figure 16.9). Additional spots outside the four corners of the rectangular area should be marked by tape (points A, B, D, and E in Figure 16.9).

The student starts at A facing away from the basket. On the signal "Ready, go," the performer slides to the left (without crossing the feet) to

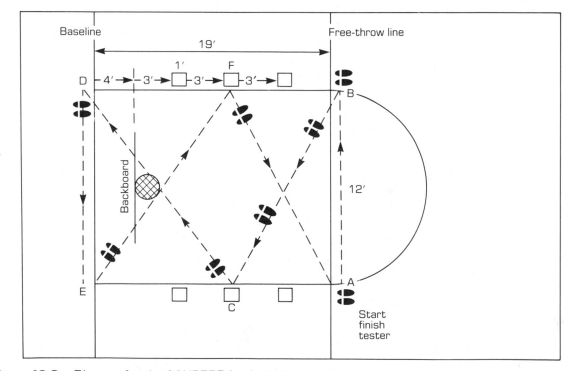

Figure 16.9. Diagram for the AAHPERD basketball defensive movement test (Reproduced from the *AAHPERD Basketball Skills Test Manual for Boys and Girls.* Reston, Va.: AAHPERD, 1984. Used by permission)

marker B, touches the floor outside the lane with the left hand, performs a dropstep[3] (Figure 16.10), and slides to point C and touches the floor outside the lane with the right hand. The student continues the course as shown in Figure 16.9 until both feet cross the finish line. Three timed trials are given. The first is practice; the last two are recorded.

Scoring: The score is the elapsed time (to the nearest tenth of a second) for each trial. The final score is the sum of the two trials. Percentile norms are given in Table 16.11. *T*-score norms are provided in the AAHPERD manual.

Penalties: Penalties include footfaults—crossing the feet during the slide or turning and running (the trial is stopped and repeated); failure to touch the hand to the floor outside the lane (the trial is stopped and repeated); and executing the dropstep before the hand touches the floor (the trial is stopped and repeated).

LSU Long and Short Test (Basketball: Nelson, 1967)

Objective: To measure the ability to shoot long and short shots in basketball, and to a certain extent, to measure ball-handling and dribbling skills.

---

3. The dropstep is a basic defensive maneuver used to stop penetration to the basket by an offensive player. It consists of changing defensive direction by moving the trailing foot in a sliding motion in the direction of the offensive move.

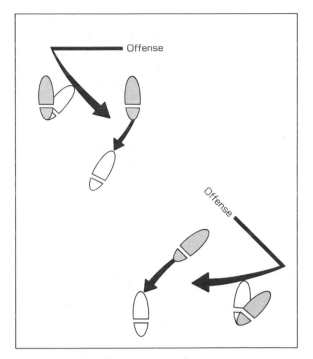

Figure 16.10. Diagram for the dropstep for the AAHPERD defensive movement test (Reproduced from the *AAHPERD Basketball Skills Test Manual for Boys and Girls*. Reston, Va.: AAHPERD, 1984. Used by permission)

Sex: Both sexes.

Age Level: Elementary school through college age.

Equipment and Materials: A basketball; a stopwatch; a regulation basket and backboard; and a string and chalk for marking the floor.

Table 16.11. Percentile Norms for Defensive Movement

PERCENTILE	AGE							
	10	11	12	13	14	15	16–17	College
GIRLS								
95	10.5	10.3	9.5	10.0	9.6	9.7	9.6	8.7
75	11.8	11.8	11.5	11.5	11.0	11.0	11.1	10.3
50	13.2	13.0	12.8	12.5	12.0	12.0	12.0	11.0
25	14.6	14.3	14.1	13.6	13.2	13.4	13.2	12.0
5	19.6	17.4	17.0	16.8	16.4	16.4	16.4	14.5
BOYS								
95	10.0	9.0	8.9	8.9	8.7	7.9	7.3	8.4
75	11.5	10.9	10.7	10.3	10.1	9.3	9.6	9.4
50	12.7	12.0	11.9	11.4	11.3	10.3	10.3	10.3
25	13.9	13.7	13.0	12.8	12.4	11.3	11.5	11.2
5	18.7	17.2	17.0	16.6	15.8	14.0	15.2	12.9

Source: *AAHPERD Basketball Skills Test Manual for Boys and Girls*. Reston, Va.: AAHPERD, 1984. Used by permission.

Directions: A string is stretched from directly under the basket to the top of the free-throw circle. With the string taut, an arc is made with chalk from the top of the free-throw circle to the end line on either side of the basket. This is the restraining line for the long shots.

The subject stands in back of the restraining line holding the ball. On the signal to begin he or she shoots from behind the restraining line, then rushes in to get the rebound, and shoots a short shot. After attempting the lay-up, the subject runs back behind the restraining line and shoots a long shot, recovers the ball, and shoots a short shot. He or she thus continues alternating a long and short shot until the whistle blows at the end of 1 min. The ball must be dribbled, not picked up, regardless of the distance to cover. The short shot may be shot from anywhere—it does not have to be a lay-up; the long shot has to be shot from behind the restraining line. Two complete trials are given, with a short rest in between.

Scoring: The watch is started on the signal to begin and is stopped at the end of 1 min. A long shot counts 2 points and a short shot counts 1 point. The score is the total number of points made in the two trials. Table 16.12 presents a scoring scale.

Additional Pointers:

1. The distance from the basket for the long shot can be varied depending on the age of the performer and the type of shot being stressed.

2. The type of shot may be varied; for example, the teacher or coach may want subjects to shoot a jump shot, then rush in and recover and shoot a lay-up or a short jump shot.

3. The arc may be shortened to test shooting left-handed, then right-handed, or vice versa, depending on the particular student's dom-inant hand, with the higher point value given for baskets made with the nondominant hand.

4. The test works well as a drill and provides for individual competition among players while they practice, much like the familiar game of twenty-one.

Bowling

The game of bowling is, in itself, objective measurement. Consequently, most of the work done in this area has been the construction of norms. Phillips and Summers developed norms for college women based on initial levels of ability. Ratings were established for the different levels of ability as to progress in the course up through 25 lines of bowling. Martin and Keogh published bowling norms for college men and women in elective physical education classes. The bowlers were classified as experienced or nonexperienced. Separate norms for superior, good, average, poor, and inferior performance were constructed for experienced and nonexperienced bowlers.

Football

AAHPERD Football Skills Test (Football: AAHPERD 1965)

Ten tests have been presented as part of the AAHPERD Sports Skills Tests Project to measure the fundamental skills of football. Each test purports to measure a single basic skill.

The tests are the following: (1) forward pass for distance, (2) 50-yard dash with football, (3) blocking, (4) forward pass for accuracy, (5) football punt for distance, (6) ball-changing zigzag run, (7) catching the forward pass, (8) pullout, (9) kickoff, and (10) dodging run. All the tests except the blocking test may also be used to eval-

Table 16.12. LSU Long and Short Test Scoring Scale, College Students[a]

PERFORMANCE LEVEL	SCORE	
	Men	Women
Advanced	18 and above	14 and above
Advanced intermediate	14–17	12–13
Intermediate	7–13	4–11
Advanced beginner	3–6	2–3
Beginner	0–2	0–1

[a]Based on the scores of a limited number of men and women students, Corpus Christi State University, Corpus Christi, Tex., 1976.

uate basic skills in touch or flag football. All the tests are for boys. Norms are provided in Tables 16.13 through 16.21. The dodging run is presented in the chapter on agility, Chapter 13.

Forward Pass for Distance

Directions and Scoring: This test is administered and scored in the same manner as the softball throw for distance in the *AAHPERD Softball Skills Test Manual* (best of three trials, 6-ft restraining area, distance measured to the last foot passed and measured at right angles to the throwing line, not arcing from the point from which the throw was made). Table 16.13 contains norms in both feet and meters.

50-Yard Dash With Football

Directions: The subject runs as fast as possible for 50 yd carrying a football. Two trials are given, with a rest between.

Scoring: When the starter shouts "go" and simultaneously swings a white cloth down with the arm, the timer starts the watch. The time is stopped when the runner crosses the finish line. The better time of two trials to the nearest tenth of a second is used as the score. Table 16.14 shows norms.

Blocking

Directions: On the signal "go," the subject runs forward and executes a cross-body block against a blocking bag. He immediately recovers and charges toward a second bag placed 15 ft directly to the right of the first bag (Figure 16.11). After cross-body blocking the bag clear to the ground, he scrambles to his feet and races toward the third bag. The third bag is 15 ft away in the direction of the starting line, but at a 45-degree angle to the line from bags 1 and 2 (Figure 16.11) (this places the bag about 5 ft from the starting line). The subject blocks this third bag to the ground with a cross-body block and then runs across the starting line. Two trials are given. The blocking bags must be blocked clear to the ground.

Scoring: The time from the signal "go" until the student crosses back over the line is measured to the nearest tenth of a second. The better of the two trials is recorded as the score. Table 16.15 shows norms.

Forward Pass for Accuracy

Directions: A target is painted on an 8- × 11-ft canvas, which is hung from the crossbar of the goal posts. The center circle is 2 ft in diameter,

the middle circle 4 ft, and the outer circle 6 ft in diameter. The bottom of the outer circle is 3 ft from the ground. It is recommended that a wooden or metal bar be inserted in a channel sewn along the bottom of the canvas, and then the channel be tied to the goal posts to keep the canvas stretched taut. A restraining line is drawn 15 yd from the target. The player takes two or three small running steps along the line, hesitates, then throws the football at the target. The player may go either to the right or left, but he must stay behind the restraining line. He should pass the ball with good speed. Ten trials are given.

Scoring: The target circles score 3, 2, and 1 point for the inner, middle, and outer circles, respectively. Passes hitting on a line are given the higher value. The point total for the ten trials is the score. Table 16.16 shows norms.

Football Punt for Distance

Directions and Scoring: The player takes one or two steps within the 6-ft kicking zone and punts the ball as far as possible. Administration and scoring of the test are the same as for the forward pass for distance test. Table 16.17 shows norms.

Ball-Changing Zigzag Run

Directions: Five chairs are placed in a line, 10 ft apart, and all facing away from the starting line (Figure 16.12). The first chair is 10 ft in front of the starting line. Holding a football under his right arm, the subject starts from behind the starting line on the signal "go." He runs to the right of the first chair, then changes the ball to his left arm and runs to the left of the second chair. He continues running in and out of the chairs in this manner, changing the position of the ball to the outside arm as he passes each chair. The inside arm should be extended as in stiff-arming. He circles around the end chair and runs in and out of the chairs back to the starting line. He is not allowed to hit the chairs. Two timed trials are given.

Scoring: The time from the signal "go" until the subject passes back over the starting line is recorded to the nearest tenth of a second for the better of the two trials. Table 16.18 shows norms.

Catching the Forward Pass

Directions: A scrimmage line is drawn with two *end* marks located 9 ft to the right and to the left of the center (Figure 16.13). At a distance of 30 ft in front of these marks are *turning points*. The subject lines up on the right end mark facing the

Table 16.13. Norms in Feet and Meters for AAHPERD Football Test, Forward Pass for Distance, Boys[a]

PERCENTILE	AGE															
	10		11		12		13		14		15		16		17–18	
	ft	m	ft	m	ft	m	ft	m	ft	m	ft	m	ft	m	ft	m
95	71	21.6	83	25.3	99	30.2	115	35.1	126	38.4	135	41.2	144	43.9	152	46.3
75	61	18.6	68	20.7	79	24.1	91	27.7	105	32.0	115	35.1	123	37.5	129	39.3
50	53	16.2	59	18.0	68	20.7	78	23.8	91	27.7	99	30.2	108	32.9	114	34.8
25	45	13.7	48	14.6	58	17.7	65	19.8	77	23.5	85	25.9	93	28.4	98	29.9
5	33	10.1	36	11.0	40	12.2	46	13.1	53	16.2	62	18.9	70	21.3	67	20.4

[a]Percentile scores based on age.
Source: *AAHPERD Football Skills Test Manual.* Reston, Va.: AAHPERD, 1965. Complete norms are in manual. Used by permission.

Table 16.14. Norms in Seconds for AAHPERD Football Test, 50-Yard Dash With Football, Boys[a]

PERCENTILE	AGE							
	10	11	12	13	14	15	16	17–18
95	7.7	7.4	7.0	6.4	6.4	6.2	6.0	6.0
75	8.3	7.9	7.5	7.1	7.0	6.6	6.5	6.3
50	8.7	8.4	8.0	7.5	7.4	7.0	6.8	6.7
25	9.2	8.9	8.4	8.1	7.9	7.4	7.3	7.1
5	9.8	9.5	9.3	9.0	8.8	8.4	8.0	7.8

[a]Percentile scores based on age.
Source: *AAHPERD Football Skills Test Manual.* Reston, Va.: AAHPERD, 1965. Complete norms are in manual. Used by permission.

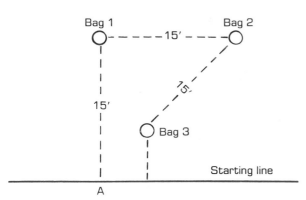

Figure 16.11. Diagram for the AAHPERD football blocking test (Reproduced from *AAHPERD Football Skills Test Manual*. Reston, Va.: AAHPERD, 1965. Used by permission)

turning point 30 ft directly in front of him. On the signal "go," he runs straight ahead, cuts around the turning point and runs to receive the pass 30 ft away at the *passing point*. On the signal "go," the center snaps the ball 15 ft to the passer, who takes one step, then passes the ball directly over the passing point above head height. The passer must be able to pass the ball in a mechanical manner to the passing point without paying attention to the receiver. A similar passing point is

located 30 ft to the left of the left turning point. Ten trials are given to the right and ten trials to the left. The player need not try for poorly thrown passes, but he must go around the turning point before proceeding to the passing point.

Scoring: One point is given for each pass caught. The sum of passes caught from both sides is recorded as the score. Table 16.19 shows norms.

Additional Pointer: Considerable practice and skill are needed on the part of the passer to be able to time the pass so that the subject can reach the passing point in a controlled manner and get his hands on the ball.

Pullout

Directions: The subject lines up in a set position halfway between two goal posts. On the signal "go," he pulls out and runs parallel to the imaginary line of scrimmage, cuts around the right-hand goal post, and races straight ahead across a finish line 30 ft from and parallel to the goal posts. Two timed trials are given.

Scoring: The score is the better of the two trials, measured in seconds and tenths of seconds from

Table 16.15. Norms in Seconds for AAHPERD Football Test, Blocking, Boys[a]

PERCENTILE	AGE							
	10	11	12	13	14	15	16	17–18
95	7.5	6.6	6.6	5.9	5.8	6.0	5.9	5.5
75	8.3	8.3	7.9	7.2	7.0	6.7	6.7	6.2
50	9.8	9.9	9.0	8.1	7.8	7.5	7.8	7.2
25	11.3	11.1	9.9	9.1	8.7	8.5	9.1	8.2
5	14.4	13.1	11.6	11.2	10.3	10.4	10.7	10.8

[a]Percentile scores based on age.
Source: *AAHPERD Football Skills Test Manual*. Reston, Va.: AAHPERD, 1965. See text for description of the test. Complete norms are in manual. Used by permission.

Table 16.16. Norms in Points for AAHPERD Football Test, Forward Pass for Accuracy, Boys[a]

PERCENTILE	AGE							
	10	11	12	13	14	15	16	17–18
95	14	19	20	21	21	20	21	22
75	8	12	15	16	16	16	16	18
50	3	7	11	12	12	12	13	14
25	0	3	6	8	8	8	9	10
5	0	0	1	2	2	3	4	5

[a]Percentile scores based on age.
Source: *AAHPERD Football Skills Test Manual*. Reston, Va.: AAHPERD, 1965. Complete norms are in manual. Used by permission.

Table 16.17. Norms in Feet and Meters for AAHPERD Football Test, Football Punt for Distance, Boys[a]

PERCENTILE	AGE															
	10		11		12		13		14		15		16		17–18	
	ft	m	ft	m	ft	m	ft	m	ft	m	ft	m	ft	m	ft	m
95	75	22.9	84	25.6	93	28.4	106	32.3	119	36.3	126	38.4	140	42.7	136	41.5
75	56	17.1	68	20.7	77	23.5	87	26.5	98	29.9	105	32.0	109	33.2	115	35.1
50	48	14.6	57	17.4	66	20.1	73	22.3	84	25.6	91	27.7	95	29.0	98	29.9
25	40	12.2	45	13.7	52	15.9	61	18.6	70	21.3	76	23.2	79	24.1	81	24.7
5	22	6.7	27	8.2	35	10.7	33	10.1	44	13.4	54	16.5	56	17.1	53	16.2

[a]Percentile scores based on age.
Source: *AAHPERD Football Skills Test Manual.* Reston, Va.: AAHPERD, 1965. Complete norms are in manual. Used by permission.

Table 16.18. Norms in Seconds for AAHPERD Football Test, Ball-Changing Zigzag Run, Boys[a]

PERCENTILE	AGE							
	10	11	12	13	14	15	16	17–18
95	9.9	7.7	7.8	8.0	8.7	7.7	7.7	8.4
75	10.7	9.3	8.8	9.0	9.5	8.6	8.7	9.0
50	11.5	10.3	9.6	9.7	10.0	9.1	9.3	9.6
25	12.5	11.3	10.5	10.3	10.7	9.9	10.1	10.3
5	15.8	14.2	12.3	12.1	12.0	11.5	12.2	12.1

[a]Percentile scores based on age.
Source: *AAHPERD Football Skills Test Manual.* Reston, Va.: AAHPERD, 1965. See text for description of the test. Complete norms are in manual. Used by permission.

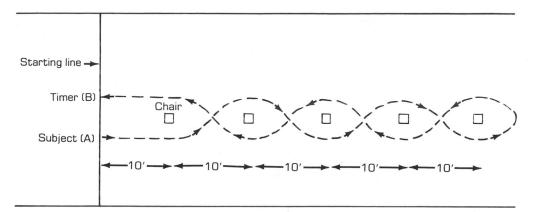

Figure 16.12.   Placement of chairs and diagram of movement for the AAHPERD ball-changing zigzag run test (Reproduced from the *AAHPERD Football Skills Test Manual.* Reston, Va.: AAHPERD, 1965. Used by permission)

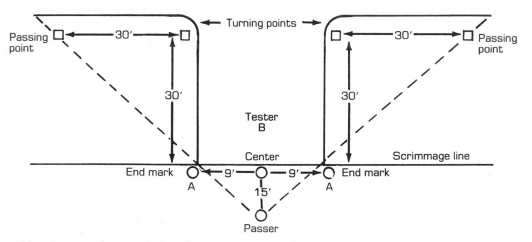

Figure 16.13.   Diagram for the AAHPERD football forward pass catching test. "A" is the starting position of the subject (Reproduced from the *AAHPERD Football Skills Test Manual.* Reston, Va.: AAHPERD, 1965. Used by permission)

Table 16.19.   Norms in Numbers Caught for AAHPERD Football Test, Catching the Forward Pass, Boys[a]

PERCENTILE	AGE							
	10	11	12	13	14	15	16	17–18
95	19	19	19	20	20	20	20	20
75	13	14	16	17	17	18	18	18
50	7	10	13	13	14	15	15	15
25	4	6	10	9	9	10	10	11
5	1	1	5	4	4	6	4	6

[a]Percentile scores based on age.
Source: *AAHPERD Football Skills Test Manual.* Reston, Va.: AAHPERD, 1965. See text for description of the test. Complete norms are in manual. Used by permission.

the signal "go" until the subject crosses the finish line. Table 16.20 shows norms.

Kickoff

Directions: A kicking tee is placed in the center of one of the lines running across the field. The ball is positioned so that it tilts slightly back toward the kicker. The player takes as long a run as he wants and kicks the ball as far as possible. Three trials are given.

Scoring: Same as for the forward pass and the punt for distance tests. Table 16.21 shows norms.

Table 16.20. Norms in Seconds for AAHPERD Football Test, Pullout, Boys[a]

PERCENTILE	AGE							
	10	11	12	13	14	15	16	17–18
95	2.9	2.5	2.8	2.8	2.7	2.5	2.5	2.6
75	3.5	2.9	3.1	3.1	3.0	3.0	2.9	2.9
50	3.8	3.4	3.4	3.3	3.2	3.2	3.2	3.1
25	4.0	3.9	3.8	3.6	3.5	3.5	3.4	3.3
5	4.4	4.4	4.2	4.0	4.0	4.1	4.3	3.9

[a]Percentile scores based on age.
Source: *AAHPERD Football Skills Test Manual*. Reston, Va.: AAHPERD, 1965. Complete norms are in manual. Used by permission.

Table 16.21. Norms in Feet and Meters for AAHPERD Football Test, Kickoff, Boys[a]

PERCENTILE	AGE															
	10		11		12		13		14		15		16		17–18	
	ft	m	ft	m	ft	m	ft	m	ft	m	ft	m	ft	m	ft	m
95	69	21.0	79	24.1	98	29.9	106	32.3	118	36.0	128	39.0	131	39.9	138	42.1
75	55	16.8	60	18.3	70	21.3	81	24.7	94	28.7	104	31.7	108	32.9	113	34.5
50	45	13.7	50	15.2	57	17.4	67	20.4	77	23.5	87	26.5	93	28.4	95	29.0
25	35	10.7	40	12.2	42	12.8	52	15.9	62	18.9	69	21.0	75	22.9	74	22.6
5	21	6.4	24	7.3	22	6.7	26	7.9	38	11.6	40	12.2	47	14.3	43	13.1

[a]Percentile scores based on age.
Source: *AAHPERD Football Skills Test Manual*. Reston, Va.: AAHPERD, 1965. Complete norms are in manual. Used by permission.

Golf

Clevett's Putting Test (Golf: Clevett 1931)

Clevett devised four tests of golf employing the brassie, midiron, mashie, and putter. The putting test is described here.

Equipment and Materials: A smooth carpet 20 ft long and 27 in. wide marked as shown in Figure 16.14; a putter; and at least ten golf balls in good condition.

Directions: The subject putts at a distance of 15 ft from the hole. It can be seen from Figure 16.14 that the subject is encouraged to putt long for the hole rather than be too cautious. Ten trials are given.

Scoring: The number in the square where the ball stops is the score for that putt. The total of the ten trials is the final score. Balls resting on a line are given the higher point value.

Additional Pointers:

1. The test can be decidedly improved by cutting an actual hole in the carpet. Several movable putting surfaces can be constructed with use of carpeting stretched over plywood, thus enabling a hole to be formed. In this case the scoring points should be altered, the points for squares beyond the hole being slightly reduced in value.

2. To make the test more functional, the distances could be varied.

3. The use of synthetic grass would undoubtedly improve the test.

Nelson Pitching Test (Golf: Nelson 1967)

Objective: To measure the ability of a golfer to use the short irons in pitching close to the pin.

Age and Sex: Suitable for both boys and girls at the secondary school and college age levels.

Reliability: Using odd–even trials and the Spearman–Brown prophecy formula, a coefficient of reliability of .83 was found with men and women college students.

Validity: A correlation of .86 was obtained with judges' ratings of ability. An *r* of .79 was found between the test scores and actual golf scores.

Equipment and Materials: The appropriate golf club, usually the eight iron, nine iron, or wedge; preferably four baskets, each with 13 balls in good condition (although two baskets will suffice if only one person is being tested at a time); a flag stick for the center of the target; two flags or markers for the restraining line; tape measure and lime or other field-marking materials.

Directions: The target is marked as shown in Figure 16.15. The inner circle is 6 ft in diameter. Proceeding out from the center, each circle's radius is 5 ft wider than the previous one. The diameters are 6, 16, 26, 36, 46, 56, and 66 ft. The target is divided into equal quadrants. A restraining line is marked 20 yd from the flag, and the hitting line is 40 yd from the flag. The point values for each circle (and sections of circle) are shown in the figure.

Preferably two students are tested at a time, who take turns hitting. A spotter is assigned for each subject. The instructor acts as the recorder. The instructor and the spotters stand near the target. The subject is given three practice shots, then ten trials, attempting to have each ball come to rest as near the flag as possible. The ball must be airborne until it passes the restraining line to be a good shot and to prevent the ball rolling all the way. A swing and miss counts as a trial. Any swing, regardless of how far the ball goes, counts as a trial. After the two subjects finish, they retrieve their balls and the spotters prepare to be tested next. Two new spotters are then called.

Scoring: The point value for the area in which the ball comes to rest is called out to the recorder.

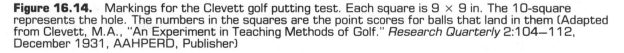

Start			1	1	1	1	2	2	2	2	6	7	7	5	5	3	3	3
			1	1	1	1	2	2	2	6	6	10	8	8	8	4	4	4
			1	1	1	1	2	2	2	2	6	7	7	5	5	3	3	3

←———— 8' ————→

Figure 16.14. Markings for the Clevett golf putting test. Each square is 9 × 9 in. The 10-square represents the hole. The numbers in the squares are the point scores for balls that land in them (Adapted from Clevett, M.A., "An Experiment in Teaching Methods of Golf." *Research Quarterly* 2:104–112, December 1931, AAHPERD, Publisher)

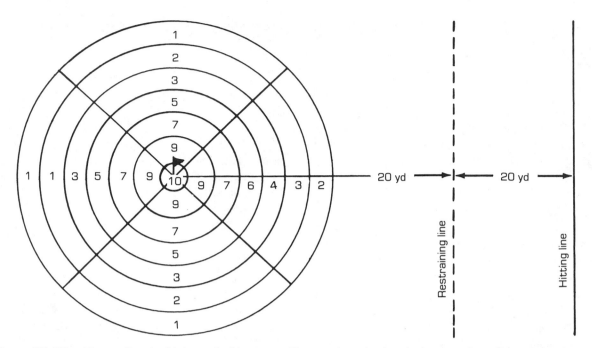

Figure 16.15.   Target for the Nelson pitching test. The numbers in the circles are the point scores for balls that land in the circles or the section of circle

The spotter calls out his or her subject's name and score—for example, "Smith, seven." The recorder enters each score. It is not difficult for the recorder to see every score, but the spotters aid in double checking and in avoiding errors in entering scores for the proper person. A ball resting on a line is given the higher point value. The score is the total point value for the ten trials.

Additional Pointers:

1. Using different colored golf balls, three subjects can easily be tested at a time without spotters being needed. The instructor stands back at the hitting line. After all subjects have finished, the instructor goes to the target area to record the scores for each subject by noting the zone in which each particular colored ball is resting.

2. The subjects must take turns hitting so as to not bother one another. If a subject is particularly slow in hitting, he or she may be tested alone at the end or with another equally slow player.

3. Balls that hit the ground before passing the restraining line are immediately removed so that they will not be mistakenly counted if they should roll onto the target.

4. It is sometimes of help to the subject if the score is called out if, because of uneven ground, he or she cannot see the exact position of the previous shot.

5. The test works well as a practice drill, enabling each student to have an objective record of progress. For this reason it is best to permanently mark the circles by burning the lines in the grass or etching them in the ground.

6. The hitting distance can be varied for more functional practice and more effective testing.

7. If time is pressing, very little reliability is lost by having the student hit ten balls and the instructor discard the three lowest trials and total the remaining seven.

Plastic Ball Golf Iron Test (Golf: Cotten, Thomas, and Plaster 1972)

Objective: To measure ability to hit the irons in golf.

Sex and Age Level: Both sexes of high school and college age.

Reliability: The test–retest reliability coefficients were .72, .69, .72, and .70 for the three, five, seven, and nine irons, respectively. Reliability coefficients were also determined for wind conditions for each iron. The coefficients ranged from .74 to .96, which indicated that the battery could be used effectively under wind conditions.

Validity: The test with the three, five, seven, and nine irons correlated .82 with judges' ratings and tee-to-green scores. The seven iron alone correlated .75 with judges' ratings and .76 with tee-to-green scores.

Equipment and Materials: A sufficient number of plastic whiffle golf balls (at least ten for each station); an appropriate golf club or clubs for each station; and a target grid.

Directions: The target grid is divided into 12 sections (see Figure 16.16) with a point value assigned for each section. The three grid sections farthest from the subject have no distance limits. Each section is fifteen ft wide. The hitting line is 30 ft from the first scoring section. More than one testing station may be set up, using adjacent or overlapping target grids (Figure 16.16). A flag or target object may be placed in the center of the 4-point section.

The subject is given ten swings with each iron. Preferably, more than one student can be tested at a time. A scorer for each subject should be stationed at the rear of the 4-point section of the target grid. A swing and miss counts as a trial.

Scoring: Each ball receives the value of the grid section in which it first strikes the ground, not the point to which it rolls. A topped ball that rolls into the scoring area, however, receives 1 point less than the value of the section in which it stops. A ball hitting a line receives the higher point value. A ball that does not reach the scoring area receives no points, nor does a ball that hits to the left or right of the grid. The final score is the cumulative points for the ten trials. A perfect score is 40 points for each iron. Table 16.22 gives a scoring scale.

Additional Pointers:

1. To conserve testing time, the seven iron alone could be used, since the addition of the other iron scores did not raise the predictive value of the test battery significantly above that of the seven iron alone.

2. The existing markings of a football field may be used conveniently for the 15-ft widths of the target grid.

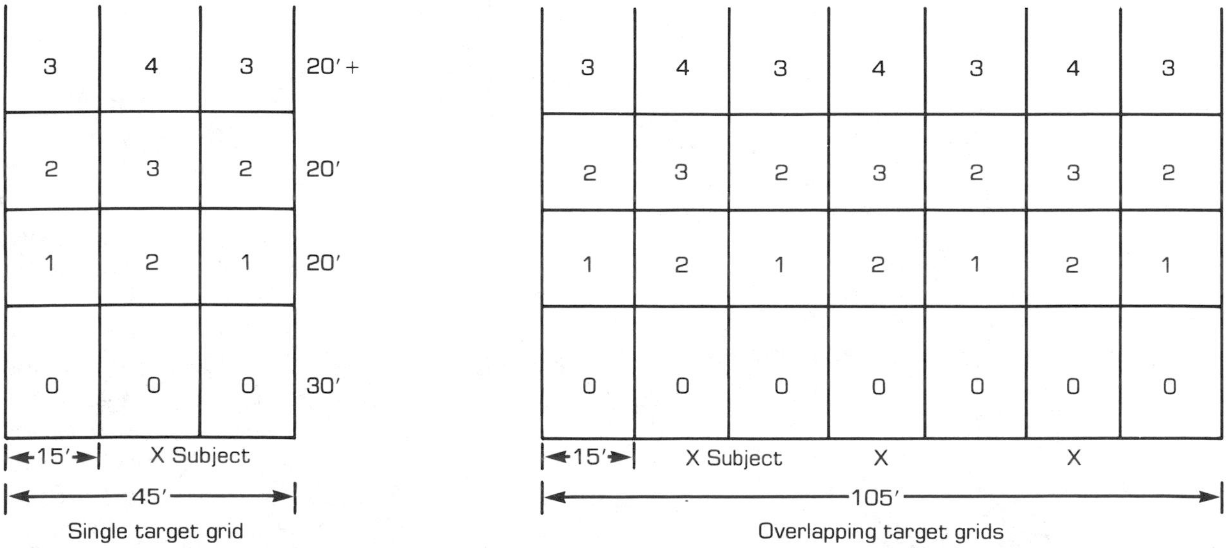

Figure 16.16. Target grid for plastic ball golf iron test. The numbers in the squares are the point scores for balls that land in the squares

Table 16.22. Plastic Ball Golf Iron Test Scoring Scale[a]

PERFORMANCE LEVEL	NO. SEVEN IRON TEST	TOTAL OF ALL FOUR IRONS
Advanced	25	94
Advanced intermediate	20	76
Intermediate	15	58
Advanced beginner	10	40
Beginner	5	22

[a]Based on the scores of 70 boys and girls as reported by D. Cotten and J. Thomas at Georgia Southern College, Stateboro, Ga., 1971. See text for description of scoring.

3. The test could be given indoors in a gymnasium, with students hitting from golf mats.

Gymnastics

Beginner Gymnastic Stunts (Gymnastics: Johnson and Garcia 1976)

Objective: To measure individual gymnastic stunt performance.

Age Level: Junior high school through college age.

Sex: Satisfactory for boys and girls as per event.

Evaluation: Beginner gymnastic stunts were compiled and rated for difficulty on a 5-point scale. Experienced men and women students from four different classes rated the stunts independently of each other. Statistical treatment revealed that the difficulty ratings of the four classes were significantly related. Moreover, the relationship between the instructor's ratings and the average ratings of the students also was significant.

Equipment and Materials: A complete gymnastic facility for boys and girls or the specific equipment for selected events in gymnastics.

Directions: Stunts are listed in Table 16.23 with the average difficulty rating and a suggested upper and lower limit as based on a 5-point scale. Students select two stunts to do from each of the five categories.

Scoring: When a student performs a chosen stunt poorly, deductions are made from the average difficulty rating score to the lower limit. When a student performs a stunt exceedingly well, additions are made to the upper limit of the rating score. The maximum score possible on a ten-stunt test would be 99.75.

Additional Pointers:

1. This test should be given only after adequate instruction and practice.
2. It is recommended that students be allowed to choose the stunts they wish to present.

Handball

Cornish Handball Test (Handball: Cornish 1949)

Objective: To measure handball ability through five test items: 30-second volley, front-wall placement, back-wall placement, service placement, and power test.[4]

Age and Sex: College men.

Validity: A criterion consisting of total points scored by each student minus points scored by the opponent was used in the statistical procedures for test selection. The r for the five tests with the criterion was .694. The power test correlated highest with the criterion ($r = .58$). This test, in combination with the 30-second volley, correlated nearly as high with the criterion (.667) as did the five items. Consequently, in the interest of time and ease of administration, only these two tests are recommended.

Equipment: Several handballs in good condition and comparable in liveliness and a stopwatch.

Court Markings: Only the power test and 30-second volley will be described here; other markings are needed for the three placement tests. The service line is the only marking necessary for the volley test. For the power test, a line is drawn on the front wall at a height of 6 ft. Lines also are drawn on the floor as follows: The first line is 18 ft from the front wall; the second line is 5 ft behind the first; the third, fourth, and fifth lines are each 5¾ ft apart. These lines form six scoring zones. The area from the front wall to the first line scores 1 point, as does the first of the five zones behind. The second, third, fourth, and fifth zones score 2-, 3-, 4-, and 5-points, respectively.

Power Test Directions: The subject stands in the service zone and throws the ball against the front wall, letting it hit the floor on the rebound before striking it. He then hits the ball as hard as possible, making sure that it strikes the front wall *below* the 6-ft line. He throws the ball against the wall prior to each power stroke. Five trials are given for each hand. A retrial is allowed for any attempt in which the subject steps into the front court or fails to hit the wall below the 6-ft line.

Power Test Scoring. The value of the scoring zone in which each ball first touches the floor is recorded. The score is the total points for the 10 trials.

---

4. Pennington and colleagues constructed a test of handball ability consisting of service placement, a total wall volley score, and back-wall placement tests. These were selected by the Wherry–Doolittle test selection method from 17 strength, motor ability, and handball skills test items. This test was constructed for use of a larger ball than regulation, with fewer rebound characteristics, and on a smaller-than-regulation court. For this reason it is not described here. However, because of the test's high validity coefficient, we recommend that these items be studied as to their applicability with the regulation court and ball.

Table 16.23.   Difficulty Scoring Scale for Gymnastic Stunts

TUMBLING	LOWER LIMIT	AVERAGE	UPPER LIMIT
Forward roll	1.50	1.75	2.00
Shoulder roll	2.25	2.50	2.75
Dive roll	2.50	3.00	2.75
Backward roll	3.25	3.50	3.75
Cartwheel	3.25	3.50	3.75
Cartwheel ¼ turn	3.75	4.00	4.25
Kip-up	3.75	4.00	4.25
Forward roll to straddle stand	3.25	3.50	3.75
Headspring	4.25	4.50	4.75
Handspring	4.50	4.75	5.00
Front walkover	4.50	4.75	5.00
Back walkover	4.50	4.75	5.00
BALANCE AND FLEXIBILITY SKILLS			
Tripod balance	.75	1.00	1.25
Tip-up balance	2.00	2.25	2.50
Headstand	2.75	3.00	3.25
Head and forearm balance	3.25	3.50	3.75
Forearm balance	3.75	4.00	4.25
Handstand	4.00	4.50	5.00
"V" seat balance	3.25	3.50	3.75
"L" balance	3.50	3.75	4.00
Front scale	3.00	3.25	3.50
Side scale	3.25	3.50	3.75
Front splits	3.50	4.00	4.50
Side splits	4.00	4.50	5.00
VAULTING			
Front vault	2.25	2.50	2.75
Flank vault	2.25	2.50	2.75
Rear vault	3.25	3.50	3.75
Thief vault	4.25	4.50	4.75
Squat vault	3.00	3.25	3.75
Straddle vault	4.00	4.25	4.50
Wolf vault	3.25	3.50	3.75
Stoop vault	4.50	4.75	5.00
Straddle vault ½ turn	4.00	4.50	5.00
Front vault ½ turn outward	4.00	4.50	5.00
Rear vault ½ turn inward	4.00	4.50	5.00
TRAMPOLINE			
Tuck bounce	1.25	1.50	1.75
Pike bounce	1.50	1.75	2.00
Straddle bounce	1.50	1.75	2.00
Seat drop	1.00	1.25	1.50
Knee drop	1.50	1.75	2.00
Hands and knee drop	2.25	2.50	2.75
Knee drop—front drop	2.75	3.00	3.25
Front drop	3.25	3.50	3.75
Back drop	3.25	3.50	3.75
Half twist to back drop	3.75	4.00	4.25
Half twist to front drop	3.75	4.00	4.25
Combination front drop to back drop	4.00	4.25	4.50
Combination back drop to front drop	4.00	4.25	4.50
Seat drop ½ twist to feet	2.50	2.75	3.00

continued

Table 16.23. (continued)

TRAMPOLINE	LOWER LIMIT	AVERAGE	UPPER LIMIT
Seat drop ½ twist to seat drop	4.00	4.25	4.50
Back drop ½ twist to feet	3.25	3.50	3.75
Back drop ½ twist to seat drop	4.25	4.50	4.75
Back drop ½ twist to back drop	4.00	4.50	5.00
One-half turntable	4.00	4.50	5.00
Front somersault	4.00	4.50	5.00
Back pullover	4.00	4.50	5.00

BALANCE BEAM			
Front support mount to "L" position	2.00	2.25	2.50
Fence vault mount	2.75	3.00	3.25
Crotch seat mount	3.25	3.50	3.75
Pivot to stand from "L" position	3.00	3.25	3.50
Cast to knee scale and return to stand	2.75	3.00	3.25
Squat rise from "V" seat position	3.50	4.00	4.50
Walk	1.00	1.25	1.50
Step turn	2.00	2.25	2.50
Pirouette turn	3.00	3.25	3.50
Arabesque turn	2.00	2.25	2.50
Squat turn	2.25	2.50	2.75
Skip step	2.00	2.25	2.50
Cat leap	3.00	3.50	4.00
Leap	3.75	4.25	4.75
Squat leap	3.50	3.75	4.00
Scissor leap	3.75	4.25	4.75
Front scale	2.75	3.00	3.25
Attitude	2.25	2.50	2.75
"V" seat balance	2.25	2.75	3.25
Splits	4.50	4.75	5.00
Straddle-touch dismount	4.00	4.25	4.50
Pike-touch dismount	4.00	4.25	4.50
Front dismount	3.25	3.50	3.75
Forward roll	4.00	4.50	5.00
Back shoulder roll	4.25	4.50	4.75
Backward roll	4.00	4.50	5.00
Roundoff or cartwheel dismount	4.00	4.50	5.00

UNEVEN BARS			
German hang	2.25	2.50	2.75
Crotch seat mount	3.00	3.25	3.50
German hang with simple turn	3.25	3.50	3.75
One-leg squat rise and combination movements	1.50	1.75	2.00
Back pullover (low bar)	3.25	3.50	3.75
Knee kip-up	3.50	3.75	4.00
Swan balance	2.75	3.00	3.25
Back pullover (high bar)	3.50	3.75	4.00
Help-kip	3.75	4.00	4.25
Forward roll to knee circle dismount	3.00	3.25	3.50
Underswing dismount	3.75	4.00	4.25
Underswing dismount over low bar	4.00	4.25	4.50
Underswing dismount ¼ turn over low bar	4.25	4.50	4.75
Half turn from low bar to high bar	1.75	2.00	2.25
Back hip circle	4.00	4.25	4.50
Forward hip circle	4.00	4.50	5.00
Forward roll down ½ turn to low bar	3.50	3.75	4.00
Quarter-turn dismount over low bar	4.00	4.50	5.00

Table 16.23. (continued)

HORIZONTAL BAR	LOWER LIMIT	AVERAGE	UPPER LIMIT
German hang	1.25	1.50	1.75
German hang—full turn	2.50	2.75	3.00
Back pullover	3.00	3.25	3.50
Knee kip-up	3.00	3.25	3.50
Underswing dismount	3.25	3.50	3.75
Pick-up swing and simple back dismount	3.25	3.50	3.75
Kip-up	4.00	4.50	5.00
Drop kip	4.25	4.50	5.00
Back-hip circle	4.00	4.25	4.50
Forward hip circle	4.25	4.50	4.75
Circus kip	4.50	4.75	5.00
Back uprise	4.00	4.50	5.00
Back kip-up	4.50	4.75	5.00
Pike seat rise	4.50	4.75	5.00
Back leanover dismount	4.25	4.50	4.75
Underswing dismount ½ turn	4.25	4.50	4.75

PARALLEL BARS			
Cross-straddle seat travel	1.00	1.25	1.50
Front dismount	3.00	3.25	3.50
Rear dismount	3.00	3.25	3.50
Front dismount—half turn	4.00	4.25	4.50
Rear dismount—half turn	4.25	4.50	4.75
Single-leg cut and catch	3.50	3.75	4.00
Flank cut and catch	4.50	4.75	5.00
Straddle cut and catch	4.50	4.75	5.00
Straddle dismount	4.00	4.25	4.50
Flank mount	4.00	4.25	4.50
Forward roll in straddle position	3.75	4.00	4.25
Shoulder stand	4.25	4.50	4.75
Single-leg cut—half turn	4.25	4.50	4.75
Back uprise	4.00	4.25	4.50
Hip-kip straddle	3.75	4.00	4.25
Hip-kip-up	4.00	4.25	4.50
Drop kip	4.50	4.75	5.00
Single-leg cut and catch (center of bars)	4.50	4.75	5.00
"L" position	4.00	4.25	4.50

STILL RINGS			
German hang	.75	1.00	1.25
Bird's nest	.75	1.00	1.25
Inverted hang	1.00	1.25	1.50
Single-leg cut dismount	3.00	3.25	3.50
Single-leg straddle dismount	3.00	3.50	4.00
Double-leg cut dismount	4.00	4.50	5.00
Double-leg straddle dismount	4.00	4.50	5.00
Single-leg kip-up	4.25	4.50	4.75
Dislocate	4.50	4.75	5.00
Inlocate	4.50	4.75	5.00
Muscle-up	4.00	4.50	5.00
Double-leg kip-up	4.50	4.75	5.00
"L" position	4.00	4.25	4.50
Single-leg front lever	4.50	4.75	5.00
Beginner's cross	4.50	4.75	5.00
Shoulder stand	4.50	4.75	5.00
Swinging to tuckover dismount	3.75	4.00	4.25

continued

Table 16.23. *(continued)*

SIDE HORSE	LOWER LIMIT	AVERAGE	UPPER LIMIT
Squat mount to "L"	2.25	2.50	2.75
Feint swings	2.00	2.25	2.50
Single-leg half circles	3.00	3.50	4.00
Single-leg full circle	3.25	3.75	4.25
Double-leg half circles	3.50	4.00	4.50
Double-leg half-cut mount to single-leg half circles	4.00	4.25	4.50
Single rear dismount	3.75	4.00	4.25
Single-leg travel	4.00	4.25	4.50
Double rear dismount	4.00	4.50	5.00
Front scissors	4.00	4.50	5.00
Rear scissors	4.00	4.50	5.00
Beginner's baby moore	4.50	4.75	5.00
Baby loop mount	4.25	4.50	4.75
Hop turn travel	4.50	4.75	5.00

30-Second Volley Directions: The subject stands behind the service line, drops the ball, and begins rallying it against the front wall for 30 sec. The subject should hit all strokes from behind the service line. In case the ball fails to return past this line, the subject is allowed to step into the front court to hit the ball, but he must get back behind the line for the succeeding stroke. If the subject misses the ball, he is handed another ball by the instructor and continues rallying.

Scoring: The score is the total number of times the ball hits the front wall in 30 sec.

Racquetball

Racquetball Skills Test (Racquetball: Hensley, East, and Stillwell 1979)

Objective: To measure basic racquetball skills.

Age and Sex: College men and women but suitable also for younger students.

Reliability: Reliability coefficients using intraclass correlation in which trial-to-trial and day-to-day variances were identified ranged from .76 to .86 for the short wall volley and long wall volley for men and women.

Validity: Concurrent validity was established using instructor ratings as the criterion. Validity coefficients were .79 for the short wall volley and .86 for the long wall volley.

Equipment: A racquet; four new racquetballs; colored floor marking tape; and a stopwatch.

Court Markings: The short wall volley test uses the short line as the only court marking. The long wall volley test requires a line drawn 12 ft behind and parallel to the short line.

Short Wall Volley Test Directions: The student receives explanation and demonstration and then is given 5 min of practice in an adjacent court. When the student enters the court for testing, he or she is given an additional 1 min of practice for familiarization. The wall volley test consists of two 30-sec trials. The student begins holding two racquetballs. Two additional balls are held by a scorer located near the back wall (or the balls may be placed in the sidewall crease behind the doubles service box). To begin the test, the student drops a ball and volleys it against the front wall for 30 sec. The student must hit all strokes from behind the short line. The ball may be hit in the air or after bouncing (no restrictions on number of bounces). Any stroke may be used to keep the ball in play. If the ball does not return past the short line, the student may step into the front court to retrieve it, but must return behind the short line to hit the next stroke. If the student misses the ball, a second ball may be put into play, or the student may retrieve the missed ball and continue to volley it. If both balls are missed, he or she may get a new ball from the scorer (or along the wall), or may elect to retrieve a missed ball. Each time the volleying is interrupted, the ball must be put into play by being bounced behind the short line. Two trials are given.

Long Wall Volley Test Directions: The directions for this test are the same as for the short wall volley test, except that the student must volley from behind a restraining line drawn 12 ft behind the short line. Two extra balls are placed in the crease of the back wall. No scorer should be in the court in this test. Both tests require about 2 to 3 min per student. If only one test is to be used, the long wall volley test is recommended. Two trials are given.

Scoring: One point is given each time the ball legally hits the front wall during the 30-sec period. The score is the sum of the legal hits for the two trials. The watch is started for each trial when the student drops the ball to begin volleying.

T-score norms for college men and women are provided in Table 16.24.

Soccer

McDonald Soccer Test (Soccer: McDonald 1951)

Objective: To measure general soccer ability.

Age and Sex: College men and women.

Validity: Validity coefficients were computed for college varsity players, junior varsity players, and freshman varsity players and for the combined groups. The scores of these groups were correlated with coaches' ratings and the resulting coefficients were .94, .63, .76, and .85, respectively.

Equipment and Materials: A wall or backboard 30 ft wide and 11½ ft high (a restraining line is drawn 9 ft from the wall); a stopwatch; and three soccer balls, properly inflated and in good condition.

Directions: The two spare balls are placed 9 ft behind the restraining line. At the signal "go,"

the subject begins kicking the ball from behind the 9-ft restraining line against the wall as many times as possible in 30 sec. The subject may kick it on the fly or on the bounce. He or she may retrieve the ball using the hands or kicking it, but for the kick to count as a hit it must be made from behind the restraining line. If the ball gets out of control, the subject has the option of playing one of the spare balls instead of retrieving the loose ball. He or she may use the hands to get a spare ball in position. Four trials are allowed.

Scoring: The score is the highest number of legal kicks in the best of the four trials. Table 16.25 shows norms.

Johnson Soccer Test (Soccer: Johnson 1963)

Objective: To measure general soccer ability by a single-item test.

Age and Sex: College men.

Reliability: A reliability coefficient of .92 was found for consecutive trials.

Validity: A coefficient of correlation of .98 between test scores and ratings by the investigator was found for physical education service class students; an *r* of .94 was obtained for physical education majors; and correlations of .58, .84, and .81 were found for varsity players on the first, second, and third teams.

Table 16.24. *T*-Score Norms for Short Wall and Long Wall Volley Tests, College Men and Women[a]

T SCORE	SCORE			
	Short Wall Volley Test		Long Wall Volley Test	
	Men	Women	Men	Women
80	53	44	40	31
75	49	41	38	29
70	46	38	35	27
65	43	35	33	25
60	40	32	30	23
55	36	29	28	21
50	33	26	25	19
45	30	23	23	17
40	27	20	20	15
35	24	17	18	13
30	20	14	15	11
25	17	11	13	9
20	14	8	10	7

[a]Scores represent the sum of two trials. See text for computation of scores.
Source: L. D. Hensley, W. B. East, and J. L. Stillwell, "A Racquetball Skills Test." *Research Quarterly* 50:114–118, March 1979. AAHPERD, Publisher. Reprinted by permission.

Table 16.25. Norms for McDonald Soccer Test, College Students[a]

PERFORMANCE LEVEL	SCORE	
	Men	Women
Advanced	24 and above	18 and above
Advanced intermediate	20–23	15–17
Intermediate	11–19	7–14
Advanced beginner	8–10	2– 6
Beginner	0– 7	0– 1

[a]Based on the scores of 50 students in each category as reported by Leroy Scott at Northeast Louisiana University, Monroe, 1973. See text for description of test and scoring.

Equipment and Materials: Soccer balls; a stopwatch; and a backboard 24 ft wide and 8 ft high. This target has the same dimensions as a regulation soccer goal. A restraining line is marked 15 ft from the wall. A ball box for spare balls is located 15 ft behind the restraining line.

Directions: The subject holds a soccer ball while standing behind the restraining line. On the signal to begin, the subject kicks the ball against the backboard (either on the fly or after bouncing it). The ball is kicked against the backboard as many times as possible in 30 sec. The ball must be kicked from behind the restraining line; regulation soccer rules pertaining to kicking the ball are followed. Assistants retrieve the loose balls if the subject elects to use a spare ball instead of chasing the loose ball. Three 30-sec trials are given.

Scoring: The score is the total number of legal hits on the three trials.

Speedball

Buchanan Speedball Skill Test (Speedball: Buchanan 1942)

Objective: To measure fundamental skills used in speedball by means of four test items: lift to others, throwing and catching, dribbling and passing, and kick-ups. A complete description of this test, along with diagrams and achievement scales, may be found in Weiss and Phillips (Speedball: Weiss and Phillips 1954).

Lift to Others

A net (volleyball, tennis, or badminton) is stretched between two standards so that the top of it is 2½ ft from the ground. Standing behind a line 6 ft from the net, the subject lifts the ball with either foot and attempts to pass it so that it crosses the net and lands within a 3-ft square diagonally opposite the subject. Ten trials are given, 1 point being scored for each pass that lands in the proper square. The test is designed for partners to score one another and to alternate turns from each side of the net.

Throwing and Catching

A restraining line is drawn 6 ft from and parallel to an unobstructed wall space. On the signal "ready, go," the subject throws the ball and catches the rebound as many times as possible in 30 sec. The score is the average number of catches made in each of five trials.

Dribbling and Passing

A starting line is marked 60 yd from the end line of the field. Five Indian clubs or other objects are placed in a line 10 yd apart. At the end line, two goal areas are marked, one to the right and one to the left of the dribbling course. The goal areas are 6 yd long, and their inner borders are 4 ft to the left and 4 ft to the right of the dribbling line. The subject stands behind the starting line and on the signal "ready, go," starts dribbling down the field. The subject dribbles to the right of the first Indian club and to the left of the second, and so on. Immediately after dribbling to the right of the last club, the subject attempts to kick the ball to the left into the goal area. Ten trials are given, five to the right and five to the left. Three scores are obtained: The combined score is the time needed for the ten trials, in seconds, minus ten times the number of accurate passes to the goal on the ten trials; the dribbling score is the time of the ten trials, in seconds; and the passing score is the number of accurate passes made in ten trials.

Kick-ups

Each testing station for this test item consists of a 2-ft square, with the inner side 3 ft from the side line. A starting line is drawn 4 ft from the outside corner of the square, following an imaginary extension of the diagonal of the square. Partners are used for this test; one student throws the ball and the other kicks it. The thrower tosses the ball from behind the side line directly opposite the square from overhead so that it lands in the 2-ft square. The subject stands behind the starting line until the thrower releases the ball; at that instant the subject runs forward and executes a kick-up to himself or herself. The score is the number of successful kick-ups in ten trials.

Softball and Baseball

Generally, the tests suggested here for the AAHPERD Softball Skills Tests represent items that have been employed in previous tests. Test descriptions, diagrams, and percentile norms are provided by the AAHPERD manuals.

AAHPERD Softball Skills Test (Softball and Baseball: AAHPERD 1966a, 1966b)

Objective: To measure fundamental softball skills of boys and girls.

Validity and Reliability: Evidently, face validity is accepted. In the criteria for the Sports Skills Tests Project, it was decided that the reliability coefficients should not be less than .80 for events scored on distance and not less than .70 for events scored on the basis of accuracy and form.

Test Items:

1. Overhand throw for accuracy
2. Underhand pitching
3. Speed throw
4. Fungo hitting
5. Base running
6. Fielding ground balls
7. Softball throw for distance

The items are identical for both boys and girls except that the throwing distances for the throw for accuracy and underhand pitching are shorter for girls.

Overhand Throw for Accuracy

Directions: The subject throws a softball from a distance of 65 ft (boys) or 40 ft (girls) at a target with the following dimensions: three concentric circles with 1-in. lines, the center circle measuring 2 ft in diameter, the next circle 4 ft, and the outer circle 6 ft in diameter. The bottom of the outer circle is 3 ft from the floor. The target may be marked on a wall or, preferably (to conserve softballs), on canvas against a mat hung on the wall. (This target is the same as that used in the AAHPERD football battery.) The subject throws the ball ten times after one or two practice throws.

Scoring: The center circle counts 3 points, the second circle counts 2 points, the outer circle counts 1 point. The total points made on ten throws is the score. Balls hitting a line are given the higher point value. Table 16.26 shows norms.

Underhand Pitching

Directions: For this test the target, representing the strike zone, is rectangular. The bottom of the target is 18 in. from the floor. The outer lines are 42 in. long and 29 in. wide. An inner rectangle is drawn 30 × 17 in. A 24-in. pitching line is drawn 46 ft (boys) or 38 ft (girls) from the target. The subject takes one practice pitch, and then pitches 15 times, underhand, to the target. He or she must keep one foot on the pitching line while delivering the ball but can take a step forward. Only legal pitches are scored. A mat behind the target helps prevent damage to the softballs.

Scoring: Balls hitting the center area or its boundary line count 2 points, balls hitting the outer area count 1 point. The score is the sum of the points made on 15 pitches. Table 16.27 shows norms.

Speed Throw

Directions: The subject, holding a softball, stands behind a line drawn on the floor 9 ft from a smooth wall. On the signal "go," he or she throws the ball overhand against the wall, catches the rebound, and repeats this as rapidly as possible until 15 hits have been made against the wall. Balls that fall between the wall and the restraining line can be retrieved, but the subject must get behind the line before continuing. If the ball gets entirely away, the subject is given one new trial. A practice trial is allowed and two trials are then given for time.

Scoring: The watch is started when the first ball hits the wall and is stopped when the fifteenth throw hits the wall. The score is timed to the nearest tenth of a second and is the better of the two trials. Table 16.28 shows norms.

Table 16.26. Norms in Points for AAHPERD Softball Test, Overhand Throw for Accuracy[a]

PERCENTILE	AGE						
	10–11	12	13	14	15	16	17–18
				BOYS			
95	14	17	18	19	20	20	21
75	8	11	12	14	14	15	16
50	5	8	9	10	10	11	13
25	2	4	5	7	7	8	9
5	0	0	1	3	3	4	4
				GIRLS			
95	17	17	18	19	19	22	20
75	11	12	13	13	14	16	15
50	6	8	9	9	10	11	10
25	2	4	5	5	6	6	5
5	0	0	0	1	1	1	1

[a]Percentile scores based on age.
Source: *AAHPERD Softball Skills Test Manual for Boys (and for Girls).* Reston, Va.: AAHPERD, 1966. See text for description of scoring. Complete norms are in manual. Reprinted by permission.

Table 16.27. Norms in Points for AAHPERD Softball Test, Underhand Pitching[a]

PERCENTILE	AGE						
	10–11	12	13	14	15	16	17–18
				BOYS			
95	12	14	15	16	18	19	19
75	7	9	10	12	13	13	14
50	4	6	7	8	9	9	10
25	2	3	4	5	5	6	7
5	0	0	1	2	2	2	3
				GIRLS			
95	12	14	16	17	16	19	21
75	6	9	10	12	11	12	14
50	4	5	7	8	6	8	9
25	1	2	4	4	3	5	5
5	0	0	1	1	0	0	2

[a]Percentile scores based on age.
Source: *AAHPERD Softball Skills Test Manual for Boys (and for Girls).* Reston, Va.: AAHPERD, 1966. See text for description of scoring. Complete norms are in manual. Reprinted by permission.

Fungo Hitting

Directions: The subject selects a bat and stands behind home plate with a ball in the hand. When ready, the student tosses the ball up and tries to hit a fly ball into right field. The next ball is hit into left field. The batting attempts are alternated to right and left fields until ten balls have been hit in each direction. Every time the bat touches the ball is considered a trial. Regardless of where the ball goes, the subject must hit the next ball to the opposite (right or left) field. Practice trials are allowed to each side. Hits to a specific side must cross the baseline between second and third or first and second base.

Scoring: Two misses in a row are considered as one trial; otherwise a complete miss is not counted. A fly ball that goes to the proper field counts 2 points, a ground ball counts 1 point. No score is given for a ball that lands in the wrong field. The point value for each trial is recorded and summed

Table 16.28. Norms in Seconds for AAHPERD Softball Test, Speed Throw[a]

PERCENTILE	AGE						
	10–11	12	13	14	15	16	17–18
	BOYS						
95	16.1	15.3	14.9	13.0	13.5	12.5	12.1
75	18.6	17.6	16.8	15.6	14.9	14.5	13.9
50	21.3	19.8	18.4	17.3	16.7	16.4	15.3
25	25.7	23.1	12.2	19.5	18.9	18.8	17.6
5	34.7	29.5	26.4	25.1	22.2	23.0	21.2
	GIRLS						
95	20.1	13.8	13.0	13.0	15.6	15.8	15.0
75	25.2	19.8	19.4	17.6	18.6	18.5	17.6
50	29.8	24.1	22.7	20.7	21.1	21.4	19.8
25	35.9	29.8	27.5	24.6	25.4	26.1	23.3
5	55.2	40.8	38.5	33.5	37.4	36.9	28.9

[a]Percentile scores based on age.
Source: *AAHPERD Softball Skills Test Manual for Boys (and for Girls)*. Reston, Va.: AAHPERD, 1966. See text for description of scoring. Complete norms are in manual. Reprinted by permission.

at the end. The maximum is 40 points. Table 16.29 shows norms.

Base Running

Directions: The subject stands holding a bat in the right-hand batter's box. On the signal to hit, the subject swings at an imaginary ball, then drops the bat, and races around the bases. The bat must not be thrown or carried, and the subject must take a complete swing before beginning to run.

Each base must be touched in proper sequence. A practice and two timed trials are given.

Scoring: The watch is started on the signal "hit" and is stopped when the runner touches home plate. The better time of the two trials to the nearest tenth of a second is the score. Table 16.30 shows norms.

Fielding Ground Balls

Directions: A rectangular area 17 × 60 ft is marked off as shown in Figure 16.17. Two lines

Table 16.29. Norms in Points for AAHPERD Softball Test, Fungo Hitting[a]

PERCENTILE	AGE						
	10–11	12	13	14	15	16	17–18
	BOYS						
95	35	36	38	35	39	38	39
75	26	29	30	30	31	33	34
50	19	23	24	24	24	26	28
25	11	15	16	16	16	17	19
5	3	7	9	11	9	9	11
	GIRLS						
95	21	28	30	31	30	30	31
75	13	18	20	21	22	22	23
50	9	13	14	15	16	16	17
25	5	8	10	10	11	11	13
5	0	2	4	3	4	5	6

[a]Percentile scores based on age.
Source: *AAHPERD Softball Skills Test Manual for Boys (and for Girls)*. Reston, Va.: AAHPERD, 1966. See text for description of scoring. Complete norms are in manual. Reprinted by permission.

Table 16.30. Norms in Seconds for AAHPERD Softball Test, Base Running[a]

PERCENTILE	AGE						
	10–11	12	13	14	15	16	17–18
	BOYS						
95	12.9	12.4	11.7	11.5	11.6	11.3	11.1
75	14.3	13.7	13.2	12.7	12.5	12.1	11.9
50	15.2	14.7	14.1	13.4	13.2	12.8	12.6
25	16.2	15.7	15.1	14.2	13.9	13.6	13.2
5	18.2	17.4	16.7	15.8	15.0	15.3	14.9
	GIRLS						
95	13.1	13.4	12.6	12.7	12.9	13.2	13.6
75	14.9	14.5	13.9	13.8	14.1	14.6	14.8
50	16.0	15.3	14.8	14.8	15.0	15.5	15.7
25	17.3	16.2	16.0	15.7	16.1	16.2	16.9
5	19.9	18.2	18.0	17.8	18.1	18.4	19.2

[a]Percentile scores based on age.
Source: *AAHPERD Softball Skills Test Manual for Boys (and for Girls).* Reston, Va.: AAHPERD, 1966. See text for description of scoring. Complete norms are in manual. Reprinted by permission.

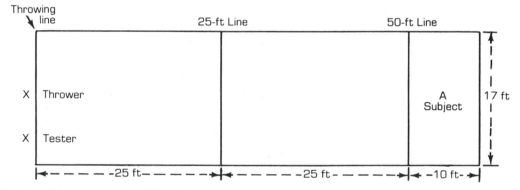

Figure 16.17. Diagram for AAHPERD fielding ground balls test (Reproduced from *AAHPERD Softball Skills Test Manual.* Reston, Va.: AAHPERD, 1966. Used by permission)

are drawn across the area 25 and 50 ft from the front, or throwing, line. This results in three areas. The subject stands in the 17- × 10-ft area at the end of the rectangle. The thrower stands behind the throwing line with a basket of ten balls. On the signal to begin, the thrower begins throwing ground balls at exactly 5-sec intervals into the first 17- × 25-ft zone. The throw is made in an overhand manner with good speed. Each throw must hit the ground inside the first area for at least one bounce. Some variation in direction is desirable, but the thrower should not try to make the subject miss. A throw that does not land as specified should be redone. The subject attempts to field each ball cleanly, holds it momentarily, then tosses it aside. The subject starts behind the 50-ft line, but thereafter he or she may field the ball anywhere in back of the 25-ft line. A practice trial and then 20 trials for score are given.

Scoring: The scoring is on a pass–fail basis. Each throw scores 1 point or zero. The maximum score is 20. Table 16.31 shows norms.

Softball Throw for Distance

Directions: A football field marked in 5-yd intervals serves nicely for this event. The subject throws a softball from within a 6-ft restraining area, which is drawn parallel to the 5-yd field markers. The ball's point of contact is marked with a metal or wooden marking stake. Three trials are given. If the second or third throw is farther, the marker is moved. It is advised that a group of approximately five students be tested together, and after completing the third throw, each subject jogs out and stands at his or her marker while the measurements are being taken. This reduces the possibility of the wrong score being recorded.

Table 16.31. Norms in Points for AAHPERD Softball Test, Fielding Ground Balls[a]

PERCENTILE	AGE						
	10–11	12	13	14	15	16	17–18
	BOYS						
95	19	20	20	20	20	20	20
75	17	18	18	18	18	19	19
50	14	15	15	15	15	17	17
25	10	12	12	10	11	13	14
5	4	6	6	6	7	8	9
	GIRLS						
95	18	20	20	20	20	20	20
75	15	18	18	18	18	19	19
50	11	14	16	16	16	17	17
25	8	9	12	12	13	14	14
5	3	5	8	8	9	8	9

[a]Percentile scores based on age.
Source: *AAHPERD Softball Skills Test Manual for Boys (and for Girls)*. Reston, Va.: AAHPERD, 1966. See text for description of scoring. Complete norms are in manual. Reprinted by permission.

Scoring: The distance to the nearest foot of the best of three trials is the score. The measurement is made at right angles from the point of landing to the restraining line (the tape is not swung in an arc for each throw). Tables 16.32 and 16.33 show norms.

Elrod Fielding and Throwing Test (Softball and Baseball: Elrod 1969)

Objective: To measure skill in fielding grounders and throwing accurately to first base.

Sex and Age Level: Appropriate for both sexes for junior and senior high school and college students.

Validity and Reliability: The validity coefficient was .67 with judges' ratings as the criterion. The test–retest correlation was .69 for reliability.

Facilities, Equipment, and Materials: A regulation softball diamond or any area sufficiently large to simulate a triangular area of home plate to shortstop position to first base; and a target with a 6- × 6-ft frame covered with canvas, the canvas marked with a 3- × 3-ft square in the center; regulation softballs; and a bat or fungo.

Directions: The target is placed upright at first base. The subject stands at a distance from home plate and first base that corresponds to the normal shortstop position. The tester hits ten ground balls, three to the subject's left, three to the right, and four directly at him or her. These are done in random order. The subject fields each grounder and throws to the target area at first base. Imme-diately after the throws or if the grounder is missed, the subject returns to position for the next trial.

Scoring: Two separate scores may be obtained, or they can be combined into one score.

Fielding: Two points are awarded for each ball cleanly fielded, 1 point is given if the ball is knocked down but is then thrown to first base within a 5-sec period from the time the ball is batted, and zero points are given if the subject misses the ball or knocks it down but cannot make the play within the 5-sec period. A perfect score for ten trials is 20.

Throwing: Three points are given for a ball that hits within the 3- × 3-ft center area (or lines that outline the square), 2 points are given if the ball hits the target outside the 3- × 3-ft center area, and 1 point is given if the ball hits anywhere on the target on the first bounce. A perfect score for ten trials is 30.

A perfect score for the combined fielding and throwing score is 50. Tentative norms for the combined test are shown in Table 16.34.

Additional Pointers:

1. The subject is informed about the 5-sec time period. The tester explains that in a game it is sometimes possible to throw a runner out even when the ball is not fielded cleanly.

2. The 5-sec time period is counted by an assistant or by the tester.

3. The target may be held by assistants or may be braced so that it stands by itself.

Table 16.32. Norms for AAHPERD Softball Test, Softball Throw for Distance[a]

| | AGE | | | | | | | | | | | | |
| | 10–11 | | 12 | | 13 | | 14 | | 15 | | 16 | | 17–18 | |
PERCENTILE	ft	m	ft	m	ft	m	ft	m	ft	m	ft	m	ft	m
							BOYS							
95	154	47.0	163	49.7	185	56.4	208	63.4	231	70.4	229	69.8	229	69.8
75	118	36.0	135	41.2	154	47.0	178	54.3	187	57.0	202	61.6	207	63.1
50	103	31.4	118	36.0	135	41.2	154	47.0	167	50.9	183	55.8	188	57.3
25	91	27.7	102	31.1	117	35.7	137	41.8	148	45.1	164	50.0	169	51.5
5	62	18.9	76	23.2	97	29.6	113	34.5	119	36.3	140	42.7	140	42.7
							GIRLS							
95	99	30.2	113	34.5	133	40.6	126	38.4	127	38.7	121	36.9	120	36.6
75	68	20.7	89	27.1	94	28.7	99	30.2	97	29.6	94	28.7	93	28.4
50	55	16.8	70	21.3	76	23.2	82	25.0	77	23.5	79	24.1	80	24.4
25	43	13.1	55	16.8	62	18.9	66	20.1	64	19.5	63	19.2	66	20.1
5	31	9.5	37	11.3	43	13.1	43	13.1	49	14.9	45	13.7	50	15.2

[a]Percentile scores based on age.
Source: *AAHPERD Softball Skills Test Manual for Boys (and for Girls)*. Reston, Va.: AAHPERD, 1966. See text for description of scoring. Complete norms are in manual. Reprinted by permission.

Table 16.33. Norms for Softball Throw, Elementary School Children[a]

PERCENTILE	SEX	AGE											
		6		7		8		9		10		11	
		ft	m	ft	m	ft	m	ft	m	ft	m	ft	m
99	Boys	69	21.0	93	28.4	115	35.1	121	36.9	123	37.5	130	39.6
	Girls	39	11.9	72	21.9	58	17.7	102	31.1	101	30.8	90	27.4
90	Boys	60	18.3	74	22.6	88	26.9	101	30.8	110	33.5	115	35.1
	Girls	38	11.6	41	12.5	49	14.9	66	20.1	79	24.1	86	26.2
80	Boys	53	16.2	66	20.1	81	24.7	95	29.0	102	31.1	110	33.5
	Girls	28	8.5	35	10.7	45	13.7	59	18.0	65	19.8	80	24.4
70	Boys	50	15.2	62	18.9	75	22.9	90	27.4	96	29.3	103	31.4
	Girls	25	7.6	31	9.5	42	12.8	53	16.2	58	17.7	76	23.2
60	Boys	43	13.1	60	18.3	71	21.6	85	25.9	92	28.1	98	29.9
	Girls	24	7.3	28	8.5	39	11.9	49	14.9	53	16.2	70	21.3
50	Boys	40	12.2	54	16.5	65	19.8	81	24.7	88	26.8	95	28.9
	Girls	23	7.0	27	8.2	36	11.0	45	13.7	51	15.5	62	18.9
40	Boys	34	10.4	49	14.9	62	18.9	75	22.9	85	25.9	90	27.4
	Girls	20	6.1	24	7.3	32	9.8	42	12.8	50	15.2	60	18.3
30	Boys	31	9.5	45	13.7	58	17.7	70	21.3	80	24.4	85	25.9
	Girls	17	5.2	22	6.7	30	9.1	39	11.9	46	14.0	54	16.5
20	Boys	29	8.8	42	12.8	52	15.9	63	19.2	72	22.0	73	22.3
	Girls	15	4.6	20	6.1	28	8.5	34	10.4	41	12.5	49	14.9
10	Boys	28	8.5	36	11.0	46	14.0	54	16.5	66	20.1	65	19.8
	Girls	13	4.0	17	5.2	25	7.6	26	7.9	36	11.0	41	12.5
N	Boys	27	8.2	116	35.4	126	38.4	203	61.9	149	45.4	50	15.2
	Girls	31	9.5	101	30.8	113	34.5	100	30.5	82	25.0	32	9.8

[a]Percentile scores based on age. The best score of two, recorded by D. H. Hardin and J. Ramirez, University of Texas at El Paso, 1972.

Table 16.34. *T*-Scale Norms for Elrod Fielding and Throwing Test and Batting Test[a]

T SCORE	FIELDING AND THROWING RAW SCORE	BATTING RAW SCORE
80	48–50	38–40
75	44–47	35–37
70	41–43	33–34
65	37–40	30–32
60	34–36	28–29
55	30–33	25–27
50	27–29	23–24
45	23–26	20–22
40	20–22	18–19
35	16–19	15–17
30	13–15	13–14
25	9–12	10–12
20	6– 8	8– 9

[a]Norms based on 100 high school boys. See text for description of scoring.

4. Any ball that cannot be fielded owing to a bad bounce or that is poorly hit does not count and the trial is taken over.

Elrod Batting Test (Softball and Baseball: Elrod 1969)

Objective: To measure skill in batting pitched balls.

Sex and Age Level: Boys in high school and college. The scoring zones could be adjusted for girls and for younger boys.

Validity and Reliability: The validity coefficient was .61 with judges' ratings. A reliability coefficient of .57 was reported on test–retest.

Facilities, Equipment, and Materials: A softball diamond with at least foul lines, home plate, and pitching rubber indicated; a stake and 300 ft ball of cord; approximately three dozen small markers, such as tongue depressors; regulation softballs and bats; and ribbon or tape to mark 80-ft intervals on cord.

Directions: A stake is driven behind home plate and serves as a pivot point. The cord is attached to the stake and is stretched from home plate to the outfield. One ribbon or a piece of tape or other type of marker is attached to the cord 80 ft from home plate, and another is attached 80 ft beyond the first.

A tester or an assistant who can consistently pitch balls across the plate pitches to the subject for ten trials. The subject attempts to hit the ball into the outfield. Each swing counts as a trial, but the subject does not have to swing at a bad pitch. Spotters place a marker at the spot at which each hit lands in fair territory.

Scoring: When the subject has had ten trials, an assistant grabs the far end of the cord and walks from one foul line to the other. As the outstretched cord passes over each marker, the point value for that marker is called out. Two points are given for a ball that hits in the first 80-ft zone, 3 points for a ball beyond that zone, and 4 points for a ball beyond that zone. One point is given for a foul ball. A swing and a miss counts as a trial and receives a zero. The maximum score for the ten trials is 40. Tentative norms are shown in Table 16.34.

Additional Pointers:

1. To facilitate testing and prevent the batter from being too selective, a trial is counted if the subject allows two pitches to go by in the strike zone without swinging.

2. The stake and cord method greatly facilitates testing in eliminating the need for elaborate field markings.

3. The use of a pitcher does detract from objectivity, but the only way batting skill can be tested accurately is for a pitched ball to be hit.

Swimming and Diving

Hewitt constructed achievement scales for college men (Swimming and Diving: Hewitt 1948) and for high school boys and girls (Swimming and Diving: Hewitt 1949) for the purposes of classifying students into homogeneous swimming groups and measuring improvement in performance.

College Swimming Achievement Scales

15-Minute Endurance Swim

The subject swims for 15 min, counting the number of lengths of the pool covered. The lengths are converted into yards. No score is given if the subject fails to swim for 15 min.

20- and 25-Yard Underwater Swims

From a regulation start, using any type of stroke, the subject swims the entire distance underwater. The score is time to the nearest tenth of a second.

25- and 50-Yard Swims Using Crawl, Breast, and Back-Crawl Strokes

From a regulation start, the subject swims the distances using each of the strokes. The score is time to the nearest tenth of a second.

50-Yard Glide Relaxation Swims Using Elementary Back Stroke, Side Stroke, and Breast Stroke

The score for each of these events is the number of strokes taken to cover the distance. All starts are made in the water.

High School Swimming Achievement Scales

50-Yard Crawl

The subject starts from a racing dive. The score is time to the nearest second.

25-Yard Flutter Kick With Polo Ball

The subject holds on to the side with one hand and the ball with the other until given the signal to go. He or she then pushes off and kicks to the other end (25 yd) of the pool. The score is time to the nearest tenth of a second.

25-Yard Glide Relaxation Swims Using Elementary Back Stroke, Side Stroke, and Breast Stroke

Same testing procedures as in the college test except for the distance. The score is the number of strokes taken.

Rosentsweig's Revision of the Fox Swimming Test (Swimming and Diving: Rosentsweig 1968)

Objective: To measure form and power on five basic strokes of swimming.

Age Level: Could be used in junior high school through college.

Sex: Satisfactory for boys and girls.

Reliability: The test–retest reliability was found to be satisfactory for each of the five strokes, with rs ranging from .89 to .96.

Validity: While face validity is acceptable for this test, Rosentsweig reported rs of .63 to .83 between the best power scores and the judges' ratings. These correlations were not intended as a validity measure.

Equipment and Materials: Marking tape and string stretched the length of the pool and marked off in 1-yd units beginning 8 ft from the shallow end. The first marker is the starting line, and the tape markers are stapled to the string.

Directions: A partner stands to the side of the performer and, with one of the forearms, cradles the legs of the performer up to the surface of the water. The shoulders of the performer are lined up on the first deck marker (starting line). The performer is allowed to scull or float in the starting position until taking the first arm stroke. If a kick is made prior to the first arm stroke, the trial is immediately stopped. The performer takes 12 arm strokes, or six cycles, depending on the type of stroke measured. The teacher rates the performer on a 5-point scale (A–F) and then notes distance covered in the 12 strokes by again using the shoulders as a reference point with the distance marker.

Scoring: The two measures of form and distance are combined into a grade for each student.

Tennis

Overhead Smash Test (Tennis: B. L. Johnson 1972)

Objective: To measure the effectiveness of the overhead smash stroke.

Age Level: Junior high school through college age level.

Sex: Satisfactory for both boys and girls.

Reliability: An r of .96 was reported by Stan Johnson, Northeast Louisiana University, Monroe, 1973.

Objectivity: An r of .98 was reported by Mike Recio and Charles Prestidge, Northeast Louisiana University, Monroe, 1972.

Validity: Since the overhead smash is one of the most vital shots in tennis, this test is accepted for its face validity.

Equipment and Materials: The tennis and badminton set-up machine[5]; several tennis balls; and a tennis racket.

Directions: The tennis set-up machine is placed in a position where the ball will fall at the junction of the center service line and the service line. The subject assumes the proper position for the smash and strikes the ball as it drops from the top pulley of the machine (Figure 16.18). The subject is allowed three practice trials, and then ten trials are administered for the test. The student tries to smash the ball across the net and into the singles playing court.

Scoring: One point is given for each successful smash into the opposing playing court. The maximum score is 10 points. Table 16.35 shows norms for college men.

---

5. The Tennis Set-Up Machine, Model M4, patent pending 1972, by B. L. Johnson, Corpus Christi State University, Corpus Christi, TX 78412. The tennis set-up machine is an inexpensive device used for testing and training purposes in the sport of tennis. It provides for overhead stroke practice and has pitch-out capabilities. Models may be either automatic or manual.

Figure 16.18. Tennis Set-Up Machine, Model M4, shown in use indoors with a shag net. This machine was invented by B. L. Johnson of Corpus Christi State University, Corpus Christi, Tex. Appendix J provides plans for such a machine

Table 16.35. Raw Score Norms for Overhead Smash Test with Johnson's Tennis and Badminton Set-Up Machine, College Men[a]

PERFORMANCE LEVEL	SCORE
Advanced	9–10
Advanced intermediate	7– 8
Intermediate	5– 6
Advanced beginner	3– 4
Beginner	0– 2

[a]Based on the scores of a limited number of college men as reported by Mike Recio and Charles Prestidge, Northeast Louisiana University, Monroe, 1972.

Additional Pointers:

1. Trials in which the subject fails to execute satisfactory form and force for a smash are not counted and must be repeated.

2. The test can be administered on a backboard with the net line drawn. This procedure is especially recommended for practice sessions during the class period.

3. If a repeated trial is also incorrect, the trial is scored as zero.

Hewitt's Revision of the Dyer Backboard Tennis Test (Tennis: Hewitt 1965)

Objective: To classify beginning and advanced tennis players.

Age and Sex: May be used for both sexes at the college and high school levels.

Reliability: With use of the test–retest method, the reliability coefficients were .93 for the advanced players and .82 for the beginners.

Validity: Rank order correlations were computed using the results of round-robin tournaments and scores made on the Hewitt revision test for beginning and advanced tennis players. Rhos were converted to *r*s and were found to range from .68 to .73 for the beginner classes and .84 to .89 for the advanced classes.

Equipment and Materials: A wall 20 ft high and 20 ft wide; a tennis racket; a stopwatch; a basket; at least a dozen new tennis balls; and masking tape for marking lines.

Directions: A line 1 in. wide is marked on the wall at a height of 3 ft and 20 ft long to simulate the net. A restraining line 20 ft long and 1 in. wide is marked 20 ft from the wall. The subject starts with two tennis balls behind the 20-ft restraining line and serves the ball against the wall. Any type of serve may be used. The watch is started when the served ball hits above the net line on the wall. The subject then rallies from behind the restraining line against the wall, using any type of stroke. If the ball should get away from the student, he or she may take another ball from the basket. Each time a new ball is taken, the subject must serve the ball again. Hitting continues for 30 sec. Three trials are given.

Scoring: One point is given each time the ball hits above the 3-ft net line. No score is counted when the subject steps over the restraining line or when the ball is hit below the net line. Balls that hit the line are counted. The average of the three trials is the score.

Hewitt's Tennis Achievement Test (Tennis: Hewitt 1966)

Hewitt constructed an achievement test for measuring the service and forehand and backhand drives. Beginners, advanced, and varsity tennis players were used in validating the test and establishing achievement scales.

Validity coefficients ranged from .52 to .93, and reliability coefficients ranged from .75 to .94. It was found that the service placement test had the highest predictive value for the varsity players; the revised Dyer wall test had the highest validity coefficient for the advanced players; and the speed of service test had the highest validity coefficient for beginners.

Hewitt recommended the revised Dyer test as being the best test because of its simplicity and ease of administration. Its validity coefficients were .87, .84, and .73 for varsity, advanced, and beginning players, respectively. If no wall is available, Hewitt suggested that the Hewitt Tennis Achievement Test be used.

The service placement test, the speed of service test, and the forehand and backhand drive tests are briefly described here. Complete descriptions are provided in the original reference.

Service Placement Test

Court Markings: The right service court is marked as shown in Figure 16.19. Point values from 1 to 6 are also shown in the figure. A quarter-inch rope is stretched above the net at a height of 7 ft.

Directions: After a demonstration by the instructor and a 10-min warm-up on another court, the subject serves ten balls into the marked right service courts. He or she must serve the ball between the net and the rope.

Scoring: The point value for the zone in which each ball hits is the score. The final score is the points for all ten trials. Balls going over the rope are given a score of zero. Table 16.36 shows a scoring scale for college students.

Speed of Service Test

Hewitt found that the distance the ball bounced after it hit the service court was a good indication of the speed of service. The type of serve had little effect on this distance.

Court Markings: Four zones are formed. Zone 1 is the backcourt area to the baseline; zone 2 is the area 10 ft beyond the baseline; zone 3 consists of the area from 10 to 20 ft beyond the baseline; and zone 4 is the area 20 ft beyond the baseline, or the fence in most courts (Figure 16.19).

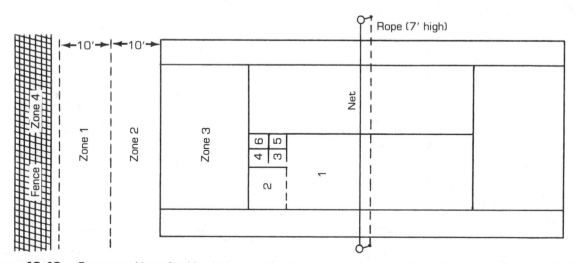

Figure 16.19. Court markings for Hewitt's service placement and speed of service tests (Redrawn from J. E. Hewitt, Hewitt's Tennis Achievement Test. *Research Quarterly* 37:231–240, May 1966, AAHPERD Publishers, by permission)

Table 16.36. Scoring Scale for Hewitt's Service Placement Test, College Students[a]

PERFORMANCE LEVEL	SCORE	
	Men	Women
Advanced	20–60	14–60
Advanced intermediate	16–19	10–13
Intermediate	7–15	4– 9
Advanced beginner	3– 6	1– 3
Beginner	0– 2	0

[a]Based on a limited number of beginning students in tennis, as reported by Stan Johnson, Northeast Louisiana University, Monroe, 1973.

Directions: This test can be conducted at the same time as the service placement test. For each of the good-serve placements (in other words, those that hit in the service court), the zone in which the ball hits on the second bounce is noted.

Scoring: The point values for zones 1, 2, 3, and 4 are 1 point, 2 points, 3 points, and 4 points, respectively.

Forehand and Backhand Drive Tests

Court Markings: With the service line as one of the lines for the test, three chalk lines are drawn 4½ ft apart between the service line and the baseline. Figure 16.20 shows the court markings and the point value for each zone. A quarter-inch rope is stretched above the net at a height of 7 ft.

Directions: The subject stands at the center mark of the baseline. With a basket of balls, the instruc-

tor takes a position across the net at the intersection of the center line and the service line. The instructor hits five practice balls to the student just beyond the service court. Then ten trials are given for the forehand and ten for the backhand. The student may choose which ten balls to hit forehand and which to hit backhand. The student tries to hit the ball between the net and the rope so that the ball goes deep into the court. The same instructor should hit to all students to standardize the testing as much as possible. A ball-throwing machine, if available, would be very effective. Net balls are repeated.

Scoring: The point values for the scoring zones in which the forehand and backhand trials hit are recorded. Balls that pass over the rope receive half the point value of the respective zone.

The ARTST Tennis Serve Test (Tennis: Avery, Richardson, and Jackson 1979)

Objective: To measure both placement and speed and spin of the tennis serve.

Age and Sex: College men and women of beginning and intermediate playing skill. The test could be given to younger students of both sexes.

Reliability: Cronbach alpha coefficients ranged from .64 to .81 for beginning and intermediate players.

Validity: Construct validity was established using the known difference-in-groups procedure. Intermediate players scored significantly higher than beginning players.

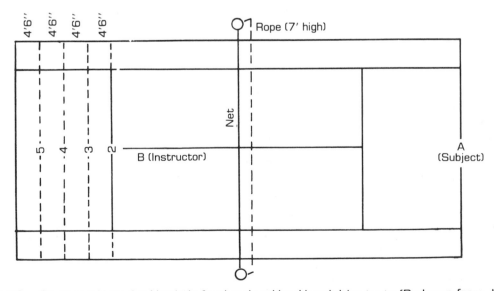

Figure 16.20. Court markings for Hewitt's forehand and backhand drive tests (Redrawn from J. E. Hewitt, Hewitt's Tennis Achievement Test. *Research Quarterly* 37:231–240, May 1966, AAHPERD Publishers, by permission)

Equipment and Materials: Tennis balls, preferably new or nearly new for uniformity of bounce; a racket; chalk to mark the court; scoresheets; and a court.

Court Markings: The tennis court with net is marked as in Figure 16.21. The lines for measuring speed and spin extend sideward at 45-degree angles for 12 ft, and the last line is 9 ft in back of the baseline.

Directions: Each student is given two practice serves to the right service court and two to the left prior to the test. The student then serves 20 trials in the following order:

Five trials to the left half of the right service court

Five trials to the right half of the right service court

Five trials to the left half of the left service court

Five trials to the right half of the left service court

A trial consists of two attempts to serve the ball to the specified half of the proper service court. If the first attempt lands within the proper court, it is scored according to placement when it hits and its speed and spin—which are measured by where the ball hits on the second bounce.

If the first attempt does not land in the proper court, a second service is given (as in a game); if this ball lands in the proper court it is scored

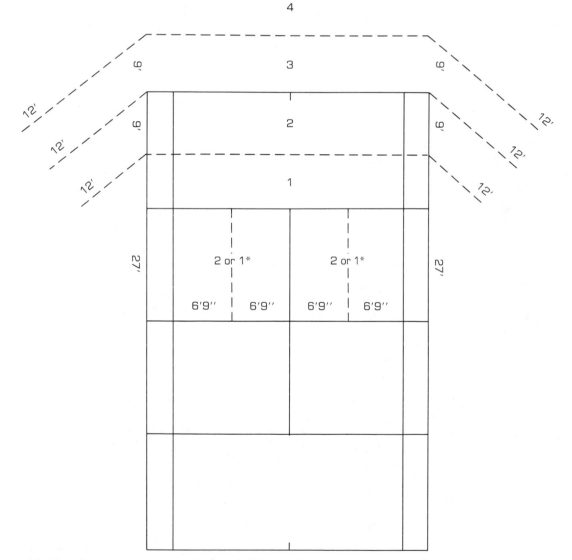

Figure 16.21.   Court markings and scoring for the ARTST tennis serve test (Reproduced from C. A. Avery, P. A. Richardson, and A. W. Jackson, "A Practical Tennis Serve Test: Measurement of Skill Under Simulated Game Conditions." *Research Quarterly* 50:554–564, December 1979, AAHPERD Publishers, by permission)

for both placement and speed and spin. Foot faults are considered attempts, and all lets are repeated.

Scoring: On each successful trial, two scores are given, one for placement and one for speed and spin, as follows:

Placement: Each service court is divided into a right and a left half (Figure 16.21). When a performer is serving to a designated half and it lands in that half, 2 points are given for placement. If it lands in the other half of that service court, 1 point is given for placement. If the student fails in two attempts, a score of zero is given for both placement and speed and spin.

Speed and Spin: The zone in which the ball hits on the second bounce is given the point value for that zone for the speed and spin score (zones 1, 2, 3, and 4 in Figure 16.21). The ball must land in the proper court on the first bounce before it can be given any points for speed and spin. If the ball should bounce a second time in the service court, 1 point is given. A ball that hits on the line is given the higher point value.

The angled lines extending sideward allow for giving credit for a spin or slice serve. A spin or slice serve does not have to travel as far after the first bounce as a flat serve to get the same score.

One scorer should stand directly to one side of the service courts, even with the back service line, to score the first hit or to yell "fault" or "let." The scorer gives a successful attempt a score of 1 or 2 according to the designated half for placement. Another scorer stands behind the baseline near the center mark and calls out the appropriate point value for the second bounce (speed and spin).

On each trial the zone score is added to the placement score. The maximum score for the test is 120. The test requires about 8 min for each student. Abbreviated norms are provided in Table 16.37. The original reference contains both *T* scores and percentile ranks.

Volleyball

The volleyball set-up machine[6] (Figure 16.22) is an inexpensive device used for testing and training in the sport of volleyball. It can be used as the thrower on the AAHPERD volleyball passing test and set-up test. It is also an ideal set-up device for spiking tests, since each set-up delivery is identical.

AAHPERD Volleyball Skills Test (Volleyball: AAHPERD 1969)

Objective: To measure the fundamental skills of volleyball by means of four tests: volleying, serving, passing, and set-ups.

Volleying

This test is essentially the same as the Brady–Wally volley except that the line on the wall is 11 ft above the floor and is 5 ft long, and vertical lines extend upward from each end of the line 3 or 4 ft. The subject volleys the ball against the wall as many times as possible in 1 min. A score of 50 is maximum. Table 16.38 shows norms.

---

6. Volleyball Set-Up Machine, Patent Pending 1972, by B. L. Johnson, Corpus Christi State University, Corpus Christi, TX 78412.

Table 16.37. Abbreviated Percentile Norms for the ARTST Tennis Serve Test

PERCENTILE	BEGINNERS		INTERMEDIATE	
	Males	Females	Males	Females
95	88	81	103	93
75	78	68	90	82
50	68	59	79	71
25	56	48	67	63
5	36	31	47	48

Source: Partial norms abstracted from C. A. Avery, P. A. Richardson, and A. W. Jackson, "A Practical Tennis Serve Test: Measurement of Skill Under Simulated Game Conditions." *Research Quarterly* 50:554–564, December 1979, AAHPERD Publishers, by permission.

Figure 16.22. Volleyball Set-Up Machine, Model M-2, for the spike test. This machine was invented by B. L. Johnson of Corpus Christi State University, Corpus Christi, Tex. Appendix J provides plans for such a machine

Serving

The server stands at "X" in Figure 16.23 and serves across the net ten times. The score is the total points made according to the value of the zone in which the serve lands (Figure 16.23). For children below 12 years of age, the serving line should be 20 ft from the net instead of 30. Table 16.39 shows norms.

Passing

A thrower (T in Figure 16.24) tosses a high pass to the passer (P in diagram) who attempts to execute a legal volleyball pass over the rope into the marked area. Twenty trials are given alternately to the right and left. The trial counts but no points are given for any ball that hits the rope or net or falls outside the target area. The maximum score is 20. Table 16.40 shows norms.

Set-up

A thrower (T in Figure 16.25) tosses a high pass to the subject (S in diagram) who executes a set-up over the rope and into the target area. Two subjects can be tested simultaneously, one setting up to the right and the other to the left. Ten trials are given to the right and ten to the left. Any ball that touches the rope or net or does not hit the target receives zero for the trial. Any throw from T that does not fall into the 6- × 5-ft area is to be repeated. The maximum score is 20. Table 16.41 shows norms.

Table 16.38. Norms in Points for AAHPERD Volleyball Test, Volleying[a]

PERCENTILE	AGE						
	10–11	12	13	14	15	16	17–18
	BOYS						
95	24	31	35	39	42	44	45
75	13	19	24	29	32	34	40
50	7	13	17	21	25	26	32
25	3	7	9	13	17	18	20
5	0	2	3	5	6	11	11
	GIRLS						
95	21	29	31	32	37	40	40
75	6	13	15	17	18	22	23
50	2	6	8	10	11	12	12
25	0	2	3	5	6	6	6
5	0	0	0	0	1	2	2

[a]Percentile scores based on age.
Source: *AAHPERD Volleyball Skills Test Manual for Boys and Girls*. Reston, Va.: AAHPERD, 1969. Complete norms are in manual. Reprinted by permission.

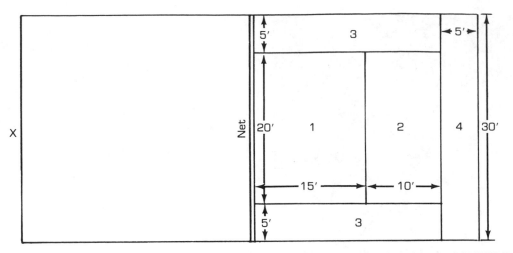

Figure 16.23. Point zones for the AAHPERD volleyball serving test (Reproduced from *AAHPERD Volleyball Skills Test Manual*. Reston, Va.: AAHPERD, 1969, by permission)

Table 16.39. Norms in Points for AAHPERD Volleyball Test, Serving[a]

PERCENTILE	AGE						
	10–11	12	13	14	15	16	17–18
	BOYS						
95	29	31	32	34	36	37	37
75	22	23	24	25	28	29	30
50	16	16	19	20	22	23	24
25	11	11	13	15	16	17	17
5	4	5	5	8	9	10	11
	GIRLS						
95	24	26	26	28	30	31	32
75	15	16	17	20	20	21	21
50	10	11	11	13	14	16	16
25	5	5	5	7	9	11	11
5	0	0	0	1	2	4	4

[a]Percentile scores based on age.
Source: *AAHPERD Volleyball Skills Test Manual for Boys and Girls*. Reston, Va.: AAHPERD, 1969. Complete norms are in manual. Reprinted by permission.

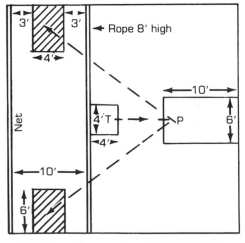

Figure 16.24. Diagram for AAHPERD volleyball passing test. P, passer; T, thrower (Reproduced from *AAHPERD Volleyball Skills Test Manual*. Reston, Va.: AAHPERD, 1969, by permission)

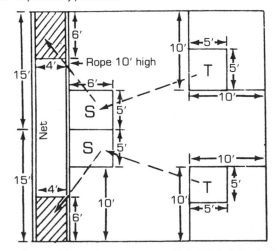

Figure 16.25. Diagram for AAHPERD volleyball set-up test. T, thrower; S, subject (Reproduced from *AAHPERD Volleyball Skills Test Manual*. Reston, Va.: AAHPERD, 1969, by permission)

Table 16.40. Norms in Points for AAHPERD Volleyball Test, Passing[a]

PERCENTILE	AGE						
	10–11	12	13	14	15	16	17–18
	BOYS						
95	12	14	16	17	17	17	17
75	7	10	12	13	13	13	13
50	3	6	8	10	10	11	11
25	1	2	4	6	6	7	8
5	0	0	1	2	2	2	2
	GIRLS						
95	10	12	12	13	13	14	15
75	5	6	7	8	8	8	9
50	2	3	4	5	5	6	6
25	0	1	1	2	2	3	3
5	0	0	0	0	0	0	0

[a]Percentile scores based on age.
Source: *AAHPERD Volleyball Skills Test Manual for Boys and Girls.* Reston, Va.: AAHPERD, 1969. Complete norms are in manual. Reprinted by permission.

Table 16.41. Norms in Points for AAHPERD Volleyball Test, Set-up[a]

PERCENTILE	AGE						
	10–11	12	13	14	15	16	17–18
	BOYS						
95	10	14	16	16	16	17	17
75	6	9	11	11	11	12	13
50	4	6	7	7	7	7	9
25	2	4	4	4	4	4	6
5	0	1	1	1	1	1	2
	GIRLS						
95	11	13	14	14	14	15	15
75	5	7	8	9	9	9	10
50	3	4	5	5	5	6	6
25	1	2	2	2	2	3	3
5	0	0	0	0	0	1	1

[a]Percentile scores based on age.
Source: *AAHPERD Volleyball Skills Test Manual for Boys and Girls.* Reston, Va.: AAHPERD, 1969. Complete norms are in manual. Reprinted by permission.

FINDINGS AND CONCLUSIONS FROM SPORTS SKILLS MEASUREMENT AND RESEARCH

The literature concerning sports skills generally pertains to methodology used in sports skills acquisition and measurement or to analysis of performance in sports. Needless to say, countless studies have been conducted that could conceivably fall under the heading of sports skills. The following is a sampling of research done since 1960 in this field. The discussion follows the divisions of the bibliography.

Archery

Zabik and Jackson concluded that the modified Chicago round and the modified Flint round were reliable measures of archery achievement of college men. Furthermore, the relationship between the two rounds was sufficiently low to warrant use of both measures. Eckert and Wendt found no relationship between kinesthetic perception of a comfortable pull and the actual pull required to comfortably draw the bow.

Barnett and Stanicek compared group conference with goal setting to group conference only on achievement in archery. The goal-setting group achieved significantly higher scores. Shifflett and Schuman constructed and evaluated a criterion-referenced test for beginning archery. Each arrow was considered a trial; the trial scored zero if the arrow got a score of 1 or 3 and it scored 1 if the arrow got a score of 5 or higher. The validity estimate was .73 and reliability estimates were k = .73 and P = .87. Misclassifications of masters and nonmasters were minimized.

Badminton

In a study by Burdeshaw, Spragens, and Weis, evidence failed to support the concept that a basic skills course in a specific sport facilitates subsequent performance. The study involved two groups of college women of low motor ability. One group participated in badminton while the control group took part in another sport. Both groups then received badminton instruction. There was no difference in performance despite the prior badminton experience of the one group. Gray and Brumbach reported that daylight viewing of loop films of specific skills appeared to accelerate learning in beginning badminton, although the learning advantage was not maintained as the subjects continued.

Basketball

Hopkins (1977) utilized factor analysis in an attempt to define the domain of basketball-playing ability and to identify skills tests that would measure this domain. The dimensions delineated were shooting, passing, jumping, and movement with and without the ball. Hopkins recommended the speed pass, dribble, jump and reach, and front shot from the AAHPERD battery as quick and objective measures of basketball skills. In a later study, Hopkins (1979) analyzed the relationship of 21 basketball skills tests to successful performance as determined by judges' ratings. Through discriminant analysis, the following six items were recommended to objectively measure basketball-playing ability and discriminate between successful and unsuccessful performers: speed pass, zig-zag run, free jump, side step, front shot, and zig-zag dribble. Gaunt also investigated the factor structure of basketball skills with high school girls as subjects. The multidimensional model was best represented by dribbling, explosive leg strength, lay-up shooting, and passing. The January 1983 *Journal of Physical Education, Recreation, and Dance* contains several articles on tests for offen-

sive and defensive techniques, adaptations, and conditioning for basketball.

Field Hockey

Chapman constructed an indoor field hockey test that is easily administered and requires little space and equipment. The timed test requires the player to send the ball into and out of a circular target by tapping it with the stick. Satisfactory reliability (.89) and content, construct, concurrent, and predictive validity were demonstrated.

Football

Various characteristics of football players have been studied including psychologic factors (Miller 1978), somatotype and body composition (Carter 1968; Smith and Byrd 1976), power (Costill et al. 1968), endurance (Wilmore and Haskell 1972), and response time (Sells 1977). McDavid reported on the validity of a test battery for predicting potential for playing football. The test battery, originally developed by McDavid and Slay (Slay 1980), includes measures of response time, agility, speed, power, strength, work capacity, and body size. The battery was subsequently modified by each of the authors. Slay tested over 1600 football players and concluded that the most significant measures for success are size, body mass index, 5-yd speed, power, and speed to the left and right.

Golf

Alderman compared two grips in teaching beginning golf and reported no differences in range, angle of impact, and velocity after 6 weeks of instruction. Purdy and Stallard found the whole method of learning to be more effective than the part method in improving accuracy and general golf ability, and the overlapping grip to be more effective when the whole method was used. DeBacy concluded that self-viewing by video tapes is beneficial in improving accuracy of self-assessment in beginning golf. A study by Thompson revealed that immediate external feedback through the use of the graph-check-sequence facilitates learning of golf skills. Bowen concluded that putting success for beginning golfers is not related to the use of a particular point of aim. In a theoretical analysis of aggressive golf putts, Mahoney detected a sharp distinction between defensive and aggressive strategies. She noted that the probability of success of an aggressive putt increases when the attempt is downhill and the green is fast, exactly the conditions that cause most golfers to be defensive. Budney and Bellow (1979) concluded from kinetic analysis of the golf swing that adding weight to the handle of a club has little effect on the forces exerted by a golfer. They also found that for the same club head speed, a graphite driver requires less effort than an ordinary driver. Budney and Bellow (1982) also compared mass distribution features of matched golf clubs with regard to physical exertion of the golfers. They found that maximal driving force is relatively the same for a specific golfer using a variety of clubs.

Gymnastics

M. Johnson (1971) conducted a 20-year follow-up study on objectivity of gymnastics judging and recommended reevaluation of the rules, judging procedures, and selection of skills for compulsory routines to permit greater discrimination between performances.

Bard and associates compared expert and novice gymnastics judges on the number and location of ocular fixations and number of errors. Expert judges detected twice as many errors as the novice judges. Experts tended to have more fixations on the upper body, while novices concentrated more on the legs of the gymnasts. Dainis (1979) analyzed kinematic variables and energy changes for the preflight, contact, and after-flight phases of the handspring vault. While preflight variables were similar, vertical velocities at initial horse contact varied considerably, with the poorest vaults showing downward velocities. Dainis (1981) developed a mathematical model describing the motions for gymnastic vaulting. The take-off velocity and initial distance from the horse were found to be the principal variables affecting the outcome of the vault.

Handball and Racquetball

Karpman and Isaacs reported a modification of the racquetball test by Hensley, East, and Stillwell whereby a backhand test is added. A subject's score is the number of strokes hit behind the 12-ft restraining line (the long-wall volley test dimensions) with only the backhand. Two 30-sec trials are given.

Swimming and Diving

Asprey, Alley, and Tuttle reported no adverse effects on swimming performances in the 1-mile freestyle from consumption of a meal of cereal and milk at ½ hr, 1 hr, or 2 hr prior to swimming. Maglischo and Maglischo compared three racing starts in competitive swimming and reported evidence favoring the circular-backswing start.

However, Piscopo and Baley reported that recent studies support the grab start as a faster technique for leaving the platform than the conventional styles.

Groves and Roberts identified the optimum angle of projection for the racing start to be 13 degrees downward from the horizontal. McCatty concluded that the use of a flotation device does not accelerate the learning process for nonswimmers.

Sharp, Troup, and Costill found that arm power as measured by a specially designed apparatus that mimics arm action in swimming offers an objective assessment of a component essential for success in sprint swimming.

Tennis

Cotten and Nixon failed to find any evidence in support of the hypothesis that learning to serve in beginning tennis is facilitated by initial practice close to the net. Anderson compared the muscle patterning in the overarm throw with the tennis serve, using skilled and less skilled subjects. Differences between the two skills were found in regard to duration of muscle activity and in muscle patterning during the force-production phase in both skills. She concluded that because of temporal differences in the two skills, reference to or practice in throwing may not be a good method to improve skill in the serve.

Surbury found that the presentation of audio, visual, and audiovisual instructions in conjunction with mental practice significantly improved performance in the forehand drive in tennis. Mariani compared the command and task methods of teaching in tennis, and concluded that the task method is superior in teaching the backhand and in retention for both the forehand and backhand. Neuman and Singer compared traditional and programmed methods on various measures of tennis skills. There was no difference in general skill level of the groups, although the traditionally taught group made significant improvement in general skills while the programmed group did not. Better subjective rating scores on form were obtained by the programmed group. Farrell also found apparently equal effectiveness in use of programmed and teacher-directed instruction;

therefore, she concluded that programmed instruction is an effective teaching device for beginning tennis. Woods investigated the comparative effectiveness of emphasis of velocity and accuracy in a tennis skill. Equal and simultaneous emphasis was found to be most desirable. Initial emphasis on velocity followed by accuracy was deemed to be superior to an initial emphasis on accuracy.

Elliott, Blanksby, and Ellis, through stroboscope photography and accelerometry techniques, concluded that the vibration and rebound velocity characteristics of the oversized tennis rackets provide support for the practical benefits of this type of racket. Elliott studied the effect of grip firmness on reaction impulse and rebound velocity in tennis. A tight grip increased both, and should be advocated by tennis instructors as one of the factors that determine the effectiveness of strokes relying on rebound velocities.

Female novice tennis players were assigned to one of three videotape replay conditions by Cooper and Rothstein to ascertain whether the treatments differentially affected open (ground strokes) and closed (serve) skills. The results indicated that the combination of performance information feedback (PIF) and environmental information feedback (EIF) or PIF alone should be used in the serve and that EIF or the combination of both should be used for ground strokes. Lindquist and Witte found no differences among three different practice schedule arrangements in learning of tennis skills as measured by skills tests and written and verbal tests.

Purcell constructed a tennis forehand–backhand drive skill test that measures both ball control and speed of the drive. The latter is determined by time in flight. The time factor is used to correct the target value total, thus rewarding the more skilled player who can stroke the ball more firmly with control. The test has a test–retest reliability of .84 and a validity coefficient of .83 with judges' ratings as a criterion.

Vodak and associates determined physiologic profiles of middle-aged men and women tennis players. Their results indicated that either physically superior individuals choose to play tennis or that regular tennis participation produces above-average levels of fitness or both. Powers and Walker found highly skilled junior female tennis players to have higher maximum oxygen consumption, relatively higher grip strength, and higher ventilatory capacity than untrained subjects of the same age group.

Volleyball

Shick investigated the effects of mental practice on selected volleyball skills. Inconsistent results were obtained with regard to the effectiveness of mental practice in the serve and wall volley.

Cox, Noble, and Johnson found the jab cross-over step to be superior to the slide step in getting the volleyball player's body off the ground and into a blocking position quickly. Morrow and colleagues analyzed various anthropometric strength and speed variables in 180 intercollegiate women volleyball players who participated in a regional round-robin tournament. Upper body strength and fat weight were identified as most important in differentiating between players of the most and least successful teams. Puhl and associates examined the physical and physiologic characteristics of elite volleyball players of both sexes. Few differences were found between the elite players and players of less skill, suggesting that total time playing the game is the most important factor rather than innate physical characteristics. Sex differences were minimal when performances were made relative to body weight or lean body mass. Spence and colleagues developed descriptive profiles for members of the U. S. Women's National Volleyball Training Team using anthropometric, strength, physiologic, and motor performance measures. The players selected for the Pan-American Team were taller and heavier and had greater motor ability than the nonselectees.

Wrestling

Singer and Weiss concluded that wrestlers may lose up to 7% of body weight without adverse effects on selected anthropometric, physical, and performance measures. Ribisl and Herbert reported that a 5% loss in body weight within 48 hr owing to dehydration significantly reduced the physical working capacity of wrestlers, although rehydration restored capacity.

A psychophysiologic assessment of elite wrestlers was performed by Silva and associates. The variables of anger, tension, total grip strength, dynamic muscular endurance, relative muscular endurance, and minute ventilation were found to discriminate most accurately between wrestlers who qualified for the touring U. S. team and non-qualifiers. Sady and colleagues found that experienced wrestlers 9 to 12 years of age had significantly less fat than a comparable group of elementary school children.

BIBLIOGRAPHY

Archery

AAHPERD Skills Test Manual: Archery. David Brace, test consultant. Reston, Va.: AAHPERD, 1967.

Barnett, M. L., and J. A. Stanicek, "Effects of Goal Setting on Achievement in Archery." *Research Quarterly* 50:328–332, October 1979.

Bohn, R. W., "An Achievement Test in Archery." Unpublished master's thesis, University of Wisconsin, Madison, 1962.

Eckert, H. M., and D. M. Wendt, "Relationship Between Perception of Pull and Draw in Archery." *Research Quarterly* 38:544–549, December 1967.

Hyde, E. I., "An Achievement Scale in Archery." *Research Quarterly* 8:109, May 1937.

Shifflett, B., and B. J. Schuman, "A Criterion-Referenced Test for Archery." *Research Quarterly for Exercise and Sport* 53:330–335, December 1982.

Zabik, R. M., and A. S. Jackson, "Reliability of Archery Achievement." *Research Quarterly* 40:254–255, March 1969.

Badminton

Burdeshaw, D., J. E. Spragens, and P. A. Weis, "Evaluation of General Versus Specific Instruction of Badminton Skills to Women of Low Motor Ability." *Research Quarterly* 41:472–477, December 1970.

Davis, P. R., "The Development of Combined Short and Long Badminton Service Skill Test." Unpublished master's thesis, University of Tennessee, Knoxville, 1968.

French, E., and E. Stalter, "Study of Skill Tests in Badminton for College Women." *Research Quarterly* 20:257–272, October 1949.

Gray, C. A., and W. B. Brumbach, "The Effect of Daylight Projection of Film Loops on Learning Badminton." *Research Quarterly* 38:562–569, December 1967.

Hale, P. A., "Construction of a Long Serve for Beginning Badminton Players." Microcarded master's thesis, University of Wisconsin, Madison, 1970.

Hicks, J. V., "The Construction and Evaluation of a Battery of Five Badminton Skill Tests." Unpublished doctoral dissertation, Texas Woman's University, Denton, 1967.

Johnson, R. M., "Determination of the Validity and Reliability of the Badminton Placement Test."

Unpublished master's thesis, University of Oregon, Eugene, 1967.

Kowert, E. A., "Construction of a Badminton Ability Test for Men." Unpublished master's thesis, University of Iowa, Iowa City, 1968.

Lockhart, A., and F. A. McPherson, "Development of a Test of Badminton Playing Ability." *Research Quarterly* 20:402–405, December 1949.

McDonald, E. D., "The Development of a Skill Test for the Badminton High Clear." Unpublished master's thesis, Southern Illinois University, Carbondale, 1968.

Miller, F. A., "A Badminton Wall Volley Test." *Research Quarterly* 22:208–213, May 1951.

Poole, J., *Badminton.* Pacific Palisades, Calif.: Goodyear Publishing, 1969, pp. 30–32.

———, and J. Nelson, "Construction of a Badminton Skills Test Battery." Unpublished study, Louisiana State University, Baton Rouge, 1970.

Scott, M. G., and E. French, *Measurement and Evaluation in Physical Education.* Dubuque, Iowa: William C. Brown, 1959, Chapter VI.

———, A. Carpenter, E. French, and L. Kuhl, "Achievement Examination in Badminton." *Research Quarterly* 12:242–253, May 1941.

Washington, J., "Construction of a Wall Volley Test for the Badminton Short Serve, and the Effect of Wall Practice on Court Performance." Unpublished master's thesis, North Texas State University, Denton, 1968.

Basketball

AAHPERD Skills Test Manual: Basketball for Boys and Girls. D. R. Hopkins, J. Shick, and J. J. Plack, Eds. Reston, Va.: AAHPERD, 1984.

Barrow, H. M., "Basketball Skill Test." *Physical Educator* 16:26–27, March 1959.

Cunningham, P., "Measuring Basketball Playing Ability of High School Girls." Unpublished doctoral dissertation, University of Iowa, Iowa City, 1964.

Edgren, H. D., "An Experiment in the Testing of Ability and Progress in Basketball." *Research Quarterly* 3:159, March 1932.

Gaunt, S. J., "Factor Structure of Basketball Playing Ability." Unpublished doctoral dissertation, Indiana University, Bloomington, 1979.

Gilbert, R. R., "A Study of Selected Variables in Predicting Basketball Players." Unpublished master's thesis, Springfield College, Springfield, Mass., 1968.

Hopkins, D. R., "Factor Analysis of Selected

Basketball Skill Tests." *Research Quarterly* 48:535–540, October 1977.

———, "Using Skill Tests to Identify Successful and Unsuccessful Basketball Performers." *Research Quarterly* 50:381–387, October 1979.

Knox, R. D., "Basketball Ability Test." *Scholastic Coach* 17:45, 1947.

Lehsten, N., "A Measure of Basketball Skills in High School Boys." *Physical Educator* 5:103–109, December 1948.

Leilich, A., "The Primary Components of Selected Basketball Tests for College Women." Unpublished doctoral dissertation, Indiana University, Bloomington, 1952.

Matthews, L. E., "A Battery of Basketball Skills Tests for High School Boys." Unpublished master's thesis, University of Oregon, Eugene, 1963.

Miller, W. K., "Achievement Levels in Basketball Skills for Women Physical Education Majors." *Research Quarterly* 25:450–455, December 1954.

Mortimer, E. M., "Basketball Shooting." *Research Quarterly* 22:234–243, May 1951.

Nelson, J. K., "The Measurement of Shooting and Passing Skills in Basketball." Unpublished study, Louisiana State University, Baton Rouge, 1967.

Peters, G. V., "The Reliability and Validity of Selected Shooting Tests in Basketball." Unpublished master's thesis, University of Michigan, Ann Arbor, 1964.

Plinke, J. F., "The Development of Basketball Physical Skill Potential Test Batteries by Height Categories." Unpublished doctoral dissertation, Indiana University, Bloomington, 1966.

Stubbs, H. C., "An Explanatory Study of Girls Basketball Relative to the Measurement of Ball Handling Ability." Unpublished master's thesis, University of Tennessee, Knoxville, 1968.

Thornes, A. B., "An Analysis of a Basketball Shooting Test and Its Relation to Other Basketball Skill Tests." Unpublished master's thesis, University of Wisconsin, Madison, 1963.

Walton, R. J., "A Comparison Between Two Selected Evaluative Techniques for Measuring Basketball Skill." Unpublished master's thesis, Western Illinois University, Macomb, 1968.

Bowling

Johnson, N. J., "Tests of Achievement in Bowling for Beginning Girl Bowlers." Unpublished master's thesis, University of Colorado, Boulder, 1962.

Martin, J. L., "A Way to Measure Bowling Success." *Research Quarterly* 31:113–116, March 1960.

———, and J. Keogh, "Bowling Norms for College Students in Elective Physical Education Classes." *Research Quarterly* 35:325–327, October 1964.

Olson, J., and M. R. Liba, "A Device for Evaluating Spot Bowling Ability." *Research Quarterly* 38:193–201, May 1967.

Phillips, M., and D. Summers, "Bowling Norms and Learning Curves for College Women." *Research Quarterly* 21:377–385, December 1950.

Field Hockey

Benedict, J. S., "An Investigation of Selected Variables Which Best Determine the Winner of a Tie Game in Field Hockey." Unpublished master's thesis, Southern Illinois University, Carbondale, 1977.

Chapman, N. L., "Chapman Ball Control Test— Field Hockey." *Research Quarterly for Exercise and Sport* 53:239–242, September 1982.

Craft, D. L., "Competitive Ability, Physical Size, and Self-Concept of Physical Size of Selected College Women Field Hockey Players." Unpublished master's thesis, University of Wisconsin-LaCrosse, 1977.

Garman, L. K., "A Cinematographical and Mechanical Analysis of the Push Pass in Field Hockey." Unpublished master's thesis, Pennsylvania State University, University Park, 1977.

Klatt, L. A., "Kinematic and Temporal Characteristics of a Successful Penalty Corner in Women's Field Hockey." Unpublished doctoral dissertation, Indiana University, Bloomington, 1977.

Sabatino, M. L., "Differences in the Preferred and Non-preferred Hand Performance for the Floor Hockey Snap Shot." Unpublished master's thesis, Springfield College, Springfield, Mass., 1979.

Football

AAPHERD Skills Test Manual: Football. David K. Brace, test consultant. Reston, Va.: AAHPERD, 1965.

Carter, J. E. L., "Somatotypes of College Football Players." *Research Quarterly* 39:476–481, October 1968.

Costill, D. L., et al., "Maximum Anaerobic Power Among College Football Players." *Journal of Sports Medicine and Physical Fitness* 8:103–106, 1968.

Cowell, C. C., and A. H. Ismail, "Validity of a Football Rating Scale and Its Relationship to Social Integration and Academic Ability."

Research Quarterly 32:461–467, December 1961.

Lee, R. C., "A Battery of Tests to Predict Football Potential." Unpublished master's thesis, University of Utah, Salt Lake City, 1965.

McDavid, R. F., "Predicting Potential in Football Players." *Research Quarterly* 48:98–104, March 1977.

Miller, K. W., "An Examination of Attentional Style and Selected Performance Variables of Intercollegiate Football Players." Unpublished master's thesis, Pennsylvania State University, University Park, 1978.

Sells, T. D., "Selected Movement and Anthropometric Variables of Football Defensive Tackles." Unpublished doctoral dissertation, Indiana University, Bloomington, 1977.

Slay, B. B., *The Measurement of Motor Function Components in Football Players.* Hattiesburg, Miss.: School of Health, Physical Education, and Recreation, University of Southern Mississippi, 1980.

Smith, D. P., and R. J. Byrd, "Body Composition, Pulmonary Function, and Maximal Oxygen Consumption of College Football Players." *Journal of Sports Medicine and Physical Fitness* 16:301–308, 1976.

Wilmore, J. H., and W. L. Haskell, "Body Composition and Endurance Capacity of Professional Football Players." *Journal of Applied Physiology* 33:564–567, 1972.

Golf

Alderman, R. B., "A Comparative Study on the Effectiveness of Two Grips for Teaching Beginning Golf." *Research Quarterly* 38:3–9, March 1967.

Bowen, R. T., "Putting Errors of Beginning Golfers Using Different Points of Aim." *Research Quarterly* 39:31–35, March 1968.

Budney, D. R., and D. G. Bellow, "Kinetic Analysis of a Golf Swing." *Research Quarterly* 50:171–179, May 1979.

———, ———, "On the Swing Mechanics of a Matched Set of Golf Clubs." *Research Quarterly for Exercise and Sport* 53:185–192, September 1982.

Clevett, M. A., "An Experiment in Teaching Methods of Golf." *Research Quarterly* 2:104–112, December 1931.

Cochrane, J. F., "The Construction of an Indoor Golf Skills Test as a Measure of Golfing Ability." Unpublished master's thesis, University of Minnesota, Minneapolis, 1960.

Cotten, D. J., J. R. Thomas, and T. Plaster, "A Plastic Ball Test for Golf Iron Skill." Paper presented at AAHPERD National Convention, Houston, Tex., March 24, 1972.

DeBacy, D., "Effect of Viewing Video Tapes of a Sport Skill Performed by Self and Others on Self-Assessment." *Research Quarterly* 41:27–31, March 1970.

Mahoney, J. F., "Theoretical Analysis of Aggressive Golf Putts." *Research Quarterly for Exercise and Sport* 53:165–171, March 1982.

McKee, M. E., "A Test for the Full-Swing Shot in Golf." *Research Quarterly* 21:40–46, March 1950.

Nelson, J., "An Achievement Test for Golf." Unpublished study, Louisiana State University, Baton Rouge, 1967.

Purdy, B. J., and M. L. Stallard, "Effect of Two Learning Methods and Two Grips on the Acquisition of Power and Accuracy in the Golf Swing of College Women." *Research Quarterly* 38:474–479, October 1967.

Roberts, J. A., "The Effect of a Particular Practice Technique on the Golf Swing." Unpublished thesis, University of Iowa, Iowa City, 1966.

Thompson, D. H, "Immediate External Feedback in the Learning of Golf Skills." *Research Quarterly* 40:589–594, October 1969.

Vanderhoof, E. R., "Beginning Golf Achievement Tests." Unpublished master's thesis, State University of Iowa, Iowa City, 1956.

West, C., and J. A. Thorpe, "Construction and Validation of an Eight-Iron Approach Test." *Research Quarterly* 39:1115–1120, December 1968.

Gymnastics

Amateur Athletic Union (AAU), *Gymnastics Guide.* AAU, 231 W. 58th Street, New York (publication updated regularly).

Bard, C., M. Fleury, L. Carriere, and M. Halle, "Analyses of Gymnastics Judges' Visual Search." *Research Quarterly for Exercise and Sport* 51:267–273, May 1980.

Bowers, C. O., "Gymnastic Skill Test for Beginning to Low Intermediate Girls and Women." Unpublished master's thesis, Ohio State University, Columbus, 1965.

Dainis, A., "Cinematographic Analysis of the Handspring Vault." *Research Quarterly* 50:341–349, October 1979.

———, "A Model for Gymnastics Vaulting." *Medicine and Science in Sports and Exercise* 13:34–43, 1981.

Division of Girls' and Women's Sports (DGWS), *Gymnastic Guide.* Reston, Va.: AAHPERD (publication updated regularly).

Harris, J. P., "A Design for a Proposed Skill Proficiency Test in Tumbling and Apparatus for Male Physical Education Majors at the University of North Dakota." Unpublished master's thesis, University of North Dakota, Grand Forks, 1966.

Johnson, B. L., "A Screening Test for Pole Vaulting and Selected Gymnastic Events." JOHPER, 44:71–72, May 1973.

———, and M. J. Garcia, *Gymnastics for the Beginner.* Manchala, Tex.: Sterling Swift, 1976, pp. 134–138.

Johnson, M., "Objectivity of Judging at the National Collegiate Athletic Association Gymnastic Meet: A Twenty-Year Follow-Up Study." *Research Quarterly* 42:454–455, December 1971.

Landers, D. M., "A Comparison of Two Gymnastic Judging Methods." Unpublished master's thesis, University of Illinois, Urbana-Champaign, 1965.

National Collegiate Athletic Association (NCAA), *Official Gymnastics Rules.* NCAA, 394 East Thomas Road, Phoenix (publication updated regularly).

United States Gymnastic Federation (USGF), *Age Group Workbook.* USGF, P.O. Box 4699, Tucson (publication updated regularly).

Handball and Racquetball

Cornish, C., "A Study of Measurement of Ability in Handball." *Research Quarterly* 20:215–222, May 1949.

Griffith, M. A., "An Objective Method of Evaluating Ability in Handball Singles." Unpublished master's thesis, University of North Carolina, Chapel Hill, 1949.

Hensley, L. D., W. B. East, and J. L. Stillwell, "A Racquetball Skills Test." *Research Quarterly* 50:114–118, March 1979.

Karpman, M. B., and L. D. Isaacs, "An Improved Racquetball Test." *Research Quarterly* 50:526–527, October 1979.

Montoye, H. J., and J. Brotzman, "An Investigation of the Validity of Using the Results of a Doubles Tournament as a Measure of Handball Ability." *Research Quarterly* 22:214–218, 1951.

Pennington, G. G., J. A. P. Day, J. N. Drowatzky, and J. F. Hanson, "A Measure of Handball Ability." *Research Quarterly* 38:247–253, May 1967.

Soccer and Speedball

Buchanan, R. E., "A Study of Achievement Tests in Speedball for High School Girls." Unpublished master's thesis, State University of Iowa, Iowa City, 1942.

Crew, V. N., "A Skill Test Battery for Use in Service Program Classes at the University Level." Unpublished master's thesis, University of Oregon, Eugene, 1968.

Johnson, J. R., "The Development of a Single-Item Test as a Measure of Soccer Skill." Microcarded master's thesis, University of British Columbia, Vancouver, 1963.

MacKenzie, J., "The Evaluation of a Battery of Soccer Skill Tests as an Aid to Classification of General Soccer Ability." Unpublished master's thesis, University of Massachusetts, Amherst, 1968.

McDonald, L. G., "The Construction of a Kicking Skill Test as an Index of General Soccer Ability." Unpublished master's thesis, Springfield College, Springfield, Mass., 1951.

Mitchell, J. R., "The Modification of the McDonald Soccer Skill Test for Upper Elementary School Boys." Unpublished master's thesis, University of Oregon, Eugene, 1963.

Smith, G., "Speedball Skill Tests for College Women." Unpublished study, Illinois State University, Normal, 1947.

Streck, B., "An Analysis of the McDonald Soccer Skill Test as Applied to Junior High School Girls." Unpublished master's thesis, Fort Hays State College, Fort Hays, Kan., 1961.

Weiss, R. A., and M. Phillips, *Administration of Tests in Physical Education.* St. Louis: C. V. Mosby, 1954, pp. 253–257.

Softball and Baseball

AAHPERD Skills Test Manual: Softball for Boys. David K. Brace, test consultant. Reston, Va.: AAHPERD, 1966a.

AAHPERD Skills Test Manual: Softball for Girls. David K. Brace, test consultant. Reston, Va.: AAHPERD, 1966b.

Elrod, J. M., "Construction of a Softball Skill Test Battery for High School Boys." Unpublished master's thesis, Louisiana State University, Baton Rouge, 1969.

Everett, P. W., "The Prediction of Baseball Ability." *Research Quarterly* 23:15–19, March 1952.

Fox, M. G., and O. G. Young, "A Test of Softball Batting Ability." *Research Quarterly* 25:26–27, March 1954.

Hardin, D. H., and J. Ramirez, "Elementary School Performance Norms." *TAHPER Journal*, February 1972, pp. 8–9.

Kelson, R. E., "Baseball Classification Plan for Boys." *Research Quarterly* 24:304–309, October 1953.

O'Donnell, D. J., "Validation of Softball Skill Tests

for High School Girls." Unpublished master's thesis, Indiana University, Bloomington, 1950.

Shick, J., "Battery of Defensive Softball Skills Tests for College Women." *Research Quarterly* 41:88–94, March 1970.

Swimming and Diving

Arrasmith, J. L., "Swimming Classification Test for College Women." Unpublished doctoral dissertation, University of Oregon, Eugene, 1967.

Asprey, G. M., L. E. Alley, and W. W. Tuttle, "Effect of Eating at Various Times on Subsequent Performances in the One-Mile Freestyle Swim." *Research Quarterly* 39:231–234, May 1968.

Bennett, L. M., "A Test of Diving for Use in Beginning Classes." *Research Quarterly* 13:109–115, March 1942.

Burdeshaw, D., "Acquisition of Elementary Swimming Skills by Negro and White College Women." *Research Quarterly* 39:872–879, December 1968.

Burris, B. J., "A Study of the Speed-Stroke Test of Crawl Stroking Ability and Its Relationship to Other Selected Tests of Crawl Stroking Ability." Unpublished master's thesis, Temple University, Philadelphia, 1964.

Durrant, S. M., "An Analytical Method of Rating Synchronized Swimming Stunts." *Research Quarterly* 35:126–134, May 1964.

Fox, M. G., "Swimming Power Test." *Research Quarterly* 28:233–237, October 1957.

Groves, R., and J. A. Roberts, "A Further Investigation of the Optimum Angle of Projection for the Racing Start in Swimming." *Research Quarterly* 43:167–173, May 1972.

Hewitt, J. E., "Swimming Achievement Scale Scores for College Men." *Research Quarterly* 19:282–289, December 1948.

———, "Achievement Scale Scores for High School Swimming." *Research Quarterly* 20:170–179, May 1949.

Kilby, E. L. J., "An Objective Method of Evaluating Three Swimming Strokes." Unpublished doctoral dissertation, University of Washington, Seattle, 1956.

Maglischo, C. W., and E. Maglischo, "Comparison of Three Racing Starts Used in Competitive Swimming." *Research Quarterly* 39:604–609, October 1968.

McCatty, C. A. M., "Effects of the Use of a Flotation Device in Teaching Non-swimmers." *Research Quarterly* 39:621–626, October 1968.

Munt, M. R., "Development of an Objective Test to Measure the Efficiency of the Front Crawl for College Women." Unpublished master's thesis, University of Michigan, Ann Arbor, 1964.

Piscopo, J., and J. A. Baley, *Kinesiology—The Science of Movement*. New York: John Wiley, 1981, p. 378.

Rosentsweig, J., "A Revision of the Power Swimming Test." *Research Quarterly* 39:818–819, October 1968.

Sharp, R. L., J. P. Troup, and D. L. Costill, "Relationship Between Power and Sprint Freestyle Swimming." *Medicine and Science in Sports and Exercise* 14:53–56, 1982.

Tennis

Anderson, M. B., "Comparison of Muscle Patterning in the Overarm Throw and Tennis Serve." *Research Quarterly* 50:541–553, December 1979.

Avery, C. A., P. A. Richardson, and A. W. Jackson, "A Practical Tennis Serve Test: Measurement of Skill Under Simulated Game Conditions." *Research Quarterly* 50:554–564, December 1979.

Broer, M. R., and D. M. Miller, "Achievement Tests for Beginning and Intermediate Tennis." *Research Quarterly* 21:303–321, October 1950.

Cobane, E., "Test for the Service." In *AAHPERD, Tennis and Badminton Guide—June 1962–June 1964*. Reston, Va.: AAHPERD, pp. 46–47.

Cooper, L. K., and A. L. Rothstein, "Videotape Replay and the Learning of Skills in Open and Closed Environments." *Research Quarterly for Exercise and Sport* 52:191–199, March 1981.

Cotten, D. J., and J. Nixon, "A Comparison of Two Methods of Teaching the Tennis Serve." *Research Quarterly* 39:929–931, December 1968.

DiGennaro, J., "Construction of Forehand Drive, Backhand Drive, and Serve Tennis Tests." *Research Quarterly* 40:496–501, October 1969.

Dyer, J. T., "Revision of the Backboard Test of Tennis Ability." *Research Quarterly* 9:25–31, March 1938.

Edwards, J., "A Study of Three Measures of the Tennis Serve." Unpublished master's thesis, University of Wisconsin, Madison, 1965.

Elliott, B. C., "Tennis: The Influence of Grip Tightness on Reaction Impulse and Rebound Velocity." *Medicine and Science in Sports and Exercise* 14:348–352, 1982.

———, B. A. Blanksby, and R. Ellis, "Vibration and Rebound Velocity Characteristics of Conventional and Oversized Tennis Rackets." *Research Quarterly for Exercise and Sport* 51:608–615, December 1980.

Farrell, J. E., "Programmed Versus Teacher-Directed Instruction in Beginning Tennis for Women." *Research Quarterly* 41:51–58, March 1970.

Hewitt, J. E., "Revision of the Dyer Backboard Tennis Test." *Research Quarterly* 36:153–157, May 1965.

————, "Hewitt's Tennis Achievement Test." *Research Quarterly* 37:231–237, May 1966.

————, "Classification Tests in Tennis." *Research Quarterly* 39:552–555, October 1968.

Hubbell, N. C., "A Battery of Tennis Skill Tests for College Women." Unpublished master's thesis, Texas Woman's University, Denton, 1960.

Johnson, B. L., "The Tennis Overhead Smash Test." Unpublished study, Northeast Louisiana University, Monroe, 1972.

Johnson, J., "Tennis Serve of Advanced Women Players." *Research Quarterly* 28:123–131, May 1957.

Jones, S. K., "A Measure of Tennis Serving Ability." Unpublished master's thesis, University of California, Los Angeles, 1967.

Kemp, J., and M. F. Vincent, "Kemp-Vincent Rally Test of Tennis Skill." *Research Quarterly* 39:1000–1004, December 1968.

Lindquist, E. L., and F. Witte, "Comparison of Women's Beginning Tennis Skills Under Three Different Time Schedules." *Research Quarterly* 48:85–92, March 1977.

Mariani, T., "A Comparison of the Effectiveness of the Command Method and the Task Method of Teaching the Forehand and Backhand Tennis Strokes." *Research Quarterly* 41:171–174, May 1970.

Neuman, M. C., and R. N. Singer, "A Comparison of Traditional Versus Programmed Methods of Learning Tennis." *Research Quarterly* 39:1044–1048, December 1968.

Powers, S. K., and R. Walker, "Physiological and Anatomical Characteristics of Outstanding Female Junior Tennis Players." *Research Quarterly for Exercise and Sport* 53:172–175, March 1982.

Purcell, K., "A Tennis Forehand-Backhand Drive Skill Test Which Measures Ball Control and Stroke Firmness." *Research Quarterly for Exercise and Sport* 52:238–245, May 1981.

Recio, M., and C. Prestidge, "The Overhead Smash Test Utilizing the Johnson Tennis and Badminton Machine." Unpublished study, Northeast Louisiana University, Monroe, 1972.

Surbury, P. R., "Audio, Visual and Audio-Visual Instruction With Mental Practice in Developing the Forehand Tennis Drive." *Research Quarterly* 39:728–734, October 1968.

Timmer, K. L., "A Tennis Test to Determine Accuracy in Playing Ability." Unpublished master's thesis, Springfield College, Springfield, Mass., 1965.

Vodak, P. A., W. M. Savin, W. L. Haskell, and P. D. Wood, "Physiological Profile of Middle-Aged Male and Female Tennis Players." *Medicine and Science in Sports and Exercise* 12:159–163, 1980.

Woods, J. B., "The Effect of Varied Instructional Emphasis Upon the Development of a Motor Skill." *Research Quarterly* 38:132–141, March 1967.

Volleyball

AAHPERD Skills Test Manual: Volleyball. Clayton Shay, test consultant. Reston, Va.: AAHPERD, 1969.

Blackmon, C. J., "The Development of a Volleyball Test for the Spike." Unpublished master's thesis, Southern Illinois University, Carbondale, 1968.

Brady, G. F., "Preliminary Investigations of Volleyball Playing Ability." *Research Quarterly* 16:14–17, March 1945.

Brumbach, W. B., C. M. McGowan, and B. A. Borrevik, *Beginning Volleyball.* Eugene, Ore.: Wayne Brumbach (distributed by University of Oregon Cooperative Store), 1972.

Chaney, D. S., "The Development of a Test of Volleyball Ability for College Women." Unpublished master's thesis, Texas Woman's University, Denton, 1966.

Clifton, M. A., "Single Hit Volley Test for Women's Volleyball." *Research Quarterly* 33:208–211, May 1962.

Cox, R. H., L. Noble, and R. E. Johnson, "Effectiveness of the Slide and Cross-Over Steps in Volleyball Blocking—A Temporal Analysis." *Research Quarterly for Exercise and Sport* 53:101–107, June 1982.

Cunningham, P., and J. Garrison, "High Wall Volley Test for Women's Volleyball." *Research Quarterly* 39:480–490, October 1968.

Jackson, P., "A Rating Scale for Discriminating Relative Performance of Skilled Female Volleyball Players." Unpublished master's thesis, University of Alberta, Edmonton, 1967.

Johnson, J. A., "The Development of a Volleyball Skill Test for High School Girls." Unpublished master's thesis, Illinois State University, Normal, 1967.

Kissler, A. A., "The Validity and Reliability of the Sandefur Volleyball Spiking Test." Unpublished master's thesis, California State University, Long Beach, 1968.

Kronquist, R. A., and W. B. Brumbach, "A Modification of the Brady Volleyball Skill Test for High School Boys." *Research Quarterly* 39:116–120, March 1968.

Lamp, N. A., "Volleyball Skills for Junior High School Students as a Function of Physical Size and Maturity." *Research Quarterly* 25:189, May 1954.

Liba, M. R., and M. R. Stauff, "A Test for the Volleyball Pass." *Research Quarterly* 34:56–63, March 1963.

Lopez, D., "Serve Test." In Division of Girls' and Women's Sports (DGWS), *Volleyball Guide— 1957–1959*. Reston, Va.: AAHPERD, 1957.

Michalski, R. A., "Construction of an Objective Skill Test for the Underhand Volleyball Serve." Unpublished master's thesis, University of Iowa, Iowa City, 1963.

Mohr, D. R., and M. V. Haverstick, "Repeated Volleys Test for Women's Volleyball." *Research Quarterly* 26:179, May 1955.

Morrow, J. R., A. S. Jackson, W. W. Hosler, and J. K. Kachurik, "The Importance of Strength, Speed, and Body Size for Team Success in Women's Intercollegiate Volleyball." *Research Quarterly* 50:429–437, October 1979.

Puhl, J., S. Case, S. Fleck, and P. VanHandel, "Physical and Physiological Characteristics of Elite Volleyball Players." *Research Quarterly for Exercise and Sport* 53:257–262, September 1982.

Ryan, M. F., "A Study of Tests for the Volleyball Serve." Unpublished master's thesis, University of Wisconsin, Madison, 1969.

Shavely, M., "Volleyball Skill Tests for Girls." In Division of Girls' and Women's Sports (DGWS), *Selected Volleyball Articles*. Reston, Va.: AAHPERD, 1960.

Shick, J., "Effects of Mental Practice on Selected Volleyball Skills for College Women." *Research Quarterly* 41:88–94, March 1970.

Spence, D. W., J. G. Disch, H. L. Fred, and A. E. Coleman, "Descriptive Profiles of Highly Skilled Women Volleyball Players." *Medicine and Science in Sports and Exercise* 12:299–302, 1980.

Wrestling

Ribisl, P. M., and W. G. Herbert, "Effects of Rapid Weight Reduction and Subsequent Rehydration Upon the Physical Working Capacity of Wrestlers." *Research Quarterly* 41:536–541, December 1970.

Sady, S. P., W. H. Thompson, M. Savage, and M. Petratis, "The Body Composition and Physical Dimensions of 9- to 12-Year-Old Experienced Wrestlers." *Medicine and Science in Sports and Exercise* 14:244–248, 1982.

Silva, J. M., 3rd, B. B. Shultz, R. W. Haslam, and D. Murray, "A Psychophysiological Assessment of Elite Wrestlers." *Research Quarterly for Exercise and Sport* 52:348–358, October 1981.

Singer, R. N., and S. A. Weiss, "Effects of Weight Reduction on Selected Anthropometric, Physical and Performance Measures of Wrestlers." *Research Quarterly* 39:361–368, May 1968.

CHAPTER 17

THE MEASUREMENT OF RHYTHM AND DANCE

OBJECTIVES

After reading this chapter, the student should be able to:

1. Appreciate the subjective nature of evaluation in the areas of rhythm and dance

2. Understand some of the problems associated with the measurement of rhythm and dance

3. Follow directions for administering practical tests of rhythm and dance

---

Evaluation in the area of rhythm and dance has depended mainly on rating scales. This dependence has been of necessity, since few tests are available in this area that can be used in the classroom. Authorities in the field have found rhythm as difficult to define as it is to measure. Existing definitions of rhythm from various sources have consistently been in such terms as flow, movement, repetition, and beat. Thus, rhythm may be thought of as the flow of movement with the regular repetition of beat in grouping movements for the successful execution of a pattern or a skill. Physical educators frequently think of rhythm as that pattern that makes performance, even difficult performance, look easy and graceful. Rhythm is closely associated with kinesthesis, speed, and agility and is important in any skill that requires a series of successive movements. In the execution of a dance, the individual moves the body while listening to music. Dance is therefore complicated in that body movement is related to a rhythmic pattern of the music. Some instructors insist that students move in time with the music, while other instructors feel that stu-

dents should not be penalized for inability to pick up a rhythmic pattern of music.[1]

USES OF RHYTHM AND DANCE TESTS

Tests of rhythm and dance may be used in physical education as follows:

1. As a means to further the learning process by stimulating students to devote their maximum effort toward rhythmic interpretation and performance (Testing should be followed by a critique so students benefit from their mistakes)

2. As a means to help students recognize rhythmic patterns in sports activities or improve fundamental skills such as walking, running, and jumping

3. As a measure for determining achievement

---

1. We are indebted to I. F. Waglow, University of Florida, Gainesville, Fla., for assistance in writing this introduction.

and grades in dance classes (Rhythmic action is also a consideration in grading of gymnastics stunts and swimming skills)

4. As a means for evaluating prospective members of physical education exhibition groups in such activities as synchronized swimming, gymnastics, and dance

PROBLEMS AND LIMITATIONS OF RHYTHM AND DANCE MEASUREMENT

The problems and limitations that have existed in the measurement of rhythm and dance are identified and briefly discussed here.

1. Most testing accomplished in the area of rhythm and dance has pertained to the gathering of facts and data for research purposes rather than to development of practical tests for the measurement of rhythm and dance ability in the classroom. Thus, there appears to be a great need for objective rhythm and dance tests that are practical for use by the classroom teacher. Graduate students and professional researchers should be encouraged to devote time and effort to the innovation of simple tests of rhythm and dance for this purpose.

2. Certain rhythm tests are limited in use because they require complicated or expensive equipment or both. Since commercial recordings are impractical for use owing to lack of variety and proper arrangement, considerable time and expense are needed to make recordings for testing purposes. However, greater use should be made of the tape recorder for development of suitable recordings.

3. Some of the well-known rhythm tests require only small muscle response, which limits their use in physical education dance classes. Tapping tests and tests that require only a written response are in this category.

4. A perplexing problem to the tester is that some students do not do their best in front of a group, owing to embarrassment. Further, the rating of students one at a time takes considerable class time. On the other hand, when several students are rated at the same time, the poor student has an opportunity to get cues from the more adept ones.

PRACTICAL TESTS OF RHYTHM AND DANCE

Since tests of rhythm and dance are quite limited, the test items discussed here are the most practical found at the present time. Moreover, the word *practical* is used somewhat apologetically for this section. For each of the various dance areas, it is important for the instructor to inform students what he or she is looking for in rating the performance and for students to understand the rating scale to be used. A few of the criteria and ideas to be considered in various types of dance were suggested by Waglow[2] as follows:

Folk Dance.   Three criteria should be considered in rating students: (1) the style of execution of the movement, (2) the knowledge of steps and sequence as related to the music—in general, the student should have memorized this movement, and (3) the rhythm of the student in keeping in time with the music.

Modern Dance.   If the instructor uses set patterns of movement (exercises) in preparing the student for self-expression in modern dance, these movements could be used to evaluate the student. A second area of evaluation is in the performance of a dance, whether it be to a poem or music. In judging an original composition of the student, the instructor might look for difficulty and combination of movements and judge the execution and form. Many instructors find it desirable to bring in other experts in the area of dance to judge the performance of students.

Social Dance.   The instructor may require students to execute a series of variations while they are being rated. Students often memorize their series of variations and provide the instructor with a statement about what variations they will do. Another way of judging would be to require students to make up variations that were not learned in class and to evaluate these variations. In social dance it is important that students dance in time with the rhythmic pattern of the music and that the style of movement be appropriate for the rhythm being played.

Square Dance.   As the student performs square dance movements, the following three criteria should be considered: (1) How well does the

2. Submitted by I. F. Waglow, University of Florida, Gainesville, Fla.

performer respond to the caller? (2) How well does the performer execute the movement that is called for? (3) Does the dancer move according to the rhythmic pattern of the music? The instructor could make use of a record with a caller or the instructor could be the caller and have other instructors do the evaluating.

Tap Dance. In evaluating a student in tap dancing, the following three areas should be considered: (1) Are the movements executed properly? (2) Is the memorized routine of the dance performed correctly? (3) Is the dance performed in rhythm with the music that is being played?

Waglow's Social Dance Test (Waglow 1953)

Objective: To measure the ability of a student to execute a dance step in time with music.

Age Level: Satisfactory for the secondary school and college level.

Sex: Satisfactory for both boys and girls.

Reliability: Recent refinements have raised the reliability of this test to $r = .82$. This is considerably higher than the reliability indicated in the original report in the literature.

Validity: The validity for this test has been found to be .76 in recent studies. The criterion was the combined subjective ratings of two judges.

Equipment and Materials: Music transcribed from records to a tape; chalk for marking a spot on the floor; and small score cards and pencils.

Directions for the Tester: With the tape recorder turned on, the rhythm is identified. The tape then indicates how many measures the student will wait before starting to move. For example, the tape would say "waltz," a short pause would ensue, and then "six measures," another short pause, and then the tape would play the number of measures

the student is to dance. The instructor must decide how many measures of music the students are to dance when making the tape. When the desired number of measures has gone by, the tape recorder ceases to play. There is a 15-sec pause and then the same procedure begins for another rhythm.

Directions to Students: Students are instructed to listen for the rhythm that is to be played and also the number of measures they are to wait before beginning to move. As the tape is played out, students are informed by the instructor that they are not to move until the end of the introductory measures, and then they are to continue moving until the music stops. The forward and backward pattern is to be followed where applicable.

Scoring: Students must be paired whether or not there are equal numbers of males and females. The student performing makes a mark on the floor and the partner is seated in front of the performer with a score card and pencil. The scorer counts the number of times that the performer leaves and returns to the chalk mark. Each return to the chalk mark receives a score of 1. When the music stops, the scorer totals up the score and computes the difference between that score and the correct number of measures for that rhythm. Plus and minus signs are disregarded in scoring. For example, if the correct answer is four and the student performed three steps, the score would be -1; whereas if the student performed five steps, the score would be $+1$. Therefore, the positive and negative scores are added together, disregarding the signs, for a composite score. When the scores are added, the performers with the lowest deviations from the true score are the better performers. Table 17.1 shows norms.

Additional Pointers:

1. In practicing to take the test, students should be told to practice doing the steps as neatly

Table 17.1. *T*-Score Norms for the Waglow Social Dance Test at the College Level

T SCORES	RAW SCORES[a]	*T* SCORES	RAW SCORES	*T* SCORES	RAW SCORES
71	0.5	48	4.5	38	8.5
67	1.0	47	5.0	36	9.5
62	1.5	45	5.5	34	10.5
58	2.0	43	6.0	33	11.0
55	2.5	42	6.5	32	11.5
53	3.0	41	7.0	31	12.0
52	3.5	40	7.5	30	12.5
50	4.0	39	8.0	29	13.0

[a]Raw scores based on performance deviations.
Source: I. F. Waglow, University of Florida, Gainesville, Fla.

as possible so the scorer will not have questions about whether the performer left the chalk mark.

2. Music used during the teaching of the course should be used to construct the test.

3. The performer might finish some distance from the chalk mark, in which case the score would be a half count. For example, if exactly eight measures of waltz music were played and a box step was performed, a correct score would be 4. Completion of five box steps would indicate that the student danced two measures too fast. Completion of three box steps would indicate that the student performed too slow. In such cases, one score is as poor as the other.

Tempo Test (Lemon and Sherbon 1934)

Objective: To measure the ability to repeat a given tempo.

Age Level: Age 10 through college age.

Sex: Satisfactory for both boys and girls.

Reliability: Reliability was not reported for this test. A study of the reliability of the scoring procedure presented here is needed.

Validity: This test is accepted at face validity.

Equipment and Materials: A metronome and either a stopwatch or a wristwatch with a second hand.

Directions: Three tempos are sounded on the metronome with settings of 64, 120, and 184, so that the three speeds will give 12, 22, and 32 beats, respectively, in 10 sec. The performer listens to the metronome at each speed and then steps as nearly as possible in the same tempo while the partner counts the steps for 10 sec. The metronome is not in use during each 10-sec testing.

Scoring: The score is the total number of deviations from the specified beats for the three speeds. Table 17.2 shows norms for college students.

Ashton Practical Rhythm Test (Ashton 1953)

Objective: To measure ability to perform rhythmic movement in response to selected musical excerpts.

Age Level: Age 12 through college age.

Sex: Satisfactory for both boys and girls.

Reliability: Reportedly as high as .86.

Validity: Face validity is accepted for this test.

Equipment and Materials: A tape recording of

Table 17.2. Raw Score Norms for the Tempo Test, College Students[a]

PERFORMANCE LEVEL	SCORE[b]
Excellent	2–0
Good	4–3
Average	7–5
Poor	9–8
Very poor	10 and above

[a]Based on the scores of 100 students with minimal rhythm training in 1970 and with similar results of 35 students in 1976.
[b]Score is total number of deviations from the specified beat for three speeds.

the musical excerpts listed in Figure 17.1 or of similar excerpts.

Directions: Students are informed that the first section of the recording has music for walking, running, and skipping. Each musical excerpt is played twice, and students listen to the first one and then perform as it is replayed, until the music stops.

During the musical excerpts in the second section of the record, students show movements they think fit the music. Students may restrict movements to walking, running, and skipping; however, they should show their best movements, since any movement will be accepted and judged for its value.

The third section of the recording has music for the schottische, waltz, and polka, with more than one piece of music being played for some movements. Students are told what to do by the tester's voice on the recording.

Scoring: The rhythm rating scale in Figure 17.2 is used for all parts of the test. The final score is the total of points made on the test. Table 17.3 shows norms for college students.

Dance Leap Test

Objective: To determine the power of the legs in performing a dance leap for horizontal distance.

Age Level: Junior high school through college age.

Sex: Satisfactory for girls and women.

Reliability: An r of .89 was found when the subjects were tested on separate days by Alita Robnak, Northeast Louisiana University, Monroe, 1971.

Objectivity: An r of .99 was obtained when the subjects were tested by Sara Stockard and Alita Robnak, Northeast Louisiana University, Monroe, 1971.

	Measures	Metronome Setting	Time (sec)
Form #1			
Section 1			
Walk—*Wisconsin Blueprint*	12	112	21.9
Skip—Davies	16	192	19.7
Run—Huerter—*Fire Dance*	24	192	29.3
Section 2			
Skip—*Kerry Dance*	20	208	21.6
Run—Concone—*Study*	16	208	24.8
Fast Walk—Prokofiev	32	132	29.0
Slow Walk—Beethoven	16	104	33.1
Skip—*New Mown Hay*	24	192	37.2
Run—Reinhold—*Gnomes*	32	208	27.6
Section 3			
Schottische—*Jubilee*	16	192	24.7
Slow Waltz—Tschaikowsky—*Waltz from Sleeping Beauty*	32	138	36.1
Mod. Waltz—Schubert, No. 7	32	168	29.0
Polka—Lichner	32	208	24.3
Form #2			
Section 1			
Walk—Davies	12	128	20.3
Skip—*Queen of Sheba*	16	208	32.5
Run—*Wisconsin Blueprint*	12	184	14.4
Section 2			
Skip—Schumann—*Sicilianish*	24	132	21.8
Run—Moszkowski—*Scherzino*	12	208	22.3
Fast Walk—Handel—*Joshua*	16	196	21.0
Slow Walk—Hollaender March	17	116	31.6
Skip—*Marche Lorraine*	32	132	28.8
Run—Delibes—*Passapied*	24	208	25.5
Section 3			
Schottische—*Faust-up-to-Date*	24	168	35.1
Slow Waltz—Gurlit—*First Dance*	32	138	35.7
Mod. Waltz—Tschaikowsky—*Waltz of the Flowers*	32	168	27.2
Polka—*Plantation Dance*	24	200	25.3

Figure 17.1. List of musical excerpts to be used for Ashton practical rhythm test (Ashton 1953)

Validity: Face validity is accepted for this test.

Equipment and Materials: Tape measure and marking material.

Directions: Starting with the toes of the right foot behind a starting line, the performer swings the left leg forward and leaps from the right leg as far forward as possible. Thus, the leap is made from one foot to the other foot while the performer splits the legs in the air. The landing on the left foot should be cushioned by landing on the ball of the foot giving in to the heel and by bending the knee. The right foot should then be brought forward to save the balance (Figure 17.3).

Scoring: The measurement is made from the starting line to the back of the heel of the left foot. The best of three trials as measured to the nearest quarter of an inch is recorded as the score.

A penalty of 1 in. is subtracted from the score for each occurrence of the following errors: (1) failure to extend the legs and point the toes during the leap, (2) failure to make a steady landing, and (3) landing flat-footed. Table 17.4 shows norms for college women.

Table 17.3. Raw Score Norms for Ashton Practical Rhythm Test, College Students

PERFORMANCE LEVEL	TOTAL POINTS[a]
Excellent	92 and above
Good	66–91
Average	40–65
Poor	14–39
Very poor	0–13

[a]Scoring scale projected on basis of a 0- to 4-point scale with 26 measured items. See Figure 17.2 for rating scale.

Point	Explanation
0	No response or incorrect response. Correct beat and accent only through chance. Step and rhythm incorrect. Attempts to start self in motion; undecided as to correct step. Starts a preliminary faltering movement, then stops.
1	Correct step but not correct beat (unable to pick up new beat or tempo). Correct movement only by imitation of another student. Awkward, uncoordinated movement. Ability to start self in movement maintained only for a measure or two. Difficulty in changing direction.
2	Step and rhythm pattern correct. Reaction time slow. Movement uncertain—lapses occasionally into incorrect beat. Movements consistently heavy; shows tension. Maintenance of movement is short; phrase. Movement is forced, mechanical. Lacking in style. Prosaic—no variety.
3	Uses correct step, beat, and accent. If loses accent and gets off beat, is aware of it and able to get back on beat. Ability to maintain movement throughout excerpt. Varies direction with effort but is able to maintain movement. Shows ability in simple movement. Movement has direction but is not alive and spirited.
4	Immediate response with correct step, beat, and accent. Ability to maintain movement throughout excerpt. Ability to vary movement (turns, etc.) Confidence shown in movement. Movements definite, spirited, and easily accomplished. Student is relaxed.

Figure 17.2. Rhythm rating scale for Ashton practical rhythm test (Ashton 1953)

Rhythm Run Dance Test

Objective: To measure coordination and control in running a given distance at one level.

Age Level: Junior high school through college age.

Sex: Girls and women.

Reliability: An *r* of .85 was determined when the test was administered on two separate days by Alita Robnak, Northeast Louisiana University, Monroe, 1971.

Figure 17.3. Dance leap test

Table 17.4. Raw Score Norms for Dance Leap Test, College Women[a]

PERFORMANCE LEVEL	SCORE	
	Inches	Centimeters
Excellent	64¼ and above	163.2 and above
Good	54 –64	137.2–162.6
Average	42¼–53¾	107.3–136.5
Poor	35 –42	88.9–106.7
Very poor	0 –34¾	0 – 88.3

[a]Based on the scores of 100 women as reported by Elizabeth Greenwood. Northeast Louisiana University, Monroe, 1972.

Objectivity: An *r* of .89 was obtained by Sara Stockard and Alita Robnak, Northeast Louisiana University, Monroe, 1971.

Validity: Face validity is accepted for this test.

Equipment and Materials: One roll of crepe paper (2 in. wide); marking tape; and two poles or standards.

Directions: The crepe paper is tied between the two poles or standards, which are 40 ft apart. The crepe paper should be stretched so that it is at eye level at the center between the two poles. It should be adjusted evenly on both sides or be kept as straight as possible between the two poles. The floor is marked off every 10 ft under the crepe paper. The performer starts at one standard (pole) and performs a low run under the length of the crepe paper (Figure 17.4).

Scoring: A maximum of 100 points is possible. Points are lost as follows: (1) For each 10-ft zone that the performer tilts her head forward while running, there is a 10-point penalty. (2) There is a 10-point penalty for stepping rather than running for each 10-ft dimension. (3) There is a 5-point penalty for each time the performer touches her head to the crepe paper. Table 17.5 shows norms for college women.

Additional Pointers:

1. The performer should keep the knees flexed at all times during the rhythm run.

2. The performer should start the extension of the leg from the hip to avoid stepping.

3. The use of a drumbeat is helpful during the test.

Figure 17.4. Rhythm run dance test

Table 17.5. Raw Score Norms for Rhythm Run Dance Test, College Women[a]

PERFORMANCE LEVEL	SCORE (POINTS)[b]
Excellent	96–100
Good	83– 95
Average	61– 82
Poor	48– 60
Very poor	0– 47

[a]Based on the scores of 100 women as reported by Pam Carmichael Holt, Northeast Louisiana University, Monroe, 1972.
[b]See text for description of scoring.

Fall and Recovery Test of Dance Agility

Objective: To determine agility in falling and recovering in a dance movement.

Age Level: Junior high school through college age.

Sex: Satisfactory for women students.

Reliability: An *r* of .92 was found when subjects were tested on separate days by Alita Robnak, Northeast Louisiana University, Monroe, 1971.

Objectivity: An *r* of .68 was obtained when the subjects were tested by Sara Stockard and Alita Robnak, Northeast Louisiana University, Monroe, 1971.

Validity: Face validity is accepted for this test.

Equipment and Materials: A stopwatch and a mat.

Directions: The performer begins from a front-standing position and pushes off from the right foot, extending it as the left leg flexes and turns out. The arms are extended overhead. This completes phase one (Figure 17.5a). She then brings the left knee behind the right knee while allowing the right to bend, thus lowering herself to the floor on the left thigh (Figure 17.5b). The performer continues to a complete extended position on the left side on the floor (Figure 17.5c). This completes phase two. Phase three is the recovery phase, where the performer sits up and brings the right leg over the left (Figure 17.5d) and then returns to a standing position.

Scoring: The performer is timed for 15 sec and receives 1 point for each phase of the movement performed correctly. Norms are shown in Table 17.6.

Additional Pointers:

1. To assume extension in phase one, the performer must push off the right leg (in flexion) to an extended position.

2. To prevent injury to the kneecap in phase two, the performer lowers herself to the floor, rotating the leg outward, thus sliding onto the leg rather than onto the knee itself.

3. To get a better score, the performer should immediately go from phase three to phase one without hesitation.

FINDINGS AND CONCLUSIONS FROM RHYTHM AND DANCE MEASUREMENT AND RESEARCH

The Seashore test, a frequently used written test of rhythm, has been correlated with various measures of motor performance (Annett 1932; Benton 1944; Dillon 1952; Lemon and Sherbon 1934). Such correlations ranged from − .10 to .48. Two investigators concluded that written sensory tests are not adequate for the type of rhythm emphasized in physical education classes (Lemon and Sherbon 1934; Simpson 1958).

Several investigators have tested the hypothesis that the rhythm found in music has a positive effect on the learning and performance of physical skills (Dillon 1952; Diserens 1926; Estep 1958; Lowenthal 1948). While the findings of such studies have revealed a positive effect, Nelson found that pure rhythmic tones, or music intensity, had no favorable or unfavorable effects on an endurance performance test.

Two studies (Johnson 1963, 1965) have shown that when music is used in conjunction with the presence of other people and with competition, endurance and strength performance are improved. This may be true of pure rhythmic tones or musical intensity (Nelson 1963).

It has been frequently assumed that Negroes are superior to whites in motor rhythm. Several investigators tested this hypothesis, and the consensus of results indicates that Negroes do not show a statistically significant superiority in rhythm to whites (Johnson 1931; Muzzey 1933; Peterson and Lanier 1929; Sanderson 1933; Streep 1931).

Concerning the use of rhythm for faster reaction time and movement time, Miles and Graves, Thompson and associates, and Wilson found faster starts when a stimulus was presented in a rhythmic rather than a nonrhythmic series. Thompson further noted that the speed of movement initiated by reaction is not influenced by rhythmicity or nonrhythmicity.

Controversy exists among investigators concerning the question as to whether rhythm is innate or acquired. McCristal and Swindle concluded

Figure 17.5. Fall and recovery test of dance agility. (a) Phase one, (b) and (c) Phase two, (d) Phase three

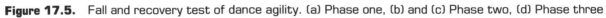

Table 17.6. Raw Scores for Fall and Recovery Test, College Women[a]

PERFORMANCE LEVEL	SCORE[b]
Excellent	15 and above
Good	12–14
Average	10–11
Poor	6– 9
Very poor	0– 5

[a]Based on the scores of 100 women as reported by Elizabeth Greenwood, Northeast Louisiana University, Monroe, 1973.
[b]See text for description of test and scoring method.

that rhythm increases with the amount of training acquired and is not an inherited quality. On the other hand, results of studies by Haight and Lemon and Sherbon revealed that rhythmic ability was more the result of innate tendencies. Other studies indicated the importance of practice and development to the improvement of motor rhythm. For example, Muzzey concluded that motor rhythm is a function of school age, with each grade showing superiority to the previous one, while Annett found that the earlier a child begins activities related to motor rhythm, everything else being equal, the better dancer he or she will become. Thus, from a study of previous research, it appears that rhythm is innate to a certain extent, but can be greatly improved through consistent practice and training.

Contrary to popular belief, there are tests and measurements instruments that enable the tester to evaluate objectively a student's rhythmic performance. Some tests involve specially constructed apparatus, and these are not only complicated but rarely found in physical education departments (Baldwin and Stecher 1924; Bond 1959; Buck 1936; Heinlein 1929; Patterson et al. 1930; Simpson 1958; Smoll 1973). Other objective tests have been devised that are practical from the standpoint of equipment involved but take too much time to administer (McCulloch 1955; Shambaugh 1935).

Benton, testing the hypothesis that dance movement involves more than just rhythm, found that other elements involved are static balance, motor educability, agility, and strength. While no single measure was found of value in predicting dance skill, a combination of several motor tests revealed a high relationship with criterion ratings (sum of three judges' scores for each subject) of dance movement technique.

Bond found that several of the senses (tactile, aural, and visual) are capable of experiencing rhythmic patterns, but she failed to find a significant relationship between scores from sensory rhythmic perception tests and measures of motor performance.

BIBLIOGRAPHY

Annett, T., "A Study of Rhythmic Capacity and Performance in Motor Rhythm in Physical Education Majors." *Research Quarterly* 3:190, May 1932.

Ashton, D., "A Gross Motor Rhythm Test." *Research Quarterly* 24:253–260, October 1953.

Baldwin, B. T., and L. I. Stecher, *The Psychology of the Pre-school Child*. New York: D. Appleton, 1924, pp. 141–145.

Benton, R. J., "The Measurement of Capacities for Learning Dance Movement Techniques." *Research Quarterly* 15:139–140, May 1944.

Blake, P. A., "Relationship Between Audio-Perceptual Rhythm and Skill in Square Dance." *Research Quarterly* 31:231, May 1960.

Bond, M. H., "Rhythmic Perception and Gross Motor Performance." *Research Quarterly* 30:259, October 1959.

Buck, N., "A Comparison of Two Methods of Testing Response to Auditory Rhythms." *Research Quarterly* 7:37–43, October 1936.

Cooper, J. M., and R. B. Glassow, *Kinesiology*. St. Louis: C. V. Mosby, 1963, pp. 278–279.

Dillon, E. K., "A Study of the Use of Music as an Aid in Teaching Swimming." *Research Quarterly* 23:8, March 1952.

Diserens, C. M., *The Influence of Music on Behavior*. Princeton, N.J.: Princeton University Press, 1926, p. 224.

Estep, D. P., "The Relationship of Static Equilibrium to Ability in Gross Motor Activities." Unpublished master's thesis, University of California, 1958.

Haight, E. C. "Individual Differences in Motor Adaptations to Rhythmic Stimuli." *Research Quarterly* 15:42, March 1944.

Heinlein, C. P., "A New Method of Studying Rhythmic Responses of Children Together With an Evaluation of the Method of Simple Observation." *Journal of Genetic Psychology* 36:205–229, June 1929.

Johnson, B. L., "The Effect of Motivational Testing Situations on an Endurance Test." Laboratory experiment, Northeast Louisiana University, Monroe, 1963.

———, "The Effect of Applying Different Motivational Techniques During Training and in

Testing Upon Strength Performance." Microcarded doctoral dissertation, Louisiana State University, Baton Rouge, 1965.

Johnson, G. B., "A Summary of Negro Scores on the Seashore Music Talent Tests." *Journal of Comparative Psychology* 11:383–393, 1931.

Lemon, E., and E. Sherbon, "A Study of the Relationship of Certain Measures of Rhythmic Ability and Motor Ability in Girls and Women." *Research Quarterly Supplement* 5:85, March 1934.

Lowenthal, E., "Rhythmic Training." *JOHPER* 19(7):474, 1948.

McCristal, K. J., "Experimental Study of Rhythm in Gymnastics and Tap Dancing." *Research Quarterly* 4:74–75, May 1933.

McCulloch, M. L., "The Development of a Test of Rhythmic Response Through Movement of First Grade Children." Microcarded doctoral dissertation, University of Oregon, Eugene, 1955.

Miles, W. R., and B. J. Graves, "Studies in Physical Exertion. III. Effect of Signal Variation on Football Charging." *Research Quarterly* 2:31, October 1931.

Muzzey, D. M., "Group Progress of White and Colored Children in Learning a Rhythm Pattern." *Research Quarterly* 4:62–70, October 1933.

Nelson, D. O., "Effect of Selected Rhythms and Sound Intensity on Human Performance as Measured by the Bicycle Ergometer." *Research Quarterly* 34:488, May 1963.

Patterson, D. G., et al., *Minnesota Mechanical Ability Tests*. Minneapolis: University of Minnesota Press, 1930.

Peterson, J., and L. H. Lanier, "Studies in the Comparable Abilities of Whites and Negroes." *Mental Measurement Monograph 5*, No. 4, 1929, p. 156.

Sanderson, H. E., "Differences in Musical Ability in Children of Different National and Racial Origin." *Journal of Genetic Psychology* 42:100–120, 1933.

Shambaugh, M. E., "The Objective Measurement of Success in the Teaching of Folk Dancing to University Women." *Research Quarterly* 6:52, March 1935.

Simpson, S. E., "Development and Validation of an Objective Measure of Locomotor Response to Auditory Rhythmic Stimuli." *Research Quarterly* 29:342, October 1958.

Smoll, F. L., "A Rhythmic Ability Analysis System." *Research Quarterly* 44:232, May 1973.

Streep, R. L., "A Comparison of White and Negro Children in Rhythm and Consonance." *Journal of Applied Psychology* 15:52–71, 1931.

Stupp, L. L., "A Correlation of Musical Ability and Dancing Ability." Unpublished master's thesis, University of Wisconsin, 1922, p. 43.

Swindle, P. F., "On the Inheritance of Rhythm." *American Journal of Psychology* 24:180–203, April 1913.

Thompson, C. W., et al., "Football Starting Signals and Movement Times of High School and College Football Players." *Research Quarterly* 29:230, May 1958.

Waglow, I. F., "An Experiment in Social Dance Testing." *Research Quarterly* 24:100–101, March 1953.

Wilson, D. J., "Quickness of Reaction and Movement Related to Rhythmicity or Nonrhythmicity of Signal Presentation." *Research Quarterly* 30:109, March 1959.

ADDITIONAL SOURCES

Austin, S. D., "The Relationship of Modern Dance Performance to Strength, Coordination, and Kinesthetic Perception." Unpublished master's thesis, Smith College, Northampton, Mass., 1969.

Brennen, M. A., "A Comparative Study of Skilled Gymnasts and Dancers on Thirteen Selected Characteristics." Unpublished master's thesis, University of Wisconsin, Madison, 1967.

Briggs, R. A., "The Development of an Instrument for Assessment of Motoric Rhythmic Performance." Unpublished master's thesis, University of Missouri, Columbia, 1968.

Bucklin, E. P., "Skills Tests and Pressure Perception Related to Social Dance." Unpublished master's thesis, Washington State University, Pullman, 1969.

Bushey, S. R., "Relationship of Modern Dance Performance to Agility, Balance, Flexibility, Power, and Strength." *Research Quarterly* 37:313–316, October 1966.

Coppock, D. E., "Development of an Objective Measure of Rhythmic Motor Response." *Research Quarterly* 39:915–921, December, 1968.

Dvorak, S. E., "A Subjective Evaluation of Fundamental Locomotor Movement in Modern Dance Using a Five-Point Scale." Unpublished master's thesis, South Dakota State University, Brookings, 1967.

Frial, P. I. S., "Prediction of Modern Dance Ability Through Kinesthetic Tests." Unpublished doctoral dissertation, University of Iowa, Iowa City, 1965.

Imel, E. C., "Construction of an Objective Motor Rhythm Skill Test." Unpublished master's thesis, University of Iowa, Iowa City, 1963.

Lang, L. M., "The Development of a Test of Rhythmic Response at the Elementary Level." Unpublished master's thesis, University of Texas, Austin, 1966.

Lockhart, A., and E. Pease, *Modern Dance: Building and Teaching Lessons*. 3rd ed. Dubuque, Iowa: William C. Brown, 1966.

Schwanda, N. A., "A Study of Rhythmic Ability and Movement Performance." *Research Quarterly* 40:567–574, October 1969.

Withers, M. R., "Measuring Creativity of Modern Dancers." Unpublished master's thesis, University of Utah, Salt Lake City, 1960.

Wurster, S. L. J., "The Scientific Authenticity of the Dvorak Evaluation Test of Fundamental Locomotor Movement for Beginners in Modern Dance." Unpublished master's thesis, South Dakota State University, Brookings, 1969.

CHAPTER 18

PERCEPTUAL-MOTOR PERFORMANCE AND MOTOR PERFORMANCE OF THE HANDICAPPED

OBJECTIVES

After reading this chapter, the student should be able to:

1. Describe some of the types of tests used to assess perceptual motor abilities and some of the types of tests that have been developed for evaluating motor performance of persons who are handicapped

2. Understand some of the problems associated with the measurement of perceptual motor ability in young children

3. Follow the directions for administering practical tests of perceptual motor ability

4. Understand and anticipate some of the problems associated with the measurement of motor performance of persons who are handicapped

5. Follow the directions for administering practical tests of motor performance with persons who are handicapped

Although theories advocating the value of motor activity experiences in a child's perceptual development are by no means new, there has been a great upsurge of interest recently among physical educators in the relationship between basic motor patterns and intellectual growth. Much of this interest was stimulated by the work of Kephart and of Delacato, who utilized motor therapy with children with language and reading-readiness problems.

Much controversy has ensued as to the relative merits of the various therapeutic programs that emphasize developmental movement experiences and the practice of basic locomotor activities. Evidence is contradictory, due largely to a lack of objective evidence. The instruments used in assessing movement behavior and perceptual functions have been questioned with regard to their validity and reliability (Smith 1968). Other facets of the controversy concern the appropriate age level, whether all children should be involved or just slow learners, and the kinds of motor activities that should be incorporated in the programs.

In studies concerning the slow learner, many of the children were found to be of normal or above-normal intelligence; yet they performed poorly on motor ability test items. According to Kephart, poor motor coordination involving laterality and directionality must be overcome through practice of various movement patterns if the child is to be able to cope with the more complex activities of reading, writing, and arithmetic.

It has been said that the children of today are denied many opportunities to climb, run, jump, explore, and manipulate their environment that were afforded children of previous generations. Hence, some workers in this area maintain that a

338

real need exists for a wide variety of movement experiences for all preschool and primary grade children.

Space does not permit us to present an adequate discussion of the rationale behind the perceptual—motor "movement" and the research evidence supporting or discounting the claims that cognitive functioning can be improved through motor activities. It will suffice to say that there is general agreement that a child's self-image and level of aspiration may be aided through improved motor skills and that because of the interaction between perception and motor functions, certain parts of the overall educational program may be affected positively through movement activities (Cratty 1967). Although disagreement may exist as to the extent of direct and indirect enhancement of intellectual functioning as a result of movement, perceptual—motor activities should be provided for all young children.

The stated objectives in the various perceptual—motor programs may differ in terms of emphasis, but essentially they seek to provide the following (Clifton 1970):

1. Development and use of skills of locomotor movement such as walking, running, jumping, hopping, sliding, skipping, and climbing

2. Development and use of eye-hand and foot-hand coordination skills of throwing, catching, striking, and kicking

3. Development of skills basic to movement and gross motor performance such as balance, agility, flexibility, strength, and endurance

4. Development of a functional concept of body size and space requirements in terms of height, depth, and breadth for the body to perform in a variety of situations

5. Opportunities for use of various sense modalities, such as auditory, visual, tactile, and proprioceptive, in gross motor activities

As was mentioned, one of the problems in establishing evidence of the effectiveness of perceptual—motor programs is the lack of precise measuring devices for evaluation. This is certainly understandable, since the teacher is interested in the quality of the movements perhaps more than in the quantity. In other words, the evaluative criteria may stress the "how" of performance as well as the "what." The teacher is interested in observing a child's performance in terms of confidence, coordination, and relaxation and not just in terms of time needed to nego-

tiate the task. The assessment of quality is by necessity largely subjective. A child's performance has generally been scored as "pass" or "fail" or on a "good," "average," "fair," or "failure" basis.

We are not condemning these evaluation methods; on the contrary, subjective judgment is fundamental in teaching motor skills. It requires a skilled examiner, preparation, and practice. In view of the dearth of tests in the area of perceptual-motor performance, we can only present some tests that have been used that may prompt the interested individual to modify existing tests or devise better ones.

MOTOR PERFORMANCE OF THE HANDICAPPED

In recent years, federal mandates, state and local legislation, and pressure and support from various agencies and organizations concerned with special education have reinforced the role of physical education in the curriculum for children with handicaps. The commitment to equal opportunities in education for such children involves the development and implementation of individual programs in physical education, recreation, and related services. Continuous evaluation is an integral part of program development and implementation.

Measurement is involved in each phase of the handicapped child's program, from the initial assessment of the need for special education, to determining the nature of the child's program, to formulating annual goals and objectives, and to the periodic reevaluation to ascertain progress toward the attainment of the specified goals. The success of the educational program rests heavily on the skill and knowledge of the teacher and the teacher's use of various forms of evaluation.

A comprehensive coverage of tests for assessing motor performance of children with handicaps is beyond the scope of this text. The many different forms and levels of impairment, disability, and handicap would necessitate several books to discuss adequately evaluation of the various conditions.

Some practical tests used in the evaluation of children who are handicapped are presented here. Descriptions or summaries are given for tests for the mentally retarded, auditory impaired, visually impaired, emotionally disturbed, and orthopedically impaired.

PROBLEMS ASSOCIATED WITH THE MEASUREMENT OF PERCEPTUAL–MOTOR PERFORMANCE AND MOTOR PERFORMANCE OF THE HANDICAPPED

Some problems associated with the measurement and evaluation of the motor proficiency of handicapped and nonhandicapped children, along with some suggestions for testing the very young child and the handicapped child, are as follows:

1. The problem of specificity is a major factor confronting perceptual–motor training programs. No evidence shows that experiences in one type of gross motor skill will transfer to another. This problem pervades in any attempt to measure perceptual–motor abilities. The results are thus limited in that the performance being assessed is specific. However, most research evidence indicates this is true with any measurement. A possible approach is the use of a problem-solving test in which the child must negotiate a series of tasks or type of obstacle course that comprises tasks similar to the specific items that the child has practiced.

2. Since quality of performance is of great importance in perceptual–motor evaluation, the scoring of tests in this area is complicated. Research is needed to devise scoring scales that might combine ratings or errors along with quantitative measures such as distance and time.

3. Practice trials might also be interwoven into the measurement of perceptual–motor performance. Perhaps some scoring system could be developed such as that discussed by McCraw in which the amount of improvement made is related to the amount of improvement possible.

4. Crafts made some observations about perceptual–motor assessment instruments concerning validity. She cautioned that perhaps in some tests the child's ability to learn various patterns of behavior, the ability to interpret feedback and then correct errors, the attention span, self-confidence, and other factors may be what are actually being reflected in the score rather than perceptual–motor ability.

5. Norms for perceptual–motor performance are practically nonexistent. If certain basic skills could be agreed on by clinicians in this area, norms for different age levels could be set up that would be of great help for teachers of preschool and elementary school children.

6. Without question, the role of the tester is different and much more important in the measurement of the handicapped than in that of the nonhandicapped. For example, it is essential that the teacher establish good rapport with the child. It is worth the extra time for the teacher to get well acquainted with the child prior to testing. The creativity, sensitivity, patience, and insight of the tester may well be the most critical aspect of a test's validity. It is extremely important that the teacher remain positive and supportive when testing the handicapped child.

7. It is much more difficult to obtain reliable measurements on young children and on certain handicapped children than on older nonhandicapped children. Thus, the teacher should strive for multiple assessments rather than relying on only one or two tests.

8. One of the most logical and effective ways to deal with inconsistent performance on tests is to use checklists. Thereby the teacher can observe a child's performance and behavior tendencies on different occasions over a period of weeks (Thomas and Thomas 1984).

9. More practice trials and test trials are often needed by the handicapped to give an accurate performance. The two or three trials usually allotted to a nonhandicapped child may not be sufficient to secure the best efforts of a very young child or a handicapped child.

10. The tester must be very careful in the use of terms in the test instructions, and should be alert to the need for simplified expressions, demonstrations, and manual guidance. In most motor performance tests, the teacher is not trying to assess the child's cognitive ability to understand directions but to evaluate physical performance. A child who does not perform well because of obvious misunderstanding should be retested.

11. As with any testing, the more knowledgeable and experienced the tester is with the student's capacities the better the results.

For example, in tests such as speed of running, use of a "false" finish line farther than the actual finish line is advisable. In other words, to compensate for the child's tendency to begin slowing down or stopping at the finish line, a false end line is marked beyond the point at which the time is actually taken. Another point is that young children have a tendency to quit or give up on difficult or strenuous tasks (Thomas and Thomas, 1984).

12. The testing area should be free of possible distractions, and added safety precautions are usually necessary.

13. The teacher should always be cognizant of the danger of attributing changes (improvement) in motor performance to the program, when in fact they are due to maturation and the improved fitness and motor control that accompanies maturation (Thomas and Thomas 1984).

PERCEPTUAL—MOTOR TEST BATTERIES

A few batteries of simple to complex activities have been devised to assess perceptual—motor performance. Some are scored on a pass—fail basis, others on a rating scale of the quality of the performance, and still others on a more objective basis. Some investigators have established obstacle courses to appraise children's ability to solve perceptual—motor "problems" that they find in their path. Such courses have the advantage of being motivating, since they present a challenge and provide knowledge of results as to improvement over previous performances. A variety of tasks can be provided in a test battery, and the

tester can evaluate the child's abilities as he or she performs the different types of movement patterns required.

The following batteries are presented as examples of tests that provide an objective score, even though a number of the items may be evaluated subjectively.

Fisher Motor Performance Test (Fisher 1970)

Objective: To measure various aspects of motor performance of preschool and primary grade children.

Age Level: Kindergarten and primary grades.

Sex: Both boys and girls.

Reliability: An r of .82 was found on test—retest with kindergarten children.

Equipment and Materials: Ten stations as shown in Figure 18.1. In Fisher's study, the children were told to imagine that a wild animal was chasing them, with the various test stations representing rivers, tunnels, mountains, cliffs, and so on. Considerable ingenuity was manifested in the construction and painting of the test stations. This is not necessary for the accomplishment of the tasks.

The specific equipment and materials needed are described with the test directions for the different stations.

Station 1. Ball Bounce

Equipment and Materials: A 10-in. playground ball and a stopwatch.

Directions: The child bounces the ball ten times before proceeding to the next station. If the ball gets away he or she must retrieve it and continue bouncing. *Note*: The stopwatch is started when the child bounces the ball the first time and it

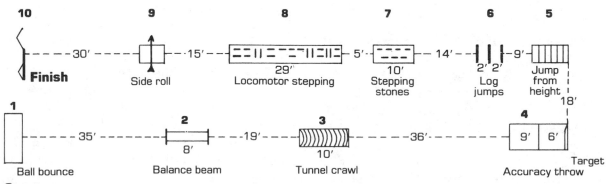

Figure 18.1.   Diagram for Fisher Motor Performance Test. Numbers 1 through 10 refer to the stations

continues to run until the child crosses the finish line (station 10).

Station 2.   Balance Beam

Equipment and Materials: A 4-in. balance beam 8 ft long and about 6 in. above the ground.

Directions: The child runs from station 1 a distance of 35 ft and crosses the "river" as quickly as possible, being careful not to fall into the "water." If the child falls off, he or she gets back up at that point and continues across.

Station 3.   Tunnel Crawl

Equipment and Materials: A cloth tunnel 10 ft long, approximately 2 ft wide and 2 ft high.

Directions: The child runs from station 2 a distance of 19 ft, and crawls on hands and knees as quickly as possible through the tunnel.

Station 4.   Accuracy Throw

Equipment and Materials: A target made of poster paper 28 × 36 in. in size (in Fisher's study, the target was a tiger drawn on the paper, the bottom of which was 54 in. from the ground); at least two 10-in. playground balls; and a restraining line 6 ft from the target and another line 15 ft from the target drawn with chalk or made by ropes or string.

Directions: The child runs 36 ft from station 3 and is told to throw the ball at the target from behind the 6-ft restraining line. He or she tries to hit the target three times, but, if unsuccessful, three more trials are given. The second line, 15 ft from the target, is the out-of-bounds line. If the ball, rebounding from the target, stays between the 6-ft and 15-ft lines, the child must retrieve it and run back to the 6-ft line to throw again. If the ball gets away beyond the lines, he or she is handed another ball.

Station 5.   Jump From Height

Equipment and Materials: A ramp about 3 ft wide and 8 ft long made of boards sloping up to a height of 2 ft (in Fisher's study, a set of four stairs was constructed up to a platform 4 ft square).

Directions: The child runs 18 ft from station 4 and then runs up the ramp and jumps to the ground.

Station 6.   Logjump

Equipment and Materials: Three "logs" approximately 6 in. high spaced 2 ft apart. The "logs" can be cardboard, metal, or wood.

Directions: The child runs 9 ft from station 5 and jumps three times in succession over the "logs," being instructed to use both feet for takeoff and landing on each jump.

Station 7.   Stepping Stones

Equipment and Materials: Nine blocks approximately 2 in. high and 4 × 7 in. in size are staggered in two lines, each equidistant across a 10-ft space (Figure 18.1).

Directions: The child runs 14 ft from station 6 and is instructed to walk across the "river," stepping on each "stone," as quickly as possible without falling off. If the child falls off he or she gets back up on that block and continues across.

Station 8.   Locomotor Stepping

Equipment and Materials: A paper cloth or canvas 29 ft long, with right and left footprints drawn on it in such a manner that the child must jump and hop turning right and left.

Directions: The child runs 5 ft from station 7 and is instructed to "do what the feet tell you to do as quickly as you can." The object of the test is to have the child jump and hop on one and two feet, turning left and right as he or she moves along as rapidly as possible. If the child should slightly miss a footprint, he is not stopped, but if he fails to execute the prescribed jump or goes completely off the sheet, he must start at that point and continue on.

Station 9.   Side Roll

Equipment and Materials: A small mat and a board of sufficient length supported by two sawhorses, which place the board 21 in. above the mat.

Directions: The child runs 15 ft from station 8 and rolls on his or her side (either right or left, or tester can specify) under the board as quickly as possible and scrambles up to run to the finish line.

Station 10.   Finish Line

Equipment and Materials: A chalk line (in Fisher's study, a doorway was built to represent a house and "safety" from the pursuing animal).

Directions: The child runs as fast as possible the 30 ft from station 9 to cross the finish line. The stopwatch is stopped at the moment the line is crossed.

Scoring: The score is the elapsed time, to the nearest tenth of a second, from the first ball bounce at station 1 to the crossing of the finish line at station 10. The total distance is approximately 250 ft. The average of four trials is the score.

Additional Pointers:

1. It is desirable to have two assistants, one to assist at the accuracy throw and the other between the two ends of the course to encourage the child.

2. A second child can start the course when the first child finishes throwing at the accuracy throw. Two stopwatches then are needed.

3. Considerable imagination can be used in devising the test stations to help motivate and challenge the children.

4. Strict adherence to the exact distances between test stations is not of great importance. The distances established by Fisher were determined by several factors such as the configuration of the grounds and the space requirements of the individual test stations.

Perceptual—Motor Obstacle Course (Nelson 1972)

Objective: To measure various aspects of perceptual—motor performance of preschool and primary grade children and to use for practice.

Reliability and Validity: Reliability and validity coefficients and norms are not yet available.

Directions: The child is instructed to proceed through the course as quickly and correctly as possible. The stopwatch is started when the child leaves the starting line and is stopped when he or she crosses the finish line.

Scoring: The score is the elapsed time for completion of the entire course. A scoring system combining errors and time is also being considered.

Station 1. Foot—Eye Coordination

Equipment and Materials: A canvas, sheet, or paper with footprints or some type of marking to denote the foot placement pattern. The pattern could be painted on a blacktop or concrete play area. The footprints are about 12 to 15 in. apart (Figure 18.2).

Directions: The child is told to hop according to the footprints as quickly as possible.

Scoring: If errors are to be counted, the number of times the child fails to hit the indicated footprints is recorded. If time only is considered, the

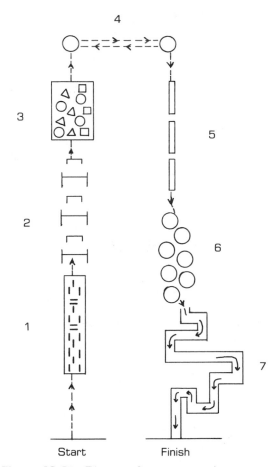

Figure 18.2. Diagram for perceptual—motor obstacle course. Numbers refer to the stations

child must start again at the point at which he or she missed.

Station 2. Over and Under (Body Space)

Equipment and Materials: Barriers and hurdles constructed with light wood, preferably in such a way that the crossbar falls off easily when bumped. The barriers are approximately 2½ ft from the ground, and the hurdles are 12 in. high (Figure 18.2).

Directions: The child is instructed to stoop under and jump over the barriers and hurdles as quickly as possible.

Scoring: Same as for station 1.

Station 3. Form Discrimination

Equipment and Materials: A pattern of squares, triangles, and circles drawn on a canvas or surface. Each figure is about 12 in. in diameter and the distance between similar forms is about 15 in.

Directions: The child is told to jump placing both feet on the specified form, that is, on a triangle, on a square, or on a circle. The specific form can vary with different trials.

Scoring: Same as for station 1.

Station 4. Ball Transfer (Eye–Hand Coordination)

Equipment and Materials: Two boxes or other containers large enough to hold at least five 10-in. playground balls. The distance between the boxes should be at least 15 ft.

Directions: The child takes the balls out of the box one at a time on the left and places them in the box at the right. The manner in which he or she deposits the balls in the box depends on the nature and level of skill desired. The teacher may want the child to (1) simply place the balls in the basket, (2) toss them from a specified distance, (3) toss them over a barrier, (4) bounce them in, (5) bank them in, or other method. The size and number of balls can be altered also.

Scoring: The score can be the number of correct trials or the elapsed time for a certain number of trials.

Station 5. Balance and Locomotor Movement

Equipment and Materials: Three balance beams, made from 2 × 4s, each about 8 ft in length set up on edge or placed flat, to vary the width of the beam depending on the age and skill level of the children. The height of the beams from the ground can also be varied.

Directions: The child is instructed to cross the first beam in a sideward sliding movement, either right or left, then to cross the second beam forward (or backward), and to cross the third in a sliding sideward movement in the opposite direction as that performed on the first beam. The child is encouraged to move as quickly as possible, but safely. The manner in which the child crosses the beams can be varied in accordance with the desired objectives.

Scoring: Same as for station 1.

Station 6. Agility Tire Run

Equipment and Materials: Seven automobile tires staggered with their sides touching, as shown in Figure 18.2.

Directions: The child runs through the tires as quickly as possible. He or she may be instructed to put the feet in the center of each tire or just to land on the side of each tire, depending on the wishes of the tester.

Scoring: Same as for station 1.

Station 7. The Maze

Equipment and Materials: A maze pattern drawn or taped to canvas or floor surface or, if sufficient folding mats are available, a more challenging maze constructed with the mats placed upright. The lane is 2 ft in width. An example of possible dimensions is shown in Figure 18.2.

Directions: The child is instructed to negotiate through the maze as quickly as possible without touching the boundary lines and then to run to the finish line.

Scoring: Same as for station 1.

Dayton Sensory Motor Awareness Survey for 4- and 5-Year-Olds[1]

Figure 18.3 contains the test items and scoring instructions for the Dayton Sensory Motor Awareness Survey for 4- and 5-Year-Olds.

TESTS USED IN ASSESSING MOTOR PERFORMANCE OF THE HANDICAPPED

Bruininks–Oseretsky Test of Motor Proficiency (Short Form) (Bruininks 1978)

Objective: To assess the motor proficiency of children from 4½ to 14½ years of age. The test is used to assess whether a child is handicapped, and may also be used to determine the child's long-term curriculum needs.

Sex: Boys and girls.

Reliability: Reliability estimates were obtained by test–retest and were found to be quite satisfactory. The *Examiner's Manual* contains statistical data on reliability coefficients. Standard errors of measurement for subtest and composite scores are provided also. In addition, interrater reliability (objectivity) coefficients on the eight items in Subtest 7 ranged from .63 to .97. Subtest 7 requires more subjective judgment than other items. Satisfactory reliability (and validity) characteristics of the Bruininks–Oseretsky Test (BOT) were reported by Beitel and Mead.

---

1. From Dayton Sensory Motor Awareness Survey, Dayton Public Schools, Dayton, Ohio. Used by permission of William Braley.

Date of Test_____

Name_____Sex_____Birth_____Center_____

Body Image. Score ½ point for each correct part; 9 points possible.

_____ 1. Ask the child to touch the following body parts:

Head_____	Ankles_____	Ears_____	Stomach_____
Toes_____	Nose_____	Legs_____	Chin_____
Eyes_____	Feet_____	Mouth_____	Waist_____
Wrists_____	Chest_____	Fingers_____	Shoulders_____
Back_____	Elbows_____		

Space and Directions. Score ½ point for each correct direction; 5 points possible.

_____ 2. Ask the child to point to the following directions:

Front_____Back_____Up_____Down_____Beside you_____
Place two blocks on a table about 1 in. apart. Ask the child to point:
Under_____Over_____To the top_____To the bottom_____
Between_____

Balance. Score 2 points if accomplished.

_____ 3. Have the child stand on tiptoes, on both feet, with eyes open for 8 sec.

Balance and Laterality. Score 2 points for each foot; 4 points possible.

_____ 4. Have the child stand on one foot, eyes closed, for 5 sec. Alternate feet.

Laterality. Score 2 points if the child keeps the feet together and does not lead off with one foot.

_____ 5. Have the child jump forward on two feet.

Rhythm and Neuromuscular Control. Score 2 points for each foot if accomplished six times; 4 points possible.

_____ 6. Have the child hop on one foot. Hop in place.

Rhythm and Neuromuscular Control. Score 2 points.

_____ 7. Have the child skip forward. Child must be able to sustain this motion around the room for approximately 30 ft.

Integration of Right and Left Sides of the Body. Score 2 points if cross-patterning is evident for each.

_____ 8. Have the child creep forward.

_____ 9. Have the child creep backward.

Eye-Foot Coordination. Score 2 points if done the length of tape or mark.

_____10. Use an 8-ft tape or chalk mark on the floor. The child walks in a crossover step the length of the tape or mark.

Fine Muscle Control. Score 2 points if paper is completely crumpled. Score 1 point if paper is partially crumpled. Score 0 points if child needs assistance or changes hands.

_____11. Using a half sheet of newspaper, the child picks up the paper with one hand and puts the other hand behind the back. He then attempts to crumple the paper in the hand. He may not use the other hand, the table, or the body for assistance.

Form Perception. Score 1 point for each correct match.

_____12. Using a piece of paper with 2-in. circles, squares, and triangles, ask the child to point to two objects that are the same.

Form Perception. Score 1 point if circle is identified correctly. Score 2 points if the triangle and square are identified correctly.

_____13. Ask the child to identify by saying, "Point to the circle." "Point to the square." "Point to the triangle."

Hearing Discrimination. Score 1 point if the child taps correctly each time.

_____14. Ask the child to turn her back to you. Tap the table with a stick three times. Ask the child to turn around and tap the sticks the same way. Ask the child to turn her back to you. Tap the table again with the sticks (two quick taps, pause, then two more quick taps). Have the child turn back to you and tap out the rhythm.

Eye-Hand Coordination. Score 1 point for each successful completion.

_____15. A board is used with three holes in it. The holes are ¾, ⅝, and ½ in. in diameter. The child is asked to put his finger through the holes without touching the sides.

Figure 18.3.   Dayton Sensory Motor Awareness Survey for 4- and 5-Year-Olds (Used by permission)

Validity: The methods used to establish validity are described in the *Examiner's Manual*. Construct validity was assessed by analyzing the relationship of test content to important aspects of motor development cited in the literature; relevant statistical properties such as relationships of test scores to age, internal consistency of subtests, and factor analysis were included. Construct validity was also tested by comparisons of contrast groups, such as normal subjects with mildly retarded, moderately to severely retarded, and learning-disabled children.

Subsequent support for the validity of the BOT was reported by Broadhead and Bruininks, who analyzed the raw score data of the original standardization sample and found that the age trends, sex differences, and interrelationships among test items and subtests were in line with other tests and instruments in the motor development literature.

Equipment and Materials: A test kit containing the necessary marking materials, tape measures, balance beams, pencils, mats, targets, balls, and other equipment for each of the 14 test items.

Test Description: The Bruininks–Oseretsky Test (BOT) is available in a long and a short form. There are eight subtests in both forms: (1) running speed and agility, (2) balance, (3) bilateral coordination, (4) strength (these four measure gross motor proficiency), (5) upper-limb coordination (measures both gross and fine traits), (6) response speed, (7) visual–motor control, and (8) upper-limb speed and dexterity (the last three measure fine motor proficiency).

The long form contains 46 test items; the short form has 14 items. A brief description of the short-form items is given here. The short form can be administered in about 20 min. A pretest involving throwing and kicking a tennis ball on command is used to determine arm and leg preference.

Running Speed and Agility

The child runs 15 yd, picks up a block, and runs back across the line. Two trials are given.

Balance

Standing on preferred leg on balance beam. The child stands on one leg on the balance beam, hands on hips, the other leg bent and parallel to the floor, looking at a target. The score is the time the child can balance to a maximum of 10 sec. Two trials are given.

Walking forward heel-to-toe on balance beam. The subject walks heel-to-toe with hands on hips. Six correct, consecutive steps is the maximum score for each trial. Two trials are given.

Bilateral Coordination

Tapping feet alternately while making circles with fingers. The child is given 90 sec to complete ten consecutive foot taps while sitting in a chair and making circles with the index fingers. The score is pass or fail. One trial is given.

Jumping up and clapping hands. The subject jumps as high as possible and claps the hands in front of the face as many times as possible. The maximum number is five. The number of correct claps is the score. Two trials are given.

Strength

The subject does a standing long jump, jumping forward as far as possible from a bent-knee position. The score is the maximum distance, as indicated by the point score on the tape. Three trials are given.

Upper-Limb Coordination

Catching a tossed ball with both hands. The subject stands on the test kit mat and catches a tennis ball using both hands. The ball is tossed underhand from 10 ft away. The score is the number of correct catches. Five trials are given.

Throwing a ball at a target with preferred hand. The subject receives a point each time he or she throws a tennis ball overhand and hits a target from a distance of 5 ft. Five trials are given.

Response Speed

One item measures the ability of the child to respond to a moving stimulus. The subject is seated in a chair and places the preferred hand flat on the wall next to the response stick. The stick is dropped and the subject stops it with his or her thumb. The response speed number on the stick is the score. Seven trials are given.

Visual–Motor Control

Drawing a line through a straight path with preferred hand. The child takes a pencil and tries to draw a line within the "road" in the test booklet, staying in the lines. The score is the number of errors. One trial is given.

Copying a circle with preferred hand. The child attempts to carefully trace a circle. A number of points (0 to 2) is given for the degree of accuracy of the drawing. One trial is given.

Copying overlapping pencils with preferred hand. The child tries to copy accurately a geometric shape. A point score of 0 to 2 is given for the accuracy of the drawing. One trial is given. For the last two tests, examples of good (2 points), adequate (1 point), and inadequate (0 points) are given in the *Examiner's Manual*.

Upper-Limb Speed and Dexterity

Sorting shape cards with preferred hand. The child sorts a mixed deck of red and blue cards into two piles by color. The number of cards correctly sorted in 15 sec is the score. One trial is given.

Making dots in circles with preferred hand. The subject makes as many pencil dots as possible inside a series of circles in 15 sec. The number of circles correctly dotted is the score. One trial is given.

Scoring and Norms for the BOT: Performance scores for each test item are converted to point scores on the appropriate scales. Best performance is used on test items with multiple trials. The item point scores are then summed. The *Examiner's Manual* contains norm tables for standard scores, percentile ranks, and Stanine scores.

Bruininks—Oseretsky Test of Motor Proficiency for the Hearing Impaired (Brunt and Dearmond 1981)

Children with hearing impairments generally do not differ a great deal from other children in motor performance except in cases of inner-ear problems, when balance and agility performance are impaired. The physical fitness level of hearing-impaired children may be low simply due to inactivity.

Communication poses a major problem between the physical educator and the hearing-impaired child. Brunt and Dearmond presented an illustrated communication strategy for administering the BOT that should be used in assessment of the physical education needs of hearing-impaired students.

The communication procedures for the 14 items in the short form of the BOT are shown in Figure 18.4.

Special Fitness Test for Mildly Mentally Retarded Persons

This test battery is a modification of the AAHPERD Youth Fitness Test. The test was developed under the direction of G. Lawrence Rarick (Rarick, Widdop, and Broadhead 1970) and was administered to over 4200 youngsters throughout the country.

Objective: To assess fitness levels for mildly mentally retarded children.

Age Level: Ages 8 through 18.

Sex: Boys and girls.

Equipment: Same as for the AAHPERD Youth Fitness Test (Chapter 19).

Directions and Scoring:

Flexed-Arm Hang. As described in Chapter 8.

Sit-ups. Straight leg sit-ups are used. The hands are clasped behind the head, and sit-ups are timed for 1 min. Test directions and scoring are the same as for the bent-knee sit-ups described in Chapter 8, except that no score is counted if the subject bends the knees.

Shuttle Run. As described in Chapter 13.

Standing Long Jump. As described in Chapter 12.

50-Yard Dash. As described in Chapter 15.

Softball Throw for Distance. As described in Chapter 16 with the exception that the distance is measured from the point of landing to the point of throwing, rather than at right angles from the point of landing to the restraining line.

300-Yard Run. The student uses a standing start and on the signal "ready, go!" runs (and walks, if necessary) the 300 yd. Scoring is in minutes and seconds. Two suggested courses are a 50- $\times$ 25-ft rectangular area (six times around) or a 50-yard straightway (three times up and back).

Percentile norms for the seven items for boys and girls ages 8 through 18 are provided in Tables 18.1 through 18.7.

Subtest 1: running speed and agility
Item 1, the subject runs to the end line, picks up the block, and runs back across the start/finish line.

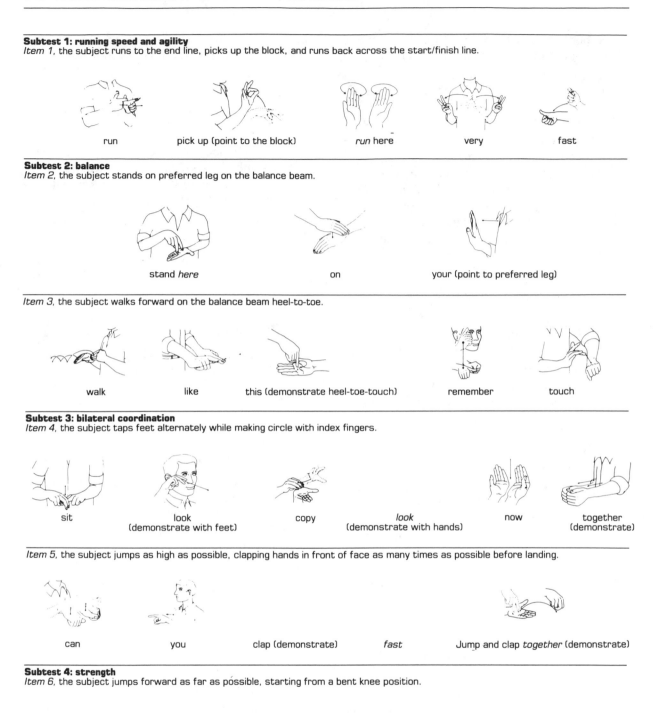

run   pick up (point to the block)   *run* here   very   fast

Subtest 2: balance
Item 2, the subject stands on preferred leg on the balance beam.

stand *here*   on   your (point to preferred leg)

Item 3, the subject walks forward on the balance beam heel-to-toe.

walk   like   this (demonstrate heel-toe-touch)   remember   touch

Subtest 3: bilateral coordination
Item 4, the subject taps feet alternately while making circle with index fingers.

sit   look (demonstrate with feet)   copy   *look* (demonstrate with hands)   now   together (demonstrate)

Item 5, the subject jumps as high as possible, clapping hands in front of face as many times as possible before landing.

can   you   clap (demonstrate)   *fast*   Jump and clap *together* (demonstrate)

Subtest 4: strength
Item 6, the subject jumps forward as far as possible, starting from a bent knee position.

stand here (demonstrate)   *jump* (demonstrate)

Figure 18.4. Hand signals for administering the Bruininks—Oseretsky Test (BOT) to children with hearing impairments (Reproduced with permission from T. J. O'Rourke, *A Basic Course in Manual Communication.* Silver Spring, Md.: National Association of the Deaf, 1978)

Subtest 5: upper-limb coordination
Item 7, the subject stands on the standing mat and, with both hands, catches a tennis ball tossed underhand from a distance of 10 feet.

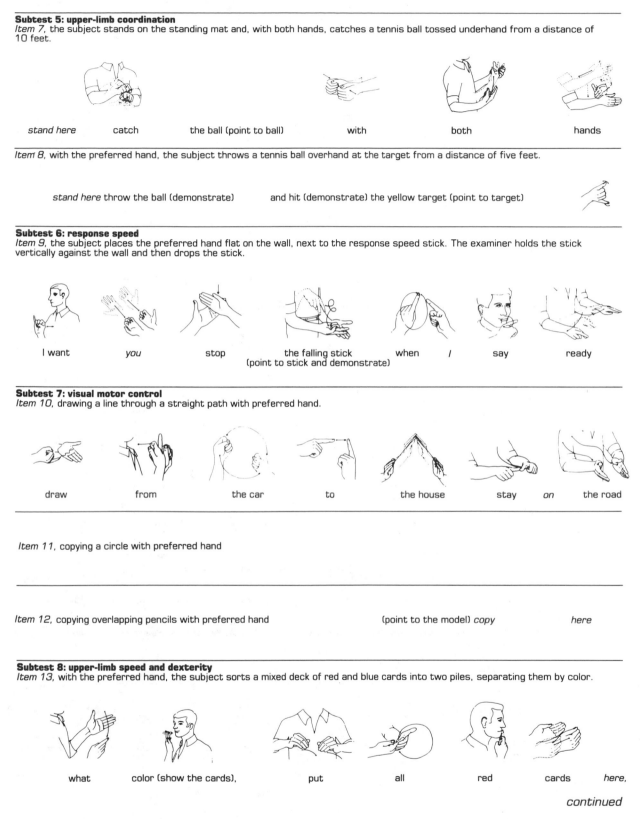

| *stand here* | catch | the ball (point to ball) | with | both | hands |

Item 8, with the preferred hand, the subject throws a tennis ball overhand at the target from a distance of five feet.

stand here throw the ball (demonstrate)   and hit (demonstrate) the yellow target (point to target)

Subtest 6: response speed
Item 9, the subject places the preferred hand flat on the wall, next to the response speed stick. The examiner holds the stick vertically against the wall and then drops the stick.

| I want | *you* | stop | the falling stick (point to stick and demonstrate) | when | *I* | say | ready |

Subtest 7: visual motor control
Item 10, drawing a line through a straight path with preferred hand.

| draw | from | the car | to | the house | stay | *on* | the road |

Item 11, copying a circle with preferred hand

Item 12, copying overlapping pencils with preferred hand   (point to the model) *copy*   *here*

Subtest 8: upper-limb speed and dexterity
Item 13, with the preferred hand, the subject sorts a mixed deck of red and blue cards into two piles, separating them by color.

| what | color (show the cards), | put | all | red | cards | *here,* |

continued

Figure 18.4   *(continued)*

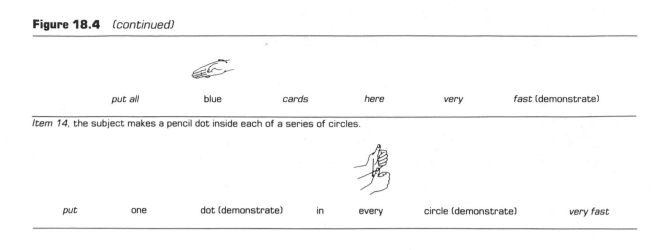

| put all | blue | cards | here | very | fast (demonstrate) |

Item 14, the subject makes a pencil dot inside each of a series of circles.

| put | one | dot (demonstrate) | in | every | circle (demonstrate) | very fast |

Table 18.1.   Percentile Norms in Seconds for Flexed-Arm Hang, Mildly Mentally Retarded Children

PERCENTILE	AGE										
	8	9	10	11	12	13	14	15	16	17	18
						GIRLS					
95	16	21	27	29	22	21	23	18	25	21	21
75	10	11	13	12	10	11	12	11	11	10	10
50	5	6	8	7	5	5	6	5	5	4	7
25	0	4	4	4	3	2	4	2	2	2	3
5	0	0	0	0	0	0	0	0	0	0	0
						BOYS					
95	32	24	35	35	38	36	53	46	50	48	68
75	11	13	16	19	19	19	22	26	29	29	39
50	7	8	8	11	12	10	13	12	17	17	25
25	4	4	5	6	6	5	7	6	9	10	15
5	0	0	0	0	0	0	0	0	0	3	3

Source: Adapted from *Special Fitness Test Manual for Mildly Mentally Retarded Persons.* Reston, Va.: AAHPERD, Rev. 1976. Used by permission.

Table 18.2.   Percentile Norms for Number of Sit-ups, Mildly Mentally Retarded Children

PERCENTILE	AGE										
	8	9	10	11	12	13	14	15	16	17	18
						GIRLS					
95	26	29	36	32	31	30	32	31	30	30	29
75	18	21	25	24	24	22	25	25	24	24	24
50	13	15	18	18	19	18	20	20	21	20	20
25	9	10	12	14	13	13	14	15	15	15	14
5	4	4	3	4	4	0	5	3	7	5	5
						BOYS					
95	26	32	34	35	37	35	38	38	43	41	42
75	20	23	26	27	30	30	30	34	34	35	36
50	16	17	20	22	24	25	26	31	29	30	31
25	10	13	14	17	19	18	19	24	24	24	24
5	0	4	6	7	10	10	9	15	14	12	18

Source: Adapted from *Special Fitness Test Manual for Mildly Mentally Retarded Persons.* Reston, Va.: AAHPERD, Rev. 1976. Used by permission.

Table 18.3. Percentile Norms in Seconds for Shuttle Run, Mildly Mentally Retarded Children

PERCENTILE	AGE										
	8	9	10	11	12	13	14	15	16	17	18
					GIRLS						
95	12.6	11.9	11.2	10.9	10.6	10.7	10.8	10.4	10.4	10.2	11.0
75	13.8	12.9	12.1	11.9	11.5	11.6	11.3	11.0	11.2	11.7	11.5
50	15.0	14.2	13.3	12.9	12.2	12.3	12.1	12.0	12.1	12.5	12.2
25	16.3	15.5	14.5	13.8	13.3	13.1	12.8	12.9	13.0	13.4	12.7
5	17.6	17.8	17.1	15.8	15.0	15.9	14.4	14.5	15.1	15.7	14.4
					BOYS						
95	11.6	11.3	10.9	10.4	10.3	10.1	9.7	9.8	9.6	9.1	9.4
75	12.6	12.1	11.8	11.1	11.0	10.8	10.4	10.7	10.2	9.8	9.9
50	14.0	13.1	12.6	11.9	11.6	11.3	11.0	11.2	11.1	10.6	10.6
25	15.3	14.8	13.9	12.8	12.5	12.0	12.0	12.0	12.2	11.4	11.5
5	18.2	16.4	15.5	14.9	14.8	13.9	13.8	13.8	14.1	13.0	13.5

Source: Adapted from *Special Fitness Test Manual for Mildly Mentally Retarded Persons.* Reston, Va.: AAHPERD, Rev. 1976. Used by permission.

Table 18.4. Percentile Norms in Feet for Standing Long Jump, Mildly Mentally Retarded Children

PERCENTILE	AGE										
	8	9	10	11	12	13	14	15	16	17	18
					GIRLS						
95	4' 2"	4' 4"	5' 0"	5' 5"	6' 0"	5' 7"	6' 0"	6' 3"	6' 3"	6' 1"	5'10"
75	3' 8"	3' 9"	4' 5"	4' 8"	4'11"	4'10"	5' 1"	5' 1"	5' 3"	5' 3"	5' 3"
50	3' 1"	3' 4"	3'10"	4' 0"	4' 3"	4' 3"	4' 6"	4' 6"	4' 8"	4' 9"	4' 9"
25	2' 5"	2'10"	3' 3"	3' 5"	3' 8"	3' 8"	3'11"	4' 0"	3'11"	4' 1"	4' 3"
5	1'10"	1' 9"	2' 2"	2' 5"	2' 8"	2' 7"	3' 0"	3' 3"	2' 9"	2' 9"	2' 9"
					BOYS						
95	4' 5"	5' 2"	5' 3"	5' 9"	6' 0"	6' 4"	7' 1"	7' 0"	7' 3"	8' 1"	7' 9"
75	3' 9"	4' 5"	4' 8"	5' 1"	5' 4"	5' 6"	5'11"	6' 4"	6' 9"	7' 2"	7' 1"
50	3' 4"	3'10"	3'11"	4' 6"	4'10"	5' 0"	5' 3"	5' 9"	6' 1"	6' 2"	6' 6"
25	2' 9"	3' 0"	3' 4"	3'10"	4' 2"	4' 4"	4' 6"	5' 3"	5' 0"	5' 6"	5'10"
5	1'10"	2' 2"	2' 4"	2'10"	3' 1"	3' 3"	3' 3"	3'11"	3'10"	3'11"	4' 6"

Source: Adapted from *Special Fitness Test Manual for Mildly Mentally Retarded Persons.* Reston, Va.: AAHPERD, Rev. 1976. Used by permission.

Table 18.5. Percentile Norms in Seconds for 50-Yard Dash, Mildly Mentally Retarded Children

PERCENTILE	AGE										
	8	9	10	11	12	13	14	15	16	17	18
					GIRLS						
95	9.3	8.2	8.1	7.8	7.4	7.4	7.4	7.4	7.1	7.2	7.2
75	10.1	9.1	8.8	8.4	8.1	8.3	8.2	8.0	8.1	8.2	8.5
50	11.3	10.5	9.3	9.1	8.8	8.9	8.7	8.6	9.0	9.0	9.0
25	12.6	11.4	10.3	9.9	9.5	9.7	9.5	9.4	10.1	10.0	9.9
5	14.1	14.2	12.3	12.0	10.9	11.3	11.1	11.1	12.2	12.5	11.0
					BOYS						
95	8.6	8.0	7.8	7.3	7.2	7.1	6.6	6.6	6.2	6.0	6.1
75	9.4	8.9	8.5	8.2	7.9	7.7	7.4	7.1	6.9	6.3	6.5
50	10.5	9.9	9.2	8.9	8.3	8.2	8.0	7.5	7.3	6.9	7.1
25	11.9	10.7	10.0	9.6	9.0	9.0	8.8	8.1	7.8	7.9	7.8
5	14.1	12.8	12.1	11.1	10.3	10.3	10.6	9.4	9.7	8.5	8.9

Source: Adapted from *Special Fitness Test Manual for Mildly Mentally Retarded Persons.* Reston, Va.: AAHPERD, Rev. 1976. Used by permission.

Table 18.6. Percentile Norms in Feet for Softball Throw, Mildly Mentally Retarded Children

PERCENTILE	AGE										
	8	9	10	11	12	13	14	15	16	17	18
						GIRLS					
95	54	64	68	88	102	97	106	111	115	118	118
75	33	46	52	65	71	72	86	84	82	81	84
50	27	34	41	46	56	57	63	65	67	62	61
25	22	22	33	35	42	42	46	46	48	50	50
5	14	14	17	21	27	28	31	29	24	30	28
						BOYS					
95	74	100	102	123	136	154	180	191	214	230	216
75	57	73	81	99	114	125	142	159	181	176	187
50	43	58	66	80	95	104	112	137	154	159	159
25	32	44	46	61	76	89	91	111	127	125	126
5	15	31	26	41	45	51	51	77	77	69	74

Source: Adapted from *Special Fitness Test Manual for Mildly Mentally Retarded Persons*. Reston, Va.: AAHPERD, Rev. 1976. Used by permission.

Table 18.7. Percentile Norms in Minutes for 300-Yard Run, Mildly Mentally Retarded Children

PERCENTILE	AGE										
	8	9	10	11	12	13	14	15	16	17	18
						GIRLS					
95	1:20	1:12	1:08	1:08	1:00	1:00	1:00	1:02	:59	1:03	1:05
75	1:28	1:24	1:16	1:15	1:09	1:10	1:08	1:12	1:11	1:13	1:11
50	1:34	1:33	1:23	1:23	1:18	1:16	1:15	1:20	1:18	1:22	1:20
25	1:50	1:43	1:34	1:32	1:28	1:25	1:26	1:30	1:26	1:35	1:30
5	2:00	2:19	2:01	1:50	1:48	1:51	1:50	1:56	1:57	2:10	1:16
						BOYS					
95	1:17	1:06	1:02	1:01	:58	:57	:50	:53	:49	:45	:47
75	1:23	1:17	1:13	1:08	1:05	1:04	1:00	:58	:55	:51	:52
50	1:33	1:24	1:20	1:15	1:12	1:10	1:07	1:01	:59	:56	:57
25	1:42	1:34	1:31	1:26	1:22	1:20	1:15	1:10	1:05	1:03	1:03
5	1:58	1:54	1:51	1:46	1:51	1:39	1:38	1:23	1:23	1:24	1:13

Source: Adapted from *Special Fitness Test Manual for Mildly Mentally Retarded Persons*. Reston, Va.: AAHPERD, Rev. 1976. Used by permission.

Motor Fitness Test for the Moderately Mentally Retarded (Johnson and Londeree 1976)

Leon Johnson and Ben Londeree developed a motor fitness test for moderately mentally retarded boys and girls. Test data were gathered on 1097 moderately mentally retarded persons aged 6 to 21 in the state of Missouri. Percentile norms are provided in the *Manual*. The test items are as follows:

Flexed-arm hang

Sit-ups (30 sec)

Standing long jump
Softball throw for distance
50-Yard dash

300-Yard run—walk

Height and weight
Sitting bob and reach
Hopping
Skipping
Tumbling progression
Target throw

Broadhead Dynamic Balance Test (Broadhead 1974)

Objective: To measure dynamic balance in special education. The test was developed with minimally brain-injured (MBI) and educable mentally retarded (EMR) children.

Age Level: Age 8 to 13, inclusive.

Sex: Boys and girls.

Reliability: Reliability was assessed using intraclass R for mean of trials and single trial estimates for boys and girls at each age level for both MBI and EMR subjects. For MBI boys and girls, mean of trial Rs ranged from .69 to .97 and .51 to .90, respectively; for EMR boys and girls, Rs ranged from .85 to .96 and .51 to .91, respectively.

Validity: Face or logical validity is assumed.

Equipment: Three wooden beams each 12 ft long connected to form a continuous 36-ft length. The first 12-ft length is 4 in. wide, the second is 12 in. wide, and the third is 1 in. wide. All beams are firmly supported with the top surface 6 in. above floor level and coated with nonslip paint.

Directions: After explanation and demonstration, the subject is asked to walk forward along the beam as far as possible without making contact with the floor or the supports of the beams. If the subject covers the full 36 ft, he or she should remain on the beam and then retrace the path backward. Three trials are allowed.

Scoring: The distance covered for the sum of three trials is the score. Mean performances for MBI and EMR boys and girls ages 8 to 13 are shown in Table 18.8.

Basic Motor Fitness Test for Emotionally Disturbed Children (Hilsendager, Jack, and Mann 1973)

Emotionally disordered children may or may not have physiologic deficiencies. Their motor fitness ranges from low to very high. Obviously their behavior problems may inhibit fitness and motor skill development. Hilsendager, Jack, and Mann developed a norm-referenced basic motor fitness test designed for emotionally disturbed children with apparent delayed motor skill development.

The test can be administered in about 20 min. Items include walking, balancing, jumping, hopping, throwing, catching, kicking, flexibility (sit and reach), sit-ups, and a 300-yard dash. The scoring method includes a "would not try" column and "not a maximum effort" column. Stand-

Table 18.8. Mean Distance Covered in Feet During Three Trials in Broadhead Dynamic Balance Test

AGE	BOYS		GIRLS	
	MBI[a]	EMR[b]	MBI	EMR
8	49.9	46.7	55.7	52.7
9	63.7	59.3	62.3	47.8
10	64.4	61.3	55.5	56.9
11	75.6	63.5	58.6	62.2
12	75.6	64.4	72.0	65.7
13	64.1	67.0	77.5	61.5

[a]MBI, minimally brain injured; 226 children tested.
[b]EMR, educable mentally retarded; 189 children tested.

ard scores are provided, based on the performance of normal children.

OTHER TESTS

Some other test batteries for measuring motor development and motor pfoficiency of handicapped and nonhandicapped children are described as follows.

AMP Index #1 (Webb, Shutz, and McMahill 1977)

This test is designed to evaluate awareness, movement, manipulation of environment, posture, and locomotion of profoundly retarded children aged 2½ through 17½. The awareness scales include avoidance, approach, and integrating memory with present stimuli. The manipulation scale includes responses to objects and commands and expression of intentionality. The posture scale involves static and dynamic posture measures.

Basic Motor Ability Test (Arnheim and Sinclair 1979)

The purpose of this test is to assess fine and gross motor skills of children aged 4 through 12. Items include:

Bead stringing	Static balance
Target throwing	Basketball throw for distance
Marble transfer	Ball striking
Back and hamstring stretch	Target kicking
Standing long jump	Agility run
Face down to standing	

Percentile norms are provided for boys and girls.

Buell AAHPERD Youth Fitness Test Adaptation for the Blind (Buell 1982)

This test measures motor fitness of visually impaired children, aged 10 through 17. Test items are:

Pull-ups (boys)	50-Yard dash
Flexed-arm hang (girls)	600-Yard run–walk
Sit-ups	Basketball throw
Standing broad jump	

The same percentile norms as in the 1975 revision of the AAHPERD Youth Fitness Test are used for the first four test items. New norms were developed for the 50-yard dash and the 600-yard run–walk. The basketball throw was developed specifically for the test battery.

Fait Physical Fitness Test for the Mentally Retarded (Fait 1978)

This test battery was designed to measure physical fitness of EMR and the majority of medium and high trainable mentally retarded children. Test items are:

25-Yard run	Static balance
Bent-arm hang	Thrusts
Leg lift	300-Yard run–walk

Norms are provided for the following age categories: 9–12, 13–16, and 17–20.

I CAN Program (Wessel 1976)

I CAN is a comprehensive developmental, physical, and associated skills program for children with special educational needs. It is designed for children with slower-than-average developmental growth, with specific learning disabilities, with social or emotional adjustment difficulties, or with economic or language disadvantages, or for any combination of these. I CAN encompasses several areas of formative evaluation and curriculum development. Diagnostic and prescriptive teaching resource materials are presented for primary skills, continuing skills, social skills, and associated skills as follows:

Primary Skills

Aquatics. Basic skills, swimming, and entry skills

Fundamental Skills. Locomotor skills and rhythms, object control

Body Management Skills. Body awareness, controlling the body

Health and Fitness Skills. Physical fitness, awareness of body posture

Social Skills

Responsibility

Cooperation

Self-Control

Continuing Skills

Dance Skills. Folk and square dance

Team Sports. Basketball, volleyball, softball

Individual and Dual Sports. Track and field, gymnastics, bowling, roller skating, badminton, horseshoes, croquet, tetherball

Outdoor Activities. Camping, cross-country skiing, backpacking and hiking

Associated Skills

Self

Environment

Participation

FINDINGS AND CONCLUSIONS FROM MEASUREMENT AND RESEARCH IN PERCEPTUAL–MOTOR PERFORMANCE AND MOTOR PERFORMANCE OF THE HANDICAPPED

A number of studies have investigated the relationship between perceptual–motor and cognitive behavior, with conflicting results. Certainly differences in results may be attributed partly to different measurements used and to the statistical analysis employed. Usually, very low relationships have been found with use of univariate statistics (Olson 1966; Singer 1968). When several measures of perceptual–motor and cognitive behavior are used and analyzed by multivariate statistics, however, the relationships have been quite significant (Chissom, Thomas, and Biasiotto 1972; Thomas and Chissom 1972). Belka and Williams administered a large battery of perceptual–motor, perceptual, and cognitive tests to prekindergarten, kindergarten, and first grade children, and through canonical correlation found that perceptual–motor and cognitive measures were significantly correlated at the kindergarten level. They concluded that the relationship between perceptual–motor and cognitive domains is relatively close for younger children but broadens as the child gets older. It has been noted in other studies that various abilities tend to become more specific with increased age (Singer 1968). Gruber and Noland found no significant relationships between perceptual–motor and scholastic achievement in emotionally disturbed elementary school children when using univariate or multivariate analysis.

Leithwood correlated simple and complex motor measures of 4-year-old children with eight dimensions of intellectual functioning and a multidimensional scale of psychosocial adjustment. He reported several significant but low relationships between intellectual abilities and motor performance. There were twice as many significant correlations between cognitive abilities and complex motor tasks as with simple motor tasks.

Fisher compared the motor ability, intelligence, and academic readiness of one group of kindergarten children who participated in a sequential, individualized perceptual–motor program with a group who received the traditional supervised free play and games. Both groups gained significantly in all measures, and there were no significant differences between the groups.

In a study by Penman, Christopher, and Wood, learning of language arts skills was facilitated by use of active games in the teaching process. Lipton reported that a 12-week perceptual program was superior to a conventional physical education program in improving perceptual–motor performance, visual perception, and reading readiness of first grade children. Other investigators have also found evidence of the contribution of perceptual–motor training to academic achievement by young children (McCormick, Schnobrick, and Footlik 1969), while others doubt the validity of such claims, pointing to the questionable nature of these studies (Rarick 1980).

Various authors have attempted to secure evidence as to the value of movement exploration and movement education. Effectiveness of movement exploration in elementary physical education was studied by Thaxton, Rothstein, and Thaxton, and they concluded it should be used in combination with traditional methods, depending on the activities.

Kindergarten children who took part in a movement program and received guided practice in overhand throwing were compared by Halverson and associates with children in the movement program who did not receive throwing practice. A control group received neither the movement program nor throwing instruction. Results showed no differences in ball-throwing velocity, indicating that specific practice did not improve throwing ability. Yet none of the groups improved in throwing velocity during the 8-week period, which led the authors to speculate about the adequacy of using just velocity as a criterion and whether enough time was provided to realize change.

No formal instruction was given to children in a study by Flinchum in which she wished to assess the effectiveness of goal-oriented practice with children 2 to 6 years of age. The children were given regular opportunity to practice, but the only instruction was to throw, kick, or swing as "hard as you can." The filmed performances of the children were compared with those of skilled adult patterns. In throwing, only 39% of the children evaluated showed improvement.

Permissive, indulgent home environments were positively associated with superior throwing skill, and jumping skill was associated with higher maternal discipline in a study by Schnabl-Dickey.

The young child is at a disadvantage in learning motor skills compared with older children and adults. Besides some physiologic limitations, an important difference is the speed of processing information between younger and older children (Chi 1977; Thomas 1980). Gallagher stressed the importance of teachers recognizing developmental differences when using memory strategies in the learning of motor skills.

Toole and Arink compared movement education and traditional instruction of first grade students on skill improvement and transfer of movement education to performance of new skills. Traditional learning (command style with demonstration) was of more help than movement education in the development of skills in the relatively short time of 20 weeks. The two teaching approaches showed no significant differences in the transfer of training effect. Three teaching styles were found by Goldberger, Gerney, and Chamberlain to be comparably effective in facilitating the learning of a motor task with fifth grade children. Williams reported that Roberton's component approach was useful in the objective and comprehensive description of actions occurring in teaching of the forward roll.

Martinek, Zaichkowsky, and Cheffers compared a teaching method in which the teacher made all the decisions with one in which the students shared in the decision-making process. The teacher-directed approach was more effective for motor skill development, but the student-sharing approach had positive effects on self-concept.

In the study of motor development, Roberton, Williams, and Langendorfer maintained that only longitudinal studies can validate developmental sequences, although cross-sectional studies can be used effectively for prolongitudinal screening. Feltz investigated the effects of age and number of demonstrations on the strategy employed and the performance on a ladder-balance task. She concluded that matching form (strategy) by the learner is more effective in the measurement of modeling effects than the inference of modeling from performance.

Keogh, Griffin, and Spector studied confidence of movement in children with respect to how different observers—adults and children—perceived the confidence of children approaching and performing a movement task. There were high levels of agreement within and between the adults and children in rating the confidence of children in filmed performance. Movements, tempo, and attention were identified as three behavioral manifestations of movement confidence.

Roberton and Halverson pointed out that the term *motor development* is not confined to early childhood. Movements continually change with age. Public Law 94–142, the "Education for All Handicapped Children Act" of 1975, has had a great impact on physical educators in the field and on the professional preparation of physical educators. The law requires that all handicapped children must be provided free, appropriate, and public physical education, involving individualized programs and mainstreaming. Knowles investigated the concerns of physical education teachers about implementing individualized instruction. She concluded that the required changes can be facilitated by teacher training that focuses on individual teacher's needs and concerns.

In the process of modifying the AAHPERD Youth Fitness Test for mentally retarded children, Rarick, Widdop, and Broadhead tested 4235 educable mentally retarded boys and girls 8 to 18 years of age. The retarded children were substantially poorer in the motor fitness items than were normal children. Age trends and sex differences paralleled those of normal children.

Physical fitness and motor proficiency of the mentally retarded are generally below those of normal children. Fitness differences between retarded and nonhandicapped children tend to widen with chronologic age (French and Jansma 1982). Dobbins, Garron, and Rarick administered a number of motor performance and anthropometric measures to EMR and normal children and found the usual superiority of normal children in motor performance. When adjustments were made for differences in body size, however, nonsignificant differences were found in 5 of the 12 test items, indicating that motor performance differences are less a function of intelligence than of body size inequalities. In an earlier study, Rarick and Dobbins found that retarded children had significantly greater body fat than nonretarded boys and girls, suggesting that the retarded child is more sedentary with respect to engaging in physical activities.

Most studies on motor fitness have used comparisons of performance of retarded children with national norms. Bruininks (1974) suggested that such comparisons do not account for the influence of differences in experience on motor development. Stein, for example, reported that mildly retarded children who receive regular, sound physical education are comparable to normative samples on the AAHPERD Youth Fitness Test.

Broadhead (1975) assessed grip strength and two-handed push and pull strength of MBI and EMR boys and girls aged 8 to 13 years. Overall, the grip tests were reliable, scores increased significantly with age, and boys outperformed girls. The performances of the MBI and EMR children were not significantly different. Bowman and Dunn found that performance in the presence of peers had a motivating effect on the psychomotor test scores of EMR children.

Matthews investigated the types of recreation activities in which the mentally retarded participated, and the frequency of such participation. He found essentially no differences between retarded and nonretarded children in frequency of participation. Socioeconomic factors were involved in choice of activities in both populations. Broadhead and Rarick examined the association between selected family characteristics and some gross motor traits of EMR and MBI children. High-quality gross motor performance, as measured by the modified AAHPERD Youth Fitness battery, tended to be associated with the larger families and with lower occupational status and education.

Highly active retarded children often are unable to maintain attention to task relevant conditions, which increases their probability of failure in learning situations (Chasey, Haygood, and Tzuriel 1977). Horgan found that stabilometer performance of mentally retarded children showed improvement only when supplementary auditory and visual feedback training techniques were used. A significant relationship between the amount of overlearning and retention and relearning of a stabilometer task by mentally retarded boys was reported by Chasey.

Additional evidence of the validity of the Bruininks–Oseretsky Test of Motor Proficiency (BOT) was reported by Broadhead and Church who, through the use of discriminant analysis, found that the BOT was effective in classifying mildly and moderately retarded children and kindergarten and first grade children.

Visually handicapped children generally are found to be less physically fit than nonimpaired children, and children with partial sight outperform totally blind children in tests of physical proficiency (Buell 1966, 1982; Winnick 1979). Buell (1966) adapted the AAPHERD Youth Fitness Test for individuals with visual handicaps. Visually handicapped youngsters perform more nearly like sighted youngsters in rather uncomplicated activities such as sit-ups and pull-ups (Winnick and Short 1982). Quite naturally, they do more poorly on throwing and running items, which undoubtedly reflects skill learning opportunities and body image differences (French and Jansma 1982). Although it has been generally accepted that blindness at birth is more handicapping than blindness occurring later in life, Winnick and Short found that age at onset of visual impairment was not a significant factor in motor proficiency.

Brunt and Broadhead assessed the motor proficiency traits of deaf children using the Bruininks–Oseretsky test. Although they found sex differences, there was considerable similarity in the performances of male and female deaf children and the performances of normal children, which supported the findings of Lindsey and O'Neal. When auditory-impaired subjects were classified as either hard of hearing or deaf, no differences were found between the classifications in 15 of the 17 test items in the UNIQUE test (Winnick and Short 1982). Thus, severity of handicapping condition was not a factor. Kraft outlined class techniques and games by which children with auditory handicaps can more easily and effectively participate in physical activities.

BIBLIOGRAPHY

Arnheim, D. D., and W. A. Sinclair, *The Clumsy Child: A Program of Motor Therapy*. 2nd ed. St. Louis: C. V. Mosby, 1979.

Beitel, P. A., and B. J. Mead, "Bruininks –Oseretsky Test of Motor Proficiency: A Viable Measure for 3–5 Year Old Children." *Perceptual and Motor Skills* 51:919–923, 1980.

Belka, D. E., and H. G. Williams, "Canonical Relationships Among Perceptual–Motor, Perceptual, and Cognitive Behaviors in Children." *Research Quarterly for Exercise and Sport* 51:463–477, October 1980.

Bowman, R. A., and J. M. Dunn, "Effect of Peer Pressure on Psychomotor Measures With EMR Children." *Exceptional Children* 48:449–451, 1982.

Broadhead, G. D., "Beam Walking in Special Education." *Rehabilitation Literature* 35:145–147, May 1974.

———, "Dynamometric Grip Strength in Mildly Handicapped Children." *Rehabilitation Literature* 36:279–283, September 1975.

———, and R. H. Bruininks, "Childhood Motor Performance Traits on the Short Form Bruininks–Oseretsky Test." *Physical Educator* 39:149–155, October 1982.

———, and G. E. Church, "Discriminant Analysis of Gross and Fine Motor Proficiency Data." *Perceptual and Motor Skills* 55:547–552, 1982.

———, and G. L. Rarick, "Family Characteristics and Gross Motor Traits in Handicapped Children." *Research Quarterly* 49:421–429, December 1978.

Bruininks, R. H., "Physical and Motor Development of Retarded Persons." In Norman R. Ellis, Ed., *International Review of Research in Mental Retardation Vol. 7*. New York: Academic Press, 1974.

———, *Bruininks–Oseretsky Test of Motor Proficiency, Examiner's Manual*. Circle Pines, Minn: American Guidance Service, 1978.

Brunt, D., and G. D. Broadhead, "Motor Proficiency Traits of Deaf Children." *Research Quarterly for Exercise and Sport* 53:236–238, September 1982.

———, and D. A. Dearmond, "Evaluating Motor Profiles of the Hearing Impaired." *JOPERD* 52:50–52, November-December 1981.

Buell, C. E., *Physical Education for Blind Children*. Springfield, Ill.: Charles E. Thomas, 1966.

———, *Physical Education and Recreation for the Visually Handicapped*. Reston, Va.: AAHPERD, 1982.

Chasey, W. C., "Motor Skill Overlearning Effects on Retention and Relearning by Retarded Boys." *Research Quarterly* 48:41–46, March 1977.

———, H. C. Haygood, and D. Tzuriel, "Effects of Various Stimuli on Activity Level and Learning by High- and Low-Active Retarded Children." *Research Quarterly* 48:265–269, May 1977.

Chi, M., "Age Differences in the Speed of Processing: A Critique." *Developmental Psychology* 13:543–544, 1977.

Chissom, B. S., J. R. Thomas, and J. Biasiotto, "Canonical Validity of Perceptual–Motor Skills for Predicting an Academic Criterion." *Educational and Psychological Measurement* 32:1095–1098, 1972.

Clifton, M., "A Developmental Approach to Perceptual–Motor Experiences." *JOHPER* 41:34–37, April 1970.

Crafts, V. R. (comments reported by R. E. McAdam), "Perceptual–Motor Assessment Instruments." In AAHPERD *Foundations and Practices in Perceptual–Motor Learning—A Quest for Understanding.* Reston, Va.: AAHPERD, 1971.

Cratty, B. J., *Movement Activities for Neurologically Handicapped and Retarded Children and Youth.* Freeport, N.Y.: Educational Activities, 1967.

Delacato, C. H., *The Diagnosis and Treatment of Speech and Readiness Problems.* Springfield, Ill.: Charles C. Thomas, 1963.

Dobbins, D. A., R. Garron, and G. L. Rarick, "The Motor Performance of Educable Mentally Retarded and Intellectually Normal Boys After Covariate Control for Differences in Body Size." *Research Quarterly for Exercise and Sport* 52:1–8, March 1981.

Fait, H. F., *Special Physical Education: Adapted, Corrective, Developmental.* 4th ed. Philadelphia: W. B. Saunders, 1978.

Feltz, D. L., "The Effect of Age and Number of Demonstrations on Modeling of Form and Performance." *Research Quarterly for Exercise and Sport* 53:291–296, December 1982.

Fisher, D. H., "Effects of Two Different Types of Physical Education Programs Upon Skills Development and Academic Readiness of Kindergarten Children." Unpublished doctoral dissertation, Louisiana State University, Baton Rouge, 1970.

Flinchum, B., "Selected Motor Patterns of Preschool Age Children." Unpublished doctoral dissertation, Louisiana State University, Baton Rouge, 1971.

French, R. W., and P. Jansma, *Special Physical Education.* Columbus, Ohio: Charles E. Merrill, 1982.

Gallagher, J. D., "The Effects of Developmental Memory Differences on Learning Motor Skills." *JOPERD* 53:36–37, 40, May 1982.

Goldberger, M., P. Gerney, and J. Chamberlain, "The Effects of Three Styles of Teaching on the Psychomotor Performance and Social Skill Development of Fifth Grade Children." *Research Quarterly for Exercise and Sport* 53:116–124, June 1982.

Gruber, J. J., and M. Noland, "Perceptual–Motor and Scholastic Achievement Relationships in Emotionally Disturbed Elementary School Children." *Research Quarterly* 48:68–73, March 1977.

Halverson, L. E., M. A. Roberton, M. J. Safrit, and T. W. Roberts, "Effect of Guided Practice on Overhand-Throw Ball Velocities of Kindergarten Children." *Research Quarterly* 48:311–318, May 1977.

Hilsendager, D. R., H. Jack, and L. Mann, *Basic Motor Fitness Tests for Emotionally Disturbed Children.* Report of National Institute of Mental Health, Grant 1-T1-MT1-8543-1,5, Philadelphia: Temple University, 1973.

Horgan, J. S., "Stabilometer Performance of Educable Mentally Retarded Children Under Differential Feedback Conditions." *Research Quarterly* 48:711–716, December 1977.

Johnson, L., and B. Londeree, *Motor Fitness Testing Manual for the Moderately Mentally Retarded.* Reston, Va.: AAHPERD, 1976.

Keogh, J. F., N. S. Griffin, and R. Spector, "Observer Perceptions of Movement Confidence." *Research Quarterly for Exercise and Sport* 52:465–473, December 1981.

Kephart, N. C., *The Slow Learner in the Classroom.* Columbus, Ohio: Charles E. Merrill, 1960.

Knowles, C. J., "Concerns of Teachers About Implementing Individualized Instruction in the Physical Education Setting." *Research Quarterly for Exercise and Sport* 52:48–57, March 1981.

Kraft, R., "Movement Experience for Children With Auditory Handicaps." *Physical Educator* 38:35–38, 1981.

Leithwood, K. A., "Motor, Cognitive, and Affective Relationships Among Advantaged Preschool Children." *Research Quarterly* 42:47–53, March 1971.

Lindsey, D., and J. O'Neal, "Static and Dynamic Balance Skills of Eight Year Old Deaf and Hearing Children." *American Annals of the Deaf* 121:49–55, 1976.

Lipton, E. D., "A Perceptual–Motor Development Program's Effect on Visual Perception and Reading Readiness of First Grade Children." *Research Quarterly* 41:402–405, October 1970.

Martinek, T. J., L. D. Zaichkowsky, and J. T. F. Cheffers, "Decision-Making in Elementary Age Children: Effects on Motor Skills and Self-Concept." *Research Quarterly* 48:349–357, May 1977.

Matthews, P. R., "The Frequency With Which the Mentally Retarded Participate in Recreation Activities." *Research Quarterly* 50:71–79, March 1979.

McCormick, C. C., J. N. Schnobrick, and S. W. Footlik, "The Effect of Perceptual–Motor Training on Reading Achievement." *Academic Therapy* 4:171–176, March 1969.

McCraw, L. W., "Comparative Analysis of Methods of Scoring Tests of Motor Learning." *Research Quarterly* 26:440–453, December 1955.

Nelson, J. K., "The Construction of a Perceptual-Motor Performance Obstacle Course for Preschool and Primary Grade Children." Unpublished study, Louisiana State University, Baton Rouge, 1972.

Olson, A. V., "Relation of Achievement Test Scores and Specific Reading Abilities to the Frostig DTVP." *Perceptual and Motor Skills* 22:179–184, 1966.

Penman, K. A., J. R. Christopher, and G. S. Wood, "Using Gross Motor Activity to Improve Language Arts Concepts by Third Grade Students." *Research Quarterly* 48:134–137, March 1977.

Rarick, G. L., "Cognitive–Motor Relationships in the Growing Years." *Research Quarterly for Exercise and Sport* 51:174–192, March 1980.

———, and D. A. Dobbins, *Basic Components in the Motor Performance of Educable Mentally Retarded Children: Implications for Curriculum Development*. Grant No. OEG-0-70-2568-610, Washington, D.C.: U.S. Office of Education, 1972.

———, J. H. Widdop, and G. D. Broadhead, "The Physical Fitness and Motor Performance of Educable Mentally Retarded Children." *Exceptional Children* 36:509–519, March 1970.

Roberton, M. A., "Stages in Motor Development." In M. Ridenour, Ed., *Motor Development: Issues and Applications*. Princeton, N. J.: Princeton Book Co., 1978.

———, and L. E. Halverson, "Motor Development: A Lifelong Process." *JOPERD* 53:31–32, May 1982.

———, K. Williams, and S. Langendorfer, "Pre-longitudinal Screening of Motor Development Sequences." *Research Quarterly for Exercise and Sport* 51:724–731, December 1980.

Schnabl-Dickey, E. A., "Relationships Between Parents' Child-Rearing Attitudes and the Throwing and Jumping Performance of Their Preschool Children." *Research Quarterly* 48:382–390, May 1977.

Singer, R. N., "Interrelationships of Physical, Perceptual–Motor and Academic Variables in Elementary School Children." *Perceptual and Motor Skills* 27:1323–1332, 1968.

Smith, H. M., "Motor Activity and Perceptual Development." *JOHPER* 39:28–33, February 1968.

Special Fitness Test Manual for Mildly Mentally Retarded Persons. Revised. Reston, Va.: AAHPERD, 1976.

Stein, J. U., "Physical Fitness of Mentally Retarded Boys Relative to National Norms." *Rehabilitation Literature* 24:230–242, 1965.

Thaxton, A. B., A. L. Rothstein, and N. A. Thaxton, "Comparative Effectiveness of Two Methods of Teaching Physical Education to Elementary School Girls." *Research Quarterly* 48:420–427, May 1977.

Thomas, J. R., "Acquisition of Motor Skills: Information Processing Differences Between Children and Adults." *Research Quarterly for Exercise and Sport* 51:158–173, March 1980.

———, and B. S. Chissom, "Relationships as Assessed by Canonical Correlation Between Perceptual–Motor and Intellectual Abilities for Pre-school and Early Elementary Age Children." *Journal of Motor Behavior* 4:23–29, 1972.

———, and K. T. Thomas, "Strange Kids and Strange Numbers: Assessing Children's Motor Development." In J. R. Thomas, Ed., *Motor Development During Childhood and Adolescence*. Minneapolis: Burgess, 1984.

Toole, T., and E. A. Arink, "Movement Education: Its Effects on Motor Skill Performance." *Research Quarterly for Exercise and Sport* 53:156–162, June 1982.

Webb, R., R. Shutz, and J. McMahill, *Manual for AMP Index #1*. 9th rev. Glenwood, Iowa: Glenwood State Hospital School, 1977.

Wessel, J. A., *I CAN*. Northbrook, Ill.: Hubbard Scientific, 1976.

Williams, K., "Developmental Characteristics of a Forward Roll." *Research Quarterly for Exercise and Sport* 51:703–713, December 1980.

Winnick, J. P., *Early Movement Experiences and Development—Habilitation and Remediation*. Philadelphia: W. B. Saunders, 1979.

———, and F. X. Short, *The Physical Fitness of Sensory and Orthopedically Impaired Youth*. Project UNIQUE, Final Report. U.S. Department of Education Grant. New York: State University of New York College at Brockport, 1982.

CHAPTER 19

MOTOR PERFORMANCE TEST BATTERIES

O B J E C T I V E S

After reading this chapter, the student should be able to:

1. Identify components represented by test items in motor performance test batteries

2. Distinguish between the terms *motor ability,* *motor performance,* and *physical fitness*

A comprehensive motor performance test battery would theoretically represent all the factors that enter into various types of physical performance. Not only would this be beyond the scope of any one test, but by and large, research has failed to support adequately the theory of "generality" of motor skills. Nevertheless, physical educators have incorrectly continued to speak in terms of general athletic ability and have sought ways of measuring it.

The test batteries presented in this chapter have frequently been used as measures of motor performance. Motor performance batteries were devised with a specific purpose in mind. For example, some were designed to measure general athletic ability (the present ability to excel in various sports events); some to measure general motor ability (the ability, both acquired and innate, to display fundamental motor skills rather than highly specialized sports skills); some to measure motor capacity (the inborn ability to learn complex motor performance); some to measure motor educability (the ability to learn quickly unfamiliar motor skills); and some to measure motor fitness (the ability to perform basic motor skills involving such elements as power, agility, speed, and balance). It should be noted, however, that while the batteries were designed with a specific purpose

in mind, the items selected or the manner in which they were administered and scored or both was not always conducive to the original purpose of the test.

The qualities that are considered motor performance qualities and that make up the majority of test items for motor performance test batteries include speed, power, agility, reaction time, hand and eye coordination, and balance. Although reaction time is recognized as a separate quality, it has not been measured as such in motor performance tests, but rather it has remained combined with speed. Other test items sometimes included are strength and endurance, although they are also classified as physical fitness components. Motor factors may be improved with practice, but essentially they are considered relatively stable. Despite the fact that motor ability has usually been found to be task specific, perhaps more generality would be found if the performer had sufficient practice. In other words, if a person possesses considerable ability in the basic skills that are thought to underlie motor performance and are represented by the test items in the general motor ability tests, then he or she should perform well in a variety of physical tasks if given enough practice to overcome initial inhibitions and to establish the specific neuromotor patterns. Cratty has proposed an interesting three-level theory of perceptual–motor behavior that is pertinent to this topic.

USES OF MOTOR PERFORMANCE TEST BATTERIES

Although more research is indicated as to the efficacy and predictability of certain motor performance tests, the tests can be used as follows:

1. As a means for preliminary classification of students into homogeneous groups

2. As a tool for diagnosis of weaknesses in particular areas of motor performance

3. As a form of motivation in that students are able to assess their own status

4. As one of a number of measures for prognostic purposes

5. As tests of physical achievement

PROBLEMS ASSOCIATED WITH MOTOR PERFORMANCE TESTING

The problems involved in the testing of general motor ability are primarily those associated with testing of the separate qualities that make up the total battery. In other words, if the motor ability test contains measures of agility, balance, power, and so on, it has the same problems as those associated with agility testing, balance testing, and power testing. The problems are not necessarily additive, however. Some of the limitations of the individual measures are actually remedied when the tests are used as part of a battery that purports to measure general motor ability. For example, the standing long jump might be questioned as a strict measure of leg power because of the arm and trunk action. For general motor ability, however, the inclusion of this coordination of the arms, trunk, and legs is desirable.

Sometimes a question arises as to whether physical fitness factors should be included in motor ability batteries. Cardiorespiratory endurance, strength, muscular endurance, and flexibility are for physical (health-related) fitness, whereas power, agility, coordination, reaction time, balance, and speed are factors essential for motor performance but not for physical fitness. We have found the criteria set up for this distinction by Johnson and Schaefer to be most satisfactory, and if this distinction is widely accepted, it would seem that new motor ability tests are needed that are based primarily on the factors just listed as motor ability factors.

Physical educators must make the decision concerning the efficacy of motor ability tests on the basis of their own situation. If only a few activities are offered in their program, testing for purposes of classification should involve tests of those specific activities. On the other hand, if a large number and wide variety of activities are taught, task-specific testing is normally not feasible. In this case the use of general motor ability tests would appear to be applicable. In all cases, the teacher should use tests in conjunction with his or her own knowledge and subjective evaluation of the attitudes and the individual needs and interests of the students.

A number of authorities in the areas of anatomy and kinesiology have objected to the performance of sit-ups with straight legs. Sit-ups done in this manner are said to involve the psoas muscles more than the abdominal muscles, and it has been observed that the psoas muscles do not ordinarily require additional exercise. More important, however, is the possible harm to the back the performance of sit-ups can cause in persons with weak abdominal muscles. Because of the attachment of the psoas to the lumbar vertebrae, straight-leg sit-ups are said to cause excessive pull and possible strain in the lumbar area. Thus, bent-knee sit-ups are recommended, since they reduce the effect of the psoas muscles and involve the abdominal muscles more. Despite these objections, motor fitness tests have often included straight-leg sit-ups.

Most motor fitness tests require little equipment, and they are also relatively easy to administer. Each local setting, whether it be a single school, all schools in a county, or all schools in a state, should strive to establish standardized testing procedures. Through clinics and workshops, the various fine points of test administration that are not covered in test directions should be agreed on. This is the principal value of the laboratory portion of a class in tests and measurements. Without actual performance of the tests and discussion of the procedures, the rigid standardization that is necessary for accurate and worthwhile results cannot be attained. For the same reasons, the teacher should exercise good judgment when using national norms. These norms are intended only for general reference. It should be obvious that under varied conditions for testing, the results will not be comparable. For example, if some testers administer the shuttle run outdoors and others use a gymnasium floor, the scores will not be comparable. Similarly, if the 50-yard dash is given in one instance on a track and in another on the grass, variations in scores will result. In most cases, authors of tests recommend that local norms be constructed. In any case, the norms should be made available to students so that the norms have maximum interpretative and motivational value. We repeat, a test should be used for evaluation by the teacher, students, parents, the administration, and the general public.

SOME MOTOR PERFORMANCE TEST BATTERIES

Barrow Motor Ability Test (Barrow 1954)

Objective: To measure motor ability for purposes of classification, guidance, and achievement.

Age and Sex: Junior and senior high school boys and college men.

Reliability: Using the test–retest method, reliability for each test item was computed. Objectivity was also established by having two persons score each subject on each test item. The six test items, the motor ability factor they represent, their reliability and objectivity coefficients, and their correlation with the criterion are presented in Table 19.1.

Validity: Twenty-nine test items measuring eight factors were administered to 222 college men. Through multiple correlation and regression equations, two test batteries were established. The first test contained six items and yielded an *r* of .950 with the criterion, which was the total score from the 29 items. The shorter test battery, containing three items (which are included in the six-item battery), was found to have an *r* of .920 with the same criterion.

Equipment and Materials:

Standing broad (long) jump. A mat 5 × 12 ft and a measuring tape if the mat is not marked off.

Softball throw. Several 12-in. inseam softballs and a target area of about 100 yd. A football field marked off in 5-yd intervals is ideal for this test.

Zigzag run. A stopwatch; five cones or obstacles; and space enough to accommodate the 16- × 10-ft course.

Wall pass. A regulation basketball; a stopwatch; and wall space.

Medicine ball put. A space approximately 90 × 25 ft and a tape measure.

60-Yard dash. A stopwatch; a whistle; and a smooth surface at least 80 yd long with start and finish lines.

Scoring: A regression equation that uses weighted standard scores is provided to determine the total general motor ability score (GMAS). The equation is as follows:

$$\text{GMAS} = 2.2 \text{ (standing broad jump score)} + 1.6 \text{ (softball throw score)} + 1.6 \text{ (zigzag run score)} + 1.3 \text{ (wall pass score)} + 1.2 \text{ (medicine ball put score)} - 60\text{-yard dash score}$$

Barrow recommended that the users of the test establish their own norms. The norms (shown here in Table 19.2) were from a sample of college students and a group of physical education majors. Barrow also developed a motor ability test for junior and senior high school boys (Barrow 1957). He used the three-item indoor battery, consisting of the standing broad jump, medicine ball put, and zigzag run, and presented norms for grades 7 through 11 as well as for college men. It should be remembered that this shortened version loses

Table 19.1. Test Item Data for the Barrow Motor Ability Test, College Men

TEST ITEM	FACTOR[a]	RELIABILITY	OBJECTIVITY	CORRELATION WITH CRITERION[b]
Standing broad jump	Power	.895	.996	.759
Softball throw	Arm-shoulder coordination	.928	.997	.761
Zigzag run	Agility	.795	.996	.736
Wall pass	Hand-eye coordination	.791	.950	.761
Medicine ball put	Strength	.893	.997	.736
60-Yard dash	Speed	.828	.997	.723

[a]Balance and flexibility were also identified as motor ability factors, but no test item for either factor was found to have a high enough coefficient of correlation with the criterion to be included in the final battery.

[b]The criterion was the total score for 29 test items measuring eight factors in 222 college men.

Source: H. M. Barrow, "Test of Motor Ability for College Men." *Research Quarterly* 25:258, October 1954.

Table 19.2. General Motor Ability Test Scores, College Men[a]

PERFORMANCE LEVEL	PHYSICAL EDUCATION MAJORS		NONMAJORS	
	Six Items[b]	Three Items[c]	Six Items	Three Items
Excellent	586 and above	197 and above	550 and above	185 and above
Good	534–585	180–196	481–549	163–184
Average	480–533	161–179	410–480	138–162
Poor	428–479	143–160	341–409	116–137
Inferior	427 and below	142 and below	340 and below	115 and below

[a]See test for method of scoring.
[b]The six items are: standing broad jump, softball throw, zigzag run, wall pass, medicine ball put, and 60-yard dash.
[c]The three items are: standing broad jump, medicine ball put, and zigzag run.
Source: H. M. Barrow, *Motor Ability Testing for College Men*. Minneapolis: Burgess Publishing, 1957. Used by permission.

very little in predictive power when compared with the six-item test. The small loss is compensated for by the increase in administrative economy. It is also significant to point out that the order of testing is unimportant, which enables the teacher to employ three testing stations.

Barrow's norms for college men are shown in Table 19.3. The norms for boys in grades 7 through 11 for each test item are presented in Tables 19.4, 19.5, and 19.6.

Standing Broad (Long) Jump

Same as the standing long jump presented in Chapter 12.

Softball Throw

Directions: The subject attempts to throw the softball as far as possible. A short run is allowed, but the subject must not step over the restraining line. Three trials are allowed.

Scoring: The best distance of the three trials, to the nearest foot, is recorded as the score.

Safety: Students who are assisting with marking and measuring of the throws must be warned to keep their eyes on the ball when it is thrown. The subject should not be allowed to throw until the field is clear. Adequate warm-up should be provided.

Additional Pointers:

1. Student helpers can be employed effectively for marking each throw, measuring, and retrieving the balls. If a football field is used, markers reading in feet can be prepared and placed at each 5-yd line.

2. One of the student helpers should be assigned to run immediately and stand at the spot at which the ball lands, while another brings the marker. A decision can then be made whether the subject has a better throw.

Table 19.3. *T* Scores for Barrow Motor Ability Test, College Men

T SCORE	STANDING BROAD JUMP (in.)	ZIGZAG RUN (sec)	MEDICINE BALL PUT (ft)
80	113 and above	20.8 and below	58 and above
75	109–112	21.6–20.9	55–57
70	105–108	22.4–21.7	52–54
65	101–104	23.1–22.5	48–51
60	97–100	23.9–23.2	45–47
55	93– 96	24.7–24.0	42–44
50	89– 92	25.5–24.8	39–41
45	85– 88	26.3–25.6	35–38
40	81– 84	27.1–26.4	32–34
35	77– 80	27.8–27.2	29–31
30	73– 76	28.6–27.9	26–28
25	69– 72	29.4–28.7	23–25
20	68 and below	29.5 and above	22 and below

Source: H. M. Barrow, *Motor Ability Testing for College Men*. Minneapolis: Burgess Publishing, 1957. Used by permission.

Table 19.4. *T* Scores for Standing Broad Jump on Barrow Motor Ability Test, High School and Junior High School Boys

T SCORE	GRADE				
	7	8	9	10	11
80	90 and above	97 and above	103 and above	105 and above	112 and above
75	86–89	92–96	98–102	101–104	107–111
70	82–85	88–91	93– 97	97–100	103–106
65	77–81	83–87	88– 92	92– 96	97–102
60	73–76	78–82	83– 87	88– 91	93– 96
55	69–72	73–77	79– 82	83– 87	88– 92
50	65–68	69–72	74– 78	79– 82	83– 87
45	61–64	64–68	69– 73	75– 78	78– 82
40	56–60	59–63	64– 68	71– 74	74– 77
35	52–55	54–58	59– 63	66– 70	69– 73
30	48–51	50–53	54– 58	62– 65	64– 68
25	44–47	45–49	49– 53	58– 61	59– 63
20	43 and below	44 and below	48 and below	57 and below	58 and below

Source: H. M. Barrow, *Motor Ability Testing for College Men.* Minneapolis: Burgess Publishing, 1957. Used by permission.

Table 19.5. *T* Scores for Zigzag Run on Barrow Motor Ability Test, High School and Junior High School Boys

T SCORE	GRADE				
	7	8	9	10	11
80	20.1 and below	17.8 and below	20.2 and below	21.6 and below	21.5 and below
75	21.4–20.2	19.5–17.9	21.3–20.3	22.7–21.7	22.6–21.6
70	22.7–21.5	21.2–19.6	22.4–21.4	23.8–22.8	23.7–22.7
65	24.0–22.8	22.8–21.3	23.5–22.5	24.8–23.9	24.7–23.8
60	25.2–24.1	24.5–22.9	24.6–23.6	25.8–24.9	25.8–24.8
55	26.5–25.3	26.2–24.6	25.7–24.7	26.9–25.9	26.8–25.9
50	27.8–26.6	27.8–26.3	26.8–25.8	27.9–27.0	27.8–26.9
45	29.0–27.9	29.5–27.9	27.9–26.9	28.9–28.0	28.9–27.9
40	30.3–29.1	31.2–29.6	29.0–28.0	29.9–29.0	29.9–29.0
35	31.6–30.4	32.8–31.3	30.1–29.1	31.0–30.0	31.0–30.0
30	32.8–31.7	34.5–32.9	31.2–30.2	32.1–31.1	32.0–31.1
25	34.1–32.9	36.2–34.6	32.3–31.3	33.1–32.2	33.0–32.1
20	34.2 and above	36.3 and above	32.4 and above	33.2 and above	33.1 and above

Source: H. M. Barrow, *Motor Ability Testing for College Men.* Minneapolis: Burgess Publishing, 1957. Used by permission.

3. Measurement from the nearest 5-yd line facilitates scoring, as opposed to the use of a tape measure from the point of the throw.

Zigzag Run

Directions: Standards are set up as shown in Figure 19.1. The student begins from a standing start on the command "go" and runs the pattern shown in the figure as quickly as he can without grasping or moving the standards. Three complete circuits are made. The stopwatch is started when the command to go is given and is stopped when the subject crosses the finish line.

Scoring: The elapsed time to the nearest tenth of a second is recorded. If the student should grasp

or move a standard, run the wrong pattern, or otherwise fail to follow directions, he should run again after a suitable rest period.

Safety: The floor should be clean. The subjects should wear proper-fitting shoes with good traction to avoid blisters and slipping. Other students should be kept well away from the perimeter of the obstacle course and, especially, away from the finishing area. Sufficient warm-up should be allowed.

Additional Pointers:

1. The instructor should demonstrate the pattern of the course and stress that three complete circuits must be made.

Table 19.6. *T* Scores for Medicine Ball Put on Barrow Motor Ability Test, High School and Junior High School Boys

T SCORE	GRADE				
	7	8	9	10	11
80	43 and above	45 and above	49 and above	50 and above	54 and above
75	38–42	43–44	46–48	47–49	51–53
70	35–37	40–42	44–45	44–46	48–50
65	33–34	37–39	41–43	42–43	46–47
60	30–32	34–36	38–40	39–41	43–45
55	27–29	31–33	35–37	37–38	40–42
50	25–26	28–30	32–34	34–36	37–39
45	22–24	25–27	29–31	32–33	34–36
40	19–21	23–24	27–28	29–31	31–33
35	17–18	20–22	24–26	27–28	28–30
30	14–16	17–19	21–23	24–26	25–27
25	12–13	14–16	18–20	22–23	22–24
20	11 and below	13 and below	17 and below	21 and below	21 and below

Source: H. M. Barrow, *Motor Ability Testing for College Men.* Minneapolis: Burgess Publishing, 1957. Used by permission.

2. Students should be allowed to jog through the course before being tested.

3. If any student believes he can improve his score, he should be given another trial after he has rested.

Wall Pass

Directions: The subject stands behind a restraining line drawn 9 ft from the wall. On the signal to begin, he passes the ball against the wall in any manner he chooses. He attempts to catch the rebound and pass it again as many times as possible for 15 sec. For any pass to be legal, both of the subject's feet must remain behind the restraining line. If the subject loses control of the ball, he must retrieve it, return to the line, and continue passing.

Scoring: The score is the number of times the ball hits the wall in the 15 sec.

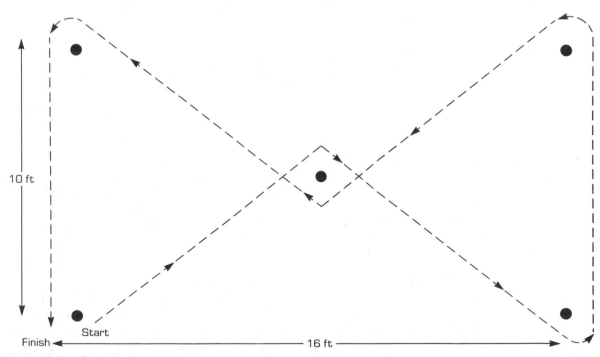

Figure 19.1. Pattern for the zigzag run in the Barrow Motor Ability Test

Additional Pointers:

1. The teacher should consider the possible variations in those cases when a subject loses control of the ball. He or she may wish to standardize the distance behind the subject by having students line up to block the ball, or have a wall of rolled mats, or some other variation.

2. The teacher should stress that the subject must maintain control of the ball and that the student will not be thrown a new ball if the rebound is missed.

6-Pound Medicine Ball Put

Directions: The subject stands between two restraining lines 15 ft apart. He then propels the medicine ball out as far as possible without stepping on or over the restraining line. He should hold the ball at the junction of his neck and shoulder and thrust it away from the body at an angle of approximately 45 degrees. Three throws are given.

Scoring: The best distance of three throws, to the nearest foot, is recorded as the score. A throw in which the subject commits a foul is not scored. If all three trials are fouls, the subject should try until he makes a fair put.

Additional Pointers:

1. Two students are needed at all times to assist in marking and measuring the throws. It is also helpful if one student is assigned to retrieve the ball. One student should quickly run to the exact spot where the ball lands, while another marks (or measures) it.

2. Any of several plans could be followed for measuring individual throws. Since the test is conducted on the gymnasium floor, small pieces of tape could be used to quickly mark each of the three trials. Another approach is to leave the tape stretched out from the restraining line and then measure each throw. One disadvantage to this method is that each throw must be recorded unless, of course, the succeeding throw or throws are not as far. The tape should be swung in an arc to ensure that the distance from the point of the throw to the spot of landing is obtained. Still another method is to have arcs marked on the floor 5 or 10 ft apart. In this way the measuring tape would not have to be as long, and it may facilitate testing.

3. The tester may wish to dust the ball with powdered chalk before each throw to obtain the exact point of landing. This procedure is ordinarily not too practical because of the time consumed and the necessity of continually wiping away the chalk marks.

60-Yard Dash

Directions: The subject starts from a standing position and on the signal "go" runs as rapidly as possible to the finish line. One trial is given.

Scoring: The time is recorded in seconds to the nearest tenth of a second, beginning at the command "go." In 60 yd there should be no appreciable time lag, owing to the relative speed of sound versus the speed of light.

Safety: The most important safety precaution has to do with pulled muscles. The teacher should make it a point to provide a thorough warm-up. The other safety features concern footwear, running surface, and adequate space beyond the finish line.

Additional Pointers:

1. The timer should be stationed parallel to the finish line to make sure an accurate score is obtained.

2. The starter should standardize the preparatory commands such as "ready," "get set," "go." If an arm signal is employed for starting, the movement of the arm must be practiced to synchronize it with the verbal command to "go."

Scott Motor Ability Test (Scott 1939, 1943)

Objective: To measure general motor ability to determine the individual needs of students and to assist in the assignment of students to classes. There are two test batteries.

Age and Sex: High school girls and college women.

Reliability: The reliability coefficients for individual test items ranged from .62 to .91. Table 19.7 presents the reliability coefficients for each test item.

Validity: Validity was established for each test battery. The criterion used was a composite score composed of ratings by experts, T scores from a variety of sports skills, and an achievement score composed of three fundamental activities. Validity coefficients of .91 and .87 were found for

Table 19.7. Validity and Reliability Data for Scott Motor Ability Test Items (Scott 1939, 1943)

TEST ITEM	VALIDITY	RELIABILITY
Basketball throw	.79 when correlated with the McCloy general motor ability test, total points scored from running, throwing, and jumping, and .78 with composite criterion of total points, other sports items, and subjective ratings	.89 on successive trials with 200 University of Iowa women
Dash	.71 and .62 with the same criteria as the basketball throw	.62 with 88 University of Iowa women
Wall pass	.47 and .54 with the same criteria as the basketball throw	.62 with 188 college women, .75 with 185 high school girls
Broad jump	.79 and .78 with the same criteria as the basketball throw	.79 with 252 college women, .92 with 144 high school girls
Obstacle race	When correlated with the longer but similar test, .94 with the same criteria as the basketball throw	.91 on two successive days

Battery 1 and Battery 2, respectively. Table 19.7 contains validity coefficients for each test item.

Test Battery 1 is made up of the following test items: basketball throw, dash, wall pass, and broad (long) jump. Test Battery 2 has three items: basketball throw, broad jump, and obstacle race. This battery is easier to administer than Test Battery 1 and may therefore be preferable. It differs very little from the larger battery in validity. Scott (1939, 1943) has found it to be accurate in predicting rate of achievement in physical education skills, and it has been used effectively for screening individuals needing special help in motor ability development.

Equipment and Materials:

Basketball Throw. Three or four regulation basketballs (although one could suffice) and measuring tape. Chalk or tape is desirable to mark the floor.

Dash. A stopwatch; a whistle; and tape, chalk, or other marking materials.

Wall Pass. A regulation basketball; a stopwatch; and unobstructed wall space.

Broad (Long) Jump. A gymnasium mat; measuring tape (or mat marked in inches); and a beat board (or 2-ft solid board).

Obstacle Race. A stopwatch; a high-jump standard; a 6-ft crossbar and supports; and chalk or tape for marking.

Basketball Throw

Directions: The subject throws the basketball as far as she can without stepping on or across the restraining line. Three trials are given. The direc-

tions emphasize that no demonstration should be given. Any technique of throwing is allowed, and the teacher is not to specify a particular one.

Scoring: The distance from the restraining line to the spot where the ball lands is measured to the nearest foot. The best of the three trials is the score.

Additional Pointers:

1. Students can help with the testing as they proceed from one station to another. One student should act as a spotter to work the landing point, while another watches for fouls at the throwing line.

2. Sufficient warm-up time should be provided.

3. The throwing area should be kept clear of traffic. On each trial, the student should not be allowed to throw until the marker and scorer are ready.

Dash

Directions: The student stands behind the starting line in any position she wishes. On the command "go," the student starts running down the lane as fast as possible until the whistle blows. The student does not have to stop on the whistle, but simply slows down and stops at her own pace. The student should be told that the running time will be 4 sec, and only one trial is given.

Scoring: The running course is marked and numbered in 1-yd zones. The zone where the student is at the sound of the whistle is quickly marked by an assistant. The distance in yards is then noted and recorded as the score.

Safety: Several factors should be considered with regard to safety. Pulled muscles and other injuries can easily occur without adequate warm-up. Another precaution is for the teacher to provide ample space at the end of the course to accommodate a gradual stop. Lack of sufficient space is not only a safety hazard but affects the validity of the test as well, if the performer starts to slow down prior to the whistle.

Adequate footwear is another factor that should be insisted on by the teacher in the interests of safety (and again validity). All obstructions must be removed from the running lane. The width of the lane itself should be at least 4 ft, and additional space along the sides of the lane should be kept clear.

Additional Pointers:

1. The first 10 yd need not be marked off in 1-yd intervals. The numbers can either be painted (or chalked) on the floor or cards can be prepared and placed along the side of the running lane. The latter is preferable, since placement has to be done only once and the cards can then be used again.

2. More than one student can be tested at the same time if provisions are made for judges. If this procedure is followed, the judges must be impressed with the importance of keeping their eyes on their assigned runner. The judges must guard against the tendency to watch to see who is ahead. At the sound of the whistle, each judge should run out and stand on the spot at which her assigned runner was when the whistle sounded.

3. The tester must be careful not to glance up at the runner or runners and thereby let the watch run past the 4 sec.

Wall Pass

Same as the wall pass test previously presented in the Barrow Motor Ability Test.

Broad (Long) Jump

Same as the standing long jump test previously presented in Chapter 12.

Obstacle Race

Directions: This test is designed to measure speed, agility, and general body coordination. The student starts in a back-lying position on the floor, with her heels at the starting line. When given the command "go," the student scrambles to her feet and runs to the first square marked on the floor (Figure 19.2). She steps on this square, and on each of the next two squares (B and C), with both feet. She then runs twice around the jump standard (D) and proceeds to dive under the crossbar (E). She then gets up and runs to the end line, touches it with her hand, runs back to line F, touches it, runs and touches the end line, runs back to line F, then sprints across the end line. One trial is given.

Scoring: The stopwatch is started at the signal "go" and is stopped when the student sprints across the end line. The score is the time to the nearest tenth of a second.

Safety: As in all speed and agility tests, the subject's footwear is an important consideration. Another possible source of injury is crawling or rolling under the crossbar. This sometimes results in a scraped knee, and the teacher should consider the use of knee guards. The crossbar itself should be made of very light material so as to not pose a danger when it is knocked down. The teacher should keep onlookers well away from the course

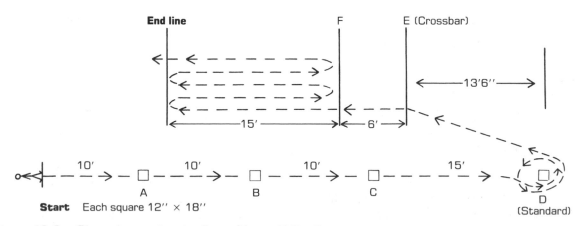

Figure 19.2. Obstacle race for the Scott Motor Ability Test

boundaries and particularly away from the finishing area. Adequate warm-up should be provided.

Additional Pointers:

1. It is suggested that the entire class be given directions at the same time, to avoid needless repetition.

2. The teacher should walk through the test, making sure students understand what is meant by stepping with both feet in the squares. It is not necessary to call the student back if the toe or heel is not completely inside the square.

3. It should not be considered a foul if the subject happens to bump and dislodge the crossbar as she passes under it.

4. The student cannot grasp the jump standard as she runs around it.

5. The teacher should emphasize the method of circling the jump standard and also stress the number of times the student must touch behind the end line and line F, as this procedure can result in some confusion if not thoroughly understood.

6. Two timers could be used to reduce the testing time. In this arrangement, the second subject is started when the first girl finishes circling the jump standard.

Scoring: T scales are available for each test item and for the composite scores (GMAS) of each test battery for high school girls and college women. These norms are presented in Tables 19.8 and 19.9.

Two methods are suggested for computing the composite score. One method is to obtain an average T score by adding the T-score values for the three or four tests given and dividing this sum by the appropriate number. For example, on Test Battery 1, a high school girl has the following T scores: 45 for the basketball throw, 55 for the dash, 52 for the wall pass, and 48 for the broad jump. The mean of these T scores is 50, which indicates that the student's overall performance on this test battery was exactly average.

Another method is to use the regression equation for the appropriate test battery, as follows:

Test Battery 1 (four items)

Score = 0.7 (basketball throw score)
       + 20 (dash score) + 10 (wall pass score)
               + 0.5 (broad jump score)

Test Battery 2 (three items)

Score = 2.0 (basketball throw score)
     + 1.4 (broad jump score) − obstacle race score

To illustrate, a college girl has the following raw scores on the three-item test battery:

Basketball throw: 47 ft

Broad jump: 72 in.

Obstacle race: 20.6 seconds

The raw scores are multiplied by their proper weightings and the products are added as follows:

$$2.0(47) + 1.4(72) - 20.6 = 174.2$$

This value is then found to represent a T score of 63, which indicates that this girl is considerably above average in motor ability.

Latchaw Motor Achievement Tests for Fourth, Fifth, and Sixth Grade Boys and Girls (Latchaw 1954; Latchaw and Brown 1962)

Objective: To measure general motor achievement.

Age and Sex: Fourth, fifth, and sixth grade girls and boys.

Reliability: The reliability coefficients for the individual test items ranged from .77 to .97. Students from 20 elementary schools in two states were tested.

Validity: Face validity is accepted for each test.

Equipment and Materials:

Basketball Wall Pass. A stopwatch; a regulation basketball; tape or marking equipment; and wall space to accommodate a target 8 ft long, 4 ft high, and drawn 3 ft from the floor. The restraining line is 8 ft long and 4 ft from the wall (Figure 19.3).

Volleyball Wall Volley. A stopwatch; a regulation volleyball; and a target identical to that for the basketball wall pass test (Figure 19.3).

Vertical Jump. Forty-eight 1-in. cloth strips, cut so that when suspended from a horizontal bar the longest strip is 5 ft from the floor and each succeeding one is 1 in. shorter, with the shortest strip being 8 ft 11 in. from the floor. The bottom of each strip should be weighted with a penny so that all strips hang even.

Standing Broad (Long) Jump. A mat and measuring tape unless the mat is marked in inches.

Shuttle Run. A stopwatch; floor markings— two ½-in. lines at least 20 ft long, parallel to each other and 20 ft apart; space to permit the 20-ft shuttle run as well as equal additional distance to allow for the subject to slow down after crossing the finish line.

Table 19.8.   *T* Scales for Scott Motor Ability Test, High School Girls

T SCORE	WALL PASS (410)[a]	BASKETBALL THROW (ft) (310)	BROAD JUMP (in.) (287)	4-SECOND DASH (yd) (398)	OBSTACLE RACE (sec) (374)
80	16	71			
79			96		
78					
77	15	68	94	27	
76		66			18.5–18.9
75		65			
74		64	92		
73	14	63			
72		61			
71		59	90	26	
70		55	88		19.0–19.4
69	13	54			
68		52	86	25	
67		51			19.5–19.9
66		50			
65		49			
64		48	84	24	20.0–20.4
63	12	47			
62		46	82		20.5–20.9
61			80		
60		45		23	
59		44	78		21.0–21.4
58	11	43			
57		42	76		21.5–21.9
56		41			
55		40	74	22	
54					22.0–22.4
53		39			
52	10		72		
51		37			22.5–22.9
50		36		21	
49		35	70		
48			68		23.0–23.4
47		34	66		
46	9	33			23.5–23.9
45		32	64	20	
44		31			24.0–24.4
43			62		
42		30			24.5–24.9
41	8	29	60	19	
40		28			
39			58		25.0–25.4
38		27	56		
37	7		54		25.5–25.9
36		26			26.0–26.4
35			52	18	26.5–26.9
34		25	50		27.0–27.4
33					

Table 19.8. *(continued)*

T SCORE	WALL PASS (410)[a]	BASKETBALL THROW (ft) (310)	BROAD JUMP (in.) (287)	4-SECOND DASH (yd) (398)	OBSTACLE RACE (sec) (374)
32		24	47		27.5–27.9
31	6	23			
30			44		28.0–28.4
29		22		17	28.5–28.9
28					29.0–29.4
27		21			29.5–29.9
26			40		30.0–30.4
25	5	20			
24				16	30.5–31.4
23		19	36		31.5–32.4
22				15	32.5–34.9
21		16			
20	4			14	35.0–36.0

[a]Number of subjects on which the scale is based.

Table 19.9. *T* Scales for Scott Motor Ability Test, College Women

T SCORE	BASKETBALL THROW	PASSES	BROAD JUMP	OBSTACLE RACE
85	75	18	86	17.5–17.9
84				
83	71	17		18.0–18.4
82				
81		16	85	
80	70	15		
79	69			18.5–18.9
78	68	14	84	
77	67		83	
76	66			
75	65		82	19.0–19.4
74	64		81	
73	62		80	
72	61	13	79	19.5–19.9
71	59			
70	58		78	20.0–20.4
69	57		77	
68	56		76	
67	55		75	20.5–20.9
66	54	12	74	
65	52			
64	51		73	21.0–21.4
63	50		72	
62	48		71	21.5–21.9
61	47			
60	46		70	
59	45	11	69	22.0–22.4

continued

Table 19.9. *(continued)*

T SCORE	BASKETBALL THROW	PASSES	BROAD JUMP	OBSTACLE RACE
58	44		68	
57	43		67	22.5–22.9
56	42			
55	41		66	23.0–23.4
54	40		65	
53	39		64	23.5–23.9
52	38	10	63	
51	37			24.0–24.4
50	36		62	
49	35		61	24.5–24.9
48			60	
47	34		59	25.0–25.4
46	33		58	
45	32	9	57	25.5–25.9
44	31			
43			56	26.0–26.4
42	30		55	
41			54	26.5–26.9
40	29		53	27.0–27.4
39	28	8	52	
38				27.5–27.9
37	27		51	28.0–28.4
36	26		50	
35			49	28.5–28.9
34	25		48	29.0–29.4
33			47	29.5–29.9
32		7	46	30.0–30.4
31			45	30.5–30.9
30	24		44	31.0–31.4
29			43	31.5–31.9
28	23		42	32.0–32.4
27	21		41	32.5–32.9
26		6	40	33.0–33.4
25	20		39	33.5–33.9
24			38	34.0–34.4
23		5	37	34.5–34.9
22			36	
21	19			35.0–35.4
20				
19			35	35.5–35.9
18				
17	18	4		
16				
15				
14				43.5–43.9
13			30	45.5–45.9

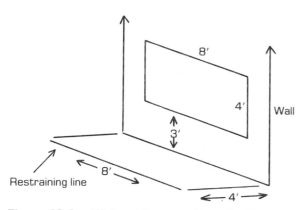

Figure 19.3. Wall and floor markings for the basketball wall pass and the volleyball wall volley tests

Soccer Wall Volley. A stopwatch; a regulation soccer ball; marking material; and wall and floor space to accommodate a wall target 4- × 2½-ft and a 4- × 2½-ft floor area (Figure 19.4).

Softball Repeated Throws. A stopwatch; a regulation softball (12-in. inseam); marking material; and wall and floor space to accommodate a wall target 10 ft high and 5½ ft wide, with the bottom 6 in. above the floor. A 5½-ft square is marked as the throwing area, 9 ft from the wall. A backstop 15 ft behind the throwing area should be 12 ft long and at least 2½ ft high (Figure 19.5).

Basketball Wall Pass

Reliability:

Grade four:	Boys .91, girls .94
Grade five:	Boys .84, girls .89
Grade six:	Boys .78, girls .83

Directions: The student stands behind the restraining line, which is 4 ft from the wall. When the teacher gives the signal to begin, the student throws the ball against the wall inside the target as many times as possible in 15 sec. The ball must be thrown from behind the restraining line to count, and it must hit completely inside the target. Balls that touch the line do not count. The student does not have to catch the ball first for the hit to be successful. In other words, the student could catch it in the air, catch it on the bounce, or run to retrieve it before throwing. If the student loses control of the ball, he or she must recover it personally. A 10-sec practice period is allowed, and two 15-sec trials are given.

Scoring: The score is the number of correct hits in the 15-sec period in the better of the two trials.

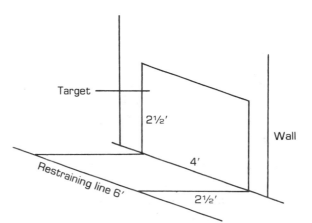

Figure 19.4. Wall and floor markings for the soccer wall volley test

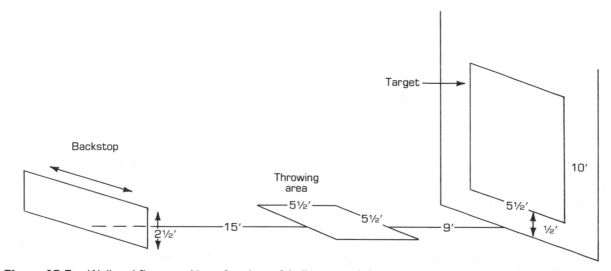

Figure 19.5. Wall and floor markings for the softball repeated throws test

Additional Pointers:

1. The instructor should ensure that the subject understands that the ball must hit inside the target area and that the throw must be made from behind the line.

2. It should also be stressed that the ball does not have to be caught in the air on the rebound and that, if the ball is lost, the subject must retrieve it as quickly as possible, since the time keeps running.

3. The test is more accurate if the person keeping the time does not have to simultaneously count hits and watch for faults.

Volleyball Wall Volley

Reliability:

Grade four:	Boys .85, girls .88
Grade five:	Boys .89, girls .92
Grade six:	Boys .91, girls .93

Directions: On the signal to begin, the subject throws the ball (from behind the restraining line) against the wall. The ball must then be hit, again from behind the restraining line, as it bounces off the wall so that it hits inside the target. If the ball gets away, the subject must recover it. For any new start, the ball throw may be against the wall to begin the volleying. Balls that are thrown or carried are not counted, nor are balls that hit the lines of the target. One 10-sec practice test is given, then the subject has four 15-sec trials.

Scoring: The best of the four trials is counted, the score being the number of legal hits inside the target.

Additional Pointers:

1. The teacher should be sure to explain the difference between a hit and a throw or carry.

2. Other procedures are the same as the basketball wall pass.

Vertical Jump

Same as for the vertical jump presented in Chapter 12, except that cloth strips are used and unlimited trials are allowed.

Standing Broad (Long) Jump

Same as for the standing long jump test presented in Chapter 12.

Shuttle Run

Reliability:

Grade four:	Boys .89, girls .84
Grade five:	Boys .89, girls .85
Grade six:	Boys .89, girls .79

Directions: The student stands behind the starting line with one foot against the line. On the command "go," he or she runs to the other line and places at least one foot on the line, then returns to the other side and touches that line with at least one foot, returns, and so on back and forth until three round trips have been completed. The subject thus finishes by crossing the same line at which he or she started. The subject may step beyond a line but is stopped any time one of the lines is missed. If stopped, the subject is given no score for the trial and, after a short rest, is tested again. If he or she fails again to follow directions, the score is zero for that trial. Two trials are given in this test.

Scoring: The better of two trials, measured to the nearest tenth of a second, is the score.

Safety: All subjects should be required to wear suitable shoes to prevent injury to the feet. Warm-up is recommended, and the area should be kept clear beyond both lines and especially at the finish line.

Additional Pointers:

1. Spotters at both ends could be assigned to watch for foot faults; however, the tester can usually do the timing, watching, and recording quite easily alone in such a small area.

2. When the student sprints across the end line at the finish of the race, the timer should be even with that line to get the most accurate score.

3. If subjects are tested in pairs, the factor of fatigue can be well handled by testing student A, then B, then A again, and finally B. Short rest periods between the two trials are thus provided without any lag in the testing.

4. If a large number of students are to be tested, chalk is unsuitable for marking the lines, as it rubs off. White washable tempera paint is recommended.

Soccer Wall Volley

Reliability:

Grade four:	Boys .82, girls .77
Grade five:	Boys .89, girls .83
Grade six:	Boys .88, girls .77

Directions: The subject stands behind the restraining line, which is an extension of 1 ft on either side of the 4-ft line on the floor area farthest from the wall, and places the ball at any place he or she chooses behind the line. When the teacher gives the signal to begin, the subject kicks the ball toward the wall in an attempt to hit inside the target. When the ball rebounds from the wall, the student attempts to kick it again inside the target. If the ball gets away, the student must recover it and bring it back into position to kick again. The hands may not be used to retrieve a ball within the 4- $\times$ 2½-ft floor area between the restraining line and the wall, but may be used to recover a loose ball outside that area. To be counted, a kick must be made from behind the restraining line, and the ball must be completely within the target area without touching any line. A practice period of 15 sec is allowed; then four 15-sec trials are given.

Scoring: The number of legal kicks in a 15-sec trial is counted and the best of the four trials is the score. A penalty of 1 point is deducted for each time a subject touches the ball with the hands while in the rectangular floor area.

Safety: All subjects should wear shoes, and the area should be kept unobstructed.

Additional Pointers:

1. While a kick made from within the 6- $\times$ 2½-ft floor area is not counted as a legal score, the student may certainly kick a ball from within this area and then kick the ball on the rebound from behind the restraining line. In this way the student can recover the ball quickly and not use the hands. This point should be stressed.

2. The suggestions that were mentioned for the basketball wall pass and volleyball wall volley also apply for this item. In all three events, the teacher may wish to regulate the degree of ball control loss. For example, if there is a large open area behind the subject, the student cannot hope to recover a loose ball and return before the trial is over. Therefore, the teacher may wish to have the students waiting to be tested stand in a line

at a prescribed distance behind the restraining line. The line of students could stop any lost ball, but they must not do anything to help or hinder the performer.

Softball Repeated Throws

Reliability:

Grade four:	Boys .82, girls .80
Grade five:	Boys .81, girls .82
Grade six:	Boys .85, girls .85

Directions: The student may stand anywhere within the 5½-ft square throwing area. On the command "go," he or she throws the ball at the target with an overhand throwing motion. The subject attempts to catch the ball as it rebounds in the air or on the bounce, so as to throw it again as quickly as possible. Each ball must be thrown from within the throwing area to be legal, and the ball must strike the wall completely within the target boundaries. Balls that hit the target lines do not count. If the student loses control of the ball, he or she must retrieve it as quickly as possible, rush back to the throwing area, and continue throwing. A practice period of 10 sec is provided, and then two 15-sec trials are given.

Scoring: The number of correct throws in the 15-sec period in the better of the two trials is the score.

Safety: All persons should be kept well away from the target area. The entire testing area from the wall to the backstop, with ample lateral distance, should be kept free of obstructions and people.

Additional Pointers:

1. The backstop may be a rolled mat, an ordinary table turned on its side, or an actual wall.

2. A wall volley test with use of a softball quickly softens and alters the shape of the ball. This can influence subsequent performance and should be a consideration in the administration of the test. The tester may wish to bring out new balls periodically or rotate them in some manner. This can be expensive. With children of the age being tested, the alteration of the ball is not nearly as serious a problem as with older students.

Norms: Norms are available in the form of *T* scores and percentile scores for each of the seven tests. Norms for fifth grade children are presented in Tables 19.10 and 19.11.

Table 19.10. Latchaw Achievement Scales, Fifth Grade Boys

T SCORES	PERCENTILE	BASKETBALL WALL PASS	VOLLEYBALL WALL VOLLEY	VERTICAL JUMP	STANDING BROAD JUMP	SHUTTLE RUN	SOCCER WALL VOLLEY	SOFTBALL REPEATED THROWS
75		27		17"	6'3"	11.2	16	
	99	26						14
70		22	20	16	6-2	11.4	15	
	97		19		6-0	11.5	14	13
65		21	17	15	5-8	11.8		
	92							
		20	14	14			13	12
60	81	19	13		5-3	12.2	12	11
		18	11	13			11	
55	69		10		5-0	12.5		10
		17		12			10	
50	50	16	8		4-9	12.8	9	9
45	30	15	7	11	4-5	13.3		8
		14	6	10			8	
		13	5		4-0	13.7		7
40	15	12	4	9			7	
		11			3-9	14.0		
35	6	10	3	8	3-8			6
		9				14.8		
30	2	8		7		15.1		
		6	2		3-7	15.9	5	5
25	1							

Source: M. G. Scott and E. French, *Measurement and Evaluation in Physical Education*. Dubuque, Iowa: William C. Brown, 1959. Modified for economy of space. Used by permission.

Table 19.11.   Latchaw Achievement Scales, Fifth Grade Girls

T SCORES	PERCENTILE	BASKETBALL WALL PASS	VOLLEYBALL WALL VOLLEY	VERTICAL JUMP	STANDING BROAD JUMP	SHUTTLE RUN	SOCCER WALL VOLLEY	SOFTBALL REPEATED THROWS
75	99	20	18	16	5'8"	11.6	15	10
70	97	19	17 / 13	15	5-7	11.8	14 / 13	9
65	92	18 / 17	12 / 11	14	5-4	12.2	12 / 11	
60	81	16 / 15	9 / 8 / 7	13 / 12	4-10	12.5	10	
55	69		6		4-5	13.0	9	8
50	50	14	5	11 / 10	4-1	13.4 / 13.5	8	
45	30	13	4		3-10	13.7	7	7
40	15	12 / 11	3	9	3-8	14.0	6	6
35	6	10 / 9 / 8 / 7	2	8 / 7	3-7 / 3-3	14.1 / 14.4 / 14.5	5	5
30	2	6	1		2-11	15.1	4	
25	1			6	2-8	15.9 / 16.0		4 / 3

Source: M. G. Scott and E. French, *Measurement and Evaluation in Physical Education*. Dubuque, Iowa: William C. Brown, 1959. Modified for economy of space. Used by permission.

AAHPERD Youth Fitness Test (AAHPERD 1976)

This test battery contains some items that measure physical fitness and some that are strictly skill related (motor fitness). The battery consists of the following items:

Pull-ups. Presented in Chapter 8 (Muscular Endurance).

Flexed Arm Hang. Presented in Chapter 8 (Muscular Endurance).

Sit-ups. Presented in Chapter 8 (Muscular Endurance).

Distance Run. Presented in Chapter 9 (Cardiorespiratory Condition). Options: 600-yard run or 1-mile or 9-minute run, boys and girls 10 to 12 years of age, or 1.5-mile or 12-minute run, children 13 years old and over.

Shuttle Run. Presented in Chapter 13 (Agility).

50-Yard Dash. Presented in Chapter 15 (Speed and Reaction Time).

Standing Long Jump. Presented in Chapter 12 (Power).

Johnson Indoor Motor Performance Test (Johnson 1976)

Objective: To provide a screening test of motor performance for college students pursuing a degree in physical education. Students who are not highly skilled or active in selected sports but who desire to major in physical education may still demonstrate average or higher level of ability in motor performance and thus show competence in this area.

Age and Sex: Intended for college-age men and women. The test can also be used for classification, guidance, and estimation of achievement with other school levels when satisfactory norms are established at each level.

Reliability: Satisfactory reliability coefficients were obtained for all items using the test–retest method. The best of three trials on two separate days were correlated.

Objectivity: All items had satisfactory objectivity when two different testers scored the same group of students.

Validity: Face validity is accepted for all test items. The battery includes a wider variety of general motor performance components than do previously published test batteries: static balance, hand–eye coordination, agility, power, and speed and reaction time.

Equipment and Materials: Given for each test item.

Inverted Balance Test for Static Balance (Short Form)

Directions: The student selects one of the five balance positions presented in Chapter 14 and attempts to hold it for a maximum of 5 sec.

Scoring: Each position has its own difficulty value, which is multiplied times the number of seconds held (up to 5 sec) for the score. The positions and values are as follows:

Tripod balance:	1 point per second
Tip-up balance:	2 points per second
Headstand:	3 points per second
Head and forearm:	4 points per second
Handstand:	5 points per second

Thus, if a student selects the headstand and holds it for 4 sec, the score would be $3 \times 4 = 12$ points. A score of 15 points is considered the minimal accepted standard for men and women physical education majors.

Softball Overhand Throw for Accuracy (Hand—Eye Coordination)

Directions: Men throw at a target from a 65-ft line, while women throw from a 40-ft line. Each student is allowed two practice throws prior to the trials. The target is of the same dimensions as that for the AAHPERD softball overhand throw for accuracy, described in Chapter 16.

Scoring: Points are given as follows:

Center circle:	3 points
Second circle:	2 points
Outer circle:	1 point

Balls hitting a line are given the higher value. A score of 13 points is the minimal accepted level for men, while a score of 16 points is required for women.

Basketball Dribble Test (Agility)

Directions: Six chairs, a basketball, and a stopwatch are needed. The chairs are placed in a straight line. The first chair is 5 ft from the starting line; the rest of the chairs are 8 ft apart. The subject stands behind the starting line, and on the command "go" begins to dribble around the right side of the first chair, then to the left of the second, and so on alternately around the rest of the chairs and back to the starting line. The ball may be dribbled with either hand, but only legal dribbles are allowed. The ball must be dribbled at least once as each chair is passed. Two trials are allowed. The time starts at the signal to go and stops as the subject crosses the starting line on the return. The better score of the two trials is recorded to the nearest tenth of a second. A score of 11.7 sec is required for men majors and of 14.0 sec for women majors.

Standing Long Jump (Athletic Power)

Directions: Same as for the standing long jump test presented in Chapter 12. Men must jump 7 ft 3 in. or better, while women must jump 5 ft 4 in. or better to meet minimal standards.

Four-Second Dash (Speed and Reaction Time)

Directions: Same as for the Scott Motor Ability Test presented earlier in this chapter.

Scoring: Table 19.12 contains point values for all test items in the Johnson Indoor Motor Performance Test and gives a rating scale for the overall score.

Division of Girls' and Women's Sports (DGWS) Physical Performance Test (Metheney 1945)

Objective: To assess muscular control and coordination, speed and agility, and strength.

Sex and Age Level: High school girls.

Validity: The Research Committee of the National Section on Women's Athletics (NSWA), later titled the Division of Girls' and Women's Sports (DGWS), selected eight items for this test. The items were selected on an empirical basis. Therefore, the items are assumed to have face validity. Some of the items were chosen to evaluate general motor ability, such as the standing long jump, the basketball throw, and the potato race. Agility measures include the 10-second squat thrust and the potato race. The strength of the arms and shoulders is represented by performance in pull-ups and push-ups, and abdominal muscle strength is measured by sit-ups. Endurance is assessed by the 30-second squat thrust. No reliability figures were given. The committee recommended that if all eight of the tests could not be administered, the battery could be shortened to the standing broad (long) jump, the basketball throw, the potato race or 10-second squat thrust, sit-ups, and push-ups or pull-ups.

Scoring: The test items were administered to over 20,000 girls, and scoring scales were constructed on the basis of data gathered from the 25 schools whose students showed the best performances.

Standing Broad (Long) Jump

Directions: Performed as described in Chapter 12 and scored in feet and inches.

Basketball Throw

Directions: The floor should be marked off in 5-ft intervals to facilitate scoring. The subject stands behind the restraining, or zero, line and throws a regulation basketball as far as possible. She may take one step in throwing, but she must not step over the restraining line. Any method of throwing may be used. Two trials are given.

Scoring: Spotters are employed to stand along the throwing lanes at a distance the girl has thrown in practice. As soon as the ball hits, a spotter immediately stands at that point. The marked zone is noted and the distance to the nearest foot is recorded. The better of two trials is the score.

Potato Race

Directions: The same as for the shuttle race in the AAHPERD Youth Fitness Test (Chapter 13). Two trials are given.

Scoring: The better score of the two trials to the nearest fifth of a second is recorded.

Sit-ups

Directions: Sit-ups are done with the legs straight and the hands clasped behind the head. There is no time limit.

Scoring: The number of sit-ups done is recorded.

Push-ups

Directions: The girl assumes a position in which the hands are placed on the mat, shoulder-width apart; the knees are in contact with the mat, with feet raised; and the body is straight from head to knees. The subject bends her arms to touch the chest to the floor and pushes up again, keeping the body as straight as possible throughout. The arms must come to complete extension, and only the chest is allowed to touch the floor. The subject repeats the exercise with no rest for as long as possible.

Scoring: The number of repetitions is recorded.

Table 19.12. Norms for Johnson Indoor Motor Performance Test, and Overall Rating Scale

PERFORMANCE LEVEL	INVERTED BALANCE TEST, SHORT FORM (points)[a]	THROW FOR ACCURACY OVERHAND (points)[b]	DRIBBLE TEST (sec)[c]	STANDING LONG JUMP (ft,in.)[d]	4-SECOND DASH (ft)[e]
MEN					
Excellent	25	20 and above	9.4 and below	8'4" and above	93 and above
Good	20	17–19	10.5– 9.5	7'9"–8'3"	88–92
Average	15	12–16	12.6–10.6	6'11"–7'8"	82–87
Poor	10	7–11	14.2–12.7	6'1"–6'10"	70–81
Very poor	5	0– 6	14.3 and above	0–6'0"	0–69
WOMEN					
Excellent	25	23 and above	11.6 and below	6'5" and above	76 and above
Good	20	21–22	12.7–11.7	5'10"– 6'4"	72–75
Average	15	14–20	15.0–12.8	4'11"– 5'9"	65–71
Poor	10	9–13	17.0–15.1	4'4"–4'10"	59–64
Very poor	5	0– 8	17.1 and above	0– 4'3"	0–58

Directions for Score
Each excellent = 5 pts
Each good = 4 pts
Each average = 3 pts
Each poor = 2 pts
Each very poor = 1 pt

Example: Jane Doe
Inverted balance: Excellent = 5 pts
Throw for accuracy: Average = 3 pts
Dribble test: Good = 4 pts
Standing long jump: Poor = 2 pts
4-Second dash: Average = 3 pts
Total: 17 pts

Overall Rating
23–25 = Excellent
18–22 = Good
13–17 = Average
8–12 = Poor
0– 7 = Very poor

[a]Chapter 14 of this text describes this test.
[b]Throw from 65 ft (men) or 40 ft (women). Data from students at Corpus Christi State University, Corpus Christi, Tex., 1976. Source: AAHPERD Sports Skills Project, 1966.
[c]Source: AAHPERD Sports Skills Project, 1966.
[d]Source: AAHPERD Youth Fitness Test, 1976.
[e]Data from students at Corpus Christi State University, Corpus Christi, Tex., 1943. Source: Scott Motor Ability Test.

Pull-ups

Directions: A horizontal bar is adjusted at a height of 3½ ft from the floor. The subject grips the bar and moves under it so that her arms are completely extended, her knees are bent to right angles, and her body is straight from the shoulders to the knees and parallel with the floor. All of her weight should be borne by her hands and feet. The subject then pulls upward, using only her arms (no leg action) until her chest touches the bar. The body moves from the knees with no bending at the hips or rounding of the back, nor is resting allowed. The arms must be completely extended after each touching of the chest.

Scoring: The number of repetitions is recorded.

Squat Thrusts

Directions: The squat thrusts are performed as described in Chapter 13.

Scoring: The number of complete movements plus extra quarter movements performed in the 10-sec or 30-sec time period is the score.

Additional Pointers:

1. The committee recommended that the test should not be given to any student who has not been given medical approval for strenuous exercise.

2. Form should be stressed instead of all-out maximum performance.

3. The test scores should be employed to evaluate the program with respect to selecting activities that provide balanced development.

4. Girls who score very poorly on the tests should be given special attention as to cause and remedial work.

Norms: The scoring table with the scale based on three standard deviations above and below the mean is given in Table 19.13.

OTHER TESTS OF MOTOR PERFORMANCE AND MOTOR EDUCABILITY

Space does not permit the description of other motor performance tests, but brief mention of some of these is made here. The references cited describe the tests and norms.

McCloy (1934) and McCloy and Young devised tests they described as being measures of general motor achievement. These tests included track and field events and strength tests. The test items

for boys consisted of pull-ups; a 50- or 100-yard dash; the running or standing long jump; the running high jump; and a shot put, basketball, or baseball throw for distance. For girls the items were modified pull-ups, a dash, a long jump, and a throw. Through the use of tables, the General Motor Ability Score (GMAS) for boys and girls is obtained with the following formulas:

GMAS (boys) = 0.1022 (total track and field
points) + 0.3928 (pull-up strength)
GMAS (girls) = 0.42 (total track and field points)
+ (number of pull-ups)

Cozen's General Athletic Ability Test has been used for measuring motor ability of college men for a number of years. Through a study of 40 activities, Cozens selected seven test items: dips, baseball throw for distance, football punt for distance, bar snap, standing long jump, dodging run, and quarter-mile run. These items, which were selected as measuring the elements of general motor ability, are weighted and totaled. Then, through use of a classification scale that takes into account body size, the score for the test battery is interpreted as superior, above average, average, below average, or inferior. The validity and reliability coefficients for this test are high. The principal disadvantage to the test is the space and time requirements for administration.

Larson developed a motor ability test for college men through factor analysis that has both an indoor and an outdoor form. The indoor test battery includes a dodging run, chinning, dipping, a vertical jump, and the bar snap. The outdoor test has the baseball throw for distance, bar snap, pull-ups, and the vertical jump. The raw scores are converted to T scores, which are weighted and totaled to be used for classification. High validity and reliability have been reported.

The Humiston Motor Ability Test (Humiston 1937) was devised to measure the motor ability of college women for the primary purpose of classifying the women for intramurals and physical education. The test contains seven test items: a dodging run, sideward roll on a mat, climb over a box, turn around in a circle, run between two barriers, a basketball throw over a rope with subsequent catch, and a 60-foot sprint. The items are arranged in the form of an obstacle course set up on a gymnasium floor. They must be executed in sequence, and the score is the elapsed time to the nearest tenth of a second.

The Newton Motor Ability Test for high school girls was developed by Powell and Howe. The test is made up of three items: the standing long

Table 19.13. Norms for Division of Girls' and Women's Athletics (DGWS) Physical Performance Test

SCALE SCORE	STANDING BROAD JUMP (ft.,in.)	BASKETBALL THROW (ft)	POTATO RACE (sec)	PULL-UPS (no.)	PUSH-UPS (no.)	SIT-UPS (no.)	10-SECOND SQUAT THRUST (no.)[a]	30-SECOND SQUAT THRUST (no.)[a]
100	7'9"	78	8.4	47	61	65	9-1	24
95	7'7"	75	8.6	45	58	61	9	23
90	7'4"	72	8.8	42	54	57	8-3	22
85	7'2"	68	9.0	39	51	54	8-1	21
80	6'11"	65	9.4	37	47	50	8	20
75	6'9"	62	9.6	34	43	46	7-3	19
70	6'7"	59	10.0	32	39	43	7-1	18-2
65	6'4"	56	10.2	29	36	39	7	18
60	6'2"	53	10.4	26	32	36	6-2	17
55	6'0"	50	10.6	24	28	33	6-1	16
50	5'9"	46	11.0	21	25	29	6	15
45	5'7"	43	11.2	18	21	25	5-2	14-2
40	5'5"	40	11.6	16	17	22	5-1	14
35	5'2"	37	11.8	13	13	18	4-3	13
30	5'0"	34	12.0	10	10	15	4-2	12
25	4'9"	31	12.4	8	6	11	4	11
20	4'7"	27	12.6	5	2	7	3-3	10
15	4'4"	24	13.0	3	1	3	3-2	9
10	4'2"	21	13.2	1	0	1	3	8-2
5	4'0"	18	13.4	0	0	0	2-3	7-2
0	3'9"	15	13.6	0	0	0	2-2	7

[a]Number completed plus extra quarter movements.
Source: E. Metheny, Chairman, "Physical Performance Levels for High School Girls." *Journal of Health and Physical Education,* June 1945, p. 309.

jump; a hurdle race in which the subject jumps over five 15-in. hurdles and then runs around the Indian club and back over the hurdles; and a scramble, which involves the subject getting to her feet from a supine position and running to tap a bell twice, then returning to the starting position, clapping her hands twice on the floor, and finally, repeating the task until the fourth double tap of the bell. Powell and Howe recommended that the test be given again on successive days and an average taken for each item to increase reliability.

Iowa–Brace Motor Educability Test (McCloy 1934, 1937)

The Iowa–Brace test represents McCloy's revision of the original Brace test. The test has 21 items, 10 of them from the Brace test. Students are scored on ten stunts without practice. Scoring is on a pass–fail basis, and two trials are allowed. If the first trial is done correctly, 2 points are awarded. If the first trial is incorrect, the subject immediately tries again and if successful, receives 1 point. A second failure scores a zero.

Three of the test items are described here.

Stork Stand

The subject stands on the left foot and places the bottom of the right foot against the inside of the left knee. The hands are on the hips. With the eyes closed, the subject holds the position for 10 sec without shifting the left foot about on the floor. A failure is loss of balance, movement of the right foot away from the knee, or opening of the eyes or removal of the hands from the hips.

Double Heel Click

The subject jumps upward, claps the feet together twice, and lands with the feet apart (any distance). A failure is lack of two claps of the feet or landing with the feet touching each other.

Full Right Turn

The subject stands with both feet together, then jumps up and makes a full (360 degrees) turn to the right, landing on about the same spot. He or she must not lose the balance on landing, causing the feet to move. A failure is not making a full right turn and thus landing facing in the original direction or losing one's balance and moving the feet after they touch the floor.

Adams Sports-Type Educability Test (Adams 1954)

Adams developed a sports-type educability test with two rather unusual items that fit the concept of testing for unfamiliar skills. Two items (from a battery of four items) are presented here.

Lying Tennis Ball Catch

The subject lies on the back and tosses a tennis ball in the air and catches it with either hand. The ball must go at least 6 ft in the air, and the subject must maintain the supine position. Ten trials are given. The score is the number of correct tosses. A perfect score is 10.

Ball Bounce Test

The subject stands in a circle that is 6 ft in diameter. Holding a softball bat one hand length from the thick end, he or she attempts to bounce a volleyball on the top end of the bat for ten consecutive bounces. The ball must bounce at least 6 in. off the top of the bat. Each attempt, whether successful or not, is a trial. Ten trials are given. A perfect score is 100.

Carpenter Motor Ability Test (Carpenter 1942a, 1942b)

The Carpenter Motor Ability Test was developed for boys and girls of grades one, two, and three. The measurements include the broad (long) jump, the (6-lb) shot put, and body weight. The scores are computed with formulas presented in the study.

Johnson–Metheny Motor Educability Test (Metheny 1938)

For this test a canvas 15 ft long is marked as shown in Figure 19.6. Every other line is 3 in. wide; the narrow lines are ¾ in. wide. The centers of the lines are 18 in. apart. A ¾-in. line is then drawn down the center of the 24-in. lane, running the length of the canvas. The canvas should be placed over a mat with the ends and sides tucked under so that the canvas is stretched taut. (The lines could be painted or chalked directly on a mat.)

Two of the four test items are presented as samples here. The numbers in parentheses refer to the number of the test item in the original Johnson test battery.

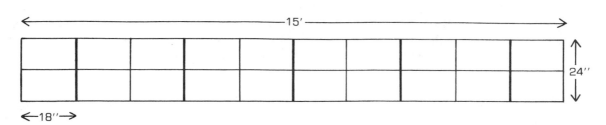

Figure 19.6. Canvas markings for the Johnson—Metheny test

Front Roll (Test No. 5)

The subject starts from a standing position at one end of the 24-in. lane and performs one front roll within the limits of the first half of the lane, then another front roll within the limits of the second half of the lane. Each roll is worth 5 points. Points are deducted as follows: (1) For each roll, 2 points are deducted if the subject strays beyond the left boundary, and a similar penalty is imposed if he or she overreaches the right boundary. (2) One point is deducted for each roll not performed within the designated half of the lane. (3) Five points are deducted for failure to perform a true roll. If the subject fails on the first attempt, he or she is allowed to try a second roll in the first half of the lane.

Jumping Half Turn (Test No. 8)

Standing on the first 3-in. line, the subject jumps upward and executes a half turn in either direction, landing on the second 3-in. line. He or she is now facing the starting line. The subject then jumps upward, making a half turn in the opposite direction from which the first jump was done, and lands on the starting line. The test proceeds in this manner, with the subject alternating directions of the turns, until four jumps are completed. Perfect execution is worth 10 points. Two points are deducted for each jump in which the subject does not land on the line with both feet or turns in the wrong direction.

California Physical Performance Test

This test contains five test items for boys and girls from 10 to 18 years of age. The items are: pull-ups for boys, knee push-ups for girls, standing long jump, knee-bent sit-ups for time, 50-yard dash, and softball throw. Nearly all the test items have been described previously. It should be noted that several of the AAHPERD Youth Fitness Test items were taken from this test. The knee push-ups are performed as outlined in the NSWA test except that the maximum is 50. Some of the unique features of the knee-bent sit-ups for time should be mentioned.

Knee-Bent Sit-ups for Time

The sit-up is accomplished in the manner described in Chapter 8. The hands are clasped behind the head, and the subject raises the trunk by lifting first the head, then the shoulders, and then the back. Each student must show correct performance by executing five sit-ups correctly for the tester before proceeding with the time trials. The following time limits are observed: 30 sec for boys and girls ages 10 and 11; 60 sec for boys 12, 13, and 14 and for all girls 15 years and over, and 90 sec for boys 14 and above.

The revised norms for the test battery are in percentiles and are based on only sex and age. Espenschade found that height and weight did not significantly affect performance any more than age alone.

Oregon Motor Fitness Test (Motor Fitness Tests for Oregon Schools 1962)

The Oregon State Department of Education provides a manual of motor fitness test batteries and norms for three age groups: intermediate boys and girls (grades 4, 5, 6); junior high school boys and girls (grades 7, 8, 9); and senior high school boys and girls (grades 10, 11, 12). For boys in grades 4 through 6, the items include the standing long jump, floor push-ups, and sit-ups. The junior and senior high school tests are pull-ups, the jump and reach test, and the 160-yard potato race. These test items, except the potato race, have been described previously.

The 160-yard potato race is conducted in an area requiring 70 ft for running plus some space for finishing. Three circles are drawn on the floor in a line; each circle is 1 ft in diameter. The first circle is drawn immediately behind the starting line. The second circle is 50 ft and the third is 70 ft away. A small block or eraser 2 × 4 in. is placed in circle two and another in circle three. The subject runs to circle two, picks up the block, and runs to place it in the first circle. He or she then runs to circle three, picks up the block, and places it in circle one. Then the first block must be returned to circle two and the second block returned to circle three. The subject finishes the race by dashing across the finish line. The score is in seconds.

The girls' battery also contains three items: standing long jump, hanging in arm-flexed position, and crossed-arm curl-ups. The hanging in arm-flexed position test is similar to the flexed-arm hang for girls in the AAHPERD Youth Fitness Test, except that the timing continues as long as there is some flexion in the elbow. The time stops as soon as the elbow is straight.

Crossed-arm curl-ups are done with the knees bent at about a 90-degree angle and with the soles of the feet flat on the floor. The feet are held down by a partner. The subject folds her arms across her chest and rises to a sitting position without using the arms in any way. She then returns to a lying position and repeats the exercise as many times as possible. It is not permissible to bounce back up, or to rest at any time.

FINDINGS AND CONCLUSIONS FROM MOTOR PERFORMANCE MEASUREMENT AND RESEARCH

Studies related to the topic of motor performance are so numerous that this brief summary can only be considered a sampling, at best. Furthermore, only studies on motor ability reported in the literature since 1950 are presented here, although a great deal of research in this area was done prior to that time. In fact, most of the motor ability tests were developed in the 1930s and 1940s. The sprinkling of studies mentioned here are merely intended to acquaint the reader with some of the information pertaining to this topic.

Although some test makers have proceeded on the assumption that motor ability is basically stable, Lafuze found that general motor ability can be significantly improved through specific practice, and Hardin and Garcia have identified diagnostic performance tests to aid in the specific practice of elementary children. Broer studied the improvement in general motor ability of students of low ability. She concluded that basic instruction is more beneficial than participation in a regular activity program and should precede participation in the regular program. In a somewhat contradictory study, Dohrmann concluded that throwing and kicking training programs, given in

addition to regular physical education programs, did not result in greater improvement in throwing and kicking ability than did the regular physical education program alone.

Burdeshaw, Spragens, and Weis studied the effects of specific versus general instruction of badminton skills in college women classified as low in motor ability, as measured by the Scott Motor Ability Test. The results supported the theory of specificity in learning motor skills and cast doubt on the worth of a basic skills course in facilitating subsequent performance in specific skills. Gallagher compared athletically high-skilled and low-skilled subjects on the learning of six novel motor skills. He found that the high-skilled group had significantly better scores on only two of the six tasks. The two tasks were athletically oriented, which again supported specificity.

Miller did not find any differences in motor ability, as measured by the Barrow Motor Ability Test, as a result of individual and team sports physical education programs. Patterson compared subjects participating in a physical education soccer class with subjects who also received supplementary exercises and found all three programs to be equally effective in significantly improving scores on the Barrow Motor Ability Test.

Some findings particularly relevant to the subject of testing and motor ability are those by Smith and Bozymowski and Singer. Smith and Bozymowski concluded that subjects who viewed warm-up as being desirable performed better when warm-up preceded performance in an activity, such as an obstacle race. Subjects who had less favorable attitudes toward warm-up did not improve significantly following warm-up. Singer found that nonathletes performed significantly better on a gross motor task than did athletes in the presence of spectators.

Landiss found that of eight activities studied, tumbling, gymnastics, and wrestling appeared most effective in developing the abilities measured in the Larson Test of Motor Ability. In a study with college women, Bennett investigated the relative effectiveness of four activities in developing specific and general motor ability. The subsequent ratings were swimming and modern dance first, basketball second, and folk dance third.

Boys were found to be superior to girls on all motor ability-educability tests and in practically all physical skills in studies by Smith and Hoffman. Bachman, however, concluded that the rate of learning in large muscle skills was independent of age and sex over the range of 6 to 26 years and that no sex differences were found in motor learning ability in that age range.

Lockhart and Mott concluded that superior performers benefit by being segregated into homogeneous ability groupings and that the majority of subjects involved preferred participation in classes composed of persons of similar ability. Walters found that above-average bowlers had higher motor ability scores than below-average bowlers. Roloff, Hoffman, and Phillips and Summers all found positive relationships between motor ability tests and kinesthesis. Athletes were found to be superior to nonathletes in performance on test items related to general motor ability and motor capacity in studies conducted by Shelley and Girolamo. Coleman, Keogh, and Mansfield reported a strong positive relationship between motor ability scores and both peer acceptance and social adjustment in boys experiencing learning difficulties.

The literature in the area of motor fitness is so extensive that it would fill volumes. Numerous studies have been reported on construction of tests, the contribution of various activities to the development of fitness, and the relationship of fitness to other traits and types of performance. The term *physical fitness* is sometimes used by the writers of the studies, but the measuring devices employed are motor fitness tests, as the term is used in this text.

Landiss investigated the contributions of eight selected physical education activities to the development of fitness. He found that the combined activities of tumbling and gymnastics were most effective in developing motor fitness and motor ability and that tennis, swimming, and boxing ranked lowest.

Davis found that a training and conditioning program for the 200-yard crawl stroke in swimming brought about significant improvement in motor fitness tests. Campbell studied the effects of supplemental weight training given to members of football, basketball, and track squads with regard to improving their motor fitness performance. His findings showed that weight training produced a significantly greater increase in fitness than did the normal conditioning program alone. A program of creative activities, studied by Estes, produced increases in muscular fitness, strength, balance, and flexibility.

B. J. Keogh compared a daily physical education program with a program that met twice a week on the development of motor fitness in third and fifth grade children. The actual time spent in class was the same for both programs, since the daily program lasted for four weeks and the two-day-a-week program continued for ten weeks. Both programs were equally effective in improving motor fitness. Fabricius found that a physical education program for fourth grade boys and girls, in which calisthenics was added to the normal program, improved fitness, as measured by the Oregon Motor Fitness Test, to a greater degree than the program without added calisthenics. Wireman concluded from his study that a knowledge of results of performance in calisthenics, games, and sports facilitates improvement in motor fitness.

Harkness compared a physical education program with a Reserve Officers Training Corps (ROTC) program on improvement in motor fitness, as measured by the JCR Test. The physical education program was significantly superior to the ROTC program in the development and maintenance of motor fitness.

Numerous studies have shown that programs of conditioning produce gains in fitness (e.g., Sills 1954). Conversely, Campney and Wehr concluded that a ten-week training period utilizing the exercises advocated by the President's Council on Physical Fitness was not likely to produce significant improvements in any of the fitness components studied except in flexibility. Kirby investigated the effects of different amounts of exercise performed in addition to the regular physical education activities on improvement of college men on the JCR Test. He found that the gains in the JCR scores were inversely proportional to the number of additional exercises. He concluded that the intensity of performing the exercises in a short time was more influential than the number of exercises performed.

BIBLIOGRAPHY

AAHPERD Youth Fitness Test Manual. Reston, Va.: AAHPERD, 1976.

Adams, A. R., "A Test Construction Study of Sport-Type Motor Educability for College Men." Microcarded doctoral dissertation, Louisiana State University, Baton Rouge, 1954.

Bachman, J. C., "Motor Learning and Performance as Related to Age and Sex in Two Measures of Balance Coordination." *Research Quarterly* 32:123–137, May 1961.

Barrow, H. M., "Test of Motor Ability for College Men." *Research Quarterly* 25:253–260, October 1954.

———, *Motor Ability Testing for College Men*. Minneapolis: Burgess, 1957.

————, and R. McGee, *A Practical Approach to Measurement in Physical Education.* Philadelphia: Lea & Febiger, 1964.

Baumgartner, T. A., and A. S. Jackson, "Measurement Schedules for Tests of Motor Performance." *Research Quarterly* 41:10, March 1970.

Bennett, C. L., "Relative Contributions of Modern Dance, Folk Dance, Basketball, and Swimming to Motor Abilities of College Women." *Research Quarterly* 27:253–261, October 1956.

Brace, D. K., *Measuring Motor Ability.* New York: A. S. Barnes, 1927.

Broer, M. R., "Evaluation of a Basic Skills Curriculum for Women Students of Low Motor Ability at the University of Washington." *Research Quarterly* 26:15–27, March 1955.

Burdeshaw, D., J. E. Spragens, and P. A. Weis, "Evaluation of General Versus Specific Instruction of Badminton Skills to Women of Low Motor Ability." *Research Quarterly* 41:472–477, December 1970.

California Physical Performance Tests, Sacramento, Calif.: Bureau of Health, Education, Physical Education, and Recreation, California State Department of Education, 1962.

Campbell, R. L., "Effects of Supplemental Weight Training on the Physical Fitness of Athletic Squads." *Research Quarterly* 33:343–355, October 1962.

Campney, H. K., and R. W. Wehr, "Effects of Calisthenics on Selected Components of Physical Fitness." *Research Quarterly* 36:393–402, December 1965.

Carpenter, A., "Strength Testing in the First Three Grades." *Research Quarterly* 13:328–335, October 1942a.

————, "The Measurements of General Motor Capacity and General Motor Ability in the First Three Grades." *Research Quarterly* 13:444–465, December 1942b.

Clarke, H. H., *Application of Measurement to Health and Physical Education.* 4th ed. Englewood Cliffs, N.J.: Prentice-Hall, 1967, Chapter 7.

Coleman, J. C., J. F. Keogh, and J. Mansfield, "Motor Performance and Social Adjustment Among Boys Experiencing Serious Learning Difficulties." *Research Quarterly* 34:516–517, December 1963.

Cozens, F. W., *Achievement Scales in Physical Education Activities for College Men.* Philadelphia: Lea & Febiger, 1936.

Cratty, B. J., "A Three Level Theory of Perceptual Motor Behavior." *Quest,* Monograph VI, May 1966, pp. 3–10.

Davis, J. F., "Effects of Training and Conditioning for Middle Distance Swimming Upon Various Physical Measures." *Research Quarterly* 30:399–412, December 1959.

Dohrmann, P., "Throwing and Kicking Ability of 8-Year-Old Boys and Girls." *Research Quarterly* 35:464–471, December 1964.

Espenschade, A. S., "Restudy of Relationships Between Physical Performances of School Children and Age, Height, and Weight." *Research Quarterly* 34:144–153, May 1963.

Estes, M. M., "The Role of Creative Play Equipment in Developing Muscular Fitness." Microcarded doctoral dissertation, State University of Iowa, Iowa City, 1959.

Fabricius, H., "Effect of Added Calisthenics on the Physical Fitness of Fourth Grade Boys and Girls." *Research Quarterly* 35:135–140, May 1964.

Gallagher, J. D., "Motor Learning Characteristics of Low-Skilled College Men." *Research Quarterly* 41:59–67, March 1970.

Girolamo, C. G., "A Comparison of General Motor Capacity of Athletes and Non-athletes." Microcarded master's thesis, State University of Iowa, Iowa City, 1956.

Hardin, D. H., and M. J. Garcia, "Diagnostic Performance Tests for Elementary Children (Grades 1–4)." *JOPERD* 53:48–49, February 1982.

Harkness, W. W., "The Contributions of AFROTC and Physical Education Experiences to Selected Components of Fitness of College Men." Microcarded doctoral dissertation, Stanford University, Palo Alto, Calif., 1957.

Henry, F., "Evaluation of Motor Learning When Performance Levels Are Heterogeneous." *Research Quarterly* 27:176–181, May 1956.

Hoffman, V., "Relation of Selected Traits and Abilities to Motor Learning." Microcarded doctoral dissertation, Indiana University, Bloomington, 1955.

Humiston, D. A., "A Measurement of Motor Ability in College Women." *Research Quarterly* 8:181–185, May 1937.

Johnson, B. L., "An Indoor Motor Performance Test for College Physical Education Majors." Unpublished study, Corpus Christi State University, Corpus Christi, Tex., 1976.

Johnson, G. B., "Physical Skill Tests for Sectioning Classes into Homogeneous Units." *Research Quarterly* 3:128–134, March 1932.

Johnson, P. B., and M. Schaefer, *Physical Education—A Problem Solving Approach to Health and Fitness.* Chicago: Holt, Rinehart, and Winston, 1966, pp. 20–27.

Keogh, B. J., "The Effects of a Daily and Two Day Per Week Physical Education Program Upon Motor Fitness of Children." Microcarded doctoral dissertation, State University of Iowa, Iowa City, 1962.

Keogh, J. F., "Motor Performance Test Data for Elementary School Children." *Research Quarterly* 41:600–602, December 1970.

Kirby, R. F., "The Effects of Various Exercise Programs Involving Different Amounts of Exercise on the Development of Certain Components of Physical Fitness." Unpublished doctoral dissertation, Louisiana State University, Baton Rouge, 1966.

Lafuze, M., "A Study of the Learning of Fundamental Skills by College Freshman Women of Low Motor Ability." *Research Quarterly* 22:149–157, May 1951.

Landiss, C. W., "Influence of Physical Education Activities on Motor Ability and Physical Fitness of Male Freshmen." *Research Quarterly* 26:295–307, October 1955.

Larson, L. A., "A Factor Analysis of Motor Ability Variables and Tests, With Tests for College Men." *Research Quarterly* 12:499–517, October 1941.

Latchaw, M., "Measuring Selected Motor Skills in Fourth, Fifth, and Sixth Grades." *Research Quarterly* 25:439–449, December 1954.

———, and C. Brown, *The Evaluation Process in Health Education, Physical Education and Recreation*. Englewood Cliffs, N.J.: Prentice-Hall, 1962, pp. 84–104.

Lockhart, A., and J. A. Mott, "An Experiment in Homogeneous Grouping and Its Effect on Achievement in Sports Fundamentals." *Research Quarterly* 22:58—62, March 1951.

Marteniuk, R. G., "Individual Differences in Motor Performance and Learning." In J. H. Wilmore, Ed., *Exercise and Sport Sciences Reviews*. Vol. 2. New York: Academic Press, 1974, pp. 103–130.

McCloy, C. H., "The Measurement of General Motor Capacity and General Motor Ability." *Research Quarterly Supplement* 5:46–61, March 1934.

———, "An Analytical Study of the Stunt Type Test as a Measure of Motor Educability." *Research Quarterly* 8:46–55, October 1937.

———, and N. D. Young, *Tests and Measurements in Health and Physical Education*. 3rd ed. New York: Appleton-Century-Crofts, 1954, Chapter 17.

Metheny, E., "Studies of the Johnson Test as a Test of Motor Educability." *Research Quarterly* 9:105–114, December 1938.

———, "Physical Performance Levels for High School Girls." *Journal of Health and Physical Education* 16:32–35, June 1945.

Miller, D. K., "A Comparison of the Effects of Individual and Team Sports Programs on the Motor Ability of Male College Freshmen." Unpublished doctoral dissertation, Florida State University, Tallahassee, 1970.

Motor Fitness Tests for Oregon Schools. Salem, Ore.: State Department of Education, 1962.

Patterson, M. L., "A Comparison of Two Methods of Training on the Improvement of General Motor Ability Performance." Unpublished doctoral dissertation, Louisiana State University, Baton Rouge, 1970.

Phillips, B. E., "The JCR Test." *Research Quarterly* 18:12–29, March 1947.

Phillips, M., and D. Summers, "Relation of Kinesthetic Perception to Motor Learning." *Research Quarterly* 25:456–469, December 1954.

Powell, E., and E. C. Howe, "Motor Ability Tests for High School Girls." *Research Quarterly* 10:81–88, December 1939.

Roberts, G. C., and R. Martens, "Social Reinforcement and Complex Motor Performance." *Research Quarterly* 41:175, May 1970.

Roloff, L. L., "Kinesthesis in Relation to the Learning of Selected Motor Skills." *Research Quarterly* 24:210–217, May 1953.

Sage, G. H., *Introduction to Motor Behavior: A Neurological Approach*. Reading, Mass.: Addison-Wesley, 1971, pp. 218–245.

Schmidt, R. A., "Retroactive Interference and Amount of Original Learning in Verbal and Motor Tasks." *Research Quarterly* 42:314, October 1971.

Scott, M. G., "The Assessment of Motor Abilities of College Women Through Objective Tests." *Research Quarterly* 10:63–83, October 1939.

———, Motor Ability Tests for College Women." *Research Quarterly* 14:402–405, December 1943.

———, and E. French, *Measurement and Evaluation in Physical Education*. Dubuque, Iowa: William C. Brown, 1959, pp. 344–350.

Shelley, M. E., "Maturity, Structure, Strength, Motor Ability, and Intelligence Test Profiles of Outstanding Elementary School and Junior High School Athletes." Microcarded master's thesis, University of Oregon, Eugene, 1960.

Sills, F. D., "Special Conditioning Exercises for Students With Low Scores on Physical Fitness

Tests." *Research Quarterly* 25:333–337, October 1954.

Singer, R. N., "Effect of Spectators on Athletes and Non-athletes Performing a Gross Motor Task." *Research Quarterly* 36:473–482, December 1965.

————, J. Llewellyn, and E. Darden, "Placebo and Competition Placebo Effects on Motor Skill." *Research Quarterly* 44:51, March 1973.

Smith, J. A., "Relation of Certain Physical Traits and Abilities to Motor Learning in Elementary School Children." *Research Quarterly* 27:220–228, May 1956.

Smith, J. L., and M. F. Bozymowski, "Effect of Attitude Toward Warm-up on Motor Performance." *Research Quarterly* 36:78–85, March 1965.

Thorpe, J., C. West, and D. Davies, "Learning Under a Traditional and an Experimental Schedule Involving Master Classes." *Research Quarterly* 42:83, March 1971.

Walters, E. C., "Motor Ability and Educability Factors of High and Low Scoring Beginning Bowlers." *Research Quarterly* 30:94–100, March 1959.

Wireman, B. O., "Comparison of Four Approaches to Increasing Physical Fitness." *Research Quarterly* 31:658–666, December 1960.

CHAPTER 20

THE MEASUREMENT OF SOCIAL QUALITIES AND ATTITUDES

OBJECTIVES

After reading this chapter, the student should be able to:

1. List four different types of tests under the heading of affective behavior

2. Recognize and describe two scales used for the scoring of responses to attitude inventories

3. Understand some of the problems associated with measuring social behavior and attitudes

---

I. SOCIAL QUALITIES

Social development is considered one of the major objectives of physical education by most physical educators. Unfortunately, social concepts such as character, sportsmanship, adjustment, personality, leadership, behavior, and acceptance are very difficult to measure objectively. Because of this difficulty, some critics have argued that social development should not be included as an objective of physical education. As has been mentioned, however, attempts to develop scientific measures in this area are still in a relatively immature stage. It is certainly logical to assume that better evaluative techniques will become available.

It seems appropriate also to point out that social concepts do exist and can be appraised. It is too often assumed that desirable changes automatically come about through athletic and physical education participation. To the contrary, games and other physical activities under poor leadership can foster undesirable social change. Therefore, regardless of the fact that present measuring tools are somewhat crude, physical educators should make a systematic, conscientious effort to evaluate this aspect of students' development as well as the more tangible area of organic efficiency and skills.

USES OF SOCIAL FACTORS MEASURING INSTRUMENTS

Social factors measuring instruments are used in physical education in the following ways:

1. To assist in the evaluation of social behavior

2. To determine the degree of acceptance or the status of individuals within the group

3. To identify group leaders and the degree to which students perceive the best course in getting along with others

4. To provide information helpful for guidance or referral to professional personnel

PROBLEMS ASSOCIATED WITH MEASUREMENT OF SOCIAL FACTORS

Several of the problems associated with social measurement are listed as follows:

1. Since physical educators are not trained observers of character and personality traits, the validity of their evaluations may be questioned. Thus, it seems important for mea-

surement to include pupil evaluations in conjunction with teacher evaluations.

2. The physical and mental condition of the teacher frequently affects the type of ratings students receive. For example, a teacher who is ill or unduly tired at the time of rating may not give the same ratings as he or she would if feeling well or in high spirits. Also, the personality of the teacher may have a bearing on the ratings, in that the teacher may rate students who exhibit similar behavior patterns as *good* and students of an opposite nature as *poor.*

3. Although sociometric tests are quite reliable and valid for the purpose they serve, they are limited in the types of information they can provide.

4. Results of sociometric tests given without consideration for feelings toward the opposite sex may not be too valid. Usually it is best to have boys rate boys and girls rate girls, and then have each rate members of the opposite sex. Otherwise, certain students may indicate only members of the opposite sex as the ones they would like to work with or have as friends.

PRACTICAL MEASUREMENTS OF SOCIAL FACTORS

Social factors are measured in three ways.[1] One is with use of social behavior and adjustment scales, to measure changes in habits or in the behavior subjects exhibit in association with others. The second is with use of sociometric measures, to determine the status or degree of acceptance of students within their group. The third is with use of leadership measurements and measurement of the student's ability to perceive getting along with others.

Social Behavior and Adjustment Scales

Blanchard Behavior Rating Scale (Blanchard 1936)

Objective: To measure the character and personality of students.

Age Level: Satisfactory for ages 12 through 17.

Sex: Satisfactory for both boys and girls.

Reliability: Reliability has been reported as high as .71.

Validity: A validity of .930 was found when intercorrelations of one trait action were made with the rest of the items in its category.

Directions: The teacher rates each student on the basis of 20 scale items. Ten of these are shown in Figure 20.1. Individual items are then analyzed for specific weaknesses.

Scoring: We have modified the scale in Figure 20.1 so that the maximum possible score is 100 points. The higher the score, the better the evaluation of character and personality.

Cowell's Social Adjustment Index (Cowell 1958)

Objective: To determine the degree of social adjustment or maladjustment of students within their social groups.

Age Level: Satisfactory for ages 12 through 17.

Sex: Satisfactory for both boys and girls.

Reliability: The reliability was reported as high as .82.

Validity: With Pupil's Who's Who ratings as the criterion, an *r* of .628 was obtained with the Social Adjustment Index.

Direction: The teacher rates each student on the basis of the degree to which the student displays the behaviors. Figure 20.2 shows Form A, positive behavior trends. Readers should consult the original reference for the whole test.

Scoring: All points are added and an average computed to compare with the descriptive scale categories for the overall rating (Figure 20.2).[2]

Sociometric Measures of Acceptance

Breck's Sociometric Test of Status (Breck 1950)

Objective: To measure the status of students within a group concerning acceptance for team membership and friendship.

Age Level: Satisfactory for age 12 through college age.

Sex: Satisfactory for both boys and girls.

Reliability: The reliability of the skill status test was reported as .894 ± .01. The reliability of

---

1. Dr. Marion Johnson, Southeastern Louisiana University, Hammond, Louisiana, kindly provided assistance for this section.

2. The original reference should be consulted for greater test accuracy.

	No opportunity to observe	Never	Seldom	Fairly often	Frequently	Extremely often	Score
Student is popular with classmates		1	2	3	4	5	
Student seeks responsibility in the classroom		1	2	3	4	5	
Student shows intellectual leadership in the classroom		1	2	3	4	5	
Student shows initiative in assuming responsibility in unfamiliar situations		1	2	3	4	5	
Student is alert to new opportunities		1	2	3	4	5	
Student shows keenness of mind		1	2	3	4	5	
Student volunteers ideas		1	2	3	4	5	
Student grumbles over decisions of classmates		5	4	3	2	1	
Student takes a justified criticism by teacher or classmate without showing anger or pouting		1	2	3	4	5	
Student is loyal to group		1	2	3	4	5	

Figure 20.1. Sample items for Blanchard Behavior Rating Scale. The scale has been modified for this text so that the maximum possible score is 100 points (Adapted from B. E. Blanchard, "A Behavior Frequency Rating Scale for the Measurement of Character and Personality in Physical Education Classroom Situations." *Research Quarterly* 7:56–66, May 1936)

POSITIVE BEHAVIOR TRENDS (Form A)	MARKEDLY (+3)	SOMEWHAT (+2)	ONLY SLIGHTLY (+1)	NOT AT ALL (+0)
1. Enters heartily and with enjoyment into the spirit of social intercourse				
2. Frank, talkative and sociable, does not stand on ceremony				
3. Self-confident and self-reliant, tends to take success for granted, strong initiative, prefers to lead				
4. Quick and decisive in movement, pronounced or excessive energy output				
5. Prefers group activities, work or play; not easily satisfied with individual projects				
6. Adaptable to new situations, makes adjustments readily, welcomes change				
7. Is self-composed, seldom shows signs of embarrassment				
8. Tends to elation of spirits, seldom gloomy or moody				
9. Seeks a broad range of friendships, not selective or exclusive in games and the like				
10. Hearty and cordial, even to strangers, forms acquaintanceships very easily				

Figure 20.2. Form A of Cowell's Social Adjustment Index. Scoring has been modified (From C. C. Cowell, "Validating an Index of Social Adjustment for High School Use." *Research Quarterly* 29:7–10, March 1958)

the friendship status test was reported as .79 ± .01.

Validity: Face validity is accepted for the two items.

Materials: Cards or paper and pencils.

Directions: Students are asked to print in order of preference the names of five students they would most prefer to have as members of their team.

Students are also directed to list the five students they would most prefer to have as friends and the five they would least like to have as friends.

Scoring: For team membership, the number of choices received by each student, minus the number of rejections by classmates, is calculated. For friendship, the number of choices received by each student is merely tabulated.

Cowell's Personal Distance Scale (Cowell 1958)

Objective: To determine a student's degree of acceptance by the group.

Age Level: Satisfactory for age 12 through college age.

Sex: Satisfactory for both boys and girls.

Reliability: The reliability has been reported as high as .93.

Validity: With Pupil's Who's Who ratings as the criterion, an r of .844 was obtained with Pupil's Personal Distance Scale.

Directions: Each student is told to rate fellow students on the basis of the scale items shown in Figure 20.3.

Scoring: Each subject's total weighted scores given by fellow students are added and the total is divided by the total number of respondents. Division is carried to two places and the decimal point is dropped. The lower the score, the greater the degree of acceptance.

Measures of Leadership and Ability to Perceive Getting Along

Modified Nelson Sports Leadership Questionnaire (Nelson 1966)

Objective: To determine athletic leaders as identified by the players.

Age Level: Satisfactory for junior high through college.

Sex: Satisfactory for both boys and girls.

Reliability: An r of .96 was reported by Lloyd Williams (Northeastern Louisiana University, Monroe) with ninth grade football players, Monroe, La., 1973. An r of .78 was reported by Pam Holt (Northeastern Louisiana University) with varsity college basketball players, Monroe, La., 1973.

Objectivity: An r of .98 was reported by Lloyd Williams and Pam Holt, Northeastern Louisiana University, 1973.

Validity: Face validity is accepted for this instrument.

WHAT TO DO:	I WOULD BE WILLING TO ACCEPT HIM:						
If you had full power to treat each student on this list as you feel, just how would you consider him? How near would you like to have him to your family? Check each student in *one* column as to your feeling toward him. Circle your own name.	Into my family as a brother	As a very close "pal" or "chum"	As a member of my "gang" or club	On my street as a "next-door neighbor"	Into my class at school	Into my school	Into my city
	1	2	3	4	5	6	7

1. _____

2. _____

3. _____

4. etc. _____

Figure 20.3.   Cowell's Personal Distance Ballot (From C. C. Cowell, "Validating an Index of Social Adjustment for High School Use." *Research Quarterly* 29:7–10, March 1958)

Materials: Pencils and questionnaires (Figure 20.4).

Directions: Students do *not* sign their name on the questionnaire. They fill in the name or names of the team members that, in their opinion, best fit the question. They should give first and second choices in all cases. *Students must not use their own name* on any of the answers. The names of the same athletes can be used any number of times. Answers are kept confidential.

Scoring: Five points are awarded for a name appearing in response A blank and 3 points for a name appearing in response B blank.

Getting Along Appraisal (Lawrence 1966)

Objective: To determine the extent to which students get along with themselves, with others, and with their surroundings.

Age Level: Grades seven, eight, and nine.

A._____ B._____	1. If you were on a trip and had a choice of the players you would share the hotel room with, who would they be?
A._____ B._____	2. Who are the most popular members of the team?
A._____ B._____	3. Who are the best scholars on the team?
A._____ B._____	4. Which players know the most about the sport, in terms of strategy, rules, etc.?
A._____ B._____	5. If the coach were not present for a workout, which athletes would be the most likely to take charge of the practice?
A._____ B._____	6. Which players would you listen to first if the team appeared to be disorganized during a crucial game?
A._____ B._____	7. When the team is behind in a close match and there is still a chance to win, who is the most likely teammate to score the winning points?
A._____ B._____	8. Of all of your teammates, who exhibits the most poise during crucial parts of the match?
A._____ B._____	9. Who are the most valuable players on the team?
A._____ B._____	10. Who are the players who play "most for the team"?
A._____ B._____	11. Who are the most consistent point makers for the team?
A._____ B._____	12. Who are the most respected performers on the team?
A._____ B._____	13. Which teammates have the most overall ability?
A._____ B._____	14. Which teammates train the hardest to improve their performance off season?
A._____ B._____	15. Who are the most likeable players on the team?
A._____ B._____	16. Which players have most favorably influenced you?
A._____ B._____	17. Which players have actually helped you the most?
A._____ B._____	18. Which teammates do you think would make the best coaches?
A._____ B._____	19. Which teammates do you most often look to for leadership?
A._____ B._____	20. Who are the hardest workers during regular practice hours?

Figure 20.4. Modified Nelson Sports Leadership Questionnaire (From D. O. Nelson, "Leadership in Sports." *Research Quarterly* 37:268–275, May 1966)

Sex: Satisfactory for both boys and girls.

Reliability: The range was .79 to .84 for Form A and .73 to .83 for Form B.

Objectivity: None reported.

Validity: High correlations were found between social adjustment ratings and raw scores.

Materials: Pencils; test questions; and answer sheets.

Directions: Students must not open the booklet until told to do so. There are 45 items in the test. Each item has two pictures with information about them (Figure 20.5). At the right of each pair of pictures is a sentence with three possible answers. Students read the sentence carefully and choose the answer they think is best.

FINDINGS AND CONCLUSIONS FROM SOCIAL FACTORS MEASUREMENT AND RESEARCH

Numerous studies have found that various physical measures (e.g., motor ability, physical fitness, being physically active, athletic ability, height, weight, and health) are significantly related to social measures (e.g., leadership ability, good adjustment, and popularity) (Betz 1956; Reaney 1914; Signorella 1963; Sperling 1942; Stogdill 1948; Wells 1958).

Concerning the characteristic of being physically active, Cowell and Ismail, Tryon, Kuhlen and Lee, and Hanley all found it to be an important factor in social acceptance.

Physical educators have long contended that participation in physical education activity brings about desirable traits or closer social integration within the group. Several studies have found support for such a contention (Blanchard 1946; Clevett 1932; Skubic 1947; Whilden 1956). While desirable changes in social status have been reported, it is feasible that physical activity participation under the wrong leadership could breed undesirable social change. Perhaps differences in leadership or emphasis on social goals were the reasons why Blanchard (1946) found girls' activity classes to be significantly superior to boys' activity classes in the acquisition of wholesome character and personality traits.

Two studies have investigated the effects of motivated activity participation on social acceptance (Nelson and Johnson 1968; Walters 1955). Walters found motivated groups to be more closely knit than nonmotivated groups in bowling classes,

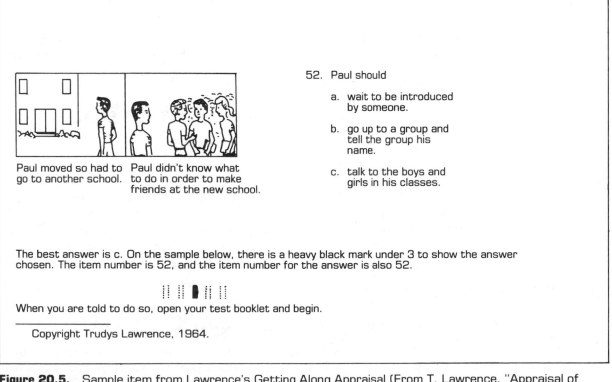

Figure 20.5. Sample item from Lawrence's Getting Along Appraisal (From T. Lawrence, "Appraisal of Emotional Health at the Secondary School Level." *Research Quarterly* 37:252–257, May 1966. Used by permission of AAHPERD)

and students to become more closely integrated socially as a result of acquaintance and group participation. Nelson and Johnson further found that motivated participation brought about positive changes in social ratings when anticohesive pairs were induced to work together.

Several studies have found that individuals do not radically shift from one position in social standing to a very different position, thus showing the stability of sociometric testing (Breck 1950; Jennings 1941; Nelson and Johnson 1968). Such testing has been used to show objective relationships between physical education and the development of groups (Breck 1950; McKenna 1948; Zeleny 1941) and the closer integration of individuals constituting those groups (Breck 1950; McKenna 1948; Robinson 1948). Moreover, some studies have been concerned with the relationships between sociometric status and skill in specific activities such as volleyball, swimming, and dancing (Breck 1947; Fulton 1950; Skubic 1949).

Members of athletic teams were found to have higher social status than boys who could not make the team or were not members of a team (Biddulph 1954; Cowell and Ismail 1962; Flowtow 1946; Lakie 1964; Ondrus 1953). Trapp and Cowell and Ismail further noted that social integration in a football squad was positive and remained so, or increased, as the time the squad played together increased.

Concerning the relationship of physical fitness and strength to social prestige, Clarke and Clarke, Yarnell, Jones (1946, 1949), and Popp found that boys who scored higher in strength and physical fitness enjoyed greater social prestige than others. Haines, however, did not find such a relationship with fifth grade students. On the other hand, Cowell and Ismail and Rarick and McKee found students who scored high in physical measures and motor achievement to be the most popular.

II. ATTITUDES

Attitudes are ideas or feelings that a person has about things as a result of past experience or as a result of imagined likes and dislikes. Attitudes may change often. When conditions or the environment changes, whether for better or worse, we can usually expect to see a change in attitudes. In physical education, the attitudes of students toward the physical education activity program as well as toward individual activities within the program are of interest. Measurement of their attitudes is valuable to see what effect various types of programs, administrative procedures, and methods of instruction have on their feelings. When such measurement is objectively conducted, avenues of approach are opened so that desirable changes can be logically brought about.

USES OF ATTITUDE TESTS

Several ways in which attitude tests can be used in physical education classes are as follows:

1. To assist in determining whether objectives are being reached

2. As a means for assembling information in a survey for administrative planning and curriculum development

3. To evaluate the effectiveness of teaching methods in helping students to enjoy physical education

SCORING ATTITUDE SCALES

The two methods most commonly used in scoring attitude scales are the Thurston and Chave method and the Likert method. A study by Adams showed how each method is applied to measurement of attitude toward physical education.

In the *Thurston and Chave method,* statements would appear as follows on the student statement list:

10. Physical education is a necessary subject.

Agree ( )　　Disagree ( )

Thus, to score the items the teacher merely considers the statements where "Agree" is checked. The other items are ignored. On the teacher's master statement list appear statement marks that were derived from judges' scores representing the average position of each statement along a favorable–unfavorable continuum ranging from 11 to 1. An example of a statement as it appears on the teacher's copy follows:

10.   Physical education is a necessary subject.

      (8.65)

Thus, if "Agree" is checked for statement number 10, the score awarded is 8.65. The final score is the sum of all of the statement scores divided by the number of "Agree" items checked. Statement scores should never appear on the student's questionnaire copy.

In the *Likert method,* each statement is followed by a scale of numbers or letters indicating degree of agreement or feeling.

10.   Physical education is a necessary subject.

      $+3 \ +2 \ +1 \quad 0 \ -1 \ -2 \ -3$

The numbers are interpreted as follows:

$+3$ = Very strongly agree

$+2$ = Strongly agree

$+1$ = Agree

$\ \ 0$ = Neither agree nor disagree

-1 = Disagree

-2 = Strongly disagree

-3 = Very strongly disagree

Positive statements are weighted, so that a favorable response results in a higher score than an unfavorable one, as seen in the following:

10.   Physical education is a necessary subject.

	$+3$	$+2$	$+1$	0	-1	-2	-3
Weighted pts	6	5	4	3	2	1	0

For negative statements, the entire procedure is reversed as follows:

15.   Physical education is of no value to students.

	$+3$	$+2$	$+1$	0	-1	-2	-3
Weighted pts	0	1	2	3	4	5	6

PROBLEMS ASSOCIATED WITH ATTITUDE TESTING

Several of the problems associated with attitude testing are listed as follows:

1.   Each statement must be worded carefully to secure the actual attitude response and to avoid giving away the desired response.

2.   There is an obvious lack of stability of attitudes of young people, especially those below the high school level. Quite commonly students change their attitudes rapidly after exposure to new experiences. Therefore, attitude results must not be regarded as permanent.

3.   The validity associated with attitude scales is sometimes questionable. If students have had limited experience with certain aspects of a program, they cannot make intelligent responses concerning these aspects.

GENERAL PHYSICAL EDUCATION ATTITUDE SCALES

Several practical attitude scales directed toward general physical education include those by Wear, Carr, and Adams.

Wear's Attitude Scale With Equivalent Forms (Wear 1955)

Objective: To measure changes in attitude toward physical education as a result of special experiences in which students might be involved.

Age Level: College age.

Reliability: The reliability of Form A was reported as .94 and the reliability of Form B was .96. The Pearson correlation coefficient between scores on the two forms was .96.

Validity: Face validity has been accepted for the two scales.

Directions: Students are directed to consider physical education only from the standpoint of its place as an activity course taught during a regular class period and to check the response that best expresses their feeling about each statement. Students are also told to let their personal experiences determine their answers and that their answers will in no way affect their grade in any course. Figure 20.6 shows some questions in Form A.

Scoring: The five possible responses to each inventory item are as follows: strongly agree,

agree, undecided, disagree, and strongly disagree. The responses are scored 5 4 3 2 1 when the item is worded positively and 1 2 3 4 5 when worded negatively. Thus, a high score indicates a favorable attitude toward physical education. (See the original source for the remainder of Form A and for Form B.

Carr Physical Education Attitude Scale (Carr 1945)

Objective: To determine the attitudes of girls as they relate to physical education.

Age Level: High school age.

Reliability: Reliability was not reported for this scale.

Validity: Face validity is accepted in addition to following selected criteria in establishing the scale.

Directions: The student indicates her attitude by placing a check mark under "Agree" or "Disagree" before each statement. Figure 20.7 shows sample statements.

Scoring: The first 37 statements of the Carr scale are indicated as desirable attitudes and the remaining 47 statements as undesirable attitudes. The final score is determined by subtracting the percentage of undesirable attitudes checked from the percentage of desirable attitudes checked. (See original source for complete list of statements.)

Adams Physical Education Attitude Scale (Adams 1963)

Objective: To provide a means for assessing individual and group attitudes toward physical education.

---

1. If for any reason a few subjects have to be dropped from the school program, physical education should be one of the subjects dropped.
2. Physical education activities provide no opportunities for learning to control the emotions.
3. Physical education is one of the more important subjects in helping to establish and maintain desirable social standards.
4. Vigorous physical activity works off harmful emotional tensions.
5. I would take physical education only if it were required.
6. Participation in physical education makes no contribution to the development of poise.
7. Because physical skills loom large in importance in youth, it is essential that a person be helped to acquire and improve such skills.
8. Calisthenics taken regularly are good for one's general health.
9. Skill in active games or sports is not necessary for leading the fullest kind of life.
10. Physical education does more harm physically than it does good.

Figure 20.6. Questions in Form A of Wear's Attitude Scale With Equivalent Forms (From C. L. Wear, "Construction of Equivalent Forms of an Attitude Scale." *Research Quarterly* 26:113–119, March 1955)

AGREE   DISAGREE

_____	_____	1. Being a leader is a fine responsibility.
_____	_____	2. I feel as if I am learning something when I play with someone who plays better than I do.
_____	_____	3. I prefer playing outdoors when the weather is good.
_____	_____	4. I like to bathe after playing hard.
_____	_____	5. I like to set a goal for my own improvement and want to practice until I reach that goal.
_____	_____	6. I like to talk to my teachers as that makes them seem like friends.
_____	_____	7. I prefer to play in a playsuit as I feel I can play more freely.
_____	_____	8. I like games that have lots of vigorous activity in them.
_____	_____	9. I like to have a place to keep my own things.
_____	_____	10. Playing games with a group is more fun than playing alone.

Figure 20.7. Sample statements for Carr Physical Education Attitude Scale (From M. G. Carr, "The Relationship Between Success in Physical Education and Selected Attitudes Expressed by High School Freshman Girls." *Research Quarterly* 16:176–191, October 1945)

Age Level: High school and college age.

Sex: Satisfactory for both boys and girls.

Reliability: An r of .71 was obtained using the Thurston and Chave scoring scale.

Validity: An r of .77 was obtained when correlating the Thurston (set 1) scoring scale against the Likert scoring scale.

Directions: Students indicate their attitude toward physical education as a college subject by placing a check mark under "Agree" or "Disagree" before each statement. Figure 20.8 shows sample statements.

Scoring: Only the "Agree" items checked are considered. The final score is the sum of all of the statement scores divided by the number of "Agree" items checked. Thus, if "Agree" is checked for items 7, 8, 9, and 12, the corresponding statement values of 8.64, 8.0, 7.71, and 10.66 (Figure 20.8) are added and the sum is divided by 4.

Additional Pointers:

1. Statement scores should never be printed on the questionnaire itself.

2. A cardboard straightedge with the appropriate numbers printed and spaced to correspond with the brackets on the original questionnaire helps with scoring.

ATTITUDE TOWARD PHYSICAL ACTIVITY SCALES

Scales by Kenyon, McPherson and Yuhansz, and Richardson are examples of scales directed toward attitudes dealing with physical activity and physical fitness.

Kenyon's Six Attitude Scales Toward Physical Activity[1, 2] (Kenyon 1968a, 1968b)

Objective: To determine attitudes toward physical activity. Kenyon recommended that the scales be restricted to use for research purposes. Figure 20.9 shows the six dimensions of the scale.

Age Level: College age.

Reliability: Hoyt reliabilities ranged from .72 to .89 for six scales.

AGREE	DISAGREE		VALUE
_____	_____	1. Physical education gets very monotonous.	3.50
_____	_____	2. I only feel like doing physical education now and then.	5.95
_____	_____	3. Physical education should be disposed of.	1.58
_____	_____	4. Physical education is particularly limited in its value.	4.50
_____	_____	5. I suppose physical education is all right but I don't much care for it.	5.03
_____	_____	6. Physical education is the most hateful subject of all.	1.02
_____	_____	7. I do not want to give up physical education.	8.64
_____	_____	8. On the whole I think physical education is a good thing.	8.0
_____	_____	9. People who like physical education are nearly always good to know.	7.71
_____	_____	10. Anyone who likes physical education is silly.	2.65
_____	_____	11. Physical education has some usefulness.	6.45
_____	_____	12. Physical education is the ideal subject.	10.66

Figure 20.8. Sample of Adams Physical Education Attitude Scale. Set I, sample of 12 items (From R. S. Adams, "Two Scales for Measuring Attitude Toward Physical Education." *Research Quarterly* 34:91—94, 1963)

1. The directions and scales may be ordered as follows: ADI Auxiliary Publications Project, Photoduplication Service, Library of Congress, Washington, DC 20540. Cite document number 9983 and enclose $1.25 for photoprints. Make checks or money orders payable to Chief, Photoduplication Service, Library of Congress.

2. A seventh scale has been developed since 1968, along with a semantic differential approach for all seven scales. For details, the reader is referred to *Values Held for Physical Activity by Selected*

Urban Secondary School Students in Canada, Australia, England and the United States. This publication can be obtained from ERIC Document Reproduction Service, P.O. Drawer O, Bethesda, MD 20014, U.S.A. Quote accession number ED 019709. The cost for a microfiche copy is 65¢ and for a hard copy, $13.16. This report contains considerable data and also complete instructions on the use of the scales and scoring.

ATTITUDE SCALE	SAMPLE STATEMENT
1. Physical Activity as a Social Experience	I like to engage in socially oriented physical activities.
2. Physical Activity as Health and Fitness	Being strong and fit is not the most important thing in my life.
3. Physical Activity as the Pursuit of Vertigo	I would enjoy engaging in those games and sports that require a defiance of danger.
4. Physical Activity as an Aesthetic Experience	The idea that every human movement is beautiful is absurd.
5. Physical Activity as Catharsis	Regular physical activity is the major prerequisite to a satisfying life.
6. Physical Activity as an Ascetic Experience	A sport is sometimes spoiled if allowed to become too highly organized and keenly competitive.

Figure 20.9. Kenyon's Six Attitude scales with sample statements (From G. S. Kenyon, "Six Scales for Assessing Attitude Toward Physical Activity." *Research Quarterly* 39:566–574, October 1968)

Validity: Scale scorers differentiated satisfactorily between strong and weak preference groups in the predicted direction for all scales except "catharsis" (recreation and relaxation).

Scoring: Likert-type scoring is used. Order photoprints for details.

Exercise and Physical Activity Scale (McPherson and Yuhansz 1968)

Objective: To measure the attitude of students toward exercise and physical activity.

Age Level: High school age through adulthood.

Reliability: An *r* of .72 was reported on a test–retest basis.

Validity: A significant difference at the .01 level occurred between a criterion group presumed to have favorable attitudes and a criterion group presumed to have unfavorable attitudes.

Directions: Students are asked to respond to 50 statements that express common opinions, beliefs, attitudes, and fallacies about exercise and physical activity. Figure 20.10 shows the scales and sample statements.

Scoring: A 5-point Likert-type scale is used. The

STRONGLY DISAGREE	DISAGREE	NEUTRAL	AGREE	STRONGLY AGREE	
( )	( )	( )	( )	( )	1. Physical exercise is beneficial to the human body.
( )	( )	( )	( )	( )	2. Exercise helps to work off emotional tensions and anxieties.
( )	( )	( )	( )	( )	3. Adults get all the physical activity they need in their daily work.
( )	( )	( )	( )	( )	4. Exercise is of little value in maintaining desirable body weight.
( )	( )	( )	( )	( )	5. Regular physical activity makes one feel better.
( )	( )	( )	( )	( )	6. Physical education should be a required subject for elementary and secondary school children.
( )	( )	( )	( )	( )	7. Exercise does more harm than good.
( )	( )	( )	( )	( )	8. Those who are physically able should take part in a daily period of physical activity.
( )	( )	( )	( )	( )	9. An individual has all the strength and stamina he needs without participating in an exercise program.
( )	( )	( )	( )	( )	10. Exercise does little to improve a person's sense of well-being.

Figure 20.10. Sample statements for Exercise and Physical Activity Scale (From B. D. McPherson and M. S. Yuhansz, "An Inventory for Assessing Men's Attitudes Toward Exercise and Physical Activity." *Research Quarterly* 39:218–219, March 1968)

scores on each item are summed, and the total score indicates the intensity of the subject's attitude toward exercise and physical activity.

Richardson Physical Fitness and Attitude Scale (Richardson 1960)

Objective: To measure the attitude of students toward physical fitness and exercise. Figure 20.11 shows sample items of the scale.

Age Level: College age, although the scale could be adapted for high school students.

Sex: Satisfactory for both boys and girls.

Reliability: A reliability coefficient derived from test–retest samplings was .83 ± .06.

Validity: Based on authoritative opinion and expert judgment.

Directions: Subjects read each item carefully and circle the number opposite each item with which they agree. They should make no marks on numbers opposite items with which they disagree. There is no time limit but students should mark rapidly. Sample statements are shown in Figure 20.11.

Scoring: The subject's score is the median value of numerical scale values of the statements marked. For example, if the subject indicated an agreement with seven items having scale values of 2.5, 2.7, 3.5, 4.1, 4.5, and 4.7, the value of 3.7 would be the score.

PSYCHOSOCIAL CONSTRUCTS (SPORTSMANSHIP SCALES)

The following scales by Johnson and Lakie pertain to the sensitivity students have in dealing with their own needs and rights and those of other people.

Johnson Sportsmanship Attitude Scales (Johnson 1969)

Objective: To measure attitudes toward sportsmanship.

Age Level: Ages 12 through 14.

Sex: Satisfactory for both boys and girls.

Reliability: A reliability of .86 was found between scores of Form A and Form B for a single test administration.

Validity: Empirical validity coefficients ranging from − .01 to .43 were found between test scores and behavior ratings.

Directions: Subjects read each statement carefully and decide whether they approve or disapprove of the action taken by the person. They then circle the ONE response category that tells the way they feel. Every item should be completed. Figure 20.12 shows sample items.

Lakie's Attitudes Toward Athletic Competition Scale (Lakie 1964)

Objective: To determine to what degree the "win-at-any-cost" attitude exists among students and groups.

Age Level: College age.

Sex: Satisfactory for both men and women.

Reliability: A reliability of .81 was reported.

Validity: Face validity is accepted for this scale.

Directions: Students are directed to circle the category that indicates their feelings toward the behavior described in each of the situations. Figure 20.13 shows sample items. The complete scales are available from Lakie.

Scoring: Except for item 6, where points should be figured in reverse order, the points are added

---

(1.1) Physical fitness activity is the lowest type of activity indulged in by man.
(1.3) Man has outgrown the need for physical fitness programs.
(1.5) Physical fitness activity programs are necessary only in wartime.
(1.7) Physical fitness activities are the least civilized of man's activities.
(1.9) Physical activity should not be stressed so much in our present culture.
(2.1) Planned physical activity programs have limited value.
(2.3) Physical fitness activity is unnecessary.
(2.5) The values of physical activity are debatable.
(2.7) Physical fitness activity should be left to the individual.
(2.9) Physical fitness programs are too soft.

Figure 20.11. Richardson Physical Fitness and Attitude Scale, Form A, sample of ten items. The scale values in parentheses are listed with decimal points only for presentation purposes. In actual testing, items are given three numbers (without decimals) for convenience in scoring. The first of the three refers to item number on the test; the last two indicate scale values. Thus, the subject sees the numbers 111, 113, 117, and so on to the left of each item. This method of numbering is used to minimize the possibility of a suggested response pattern for the subject (From C. E. Richardson, "Thurston Scale of Measuring Attitudes of College Students Toward Physical Fitness and Exercise." *Research Quarterly* 31:638–643, December 1960)

Example: A pitcher in a baseball game threw a fastball at the batter to scare him.

STRONGLY APPROVE   APPROVE   DISAPPROVE   STRONGLY DISAPPROVE

(If you strongly approve of this action by the pitcher you would circle the first response category as shown.)

Sample of Ten Items

1. After a basketball player was called by the official for traveling, he slammed the basketball onto the floor.
   STRONGLY APPROVE   APPROVE   DISAPPROVE   STRONGLY DISAPPROVE

2. A baseball player was called out as he slid into home plate. He jumped up and down on the plate and screamed at the official.
   STRONGLY APPROVE   APPROVE   DISAPPROVE   STRONGLY DISAPPROVE

3. After a personal foul was called against a basketball player, he shook his fist in the official's face.
   STRONGLY APPROVE   APPROVE   DISAPPROVE   STRONGLY DISAPPROVE

4. A basketball coach talked very loudly in order to annoy an opponent who was attempting to make a very important free-throw shot.
   STRONGLY APPROVE   APPROVE   DISAPPROVE   STRONGLY DISAPPROVE

5. After a baseball game, the coach of the losing team went up to the umpire and demanded to know how much money had been paid to "throw" the game.
   STRONGLY APPROVE   APPROVE   DISAPPROVE   STRONGLY DISAPPROVE

6. A basketball coach led the spectators in jeering at the official who made calls against his team.
   STRONGLY APPROVE   APPROVE   DISAPPROVE   STRONGLY DISAPPROVE

7. After two men were put out on a double play attempt, a baseball coach told the players in his dugout to boo the umpire's decision.
   STRONGLY APPROVE   APPROVE   DISAPPROVE   STRONGLY DISAPPROVE

8. As the basketball coach left the gymnasium after the game, he shouted at the officials, "You lost me the game; I never saw such lousy officiating in my life."
   STRONGLY APPROVE   APPROVE   DISAPPROVE   STRONGLY DISAPPROVE

9. A basketball coach put sand on the gym floor to force the opponents into traveling penalties.
   STRONGLY APPROVE   APPROVE   DISAPPROVE   STRONGLY DISAPPROVE

10. A football coach left the bench to change the position of a marker dropped by an official to indicate where the ball went out of bounds.
    STRONGLY APPROVE   APPROVE   DISAPPROVE   STRONGLY DISAPPROVE

Figure 20.12. Sample of Johnson Sportsmanship Attitude Scale (From M. L. Johnson, "Construction of Sportsmanship Attitude Scales." *Research Quarterly* 40:312–316, May 1969)

as scored. The lower the score, the greater the student agrees with a "win-at-any-cost" attitude.

SELF-ASSESSMENT SCALES

Self-assessment scales are frequently used today to obtain information about how people honestly feel about themselves in relation to skills, physical attributes, social status, and health. Such information allows the teacher to choose and develop a specific training program that is meaningful at an individual level. An example of an instrument that is available for high school students, college students, and adults is the Physical Wellness Map (PWM) program developed by Johnson and Nelson. The self-assessment instru-

ment consists of 155 items with six personal skill scales and a composite scale. The scales are:

Flexibility scale

Strength scale

Muscular endurance scale

Cardiorespiratory endurance scale

Body composition scale

General health indicators

Composite fitness scale

A sample of the PWM appears in Figure 20.14. Johnson found a test–retest reliability following a 1-week interval of .84. Individual skill scale items were selected on the basis of the ratings of five fitness experts, with scores of three out of

(1) Strongly Approve (2) Approve (3) Undecided (4) Disapprove (5) Strongly Disapprove

1 2 3 4 5   1. During a football game, team A has the ball on its own 45-yard line, fourth down and 1 yd to go for a first down. The coach of team A signals to the quarterback the play that he wants the team to run.

1 2 3 4 5   2. Team A is the visiting basketball team and each time a member of the team is given a free shot the home crowd sets up a continual din of noise until the shot has been taken.

1 2 3 4 5   3. Tennis player A frequently calls out, throws up his arms, or otherwise tries to indicate that his opponent's serve is out of bounds when it is questionable.

1 2 3 4 5   4. In a track meet, team A enters a man in the mile run who is to set a fast pace for the first half of the race and then drop out.

1 2 3 4 5   5. In a football game, team B's quarterback was tackled repeatedly after handing off and after he was out of the play.

1 2 3 4 5   6. Sam, playing golf with his friends, hit a drive into the rough. He accidentally moved the ball with his foot; although not improving his position, he added a penalty stroke to his score.

1 2 3 4 5   7. A basketball player was caught out of position on defense, and rather than allow his opponent to attempt a field goal he fouled him.

1 2 3 4 5   8. Player A, during a golf match, made quick noises and movements when player B was getting ready to make a shot.

1 2 3 4 5   9. School A has a powerful but quite slow football team. The night before playing a smaller but faster team, they allowed the field sprinkling system to remain on, causing the field to be heavy and slow.

1 2 3 4 5   10. A basketball team used player A to draw the opponent's high scorer into fouling situations.

Figure 20.13. Sample of Lakie's Attitudes Toward Athletic Competition Scale (From W. L. Lakie, "Expressed Attitudes of Various Groups of Athletes Toward Athletic Competition." *Research Quarterly* 35:497–503, December 1964)

(M) MOST DESCRIPTIVE OF ME   (S) SOMETIMES DESCRIPTIVE   (L) LEAST DESCRIPTIVE

Flexibility:
(M) (S) (L)   1. After sitting at my desk for awhile, I usually feel stiff and tight in my ankles and knees.
Strength:
(M) (S) (L)   2. My grip strength is such that at present I have difficulty maintaining a firm grasp when swinging a racquet, golf club, or bat.
Cardiovascular Endurance:
(M) (S) (L)   3. My wind endurance is such that in an emergency I could jog as far as 4 miles or more for help (nonstop).
Muscular Endurance:
(M) (S) (L)   4. My present physical condition allows me to do many repetitions of an exercise without getting sore.
Body Composition:
(M) (S) (L)   5. In the past two years I have lost some of my muscle mass and have gained some body fat.
General Health Indicators:
(M) (S) (L)   6. I usually eat three meals a day, with some snacking in between.

Figure 20.14. Sample of Physical Wellness Map Assessments (From B. L. Johnson and D. B. Nelson, *The Physical Wellness Map; A Positive Assessment and Personalized Learning Program for Developing Physical Wellness Skills*. Portland, Tex.: Brown & Littleman, 1982)

five (or higher) required for retention in a particular scale.

Once the assessment has been scored and interpreted for each participant, a comprehensive guidance and instructional program is presented so that participants end up with a personalized wellness–fitness program that is specific to their needs and adapted to their interests and capabilities.

FINDINGS AND CONCLUSIONS FROM ATTITUDE MEASUREMENT AND RESEARCH

Numerous studies have reported that students generally have favorable attitudes toward physical education as an activity course (Baker 1940; Bell and Walters 1953; Broer et al. 1955; Brumbach and Cross 1965; Kappes 1954). Brumbach and Cross further found that students who participated in a high school athletic program or who attended a small school (enrollment under 300) were more apt to have a wholesome attitude toward physical education. Moreover, both Bell and Walters and Brumbach and Cross found that the university students with the most favorable attitudes toward physical education were the ones who had had more years of physical education in high school.

Physical educators who are concerned with the social and ethical values of activities often question the contributions of varsity athletics toward such values. Both Kistler and D. E. Richardson found that varsity athletes had poorer attitudes about sportsmanship than did those students who either had not participated at the varsity level or had engaged in the less publicized sports.

While Kistler found that only a small number of students were aware of the benefits concerning social and ethical values received from participation in physical education classes, Keogh reported that students endorsed the social, physical, and emotional values of physical education, and Vincent found that college women expressed greatest appreciation for the physiologic-physical values of physical education.

Dotson and Stanley studied the values of physical activities perceived by male students and found that students of gymnastics expressed the highest positive attitude, with students of badminton, archery, and bowling the lowest. They also found that physical activity as pursuit of vertigo (thrills and excitement) and catharsis (recreation and relaxation) were the strongest perceived values, while aesthetic experience was the lowest of the six values studied with Kenyon's scales.

Straub and Felock found that nondelinquent girls scored significantly higher on the social scale of Kenyon's scales than delinquent girls.

Carr and Vincent found that attitudes held by girls do influence their success in physical education. Wessel and Nelson further found that strength among college women is significantly related to attitudes toward physical activity.

Neale and associates, however, found highly fit boys significantly higher than lesser fit boys in self-reported attraction to physical activities, but not significantly different in reported participation in voluntary physical activities.

A number of studies in the 1970s attempted to assess the psychologic characteristics of students or adults in a sport or activity setting. For example, Kay and colleagues found a positive and significant relationship between personal interest in sports measures and self-concept in seventh, eighth, and ninth grade boys, while Sonstroem (1976, 1978) found his physical estimation scale positively related to the Fleishman fitness index and somewhat related to self-esteem. Moreover, Rohrbacher, working with overweight boys in a camp setting, found that self-concept scores remained unchanged while body image scores reflected positive changes attributed to the camp program. He further found a moderate relationship between self-concept and body image.

Morgan and Pollock found that the estimation of physical ability may change as a result of vigorous training, but that attraction to physical activity is relatively stable. Shortly thereafter, Sonstroem (1974) developed the physical estimation and attraction scale (PEAS) to measure changes occurring in attraction to physical activity and in estimation of physical abilities as a result of participation in physical activity.

BIBLIOGRAPHY

Adams, R. S., "Two Scales for Measuring Attitude Toward Physical Education." *Research Quarterly* 34:91–94, March 1963.

Alderman, K. B., "A Sociopsychological Assessment of Attitude Toward Physical Activity in Champion Athletes." *Research Quarterly* 41:1–9, March 1970.

Baker, M. C., "Factors Which May Influence the Participation in Physical Education of Girls and Women." *Research Quarterly* 11:126–131, May 1940.

Bell, M., and C. E. Walters, "Attitudes of Women at the University of Michigan Toward Physical Education." *Research Quarterly* 24:379, December 1953.

Betz, R. L., "A Comparison Between Personality Limits and Physical Fitness Tests of Males 26–60." Unpublished master's thesis, University of Illinois, Urbana, 1956.

Biddulph, L. G., "Athletic Achievement and Personal-Social Adjustment of High School Boys." *Research Quarterly* 25:1–7, March 1954.

Blanchard, B. E., "A Behavior Frequency Rating Scale for the Measurement of Character and Personality in Physical Education Classroom Situations." *Research Quarterly,* 7:56–66, May 1936.

———, "A Comparative Analysis of Secondary School Boys' and Girls' Character and Personality Traits in Physical Education Classes." *Research Quarterly* 17:33–39, March 1946.

Breck, J., "A Sociometric Test of Status as Measured in Physical Education Classes." Unpublished master's thesis, University of California, 1947.

———, "A Sociometric Measurement of Status in Physical Education Classes." *Research Quarterly* 21:75–82, May 1950.

Broer, M., et al., "Attitudes of University of Washington Women Students Toward Physical Education Activity." *Research Quarterly* 26:378–384, December 1955.

Brumbach, W. B., and J. A. Cross, "Attitudes Toward Physical Education of Male Students Entering the University of Oregon." *Research Quarterly* 36:10, March 1965.

Campbell, D. E., "Students' Attitudes Toward Physical Education." *Research Quarterly* 39:456–462, October 1968.

Carr, M. G., "The Relationship Between Success in Physical Education and Selected Attitudes Expressed by High School Freshman Girls." *Research Quarterly* 16:176–191, October 1945.

Clarke, H. H., and D. H. Clarke, "Social Status and Mental Health of Boys as Related to Their Maturity, Structural, and Strength Characteristics." *Research Quarterly* 32:326, October 1961.

Clevett, M. A., "An Experiment in Physical Education Activities Related to the Teaching of Honesty and Motor Skills," *Research Quarterly* 3:121–127, March 1932.

Corbin, C., and H. Tolson, "Attitudes of College Males Toward Physical Activity." Unpublished paper, Texas A & M University, College Station, 1970.

Cowell, C. C., "Validating an Index of Social Adjustment for High School Use." *Research Quarterly,* 29:7–10, March 1958.

———, and A. H. Ismail, "Relationships Between Selected Social and Physical Factors." *Research Quarterly* 33:4, March 1962.

Dotson, C. O., and W. J. Stanley, "Values of Physical Activity Perceived by Male University Students." *Research Quarterly* 43:148–156, May 1972.

Dowell, L. J., "A Study of Selected Psychological Dimensions and Athletic Achievement of Entering College Freshmen." Paper presented at Southern District Convention of AAHPERD, Memphis, 1969.

Drinkwater, B. L., "Development of an Attitude Inventory to Measure the Attitudes of High School Girls Toward Physical Education as a Career for Women." *Research Quarterly* 31:575–580, December 1960.

Edington, C. W., "Development of an Attitude Scale to Measure Attitudes of High School Freshmen Boys Toward Physical Education." *Research Quarterly* 39:505–512, October 1968.

Flowtow, E. A., "Charting Social Relationships of School Children." *Elementary School Journal* 46:498, May 1946.

Fulton, R. E., "Relationship Between Teammate Status and Measures of Skill in Volleyball." *Research Quarterly* 21:274–276, October 1950.

Haines, J. E., "The Relationship of Kraus–Weber Minimal Muscular Fitness and Rogers' Physical Fitness Index Tests With Social Acceptance, Teacher Acceptance, and Emotional Stability in Selected Fifth Grade Pupils." Unpublished doctoral dissertation, Springfield College, Springfield, Mass., 1957.

Hanley, C., "Physique and Reputation of Junior High School Boys." *Child Development* 22:247, 1951.

Jaeger, E., "An Investigation of a Projective Test in Determining Attitudes of Prospective Teachers of Physical Education." Unpublished doctoral dissertation, State University of Iowa, Iowa City, 1952.

Jennings, H. H., "Sociometry and Social Theory." *American Sociological Review* 6:512–522, 1941.

Johnson, B. L., and D. B. Nelson, *The Physical Wellness Map.* Portland, Tex.: Brown & Littleman, 1982.

Johnson, M. L., "Construction of Sportsmanship Attitude Scales." *Research Quarterly* 40:312–316, May 1969.

Jones, H. E., "Physical Ability as a Factor in Social Adjustment in Adolescence." *Journal of Educational Research* 4:287, 1946.

———, "Motor Performance and Growth." Berkeley, Calif.: University of California Press, 1949.

Kappes, E. E., "Inventory to Determine Attitudes of College Women Toward Physical Education and Student Services of the Physical Education Department." *Research Quarterly* 25:429–438, December 1954.

Kay, R. S., et al., "Sports Interests and Abilities as Contributors to Self-Concept in Junior High School Boys." *Research Quarterly* 43:208–215, May 1972.

Kenyon, G. S., "A Conceptual Model for Characterizing Physical Activity." *Research Quarterly* 39:96–105, March 1968a.

———, "Six Scales for Assessing Attitude Toward Physical Activity." *Research Quarterly* 39:566–574, October 1968b.

Keogh, J., "Analysis of General Attitudes Toward Physical Education." *Research Quarterly* 33:239–248, May 1962.

Kistler, J. W., "Attitudes Expressed About Behavior Demonstrated in Certain Specific Situations Occurring in Sports." In *60th Annual Proceedings, National College Physical Education Association,* 1957, pp. 55–59.

Kuhlen, R. G., and B. J. Lee, "Personality Characteristics and Social Acceptability in Adolescence." *Journal of Educational Psychology* 34:321, 1943.

Lakie, W. L., "Expressed Attitudes of Various Groups of Athletes Toward Athletic Competition." *Research Quarterly* 35:497–503, December 1964.

Langston, K. F., "The Relationship Between Body Image and Body Composition of College Females." Unpublished doctoral dissertation, University of Houston, Houston, Tex., 1979.

Lawrence, T., "Appraisal of Emotional Health at the Secondary School Level." *Research Quarterly* 37:252–257, May 1966.

McCloy, C. H., "Character Building Through Physical Education." *Research Quarterly* 1:41–61, October 1930.

———, and F. Hepp, "General Factors or Components of Character as Related to Physical Education." *Research Quarterly* 28:269–278, October 1957.

McCraw, L. W., and J. W. Tabert, "Sociometric Status and Athletic Ability of Junior High School Boys." *Research Quarterly* 24:72–78, March 1953.

McKenna, H. M., "The Effects of Two Methods of Grouping in Physical Education Upon the Social Structure of the Group." Unpublished master's thesis, University of California, 1948.

McPherson, B. D., and M. S. Yuhansz, "An Inventory for Assessing Men's Attitudes Toward Exercise and Physical Activity." *Research Quarterly* 39:218–219, March 1968.

Morgan, W. P., and M. L. Pollock, "Physical Activity and Cardiovascular Health: Psychological Aspects." Presented at the International Congress of Physical Activity Sciences, 1976.

Neale, D. C., et al., "Physical Fitness, Self-Esteem and Attitudes Toward Physical Activity." *Research Quarterly* 40:743–749, December 1969.

Nelson, D. O., "Leadership in Sports." *Research Quarterly* 37:268–275, May 1966.

Nelson, J. K., and B. L. Johnson, "Effects of Varied Techniques in Organizing Class Competition Upon Changes in Sociometric Status." *Research Quarterly* 39:634–639, October 1968.

O'Bryan, M. H., and K. G. O'Bryan, "Attitudes of Males Toward Selected Aspects of Physical Education." *Research Quarterly* 40:343–352, May 1969.

Ondrus, J., "A Sociometric Analysis of Group Structure and the Effect of Football Activities on Inter-personal Relationships." Unpublished doctoral dissertation, New York University, New York, 1953.

Peterson, J. A., and R. Martens, "Success and Residential Affiliation as Determinants of Team Cohesiveness." *Research Quarterly* 43:62–75, March 1972.

Popp, J., "Case Studies of Sophomore High School Boys with High and Low Physical Fitness Indices." Unpublished master's thesis, University of Oregon, Eugene, 1959.

Rarick, G. L., and R. McKee, "A Study of Twenty Third-Grade Children Exhibiting Extreme Levels of Achievement on Tests of Motor Proficiency." *Research Quarterly* 20:142–152, May 1949.

Reaney, M. J., "The Correlation Between General Intelligence and Play Ability as Shown in Organized Group Games." *British Journal of Psychology* 7:226–252, 1914.

Richardson, C. E., "Thurston Scale of Measuring Attitudes of College Students Toward Physical Fitness and Exercise." *Research Quarterly* 31:638–643, December 1960.

Richardson, D. E., "Ethical Conduct in Sport Situations." In *66th Annual Proceedings, National College Physical Education Association,* 1962, pp. 98–104.

Robinson, V. R., "A Study of the Effects of Two Methods of Teaching Physical Education as Measured by a Sociometric Test." Unpublished master's thesis, University of California, 1948.

Rohrbacher, R., "Influence of a Special Camp Program for Obese Boys on Weight Loss, Self-Concept, and Body Image." *Research Quarterly* 44:150–157, May 1973.

Schultz, R. W., and F. L. Smoll, "Equivalence of Two Inventories for Assessing Attitudes Toward Physical Activity." *Psychological Reports* 40:1031–1034, 1977.

Seaman, J. A., "Attitudes of Physically Handicapped Children Toward Physical

Education." *Research Quarterly* 41:439–445, October 1970.

Signorella, M., "Social Adjustment and Athletic Participation." Unpublished study, Purdue University, Lafayette, Ind., 1963.

Simon, J. A., and F. L. Smoll, "An Instrument for Assessing Children's Attitudes Toward Physical Education." *Research Quarterly* 45:407–415, December 1974.

Singer, R. N., "Personality Differences Between and Within Baseball and Tennis Players." *Research Quarterly* 40:582–588, October 1969.

Skubic, E., "A Study in Acquaintanceship and Social Status in Physical Education Classes." *Research Quarterly* 20:80–87, March 1949.

Sonstroem, R. J., "Attitude Testing Examining Certain Psychological Correlates of Physical Activity." *Research Quarterly* 45:93–103, May 1974.

———, "The Validity of Self-Perceptions Regarding Physical and Athletic Ability." *Medicine and Science in Sports* 8:126–132, 1976.

———, "Physical Estimation and Attraction Scales: Rationale and Research." *Medicine and Science in Sports* 10:97–102, 1978.

Sperling, A. P., "The Relationship Between Personality Adjustment and Achievement in Physical Education Activities." *Research Quarterly* 13:351–363, October 1942.

Stogdill, R. M., "Personal Factors Associated with Leadership: A Survey of Literature." *Journal of Psychology* 25:35–71, 1948.

Straub, W. F., and T. Felock, "Attitudes Toward Physical Activity of Delinquent and Non-delinquent Junior High School Girls." *Research Quarterly* 45:21–27, March 1974.

Trapp, W. G., "A Study of Social Integration in a College Football Squad." In *56th Annual Proceedings, National College Physical Education Association,* 1953.

Tryon, C. C., "Evaluation of Adolescent Personality by Adolescents." *Monograph of Society for Research in Child Development,* Vol. 4, 1939.

Vincent, M. F., "Attitudes of College Women Toward Physical Education and Their Relationship to Success in Physical Education." *Research Quarterly* 38:130, March 1967.

Walters, C. E., "A Sociometric Study of Motivated and Nonmotivated Bowling Groups." *Research Quarterly* 26:107–112, March 1955.

Wear, C. L., "Construction of Equivalent Forms of an Attitude Scale." *Research Quarterly* 26:113–119, March 1955.

Wells, H. P., "Relationship Between Physical Fitness and Psychological Variables." Unpublished doctoral dissertation, University of Illinois, Urbana, 1958.

Wessel, J., and R. Nelson, "Relationship Between Strength and Attitudes Toward Physical Education Activities Among College Women." *Research Quarterly* 35:562–568, December 1964.

Whilden, P. P., "Comparison of Two Methods of Teaching Beginning Basketball." *Research Quarterly* 27:235–242, May 1956.

Yarnell, C. D., "Relationship of Physical Fitness to Selected Measures of Popularity." *Research Quarterly* 37:287, May 1966.

Zeleny, L. D., "Status: Its Measurement and Control in Education." *Sociometry* 4:193–204, 1941.

CHAPTER 21

THE MEASUREMENT OF KNOWLEDGE

OBJECTIVES

After reading this chapter, the student should be able to:

1. Construct a table of specifications and explain its use

2. List at least two strengths and two weaknesses of the different types of test items

3. Calculate item difficulty and index of discrimination for objective test items

The measurement of knowledge in physical education activity classes is just as important as its measurement in other subject areas. When physical educators elect to not secure a measure of knowledge, they ignore one of the major objectives of our field and fail to capitalize on the potential of such tests to further the learning process. Evaluation of students' knowledge of rules, strategy, etiquette, and other pertinent information should be considered an integral and vital part of every teaching unit.

The tools employed in the measurement of knowledge should be so designed that the teacher can easily determine what the students have learned from laboratory participation and from facts and materials presented within the unit. Knowledge tests consist of several types. The most common and practical type used in the classroom is the teacher-made test, which may be either objective or subjective in nature. The objective test calls for a brief response and, if properly constructed, has higher reliability and objectivity than the subjective or essay test, which usually calls for a long and detailed response.

A standardized test is one that has been subjected to rigorous steps and procedures in construction and is usually accompanied by norms.

Most standardized tests are objective, consisting of true–false, matching, and multiple choice questions. Standardized tests have not had widespread use in physical education, at least not on the national level.

USES OF KNOWLEDGE TESTS

Several ways in which knowledge tests in physical education classes may be used are as follows:

1. To determine the needs of students as to what information should be imparted

2. To evaluate student achievement and form the basis for determining grades at the end of an instructional unit

3. To evaluate teaching effectiveness; when a class as a whole fails to respond as expected, some inadequacy on the part of the teacher may be noted

4. To motivate students to learn the information deemed important by the teacher and perhaps undertake more comprehensive study on the subject

5. To further the learning process by giving students knowledge of results (when reports

are provided immediately, the desired responses are more apt to be learned than when results are delayed or when tests are not returned at all)

PROBLEMS AND LIMITATIONS OF KNOWLEDGE MEASUREMENT

1. Most standardized knowledge tests in physical education are not available on a commercial basis and consequently must be located from various sources and be prepared for distribution. There appears to be a definite need for the encouragement of commercial interest in physical education knowledge tests.

2. Standardized tests do not always fit the local situation. They may cover materials not covered in some schools owing to limited time, equipment, facilities, or emphasis.

3. Knowledge tests require careful security measures to ensure that all students are exposed to the test at the same time. Students sometimes use ingenious methods to gain an unfair advantage and ensure their success on knowledge tests. Students can also pass on information about the test from one class to another.

4. Norms for standardized knowledge tests are of doubtful value, since they depend on such specific factors as age group, unit of instruction, length of unit, and content presented, factors that can vary greatly. Such norms are seldom applicable to many groups.

5. The standardized test frequently encourages the teacher to emphasize the information covered in the test and to leave out other important but not covered information. This practice is often referred to as *teaching for testing,* with the obvious purpose of helping students and thus of making the teacher look good on norm comparisons.

6. The construction of good tests is a much more difficult task than it might appear. The tests must be valid, and the teacher must continually question whether the items are fair and pertinent to the material covered in class.

7. The writing of good test questions requires skill in expression which, unfortunately, many physical educators lack.

8. The physical educator must guard against the temptation to make the questions too comprehensive and difficult, in an unconscious attempt to prove that physical education is not easy.

9. One of the biggest mistakes teachers make is failing to prepare a test blueprint or table of specifications concerning the area to be tested, how much weighting each area deserves, and the levels of cognition desired. Some teachers simply start writing questions as they come to mind. The easiest items to write are those that deal with facts such as rules, dimensions, dates, and so on. When the teacher has run out of ideas, it may be that most of the test items pertain to an area or areas that received relatively little attention in class, but about which questions were easy to write. A table of specifications can help teachers to avoid this pitfall.

PLANNING OF THE TEST

Good tests require careful planning and preparation. The teacher should not wait until the day before the test and then hurriedly throw together some questions, relying on memory as to what was covered, or scanning the text for test item ideas. One of the reasons essay test questions are used (and abused) to the extent they are is because some teachers wait until the last minute to prepare the test. This is not to say that good essay questions cannot be generated in a short time, but teachers often falsely assume that they can come up with a few questions quickly and then place the burden on the student to adequately cover the course content. Indeed, one of the reasons essay questions tend to be less reliable than other test items is that they are not carefully planned.

We should hasten to say that essay questions are not the only types of questions that suffer from improper planning. Most of the weak points associated with completion, multiple choice, true–false, and matching questions that are later described in this chapter are the results of improper preparation.

Aside from the deleterious effects on the reliability of the test questions, improper planning can seriously impair the content validity of the entire test. We mentioned previously in this chapter that a common mistake in preparation of a knowledge test is to simply start writing items that come to mind easily from scanning the text. Such items are usually factual in nature and require the student only to memorize and repeat.

They often tend to be trivial as well. Consequently, the teacher must carefully and thoroughly plan the test to ensure complete coverage and balance as to the relative importance of the different areas covered in the course (Shick 1981).

TABLE OF SPECIFICATIONS

The first step in sound test construction is the preparation of a test blueprint, called a table of specifications. The table has two dimensions, one being the type of cognition or thought process desired, and the other the content of the test. Typically the latter dimension is on the vertical axis, and the type of cognition or desired behaviors is on the horizontal axis.

The nature of the desired thought processes (horizontal dimension) will, of course, vary considerably with the nature of the subject matter. Many test makers have utilized the behaviors of the Bloom taxonomy (Bloom 1956), which are knowing, comprehending, applying, analyzing, synthesizing, and evaluating. Other testers may use desired behaviors such as criticizing and expressing. Still other teachers may wish to have fewer levels, such as remembering, understanding, and applying or thinking, and so on. In the hierarchy of levels of cognition, knowing or remembering is lowest. In other words, the student merely has to recognize a fact or recall a specific piece of information. As was mentioned earlier, these items are easiest for the teacher to write. Questions aimed at higher levels of cognition such as analyzing, synthesizing, and evaluating are much more difficult to write. Hence, they are often omitted.

The vertical dimension in the table of specifications deals with objectives (i.e., the areas covered in the course). A knowledge test in an activity course, for example, might have areas such as history of the sport, rules, equipment, techniques, and strategies listed on the vertical dimension. A unit on conditioning exercises might include physiologic principles, training procedures, conditioning facts and fallacies, alternate exercise programs, and other objectives. In any event, this enables the teacher to make sure that (1) questions are directed toward each of the areas and (2) a proper balance is achieved with regard to the number of questions concerning each area in relation to the amount of emphasis that was accorded each area.

Once the table of specifications is created, the teacher carefully examines lecture notes, textbooks, previous examinations, and other sources for relevant ideas for questions. The teacher must decide on the type of questions to be used and, of course, the type of cognitive response desired.

As questions are developed, the teacher tallies them in the appropriate cells in the table, which are the intersections of content areas and levels of cognition. Table 21.1 shows a sample table of specifications.

Some examples of questions and their assignment to content areas and desired thought processes are given here. The letter of the correct response is capitalized. The question number is circled in the table of specifications (Table 21.1).

Question 1. Major Walter C. Wingfield introduced what is officially known as lawn tennis in
a. 1853
B. 1873
c. 1881
d. 1910

Question 1 is related to the history of tennis and is clearly at the knowledge (or remembering) level of cognition.

Question 15. Player A's first serve is a fault. The second serve is good but a player from the

Table 21.1. Table of Specifications

CONTENT	NUMBER OF QUESTIONS (% of total)	THOUGHT PROCESSES (QUESTION NUMBERS)			
		Knowledge	Comprehension	Application	Analysis
History	3 (10%)	①6,12			
Rules and score keeping	12 (40%)	3,8,10,11,17	20,㉔,27,28	⑮,19,22	
Equipment	3 (10%)	2,9	14		
Techniques and strategy	12 (40%)	4,5	7,30	13,16,25,29	18,㉑,23,26

next court, in attempting to retrieve a ball, accidentally interferes with the receiver (player B). What is the ruling?

a. The point is awarded to player B because of interference
b. The second serve is reserved
C. The entire point is replayed, with the server being allowed two serves
d. The play continues despite the interference

Question 15 pertains to rules, but requires the student to understand the rules concerning service and interference and to apply this knowledge. Thus, it is assigned to the application cell.

Question 21. Which of the following strokes would you use when you are in the backcourt against an opponent who is at the net?

a. A lob to his or her baseline
b. A short top-spin across court
c. A drop shot to either side
D. Both a and b
e. a, b, and c

Question 21 pertains to strategy and requires analysis of the situation and the appropriate action.

Question 24. Players should change ends of the court when the score is

a. 4-6, 6-3, 1-3
B. 6-3, 5-2
c. 6-0
d. Both a and b
e. a, b, and c

Question 24 deals with score keeping and involves more than just knowledge of when to change ends of the court; it also demands comprehension of the rule.

PRACTICAL TEST ITEMS FOR KNOWLEDGE MEASUREMENT

The most common types of test questions are completion, multiple choice, matching, true–false, and essay. Each of these methods is discussed briefly by presenting some sample questions and listing strong points and weak points.

Completion Items

These items require that the student supply a word or phrase in a blank to complete a sentence. Figure 21.1 shows samples. Only key words or phrases should be asked for, since trivial information serves little instructional purpose.

Strong Points:

1. These items reduce the problem of guessing.
2. Completion items can be used in a variety of ways to obtain the desired answers.
3. These items require intensive study on the part of students in that they must recall and reproduce material rather than merely recognize it.
4. Completion items are relatively easy to prepare.

Weak Points:

1. Subjective judgment is needed by the teacher as to what specific items are most important.
2. Different answers may be obtained, each of which could be appropriate owing to the wording of the statement.
3. There is a tendency for teachers to test on isolated facts, to confine the answers to one word.

_____ 1. The (1) event is conducted in a square area approximately 40 × 40 ft on the floor.
_____ 2. The two American gymnastics events that are not contested
_____ 3. as part of the all-around competition are (2) and (3).
_____ 4. (4) refers to assisting or helping someone during the performance of a stunt.
_____ 5. Strength is a term used to denote (5) being exerted against a resistance.

Figure 21.1. Sample completion questions

Multiple Choice Items

Questions of this type consist of an incomplete statement (stem) followed by several answers, one of which is the correct one. In some cases the student may be directed to pick the only incorrect answer or to pick the one best answer from among all correct responses. Figure 21.2 shows sample questions.

Strong Points:

1. Multiple choice items can be applied to most types of material and information.

2. Such items are easy to score.

3. Such items can be used at practically all educational levels.

4. Guessing is discouraged if the questions are well constructed.

Weak Points:

1. Good multiple choice items are relatively difficult to prepare.

2. Too much emphasis is frequently placed on isolated facts.

3. It is difficult to avoid ambiguity when the tester tries to confine the choices to short statements.

Matching Items

A matching item usually consists of two columns of words or partial sentences, and the student is directed to associate the responses of one column correctly with those of the other. The usual form is for letters next to the responses in the right-hand column to be placed in blanks next to the numbers in the left-hand column. Sample matching items are shown in Figure 21.3.

_____ 1. Tonus is decreased by:
  a. Worry
  b. Exercise
  c. Lack of sleep
  d. Colds
  e. Inactivity

_____ 2. The normal college student needs:
  a. Light exercise
  b. Vigorous exercise
  c. No exercise
  d. Mainly team sports
  e. Infrequent exercise

_____ 3. One of the best measurements of physical fitness is through:
  a. Mental tests
  b. Blood tests
  c. Muscular strength tests
  d. Tests of agility
  e. Tests of balance

_____ 4. The inability of a muscle to contract as a result of continual contraction indicates:
  a. Nervous block
  b. Poor nutrition
  c. Malfunction of nerve impulse
  d. Destruction of end plate
  e. Fatigue

_____ 5. A person develops neuromuscular skill through:
  a. Occasional sports activity
  b. Studying films of movement
  c. Watching others perform
  d. Repeated practice of skills
  e. A corrective program of physical education

Figure 21.2. Sample multiple choice questions

_____ 1. Rectus abdominis
_____ 2. Trapezius
_____ 3. Rhomboid
_____ 4. Pectoralis major
_____ 5. Biceps
_____ 6. Triceps
_____ 7. Sternocleidomastoid
_____ 8. Biceps femoris

a. Flexion of neck
b. Flexion of ankle
c. Trunk flexion
d. Upward rotation of scapula
e. Downward rotation of scapula
f. Abduction of humerus
g. Flexion of forearm
h. Extension of hip
i. Extension of forearm
j. Abduction of femur

Figure 21.3. Sample matching questions

Strong Points:

1. The matching items are usually quick and relatively easy to prepare.

2. Such items usually cover a maximum amount of material in a minimal amount of space.

3. The test is easy to score.

Weak Points:

1. The test is time consuming on the part of students if the list is lengthy.

2. Matching items are limited in that they measure only recognition.

3. The choices should outnumber the questions or students may achieve the correct match through elimination.

True–False Items

These items are statements that confront the student with two possible answers (either negative or positive). Figure 21.4 shows some samples.

Strong Points:

1. A wide range of topics can be covered in a short period of time.

2. True–false items provide coverage of material that does not lend itself to coverage by other test items.

3. This type of test is objective and easy to score.

Weak Points:

1. True–false items encourage guessing.

2. There is a tendency for teachers to test on isolated facts and to insert "trick" words, which tend to trap students who actually know the material.

3. Better students tend to read things into such statements and consequently may do worse than weaker students on true–false questions.

4. Students can develop a certain knack in taking true–false tests by identifying certain keys that are typical of this test form. For example, short sentences are more apt to be false and long sentences true, and questions containing words such as *never* and *always* are almost always false.

Essay Questions

Essay questions are statements that direct the student to discuss, with some detail and organization, a particular topic. They are often referred to as short-question–long-answer items. Such questions usually direct the student to summarize, contrast, compare, describe, or explain some subject. Samples are shown in Figure 21.5.

Strong Points:

1. Essay questions can be quickly constructed.

2. Essay tests require the learning of large units of subject matter, rather than isolated facts.

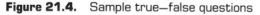

     1. Walking in a handstand is considered a weakness or fault in gymnastic competition.
     2. In performing a headstand, most of the weight should rest on top of the head.
     3. In performing a backward roll, the hands should be placed on the mats so that the little fingers are next to the ears.
     4. Static balance is directly proportional to the area of the base on which the body is supported.
     5. A body will turn faster when the length of the radius of rotation about the center of gravity is increased.

Figure 21.4.   Sample true–false questions

---

1. Summarize the contributions of early German gymnastic instructors to the development of the sport of gymnastics.
2. Compare the Swedish system of gymnastics with the German system.
3. Name four organizations that have contributed to the development of gymnastics in the United States, and discuss the importance of each organization's contributions.
4. Identify the present Olympic gymnastics events and briefly summarize their description, characteristics, and values.
5. List and explain four scientific principles of balance.

Figure 21.5.   Sample essay questions

3. Essay items are effective in testing such skills as synthesizing pertinent information, organizing, and relating the facts and material that have been learned.

4. Guessing is held to a minimum in essay items.

5. Essay items allow for greater freedom of response and permit variety in expression.

Weak Points:

1. Essay tests have low objectivity and reliability.

2. Essay tests require considerable time to grade.

3. Bluffing and rambling are inherent dangers in essay tests.

4. Students who write slowly or have difficulty organizing their answers are severely penalized by essay questions.

TEST EVALUATION

Teachers rarely take the time to analyze the results of a test to determine its effectiveness. In other words, we seldom "test our tests." Certainly, a teacher's time is limited, and a teacher cannot be expected to undertake the elaborate checking methods used by publishers of standardized tests. Nevertheless, teachers can and should find time to utilize some of the simpler techniques to establish whether their tests can, so to speak, withstand testing.

Three important criteria in test evaluation are usability, reliability, and validity. Usability can be determined as the test is being administered and scored, since it pertains to satisfactory completion time, ease of interpretation of directions, and ease of scoring. However, determination of reliability and validity requires an analysis of test scores and the individual items of the test.

Reliability

There are several methods a teacher might use to determine whether a written test reliably measures student achievement. The *test–retest* method, which is used frequently in physical performance measurement, is rarely used for written tests for obvious reasons. The *parallel* or *alternate-forms* method involves the construction of two or more tests that supposedly represent similar samples of test items from a "universe" of possible items. The two forms are administered to the same group of subjects and the scores are correlated to obtain

a reliability coefficient. The preparation of alternate forms of a test requires care and skill to attain equivalent tests.

One of the most commonly used methods of establishing reliability of written tests is the *split-half* method. This method involves *internal consistency,* since it is based on a single administration of the test, whereas the test–retest and alternate-forms methods require two test administrations. The split-half method that is used most often is the odd–even splitting of the test. The number of correct odd-numbered items and the number of correct even-numbered items are tabulated for each student, and a correlation is computed for the two sets of scores. Since the resulting correlation is based on two halves of the test, it is necessary to correct for the length. It should be recalled that reliability is directly related to the length of a test. The Spearman–Brown formula is used for this purpose:

$$rtt = \frac{2\ rht}{1 + rht}$$

where rtt is the reliability coefficient for total test and rht is the coefficient of correlation between the two halves. If, for example, the correlation between the odd-numbered items and the even-numbered items is .85, the estimated reliability for a test twice that length would be as follows:

$$rtt = \frac{2\ (.85)}{1.00 + .85} = \frac{1.70}{1.85} = .92$$

The odd–even method cannot be used for speed tests.

The *Kuder–Richardson Formula* (Kuder and Richardson 1937) is also a method of establishing a reliability coefficient from one test administration. Actually, Kuder and Richardson proposed several formulas for this purpose. The simplest and perhaps the most widely used Kuder–Richardson formula is the K-R 21:

$$\text{K-R } 21 = 1.00 - \frac{\overline{X}\ (N - \overline{X})}{Ns^2}$$

where $\overline{X}$ is the mean of the test, N is the number of test items, and s is the standard deviation of the test (s^2 is the variance).

As an illustration of the use of this formula, let us assume we have a test of 80 questions; the mean score is 62 correct and the standard deviation is 11. The reliability coefficient for this test is .88.

$$K\text{-}R\ 21\ =\ 1.00\ -\ \frac{62\ (80-62)}{80\ (11)^2}$$
$$=\ 1.00\ -\ \frac{1116}{9680}$$
$$=\ 1.00\ -\ .12\ =\ .88$$

Another formula, the K-R 20, is more accurate but more complicated than the K-R 21. The K-R 20 is computed from the proportion of students passing each item and from the standard deviation. It provides a coefficient that is equal to the average of all possible split-half coefficients. It is a good approximation of an alternate-form correlation.

Validity

As we learned earlier, validity is the degree to which we measure what we intend to measure. There are different methods for establishing validity with knowledge tests, just as there are with physical performance tests. For example, construct validity might be established by giving the test to groups known to be different in knowledge, such as experienced and inexperienced performers, older and younger subjects, and so on. Concurrent validity could be assessed by correlating the results of a "homemade" test with those of a standardized test. The predictive validity of knowledge tests is exemplified by the ability of the college entrance examination to predict future college success.

For most teachers, content validity is the most important type of validity with regard to knowledge testing. One method of trying to assure content validity is in the development of the table of specifications, by means of which the teacher ascertains that questions concerning the various areas (objectives) of course content are included in the test in proper balance. Another method is having persons knowledgeable in the field rate the test regarding content validity.

Item Analysis

Item analysis is a procedure used to assure greater reliability and validity of a test. It entails examination of each test item for its level of difficulty and its power to discriminate between students who presumably have learned the material to a high degree and those who have not learned the material as well. In essence, this is a measure of internal validity in that a knowledge test is designed to discriminate among students of different levels of achievement.

Thus, each item is analyzed as to how difficult it is and the degree to which students who get the item correct also score well on the total test.

Item Difficulty

For the typical teacher, the analysis of difficulty of each item on a written test is easily done. The teacher simply divides the number of students who got each question correct by the number of students who answered that item. For example, if 50 students answered question 1 and 25 marked it correctly, the difficulty index is 25 / 50 or .50. A hard item has a low difficulty index (i.e., if only 5 of 50 answered a question correctly, the difficulty index is 5 / 50 = .10). Test items that everyone misses or everyone gets correct do not tell the teacher anything about pupil differences in learning.

The best questions are those that have a difficulty index of around .50. Most test authorities recommend that questions with an index below .10 or over .90 be eliminated.

Although pure test construction theorists may disagree, it sometimes is appropriate to retain a *few* easy items. Since they are easy, they can have motivational value, and since they are answered correctly by both high and low scorers, they do not affect the relative position of the scores (Tuckman 1978). Moreover, a teacher may want to check that some important basic concepts are mastered by all students (Hills 1976).

Item Discrimination

As mentioned before, item discrimination determines how each question differentiates between students who do well on the entire test from those who do poorly. An index of discrimination can be derived in several ways. With a large number of scores, the index of discrimination is usually computed by taking a certain percentage of the papers, such as the upper and lower 25%, 27%, or 30%, and subtracting the proportion of low-ability students who answered each question correctly from the proportion of high-ability students who answered the item correctly.

The simplest method for deriving an index is to divide the test papers into a high and a low group and use the following formula:

$$\text{index of discrimination}\ =\ \frac{N_H\ -\ N_L}{N}$$

where N_H is the number of high scorers who answered the item correctly, N_L is the number of low scorers who answered the item correctly, and N is the number in either the high or the low group. Thus, if there were 20 high scorers and 20 low scorers and 15 of the high scorers answered correctly while only 5 of the low scorers answered correctly, the index of discrimination would be .50.

$$\frac{15 - 5}{20} = \frac{10}{20} = .50.$$

A general rule is that items with an index of discrimination of .40 or above are excellent items; items with an index below .20 (or a negative index) are poor items and should be discarded or revised.

In Table 21.2, six questions are analyzed for difficulty and discrimination. In this example, 60 papers were divided into the upper and the lower 50%, that is, the 30 high and the 30 low scorers. We can see that a test item has to have both properties of suitable difficulty level and discrimination.

The analysis for the six questions is as follows:

Question 1. The difficulty is "perfect" (.50) but there is no discrimination, and thus the item is unacceptable.

Question 2. The discrimination is suitable but the item is very difficult. Contrary to some teachers' viewpoints, hard items are not good items.

Question 3. The difficulty is satisfactory but the discrimination is negative. The question needs rewording if more low scorers than high scorers answer it correctly.

Question 4. The difficulty is unsatisfactory, since 92% of the class got the correct answer, and the discrimination is inadequate.

Questions 5 and 6. Good items for both difficulty and discrimination.

Hills gave this advice for teachers: "(a) Never try to write hard items and (b) never aim to have test items of varied difficulty."

Writing good test questions takes time, effort, and deliberation. A wise teacher will establish a pool of questions that have successfully met the criteria of difficulty and discrimination. Thus, the teacher can accumulate test items in different subject areas that require different levels of cognition. The creation of a test subsequently becomes much easier when the teacher can choose from a number of proven items. The task becomes easier still if the pool of items can be stored on a computer or microcomputer. Then the test items can be selected according to the table of specifications and even put together by the computer.

SOURCES FOR PHYSICAL EDUCATION KNOWLEDGE TESTS

The knowledge tests we list here represent the majority of studies conducted for the purpose of constructing test items for use in physical education activity classes. Although a number of these tests are now out of date, they may still be valuable in giving teachers ideas about new test items, as well as serving as examples of procedures utilized in constructing tests. The knowledge tests are presented in alphabetical order according to activities.

Archery

Ley, K. L., "Constructing Objective Test Items to Measure High School Levels of Achievement in Selected Physical Education Activities." Microcarded doctoral dissertation, University of Iowa, Iowa City, 1960.

Snell, C., "Physical Education Knowledge Tests." *Research Quarterly* 6:83–86, October 1935.

Badminton

Fox, K., "Beginning Badminton Written Examinations." *Research Quarterly* 24:135–146, May 1953.

Table 21.2. Sample Test Item Analysis[a]

QUESTION	NUMBER IN UPPER 50% CORRECT	NUMBER IN LOWER 50% CORRECT	ITEM DIFFICULTY	INDEX OF DISCRIMINATION
1	15	15	.50	.00
2	9	0	.15	.30
3	10	18	.47	-.27
4	29	26	.92	.10
5	25	5	.50	.67
6	24	10	.57	.47

[a]A total of 60 papers were separated into the upper and lower 30 scorers.

French, E., "The Construction of Knowledge Tests in Selected Professional Courses in Physical Education." *Research Quarterly* 14:406–424, December 1943.

Goll, L. M., "Construction of Badminton and Swimming Knowledge Tests for High School Girls." Microcarded master's thesis, Illinois State University, Normal, 1956, pp. 656–75.

Hennis, G. M., "Construction of Knowledge Tests in Selected Physical Education Activities for College Women." *Research Quarterly* 27:301–309, October 1956.

Hooks, E. W., Jr., "Hooks' Comprehensive Knowledge Test in Selected Physical Education Activities for College Men." *Research Quarterly* 37:506, December 1966.

Ley, K. L., "Constructing Objective Test Items to Measure High School Levels of Achievement in Selected Physical Education Activities." Microcarded doctoral dissertation, University of Iowa, Iowa City, 1960.

Phillips, M., "Standardization of a Badminton Knowledge Test for College Women." *Research Quarterly* 17:48–63, March 1946.

Scott, G. M., "Achievement Examination in Badminton." *Research Quarterly* 12:242–253, May 1941.

Baseball

Goldberg, I. H., "The Development of Achievement Standards in Knowledge of Physical Education Activities." Microcarded doctoral dissertation, New York University, New York, 1953.

Hemphill, F., "Information Tests in Health and Physical Education for High School Boys." *Research Quarterly* 3:82, December 1932.

Rodgers, E. G., and M. L. Heath, "An Experiment in the Use of Knowledge and Skill Tests in Playground Baseball." *Research Quarterly* 2:128–130, December 1931.

Snell, C., "Physical Education Knowledge Tests." *Research Quarterly* 7:87–91, May 1936.

Basketball

Bliss, J. G., *Basketball*. Philadelphia: Lea & Febiger, 1929.

Fisher, R. B., "Tests in Selected Physical Education Service Courses in a College." Microcarded doctoral dissertation, State University of Iowa, Iowa City, 1950, pp. 158–181.

French, E., "The Construction of Knowledge Tests in Selected Professional Courses in Physical Education." *Research Quarterly* 14:406–424, December 1943.

Goldberg, I. H., "The Development of Achievement Standards in Knowledge of Physical Education Activities." Microcarded doctoral dissertation, New York University, New York, 1953.

Hemphill, F., "Information Tests in Health and Physical Education for High School Boys." *Research Quarterly* 3:82, December 1932.

Hennis, G. M., "Construction of Knowledge Tests in Selected Physical Education Activities for College Women." *Research Quarterly* 27:301–309, October 1956. (Also see physical education microcards.)

Ley, K. L., "Constructing Objective Test Items to Measure High School Levels of Achievement in Selected Physical Education Activities." Microcarded doctoral dissertation, University of Iowa, Iowa City, 1960.

Schwartz, H., "Knowledge and Achievement Tests in Girls' Basketball on the Senior High Level." *Research Quarterly* 8:153–156, March 1937.

Snell, C., "Physical Education Knowledge Tests." *Research Quarterly* 7:79–82, March 1936.

Body Mechanics

French, E., "The Construction of Knowledge Tests in Selected Professional Courses in Physical Education." *Research Quarterly* 14:406–424, December 1943.

Bowling

Hennis, G. M., "Construction of Knowledge Tests in Selected Physical Education Activities for College Women." *Research Quarterly* 27:301–309, October 1956.

Ley, K. L., "Constructing Objective Test Items to Measure High School Levels of Achievement in Selected Physical Education Activities." Microcarded doctoral dissertation, University of Iowa, Iowa City, 1960.

Canoeing

French, E., "The Construction of Knowledge Tests in Selected Professional Courses in Physical Education." *Research Quarterly* 14:406–424, December 1943.

Dance and Rhythm

French, E., "The Construction of Knowledge Tests in Selected Professional Courses in Physical Education." *Research Quarterly* 14:406–424, December 1943.

Garcia, M. J., *An Objective Knowledge Test of Aerobic Dance and Fitness*. Portland, Tex.: Brown and Littleman, 1978.

Murry, J. K., "An Appreciation Test in Dance." Unpublished master's thesis, University of California, 1943.

Stockard, S., "The Development and Evaluation of an Information Test in Beginning Modern Dance for Undergraduate College Students." *LAHPER Journal*, Fall Issue, 1972, p. 29.

Football

Goldberg, I. H., "The Development of Achievement Standards in Knowledge of Physical Education Activities." Microcarded doctoral dissertation, New York University, New York, 1953.

Hemphill, F., "Information Tests in Health and Physical Education for High School Boys." *Research Quarterly* 3:82, December 1932.

Fundamentals

Snell, C., "Physical Education Knowledge Tests." *Research Quarterly* 6:79–83, October 1935.

Golf

French, E., "The Construction of Knowledge Tests in Selected Professional Courses in Physical Education." *Research Quarterly* 14:406–424, December 1943.

Ley, K. L., "Constructing Objective Test Items to Measure High School Levels of Achievement in Selected Physical Education Activities." Microcarded doctoral dissertation, University of Iowa, Iowa City, 1960.

Snell, C., "Physical Education Knowledge Tests." *Research Quarterly* 7:79–80, May 1936.

Waglow, I. F., and C. H. Rehling, "A Golf Knowledge Test." *Research Quarterly* 24:463–470, December 1953.

Gymnastics

Fisher, R. B., "Tests in Selected Physical Education Service Courses in a College." Microcarded doctoral dissertation, State University of Iowa, Iowa City, 1950, pp. 145–156.

French, E., "The Construction of Knowledge Tests in Selected Professional Courses in Physical Education." *Research Quarterly* 14:406–424, December 1943.

Gershon, E., "Apparatus Gymnastics Knowledge Test for College Men in Professional Physical Education." *Research Quarterly* 28:332, December 1957.

Johnson, B. L., *An Objective Knowledge Test of Gymnastics (Including Tumbling and Trampoline)*. Portland, Tex.: Brown and Littleman, 1977.

Nipper, J., "A Knowledge Test of Tumbling and Gymnastics." Unpublished study, Northeast Louisiana University, Monroe, 1966.

Handball

Phillips, B. E., *Fundamental Handball*. New York: A. S. Barnes, 1937.

Hockey

Dietz, D., and B. Trech, "Hockey Knowledge Test for Girls." *JOHPER* 11:366, 1940.

French, E., "The Construction of Knowledge Tests in Selected Professional Courses in Physical Education." *Research Quarterly* 14:406–424, December 1943.

Grisier, G. J., "The Construction of an Objective Test of Knowledge and Interpretation of the Rules of Field Hockey for Women." *Research Quarterly Supplement* 5:79–81, March 1943.

Hennis, G. M., "Construction of Knowledge Tests in Selected Physical Education Activities for College Women." *Research Quarterly* 27:301–309, October 1956. (Also see physical education microcards.)

Kelly, E. D., and J. E. Brown, "The Construction of a Field Hockey Test for Women Physical Education Majors." *Research Quarterly* 23:322–329, October 1952.

Snell, C., "Physical Education Knowledge Tests." *Research Quarterly* 6:86–89, October 1935.

Horseback Riding

Snell, C., "Physical Education Knowledge Tests." *Research Quarterly* 7:80–84, May 1936.

Physical Fitness

Johnson, B. L., and M. J. Garcia, *An Objective Knowledge Test of Conditioning, Fitness and Performance*. Portland, Tex.: Brown and Littleman, 1982.

Stradtman, A. D., and T. K. Cureton, "A Physical Fitness Knowledge Test for Secondary School Boys and Girls." *Research Quarterly* 21:53–57, March 1950.

Recreational Sports

Fisher, R. B., "Tests in Selected Physical Education Service Courses in a College." Microcarded doctoral dissertation, State University of Iowa, Iowa City, 1950, pp. 285–319.

French, E., "The Construction of Knowledge Tests in Selected Professional Courses in Physical Education." *Research Quarterly* 14:406–424, December 1943.

Soccer

Fisher, R. B., "Tests in Selected Physical Education Service Courses in a College." Microcarded doctoral dissertation, State University of Iowa, Iowa City, 1950, pp. 123–143.

French, E., "The Construction of Knowledge Tests in Selected Professional Courses in Physical Education." *Research Quarterly* 14:406–424, December 1943.

Heath, M. L., and E. G. Rodgers, "A Study in the Use of Knowledge and Skill Tests in Soccer." *Research Quarterly* 3:33–53, October 1932.

Knighton, M., "Soccer Questions." *Journal of Health and Physical Education,* Vol. 1, October 1930.

Ley, K. L., "Constructing Objective Test Items to Measure High School Levels of Achievement in Selected Physical Education Activities." Microcarded doctoral dissertation, University of Iowa, Iowa City, 1960.

Snell, C., "Physical Education Knowledge Tests." *Research Quarterly* 7:76–79, March 1936.

Softball

Fisher, R. B., "Tests in Selected Physical Education Service Courses in a College." Microcarded doctoral dissertation, State University of Iowa, Iowa City, 1950, pp. 254–270.

French, E., "The Construction of Knowledge Tests in Selected Professional Courses in Physical Education." *Research Quarterly* 14:406–424, December 1943.

Hennis, G. M., "Construction of Knowledge Tests in Selected Physical Education Activities for College Women." *Research Quarterly* 27:301–309, October 1956. (Also see physical education microcards.)

Hooks, E. W., Jr., "Hooks' Comprehensive Knowledge Test in Selected Physical Education Activities for College Men." *Research Quarterly* 37:506, December 1966.

Ley, L., "Constructing Objective Test Items to Measure High School Levels of Achievement in Selected Physical Education Activities." Microcarded doctoral dissertation, University of Iowa, Iowa City, 1960.

Waglow, I. F., and F. Stephens, "A Softball Knowledge Test." *Research Quarterly* 26:234–237, May 1955.

Sportsmanship

Haskins, M. J., "Problem-Solving Test of Sportsmanship." *Research Quarterly* 31:601–605, December 1960.

Swimming

Fisher, R. B., "Tests in Selected Physical Education Service Courses in a College." Microcarded doctoral dissertation, State University of Iowa, Iowa City, 1950, pp. 182–253.

French, E., "The Construction of Knowledge Tests in Selected Professional Courses in Physical Education." *Research Quarterly* 14:406–424, December 1943.

Goll, L. M., "Construction of Badminton and Swimming Knowledge Tests for High School Girls." Microcarded master's thesis, Illinois State University, Normal, 1956.

Scott, M. G., "Achievement Examinations for Elementary and Intermediate Swimming Classes." *Research Quarterly* 11:104–111, May 1940.

Team-Game Activities

Rodgers, E. G., "The Standardization and Use of Objective Type Information Tests in Team Game Activities." *Research Quarterly* 10:103, March 1939.

Tennis

Broer, M. R., and D. M. Miller, "Achievement Tests for Beginning and Intermediate Tennis." *Research Quarterly* 21:303–313, October 1950.

Fisher, R. B., "Tests in Selected Physical Education Service Courses in a College." Microcarded doctoral dissertation, State University of Iowa, Iowa City, 1950, pp. 271–284.

French, E., "The Construction of Knowledge Tests in Selected Professional Courses in Physical Education." *Research Quarterly* 14:406–424, December 1943.

Hennis, G. M., "Construction of Knowledge Tests in Selected Physical Education Activities for College Women." *Research Quarterly* 27:301–309, October 1956. (Also see physical education microcards.)

Hewitt, J. E., "Comprehensive Tennis Knowledge Test." *Research Quarterly* 8:74–84, October 1937.

———, "Hewitt's Comprehensive Tennis Knowledge Test." *Research Quarterly* 35:149–154, May 1964.

Hooks, E. W., Jr., "Hooks' Comprehensive Knowledge Test in Selected Physical Education Activities for College Men." *Research Quarterly* 37:506, December 1966.

Miller, W. K., "Achievement Levels in Tennis Knowledge and Skill for Women Physical Education Major Students." *Research Quarterly* 24:81–89, March 1953.

Scott, M. G., "Achievement Examinations for Elementary and Intermediate Tennis Classes." *Research Quarterly* 12:40–49, March 1941.

Snell, C., "Physical Education Knowledge Tests." *Research Quarterly* 7:84–87, May 1936.

Track and Field

French, E., "The Construction of Knowledge Tests in Selected Professional Courses in Physical Education." *Research Quarterly* 14:406–424, December 1943.

Volleyball

Fisher, R. B., "Tests in Selected Physical Education Service Courses in a College." Microcarded doctoral dissertation, State University of Iowa, Iowa City, 1950, pp. 82–122.

French, E., "The Construction of Knowledge Tests in Selected Professional Courses in Physical Education." *Research Quarterly* 14:406–424, December 1943.

Hennis, G. M., "Construction of Knowledge Tests in Selected Physical Education Activities for College Women." *Research Quarterly* 27:301–309, October 1956.

Hooks, E. W., Jr., "Hooks' Comprehensive Knowledge Test in Selected Physical Education Activities for College Men." *Research Quarterly* 37:506, December 1966.

Langston, D. F., "Standardization of a Volleyball Knowledge Test for College Men Physical Education Majors." *Research Quarterly* 26:60–66, March 1955.

Ley, K. L., "Constructing Objective Test Items to Measure High School Levels of Achievement in Selected Physical Education Activities." Microcarded doctoral dissertation, University of Iowa, Iowa City, 1960.

Snell, C., "Physical Education Knowledge Tests." *Research Quarterly* 7:73–76, March 1936.

FINDINGS AND CONCLUSIONS FROM KNOWLEDGE MEASUREMENT AND RESEARCH

Numerous tests of knowledge in physical education activities have been available for years; however, test authors have been quick to point out that such tests should only be used in situations where the distribution of factual information is in relatively close agreement with the specifications of the published test (Hennis 1956; Ley 1960). Many knowledge tests are presented in their entirety in professional publications and can serve as guides for constructing teacher-made tests (Fisher 1950; Fox 1953; French 1943; Goll 1956; Hills 1976).

A number of test authors have established norms that may be used for comparative purposes when the test is used in its entirety (Gershon 1957; Hemphill 1932; Hennis 1956; Hooks 1966; Langston 1955; Miller 1953). As previously pointed out, however, so many specific factors are involved that norms are seldom applicable.

Concerning a possible relationship between knowledge about an activity and skill in the activity, Scott noted that a direct relationship did not exist in tennis measurement. Hewitt, however, found a high relationship between knowledge in tennis and playing experience in tennis. We have often noted that students who are highly skilled in an activity frequently take for granted their knowledge of the activity and do not do as well on the activity knowledge test as students who are less skilled in the activity.

In 1960, Ley studied objective knowledge test items in selected physical education activities, and some of her comments might prove valuable to future test authors. They are paraphrased as follows:

1. Test constructors since 1940 have not used any particular method of determining the relevance level of individual items.

2. Knowledge test studies have contained too many factual items while neglecting items in the generalization, understanding, application, and interpretation categories.

3. Examinations by committee groups are not superior to those by an individual in regard to topical content, relevance level, and the worth of the individual items.

4. Rules of play have dominated physical education knowledge tests, and it is doubtful

that such a practice can be justified in many situations.

5. If accurate, pictures and diagrams are of value in developing test items.

6. Highly relevant items can be written for all topical areas found in physical education activity knowledge tests.

Ley found that physical education major students scored significantly higher than nonmajor students in only one of six physical activity knowledge tests. If this finding is characteristic of physical education majors across the nation, then greater emphasis should be placed on a more thorough understanding of *what is what* in physical activities for majors.

Several investigators have researched the effect of knowledge on learning to perform skills in various activities or tasks. Operating on the hypothesis that exposing students to an understanding and application of mechanical principles will bring about greater improvement than instruction without reference to these principles, Mohr and Barrett, Broer, Ruger, and Colville found such knowledge to be beneficial.

Numerous investigators have used such knowledge measures as grade point average, standard achievement test scores, and intelligence scores to determine the relationship between mental ability and physical ability. Most results of such studies have varied, with some reports indicating little or no relationship (Bond 1959; Brace 1941; Burley and Anderson 1959; Kuder and Richardson 1937), while others indicated a low but positive relationship (Distefano et al. 1958; Johnson 1942; McMillan 1961; Weber 1953). However, Clarke and Jarman have pointed out that most investigations that showed little or no relationship did not allow for variances in the intelligence of the subjects. Along this line, we would like to stress the fact that one needs extremes in the variables concerned to obtain a high coefficient of correlation. If the sample is too homogeneous in the variables, it is simply mathematically unrealistic to expect high correlations even though a significant relationship could exist.

Through the years, various physical educators and researchers have held the belief that physical fitness improves the effectiveness of the individual's mental capabilities. Research that supports this contention is presented as follows:

1. Studying two groups of college men with nearly equal intelligence quotient averages, Rogers found the scholarship in the physically stronger group to be considerably higher than that in the low-strength group.

2. Terman noted that symptoms of general weakness were reported 30% less frequently for gifted students than for nongifted students.

3. Brace (1933) reported studies from England that revealed that only 2.35% of students who were above average in scholarship were below average in body build, as compared with 39.7% of students with poor scholarship who were below average in body build.

4. A report from Massachusetts (Report of the School Committee and Superintendent of Brookline, Mass. 1941) revealed that the average physical fitness index for 126 high school honor students attending Brookline public schools was 117, which is 2 points above the national third quartile score.

5. Studying one group of children high and one group low in motor proficiency, Rarick and McKee found that the high motor proficiency group demonstrated better scholastic adjustment than the low group in reading, writing, and comprehension.

6. Two studies noted that male freshmen at large universities with low physical fitness indexes were also low in scholastic accomplishment as compared with other students, in spite of the fact that these same low-fitness students were above average in scholastic aptitude (Coefield and McCollum 1955; Page 1940).

7. Shaffer found that as intelligence increased, failures on the Kraus–Weber test decreased.

8. Popp compared boys of low physical fitness with boys of high physical fitness and noted that 8 of 20 in the low-fitness group failed to graduate from high school, whereas only 2 of 20 in the high-fitness group failed to graduate.

9. Clarke and Jarman found that subjects high in physical fitness measures had a consistent and significant tendency to have higher means on knowledge measures than subjects low in physical fitness measures. The groups were previously equated by intelligence scores.

10. Two studies indicated that physical fitness is an important factor in the improvement of mental tasks (Gutin 1966; Hart and Shay 1964).

BIBLIOGRAPHY

Barrow, H. M., and R. McGee, *A Practical Approach to Measurement in Physical Education*. Philadelphia: Lea & Febiger, 1964, p. 358.

Bloom, B. E., *Taxonomy of Educational Objectives: Handbook I: Cognitive Domain*. New York: McKay, 1956.

Bond, M. H., "Rhythmic Perception and Gross Motor Performance." *Research Quarterly* 30:259–265, October 1959.

Brace, D. K., "Some Objective Evidence of the Value of Physical Education." *Journal of Health and Physical Education* 4:36, April 1933.

———, "Studies in the Rate of Learning Gross Bodily Skills." *Research Quarterly* 12:181–185, May 1941.

———, "Motor Learning of Feeble-Minded Girls." *Research Quarterly* 19:269–275, December 1948.

Broer, M., "Effectiveness of a General Basic Skills Curriculum for Junior High School Girls." *Research Quarterly* 29:379–388, December 1958.

Burley, L., and R. L. Anderson, "Relation of Jump and Reach Measures of Power to Intelligence Scores and Athletic Performance." *Research Quarterly* 30:259–265, March 1959.

Clarke, H., and B. O. Jarman, "Scholastic Achievement of Boys 9, 12, and 15 Years of Age as Related to Various Strength and Growth Measures." *Research Quarterly* 32:155, May 1961.

Coefield, J. R., and R. H. McCollum, "A Case Study Report of Seventy-Eight University Freshmen Men With Low Physical Fitness Indices." Microcarded master's thesis, University of Oregon, Eugene, 1955.

Colville, F., "The Learning of Motor Skills as Influenced by a Knowledge of General Principles of Mechanics." Unpublished doctoral dissertation, University of Southern California, Los Angeles, 1956.

Distefano, M. K., et al., "Motor Proficiency in Mental Defectives." *Perceptual and Motor Skills* 8:231–234, 1958.

Fisher, R. B., "Tests in Selected Physical Education Service Courses in a College." Microcarded doctoral dissertation, State University of Iowa, Iowa City, 1950, p. 72.

Fox, K., "Beginning Badminton Written Examinations." *Research Quarterly* 24:135, May 1953.

French, E., "The Construction of Knowledge Tests in Selected Professional Courses in Physical Education." *Research Quarterly* 14:406–424, December 1943.

Gershon, E., "Apparatus Gymnastics Knowledge Test for College Men in Professional Physical Education." *Research Quarterly* 28:332, December 1957.

Goll, L. M., "Construction of Badminton and Swimming Knowledge Tests for High School Girls." Microcarded master's thesis, Illinois State University, Normal, 1956, p. 54.

Gutin, B., "Effect of Increase in Physical Fitness on Mental Ability Following Physical and Mental Stress." *Research Quarterly* 37:211, May 1966.

Hart, M. E., and C. T. Shay, "Relationship Between Physical Fitness and Academic Success." *Research Quarterly* 35:445, October 1964.

Hemphill, F., "Information Tests in Health and Physical Education for High School Boys." *Research Quarterly* 3:82, December 1932.

Hennis, G. M., "Construction of Knowledge Tests in Selected Physical Education Activities for College Women." *Research Quarterly* 27:301–309, October 1956. (Also see physical education microcards.)

Hewitt, J. E., "Hewitt's Comprehensive Tennis Knowledge Test—Form A and B Revised." *Research Quarterly* 35:147–155, May 1964.

Hills, J. R., *Measurement and Evaluation in the Classroom*. Columbus, Ohio: Charles E. Merrill, 1976, p. 55.

Hooks, E. W., Jr., "Hooks' Comprehensive Knowledge Test in Selected Physical Education Activities for College Men." *Research Quarterly* 37:506, December 1966.

Johnson, G. B., "Study of the Relationship That Exists Between Physical Skill as Measured, and the General Intelligence of College Students." *Research Quarterly* 13:57–59, March 1942.

Kuder, G. F., and M. W. Richardson, "The Theory of the Estimation of Test Reliability." *Psychometrika*, September 1937, pp. 151–160.

Langston, D. F., "Standardization of a Volleyball Knowledge Test for College Men Physical Education Majors." *Research Quarterly* 26:60–66, March 1955.

Ley, K. L., "Constructing Objective Test Items to Measure High School Levels of Achievement in Selected Physical Education Activities." Microcarded doctoral dissertation, University of Iowa, Iowa City, 1960, p. 25.

McMillan, B. J., "A Study to Determine the Relationship of Physical Fitness as Measured by the New York State Physical Fitness Test to the Academic Index of High School Girls." Unpublished master's thesis, Springfield College, Springfield, Mass., 1961.

Miller, W. K., "Achievement Levels in Tennis Knowledge and Skill for Women Physical Education Major Students." *Research Quarterly* 24:81–89, March 1953.

Mohr, D. R., and M. E. Barrett, "Effect of Knowledge of Mechanical Principles in Learning to Perform Intermediate Swimming Skills." *Research Quarterly* 33:574, December 1962.

Page, C. G., "Case Studies of College Men With Low Physical Fitness Indices." Unpublished master's thesis, Syracuse University, Syracuse, N.Y., 1940.

Popp, J., "Case Studies of Sophomore High School Boys With High and Low Physical Fitness Indices." Microcarded master's thesis, University of Oregon, Eugene, 1959.

Rarick, L. G., and R. McKee, "A Study of Twenty Third-Grade Children Exhibiting Extreme Levels of Achievement on Tests of Motor Efficiency." *Research Quarterly* 20:142, May 1949.

Report of the School Committee and Superintendent of Brookline, Massachusetts, December 31, 1941. Available from Brookline High School, Brookline, Mass.

Rogers, F. R., "The Scholarship of Athletes." Unpublished master's thesis, Stanford University, Stanford, Calif., 1922.

Ruger, H. A., "The Psychology of Efficiency." *Archives of Psychology* 2:85, 1910.

Scott, M. G., "Achievement Examinations for Elementary and Intermediate Tennis Classes." *Research Quarterly* 12:40–49, March 1941.

Shaffer, G., "Interrelationship of Intelligence Quotient to Failure on Kraus–Weber Test." *Research Quarterly* 30:75–86, March 1959.

Shick, J., "Written Tests in Activity Classes." *JOPERD* 52:21–22, April 1981.

Terman, L. M., Ed., "Genetic Studies of Genius." In *Mental and Physical Traits of a Thousand Gifted Children.* Stanford, Calif.: Stanford University Press, 1926.

Tuckman, B. W., *Conducting Educational Research.* 2nd ed. New York: Harcourt Brace Jovanovich, 1978, p. 178.

Weber, R. J., "Relationship of Physical Fitness to Success in College and to Personality." *Research Quarterly* 24:471–474, December 1953.

CHAPTER 22

THE MEASUREMENT OF POSTURE

OBJECTIVES

After reading this chapter, the student should be able to:

1. Describe the body segment points through which a plumb line should fall for "correct" alignment

2. Recognize the difference between static and dynamic postural assessment

3. Recognize the problems associated with posture evaluation

The evaluation of posture has been a problem for tests and measurements people for nearly a century. The problem has been attacked in a variety of ways, with use of rating charts, posture screens, photographs, silhouettes, plumb lines, aluminum pointers, angle irons, and adhesive tape. Unfortunately, even the most sophisticated techniques of photographic analysis with body landmarks, angles, and others have not met with a great deal of success. Primarily this failure is because posture experts cannot agree on what constitutes good posture. This is not meant as criticism, it merely points up the fundamental complexity of the problem: What is good posture?

We cannot presume to answer this question; we can only adopt a working concept on which to base our approach to measurement. It is generally recognized that posture involves mechanical considerations, such as the alignment of body segments, the strength and stress of the muscles and ligaments, and the effects of gravity on the body parts. It is also acknowledged that posture has an aesthetic component as well as being a reflection of the individual's total being, self-image, physical state, and self-concept in relation to the environment. Above all, it should be realized that posture, like all human characteristics, involves

not only differences among individuals but also differences within the individual. Posture is not just the ability of individuals to stand in one position in front of a plumb line while someone examines them from various angles. The evaluation of posture should include the appraisal of posture while the person is walking, running, climbing, descending, sitting, and standing. Moreover, the appraisal should be in accordance with the individual's skeletal architecture and body build (McCloy and Young 1954).

USES OF POSTURE TESTS

Primarily, posture tests are employed for either remedial work in an adaptive program or as a means of providing information and motivation for the student in a planned program of posture improvement. Adaptive work requires a specialist. In analyzing a student's posture, a tester must be able to identify abnormalities and determine whether improvements can be made by the strengthening and stretching of certain muscles. If the tester is not well prepared in this area, no objective tests will enable him or her to evaluate posture intelligently. If the tester is well qualified, it is doubtful that any objective measuring device will provide more information than do the eyes and hands (Smithells and Cameron 1962). However, the tester may well want to utilize objective devices as teaching aids in attempting to motivate the student to strive for improvement.

In selecting posture tests, the physical education teacher should be guided primarily by the needs of the program, personal preparation and competence, and of course the cost and administrative feasibility of the tests.

PROBLEMS ASSOCIATED WITH THE MEASUREMENT OF POSTURE

The problems and limitations of posture appraisal have been discussed at length in various meetings, in professional journals, and in books. While there is considerable disagreement about various aspects of posture measurement, there is consensus that posture is difficult to measure. Some of the problems of posture appraisal are listed here:

1. Probably the greatest problem is the inability of workers to establish standards of posture that will take into account individual differences.

2. Individuals tend to assume an unnatural pose when they know they are being tested for posture.

3. Problems are sometimes encountered in retesting and scoring because of the difficulty subjects have in standing in exactly the same pose as before.

4. In terms of administration and analysis, the techniques for posture appraisal are generally quite time consuming, and some of the devices are expensive.

5. The use of photographs and silhouettes has in the past required considerable skill in areas such as lighting and lens adjustment in order to obtain clear and well-defined pictures. Recent advances in photographic equipment, however, such as development of Polaroid cameras and of equipment with automatic adjustments, have alleviated this problem considerably.

6. The subjective ratings of posture have generally been criticized for low reliability and objectivity.

7. Because of the many variables involved in posture, doubts have often been expressed concerning the accuracy of its measure. Even more basic are the questions raised as to the real significance of the measures once they are obtained.

Despite the many problems associated with posture appraisal, a skilled and imaginative teacher can do much to help students become conscious of posture and strive for improvement. To conclude that posture work is a waste of time because of the problems of measurement is just as indefensible as concluding that social adjustment is not important because it too does not lend itself readily to measurement.

The evidence, while contradictory, does tend to indicate that posture is related to certain physiologic and emotional factors that make up the general health status of the individual. Clarke (1967) suggested that perhaps many of the contradictory findings in the literature could be due to lack of precision of the measuring instruments. Nevertheless, even if there were no relationship whatsoever between posture and physical health, a posture improvement program could well be justified for aesthetic purposes alone. Physical education has the same basic goals as general education, and the program should thus be based on the needs of students. Not everyone can have the physique of a superb athlete or the looks of a glamorous movie star. Everyone does, however, have the opportunity and perhaps even the obligation to do the best with what he or she has. Physical education should profit from the subtle teachings of movies and television concerning the importance of posture and graceful carriage for good appearance.

Perhaps herein lies the key to the rather difficult task of fostering posture consciousness. For some students, it may be effective to simply lead them to the realization that frequently persons who seem very attractive are actually quite plain— their grace, poise, and beauty of movement completely overshadow any flaws in face or form. For other students, a more direct and personal approach is needed. One of the most powerful and effective motivating techniques is the use of video replay. In most cases the student has no idea what he or she looks like while moving.

A modified version of *candid camera* was employed in a high school health class. Motion pictures were taken secretly of each class member and then shown during class for analysis and discussion of posture. In each instance the student was unaware of the picture taking. Some of the pictures were obtained away from the school grounds. There was a great deal of interest in the project. No appreciable expense was involved, as the camera was borrowed and the class members each contributed a small amount for film. While the project brought about no drastic changes, it was very effective in calling attention to posture, and students derived considerable value from the discussions. As a result of the unit, three class members began exercise programs in an attempt at reeducation of posture habits, and two individuals began dieting.

The elementary grades are undoubtedly the most important in terms of being able to identify and then help to remedy faulty posture. This is where concentrated efforts should be made to install posture screening programs. Well-planned motivational devices should be employed to create favorable attitudes toward good posture and body mechanics, rather than the teacher relying on the typical nagging admonition to sit up straight.

In conclusion, the ratings and objective measuring devices used for posture evaluation have not met with a great deal of success insofar as being generally accepted by the profession. Posture and body mechanics are, however, important facets of physical education. Until better measuring tools are developed, the logical approach would seem to be to begin planned posture screening and improvement programs early in the elementary grades and to strive to diagnose and evaluate posture in relation to each individual's structure and capacity for improvement.

MEASURES OF POSTURE (RATING SCALES)

Iowa Posture Test[1]

This test is recommended for use in classes. Groups of ten students can be rated at a time. The posture ratings are subjective, but the examiner has specific criteria on which to evaluate the elements in posture during standing, walking, running, sitting, and stair climbing. This test represents a practical approach to the problem of assessing posture when the individual is moving and performing daily activities rather than just standing in a fixed position.

---

1. Mimeographed form published by the Department of Physical Education for Women, University of Iowa, Iowa City. The test and scoring charts are also presented in M. G. Scott and E. French, *Measurement and Evaluation in Physical Education*. Dubuque, Iowa: William C. Brown, 1959.

Validity and Reliability: No coefficients are given, although Moriarity and Irwin reported a reliability coefficient of .965 using dual but independent ratings.

Test Equipment and Floor Space: Ten chairs arranged in a row about 2 ft apart and open floor space so students can walk ten or more steps away from the chair. Stairs may be constructed or real ones used. The stairs should be sufficiently wide to accommodate two students at a time. The subjects should be dressed in swimsuits or leotards and should also be barefoot.

Foot Mechanics Test

Directions: Students take turns walking approximately ten steps forward and then back to their chair. The examiner stands at the side and rates each subject on heel contact, weight transfer, and toe drive.

The examiner then stands in front of each subject, who walks first toward the examiner and then away as the examiner assesses foot alignment and the absence or presence of pronation.

Scoring: The suggested 3-point scoring scale is based on ratings of good, fair, and poor, which are given point values of 3, 2, and 1, respectively. More specific criteria for making each rating are presented here, as provided by McCloy and Young.

Criteria for Scoring Foot Mechanics Test

1. Heel-toe walking
   a. Heel contacts ground first
   b. Weight transferred through outside of foot and then diagonally across to ball of foot
   c. Toes used in gripping action
   d. Walk has spring in it
2. Absence of pronation
   a. No bony bulge in front of and below medial malleolus
   b. No noted inward protrusion of navicular
   c. Heel cord not noticeably turned outward
   Scoring: No pronation = 3, some pronation = 2, marked pronation = 1.
3. Feet parallel
   a. Slight angle of toeing out (considered good)
   b. Some degree of toeing in (permissible but unattractive)
   Scoring: Normal = 3, moderate toeing out = 2, marked toeing out = 1.

Standing Position Test

Directions: Subjects stand with their left side toward the front of their chair. The tester, viewing from the side, rates the alignment of the body segments and the weight distribution.

Criteria for Scoring Correct Alignment of Body Segments

1. Axis approximating straight line runs through head, neck, trunk, and legs

2. Head and neck erect (although there may be some slight forward inclination)

3. Chest high, abdomen flat

4. Slight roundness of upper back and slight hollow of lower back (i.e., normal curves)

5. Overall impression of ease and balance
   Scoring: Good alignment = 3, slight general deviation = 2, marked general deviation = 1.

Walking Test

Directions: Subjects walk around the row of ten chairs, keeping 5 or 6 ft from one another. The tester stands to the side and checks for body alignment, weight distribution, stiffness, and unnecessary movements while walking.

Criteria for Scoring Walking Test

1. Alignment of body segments while walking (rating is the same as for standing)
   Scoring: Same as for walking—3, 2, and 1.

2. Weight distribution (weight should be carried farther forward than in standing position, but only slightly. No forward or backward deviations from perpendicular)
   Scoring: Good weight distribution = 3, some deviation = 2, marked deviation = 1.

Sitting Test

Directions: The examiner stands at the side and rates each subject in the sitting position. The subject then is instructed to lean forward about 30 degrees and is rated in this position. After this rating the subject rises and walks forward a few steps. Body mechanics and carriage while rising from a sitting position are assessed during this movement. If desired, the tester could rate the subject's performance in sitting down as well.

Criteria for Scoring Sitting Test

1. Sitting position
   a. Upper trunk balanced over pelvis

   b. Head erect, chest high, shoulders back (but not stiff)
   c. Abdomen controlled and normal upper back curve
   d. Hips well back, and back of chair utilized for support
   Scoring: Correct position = 3, some deviation = 2, marked deviation = 1.

2. Rising from sitting position
   a. One foot slightly under chair, other foot slightly in advance, trunk inclined from hips, and arms relaxed
   b. Hips well under body during rising, with no appreciable bending of back or dropping of head
   c. Movement smooth and graceful with no stiffness
   Scoring: Good = 3, fair = 2, poor = 1.

Stooping to Pick Up Light Object Test

Directions: A small object is placed on the floor a few feet in front of the subject. The subject is instructed to walk to the object, pick it up, and then return it to the floor. The examiner views the subject from the side.

Criteria for Scoring Picking Up Light Object Test

1. Subject bends mainly at knees with slight bend from hips

2. Feet and hips well under body with one foot slightly ahead of other

3. Trunk forms relatively straight line, but arms are relaxed and back controlled, so appearance is not stiff

4. Object picked up (and replaced) slightly ahead of foot (movement should be smooth with good balance maintained throughout)
   Scoring: Good = 3, fair = 2, poor = 1.

Ascending and Descending Stairs Test

Directions: Each subject ascends and descends eight or ten stairs. The examiner stands at the side and rates the subject's carriage separately for ascending and descending.

Criteria for Scoring Ascending and Descending Stairs Test

1. Ascending
   a. Weight only slightly forward and bend from ankles not hips

b. Push-up from ankles and knees with no swinging of hips
Scoring: Good = 3, fair = 2, poor = 1.

2. Descending
   a. Weight lowered in a controlled manner (not a relaxed drop)
   b. Movement smooth with no bobbing
   Scoring: Good = 3, fair = 2, poor = 1.

Additional Pointers:

1. If desired, the physical educator could include running, picking up and carrying heavy objects, jumping, and other movements.

2. The desired mechanics for each test may be explained or not, depending on whether the teacher wishes to evaluate students' normal behavior or their performance after instruction.

3. The teacher may also wish to devise a system in which each subject is evaluated covertly, as, for example, while another student is performing or during a pause between tests.

New York State Posture Rating Test (New York State Physical Fitness Test 1966)

Posture evaluation is included in the New York State Physical Fitness Test. This assessment involves 13 areas of the body. The rating chart (Figure 22.1) shows three profiles: the correct position (5 points), a slight deviation (3 points), and a pronounced deviation (1 point) from the correct position for each of the 13 areas. The examiner rates each area on a 5-3-1 basis, and the total point value is the student's score. A perfect score is 65.

The testing area consists of a plumb line suspended over a line on which the subject stands, which is 3 ft in front of a screen. Another line is drawn at a right angle to the first line and extends 10 ft farther back from the screen (a total of 13 ft). The examiner is positioned here to view the subject against the screen.

The subject is rated from two viewpoints. In one position the subject stands facing the screen, so that the plumb line bisects the back of the head, runs down the spine, and passes down between the legs and feet. Lateral deviations are assessed from this position.

The subject then turns to the left and stands sideward so that the plumb line passes in a line through the ear, shoulder, hip, knee, and ankle. The left lateral malleolus must be in line with the plumb bob. Anteroposterior posture is rated from this position.

The student's cumulative posture ratings from grades 4 through 12 are contained on the one chart. Reliability coefficients ranging from .93 to .98 are reported for students at different grade levels. Norms for the ratings have been established for boys and girls from grades 4 through 12, as shown in Table 22.1.

Theoretically, regular assessment of posture as an integral part of a student's overall fitness should do much to make students and teachers posture conscious. It could also make a significant contribution toward health appraisal in general and to meeting individual needs by special programs and medical referrals.

OBJECTIVE POSTURE TESTS AND INSTRUMENTS

Brief mention is made here of some of the objective tests and instruments that have been devised in the attempt to analyze and evaluate posture. Readers who desire more information and detailed descriptions of the tests are referred to the original sources. Considerable effort was expended during the 1930s and 1940s to develop objective devices. Since then there has not been a great deal of work done in the way of invention.

Cureton-Gunby Conformateur (Cureton, Wickens, and Elder 1935)

Cureton was an early leader in the attempt to develop objective, reliable instruments for measuring anteroposterior spinal curvature. Dissatisfied with the errors of exaggeration in use of silhouettes, Cureton and Gunby devised the conformateur. In this instrument, metal rods slide through holes placed in an upright. The subject stands with the back toward the upright and the metal rods are pushed through the holes so that they make contact with the subject from the head down the entire length of the spine (Figure 22.2). The rods are locked in place, thus presenting an outline of the spinal curvature. Cureton recommended that the device be used in conjunction with silhouettographs to facilitate interpretation and allow for a personal record for student motivation.

Figure 22.1. New York State Posture Rating Chart (Courtesy of the New York State Education Department)

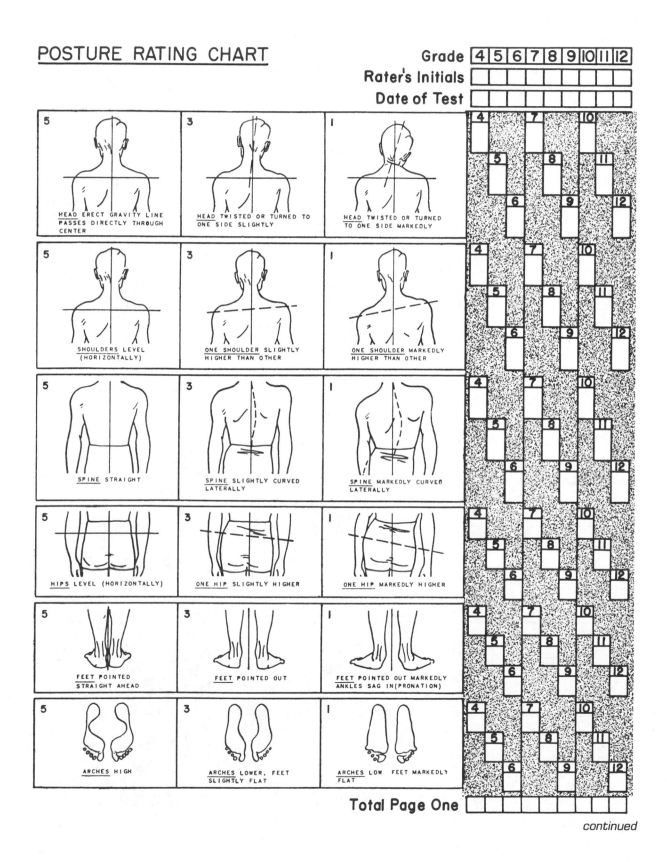

continued

Figure 22.1 (continued)

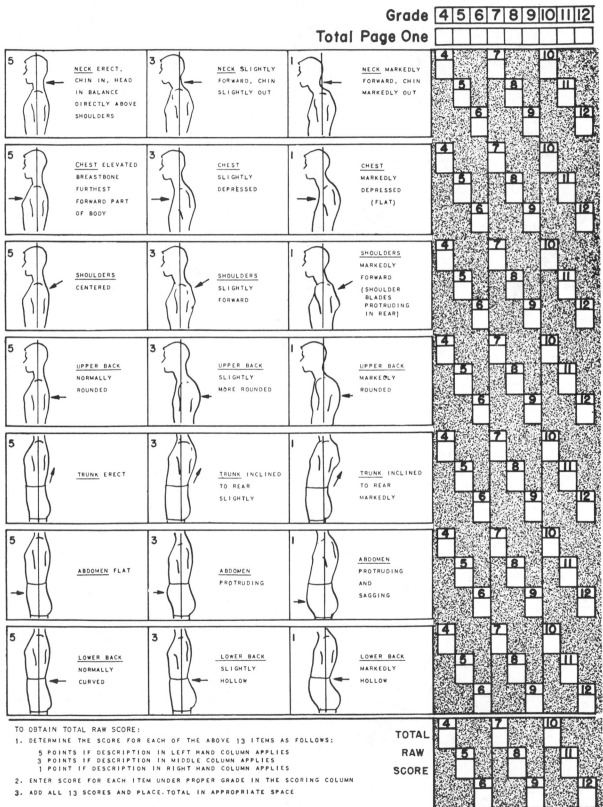

Grade 4 5 6 7 8 9 10 11 12

Total Page One

NECK ERECT, CHIN IN, HEAD IN BALANCE DIRECTLY ABOVE SHOULDERS

NECK SLIGHTLY FORWARD, CHIN SLIGHTLY OUT

NECK MARKEDLY FORWARD, CHIN MARKEDLY OUT

CHEST ELEVATED BREASTBONE FURTHEST FORWARD PART OF BODY

CHEST SLIGHTLY DEPRESSED

CHEST MARKEDLY DEPRESSED (FLAT)

SHOULDERS CENTERED

SHOULDERS SLIGHTLY FORWARD

SHOULDERS MARKEDLY FORWARD (SHOULDER BLADES PROTRUDING IN REAR)

UPPER BACK NORMALLY ROUNDED

UPPER BACK SLIGHTLY MORE ROUNDED

UPPER BACK MARKEDLY ROUNDED

TRUNK ERECT

TRUNK INCLINED TO REAR SLIGHTLY

TRUNK INCLINED TO REAR MARKEDLY

ABDOMEN FLAT

ABDOMEN PROTRUDING

ABDOMEN PROTRUDING AND SAGGING

LOWER BACK NORMALLY CURVED

LOWER BACK SLIGHTLY HOLLOW

LOWER BACK MARKEDLY HOLLOW

TO OBTAIN TOTAL RAW SCORE:

1. DETERMINE THE SCORE FOR EACH OF THE ABOVE 13 ITEMS AS FOLLOWS:

     5 POINTS IF DESCRIPTION IN LEFT HAND COLUMN APPLIES
     3 POINTS IF DESCRIPTION IN MIDDLE COLUMN APPLIES
     1 POINT IF DESCRIPTION IN RIGHT HAND COLUMN APPLIES

2. ENTER SCORE FOR EACH ITEM UNDER PROPER GRADE IN THE SCORING COLUMN

3. ADD ALL 13 SCORES AND PLACE TOTAL IN APPROPRIATE SPACE

TOTAL RAW SCORE

Table 22.1. Norms for New York State Posture Rating Test for Students in Grades 4 Through 12

PERCENTILE RANK	ACHIEVEMENT LEVEL	POSTURE SCORE[a]
99	10	65
98	9	65
93	8	63
84	7	61
69	6	59
50	5	57
31	4	53-55
16	3	49-51
7	2	43-47
2	1	39-41
1	0	13-37

[a]See text for description of test and scoring.

Source: *New York State Physical Fitness Test for Boys and Girls Grades 4-12.* Albany: New York State Education Department, 1966. Reprinted by permission.

Woodruff Body Alignment Posture Test[1]

An inexpensive device for measuring body alignment was developed by Woodruff at the University of Oregon. With the use of a wooden frame (Figure 22.3) containing nine strings running lengthwise ¾ in. apart, an objective score can be obtained of deviations in the alignment of body segments. The inventor believed this test represented a more reliable means of assessing body alignment than subjective ratings, and at the same time was less time consuming and less expensive than most of the objective devices.

Directions: The subject stands between the wall and the frame. The subject's left side is toward the frame, and the left foot is placed at the 1½-in. line that is marked on the floor. The tester then directs the subject to adjust the foot position until the baseline is directly under the instep. The tester stands 10 ft from the frame and, looking through the strings, aligns the center string with the 1-in. line drawn on the wall. The subject is instructed to stand in a *normal* position.

Scoring: This test is basically a plumb line test. The tester starts at the alignment of the ankle and the center string and proceeds upward, scoring each body segment's deviation from the one below it (not from the center line). In other words, the prescribed points at the ankle, knee, hip, shoulder, and ear are scored in terms of the number of strings they deviate in either direction from the

segment below. A perfect score is 25, and 1 point is subtracted for each deviation.

There are no published norms for this test, although Clarke (1967) reported a mean of 20 and a range of 16 to 25 for college women.

Spinograph (Cureton, Wickens, and Elder 1935)

This instrument utilizes a pointer that traces the student's spine and records the contour of the spine on a blackboard or poster board (Figure 22.4).

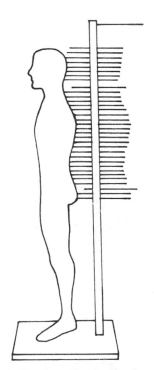

Figure 22.2. Cureton-Gunby Conformateur

---

1. Janet Woodruff, School of Health, Physical Education, and Recreation, University of Oregon, Eugene. Described in H. H. Clarke, *Application of Measurement to Health and Physical Education.* 4th ed. Englewood Cliffs, N.J.: Prentice-Hall, 1967, pp. 123-124.

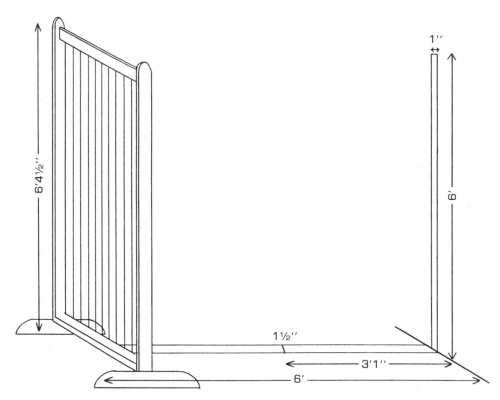

Figure 22.3. Wooden frame and markings used in Woodruff body alignment posture test

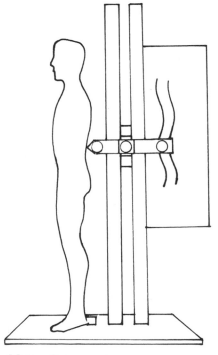

Figure 22.4. Spinograph

Wellesley Posture Test (MacEwan and Howe 1932)

With use of aluminum markers taped on the subject's sternum and spine, a method of objec-

tive measurements from photographs was developed by MacEwan and Howe. The pointers were attached at the lower end of the sternum and on the spinous process of the seventh cervical and every other vertebra down to the sacrum. After photographing the subject, the tester could draw the actual position of the spine and the chest on the photograph from knowing the actual length of the pointers. In this way, certain body parts such as the arms, breasts, back muscles, and projecting scapulae would not mask the true spinal curvature, which had heretofore been a noted weakness of silhouettes and photographs. Three measurements were taken and weighted to make up the posture grade of each subject.

Wickens and Kiphuth Posture Test (Wickens and Kiphuth 1937)

Wickens and Kiphuth developed a test by which the anteroposterior curvature of the spine could be measured objectively from photographs by use of aluminum pointers and flesh pencil markings. Markings are made on the points of the body through which the plumb line should pass with a black flesh pencil, and five pointers capture the true spinal curvature and chest position. After tiny holes are made in the picture at the sites of the pointer attachments, at the flesh pencil markings, and at the most protuberant part of the abdomen, the picture is placed facedown on an illuminated mimeoscope. Measurements are drawn on the back of the picture.

With use of a venier caliper and protractor, the position of the head and neck, the amount of kyphosis and lordosis, and the positions of the chest, abdomen, shoulders, trunk, hips, and knees are measured and evaluated.

Massey Posture Test (Massey 1943)

Massey developed a technique of assessing posture from silhouettes by means of the following angles: (1) angle of the head and neck with the trunk, (2) trunk with the hips, (3) hips with the thighs, and (4) thighs with the legs. The angles are in degrees away from a straight line. The sum of the angles is converted to a letter grade.

Howland Alignometer (Howland 1953)

The alignometer, designed by Howland, consists of two sliding pointers that are calibrated and attached to a vertical rod (Figure 22.5). These pointers are adjusted so as to fix the position of the center of the sternum and the superior border of the symphysis pubis. Howland determined from research that the structural balance of the trunk approximates the line of gravity when the upper trunk and tilt of the pelvis are in vertical alignment. Disalignment is noted on the alignometer by the difference in the readings of the two calibrated pointers. If the subject's alignment is balanced, the difference in readings will be zero.

Symmetrigraf

The Symmetrigraf Posture Chart (Figure 22.6) is used for fast screening of front and side views. If the posture of the subject is within normal range, no further analysis is necessary.

Skan-a-Graf

This instrument is used to record individualized posture measurements for future comparison to detect remedial progress, if any. It provides visual screening with the aid of an angle sight (Figure 22.7).

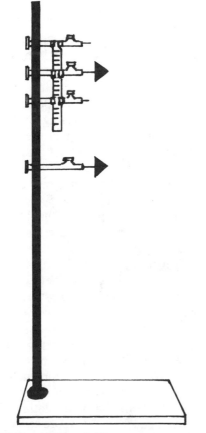

Figure 22.5. Howland Alignometer

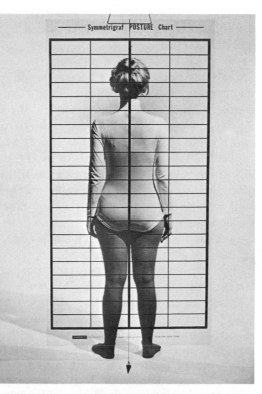

Figure 22.6. Symmetrigraf Posture Chart (Courtesy of Reedco, Inc., Auburn, New York)

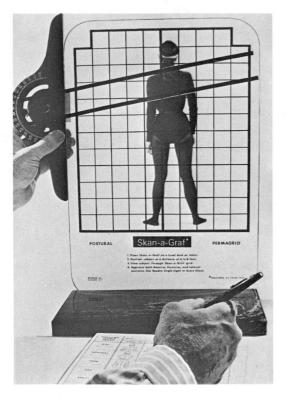

Figure 22.7.   Skan-a-Graf (Courtesy of Reedco, Inc., Auburn, New York)

FINDINGS AND CONCLUSIONS FROM POSTURE MEASUREMENT AND RESEARCH

Relatively little research has been reported in the area of posture in the United States for a decade or more. Clarke (1979) mentioned that there were six posture articles in the *Research Quarterly* in the 1950s, five articles in the 1960s, and none in the 1970s—compared with over 30 articles during 1930 to 1939. Most research in the area of posture today deals with neurophysiologic functions such as postural sway, postural hand tremors, and postural reflexes.

Although the number of research studies dealing with posture in the school setting has dropped drastically, apparently the need for posture improvement among boys and girls has not lessened. Specific exercise programs designed to improve posture have met with some success, particularly with young children. Ashe found that a posture awareness program resulted in significant improvement in static standing posture of emotionally disturbed children. Minotti reported that a 3-month exercise program specifically designed to correct postural deviations was effec-

tive in improving anteroposterior posture of third and fourth grade children. Lateral postural deviations were not improved. The effects of an exercise program on minimal idiopathic scoliosis in adolescents were assessed by Stone and associates. Although over 20% of the patients showed a decrease in scoliosis, there was no significant difference in change in curvature between the exercise group and a matched control group.

In an early study, Maple reported some observations concerning the influence of chronologic age on certain postural characteristics. Among her conclusions were that the head is not held completely erect until the age of 6 or 7; that the scapulae do not lie flat until after 10 years of age; that the sacral angle increases markedly from age 3 to 6 or 7; and that the infant is more erect than the child. In another early study, Korb found the comparograph, in which an outline of good posture was placed on the subject's picture, to be a valid, reliable, and inexpensive method for grading posture. Cureton, Wickens, and Elder in 1935 concluded that objective measurement was more precise than subjective methods.

Flint found no significant correlation between lordosis and strength of the abdominal muscles or the back extensor muscles, or between lordosis and hip or hip–trunk flexibility. The position of the center of gravity was not found to be affected by lordosis or pelvic inclinations. Flint and Diehl had previously found trunk-strength balance, abdominal strength, and back-extensor strength all significantly related to anteroposterior alignment. Hutchins found supporting evidence for these findings and concluded that the balance of strength between trunk–flexor and trunk–extensor muscles and other muscle groups is an important factor in anteroposterior alignment. She further reported that her study provided evidence in support of posture-training methods that involve specific strength and flexibility exercises. Anderson found that over 90% of the high school students in her study had posture deviations. She concluded that photography could be effectively used in posture education and that posture education resulted in improvement in posture.

Coppock reported that tightness of the pectoral muscles did not correlate significantly with round shoulders. Fox concluded that faulty pelvic tilt was not associated with any appreciable weakness in the abdominal muscles, nor was swayback related to weak abdominal musculature. She did report that dysmenorrhea was more severe among women having swayback than among a control group. Swim observed a definite pattern of body sway in females in different age groups from 3 to 22 years of age. Haynes found that body sway during 1 min of erect standing had little influence on postural alignment.

DiGiovanna, in an early investigation, studied the relationship of athletic achievement and posture. The results, although not statistically treated, indicated a fairly definite relationship between the two variables. Davies, however, found little or no relationship between motor ability and judges' ratings of postural divergencies. More recently, Miller correlated posture evaluation scores with motor performance achievement in fifth and sixth grade boys. The only significant correlation was between posture and agility performance.

Several individuals have studied the gravitational line of the body and have recommended specific points on the different segments of the body along which a plumb line should fall. Basically, the line passes through the lobe of the ear, the tip of the shoulder, and the great trochanter of the hip, behind the knee cap, and in front of the external malleolus. There has been some disagreement concerning the exact location of these body sites. For example, Phelps, Kiphuth, and Goff objected to the criterion that the mastoid bone be in line with the acromion process because of individual variations in the mobility of the shoulders. Minor differences have also been noted with regard to the point at which the gravitational line passes through the ankle. Fox and Young concluded that the line of gravity lay anterior to the center of the ankle joint and near enough to the anterior border of the tibia to be considered in line with it.

Various investigators have attempted to relate posture to health and to certain physiologic and emotional characteristics. In 1931, Alden and Top found no relationship between posture and the factors of weight, vital capacity, and intelligence. Cyriax stated that poor dorsocervical posture, which induces cardiac impairment, may cause sudden heart failure, angina, and functional heart troubles. Moriarity and Irwin reported a significant relationship between poor posture and certain physical and emotional factors, including self-consciousness, fidgeting, restlessness, timidity, fatigue, underweight, disease, heart defects, hearing problems, and asthma.

Clarke (1967) observed that in earlier days, many extravagant claims were made regarding the values of good posture, and yet evidence has not supported such claims. Clarke suggested that maybe cause and effect may have been confused, in that poor posture and various ills may be due to a third factor: poor physical fitness from sedentary living.

BIBLIOGRAPHY

Alden, F. D., and H. Top, "Experiment on the Relation of Posture to Weight, Vital Capacity and Intelligence." *Research Quarterly* 2:38–41, October 1931.

Anderson, M. K., "An Investigation of the Need for Posture Education Among High School Girls and a Suggested Plan for Instruction to Meet These Needs." Unpublished master's thesis, University of Texas, Austin, 1966.

Ashe, C. L., "Effects of a Posture Awareness Program on the Static Standing Posture of Emotionally Disturbed Children." Unpublished master's thesis, University of Wisconsin, LaCrosse, 1977.

Clarke, H. H., *Application of Measurement to Health and Physical Education.* 4th ed. Englewood Cliffs, N.J.: Prentice-Hall, 1967, p. 79.

———, ed., "Posture." *Physical Fitness Research Digest.* Series 9, January 1979.

Coppock, D. E., "Relationship of Tightness of Pectoral Muscles to Round Shoulders in College Women." *Research Quarterly* 29:146–153, May 1958.

Cureton, T., J. S. Wickens, and H. P. Elder, "Reliability and Objectivity of Springfield Postural Measurements." *Research Quarterly Supplement* 6:81–92, May 1935.

Cyriax, E., "The Relation of Dorso-Cervical Postural Deficiencies to Cardiac Disease, Especially From Middle Life Onwards." *Research Quarterly* 7:74–79, December 1936.

Davies, E. A., "Relationship Between Selected Postural Divergencies and Motor Abilities." *Research Quarterly* 28:1–4, March 1957.

DiGiovanna, V. G., "A Study of the Relation of Athletic Skills and Strengths to Those of Posture." *Research Quarterly* 2:67–79, May 1931.

Flint, M. M., "Lumbar Posture: A Study of Roentgenographic Measurement and the Influence of Flexibility and Strength." *Research Quarterly* 34:15–20, March 1963.

———, and B. Diehl, "Influence of Abdominal Strength, Back Extensor Strength and Trunk Strength Balance Upon Antero-Posterior Alignment of Elementary School Girls." *Research Quarterly* 32:490–498, December 1961.

Fox, M. G., "Relationship of Abdominal Strength to Selected Posture Faults." *Research Quarterly* 22:141–144, May 1951.

————, and O. G. Young, "Placement of the Gravital Line in Antero-Posterior Standing Posture." *Research Quarterly* 25:277–285, October 1954.

Haynes, B. A., "Postural Sway and Antero-Posterior Alignment During One Minute Erect Standing." Unpublished master's thesis, Michigan State University, East Lansing, 1966.

Howland, I. S., *Body Alignment in Fundamental Motor Skills*. New York: Exposition Press, 1953, p. 78.

Hutchins, G. L., "The Relationship of Selected Strength and Flexibility Variables to the Antero-Posterior Posture of College Women." *Research Quarterly* 36:253–269, October 1965.

Korb, E. M., "A Method to Increase the Validity of Measuring Posture." *Research Quarterly* 10:142–149, March 1939.

MacEwan, C. G., and E. C. Howe, "An Objective Method of Grading Posture." *Research Quarterly* 3:144–147, October 1932.

Malina, R. M., and F. E. Johnston, "Significance of Age, Sex, and Maturity Differences in Upper Arm Composition." *Research Quarterly* 38:219–230, May 1967.

Maple, K. N., "Chronological Variations in the Posture of Children Ages One to Seven and Ten to Thirteen." *Research Quarterly* 1:30–33, March 1930.

Martin, B., et al., "Effects of Whole-Body Vibrations on Standing Posture in Man." *Aviation, Space, and Environmental Medicine* 51:778–787, August 1980.

Massey, W. W., "A Critical Study of Objective Methods of Measuring Antero-Posterior Posture With a Simplified Technique." *Research Quarterly* 14:3–10, March 1943.

McCloy, C. H., and N. D. Young, *Tests and Measurements in Health and Physical Education*. 3rd ed. New York: Appleton-Century-Crofts, 1954, Chapter 21.

Miller, C., "A Comparison Between Postural Divergencies and Motor Achievement in Selected Motor Skills of Fifth and Sixth Grade Boys." Unpublished master's thesis, Western Illinois University, Macomb, 1977.

Minotti, L. A., "Effects of an Exercise Program on Posture Improvement." Unpublished master's thesis, Springfield College, Springfield, Mass., 1978.

Moriarity, M. J., and L. W. Irwin, "A Study of the Relationships of Certain Physical and Emotional Factors to Habitual Poor Posture Among School Children." *Research Quarterly* 23:221–225, May 1952.

New York State Physical Fitness Test for Boys and Girls Grades 4-12. Albany: New York State Education Department, 1966.

Phelps, W. W., R. J. H. Kiphuth, and C. W. Goff, *The Diagnosis and Treatment of Postural Defects*. 2nd ed. Springfield, Ill.: Charles C. Thomas, 1956, pp. 118–138.

Scott, M. G., and E. French, *Measurement and Evaluation in Physical Education*. Dubuque, Iowa: William C. Brown, 1959, pp. 414–421.

Smithells, P. A., and P. E. Cameron, *Principles of Evaluation in Physical Education*. New York: Harper, 1962, pp. 334–340.

Stone, B. S., et al., "The Effect of an Exercise Program on Change in Curve in Adolescents with Minimal Idiopathic Scoliosis: A Preliminary Study." *Physical Therapy* 59:759–763, June 1979.

Swim, C. L., "A Comparative Study of Body Sway in the Antero-Posterior Plane With Reference to the External Malleolus in Females Ages 3 Through 22. Unpublished master's thesis, University of North Carolina, Chapel Hill, 1965.

Wickens, J. S., and O. W. Kiphuth, "Body Mechanics Analysis of Yale University Freshmen." *Research Quarterly* 8:38–44, December 1937.

APPENDIX A

HEIGHT-WEIGHT TABLES

Table A.1. Average Height and Weight of Elementary and Junior High School Children

AGE (yr)	HEIGHT (in.)	WEIGHT (lb)
Boys, 5	42–46	38– 48
Girls, 5	42–46	36– 48
Boys, 6	44–48	41– 54
Girls, 6	44–48	40– 53
Boys, 7	46–50	45– 60
Girls, 7	46–50	44– 59
Boys, 8	48–53	50– 67
Girls, 8	48–52	48– 66
Boys, 9	50–55	55– 74
Girls, 9	50–54	52– 74
Boys, 10	52–57	59– 82
Girls, 10	52–57	57– 83
Boys, 11	54–59	64– 91
Girls, 11	54–59	63– 94
Boys, 12	55–61	70–101
Girls, 12	56–62	72–107

Source: Modified from American Medical Association, 535 N. Dearborn St., Chicago, IL 60610.

Table A.2. Average Height and Weight of Secondary School Students

AGE (yr)	HEIGHT (in.)	WEIGHT (lb)
Boys, 13	59–63	90–115
Girls, 13	60–64	95–115
Boys, 14	62–66	105–127
Girls, 14	62–64	105–125
Boys, 15	64–68	115–140
Girls, 15	63–65	112–130
Boys, 16	66–69	125–150
Girls, 16	63–65	117–135
Boys, 17	67–70	132–157
Girls, 17	63–65.5	118–137
Boys, 18	67–70	137–160
Girls, 18	63–65.5	120–138

Source: Modified from American Medical Association, 535 N. Dearborn St., Chicago, IL 60610.

STEPS FOR COMPUTING SQUARE ROOT

The easiest method of finding square root is to use a computer or pocket calculator. If one does not have access to these, tables are available in any school from the mathematics or science teachers or school library. Sometimes the teacher needs to be able to compute square root by hand. The following method is often taught in schools.

Problem: Find the square root of 698.4

$$\sqrt{698.4}$$

Step 1: Separate the number into two-digit units in each direction from the decimal. (Here we add zero in front of the 6 merely to demonstrate the fact that one moves to the right *and* to the left from the decimal point.)

$$\sqrt{06'98'.40'}$$

Step 2: Determine the largest number that will square itself into the first pair of digits, 06. the largest square in 06 is 2×2, or 4. Therefore, place 2 as the first digit of the square root. Then subtract 4 from 6 and bring down the next pair of digits, 98.

$$\begin{array}{r} 2 \\ \sqrt{6'98'.40'} \\ 4 \\ \hline 298 \end{array}$$

Step 3: Double the partial square root, 2, and place the sum, 4, to the left of 298:

$$\begin{array}{r} 2 \\ \overline{6'98'.40'} \\ 4 \\ \hline 4 298 \end{array}$$

Determine the next digit of the square root by dividing 298 by 10 × 4, or 40:298/40 = 6. Now place the 6 as the next digit of the square root and also add the number 6 to the 4 to make the divisor 46. Then multiply 46 by 6, subtract the product from 298, and bring down the next pair of digits. The remainder is now 2240.

$$\begin{array}{r} 2 6 . \\ \sqrt{6'98'.40'} \\ 4 \\ \hline 46 298 \\ 276 \\ \hline 2240 \end{array}$$

Step 4: Double the partial square root, 26, and place the sum, 52, to the left of 2240:

$$\begin{array}{r} 2 6 . \\ \sqrt{6'98'.40'} \\ 4 \\ \hline 46 298 \\ 276 \\ \hline 52 2240 \end{array}$$

The third digit is now determined by multiplying 52 × 10 and dividing the resulting product, 520, into 2240, which equals 4. Place 4 to the right of the decimal as the third digit in the square root and also place 4 to the right of 52 to form the divisor 524. Multiply 524 by 4 and subtract the product, 2096, from 2240. Bring down the next pair of zeros to form the remainder of 14,400.

```
        2   6.4
      √6'98'.40'00'
          4
   46  298
       276
  524   2240
       2096
       14400
```

This process may be continued as long as desired. The square root of this number carried to two more places is:

```
        2   6 . 4   2   7
      √6'98'.40'00'00'
          4
   46   298
        276
  524    2240
         2096
 5282    14400
         10564
52847    383600
         369929
         13671
```

THE MEASUREMENT OF KINESTHETIC PERCEPTION

Kinesthetic perception, the ability to perceive the position, effort, and movement of parts of the body or of the entire body during muscular action, is sometimes referred to as the sixth sense. In reality, we have more than just six senses; in fact, kinesthetic sense could be considered several senses within itself. The term *proprioceptive sense* is also used to refer to this sense. The sources of proprioceptive or kinesthetic perception are presumably located in the joints, muscles, and tendons.

Physical educators have long recognized the importance of kinesthesis. Steinhaus declared that our muscles see more than our eyes. Individuals who can observe a demonstration and perceive the significance of the sequence of movements are able to develop a physical empathy, which enables them to learn a movement much faster than others whose kinesthetic ability is not as highly developed. Kinesthetic perception can be improved through practice. Physical educators and coaches constantly urge performers to be aware of the "feel" of the correct movement, the amount of effort or force involved, and the position of the body part, racket, club, or other piece of equipment at various points in the movement.

USES OF KINESTHETIC PERCEPTION TESTS

Some of the ways physical educators might use tests of kinesthetic perception are as follows:

1. As a form of practice in establishing the feel of certain movements
2. As a means of diagnosis and interpretation
3. As a method of providing students with experiences in using this sensory modality by itself and in combination with other sensory modalities
4. As variables in demonstrating or exploring the specificity or generality or both of kinesthesis in research projects

TESTS OF KINESTHETIC PERCEPTION

Distance Perception Jump (Scott 1955)

Objective: To measure the ability to perceive distance by concentrating on the effort involved in a jump.

Age Level: Preschool and older. The distance of the jump is immaterial; if the 24-in. distance is too great for younger children, it can be reduced to 18 in. or to 15 or 12 and so on.

Sex: Both boys and girls.

Reliability: Reliability increases with an increased number of trials. A coefficient of .44 was obtained with seventh and eighth grade boys on test–retest using the total of two trials as the score. A coefficient of .61 was found with seventh and eighth grade boys using the total of ten trials as the score.

Objectivity: An r of .99 was reported by Elaine Wyatt, Northeast Louisiana University, Monroe, 1969.

Validity: With the eyes of the subject closed during the test, face validity is acceptable.

Equipment and Materials: A yardstick or tape measure; a blindfold; and chalk.

Directions: The performer is instructed to sense the distance between the two lines used in the test without a practice trial. The blindfold is then put on and the subject jumps from behind the starting line, trying to land with the heels as close to the target line as possible (Figure C.1). He or she is allowed to see the landing spot on each trial. Ten trials are given. *Note:* This is a modification of the original distance perception jump, in which only two trials were allowed. Another variation of the test is to allow the subject to jump first with the eyes open. Then he or she is blindfolded to measure the ability to duplicate the amount of effort required. However, few people can jump perfectly on the first trial; therefore, it again becomes a matter of interpreting the feedback from each jump.

Scoring: For each jump the distance to the nearest one-fourth inch from the target line to the farthest heel is measured and recorded. The score is the total for ten jumps. Table C.1 shows norms.

Figure C.1.   Distance perception jump

Table C.1.   Excellent, Average, and Poor Performance Scores on the Distance Perception Jump Test for Junior and Senior High School Boys[a]

SCHOOL LEVEL	SCORE					
	Poor		Average		Excellent	
	Inches	Centimeters	Inches	Centimeters	Inches	Centimeters
Junior high school	10¼	26	5½	13	¾	2
Senior high school	10¼	26	5¼	13	½	1

[a]Scores based on only two trials for a limited number of subjects from physical education classes in East Baton Rouge Parish, Baton Rouge, La., 1968

Shuffleboard Distance Perception Test (Johnson 1966a; Nelson 1971)

Objective: To measure the ability to perceive distance by concentrating on the effort involved in pushing a disk.

Age Level: Age 9 and over. The distance could be modified to be suitable for preschool and primary grade children as well as older children.

Sex: Satisfactory for both boys and girls.

Reliability: An r of .71 was obtained on test–retest, using seventh and eighth grade boys. An r of .66 was found with fourth grade girls on test–retest.

Validity: With the eyes of the subject closed, face validity is acceptable.

Equipment and Floor Marking: Shuffleboard cue sticks; disk; chalk or tape; a blindfold; and a tape measure. The floor is marked as shown in Figure C.2. There are three phases of the test, each from a different distance to the target (5, 10, and 15 ft from beginning of target scoring zones). The distance between each scoring zone is 6 in.

Directions: The subject is initially given four or five practice trials away from the target to get acquainted with the shuffleboard pushing motion and the movement of the disk on the floor surface. The subject is then taken to the target and positioned at starting line 1 (5 ft from beginning of the target zones) and told to sense the distance to the 10-point target zone. The subject is then blindfolded and given ten trials. After each trial he or she is allowed to see where the disk came to rest. The blindfold is then repositioned, and the next trial is executed. After ten trials at that distance, the subject is moved to starting line 2 and instructed to try to sense the distance to the 10-point zone. The subject is again blindfolded, and ten trials are given. The same procedures are repeated at starting line 3.

Scoring: The zone in which the disk stops is recorded as the score for each trial. The total points from the three distances (30 trials) are recorded as the score. Table C.2 shows norms for college students.

Additional Pointers:

1. The test can be given on cement and other hard surfaces.

2. The nature of the feedback can be altered by calling out the score of each trial, such as "seven over" or "eight under," and so on.

3. The order of testing from the different starting lines could be altered such as 15, 10, then 5, or in a random order.

4. Some aspects of transfer could be studied by, for example, having subjects practice at distances different from the distance tested.

5. Several targets can be established to expedite the administration of the test.

6. Performance with eyes open may be assessed if the instructor wishes to evaluate depth perception.

Kinesthetic Obstacle Test (Johnson 1966b)

Objective: To measure the ability to predict position during movement without the use of the eyes.

Age Level: Age 10 through college age.

Sex: Satisfactory for both boys and girls.

Table C.2. Raw Scores for Shuffleboard Distance Perception Test for College Students Limited to Ten Trials (Blindfolded) From the 15-ft Line to the First Zone[a]

PERFORMANCE LEVEL	SCORE	
	Men	Women
Excellent	95–100	95–100
Average	65– 75	70– 80
Poor	30– 40	40– 50

[a]Based on the scores of 100 men and 100 women as reported by R. Johnson and D. LeBlanc, Northeast Louisiana University, Monroe, 1967. See text for description of test and scoring.

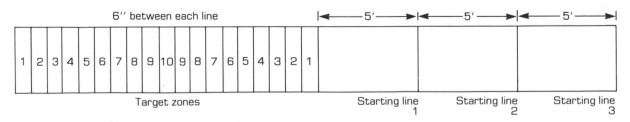

Figure C.2. Shuffleboard distance perception test

Reliability: An *r* of .30 was found for college women when test 1 was correlated with test 2. For men, an *r* of .53 was found using the same procedure.

Validity: Without the use of the eyes, the test has face validity.

Equipment and Materials: Twelve chairs (or similar objects); material for blindfolds; chalk markers or a tape marker; and tape measures.

Directions: The chairs are arranged in accordance with the floor pattern shown in Figure C.3. Each performer is allowed one practice trial walk through the course without a blindfold. Then the subject walks once through the course blindfolded for a score.

Scoring: The score is 10 points for each station successfully cleared without touching. There are ten stations and thus the maximum score is 100 points. Table C.3 shows norms for college students.

Penalty: There is a 10-point penalty if any part of the body touches any part of a chair. When such a penalty occurs, the performer is directed to the center line and one step ahead of the station where the penalty occurred. There is a 5-point penalty for each occurrence of getting outside the line or pattern of the chairs. In this case, the performer is directed back into the center of the pattern at the nearest point from which he or she went astray.

Additional Pointers:

1. The dotted line merely shows the ideal walking path and need not be drawn on the floor.

2. The two outside lines are boundary lines and should be indicated on the floor.

3. Further experimentation with scoring systems is needed, since the reliability of the test was found to be quite low.

Bass Kinesthetic Stick Test (Lengthwise) (Young 1945)

Objective: To measure the kinesthetic ability to maintain balance on a small narrow surface.

Age Level: Age 10 and over. (See additional pointers.)

Sex: Satisfactory for both boys and girls.

Reliability: A test–retest correlation of .36 was found with sixth grade boys.

Validity: With the subject's eyes closed during the test, this test has face validity.

Equipment and Materials: A stopwatch; several

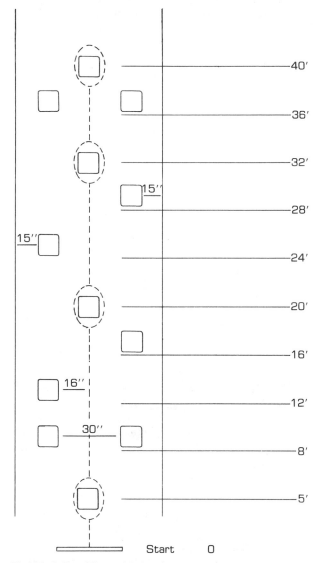

Figure C.3.   Kinesthetic obstacle test

Table C.3.   Raw Score Norms for Kinesthetic Obstacle Test, College Students[a]

PERFORMANCE LEVEL	SCORE	
	Men	Women
Excellent	90–100	80–90
Average	65– 50	60–70
Poor	40– 50	30–40

[a]Based on the scores of 100 men and 100 women as reported by B. B. Dunn and D. Washington, Northeast Louisiana University, Monroe, 1967. See text for description of test and scoring.

sticks cut to 1 in. × 1 in. × 12 in.; tape; and blindfolds. Several stations may be set up to save time.

Directions: The subject is instructed to place the dominant foot lengthwise on a balance stick and to raise the opposite foot from the floor to see how long he or she can maintain balance. One preliminary trial is given and then the subject is blindfolded for the test. The subject is timed from the moment the opposite foot is raised from the floor until balance is lost. Ten trials are given.

Scoring: The score is recorded to the nearest one-half second for each trial; the score is the total number of seconds for the ten trials. Table C.4 shows norms.

Additional Pointers:

1. This task is quite difficult even for adults. The test could be modified to make it more suitable for young children by increasing the width of the stick. A block of wood 1 in. high and 3 in. × 3 in. should be sufficient to make the child balance on the ball of one foot.

2. The Bass stick test can be done with the stick crosswise also, but this is even more difficult and the scores are usually quite low.

PROBLEMS ASSOCIATED WITH KINESTHETIC TESTING

1. Many investigators have failed to recognize the influence of tactual stimulation in the more traditional tests of kinesthesis (Slater-Hammel 1955). For example, Chernikoff and Taylor pointed out that, when a subject exerts force against a scale, body contact produces tactual stimulation. Moreover, when the subject is blindfolded and is required to move a body part to a designated point in space, the tester commonly moves the subject's body part in the preliminary trial, and this also produces tactual stimulation.

2. Many kinesthetic tests (including those in this appendix) are still in the exploratory stage and are of questionable reliability and validity. Concerning validity, however, Henry stated that a test in which muscle sense is the only possible cue for a successful response should be acknowledged as a valid test of some aspect of kinesthetics. Concerning reliability, investigators frequently test kinesthetic reliability by using the split-halves technique stepped up by the Spearman–Brown formula, but then recommend a different scoring system when testing other than for reliability. In checking such recommended scoring systems by the test–retest method on separate days, we and our assistant found considerably lower rs. Thus, there is a need for further experimentation to establish reliable and practical scoring systems.

3. Since most writers on the topic of kinesthesis agree that this sense is specific to the test and body part rather than general, it would seem appropriate to devise tests of kinesthesis with this thought in mind. For example, if a coach is trying to emphasize touch in basketball goal shooting, he or she might experiment by having a player shoot blindfolded. After each shot, the performer would receive verbal feedback and then would try to adjust the shot by feel. The use of skills tests with blindfolded subjects as a form of practice in certain activities may have considerable value in an effort to establish more reliance on proprioceptive cues and achieve consistency of performance, such as in grooving a golf swing. Common sense must prevail, but there may be merit in this procedure.

Table C.4. Excellent, Average, and Poor Performance Scores in Seconds on the Bass Kinesthetic Stick Test (Lengthwise), Junior and Senior High School Boys

SCHOOL LEVEL	SCORE		
	Poor	Average	Excellent
Junior high school	3	9	15
Senior high school	3½	10	16

[a]Scores based on one trial for a limited number of subjects from physical education classes in East Baton Rouge Parish, Baton Rouge, La., 1968.

FINDINGS AND CONCLUSIONS FROM KINESTHETIC PERCEPTION MEASUREMENT AND RESEARCH

Several investigators have concluded that there is no general kinesthetic ability but rather a number of factors specific to the task and the particular part of the body involved in the performance (Cratty 1962; Scott 1955; Start 1964; Wiebe 1954).

Although the evidence is by no means conclusive, studies have shown that the skilled performer in a specific activity tends to score higher on kinesthetic tests than the less skilled (Mumby 1953; Phillips 1941; Slater-Hammel 1957; Wiebe 1954). Two studies found no significant difference between boys and girls in kinesthetic perception (Slater-Hammel 1955; Witte 1953). Athletes score higher in kinesthetic performance than nonathletes (Wiebe 1951); however, most studies have failed to find any appreciable relationship between kinesthesis and ability in sports such as gymnastics (Wettstone 1938), bowling (Greenlee 1958), and basketball (Taylor 1933).

Laszlo, using a blood pressure cuff to reduce kinesthetic sensation, induced decreased tapping efficiency. She found that the impairment produced by the cuff on the arm resulted in loss of tactile sense of the fingers first, passive kinesthetic sense second, and then active kinesthetic sense.

In general, low relationships have been found between kinesthesis and motor performance (Greenlee 1958; Mumby 1953; Norrie 1952), motor learning (Linsay 1952; Phillips and Summers 1954; Roloff 1953), and certain psychologic and physiologic factors (Henry 1953; Slocum 1952; Start 1964).

BIBLIOGRAPHY

Bass, R. I., "Analysis of the Components of Tests of Semicircular Canal Functions and of Static and Dynamic Balance." *Research Quarterly* 10:33–52, May 1939.

Chernikoff, R., and F. V. Taylor, "Reaction Time to Kinesthetic Stimulation Resulting From Sudden Arm Displacement." *Journal of Experimental Psychology* 43:1–8, 1952.

Cratty, B. J., "Comparison of Learning a Time Motor Task With Learning a Similar Gross Motor Task Using Kinesthetic Cues." *Research Quarterly* 33:220, May 1962.

Greenlee, G. A., "The Relationship of Selected Measures of Strength, Balance, and Kinesthesis to Bowling Performance." Microcarded master's thesis, State University of Iowa, Iowa City, 1958.

Henry, F. M., "Dynamic Kinesthetic Perception and Adjustment." *Research Quarterly* 24:176–187, May 1953.

Johnson, B. L., "The Shuffle Board Control of Force Test." Unpublished study, Northeast Louisiana University, Monroe, September 1966a.

———, "A Kinesthetic Obstacle Test." Unpublished study, Northeast Louisiana University, Monroe, September 1966b.

Laszlo, J. I., "The Performance of a Simple Motor Task with Kinesthetic Sense Loss." *Quarterly Journal of Experimental Psychology* 18:1–8, 1966.

Linsay, D., "Relationship Between Measures of Kinesthesis and the Learning of a Motor Skill." Unpublished master's thesis, University of California, Berkeley, 1952.

Mumby, H. H., "Kinesthetic Acuity and Balance Related to Wrestling Ability." *Research Quarterly* 24:334, October 1953.

Nelson, J. K., "Modification of Shuffleboard and Bean Bag Kinesthesis Tests." Unpublished study, Louisiana State University, Baton Rouge, 1971.

———, "The Reliability of Selected Measures of Kinesthetic Perception With Grade School Children." Unpublished study, Louisiana State University, Baton Rouge, 1972.

Norrie, M. L., "The Relationship Between Measures of Kinesthesis and Motor Performance." Unpublished master's thesis, University of California, Berkeley, 1952.

Phillips, B. E., "The Relationship Between Certain Phases of Kinesthesis and Performance During the Early Stages of Acquiring Two Perceptuo-Motor Skills." Microcarded master's thesis, Pennsylvania State College, University Park, 1941.

Phillips, M., and D. Summers, "Relation of Kinesthetic Perception to Motor Learning." *Research Quarterly* 25:456–469, December 1954.

Roloff, L. L., "Kinesthesis in Relation to the Learning of Selected Motor Skills." *Research Quarterly* 24:210–217, May 1953.

Scott, M. G., "Tests of Kinesthesis." *Research Quarterly* 26:234–241, October 1955.

Slater-Hammel, A. T., "Comparisons of Reaction-Time Measures to a Visual Stimulus and Arm Movement." *Research Quarterly* 26:470–479, December 1955.

————, "Measurement of Kinesthetic Perception of Muscular Force With Muscle Potential Changes." *Research Quarterly* 28:153–159, May 1957.

Slocum, H. M., "The Effect of Fatigue Induced by Physical Activity on Certain Tests in Kinesthesis." Microcarded doctoral dissertation, State University of Iowa, Iowa City, 1952, pp. 39–40.

Start, K. B., "Kinesthesis and Mental Practice." *Research Quarterly* 35:316–319, October 1964.

Steinhaus, A. H., "Your Muscles See More Than Your Eyes." *JOHPER* 37:38, September 1966.

Taylor, W. J., "The Relationship Between Kinesthetic Judgment and Success in Basketball." Unpublished master's thesis, Pennsylvania State College, University Park, 1933.

Wettstone, E., "Tests for Predicting Potential Ability in Gymnastics and Tumbling." *Research Quarterly* 9:115–125, December 1938.

Wiebe, V. R., "A Factor Analysis of Tests of Kinesthesis." Microcarded doctoral dissertation, State University of Iowa, Iowa City, 1951, pp. 66–67.

————, "A Study of Tests of Kinesthesis." *Research Quarterly* 25:222–227, May 1954.

Witte, F., "A Factorial Analysis of Measures of Kinesthesis." Microcarded doctoral dissertation, Indiana University, Bloomington, 1953.

————, "Relation of Kinesthetic Perception to a Selected Motor Skill for Elementary School Children." *Research Quarterly* 33:476, October 1962.

Young, O. G., "A Study of Kinesthesis in Relation to Selected Movements." *Research Quarterly* 16:277, May 1945.

APPENDIX D

CALCULATION OF PERCENTILES

Percentiles can be determined by use of a frequency distribution. The steps for establishing a frequency distribution are described in Chapter 3. To illustrate the procedures for calculating percentiles, we will calculate the 50th percentile (the median). The median can be found in grouped data by the use of a cumulative frequency column and interpolation within the step interval. The following steps may be used in computing the median from the frequency distribution shown in Table D.1.

Step 1: Since the median is the midpoint of the scores and there are 60 scores, multiply $0.50 \times 60 = 30$ to get the halfway point.

Step 2: Establish a cumulative frequency column by starting at the bottom interval and progressively recording the total number of scores accumulated at each interval level (Table D.1).

Step 3: Identify the interval that contains the 30th score. We can quickly see from our cumulative frequency column that the 30th score falls within the 24–27 interval.

Step 4: Find the median within the interval. Although step intervals are usually set up with whole numbers, they actually begin at 0.5 below and extend up to but not including 0.5 above. Thus, the actual limits of the step interval 24–27 are 23.5–27.4. Since there are 24 scores below the 24–27 step interval, and this interval contains 13 scores, we need 6/13

Table D.1. Calculation of Percentile From a Frequency Distribution

SCORE	FREQUENCY	CUMULATIVE FREQUENCY		SAMPLE COMPUTATIONS		(ROUNDED)
52–55	1	60				
48–51	0	59				
44–47	1	59				
40–43	2	58				
36–39	5	56	P_{90}	90% of 60 = 54	$35.5 + 3/5 \times 4 = 37.90$	(38)
32–35	5	51	P_{80}	80% of 60 = 48	$31.5 + 2/5 \times 4 = 33.10$	(33)
28–31	9	46	$P_{75}(Q_3)$	75% of 60 = 45	$27.5 + 8/9 \times 4 = 31.06$	(31)
24–27	13	37	$P_{50}(MDN)$	50% of 60 = 30	$23.5 + 6/13 \times 4 = 25.35$	(25)
20–23	8	24	P_{30}	30% of 60 = 18	$19.5 + 2/8 \times 4 = 20.50$	(21)
16–19	7	16	$P_{25}(Q_1)$	25% of 60 = 15	$15.5 + 6/7 \times 4 = 18.93$	(19)
12–15	5	9	P_{10}	10% of 60 = 6	$11.5 + 2/5 \times 4 = 13.10$	(13)
8–11	2	4				
4– 7	2	2				
	N = 60					

of this interval for the 30th score. The following formula is used:

$$\text{median} = \text{ILL} + \frac{\text{SN}}{\text{IF}} \times i$$

where ILL is the interval lower limit, SN is the scores needed, IF is the interval frequency, and i is the interval width.

$$
\begin{aligned}
\text{Median} &= 23.5 + \left(\frac{6}{13} \times 4\right) \\
&= 23.5 + 1.85 \\
&= 25.35
\end{aligned}
$$

Any percentile can be calculated in the same manner. In Table D.1, the computation of certain percentile points is shown. We merely count up the cumulative frequency column to find the interval that contains the desired score. Then we compute the proportion of the scores that is needed and add that value to the lower limit of the interval.

SAMPLE STATISTICAL ANALYSIS SYSTEM (SAS) COMPUTER PROGRAM FOR CORRELATION[1]

PURPOSE OF THE STUDY

We wish to establish concurrent validity for a forehand drive tennis skills test. We are going to correlate forehand drive test scores with a criterion of judges' ratings of forehand drive skill for beginning and intermediate players of both sexes. We want to compute correlation (validity) coefficients for (1) beginning male tennis players ($n = 60$), (2) beginning female tennis players ($n = 52$), (3) intermediate male players ($n = 49$), and (4) intermediate female players ($n = 46$).

We have gathered the two sets of scores (forehand drive test scores and judges' rating scores) for all of our subjects ($N = 207$). The score sheet contained the information in the table below.

In entering the data on the cards we used the following coding:

Column	1, 2, 3	Student identification
Column	4	Sex (1 = male, 2 = female)
Column	5	Skill level (1 = beginner, 2 = intermediate)

Column	6,7	Forehand drive scores (no decimals)
Column	8,9	Judges' ratings (with last number a decimal)

Each data line represents each student's data as we coded it. So for John, Mary, Korky, Kim, and Paul the entries would be:

```
0 0 1 1 1 1 2 6 7
0 0 2 2 2 2 1 8 3
0 0 3 2 1 1 5 6 5
0 0 4 1 1 1 8 7 2
- - - - - - - - -
- - - - - - - - -
2 0 7 1 2 3 0 8 7
```

The SAS "job" would resemble the following (explanation for each line is given after the program):

1. //EXAMPLE JOB ACCT, NAME
2. //EXEC SAS
3. DATA FHVALID

---

1. Helwig, J. T. *SAS Introductory Guide*. Cary, N.C.: Statistical Analysis System Institute, Inc., 1978.

Name	ID #	Sex	Class Level	Forehand Drive	Judges' Rating
John	1	M	Beginner	12	6.7
Mary	2	F	Intermediate	21	8.3
Korky	3	F	Beginner	15	6.5
Kim	4	M	Beginner	18	7.1
—	—	—	—	—	—
—	—	—	—	—	—
Paul	207	M	Intermediate	30	8.7

4. INPUT NAME ID 1-3 SEX 4 LEVEL 5 FHDRIVE 6-7 JUDGES 8-9 1;

5. IF SEX = 1 THEN SEXN = "FEMALE";

6. IF SEX = 2 THEN SEXN = "MALE";

7. IF LEVEL = 1 THEN LEVELN = "BEGIN";

8. IF LEVEL = 2 THEN LEVELN = "INTER":

9. LIST;

10. CARDS;

11. PROC SORT:

12. BY SEX AND LEVELN;

13. PROC CORR;

14. VAR FHDRIVE JUDGES;

15. BY SEXN AND LEVELN;

16. //

Explanation:

1. User identification.

2. Tells computer what statistical package we want.

3. The name of our data set, an abbreviation of Forehand Validity. The name must be no more than eight characters.

4. The input statement tells SAS how the information is arranged on the data cards, and what the names of the variables are. The columns that each occupies are given. For judges' ratings, the input statement tells SAS to put a decimal before the last digit of each rating.

5,6. Tells SAS our code for sex of the students.

7,8. Tells SAS our code for the skill level of the subjects.

9. Tells SAS to print the information on each data card as SAS reads it.

10. Tells SAS that the cards come next.

11,
12. Tells SAS to sort and categorize males and females in beginner and intermediate classes.

13. Tells SAS that we want to use correlation.

14. Tells SAS what the variables are.

15. Tells SAS that we want four correlations: between FH drive scores and judges' ratings for beginning males, beginning females, intermediate males, and intermediate females.

16. End of program.

The computer output sheet would look something like the following:

NOTE: SAS INSTITUTE INC
SAS CIRCLE
PO BOX 8000
CARY, N.C. 27511-8000

SAS

SEX = 1   LEVEL = 1

VARIABLE	N	MEAN	STD DEV	MEDIAN	MINIMUM	MAXIMUM
FHDRIVE	60	17.166632	5.362178	16.900000	3.000000	26.000000
JUDGES	60	6.201361	2.013527	6.018123	1.624461	9.021189

CORRELATION COEFFICIENTS / PROB >] R] UNDER HO: RHO=O / N = 60

	FHDRIVE	JUDGES
FHDRIVE	1.00000	0.71428
	0.0000	0.0001
JUDGES	0.71428	1.00000
	0.0001	0.0000

SAS

SEX = 1   LEVEL = 2

VARIABLE	N	MEAN	STD DEV	MEDIAN	MINIMUM	MAXIMUM
FHDRIVE	49	23.300000	4.918284	22.824000	9.000000	35.000000
JUDGES	49	6.851193	2.137076	6.200000	2.121285	9.333333

CORRELATION COEFFICIENTS / PROB >] R] UNDER HO: RHO = O / N = 49

	FHDRIVE	JUDGES
FHDRIVE	1.00000	0.69632
	0.0000	0.0001
JUDGES	0.69632	1.00000
	0.0001	0.0000

SAS

SEX = 2   LEVEL = 1

VARIABLE	N	MEAN	STD DEV	MEDIAN	MINIMUM	MAXIMUM
FHDRIVE	52	14.429357	6.171683	13.811326	1.000000	22.000000
JUDGES	52	4.923416	1.465684	4.635086	1.033000	8.850000

CORRELATION COEFFICIENTS / PROB >] R] UNDER HO: RHO + / N = 52

	FHDRIVE	JUDGES
FHDRIVE	1.00000	0.61334
	0.0000	0.0001
JUDGES	0.61334	1.00000
	0.0001	0.0000

SAS

SEX = 2   LEVEL = 2

VARIABLE	N	MEAN	STD DEV	MEDIAN	MINIMUM	MAXIMUM
FHDRIVE	46	19.595713	4.277136	19.500000	8.000000	31.000000
JUDGES	46	5.913505	1.940321	5.375000	2.031490	9.153432

CORRELATION COEFFICIENTS / PROB >] R] UNDER HO:RHO = O / N = 46

	FHDRIVE	JUDGES
FHDRIVE	1.00000	0.83715
	0.0000	0.0001
JUDGES	0.83715	1.00000
	0.0001	0.0000

CONVERSION TABLES FOR ENGLISH AND METRIC SYSTEMS OF MEASUREMENT

LENGTH

	INCH	FOOT	YARD	MILLIMETER	CENTIMETER	METER
1 inch	1.0	0.083	0.028	25.4	2.54	0.0254
1 foot	12.0	1.0	0.33	304.8	30.48	0.3048
1 yard	36.0	3.0	1.0	914.4	91.44	0.914
1 millimeter	0.039	0.003	0.001	1.0	0.1	0.001
1 centimeter	0.3937	0.033	0.011	10.0	1.0	0.01
1 meter	39.37	3.28	1.09	1000.0	100.0	1.0

1 mile = 5280 feet
1 mile = 1760 yards
1 mile = 1609 meters
1 mile = 1.609 kilometers

1 kilometer = 1000 meters
1 kilometer = 3281.5 feet
1 kilometer = 1093.8 yards
1 kilometer = 0.6215 mile

WEIGHT

	OUNCE	POUND	GRAM	KILOGRAM
1 ounce	1.0	0.0625	28.0	0.028
1 pound	16.0	1.0	448.0	0.448
1 gram	0.035	0.0022	1.0	0.001
1 kilogram	35.2	2.2	1000.0	1.0

1 ton = .907 metric ton

1 metric ton = 1.102 tons

TEMPERATURE

32 °F = 0 °C
212 °F = 100 °C
To change centigrade to Fahrenheit:

$$°F = \frac{9}{5} °C + 32$$

To change Fahrenheit to centigrade:

$$°C = \frac{5}{9} (°F - 32)$$

CAPACITY

	FLUID OUNCE	LIQUID PINT	LIQUID QUART	CUBIC INCH	CUBIC CENTIMETER	DECILITER	LITER
1 U.S. fluid ounce	1.0	0.0625	0.0313	1.8047	29.574	0.2957	0.0296
1 U.S. liquid pint	16.0	1.0	0.5	28.875	473.18	4.7317	0.4732
1 U.S. liquid quart	32.0	2.0	1.0	57.75	946.35	9.4633	0.9463
1 cubic inch	0.554	0.0346	0.0173	1.0	16.387	0.1639	0.0164
1 cubic centimeter				(1 cubic centimeter = 1 milliliter)			
1 milliliter	0.0338	0.0021	0.0011	0.0610	1.0	0.01	0.001
1 deciliter	3.3815	0.2113	0.1057	6.103	100.0	1.0	0.1
1 liter	33.815	2.1134	1.0567	61.025	1000.0	10.0	1.0

AREA

1 square inch = 6.4516 square centimeters

1 square foot = 929.03 square centimeters

1 square foot = 0.092 square meter

1 square yard = 0.82 square meter

1 square centimeter = 0.155 square inch

1 square centimeter = 0.0011 square foot

1 square meter = 10.764 square feet

1 square meter = 1.196 square yards

WORK UNITS

1 foot-pound = 0.13825 kilogram-meter

1 kilogram-meter = 7.23 foot-pounds

ENERGY UNITS

1 kilocalorie = 3086 foot-pounds

1 kilocalorie = 426.4 kilogram-meters

(1 kilocalorie is the heat required to raise the temperature of 1 kilogram of water 1 °C. 1 kilocalorie = 1000 calories)

POWER UNITS (WORK PER UNIT OF TIME)

	HORSEPOWER	WATT	FT-LB MIN	KG-M MIN	FT-LB SEC	KG-M SEC
1 horsepower	1.0	746.0	33,000.0	4564.0	550.0	76.07
1 watt	0.0013	1.0	44.236	6.118	0.7373	0.1019
1 foot-pound/ min	0.00003	0.0226	1.0	0.1383	0.0167	0.0023
1 kilogram- meter/min	0.0002	0.1634	7.23	1.0	0.1205	0.0167

SAMPLE CHECKLIST OF PHYSICAL PERFORMANCE AND SKILLS TESTING MATERIALS AND SUPPLIES

MATERIALS FOR MEASURING DISTANCE

Yardsticks
Rulers
Tape measures (36 in.)
Tape measures for field marking
Panel mats (each panel is usually 1 ft)

MATERIALS FOR MEASURING TIME

Stopwatch
Wristwatch with second hand
Metronome
Nelson reaction timer

MARKING MATERIAL AND BOUNDARY MARKERS

Masking tape
Chalk
Flags
Chairs
Boundary cones
Rope or cord

SPECIAL EQUIPMENT

Mats
Horizontal bar (or chinning bar)
Parallel bars (or dipping bars)
Barbells and dumbbells
Benches
Weight scale
Stadiometer (for measuring height)
Springscale
Climbing rope
Medicine ball (6 lb)
Balance sticks (12 in. long, 1 in. high, 1 in. wide)

SPECIAL MATERIALS

Chains
Cane poles
Blindfold
S hooks
Chain links

NORMS FOR FLEXIBILITY FOR ELEMENTARY SCHOOL CHILDREN

The tests are described in Chapter 7.

Table H.1. Norms in Inches for Modified Sit-and-Reach Test, Grades 3 and 4[a]

PERFORMANCE LEVEL	BOYS	GIRLS
Excellent	20½ and above	20½ and above
Good	19¼–20¼	19¼–20¼
Average	17¼–19	17¼–19
Fair	16½–17	16¼–17
Poor	16¼ and below	16 and below

[a]Based on 80 scores obtained by Gary Beveridge, Corpus Christi, Tex., 1977.

Table H.2. Norms in Inches for Bridge-up Test, Grades 3 and 4[a]

PERFORMANCE LEVEL	BOYS	GIRLS
Excellent	9 and below	8¼ and below
Good	11¾– 9¼	9½– 8½
Average	15 –12	12 – 9¾
Fair	19 –15¼	14¾–12¼
Poor	19¼ and above	15 and above

[a]Based on 144 scores obtained by Gary Beveridge, and Janice Leal, Corpus Christi, Tex., 1977.

Table H.3. Norms in Inches for Front-to-Rear Splits Test, Grades 3 and 4[a]

PERFORMANCE LEVEL	BOYS	GIRLS
Excellent	6¾ and below	½–0
Good	8¼– 7	2¼– ¾
Average	11 – 8½	7½–2½
Fair	13 –11¼	8¼–7¾
Poor	13¼ and above	8½ and above

[a]Based on 64 scores obtained by Felipe Garcia, Corpus Christi, Tex., 1977.

Table H.4. Norms in Inches for Side Splits Test, Grades 3 and 4[a]

PERFORMANCE LEVEL	BOYS	GIRLS
Excellent	7½–0	1¾–0
Good	8½– 7¾	2½–2
Average	10 – 8¾	6¼–2¾
Fair	11½–10¼	9¼–6½
Poor	11¾ and above	9½ and above

[a]Based on 63 scores obtained by Steve Kurtz, Corpus Christi, Tex., 1977.

Table H.5. Norms in Inches for Shoulder-and-Wrist Elevation Test, Grades 3 and 4[a]

PERFORMANCE LEVEL	BOYS	GIRLS
Excellent	6½– 0	4¼– 0
Good	11¾– 6¾	8 – 4½
Average	15 –12	14¼– 8¼
Fair	16 –15¼	17½–14½
Poor	16¼ and above	17¾ and above

[a]Based on 67 scores obtained by Cherie Bushwar and Felipe Garcia, Corpus Christi, Tex., 1977.

Table H.6. Norms in Inches for Shoulder Rotation Test, Grades 3 and 4[a]

PERFORMANCE LEVEL	BOYS	GIRLS
Excellent	3¾– 0	1½–0
Good	5¾– 4	5 – 1¾
Average	13 – 6	9¼–5¼
Fair	14¾–13¼	14¾–9½
Poor	15 and above	15 and above

[a]Based on 67 scores obtained at St. Pius School, Corpus Christi, Tex., 1977.

Table H.7. Norms in Inches for Ankle Extension (Plantar Flexion) Test, Grades 3 and 4[a]

PERFORMANCE LEVEL	BOYS	GIRLS
Excellent	⅜ and below	¼ and below
Good	⅝– ½	½– ⅜
Average	1 – ¾	1¼– ⅝
Fair	2⅛–1⅛	1⅝– ⅜
Poor	2¼ and above	1¾ and above

[a]Based on 66 scores obtained by Felipe Garcia, Corpus Christi, Tex., 1977.

ALTERNATE FLEXIBILITY TESTS WITHOUT FLEXOMEASURE

Sit-and-Reach Test[1]

Objective: To measure hip and back flexion and extension of the hamstring muscles of the legs.

Sports Specificity: Vaulting, diving, and trampoline skills; straight arm–straight leg press to handstand in gymnastics; other gymnastic skills.

Equipment: A yardstick and tape (or the flexomeasure).

Directions: The 15-in. mark of a yardstick is lined up with a line on the floor and the stick is taped to the floor. The subject sits down and lines up the heels with the near edge of the 15-in. mark and slides the hips back beyond the zero end of the yardstick. With knees locked and heels not more than 5 in. apart, the subject stretches forward and touches the fingertips of both hands as many inches down the stick as possible. The position is held for a count of 2. The forward stretch should be slow and steady, not jerky. Three trials are given.

Additional Pointers:

1. Thorough warm-up should be done.

2. A partner should stand and brace his or her toes against the subject's heels as the subject stretches forward. This will keep the heels from slipping over the 15-in. mark.

3. Two assistants should hold the subject's knees locked.

Scoring: The best of three trials, measured to the nearest quarter of an inch, is the test score. Table I.1 shows norms for men and women.

Standing-Bending Reach Rating Test[2]

Directions: From a standing position, the subject bends forward with the knees locked and follows the applicable procedure listed in Table I.2.

Shoulder-and-Wrist Elevation Test[3]

Objective: To measure shoulder and wrist flexion.

Sports Specificity: Gymnastics (bars and floor exercise skills); butterfly stroke in swimming; wrestling.

Equipment: A ruler; a yardstick; and adhesive tape or the flexomeasure.

Directions: Adhesive tape is applied down the length of the ruler on one side. The subject assumes a prone (facedown) position with the arms straight and about shoulder-width apart. The fists, holding the ruler, press against the base of a smooth-surfaced wall. The subject raises the ruler (horizontally) as high as possible up the wall while keeping the chin on the floor and the elbows straight. An assistant measures to the top center level of the ruler. Three trials are given. The assistant then measures the subject's arm length from the acromion process (top of the arm at the joint) to the middle fingertip.

Additional Pointer: The subject should practice for the test by raising the stick as high as possible and having a partner grasp it at the center and slowly raise it to an even higher level (as the shoulders permit).

---

1. B. L. Johnson, J. K. Nelson, and M. J. Garcia, *Conditioning: Fitness and Performance for Everyone.* Portland, Tex.: Brown and Littleman, 1982, p. 75.

2. Ibid, p. 78.

3. T. K. Cureton, "Flexibility as an Aspect of Physical Fitness." *Research Quarterly Supplement* 12:388–389, May 1941.

Table I.1. Norms in Inches for Sit-and-Reach Test

PERFORMANCE LEVEL	MEN	WOMEN
Excellent	23¾ and above	25¾ and above
Good	21¼–23½	22½–25½
Average	18¾–21.0	20 –22¼
Fair	17 –18½	18 –19¾
Poor	0 –16¾	0 –17¾

Table I.2. Standing-Bending Reach Rating Test

PERFORMANCE LEVEL	MALES	FEMALES
Excellent	Touch midjoints of fingers to floor	Touch palms of hands flat to floor
Good	Touch fingertips to floor	Touch midjoints of fingers to floor
Average	Touch fingertips to top of toes	Touch fingertips to floor
Fair	Touch fingertips to top of insteps	Touch fingertips to top of toes
Poor	Touch fingertips to midpoint between knees and ankles	Touch fingertips to top of insteps

Scoring: The best of three lifts, measured in inches, is subtracted from arm length and the remainder is the score.

$$\begin{array}{rl} \text{Example: arm length} & = 30 \text{ in.} \\ - \text{arm lift} & = 16 \text{ in.} \\ \hline \text{score} & = 14 \text{ in.} \end{array}$$

The closer arm lift gets to arm length, the better the score. Thus, a score of zero would be perfect. Table I.3 shows norms.

Bridge-up Test[4]

Objective: To measure hyperextension of the spine.

Sports Specificity: Balance beam and floor exercise routine in gymnastics; modern dance and ballet movements; high jump event; butterfly event.

Equipment: A mat and tape.

Directions: The subject stands and places the toes against the base of a wall. An assistant marks the heel line. The subject then assumes a supine (back-lying) position on the mat, with the toes to the wall and the feet flat. Tilting the head back while pushing upward, the subject arches the back while walking the fingertips as far toward the heels as possible. This exercise may also be executed by the subject leaning backward until contacting a wall and then handwalking down the wall as far as possible. An assistant marks the farthest spot reached by the fingertips. Three trials are given. The subject then stretches out beside the mark, pressing the feet flat against the floor, and matches the fingertip mark to the nearest body part (shoulder blades, small of back, seat line, midthigh, or knee joint).

4. B. L. Johnson, J. K. Nelson, and M. J. Garcia, op. cit.

Table I.3. Norms in Inches for Shoulder-and-Wrist Elevation Test

PERFORMANCE LEVEL	MEN	WOMEN
Excellent	6 – 0	5½– 0
Good	8¼– 6¼	7½– 5¾
Average	11½– 8½	10¾– 7¾
Fair	12½–11¾	11¾–11
Poor	12¾ and above	12 and above

Additional Pointers:

1. The subject can practice the correct starting position by pushing upward without walking the hands and feet together. The hands should be turned so that the thumbs are next to the ears before the head and shoulders are pushed from the floor.

2. As strength increases in lifting the body to the arch position, the subject can gradually move the feet and hands closer together over a period of several weeks of training.

Scoring: The body part matched is compared with Table I.4 for level of performance. Table I.5 has heel-to-fingertip distance norms.

Trunk-and-Neck Extension Test[5]

Objective: To measure ability to extend the trunk.

Sports Specificity: Gymnastics (floor exercise, beam); butterfly stroke; wrestling.

Equipment: A yardstick; tape; and mats or the flexomeasure.

Directions: An assistant measures the subject's trunk and neck length by taking the distance (to the nearest quarter of an inch) between the tip of the nose and the seat of the subject's chair. Sitting position must be erect with chin level during the measurement. A yardstick is then taped vertically to a wall, the zero end touching the floor. The subject lies facedown on the mat with the nose touching the stick. With the hands resting at the small of the back and an assistant holding the hips down, the subject raises upward, extending the trunk and neck as high as possible, and holds for a count of 3. The reading is taken at the highest point reached by the nose. Three trials are given.

Additional Pointer: The subject can practice by performing the same movement described in the directions section but using the hands to push on the floor in raising the trunk as high as possible.

Scoring: The best score, in inches, of three lifts is subtracted from the trunk and neck length.

Example: trunk and neck length = 32 in.

− best trunk lift = 15 in.

score = 17 in.

The closer the trunk lift gets to the trunk and neck length the better the score. Thus, a score of zero would be perfect. Table I.6 shows norms.

---

5. Modified from flexibility tests described by T. K. Cureton, op. cit.

Table I.4. Bridge-up Test Rating Scale

PERFORMANCE LEVEL	MEN	WOMEN
Excellent	Fingertips to knee joint or farther	Fingertips to midcalf or farther
Good	Fingertips to seat line or farther	Fingertips to knee
Average	Fingertips to lumbar area (lower back)	Fingertips to seat line
Fair	Fingertips to scapula (shoulder blades)	Fingertips to lumbar area
Poor	Fingertips to neck line	Fingertips to scapula (shoulder blades)

Table I.5. Norms in Inches for Bridge-up Test[a]

PERFORMANCE LEVEL	MEN	WOMEN
Excellent	4¾– 0	3¾– 0
Good	12¾– 5	10¾– 4
Average	29¾–13	24¾–11
Fair	37¾–30	31¾–25
Poor	38 and above	32 and above

[a]Based on the best of three measures between the heels and fingertips. C. Macias and D. Castillo of Corpus Christi State University, Corpus Christi, Tex., provided flexibility data, 1976.

Table I.6. Norms in Inches for Trunk-and-Neck Extension Test

PERFORMANCE LEVEL	MEN	WOMEN
Excellent	3–0	2 –0
Good	6–3¼	5¾–2¼
Average	8–6¼	7¾–6
Fair	10–8¼	9¾–8
Poor	10¼ and above	10 and above

Ankle Extension (Plantar Flexion) Test[6]

Objective: To measure ability to flex and extend the ankle.

Age Level: Age 10 through college age.

Sex: Satisfactory for both boys and girls.

Reliability: Reportedly as high as .73.

Validity: Face validity is accepted for this test.

Equipment and Materials: Paper; long pencils; protractors; thumbtacks; and several cardboard squares about 18 in. high and 18 in. wide. Several stations may be set up to save time during testing.

Directions: The performer sits on the floor with the back of the knee touching the floor. Keeping the heel stationary, he or she dorsiflexes the foot as much as possible. The tester traces the outline of the foot (keeping the pencil horizontal), from just above the ankle to just beyond the big toe, on a sheet of paper placed at the side of the foot (Figure I.1). The performer then extends (plantar flexes) the foot as far as possible, and the outline is again traced on the same sheet of paper. The angle of each of the lines with the horizontal is measured with a protractor.

Scoring: The score is the measure taken from the protractor for each foot. An average score for the feet is then figured. Table I.7 shows norms.

6. T. K. Cureton, op. cit.

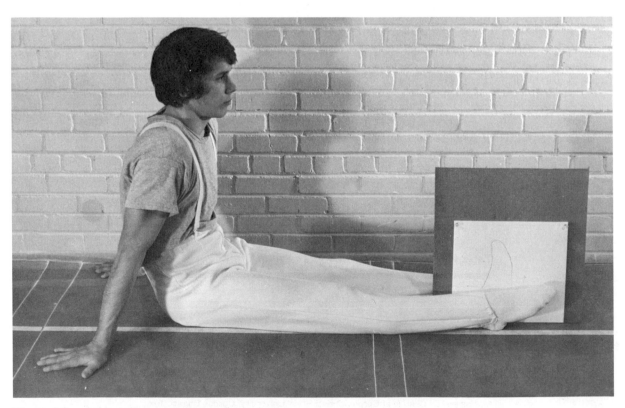

Figure I.1. Ankle extension (plantar flexion) test

Table I.7.   Norms in Angles for Ankle Extension (Plantar Flexion) Test[a]

PERFORMANCE LEVEL	MEN	WOMEN
Excellent	82 and above	84 and above
Good	67–81	71–83
Average	39–66	50–70
Fair	24–38	37–49
Poor	0–23	0–36

[a]Based on the scores of 100 men and 100 women students at Corpus Christi State University, Corpus Christi, Tex., 1977.

CONSTRUCTION OF A STROKE PRACTICE MACHINE FOR TENNIS, BADMINTON, AND VOLLEYBALL

The machine is made of 1.5-in. O.D. thickwall conduit tubing attached to a 24- × 24-in. base. It has two 4-in. pulleys with a 180-in. A-type belt and eight plastic or metal cups. A small metal handle is attached to the lower pulley. The angled upright is 13 ft from the top to the floor. As described, the model will handle both tennis balls and badminton shuttlecocks. For volleyball, there must be two pulleys at the top of the angle arm of the machine and two pulleys at the lower point of the angle arm. Also, two 180-in. A-type belts are required with the cups attached in pairs along the two belts. A small metal tab is inserted inside the cups to support the carrying of the volleyball up to the top of the angle arm. The pulleys are supported by a 7.5-in. shaft (top and bottom) inserted through a pillar block for each. The base of the machine makes use of one "T" fitting and two "L" fittings. The structure of the machine is illustrated in Figure J.1.

The cost is approximately $55.00 to build the volleyball model, which can also drop tennis balls and badminton shuttlecocks. The cost is approximately $35.00 to build a manual model for badminton and tennis. To motorize the badminton and tennis model with a Dayton gearmotor, another $35.00 is needed.

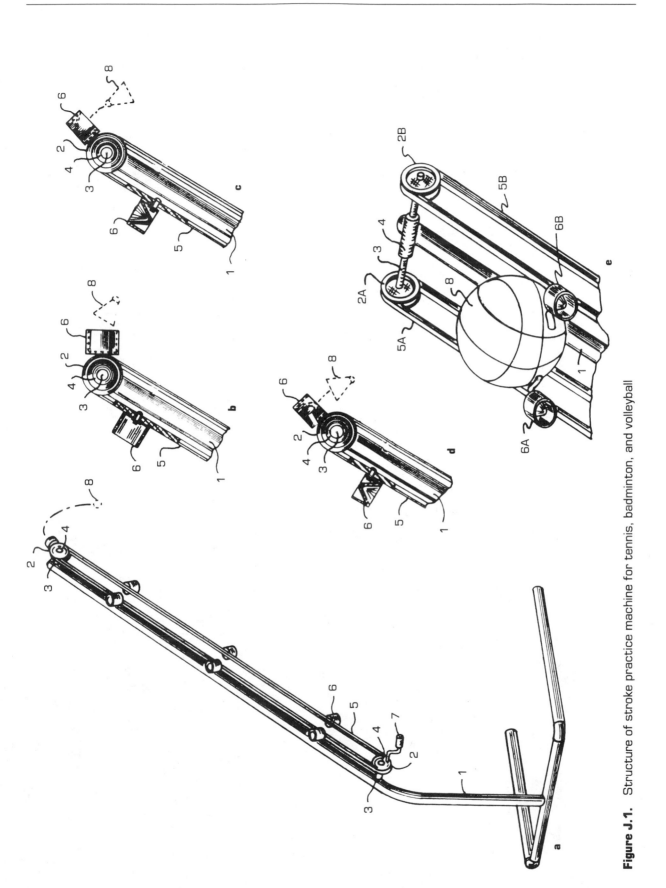

Figure J.1.   Structure of stroke practice machine for tennis, badminton, and volleyball

F DISTRIBUTION TABLES

Table K.1. The F Distribution (Values of F .05)[a]

DENOMINATOR DEGREES OF FREEDOM	NUMERATOR DEGREES OF FREEDOM												
	1	2	3	4	5	6	8	10	12	15	20	24	30
1	161	200	216	225	230	234	239	242	244	246	248	249	250
2	18.5	19.0	19.2	19.2	19.3	19.3	19.4	19.4	19.4	19.4	19.4	19.5	19.5
3	10.1	9.55	9.28	9.12	9.01	8.94	8.85	8.79	8.74	8.70	8.66	8.64	8.62
4	7.71	6.94	6.59	6.39	6.26	6.16	6.04	5.96	5.91	5.86	5.80	5.77	5.75
5	6.61	5.79	5.41	5.19	5.05	4.95	4.82	4.74	4.68	4.62	4.56	4.53	4.50
6	5.99	5.14	4.76	4.53	4.39	4.28	4.15	4.06	4.00	3.94	3.87	3.84	3.81
7	5.59	4.74	4.35	4.12	3.97	3.87	3.73	3.64	3.57	3.51	3.44	3.41	3.38
8	5.32	4.46	4.07	3.84	3.69	3.58	3.44	3.35	3.28	3.22	3.15	3.12	3.08
9	5.12	4.26	3.86	3.63	3.48	3.37	3.23	3.14	3.07	3.01	2.94	2.90	2.86
10	4.96	4.10	3.71	3.48	3.33	3.22	3.07	2.98	2.91	2.85	2.77	2.74	2.70
11	4.84	3.98	3.59	3.36	3.20	3.09	2.95	2.85	2.79	2.72	2.65	2.61	2.57
12	4.75	3.89	3.49	3.26	3.11	3.00	2.85	2.75	2.69	2.62	2.54	2.51	2.47
13	4.67	3.81	3.41	3.18	3.03	2.92	2.77	2.67	2.60	2.53	2.46	2.42	2.38
14	4.60	3.74	3.34	3.11	2.96	2.85	2.70	2.60	2.53	2.46	2.39	2.35	2.31
15	4.54	3.68	3.29	3.06	2.90	2.79	2.64	2.54	2.48	2.40	2.33	2.29	2.25
16	4.49	3.63	3.24	3.01	2.85	2.74	2.59	2.49	2.42	2.35	2.28	2.24	2.19
17	4.45	3.59	3.20	2.96	2.81	2.70	2.55	2.45	2.38	2.31	2.23	2.19	2.15
18	4.41	3.55	3.16	2.93	2.77	2.66	2.51	2.41	2.34	2.27	2.19	2.15	2.11
19	4.38	3.52	3.13	2.90	2.74	2.63	2.48	2.38	2.31	2.23	2.16	2.11	2.07
20	4.35	3.49	3.10	2.87	2.71	2.60	2.45	2.35	2.28	2.20	2.12	2.08	2.04
21	4.32	3.47	3.07	2.84	2.68	2.57	2.42	2.32	2.25	2.18	2.10	2.05	2.01
22	4.30	3.44	3.05	2.82	2.66	2.55	2.40	2.30	2.23	2.15	2.07	2.03	1.98
23	4.28	3.42	3.03	2.80	2.64	2.53	2.37	2.27	2.20	2.13	2.05	2.01	1.96
24	4.26	3.40	3.01	2.78	2.62	2.51	2.36	2.25	2.18	2.11	2.03	1.98	1.94
25	4.24	3.39	2.99	2.76	2.60	2.49	2.34	2.24	2.16	2.09	2.01	1.96	1.92
30	4.17	3.32	2.92	2.69	2.53	2.42	2.27	2.16	2.09	2.01	1.93	1.89	1.84
40	4.08	3.23	2.84	2.61	2.45	2.34	2.18	2.08	2.00	1.92	1.84	1.79	1.74
60	4.00	3.15	2.76	2.53	2.37	2.25	2.10	1.99	1.92	1.84	1.75	1.70	1.65
120	3.92	3.07	2.68	2.45	2.29	2.18	2.02	1.91	1.83	1.75	1.66	1.61	1.55
∞	3.84	3.00	2.60	2.37	2.21	2.10	1.94	1.83	1.75	1.67	1.57	1.52	1.46

[a]Abridged from M. Merrington and C. M. Thompson, "Tables of Percentage Points of the Inverted Beta (F) Distribution." *Biometrika* 33:73–88, 1943. By permission of the *Biometrika* Trustees.

Table K.2. The *F* Distribution (Values of *F* .01)[a]

DENOMINATOR DEGREES OF FREEDOM	NUMERATOR DEGREES OF FREEDOM												
	1	2	3	4	5	6	8	10	12	15	20	24	30
1	4050	5000	5400	5620	5760	5860	5980	6060	6110	6160	6210	6235	6260
2	98.5	99.0	99.2	99.2	99.3	99.3	99.4	99.4	99.4	99.4	99.4	99.5	99.5
3	34.1	30.8	29.5	28.7	28.2	27.9	27.5	27.3	27.1	26.9	26.7	26.6	26.5
4	21.2	18.0	16.7	16.0	15.5	15.2	14.8	14.5	14.4	14.2	14.0	13.9	13.8
5	16.3	13.3	12.1	11.4	11.0	10.7	10.3	10.1	9.89	9.72	9.55	9.47	9.38
6	13.7	10.9	9.78	9.15	8.75	8.47	8.10	7.87	7.72	7.56	7.40	7.31	7.23
7	12.2	9.55	8.45	7.85	7.46	7.19	6.84	6.62	6.47	6.31	6.16	6.07	5.99
8	11.3	8.65	7.59	7.01	6.63	6.37	6.03	5.81	5.67	5.52	5.36	5.28	5.20
9	10.6	8.02	6.99	6.42	6.06	5.80	5.47	5.26	5.11	4.96	4.81	4.73	4.65
10	10.0	7.56	6.55	5.99	5.64	5.39	5.06	4.85	4.71	4.56	4.41	4.33	4.25
11	9.65	7.21	6.22	5.67	5.32	5.07	4.74	4.54	4.40	4.25	4.10	4.02	3.94
12	9.33	6.93	5.95	5.41	5.06	4.82	4.50	4.30	4.16	4.01	3.86	3.78	3.70
13	9.07	6.70	5.74	5.21	4.86	4.62	4.30	4.10	3.96	3.82	3.66	3.59	3.51
14	8.86	6.51	5.56	5.04	4.69	4.46	4.14	3.94	3.80	3.66	3.51	3.43	3.35
15	8.68	6.36	5.42	4.89	4.56	4.32	4.00	3.80	3.67	3.52	3.37	3.29	3.21
16	8.53	6.23	5.29	4.77	4.44	4.20	3.89	3.69	3.55	3.41	3.26	3.18	3.10
17	8.40	6.11	5.18	4.67	4.34	4.10	3.79	3.59	3.46	3.31	3.16	3.08	3.00
18	8.29	6.01	5.09	4.58	4.25	4.01	3.71	3.51	3.37	3.23	3.08	3.00	2.92
19	8.18	5.93	5.01	4.50	4.17	3.94	3.63	3.43	3.30	3.15	3.00	2.92	2.84
20	8.10	5.85	4.94	4.43	4.10	3.87	3.56	3.37	3.23	3.09	2.94	2.86	2.78
21	8.02	5.78	4.87	4.37	4.04	3.81	3.51	3.31	3.17	3.03	2.88	2.80	2.72
22	7.95	5.72	4.82	4.31	3.99	3.76	3.45	3.26	3.12	2.98	2.83	2.75	2.67
23	7.88	5.66	4.76	4.26	3.94	3.71	3.41	3.21	3.07	2.93	2.78	2.70	2.62
24	7.82	5.61	4.72	4.22	3.90	3.67	3.36	3.17	3.03	2.89	2.74	2.66	2.58
25	7.77	5.57	4.68	4.18	3.86	3.63	3.32	3.13	2.99	2.85	2.70	2.62	2.54
30	7.56	5.39	4.51	4.02	3.70	3.47	3.17	2.98	2.84	2.70	2.55	2.47	2.39
40	7.31	5.18	4.31	3.83	3.51	3.29	2.99	2.80	2.66	2.52	2.37	2.29	2.20
60	7.08	4.98	4.13	3.65	3.34	3.12	2.82	2.63	2.50	2.35	2.20	2.12	2.03
120	6.85	4.79	3.95	3.48	3.17	2.96	2.66	2.47	2.34	2.19	2.03	1.95	1.86
∞	6.63	4.61	3.78	3.32	3.02	2.80	2.51	2.32	2.18	2.04	1.88	1.79	1.70

[a]Abridged from M. Merrington and C. M. Thompson, "Tables of Percentage Points of the Inverted Beta (F) Distribution." *Biometrika* 33:73–88, 1943. By permission of the *Biometrika* Trustees.

AUTHOR INDEX

SUBJECT INDEX

Student Survey
Barry L. Johnson and Jack K. Nelson
PRACTICAL MEASUREMENTS FOR EVALUATION IN PHYSICAL EDUCATION, Fourth Edition

Students, send us your ideas!

The author and the publisher want to know how well this book served you and what can be done to improve it for those who will use it in the future. By completing and returning this questionnaire, you can help us to develop better textbooks. We value your opinion and want to hear your comments. Thank you.

Your name (optional) _____ School _____

Your mailing address _____

City _____ State _____ ZIP _____

Instructor's name (optional) _____ Course title _____

1. How does this book compare with other texts you have used? (Check one)

   ☐ Superior ☐ Better than most ☐ Comparable ☐ Not as good as most

2. Circle those chapters you especially liked:
   Chapters: 1 2 3 4 5 6 7 8 9 10 11 12 13 14 15 16 17 18 19 20 21 22
   Comments:

3. Circle those chapters you think could be improved:
   Chapters: 1 2 3 4 5 6 7 8 9 10 11 12 13 14 15 16 17 18 19 20 21 22
   Comments:

4. Please rate the following. (Check one for each line)

	Excellent	Good	Average	Poor
Readability of text material	( )	( )	( )	( )
Logical organization	( )	( )	( )	( )
General layout and design	( )	( )	( )	( )
Up-to-date treatment of subject	( )	( )	( )	( )
Match with instructor's course organization	( )	( )	( )	( )
Illustrations that clarify the text	( )	( )	( )	( )
Selection of topics	( )	( )	( )	( )
Explanation of difficult concepts	( )	( )	( )	( )

5. List any chapters that your instructor did not assign._____

   _____

6. What additional topics did your instructor discuss that were not covered in the text?

7. Did you buy this book new or used?   ☐ New   ☐ Used
   Do you plan to keep the book or sell it?   ☐ Keep it ☐ Sell it
   Do you think your instructor should continue to assign this book?   ☐ Yes   ☐ No

8. After taking the course, are you interested in taking more courses in this field?
   ☐ Yes   ☐ No
   Did you take this course to fulfill a requirement, or as an elective?
   ☐ Required   ☐ Elective

9. What is your major?_____

   Your class rank?   ☐ Freshman   ☐ Sophomore   ☐ Junior   ☐ Senior   ☐ Other, specify:

10. GENERAL COMMENTS:

May we quote you in our advertising?   ☐ Yes   ☐ No

Please remove this page and mail to: Marketing Department
                                              Burgess Publishing
                                              7110 Ohms Lane
                                              Edina, MN 55435

THANK YOU!